Exploditions
PARADOXICA EPIDEMICA

of the time 2012-2016 with 2016-2020 to come.

of the Spiritual Oecumene

"For the spirit of enthusiasm will always be something to be taken on board and retained; and ; while it is lost, it is always to be sought; that happiness and consolation and strengthening and tranqility which are held by good affection will always be something to preserve, and these things will always need to be returned to, so that eventually they inhere more firmly; but all the words which occur are not to be taken on board in this way, in case wome untrue things be mixed in, on the ground that the bad spirit too can take the form of an angel of light. But regarding the contrary spirit and its words, we are to act in the opposite way: for this spirit is to be expelled and fled from regarding every aspect of its feelings, but not all its words; because you could accept many of these as many warnings, and on their basis become more prudent regarding human things; because many of these are true and useful, if afterwards thay are informed by another spirit. (Gerard Manley Hopkins. Collect Works V. Sermons and Spiritual Writings, 519. Commentary on the Spiritual Exercises.

AE Reiff

Histericks 2024

Copyright 2024, 2025 AE Reiff

Cover: Lesser Ury, Willows by the Lake

Contents 2012, 2013, 2014, 2015 2016, 2017, 2018, 2019, 2020

A Condition of the Eye

The association of the name Glaucus with the cloud condition of the eye, that joins the mythological figure and the medical term in the semi-opaque appearance that reflects light in a "glaucous" manner through a turbid body of water tells the blindness of the understanding of the god man.

In the *Paradiso*, I, 70, *qual si fé Glauco nel gustar de l'erba 69 che 'l fé consorto in mar de li altri dèi. 70 Trasumanar significar per verba 71*, that the "transhuman," "cannot be in words set forth" (Bergin)

The accidental similarity of the name Glaucus, fisherman turned god, with the malady of glaucoma, a literal cloudy appearance over the iris, share a *common root. The Greek* glaukos, *a range of bright, greenish-blue, or gray colors, the sort that occurs in the brain, the color of the sea, as Glaucus' skin and hair are described as having the color of the sea resembles the effects of glacouma* as looking underwater or through heavy fog. Glaucus had found a land untouched by the human, where fish once caught went back to the water. Glaucus dove in after and began *Trans-humanizing. Paradiso*, I, 70, *says, Trasumanar:*

Nel suo aspetto tal dentro mi fei, 68 qual si fé Glauco nel gustar de l'erba 69 che 'l fé consorto in mar de li altri dèi. 70 Trasumanar significar per verba 71 non si poria; però l'essemplo basti 72 a cui esperienza grazia serba. Trasumanar significar per verba, 71, means that the "transhuman," "cannot be in words set forth" (Bergin)

> To pass beyond the human, as soon as the fish touched the grass they escaped en masse back to the water. Glaucus chewed several blades of the grass and dove after, purified of his mortality (Ovid, Met. 13.900-14.69.

Transhumar is Transfer, to pass beyond human reason and social norms, made to sound authoritative and reasonable by a counter proposal. The voice does not identify itself. It sounds, much as it must have sounded in the Garden. What is the purpose of transfer? To become a god. In the best case one doesn't find out as if spirits could be exchanged. The voice is disembodied speaking of intelligence even if not known, since it is thought engineered spirit, couched in the circumstance of the moment, and presents the test to either accept or reject. Everything in the spirit world must be accepted or rejected. For it cannot be forced. It must be chosen. Had Eve rejected it nothing would have happened and it would seem to her, as it does here to us, a kind of hallucination that a beast spoke. But if not consciously rejected, accepted, life is completely changed. We don't get to see Glaucus swimming except in the poetry of Yeats. All the later culpas of a certain kind, where we think we are serving others but are serving ourselves and undertake to manipulate others because we believe it is good to do so, like our children must eat their peas, is pretty much the reasoning of those thought form controls above us, that infiltrate our minds with thought engineered spirit, so we think we are doing good when we are doing ill. But what is evil in this context of black and white and grey? Being sure ourselves or not sure? Both evils come with personality traits in ourselves that urge them, some more than others.

The child differs from the conscious adult in its first fall *after* childhood. That first, as said, was a matter of a transfer of intelligence, as if before birth. The falls that follow after are like momentary black outs. To take an analogy from the physical, none of us feel our falls. We feel the aftermath. One minute we stand the next we are down. It's hard to believe we are controlled, manipulated by ideas larger than ourselves. We just don't feel we are. If we are that type of ethical idealist who believes in doing the good, feelings are the key to our control, especially vulnerable when the controls come from our own conceptions of the good, as opposed to just doing, period.

None of this is said to rationalize the first fall, the transfer of intelligence, that had it been rejected would have changed nothing, but accepted it changed everything. The first fall transferred intelligence to promise something greater, which was less, the choice of death, destruction, hence a lie, a spirit trade of one body eternal for another, mortal, elicited by a disembodied presence that presents this considered by reason as outside the possible.

The second falls are the subject of this book.
Second Fall

If we ask to be involved in history, as though we were on the Kinder transport from Germany with Geoffrey Hartman to England in 1939, or a prisoner in camp with Levinas, Frankl or Timmerman, our own disfigured identity and character of discovery immersed in successive natural and social environments that kindle the mind before consciousness, where is an **identity of place** which we don't know but learn to know if we stick it out in the midst of our misprison concealment, this Consciousness in childhood is like a dream where we know but find it hard to act. Thus if the process of coming into the body is as if overlooking the high wall of an orphanage where inmates lament the world from behind their literal iron fence, internalizes a sensibility of **dislocation**.

But it is now in the realm of the debate of reason that the grave decision philosophers and critics underwrite in the Pascal Wager that God is the most rational choice, even without proof, because the potential gain of eternal life is infinite, while the loss from a wrong belief is minimal. But it was in the Sacrifice of Isaac, where universal ethics were suspended for sacrifice unjustified through reason or social norms, where the dilemma of the (incorporeal) transfer of responsibility of a dreadful encounter with the transcendent *mysterium* of an indiscernible (secret) encounter with the invisible in oneself, could not be reasoned. That great decisions taken and affirmed became existentially undecidable Absent the Wager and the Absurd, whether I should fight in the French Resistance or take care of my mother (Sartre) became impossible. "It is when it is not possible to know what must be done, when knowledge cannot be determined that a decision is possible as such." (Derrida, Points: Interviews, 1995 cited by Bennington.

What *Dante uses to demonstate another cloud* besides that of the blinded Glaucus, trasumanar from a place of pristine beauty (the locus amoenus) untouched by civilization to purity, mortality cleansed, immortal, answers yes and not to the undecidable decision taken on the border of the undecided, either not a decision or it is, depending. It is too much either way that involves the godding and the humanity of the man. Charles Williams considers in his *Figure of Beatrice*, of "in-othering of men and the in-Godding of men" (190), "of one who both was and was not and now is." 191 "…Being an image of the whole redeemed universe… an image of the redeemed Way." 192   "concerned to exhibit beatitude….

"The stages of the Way are marked by… the first of the eternal images…when Dante seems to himself to have entered a cloud---'lucida, spessa, solida, e polita---lucent, thick, firm, shining'---as if, living, he entered a still uncleft pearl. He impearls himself. How body enters body…our nature with God's, that is, the Incarnation, is at the root of that even physical co-inherence which is on this earth incapable of its full capacity" (Williams, 195).

 "The first heaven was a showing of rejection, of spirits in the feminine, of final vows not quite fulfilled; the second is a showing of Affirmation, of spirits in the masculine, of final vocations not quite followed." 100 "…But their desire swerved a little to themselves; it considered their own fame and honor; therefore they too in their affirmations were deflected from the eternal order.

"Man might have made satisfaction for the sin? He could not; God might 'solo per sua cortesia—only by his courtesy' have forgiven? He would not; rather he would himself become Man that Man might make satisfaction. The greater became the less, that the less might be perfect with the Creator… It is this, as one may say, handing over of the self to become another self which is the greater largesse of spirit, and this which is understood only by those adult in love." 202

"Something of this is known, on occasion, in the life of lovers… to plunge with love into each other's life---bringing power: power to resist temptation, to reject, to affirm, to purify, to pray. 'I will pray for you' is a good saying; a better—'I will pray in you.'" 204

"…This union of laughter and knowledge, modesty and magnificence, humility and infallibility, may be difficult to imagine. The alternative is a cultured female psychiatrist, with an officially spiritual smile. It will not serve. Beatrice is saying—any lover to any lover—'I know what you are thinking', only (transhumanized) she is right. The phrase is imparadised by joy; we have to learn the joy by the phrase." 201(*The Figure of Beatrice*. Charles Williams. Farrar Straus & Cudahy March 1961).

The assumption of Dante's traushumar into Thomas Paine's New Testament liberty via the American tract by Wm. Blake takes a political outcome. But before Napolean's 1799 siege of Jerusalem the millennial liberation had been declared in the American revolution in the analogy of the minor child of Thomas Paine's *Rights of Man* (part II). That provoked that the revolutionary age, till then "in bondage under the elements of the world," transferred *Galatians* 4.3 to its government. As a child, the 13 colonies, under governance before majority (of the king) had no greater authority than a servant, under the "weak and beggarly elements" of its tutors of earth, air, water and fire-- nations, states and kingdoms. Like the child who becomes a full son adopts a freedom from constraint, in this instance time, that provokes the new age of politic liberty of Paine, which inception, beyond "bondage" of the elements of the world, of the "idols" of time, above "days, months times, years" will not bow or acquiesce to time, so America, borrowed from the biblical liberation of Messias, but without him, Tom Paine was the guru who said, "thirteen American angel colonies rose from the sunken Atlantis of Bacon's New Atlantis of Troy! Hurrah! Atlantis become Troy, Rome, England, and then America! New Order politics rose from the deep. Once sunk in water, leviathan rose in fire. A thousand military bases around the globe! O my America my newfoundland, My kingdom, safeliest when with one man mann'd" (Donne. On His Mistress Going to Bed). The American colony apposite Boston mimicked the angel of Philadelphia. Parables extended dialogue of AI which had the liberty to be wrong, but not the man. In *Covalent freedom*, No Right but Wrong shares existence of independence. In shared sovereignty of equals that never quite is such, the greater shall consume the less. Subsumed, the many colonies become the one co-valence to allay, an early usurping Zarg leviathan co-valence AI. This initiation of the angel-dragon in England's "timeless apocalypse", borrowed deliverance from time as a prison, into a "change of times and laws until a time, and times, and the dividing of time" (Daniel 7.25) had begun.

> Reading the latest of these empires, the American revolution from abroad, in Imaginative literature, the "weak and beggarly elements"
> of earth, air, water and fire, nations, states and kingdoms
> tutors, when "the heir' of all things, implants these heirs by Adoption,
> at this Inception, beyond the "bondage" of the elements
> of the world, the "idols" of time. Sons above time, "days,
> months times, years" expanded to the rise of Washington away
> from the dominion of London, turned by Paine, provoke
> "change of times and laws until "a time, and
> times, and the dividing of time" (Daniel 7.25).

Metaphysical poetics are not only myth. Blake's Jerusalem after four generations in succession, would proclaim Christ's feet in England. the Lamb of God in the Cotswolds, the Holy Spirit as London fog around the dark Satanic mills.

At the beginning of our mythical days, a time out of existence reckoned in the Traushumar, The Mandarin dilemna, The Transhuman hybrid, with Wm. Burroughs' Nova, the Evangelion, Stockhausen, Godzilla, Goya, on stage. This Dante Futurum is a kind of word for a future, but opposite an Adventus., the difference being between a future of linear projection versus a future of radical arrival.

Futurum	Adventus
Refers to a predictable linear future based on the natural outcome of the past and present. where the status quo is largely maintained.	**Means "arrival" of a future that breaks into the present from an external source that can turn the present order upside down**

Secret Witnessing

"From what then do I, with all my being and above all that taste of self, have selfbeing, come?" (*Collected Works of Hopkins*, Vol 5, 350) was what Hopkins' commentary of the *Spiritual Exercises of Loyola* whether of a self existent soul, mind and consciousness, or some extrinsic cause of critics. *"To be sure, a critic resembles a poet as one pea another, the only difference being that he has no anguish in his heart and no music on his lips –* of life's great conflagration *(Kierkegaard, Diapsalmata)."*

Whether intellect is separate from the individual soul (Hopkins, 352), or partners with the so that "all things, therefore, are charged with love, are charged with God and if we know how to touch them give off sparks and take fire, yield drops and flow, ring and tell of him (Hopkins V, 346).

Thought and word of the originary cry for which there is no word, as with Dante's traushumar, "profound anguish of heart, whose lips are so fashioned that when sighs and groans pass over them they sound like beautiful music" (***Diapsalmata***. Kierkegaard *Either/Or*).

Read like so much romance after the fact of life has gone on for years in heart and mind, reached to varying degrees culminated at the approach of death and the deaths of everyone that surrounds. The agonies of spirit of these groans cannot be uttered even if paid mythic due. If romance is not the proper term for poet, suffering is, and not just the poet, but for all who stand in for the rest as more conscious of self, of a higher pitch. Hopkins says, "when I was a child I used to think, ask myself, what must it be to be someone else… "myself being, my consciousness and feeling of myself, so that I taste of myself, of I and me above and in all things.' (Hopkins 349),

This knowing of self and other after the fact, all pain and feeling gone and seen abstract "is more distinctive than the taste of ale or alum, more distinctive than the smell of walnut leaf or camphor and is incommunicable by any means to another" Hopkins 349), that 'now if it, or he, has the same intimate feeling, consciousness of all that goes on in me as I have of what goes on in my finger' (Hopkins 353)… 'I am compounded with him and that by no choice of mine,…this law of his being is unlike mine…for whatever can with truth be called a self, as persons must be…is part of this world of objects, this object world as much as one's own body, and feels and acts in the center of reference of concentric circles around it, where outside of it nothing begins from one side and ends from the other (Hopkins 353-4), leads to the window and the air, the eye and the me, where the windowpane is me and not me and the self a circumference and the fiefdom a field.

All this comes *SELVING* of the *aliquid eius* where 'incompatible frames of being exist together or are together (Hopkins 356) inset and outset that include all things," but, and this is the crux, "the self of the universal is not the self of anything else,…that is, there is no such universal….for either it is selfless or a true self." This takes us into another, which admittedly neither Hopkins says or Loyola but we are compelled, for the world then is word, expression and, the utterance of God analogous to the utterance that results in the Word one meets in and through the world that must be succored for the *Diapsalmata* originary cry of creation, the groan that cannot be uttered.

To travel thence, to hear a listening ear what none can say before the windows of the mind you know, what faces are behind, passengers or refugees, to speak the largest class, imbuement covered points of light before a thousand amenities against the window glass with alms that intervene, time traveler can't remember much. The belt of sunlight, bands of light, answers to prayers before they prayed, to wake interstices down labyrinths and fill the eyes to heal.

What we know when born is that "The first man has two faces, without their being a head of Janus, as you shall see…The sages of the Talmud prefer Psalm 139 here, from which they cite verse 5. This is the verse which would explain the unusual spelling of "he created" with two yods, when the word refers to the creation of man….(Levinas. Verses 5-10): …you hedge me before and behind. You lay Your hand upon me…"
"Always the hand of God grabs me and guides me. It is impossible to escape from God, not to be present before his sleepless gaze. ..

In the biblical passage certainly god's presence means to be besieged by God or obsessed by God. AN OBSESSION WHICH IS EXPERIENCED AS A CHOSENNESS. Read the rest of the Psalm:…

--In other words, man's humanity would be the end of interiority, the end of the subject. Everything is open. I am everywhere looked through, touched by the hand…With only a single face I have a face in the rear of the head, the occiput, in which my hidden thoughts and my MENTAL RESERVATIONS accumulate….But here, instead of the occiput, a second face! Everything is exposed, everything in me confronts and must answer. I cannot, even through sin, separate myself from this God, who looks at me and touches me…Psalm 139 tells us that this hiding place is defenseless. God crosses the shadows of sin. he does not let you go or He catches up with you again. You are always exposed! But in this spirited psalm you are discovered with joy; it is the exaltation of divine proximity that this psalm sings: a being exposed without the least hint of shadow." (Levinas, *Nine Talmud Readings*, 167).

External embodiment of the self. Totality and Infinity. Levinas.

In Heidegger the self oscillates between self revelation and self concealment, but The Il ya, two parabolas intersecting at their bases, open at the top and at the base, transcendence and transdescendence, or the apeiron

--Reading Levinas/Reading Talmud: An Introduction By Ira F. Stone:

Of the psalm, "surely darkness will conceal me, night will provide me with cover," (Ps 139.11)darkness is not dark for you, night is as light as the day. 167 In other words, man's humanity would be the end of interiority, the end of the subject. Everything is open. I am everywhere looked through, touched by the hand. Thus one can understand why Jonah could not escape his mission. This is what it means to have two faces. With only a single face, I have a place in the rear of the head, the occiput, in which my hidden thoughts and my mental reservations accumulate. Refuge which can hold my entire thought. But here, instead of the occiput, a second face! Everything is exposed, everything in me confronts (fait face] and must answer. I cannot, even through sin, separate myself from this God, who looks at me and touches me…167.

We may find them in everyday life what we can call Puppets who speak the answer to our prayers who are so bidden that in one case the disclosing whether a 65 year old man, diagnosed with a 70% blockage of the left ventral heart artery, should go as scheduled for a cardiac cath and stent, and perhaps a bypass if so judged when he is opened up, when he will have no say in those decisions, and indeed is rushed into it by situations that may seem commercial in intent rather than medical—or whether heshould he wait, deliberate, discuss, get second opinions, consider the hard work of ten years of dietary intention?

If this is not too common a dilemma, repeated over and over, it all piled upon him in the moment, the miracle cure vs. the rehab. Certainly no one who loves him can know for sure which was best, so their dilemma was the same as his, being, what to do. The secret witnessing comes about when those who only want him to live and live well consider how on one hand the nurse who works the cardiac unit and knows the outcomes and docs and specialists thinks it should be done, but the FP doc who has seen too many rushes to judgment wants to delay and consider and reconsider before the invasion. A third outcome was overheard in a public hot tub at an athletic club, by a non medical person who has no point of view from experience, -- but secretly witnesses this conversation in the hot tub the day the operation is to occur --which makes it seem orchestrated just for his benefit, as if a script had been sovereignly written and put into the mouths of strangers to be spoken in his hearing for his benefit, as if the lines had been written before, and while they were put into their mouths by intention, the speakers themselves knew nothing of that intent or his interest, as if they were puppets.

The Puppets Said out loud in the hot tub before the decision was made,

::: That Ginger had been given a stent which she later found out she did not need. Only then had she gotten a second opinion, and that the stent had been sold to her on the basis that something worse could happen, that is, by fear.

The person hearing this puppet speak has to ask if it was all made for them, which seems astonishing, the upshot being that that could exist to inform. It only remains to know that days in secret prayer brings them to the SECRET WITNESSING Kierkegaard bases on Matthew, "thy Father which seeth in secret shall reward thee openly," as "the possibility I have of keeping a secret that is visible from the interior but not from the exterior," the terrain where the giving of the gift of death permeates the New Testament sacrifice referred to in the statement, I die daily. The paradox of these statements acknowledged but not resolved of this Secret Witnessing and The Gift of Death, that *"the great decisions that must be taken and must be affirmed are taken and affirmed in this relation to the undecidable itself; at the very moment at which they are no longer possible, they become possible. These are the only decisions possible — impossible ones. Thinking of Kierkegaard's Abraham, the only decision possible is the impossible decision. It is when it is not possible to know what must be done, when knowledge is not and cannot be determining, that a decision is possible as such"* (Derrida, Points:Interviews, 1995 cited by Bennington, *A Moment of Madness*, Derrida's Kierkegaard). We are always brought up against dilemmas of faith where we cannot know for certain the outcome.

We are the sacrifice: "that same "society" [that] puts to death or allows to die of hunger and disease tens of millions of children without any moral or legal tribunal ever being considered competent to judge such a sacrifice, the sacrifice of others to avoid being sacrificed oneself" (*Gift of Death*, 86). This is based on the Abraham/Isaac account and Kierkegaard's *Fear and Trembling* for those who follow a path invisible to others,

"once I have within me... a witness that others cannot see and who is therefore at the same time other than me and more intimate with me than myself, once there is secrecy and secret witnessing within me, then what I call God exists, (there is) what I call God in me" (109).

It might be possible to humanize this paradox if we acknowledge Kierkegaard's meditation on the impossible choice Abraham was confronted with, to kill his son, all motivated by inward seeing. Indeed Kierkegaard says Abraham said nothing to Sarah. It is all background narrative (Auerbach). Kierkegaard says that Abraham feigned madness in order to save Isaac's faith. Better to think his father mad than have his son doubt the Provision of El Shaddhi.

"God, as wholly other, is to be found everywhere there is something of the wholly other. And since each of us, everyone else, each other is infinitely other in its absolute singularity, inaccessible, solitary, transcendent, nonmanifest... then what can be said about Abraham's relation to God can be said about my reaction to every other (one) as every (bit) other [*tout autre comme tout autre*], in particular my relation to my neighbor or my loved ones who are as inaccessible to me, as secret and transcendent as Jahweh". (Derrida, 78)

Abraham's fear and trembling confronts an ultimate duty which transcends conventional morality. General and absolute responsibility must, according to Derrida's analysis, stand in opposition. The critique of general convention is furthered by the recognition that society itself chooses to help one and neglect another, to align with one and war with another, all the time itself unable to justify its choices to any other but itself. Had the ram failed to appear before Abraham, he may well have killed Isaac, an act which society would deem reprehensible and condemn accordingly. And yet, Derrida points out,

"the smooth functioning of such a society, the monotonous complacency of its discourses on morality, politics, and the law, and the exercise of its rights, are in no way impaired by the fact that, because of the structure of the laws of the market that society has instituted and controls, because of the mechanisms of external debt and other similar inequities, that same "society" puts to death or allows to die of hunger and disease tens of millions of children without any moral or legal tribunal ever being considered competent to judge such a sacrifice, the sacrifice of others to avoid being sacrificed oneself" (86).

Such social order, Derrida asserts, is founded upon a bottomless chaos which will inevitably reveal itself to those who depend so heavily upon it. As an alternative to such economies of markets and debt, Derrida points to a truth he finds embedded in the Abraham narrative. In the moment Abraham embraced the paradox and submitted to absolute duty (and thereby transcended and transgressed general duty) God returned his son Isaac and thus revealed that the paradox itself yields a reward.

To uncover what such an economy might mean, and find the key in the thrice repeated promise Derrida takes up Matthew, "thy Father which seeth in secret shall reward thee". After delineating the invisible, spiritual nature of the reward in opposition to its being earthly, Derrida turns to the meaning of "seeing in secret...the clarity of divine lucidity [that] penetrates everything yet keeps within itself the most secret of secrets" (108). He proposes an understanding of God as "the name of the possibility I have of keeping a secret that is visible from the interior but not from the exterior."

But Derrida's substitution is not in the hot tub in faith, he is spinning in a darkness upon the face of the waters. "Once I have within me... a witness that others cannot see and who is therefore at the same time other than me and more intimate with me than myself, once there is secrecy and secret witnessing within me, then what I call God exists, (there is) what I call God in me, (it happens that) I call myself God. God is in me, he is the absolute "me" or "self"... And he is made manifest... when there appears the desire and power to render absolutely invisible and to constitute within oneself a witness of that invisibility". (109)

The Mandarin Decision

Many species of Mandarin thought approach the leaders of earth to propose surrender of one to be tortured forever in exchange for technology to bring perfect health and life to the whole. This sacrifice sounds made for the moment, as if volunteers would form around the block that forms when Sartre's French son asks whether he should stay home and care for his aging mother or join the French Resistance? The answer justifies neither, for the choice for one is the choice for all. So if you are tortured I am too (*Existentialism and Human Emotion*).

In this the anguish of Abraham's sacrifice of his son is opposite the public discourse whether to elect a Mandarin scapegoat or to appoint. Subverted into a democratic *auto de fe* wearing suicide vests, or monks burning themselves alive for some greater cause opposes the one offered by force, like Jacobo Timmerman tortured in Argentina, for instance. If we retain empathy we reject the Mandarin as individuals, even while our governments have accepted it and all of us live with the profit. Of course Christ's sacrifice for all humanity fulfilled the Mandarin dilemma perfectly in an ever more complete health and prosperity, but somehow in the talk of John Stuart Mill and Hayot's *The Hypothetical Mandarin*, the concern is only what happens if we sacrifice the Chinaman, or closer to home, the maquiladoras of Juárez, the machine girls. Where the merchants of the earth grow fabulously rich from their traffik and prevent choice and anguish with politic and rhetoric. The profit motives of art, history, politics and science bypass the sacrifice of all humanity and intead substitute an H+, to benefit the transhuman health and immortality from science, which choice lays bare corruption of the will. If there is no one to decide for us, says Sartre, "there is at least one being in whom existence precedes essence, a being who exists before he can be defined by any concept, and this being is man, or, as Heidegger says, human reality."

"Man, with no support and no aid, is condemned every moment to invent man."
"I ought to know that if I do not choose, I am still choosing."
"The most terrible situations of war, the worst tortures do not create a non-human state of things; there is no non-human situation. It is only through fear, flight and recourse to magical types of conduct that I shall decide on the non-human, but this decision is human, and I shall carry the entire responsibility for it" (Sartre).

What happens in the case of not-man, of death not life, Camus answers in his Sisyphus, where the choice of life itself is equal to species continuation. Have there been efforts to prevent extinction in buffalo but none for man himself?

In what he calls the complicity of all consumers Hayot says, "would you accept the death of a slave or two in return for cane sugar and cheap cotton? (14) Would you, today, admit that the miner occasionally maimed in an industrial accident is the unfortunate compensation for reduced prices on computer motherboards? Most Westerners alive in the past two centuries have answered yes to these, but the dilemma is more massive in the passive fact of living in an economic system devoted to the production of surplus value." In other words the Mandarin dilemma has been long accepted in Nike sweat shops.

Hayot adds that "it matters that the Mandarin sacrifice is Chinese, because his being Chinese means that his being Chinese doesn't matter." We would love to turn this around to say that His being Jesus does matter, that "we are all Jesus Christ and we are all crucified" as does Sherwood Anderson in his *Winesburg, Ohio*, but the paradigm will not allow. Or that as Hopkins says, Concluding that fiction allows a greater open expression, or what is called fiction even if it is as the Russians say, factura, being born for such a time as this, all the above themes are concentrated in myths of refuge and escape that in time became an extensive work with the sense of afterlife therein.

To obviate automatic algorithmic downranks of these ideas, pseudonymous identities employed to enable and speed publication, which every-men may be inferred from links of index, have appeared in the mags to brought into unity of purpose in the record of direct perception face to face with the Word in observation of the invisible.

Creator and creation speak back and forth in that instant before words and life become fact, as described in Hopkins where across <a foundering deck shone a beacon flesh fade, and world's wildfire leave but ash, [where] in a flash I am all at once what Christ is, since he was what I am, and this poor potsherd, patch, matchwood immortal>.

"The function of Chineseness is to force the transformation of the instance into a universal that retains the instance in fossil form. It appears by disappearing; it disappears by appearing."

We might rewrite this as: it matters that his being human means that his being human doesn't matter. The function of humanness thus forces the one instance into the universal so that the difference between the Chinese person and generic man is that if the universal applies only to the American, and when another designated superior, the putative Transhuman comes around, to replace the American, the human is supplanted, reduced to the particular. Still however, to make a better life inclines the American audience to vote to save more lives and justify the sacrifice. They were the first to buy cell phones.

The Transhuman Utilitarian will not doubt the value of saving thousands while millions die. If you think that is backwards, that thousands and millions are reversed, it lays bare the ethic that the Mandarin is the undercover world, millions are eliminated, thousands are saved, and the DNA of every organism is rewritten. It is just done slowly so as not to alarm. In this postscript of the Faustian bargain of supernatural powers in exchange for the soul in Faust, the mandarin meets the geoengineer changing the planet as the transhuman biologist changes the species.

How much do ethical decisions depend on distance in space and time?
The modern Mandarin is a human removed in space and time who considers a reduced price for a motherboard, cheap cotton and shoes made by maquiadores a good swap. Taken to the level of global trades, thousands of lives in New Orleans, for 100 lives in Plano does not at first seem to salt rain clouds. In Eisenhower's putative Greada Treaty of 1954, the alleged trade of human experimentation for all the overnight technology of the genome expressions of Moore's Law was the Mandarin accepted, from Adam Smith's *The Theory of Moral Sentiments*: to the panopticon AI ethical erasure debate.

Weaponizing the atmosphere, called *dry seining* back in the day of *PL3:HSTBIS*, arms electromagnetic particles well beyond the planning. What is knowable is that the belief to pull this off arrogates to itself the right to do, prescribing for all, every living being, to prosecute the greatest good for the greatest number. The geoengineer accepts the Mandarin bargain. He will decide for us, the way the government of any nation will decide to sacrifice its youth for war. Would you trade 100 lives in Plano for thousands in New Orleans? Would you trade a million youth of Ukraine to proxy the Eurasian land mass? That is, in the event that destinies could switch by seeding and spraying or warring to either negate or materialize those same clouds, to magnetize nations, defeat the atmosphere, there is no ethic at all, merely an oligarch from above.

To think that the prescribed purpose to save the earth is a mask to enslave it with digital surveillance enabled by a magnet, that scientific divination of the weather, approved by the media personalities in a way they would not approve more "primitive" kinds, in the New Orleans example inclines the debate to vote yes, do it.

We need a new word to describe the making of this new world. *Starchitects explain every form of modification and anticipate their singularity, so that biologists may make a headless frog to mine its body parts. Conclusions derived from the visible here are a fraction of the affair, like an iceberg. If we deduce a thing hides its appearance and seek the rest of its mass below, but don't seek it because we don't see it there, then chemtrails, which anybody can see--mask, not reveal—an ambition greater than imagined. "When either the spontaneous energy or the analytical intellect seeks to dominate its opposite and engages in a battle with it, and the result is "tumult." in essence," making earth into a planetary weapon, this religion recounts its followers from Dante taking myth as fact while denying the fact in literature as myth in the Abolition of Man. 19 May 2012 - 24 June 2012

There were always transformations, metamorphoses so called. The essence of Plato and classical myth through the renaissance made "their minds most monstrous" when the human was turned to a pig, whether by Circe or Spenser's Una in the *Faerie Queene*. Science today talks of "ceasing to be human" just the opposite of Nebuchadnezzar who was turned to a beast for seven years. It is not into a beast but into a god that transcendence of the human is explained by science, contra to Dante. Those remaining in the audience make appointments to have it done. It is done to them, not by them. The pretense is that human nature is different now than yesterday because the container is remade. Science and philosophy of the new head, severed from its culture and its past, remade by people who imagine everything out of their own lack, is of a love purer and stronger than anyone has ever felt, but they themselves are divorced. Pleasures, bliss, are greater too than experienced, when on the drug. Nietzsche who would transcend the animal and the human, "a roper over the abyss" to become superman, was insane.

To speak this way is not as bad as the powers who make a thousand assumptions that the paradigm of shortage is outdated since there is so much surplus food. The problem constructed is how to consume all the green rev GMO world. It could be given away except this would destroy indigenous agriculture! False plenty is poison food, hyperdrive seed stock and chemical soil. The same goes for the zero sum logic comparing chimps and men, saying apes don't have the brains, as if life were a competition to dominate the ape. Life is cooperation. Intelligence, not wisdom, redesigned viruses, genes, atmospheres under the guise of saving life while it put it to death in the minds most monstrous.

Whether it be atmospheres, plants, animals, or new technologies, the energies released in crossing produce even greater scale(r) energy hard to shield. It is the principle of dissociation to cross in manipulated personality disassociation, fragmented to multiple paradoxes that produce and release energy used for these atomic purposes, that when the new reflective atmosphere turns acidic soils alkaline beneath, requiring more engineering of GMO seeds such as Monsanto's trait technologies, 246 million acres (2007) of genetically modified corn and rice have to withstand the chemical onslaught that the spraying provokes. The catastrophic release of methane gas of the Arctic shelf, skyrocketing levels of asthma, autism, ADD and Alzheimer's, and the nano particles that easily pass the blood brain barrier are all done for your benefit citizen, to make the benefit of ionospheric heaters "one, big global space control grid." Welcome to Skynet. Global warming, global warming, global warning. Any effort to think through these contradictions looks like the crossings of sky grids after spraying. If any premise emerges it is that contradiction, crossing, releases energy.

Aluminum particulates in the atmosphere make the energy weapons work better: "barium powders let it photo-ionize from the ultraviolet sun. Barium makes aluminum-plasma more particulate dense." Aluminum particles, heated by electromagnetics, produce vertical and horizontal columns of gas plasma, orbs used as transmitters and receivers, columnar focal lenses, horizontal drift plasma antennas as Project Cloverleaf.

Weaponizing the atmosphere above, culling the herd below, matches functional genetics mutating the genome. Redesigning humans and their world, entropy, extropy, heaven, hell sounds like literature. New science asks, as if it suddenly discovered the question, what does it mean to be human, but underneath the pretty flower is a dead bird. Instead of poets - scientists and philosophers clothe themselves with challenges to our concept of human "beyond culture." They think the brain and intelligence are beyond culture, take Einstein's brain and hope, still do, to replicate it, but first oppose intelligence with animal instincts, saying that the animal will be left behind. Old hat.
August 2012 Einstein's Brain.

Kubla Khan.These tumults fall back upon the pleasure dome making new art between philosophy and poem as Coleridge does in *Kubla Khan.* Ancestral voices like waters pose as allegories of "two rapid streams" that fight against each other "within the narrow and rocky banks," an easy reference to birth and the life force of the cotyledon emerging from earth". Biology, & psychology could not make up their minds. "Kubla is a creative himself—he has built the pleasure dome… a building a union of opposite forces…thus, when either spontaneous energy or analytical intellect seeks to dominate it engages in a battle with its opposite, and the result is tumult." Each in its excess of strength threatens extinction of the other. Lizards on earlobes, tongues as eyes, a version from the Latin "rubente dextera," of Horace's *Ode* I. 2,2-3, and the "Red Right Hand" of Milton (*PL* II, 170-174) hard to compare with a rabbit jellyfish that glows in the dark to properly build a pleasure dome. A cow in a monkey, a spider in a goat, and flounder genes in a tomato bring incomprehensibility with text, until alone, A different revelation that so found makes the elves jealous who operate the Turnstile where whole assembly lines turn out. You should see what they did to their pets, that suction fingertips on Ubermensch, inject polymered 1200 IQ battery packs in roaches to transmit. Who says pleasure domes have to be gigantic? They were microscopic cloning vectors to engineer a new genetic cell. New old *Kiebsiella planticola* not readily identified, oddly dead, revived in lab. *Plantosaurus maximus pentithicatus* dinosaur made a gene to love that transplant that would reinvent the human,head, for the body was a farm of cabbage livers, tomato hearts, Brussel sprout eyes, and on all this honeydew they fed. Nanopolies formed with porcelain teeth and diamond bones. "Nano vs. polymer in a vision once I saw. Extremophiles landed microbiologists on this moon. Super man was down with Peptides wearing a flying hat for heads to land. They rolled across the floor at Daystar rise. How else talk? It's the old half remarkable question, what is it that we are part of and what is that we are?

23 June 2012

Little Boy Godzilla

First causes, what made Japan join Germany in the Axis of WW II. Had it not done so…the American military and intellectuals justified the bomb then and still do today. It is another case where they don't know what they are doing. The fallout from the flash and shock are beyond horror in the surviving society. The west thinks Japan cute but don't think it is cute because it was bombed little boyed images of the Little Boy, blinding white light, orange conflagration, pitch black rubble, rain of body parts were the costs of shock and awe known they might still be done, and that is that. But why did Japan ally with the Germans? Sure you can hear the gas. And the Chinese museums of Japan's atrocities. But consider that this is the result of the white out, the orange sun, the total dark and the rain of body parts and that that is different from the holocaust mainly because of the shock and awe, for the Nazis delivered their murder hands on, more or less medieval for the time anyway, but Hiroshima was instantly devastated from above. That this spawned Godzilla and all the monsters and giants of pop, as Murakami shows, is just another way of showing. Compare it with the ptsd and shock of IUDs among the Afgan upon the American, the disorientation, the devastation, the shocking of the brain against bone and sound and lined light, and then think of it coming sudden and immersion complete, shock waves more than felt, producing the inane patter and chatter that followed it in America, justifying…but atrocities make more.

Superflat means just that, flattened out, existence being three dimensions, and superflattened peoples dangerous to themselves, action / reaction in the shamed German nation produces woe. Godzilla to superflat to aliens. "Now the leaves are falling fast, nurses to their prams are gone and the trams go rolling on" to the the normal hiding the grotesque. Prepare the super modem superman who never died.

> "No image can replace the intuition of duration, but many diverse images, borrowed from very different orders of things, may, by the convergence of their action, direct the consciousness to the precise point where there is a certain intuition to be seized. By choosing images as dissimilar as possible, we shall prevent any one of them from usurping the place of intuition it is intended to call up."
>
> Bergson, *Introduction to Metaphysics*, 342.

Pink bunny from spacehttp://www.dailymail.co.uk/news/article-1077767/Pictured-The-giant-pink-rabbit-seenspace.html, after girl dressed as pink bunny at end of Diacon IV Confusion confirmation of the universal monster

Written during the flood: that is what they meant doecomocracy felt, fallen out of equality, correctability, sameness, monogenetically, bland. Tokyo destroyed again and again, a "persistent vision of the future in ruins." "Akira is still alive in our minds!" Kaneda tells the U.N. soldiers delivering "mutual misunderstanding between the rescued rescuer current chaos. It also pomps the circumstance out of a sense of justice. The U.S. brought fiefdom and eemocracy to the occupied, a gift?" (48).

So where does the symbolic chain of evidence in anime manga exploding art lead. Start from the beginning stylized pics of Snoopy Dog and Pretty Flower as images of La Bomba. Bomb, Bomb, Bomba, mushroom clouds ornamented with eyes and a nose, necks and arms, cute huh? Kawaii, but acht! before bombs tot turned to washing mashings, cats, bunnies and bunnies flew around to save from Bomb. Bomba transformed preventing bomba. Transformations hun-exploding subatomic subcultures. Then bombs became space ships and aliens. Those little figures flying around are Little bomblets, prepubescent, with smooth faces and sweet eyes like clouds. Litt Bloy, Little Girl! The Name of the Hiroshima bomb. The artist Okamote, says "art si explosion!" The sun is a bomb, rays of light of its aura are nuclear arms, Godzilla is a bomb, mushrooms that implode the inner world are a bomb. Godzilla Hiroshima Ultraman superpowers, super man like a snowball rolling, getting bigger, Diacon IV Bunny Girl surfing on a sword, girl bunny bomb releasing pink clouds of radioactivity reviving the black scarred word in green otaku. Destruction # 3 or 4? Over and over so many stylized bombs everywhere you should look in your underwear for la Bomba! So after the bomba blew everything up in noise, the atom fragments fell to earth in toys. Fallout! Anime toys, girl boy toys, cousin frog, all became mascots for the big companies, pharmacuticals, industrials and turned into Doraemon. Pokemon baby, baby sitting robots and Nobita. Hello Kitty! Hellow Killy, 100 thousand kittle products but kitty has no mouth just eyes and a nose because neither does La Bomb. Who will speak for kitty? *Settle not therefore before what you will answer when you are betrayed for I will give you a mouth.*

I don't know what the bill is for all the gas, the helium to pump Apocalypse, where they spray to complete the negative optical transfer. Japan contemplates the demise and gets out the mask. America wakes to find the Hiroshima bomb named Little Boy, and all Japan little boyed, its pop art enacts revenge on its humikiation, one can ask, what would you have done if Japan were a nation of warriors? Japan is a criminal enterprise like Afghanistan. Nations regard others as criminal, their heroes terrorists, their own terrorists, heroes, to sustain the bubble. Each night trucks go down the alleys spraying to decease the Schumann Resonance, to put people back to sleep. You wonder if the helium works. Just another pogram from fail safe. Weather change, coal cranks up and fracking, weather man made, Yakusa hurricanes, Yakusa and old KGB drying up leaves, driving the blue jet stream. It will set some right, seeing Dr. Strangelove drive the storm, like Roman horses with HAARP breath and cloud. Electrosmog to the transmitters, disinformation hi and lo pressures lost the ball to the NO flood on downs. Next season's American earthquake at Yakushima score that nuke plants, suitcase scalar earthquake and tsunami submarine lost, in the second half blow up Yellowstone.

Paris Hilton wears Kitty, Come to think a bubble is La Bomb. La Bubble Bubba Bugel Bagel, S&L, IT, montage mortgage loan bubba. Akira (1988) of New Tokyo 2019 a new bubble military experiment, made to take psychic powers radiated with EMP drug EMT, the bomb keeps exploding, Tokyo destroyed again, first upon a new box of bubble. Openit, nuke, nuke,nuke all the dollies, explode Akira explodes into demoscracy. Dolls are voting now. The Evangelions

In the year 2000, an expedition team led by Dr. Katsuragi, Misato's father, discovered their God of Gods, Adam. When they attempted to capture Adam by regressing him back to his embryo form, he fought back and enacted the 2nd Impact, which melted the ice cap, whipped out half of earth's population, and flooded the shorelines of the continents. Misato was the only member of the team to survive, and was saved by her father with the last of his strength, who put her in an escape pod before Adam melted the cap. Adam's embryo was found in the red waters years later by SEELE, and delivered to NERV by Kaji Ryoji.

People of Sodom Attack Angels with Evangelions created by man in man's own image. Under the aegis of the UN the Evangelions are monster machines concocted to fight the angels of judgement assuming that this scene turns on its head and side the biblical which it twists.

In the Unit episode about the Submarine Red Clover Mission the psych is asked, she has already said unconscious transference occurs with the wives and that's how the mission name surfaced: can we use thought control as a weapon? "Paramilitary organization NERV to fight monstrous beings called Angels, primarily using giant humanoids known as Evangelions piloted by select teenagers refer to events in the Biblical apocrypha among others.[9] Later episodes deconstruct the themes and motifs of the mecha genre[10] and shift focus to psychoanalysis of the main characters, who display various emotional problems and mental illnesses;[11][12] the nature of existence and reality are questioned in a way that lets Evangelion be characterized as "postmodern fantasy."[13] Hideaki Anno, the director of the anime series, suffered from clinical depression prior to creating the series, and the psychological aspects of the show are based on the director's own experiences with overcoming this illness.[14] The anime is an early example of the genre/concept "sekai-kei",[15][16] anime/manga/light novels which mirror their protagonists' lives with the end of the world." The anime here, "However, the deeply pessimistic nature of the series as well as the rarely seen huge array of problems in all the characters has drawn curiosity on why there is no real happiness in the setting's world "the climax would deal with the defeat of the final 12 Angels and not with the operation of the Human Instrumentality Project. As well, Kaworu Nagisa's initial design was a schoolboy who could switch to an "Angel form", accompanied by a pet cat.[

More direct, but less obvious myths precede the direc sea model of the vacuum as an infinite sea of particles with negative energy, properties of vacuum and found in Japanese anime mange fiction cartoons. Neon Genesis Evangelion, Visual Novel Chaos; Head, by by Ryu Mitsuse realized scalar weaponary in Manga Attack of Angels, "Nerve HQ, a biomechanical weapon named Evangelion, a monster piloted by 14 year old Shinji…keystone for the resurrection of the world" Neon Genesis Evangelelion I, Yoshiyuki Sadamoto (Gainax) tr, /Fred Burke 1998.

Anno:" "The year: 2015. A world where, fifteen years before, over half the human population perished. A world that has been miraculously revived: its economy, the production, circulation, consumption of material goods, so that even the shelves of convenience stores are filled. A world where the people have gotten used to the resurrection-yet still feel the end of the world is destined to come. A world where the number of children,

the future leaders of the world, is few. A world where Japan saw the original Tokyo destroyed, discarded and forgotten, and built a new capital in Nagano Prefecture. They constructed a new capital, Tokyo-2, then left it to be a decoy-then constructed another new capital, Tokyo-3, and tried to make it safe from attack. A world where some completely unknown enemy called the "Angels" comes to ravage the cities with Judeo-Christian symbolism including the entire structure of Adam, Lilith and the Angels – The Christian cross is often shown, frequently represented by energy beams shooting up skyward.[51] •
The Angels are a reference to the angels of God from the Old Testament (in Japanese, the word used is the same one used for apostle (or messenger), as in the New Testament). They are named after angels from Biblical angelology, including Sachiel, Shamshel, and Arael.[51] The first Angel is named Adam, just as the biblical Adam is the first man created by God.[52] The second Angel is named Lilith, a reference to the Jewish folklore in which Lilith is the first wife of Adam.[52] Lilith is shown crucified and impaled with a spear named the "Lance of Longinus", the same lance used to pierce the side of Jesus during his crucifixion,[52] according to the Gospel of Nicodemus. Eve or Eva comes from Adam's rib; similarly, most of the Evas come from the Angel first identified as Adam.[53]

The Magi supercomputers are named Melchior, Balthasar and Caspar after the names traditionally given for the Magi who were mentioned in the Gospel of Matthew as having visited Jesus in Bethlehem.[54] (often called "the three wise men", though the number of visitors is not recorded in the Gospel)

The Tree of Sephiroth (Tree of Life) is mentioned, as well as shown in the opening title sequence and on the ceiling of Gendo's office,[55] with Hebrew inscriptions on it (the terms written there are mostly Kabbalic). It also appears in The End of Evangelion during Seele's version of Instrumentality.

The Marduk Institute is a front organization for Nerv, tasked with finding the teenagers suitable for piloting Evangelion units. Marduk was the name of the chief Babylonian deity and patron god of the city of Babylon.[51] "Philosophy Existential themes of individuality, consciousness, freedom, choice, and responsibility are heavily relied upon throughout the entire series, particularly through the philosophies of Jean-Paul Sartre and Søren Kierkegaard. Episode 16's title, "The Sickness Unto Death, And…" (死に至る病、そして Shi ni itaru yamai, soshite?) is a reference to Kierkegaard's book, The Sickness Unto Death. The Human Instrumentality Project may be inspired by the philosophy developed by Georg Wilhelm Friedrich Hegel.[56] The title of Episode 4, "The Hedgehog's Dilemma", is a reference to the Hedgehog's dilemma, Arthur Schopenhauer's analogy about the challenges of human intimacy.

"Many of the characters share their names with Japanese warships from World War II (such as the Sōryū, Akagi, and Katsuragi; though the ship names and character names are written with different kanji, they share the same pronunciations.) Other characters' names refer to other works of fiction, such as the two characters named after the protagonists of Ryu Murakami's Ai to Genso no Fascism ("Fascism in Love and Fantasy"; the two main characters are named Aida Kensuke and Suzuhara Toji; Anno later directed a Murakami adaptation, Love & Pop).

Other fictive allusions to Philip K. Dick's The Divine Invasion, and "The Prisoner, Thunderbirds, Ultra Seven, UFO, The Andromeda Strain, even The Hitcher."["Human Instrumentality Project. Neon Genesis Evangelion and particularly the Human Instrumentality Project show a strong influence from Arthur C. Clarke's novel Childhood's End, an influence Anno acknowledged.[65] Similarities between the works, such as the larger themes and the declining birth rate after the Second Impact, were gleaned from this work.[citation needed] Evangelion shows influences from the science fiction author Dr. Paul Linebarger,[65] better known by his pseudonym, Cordwainer Smith. Linebarger's science fiction novels revolve around his own concept of the Instrumentality of Mankind, an all-powerful central government of humanity.[66] Like Seele, the Instrumentality of Mankind see themselves "to be shapers of the true destiny of mankind."[67] Although Anno insisted that Hokan (補完?, complementation, completion) be translated as "Instrumentality" in English, perhaps as a way to pay homage to Linebarger, the two authors' conceptions of "instrumentality" are extremely different. Probabilities of improbabilities 100%. Put it this way when tracking the opposite of reality, call it appearance, expect to find not the opposite but the unknown, wildly fantastic. That's no reason to deny the track in front of the eyes even if nobody else would say it is there, not that they look, hardly that. So take the Direc sea, model of the vacuum as an infinite sea of particles with negative energy as the starting point, something really interesting and track from there.

Evangelion had long been taken as a deeply personal expression of Hideaki Anno's personal Freudian struggles.[34] From the start, Evangelion invokes many psychological themes. Dead mothers (souls) in robots piloted by mental/psychical links with their children via the A10 nerve - Strained/parched parent-child relationships. The original anime series, the first four volumes of the manga deal with the Angel invasions, but from a much different angle. Moreover, several more mundane sub-plot tropes common to Japanese manga occur at the same time at the invasions. Phrases used in episodes, their titles, and the names of the background music frequently derive from Sigmund Freud's works,[35] in addition to perhaps some Lacanian influences in general.[36] Examples include "Thanatos", "Oral stage", "Separation Anxiety", and "Mother Is the First Other" (the mother as the first object of a child's love is the basis of the Oedipus complex). The scenery and buildings in Tokyo-3 often seem laden with psychological import, even in the first episode.[37] The connection between the Evas and their pilots, as well as the ultimate goal of the Human Instrumentality Project, bear a strong resemblance to Freud's theories on internal conflict and interpersonal communication.[38]

Piloting Eva
The Hedgehog's Dilemma described by Schopenhauer and later adopted by Freud is the subtitle of episode 4 and is mentioned in that episode by Misato Katsuragi as descriptive of her relationship with Shinji.[39] "—probing psychological questions."[40] The questions elicit unexpected answers, particularly the ones dealing with Shinji's motivation for piloting the Eva—he feels worthless and afraid of others (especially his father) if he is not piloting the Eva.[41] Asuka and Rei are also depicted in deep introspection and consideration of their

psyches. Asuka comes to the realization that her entire being is caught up in being a competent Eva pilot and that without it, she has no personal identity: "I'm the junk... I'm worthless. Nobody needs a pilot who can't control her own Eva."[42] Rei, who throughout the series has displayed minimal emotion, reveals that she does have one impulse; it is Thanatos, an inclination to death: "I am Happy. Because I want to die, I want to despair, I want to return to nothing."[42] In episode 25 Shinji and Asuka both show that they in fact suffered similar pasts and found different ways of dealing with it.

These death wishes are part of Mishima and Budo culture. How much a part honorable death in writers, sword and Religion, "the destruction of some Angels caused explosions which were cross-shaped: an example of Christian icons being used in Evangelion. The most prominent symbol inspired from Judeo-Christian sources uses iconography and themes to give the project a unique edge against other giant robot shows, that had no particular meaning,[46] and that it was not meant to be controversial (like it was[47]). Anno has said that Eva is susceptible to multiple interpretations.[48] Hiroki Sato, head of Gainax's PR department, has made similar statements,[49] as has Toshio Okada.[50]

"Were there any title proposals other than "Evangelion"? One of the names proposed by Anno was "Alcion (Arushion)". But a robot story title that doesn't have a voiced consonant sound in it just isn't catching. So I pushed "Evangelion", which had been rejected once, as sounding stronger. We had talked a lot in the beginning about wanting a title like "Space Runaway Ideon (Legendary Giant God Ideon)", so I think I did push that. And to tell the truth, the story composition is also similar. For example, Nerv can be considered the same as the Solo Ship fighting a lonely battle against both humankind and the Buff Clan, and then there are the incomprehensible robots that can only communicate with children and tend to geo berserk, etc. It might not be an exaggeration to say that if you add "Ideon" and "Devilman" together and divide by two, you get "Evangelion". (laugh) And the interview goes on and on for pages...

Burroughs, Stockhausen

When Jeremiah lived in Babylon the greatest evils were celebrated as good. Burroughs and Stockhausen are our prophets of bad weather, nano tech and scalar weapons, as if they accompany each other in concert. Both prefigure the manga of Evangelion pop. Burroughs was a trust fund baby, and while each baby is innocent, that's why some think Burroughs was not persecuted for shooting his wife in the head in Mexico. It was an exemption of state and craft since, at least Ginsburg suspected, he was a part or full time assassin for groups unnamed. They say it is the CIA but that is just a handy monster. Measured by the number of guns he owned, a gun in every room, near to hand, his aim was not so good. But his imagination was armed worse as the ravenings of *Naked Lunch* absorb, full of language as is, transliterations of Baal and Mammon, Saturn and Baal Peor. Burroughs swallowed these whole, a metaphor he would have liked, since death in life is so much sought by the desperate from Coleridge, Baudelaire, Huysmans, Rimbaud idolized by those who entrain them, what

Mr. Obama called the mass murderers of his watch. The worshipers of evil do not do as much as their gods, or their controls either. Lanza, Holmes, Loughner…are more of a chorus, not actors, to those who do not oppose them. (see Playdate Speech Duet@ *Unlikely* 2.0) If it be said that these were actors at least in the play, and the current academics are the chorus, still a cut above the audience, consumers utterly passive who parrot remnants of the death in life in their inward minds are thoroughly entrained.

Stockhausen you'd think just made odd noises, stray bits of sonar, radio, static and be done, how could that offend? But they all have two selves, the public celebrant who receives the accolades, well burnished like an idol by the lips of those who kiss, and the degraded one hidden in the unchaste hearts. What if we find Stockhausen's sounds are the accompaniment of Burroughs words, *Nova* verse sent to music? And that is not to say that they do not speak the truth about themselves or the audience, or the world, with their guns. Maybe the best use of these two is that together they give in western tones the science of Manga.

Karlheinz Stockhausen, KS said:

In 1977 I was commissioned to compose a work for the National Theatre of Tokyo, and I composed 'The Course of the Years' (Der Jahreslauf)' for gagaku orchestra and gagaku dances, and during the work on this, one day the vision came to me that this 'Course of the Years' could become one scene in a large work and I made sketches while in a temple in Kyoto of Licht. At that time I had called 'The Course of the Years' Hikari which in Japanese means 'Fast Light'.

"The sketches that I made are still valid because I composed what I call now a 'super-formula', a musical nucleus in which three formulas are vertically connected. The 'super-formula' in its original form lasts one minute and has all the chromatic tempi between 60 and 120, 12 steps of metronomic tempi which are important, and then it has 3 times 12 pitches. If one analyses all three formulas vertically, the three formulas have three very different characters. One I call the Michael formula which is a descending melody and has mainly descending and ascending fourths. Second is the Eve formula which ascends with a break in the middle and then descends and is predominantly major thirds. The third formula is called the Lucifer formula; it starts with an ascending major seventh very aggressively, descending, ascending and descending again with several tritones (dissonant intervals). There is no Adam."

KS Monday from Light deals with all the different states of water and when we performed it at La Scala Milan the stage designer and the technicians of the opera house tried to realize what was written in the score but it was very hard for them because it starts with the ocean at the beach where an enormous figure of Eve like a monument, sits in the sand and is washed and cleaned by women (female choir) after the winter and they prepare it for a spring festival. Later Eve gives birth to children and they are washed. Three sailors come with a boat and Lucifer comes out of the ocean as a Lucipolyp.

KS: Tuesday-Very strange transparent beings from the beyond appear, singing, and the musicians are so amazed that they don't dare go any further.

Wednesday from Light - The first scene is called World-Parliament. Delegates from all over the world come together for a World Parliament, they sit at tables and sing and the president is a singer himself and they all sing comments on the subject of what Love is. So they make different statements and the president responds by singing comments.

The second scene is even more difficult and nobody knows at the moment how to do it. For example 12 musicians are flying in from afar and they hover above a city, so first an oboe hovers in over a vast acoustical and optical church and then it transforms into a scene above airports, then the second musician arrives (a cello) and so on and so forth until finally there is a scene above an African jungle where you hear also all these sounds of the animals associated with these musicians, but on a different panoramic level, so you hear the sounds at different positions and the musicians play in contacts with these scenes and disappear to the back where they are flying around in a half circle.

The third scene is the Helicopter String Quartet where the four musicians of a string quartet are presented then driven to an airport or even walk to a helicopter landing place near to the opera house such as the one in Bonn with a lane around the opera house where four helicopters are waiting and the musicians board the helicopters with their instruments. They fly into the air and the music is transmitted by four times three microphones and four cameras providing a video link to the auditorium where multiple video screens are set up so the public can watch and hear the four musicians playing perfectly synchronously in four helicopters. This is possible through click track and inter-com technology. We presented this scene in Amsterdam two years ago and for the first time people were confronted with the fact that music doesn't always need to be performed in one room, but that these musicians were flying off in different directions above the city of Amsterdam, and you could see through the windows of the helicopters, the city below. All of a sudden the public realizes that the musicians play perfectly synchronously a very polyphonic and demanding music. It is a wonderful feeling to envisage music in the future which can happen in completely different places synchronously for example in space -ships where performers could be playing with other performers in other space -ships! So this is the first time in history where musicians have been flown for a performance in order to perform synchronously for a public who are watching and listening in an auditorium. The religion of pop should not be wondered at, it is space and *Urantia,* the book that inspired Harold Percival who inspired Clif High.

"The next scene which I am composing now called Michaelion a sacred futuristic meeting place of delegates from different galaxies where first a camel communicates via a short wave receiver, short wave events, to delegates who are dressed in different ways and sing in different styles and in different dialects not of this planet and they present themselves from where they come from (e.g. Alpha Centauri etc., many star names are used). Finally the camel transforms in a humorous way by fighting with its assistant, a trombone player. The two pretend to have a bull fight and finally the bull sits on the Torero and all laugh. Then the women open the zips of this camel and out comes a zen monk who is put on a stool and he begins to imitate with his voice short wave programs that he receives from all over the universe, from noises to Morse code to languages of all kinds and also sounds that we don't know where they come from . The choir singers learn from him and imitate what he does, in solos, duos, trios and different groupings, when finally six go around the public and sing the final message."

So, he 'trains' his pupils to bring to the world the news that he tries to translate as the 'operator', [like a Scientologist] after having been a camel., caneli. His Divine Weeks, (after *The Divine Weeks* of Josuah Sylvester, translated from the French, 1608f) is all a substitute of space and beings for earth and the human.

-In "Friday from Light there were a lot of objects flying in the air at the Liepzig opera, but everybody knew that it was impossible to realise this part of Licht around the public with the twelve very different objects like rockets flying, a woman in the moon, a giant syringe moving towards a woman, a huge pencil sharpener about 4 metres high as a woman and a man who is a pencil pushing himself into the pencil sharpener; an enormous male raven flying around a woman nest - how can we do all this in the 'box' of an opera house? I can imagine an auditorium but it should be built specifically for Friday from Licht. (Friday from Light is driven entirely by time-code on the tape which includes lighting cues and cues for the soloists, dancers and mimes etc. together with a 12 channel speaker distribution for the electronic music)."

"Saturday from Light is so special that in Milan, Ronconi, an excellent director and Gai Aulenti who did the stage design and costumes, had to go into the sports palace which usually seats 36,000 people for sports events, but the auditorium was in a way good for this part of Licht as the public were sitting in the center on cushions which were arranged to look like the beard of Lucifer and around the public the first scene took place half left, the second scene took place at the right where two giant mandalas about 9 meters in diameter were, and the black cat (flautist) is moving around the numbers on the mandalas which are 1 - 12 & 13 - 24 .

It is very necessary to use these visual elements in order to make the music become clear. The third scene (Lucifer's Dance) was again very difficult to realize. It is a huge human face 25 meters high and divided into five floors (levels) above each other with 82 musicians. The musicians sit at various points of the face: for example left eye, right eye, left eye brow, left cheek, right cheek, nostrils. All these parts of the giant face begin to move musically as well as visually. The musicians had to learn the choreography and movements with their instruments. Just to build that in the sports hall needed such an effort that a special hall should be built just for Saturday from Light."

"Sunday from Light not yet composed I see as an enormous planetarium system with a sun in the center and the planets of our solar system. The planets are inhabited, with traffic between the planets, a traffic of musicians, singers, dancers and performers. So this would need an enormous auditorium like an exhibition hall. There is a new one in Leipzig now which has a glass roof in a semi circle shape . It's beautiful to see the sky through this glass roof which is at least 200 yards from left to right and 400 or 500 yards from front to back. There one could perform, and we intended to perform

Wednesday from Light because the space is big enough to make objects move. Sunday needs at least such a hall if not larger. So I think the whole demand on music theatre for the future is totally different from what the traditional opera houses (even those built since the war) can provide. Licht is a very experimental undertaking." …I have to say that Pop music nowadays is not very inventive. I have several pop magazines from Germany, England, America and Scandinavia who are very interested in my work, but when I see these bands and how they look with their chains and black dress, they all look the same. I imagined that they would all look incomparably different, but their grim look is the same all over the world now, it's so uniform and I don't like uniformity. Then the public become uniformed so to speak, by these public images or models. Art is based on invention and incomparable originality and newness.

    MB: Thinking about this brings to mind Harry Partch and corporeality. Not just making music but making ritual. [Originality and newness here imbibe of Egypt and Babylon and *Urantia*. Part space opera of the fall and rise of man, part twisted on its side the biblical account]

    KS. The movement of sound and the speed of sound in space is very important .In 1954 Gesang der Jünglinge which is a 5 track composition already has diagonal movements in a hall from speaker group to speaker group and also what I call rotations - clockwise or counter-clockwise. In Kontakte this increased enormously. I found a new technique to make movements possible. Sirius was a fantastic step forward with a completely new device allowing sounds to move sometimes up to a maximum of 20 revolutions per second, so you cannot hear the revolutions anymore because they are too fast but the sound is in your body and you don't realize any longer that there are speakers involved, but the sound is everywhere and when you move yourself in space, you change the sound because you move the ears and through that you have different timbres all the time due to movements of your head.

The next step was electronic music for Friday from Light which is for 12 channels, not octophonic but in a true sense dodecaphonic which means you have 12 points in space, 12 directions. In front these move up to the highest point above the stage like a pyramid, from rear left to front ,going up and coming down to rear right, and between these 12 channels, all sorts of sound movements have been composed. This is quite fantastic but one cannot hear it if one is not in such a hall equipped.
[dodecahedron, because it is viz, the tree of life aurally translated] [Frater Achad!]

"In Octophony I have created timbres with small melodic loops which are produced electronically in a computer and then sped up with enormous speeds, let's say you have a melodic figure (already rhythmatised) which lasts 2 seconds, and then I speed it up to such a degree that there is a regular pitch, a sustained pitch of let's say a 1000 periods per second, so I would have to speed it up 2000 times to hear a timbre, and the timbre is the result of that particular micro composition. This is my aim, like in nature, to compose timbres like in atomic physics. I started this already in 1952/3 with the concept that in the end we can compose new timbres, very characteristic timbres and their variations by composing micro waves, the micro structure of vibrations. This is naturally a totally new aspect of composition and music. The layman and indeed traditional musician has no idea about this, also my composer colleagues have no idea, maybe two or three at IRCAM have practical experience with this method but that's all. This is something that will develop in the next century. You see, the devices are not here, the conservatories still think the violin or flute is the end of musical vocabulary, but we know now this is not so. Compared to atomic physics and new discoveries in astronomy, musical progression is enormously slow in developing."

Whether we feel that this music actually puts us in touch with the cosmos or not, this new way of perceiving opera, or more accurately, creative art-full expression, must surely move the spirit of any receptive musical mind.

KS. Whenever we hear sound we are changed, we are no longer the same, and this is even more the case when we hear organised sound - music.
New - means change the method - new methods change the experience - new experiences change man.
Stockhausen scalar yakusa manga: of the four manga lays bare the obvious, the loss of mother, sense of unworthiness. Eve, Michael and Lucifer, not a word for the Father, the Son and the Holy Ghost or Adam. Logics of tensor strain in co-Tangent bundles over a general Manifold for Musculpt by VirFut Q-Pro   http://anthrosites.com/m-
 Licht, (Seven Days of the Week), seven operas composed from 1977 and 2003 ENGEL-PROZESSIONEN and LICHT-BILDER sounds imaginative and at the same time aa Burroughs godfather of the beat: It sounds like gunfire if we remember that gunfire sounds like popcorn: "I Composed Kreuzspiel, or Crossplay [1951], and I knew when I wrote it that it would sound like nothing else in the world. People were quite upset when they heard it for the first time at the national summer courses for contemporary music in Darmstadt, where I conducted the piece; it was violently interrupted by the public. And since then I have composed works from one to the next, always waiting until I've found something that I had never imagined before, or that sounded like anything existing." From an interview with the composer at http://www.u.arizona.edu/~jkandell/music/stock/ks_inter.html:

Stockhausen is on the cover of the Beatles' Sgt. Pepper Hearts Club Band. John Lennon appears to have used HYMNEN as a model for his "Revolution 9." Miles Davis, was influenced by Stockhausen's music. In some circles Stockhausen is called "The Father of Techno", an honorary title he reluctantly responds to, saying that use of new technical means is one thing and musical innovation another. Björk is a huge Stockhausen fan (http://www.stockhausen.org/bjork.html).   We would call him the father of Bilbao, if Bilbao, meaning Frank Gehry, joins as a Triumvirate, Gehry, Stockhausen, Burroughs.

Sirius is the key work that leads to his LICHT (LIGHT), a cycle of seven operatic/theatre works, lasting up to 5 hours representing a 'day' of the week which Stockhausen expects to complete in the first years of the 21st century." Malcolm Ball
 Sirius is of course a code word for under culture, like the Indestructibles of Ancient Egypt: "Licht is a summation of musical and religious thought that draws inspiration from many sources including cosmology and in particular, elements drawn from 'The Urantia Book,' a cosmogony of the Urantia Brotherhood of Chicago USA where the Archangel Michael is described as the "visage of Christ" and "Creator Son", ruler of our local universe, and in Stockhausen's plot represents the progressive forces where Lucifer is the antagonist, and Eve

works towards a renewal of the 'genetic quality' of humanity through the re-creation of an essentially 'musical' human race, whereas it was political theories and racial domination that preoccupied Wagner's compositional life. Pure homogenized theosophic mush.

Musculpt

These identity states can be simulated and progressively assimilated by small human groups undergoing stress-oriented movement training with access to wireless transmission of biofeedback signals used Musculpt-equipped flotation tanks. John Lilly began inquiries into metaprogramming during the Korean War era with studies of indoctrination in deprivation environments.

Pensinger did his dolphin work right in the tank next to Lilly to Musculpt dolphin speech. Dance biofeedback research and Musculpt are necessary preliminaries to an initiative of human-dolphin communications. Humans must learn to enter identity states apropos of the dolphin pod if humans are to learn to speak Dolphin and no longer insist that dolphins learn to speak Human.. This was part of the huge Philadelphia Project on forced indoctrination. He then moved with gathering subversive potential to isolation tanks in gravity-free saltwater, and thence to whales and dolphins and dolphin-human communications.

Musculpt: Reflections 40 Years Later Derek Dillon falls through ice
http://www.oocities.org/moonhoabinh/ithapapers/music.html
The novel consists of three storylines nested inside one another. The largest loop depicts the inner growth of the American protagonist, Derek Dillon, an intelligence officer working in Saigon during the Spring of 1968. Moon of Hoh Binh µTm Scenarios, T5(M)
Dmitri Tymoczko's orbifold Chord Geometries and generalized chord-space maps are very interesting and just the sort of thing Musculptors should try as Musculpt-as-mathematical-notion evolves as a natural language. Milton Babbitt, of course, the Juilliard guru of the topological transform: To study any of this at Columbia Princeton or with Babbitt at Juilliard would have required as prerequisites mastery of an enormous range of th e totally irrelevant.

"One wonders why it took so long to progress to orbifold chord geometries from the 1958 Phillips Pavilion of the Brussels World Fair (the main piece, Metastaseis, a study in both spatialized relativistic Minkowski timeelasticity [on the metric] and aural-percept elasticity in combat due to stress-induced changes in time-rate perception, i.e., during firefights, described in Formalized Music was originally derived as a composition for [primarily] strings [if not superstrings] from a set of m-valued functions over Schrödinger's quantum wave equation, the static-hyperbolic, geometric-wavicle, Barbour-"Platonia", paraboloid form of the piece being physically constructed as the Phillips Pavilion in which Varese's Poeme Electronique premiered) -- particularly given the fact that stratified, multi-sheet, orbital manifolds have been around (at least in Japan, compliments of topologist Ichiro Satake, Japan being no surprise given the role multiple sheets of kami dust coupled by temporal operations -- musically speaking, Toru Takemitsu's orbital "November Steps" over the Noh dan mosaic-manifold -- played in traditional animistic Shinto cosmology and in laying the conceptual foundations for the whole of Japanese aesthetics) since before the Brussels World Fair, but after composition of Metastaseis." July 8, 2012

Kaznacheyev experiments

James Lovelock. Twins, Mengeles: The Kaznacheyev experiments of mirror cytopathic effects, Dr. Vlail Kaznacheyev, Director of the Institute for Clinical and Experimental Medicine in Novosibirsk experiments with twin cell cultures proved any cellular disease or death pattern can be transmitted electromagnetically, and induced in target cells absorbing the radiation. The master cellular control system responds to "coming events that cast their shadows before". In short, it responds to the upper level of the "shadow state" of a disease, still in the virtual state! (Hey, virtual particles are real, virtual photons are real, virtual ST curvatures are real - just very fleeting, only for another to immediately arise). The exchange of virtual particles is known to generate all forces in physics anyway!... "So the cellular control system responds to "shadow state" disease patterns. Enter a QP weapon application. Place a quantum potential weapon "area" on the United States, so that the entire populace is in it. The slowly introduce and bring up in the shadow state, the necrotizing fasciitis disease engine. At some point, the cellular control systems will react, and order the immune system into action.

7 July 2012

It is going to ruin the quartz jewelry industry if the longitudinal EM waves can have a healing effect because they always come in pairs called "phase conjugate pairs" and one of the pair is time reversed. This enables engineering of the waves to "pump" the cells of the body (with waves from the time domain) and actually time-reverse the cells back to a previous healthy condition in a Ritmedic recovery blanket. Frequently used in combination with Ritmscenar treatments. Enhances the effects of the treatment through a relaxing effect on the nervous system of the TMB

11 July 2012

Woke up contemplating green mason stain against Jamaica unglazed. You don't get to decide you get to act. I ended up working in factories in Pittsburgh and Philadelphia on assembly lines among blacks, immigrants of all kinds. They don't give you sensitivity training when they hand you a jack hammer and say, here. This is when I was still a teenager. But I grew up in Pittsburgh in working class schools, not the mainline of Philadelphia where my parents moved when I was 17, finishing high school there as a senior. Some dislocation. I spent much formative time in Pittsburgh in factories, bars and worse impressions beyond the pale, which nobody ever knew. The resulting grade point showed itself. Nobody knows, but if you live, you get a chance. The first assembly at Drexel we were told that they graduate 90% of their admissions, so look around and see your future grads. This was encouraging. So I went from making gunpowder in a basement lab in Pittsburgh, walking the railroad tracks with a gun, raucous untold tales of carnivals, bars, factories, fights, baseball, the Crickets, to Jim Fallon, my first college class, peering intently at the class of all males at this tech school, pushing a piece of chalk against his lower lip, delivering his first line, "I love the Greeks!" He was a PhD. candidate in philosophy at Penn as were many of the teachers in English there.

To be sure June of that summer at 17, just out of high school, I had had an all-encompassing experience in the tent of Oliver B. Greene, which though still plebian, rude, a peasant, scary to the nitwits and profs who don't hold to much, unless their own, is scary. So two months later, when Jim Fallon assigned the first paper, I asked what I should write about. He said how about "Over and above man there exists some super-human power or force, god or gods, fate or destiny." the gods and immortality? I have that paper still. Immortality is spelled immorality, but he gave it an A. The next years I took a long drink of the Bible, real long, went to Bible school at night for two years, while I went to college in the day and then went to work for Editorial Caribe in San Jose Costa Rica on a co-op term. But with a point of view things came clear, especially since the Bible is the point of view of all English lit in the positive or its negation. This bible I knew well enough by then that when I said later to Bill Ingram, who taught his Shakespeare class in his garret, what there was still to read he said the *FQ*, and assigned a paper on the allegory of evil in Book I. I got all of it without trying. I just knew it, which same thing happened in grad school at Iowa, over and over with every author from Hawthorne, Milton, Spenser…. That tent meeting gave me a PhD as well as freedom. The single most important thing in this life was the development of point of view without which I was lost. To find it was everything and entry into the mysteries and knowledge of art and the imagination.

Floods. Set out to Tuba City @ 5.30 AM to visit Aeg in Flag, taking the long way, to do a little Trading Post, but got this call just about when entering Flag of a flood (again!) so turned round, back down the mountain, driving 100, but made it finally to a pipe fitting connection showering and flooding 4 rooms. Canceled the Flag-Tuba and went straight to brooms. Before that, had gone to fix the roof and found the flood water babbling out the front door. All fixed by 11:30. Fans, wet vac, towels, dry wall gutted, pipe refitted. Best birthday! 20 July 2012

      Bizarrely sat in front of Paul van Hofwagen before he announced the new program to background check fingerprint all volunteers to safe guard children. They cannot find a pastor, none available. 25 July 2012

      Last night, 1:40 A.M., noise, went to porch, storm white light thunder transfix. Went out to move tortoise board in the rain put there so Big Guy won't get head caught again, so house won't flood, came in, dried off, searched for children taught not to answer, found Booklet 4, transposed Angel and Pismith to ms. Letters. Exhausted today. 12 Aug 2012

Goya

      There are a series of arches not in dreams but memory that dominate, the colored one of my brother, nose bleeding in the honeysuckle arbor, bees flying, yellow and white fragrant tubed flowers and tendrils lifting as he stands, but is moving, coming toward me at age 4, blood flowing from his nose, victim of the bully Chester? But this is outranked by another arch, a whitewashed tunnel at the county home in Uniontown, pa where he for some reason worked and I visited. Was I twelve, I felt six. The whitewashed tunnel is long and extends at its end to a padded door that swings massively open on its hinges, heavily metal where those most difficult of inmates were kept, but in the tunnel outside ranged, sat, stumbled, moaned the mass of others. The path was slightly elevated so that the whole could be hosed after their visitations, for they make messes where they go, but the tunnel didn't smell, for all the disinfectant. I was going down this tunnel, felt the size of a six ear old, depravity slobbering on both sides. Why? It was a visit. Seared the memory. Those who dread it think the worst would be to live sane among the mad. Transposed to 18th century asylums is not much different from early 1950 "homes" after lithium when the paroles were released. The release of the deranged may be a metaphor of society itself was progressively deranged thereafter. Madness seizes the sane? We call it the Aquarian age. Of madhouse scenes and prisons, not much different since both had common cells ruled by the inmates, we have now society, highly regulated, policed, to keep us safe, but whether that is from police or ourselves is not settled. Indeed evidence mounts that experiments continue that provoke madness in order to study the brain and to promote robotic control sources for use unnamed causes. Universities, hospitals, foundations, corporations all run by functionaries, careerists of the norm. Goya's mature madhouse, after the early ones of 1794, following his onset of deafness, are celebrated as the first depiction of fellatio (Hughes 141), which indeed provokes the notion that every madness has since been release upon society and called a class right. Porn, Namba, every sexual practice, mutation…so it goes. When weekly instances of gunfire in malls and campuses occur the bosses are at a loss to explain how the madness has been released. The Hospicio Cabañas was built as an orphanage in the early 19th century. Its deconsecrated church was decorated with a famous series of murals by Orozco in the 1930s. Galleries surrounding the huge courtyards are often given over to temporary exhibitions. The complex is a UNESCO World Heritage site.

Goya. The Black Paintings.

What makes Goya great beyond the masses of color, light and dark and the dynamism of the figures is his confrontation of evil, called by its various names, viewing these from the Old Testament, the only way it makes sense. That makes it necessary to say how, what. The witch of Endor, the lusts of Midian, worship of Mammon, meaning Saturn, the giants, book of Enoch, tortures and angels. You get the drift. It will be a while in the making. Hughes knows none of this. The phantasmagoria, the delirium of sickness, old age, alienation. Goya is 72, lives in that farmhouse four years, then heads to France. If you know nothing of the supernatural contexts, the Roman emperor worship, the war between the states of dark and light, the architectural testimonies, say the Capitol Mall, the streets, the oldest conflict between the serpent and seed of the woman, the Bohemian Grove, you're just aghast at these. He doesn't paint Balaam but Judith. Hughes reaches for de Sade to explain the darkness, but it is darker than that. What makes Goya great beyond the masses of color, light and dark and the dynamism of figure is his confrontation of evil. Black Paintings in Single Format Wikipedia.
The last paintings on plaster of his house transferred to canvas are too much for youth to take. They are of his last and if they signify madness that is too early a presumption. Lesser travesties, forms destroyed, a lower order not carried to completion so as not to celebrate death, after much pondering see in them depth, even if they are of giant forms. http://animalwilderness.blogspot.com/…So to transfer the thought to Goya, who did these in his seventies, the age when you know what comes, I got Hughes out, knowing. Those frescoes bloomed, whitened, darkened, cracked and spalled, as though the war with Neptune and all

fight had in that moment been lost, except for the patron's restoration (41). I was reading in the early pages of Hughes when the eye misread that phrase, war on Neptune, completely as though it were written to see. Later I went back and could not even find the spot where this mistake occurred. Yes it led to Troy and even more Caligula, nothing more suitable to contemplate with Goya's Saturn and his Caprichos edition of plates, an edition burned by Ruskin and one seen in the Imaginary Prisons of Giambattista Piranesi. What is meant by Old Testament is a conflict of forces of which human war is a lower order.

When the words are rods and cones maybe listen. Hear the words, but the mind, the mental fantasy is disassociation provoked by the unremembered, the unthought, the unbelieved, what you hear in the ear, shout from the housetops. The last paintings on plaster of his house transferred to canvas are too much for youth to take. They are of his last and if they signify madness that is too early a presumption. I have wrestled travesties destroyed, not carried to completion so as not to celebrate death, but after much pondering see in them depth, even if they are of giant forms. http://animalwilderness.blogspot.com/2011/10/blog-post.html So to transfer the thought to Goya, who did these in his seventies, the age when you know what comes, I got Hughes out, knowing those frescoes bloomed, whitened, darkened, cracked and spalled, as though the war with Neptune and all fight had in that moment been lost, except for the patron's restoration (41).

Is not the war with Neptune the war of the Colosi (286)? War on Neptune is however nebulous. The atmosphere swims. one cannot see feet. I was reading in the early pages of Hughes when the eye misread that phrase, war on Neptune, completely as though it were written to see. Later I went back and could not even find the spot where this mistake occurred. Yes it led to Troy and even more Caligula, nothing more suitable to contemplate with Goya's Saturn and his Caprichos edition of plates, an edition burned by Ruskin and one seen in the Imaginary Prisons of Giambattista Piranesi. Is not the war with Neptune the war of the Colosi (286)? War on Neptune is however nebulous. The atmosphere swims. one cannot see feet. Hands are ideas coming and going, to translate paint into words, but to no known purpose, as if one were to hear that it should all be banned as inappropriate nonsense, a message any writer wants to hear because it validates the kick to provoke piety from the unrighteous, to no high purpose, yet if piety is provoked that is not say without sensibility, which is of a high order even if they cannot hear. Scientists cannot see that torturing a rabbit for the good of mankind is the same as making Jesus a king by force (Jn 6.15). There is both an inappropriate analogy and a comparison. This leads to the inherent disproportion of Goya's hand in his portraits that makes the later figures so striking in their darkness, not just Saturn but the Pilgrimage of San Isidro which Hughes likens to a cobra slithering into the face of the paint, its eye a foreground guitarist, conte jondo, (18), an assault on all hearing, silence, ocher, umber, black in the background, not the insipid green trees, white clouds, blue sky formula of the Assault of Thieves and the portraits, even the repeated ritual positions of death, face down with scrabbling hands (124). These pastel unblemished faces like the Family of the Duke of Osuna are merely insipid, but the disproportion of the long faces and noses (54, 119) prepares for the assault, the distortion war of Neptune in Gehry's buildings that Goya wages throughout his greatness where idea is a misconceit housing its opposite. Now that sounds like earth except earth has moral absolutes, except where Neptune has rammed down, nearly everywhere. War does not contain peace the way a villain smile contains goodness. Transparent it becomes either deceit or itself. Do not listen to the words.

Not old enough to fathom Goya's Saturn nor his witches in Caprichos, his prisons, wars, none are, they shut the mouths of insight. What happened to Goya happened to Borges. Each had a transforming sickness (127) that produced their depth. Must this happen to them all? Shut up. Goya was struck at about 46 with deafness than took the form of delirium for several months. It changed the way he saw the world. Borges ran up a stair about age 38 and ran into a class door. The cuts became infected and he suffered at least a month with severe infection and fever, a mort. His mother read Out of the Silent Planet to him, which had just been published, 1939. The next thing he wrote was Pierre Menard and it was off to the spaces. They looked in the face of madness, sickness, evil, depravity, war. Not recommended. No one looks unless forced. I have a son who is a natural transforming artist in his youth, before the face shall we say, who is concerned he is not transformed. None of us know it till after, long after. He daily touches the depraved, the wretched, misshapen, devastated, but doesn't yet know in his mind what his heart compassed. It must be so of us all. We need not pray to be touched.

The continual images in Goya of doubt, night, owls, dark shapes, cannibalism, pederasty, witchery, simony, truly a demonic Dante, are all in some sort the dementias of reason which cannot understand because it wants to deny what is going on right by its nose, so invents all those theories of philosophy to explain to itself what it cannot bear to see, the depravity of the world alleviated only by the compassion of those who serve with sponges and rags and bowls of water, none worse than los desastres de la guerra, those licensed depravities committed by "our heroes," who we hide in graves.

I don't want to turn this apparatus on Hughes in his infantude who came to the US in 1970 from the Aussie fields, "riven" he says with certitude. He only wrote Goya after a near fatal auto accident 30 years later, where he hung between his own months and was tortured by Goya and his school with rejection, then, he wrote. That we understand. He says of ourselves that even now no voice has compassed the depravity of Little Boy, the bomb (7), or Auschwitz, but he is not Itaku. He wants the modern, irreverent attitude, skeptic against the official, the radical to deliver this insight, but turn from your wicked ways? See into the matrix, the blinding all around meaning into our own blind deaf ways? No spark of impiety against our own unrighteousness, the 50 million dead babies all good democrats want to build their homes upon. No, this doesn't go on. There is no more. Oh no. Not never.

1 September 2012

Goya. Caprichos, Black Paintings.

To get more analytical there is a triangulation in Goya, Pilgrimage of St Isidro c. 1821, what Hughes calls a cobra striking in the face of the paint, there the isosceles of St. Isidro's Meadow is perfected in the serpentine, the sinuous motion of all progress, not the black and white oppositions of Euclid, more the gradual turns of river of Chuang Tzu. Of the compositional structures reduced to geometrical formula, "he loves the diagonal and constantly uses it as the basis of his groups and figures" (206). That and the dark masses of black, ocher, umber bulked up against bodies and walls, both in the great paintings and

Caprichos via aquatint, an assault against silence from the deaf (18) painter, or against words that cannot fathom? In Equestrian Portrait of General Palafox, 1814, "the white part of the horse's body forms a rough arc, tied together (as it were) at the top by the crimson loop and knot of Palafox's sash…this major arc is echoes by a minor one above: the white fur trim of Palafox's hat." 278. Bottom line, Goya is a primitive, his portraits with few exceptions are caricature. He can't help it Goya the primitive always, sometimes escaped, but back home his Water Carrier, Knife Grinder, The Forge are of the same time as The Colossus (1810), "low-class, low-origin, lowbrow" 285, just the kind of people we like, of the earth, without pretense. The Giant above and beyond in stature is of this origin which explains its appeal.

The primitive is so much greater than the mannered, Pollack carrying around in his trunk the dead body of woman he killed in an alcoholic frenzy with his car. You do not want to be an artist. Get a job. Hughes cites Terence of the cosuffering of Dickens, Tolstoy, "I think nothing human alien to me." 26 It is like so many of Goya's paintings scraped off walls, mounted, repainted, the Aula Dei, 50f, the Saturn…all parts of the not whole, like the Inquisition, prison scenes Hughes has to cite Foxes Martyrs from, 57, nice water boarding, like the semi erect penis of Saturn the restorer Martin Cubells reshaped to public taste (17) while Saturn is following the rites of Presidents in their secret Bohemian grottoes, oh reshape that one too. It's not the penis but the man who offends, these symbols abound, that's why Blake was burned in his brazier to hide the equally offending black member of Milton. Not one word here about Dick Cheney, Clinton, Bush, Obama. Misshapen. The difference between the pornographers of England say and Goya is he is believable in suffering as Blake's torments, but not Gillray, Rowlandson, 128, or the writers celebrated by Thomas Mish who I shared a table with in the Folger. Truth they are more the torturers than the tortured, yet who is unscathed? Rather who is aware. Of the architectural functions of Goya's church frescoes or his tauromachies, 130f, pass over to the effects of trauma, not Kubler-Ross's five stages, hollow lies, she became a medium, but of what, of silence, the mouth open in scream, paint dripping like blood or glaze melting down sides. Hughes says "any trauma makes you think of worse trauma: it sets the mind worrying and fantasizing about what else might be in store…what Goya had been through in his sudden illness was not a fantasy, but it was a mystery" 137.

You hear Hughes on Goya speaking from experience. Purify my heart, make it as gold, my soul does magnify my Savior. But if Hughes has been to the bed he has not been to barn where they keep the mad 'gabbling opaquely like one of Swift's Yahoos, 139, no lessons there from the Zaragoza Madhouse, 1812, (140) the Interior of a Prison, Manicomio o Casa de locos. Neither comprehends what means one quarter of Caprichos concerning witches, feeble talk of satire, infant mortality, disease, poor nutrition, "only one son Javier survived beyond childhood", 153. Child snatchers, kidnappers, Elizabeth Smart. Goya can't explain it either. The ad in Diario de Mardrid 1799 about foibles and follies of ignorance, satire 181 has no more understanding than I of my neighbor.

After Hawthorne nothing can be understood, unless you posit all ecclesiastical, social government leadership are witches, hidden though, not bald like she with the gold pentagram on her door, never actually seen, moved finally by her father and mother in their 60′s, she of Wiccan clergy with a car sticker, who sat finally on the grass and watched them load. This today passes as normal. The neighbors then came and cut her lawn. The roof was falling in. The previous owner was a religion prof who died in the middle of talking. Outside the gates in Revelations 18 and beyond, where such habitat is landscape, the communal trash barrels are filled. Each pickup the can people and rag people patrol to find what they can from the barrels, but when the witch dismounted, and the portents cleaned, there were three rag pickers dead unconscious around the barrel from the smell. There were black flies at 6 AM.

I used another can that day, one with clean trash. You probably think this symbolic but it fact, as much fact as that a set of the 80 prints went for one ounce of gold, and 27 of 300 sets sold over four years. As said, John Ruskin burned his. Who can blame him: 52, Lo que puede un sastre, a giant, arms frighteningly raised in clerical cloth, women kneeling before, 79, Nadie nos ha visto friars gorging "unleashed cannibal orality" 195. "The old men of the Church actually eat their flock." Desolation donkey satire 37-42, must be a parable of higher education, donkeys riding students, 42, Tu que no puedes, "the donkeys are the rich, whose burden the poor carry" so say the Obama team. How many trips to Denver has he made in this lifetime anyway? Goya thought clergy were brujos, now it is politicos, dark seminarians. I guess you don't read those sites. Linda maestra, 68. 23 Aug 2012

Goya was buried in Bordeaux at the cemetery of the Chartreuse in 1828. He was reburied in Madrid in 1901, then in 1929 re-reburied under the floor of Santa Maria de la Florida, missing his skull, since found enshrined near Einstein's. Not. The point is resurrection, the raising of the dead man in The Miracle of St. Anthony of Padua, 1798, 211, I mean in the landscape itself. These colors the white, blues, browns are not the colors of death, so when I see them in the Black Paintings, the Fight with Cudgels, Procession of the Holy Office, Cabezas de paisaje, for example, they attract health, life, (and are all colors duplicated ceramically!) suggesting more than just images of death transpire, which with the overpainting of The Dog looking up at the overpainted woman in a dress, and possibly a man's head, reaching up an arm in Peregrinacion (only seen in magnification), the subtext can be more than overpainting, which Goya did a lot of. Resurrection, reburying is a kind of overpainting, like in a way his repetition of poses (275).

There is more underpainting in Pilgrimage of San Isidro, in "an open view of a river reflcting a three-span bridge… Saturn eating his son, there are traces of a dancing figure with one foot raised…funeral overtones at the beginning [of Leocadia Weiss as a widow leaning on a tomb] was simply a a woman leaning on a mantelpiece." 375f.

As court painter to three Spanish kings Goya brings the Bourbon empire into relief, like celebrating presidents and hobnobbing with celebrities, strictly a pop art endeavor, producing little of the passion we seek. Maybe the "murders, kidnappings, rapes, intrigues, adulteries, deceptions, cannibalism" 216 denoting lawlessness are escapes from having to do tapestries. Goya was lucky to live in such lawlessness and that it also appealed to his macabre instincts, but that IS the essence of pop, like it or not. So the fall of the Bourbons is like a bandit poem, Bandit Stripping a Woman, Bandits Attack III, Cannibals Beholding, 220f, good TV but way more real in its prurience. Hughes offers Marat Sade, but knows nothing of the comprachicos. It is not possible for the top of society to comprehend the bottom, unless of course it is the bottom, a la Cathy O'Brien. As Hughes says, "nobody had painted such scenes before" 223, not that it did anybody any good, they all thought it was them other guys not

themselves. Cannibalism in the Caprichos, impaled bodies in Desastres, pop art at its finest. The Horror, the horror, Poe, Conrad, who you like? "Gentility, mercy, and a sense of justice toward others are, if not false masks or lies, then certainly the product of consideration: which is to say, artifice.' 224 They for sure are to thems as live in their hat, as Goya would know since the corrupt cabinet minister Godoy "became the most consistent and enthusiastic client Goya had in the first decade of the 19th century." 240. See Manuel Godoy, Duke of Alcudia, "Prince of the Peace," 1801. That's how you get money, but nothing beside
The Dead Turkey, 258. Was Godoy what they said he was. He proposed the far future plans of Johann Pestalozzi in Madrid whose pupils,"when he paid them a visit, would chant in unison:" 232

> Viva, viva, viva
> Nuestro protector,
> De la infancia padre,
> De lat patria honor,
> Y del instituto
> Noble creador.

("Viva, viva, viva, our protector, father of our childhood, honor of the countgry, and noble creator of our institute") which with a few names change could have been chanted in Babylon, Rome and Washington D.C.

Napoleon fought Spain for six years from 1808, producing Goya's etchings Los desastres de la guerra, The Disasters of War, which together with his Inquisition Album are way over the line of perception, need independent study. See though Lux et tenebris, 1812 and allegory of the Constitution of 1812. Goya is as prophetic as Blake against empire, but more bloody by far, Blake without the spiritual side of vision, but with the outrage of the blood. Not one of the Disasters of War were issued in Goya's lifetime (273). The title page reads, Tristes presentimientos. These are all such astonishing and detailed things that come with calling Goya the last master. A little like Van Gogh's extensive drawings they must impact his later painting, but are left behind for the broad stroke that portray the ruin massively not linearly, almost not figurative. I guess we want to escape them so bad we can say they're not paintings and take flight that way. They are etchings, but just look at This Isn't the Least, of Disasters 67 or even more Might She Revive (303). Hughes says the Disasters portray "a pessimism so vast and desolating that can fairly be called Shakespearean" 302, but really folks, Shakespeare in this can be called Goyaean, "the greatest anti-war manifesto in the history of art" 304. It should be taught in high school. That would do it, The Third of May, 1808 (1814), "he kneels before the firing squad, but not in a posture of submission. it is more like devotion" 314, it is an act of charism, he is praising God as the bullets fly. Will they never fire as long as his hands are raised? Ask Moses. Hughes discussion of this is excellent, 314f.

The only difference between A Process of Flagellants 1814 and the later Black Paintings is the smaller brush strokes and detail, on a panel, the same with the Inquisition scene of 1816. These horrors with the Disasters of War, the thief scenes, the Caprichos Hughes happily calls "carceral torments" 339. in this case "human consciousness beset by forces of chaos, secrecy, anonymity" 340, all of which would be taken for encouragements by those wars advertised but not yet come of apocalypse, human hybrids and robots. Hughes describes Goya at 72 in his Self-Portrait, 1815, "his forehead is like a cannonball," 343. The last of these would be his Suenos or Dreams and Proverbios (Proverbs) of unbelievable power of this "grotesque and pathetic group…Goya talking about himself" 368.

In 1814 Ferando VII, Goya's third king sought to stamp out all liberal French sympathizers from the mind of the populacho. This ditty was sung:
Vivan las cadenas, Viva la opresion; *Viva el rey Fernando, Muera la Nacion!*
(Long live our chains, long live oppression; long live King Fernando, death to the Nation!) Hughes 325f. 5 September 2012

When events track a line they point a trend. Too good to be true, societal shaking events, 9/11 enabling the terrorist movement, Hurricane Sandy enabling the re-election of Obama, The murder of children enabling disarmerment.

Consumed by appetite. Usually we say appetite consumed, but when the self spends its resources to gain the whim of the moment, and all its resources are gone, then appetite consumes. Undated paper Found while cleaning on top of scanner. 2 women, mother /daughter naked in a limo with bed. 17 Dec 2012 19 December 2012

The Name

It would be like introducing German words into the French language, for the French pride them purity of language, that introduction of Celtic, words into the original pure Latin, but these are only analogues of our story of the vulgate that occurred when myth was introduced into science, but that is not our story either, because these are all analogues to the introduction into the human genome of animal, plant and, yes it is a making of hybrids we shall say. Our fiction requires us to believe that once upon a time, at the very beginning of time, a fictional war began between the ancient origins of man and some forces opposed to him, his enemy. It was the intent of these forces to corrupt his culture, his mind, his thought, his very being into some thing foreign to his birth. The ultimate skirmish of this was at the last his genome. These forces were known as the gods.There are no literary works written in vulgar, a hybrid of the streets of the Roman empire. 23 December 2012

Animation is a form of animism, anime pretending that a car is a girl or Disney studios, inhabiting the machine with a personality, preparation for what future event AI event. Animism says the tree has a spirit is a spirit a kind of person. Anime says that of a train. 31 December 2012

2013

Having finished *Road Notes* and reread to some extent its precursors, seeking a voice to tell a story against a background of love of the lyric I admit I learned little, absorbed less, except maybe the daring, of Kyd's Geronimo, Marlow, Donne, euphuisms, Spenser, intrigues, Raleigh, in ferment with absurd asides into the Grammars, the Schoolmaster, the propagandists, Martin Marprelate, Henry Peachum and maybe this is CS Lewis but more from Bill Ingram, the Faerie Queene and the Bible, the earlier religious history of England, the Testaments, Knox, Tyndale, the Puritans in Prison, the Coverdale versions, the bishops at bowls. Shakespeare not really at the center of it as much as could be wished, but more the propaganda of the extreme image in the Bower of Bliss or Cervantes, absurdity ending in the lyricism, complaint and wrestling of Donne against death and Milton's Lost Paradise, Traherene's songs of wheat. I still care as deeply and as fully about whatever caused this as then, more so, more, more, with others like Blake and Wordsworth and Yeats and the list goes ever on.

Rhine Gold Giants

The message of the words is conveyed in tones, voice, all sounds, music, not in the words. The depth of meaning has been severed. In the imagination of Sarah Weddington the baby died, followed by that baby'[s still alive in there because it's only in her imagination, the irony is severed. There is no irony, wit or nuance, ther is only sensationalism to evoke feelings. These are then rhetorically directed. There is no individual thought. "A world where nearly everything that passes for art is tinny and commercial and often, in addition, hollow and academic (*Moral Fiction*, 5)

Black rotting teeth down to the roots, 85% of rural El Salvador from Coke, Pepsi, Fritos in the last 30 years. Mothers are powerless against the corporate forces of addiction in commercials that destroy their children.

Bob Dylan condemned the practice, saying: "You listen to these modern records, they're atrocious, they have sound all over them. There's no definition of nothing, no vocal, no nothing, just like— static." Loudness War, Brick Wall.

The Rhine gold giants of children's books, who balloon up caps and warm canyons with fluffy heads, are clouds till beanstalks shoot out of their beds.
Giants mistake their work, that those who feed them should be their food. Tidy up bibs when they throw up, and after a hot meal clean up stuff is where the company of little dogs comes in, kept by the giants, but consumed at times like candy bits. PupPots, they are called, but the more they eat the bigger giants get and breed more.

PupPots aim to make the giants seen, but this reduces sanitation. Distracted from the cleanup of stumps and littered dens PupPots can't say what's not and at the same time clean up what is. Do giants want to appear or not? PupPots follow their imprints to the stalk where they chant the not, and squirm in its direction.

PupPots catch giants in a net like wind, but giant Cephalites are only visible from craters on the moon. Whenever there's a hole PupPots cast a crater impact of those slumps. O cognentis solipsis, if you have seen them all! You might think nothing's there, but PupPots sound the metaverse, they soar the sonar void and verse of how it breeds, what eats. This amazes only if you know.   Rhine Gold Giants and trained PupPots produce those hydrocephalic obesities on farms of readers in towns, who force their chickens and cows as we do herds, pasture feedlot libraries, slaughterhouse universities. The mind is after all the flesh the monoploid eats. As they say on buildings, "Read the Mind." Disciplines and schools of Industry enlarge the dole. Eight billion today, eleven billion tomorrow, giants multiply and need more herds. Measuring population by the feed bowl first we plead for better crops. The food base grows too slow. Giants from other planets have been assigned. There's a need to colonize. At least that's the line. No food is greater than this need.

Archeology, Biology, philosophy of myth. Beowulf's theory of Cain and the shadowlands may be better told than Enoch behind these myths where every media event is staged for effect. Actors perform their lines for limelight and the illusion of power, because people "listen" when they speak, play commit every worst imagined deed and then wail when does for real. Suppose this venture models souls? It is not necessary to be brutal. Outside the media babies are being born and men and women are marrying. People are digging gardens, talking to neighbors about the weather and the street. The stars at night and the sun during the day are not overcome. Life defeats death.

Bread

    5 Jan 13

We were telling Christmas Eve of Morning Star trip and Reading Flann Obrien's Third Policeman Ch. 3, his walk on the road, his soul's offering names, reminds me of the high pitched songs that came down from the mountain that foggy morning that burned off. But the meditation of Judah's wound last night and the compress, the poultice of the healing blood placed upon his blood is my rescue. It connects to all the organs, the code of the whole in each cell.

Russian Futurists Natalia Goncharova Alexei Kruchenykh Penn Sound Readings in Russian and English Steve McCaffery Christian Bok, Grain Boundaries 8 Jan 2013 The bread projected on the screen was a loaf of Safeway bread, mass produced, puffed, tasteless so even the symbols are gone, for this is the bread of death. If water is acid and bread poison, wine must be fire, not blood and air toxic in earth. All the children came forward with a surprise in a bag, a bow, of which the preacher said, holding it up and drawing the string at the ceiling, if God breaks his promise we can shoot him in the heart with this bow!

Prufrock Tapes

I woke up somewhere off Terra del Fuego swimming in ultra clear water where I saw 2 large brown donkeys or horses walking on the bottom and swimming up. Listened to 1984 tape of precursors to 20th cent lit, 1984 World Lit II class. Had dreamed of the Wuantum Theory of J. Alfred Prufrock the night before, listened to both. Today Tao Lin loaded to FB a tape of McKenna, The World Could be Anything, 1990 which is an mp3 essentially, with just a photo mounted as video. http://www.youtube.com/watch?v=vksUEeMh-G0

But The Experiment at Petaluma is a tweated, solarized video
http://www.youtube.com/watch?v=VXXG3w6LHrQ

(William Moloney) Chromozoid-http://www.chromazoid.com/ .

Poets, physicists, artist prophets. Negative transformation. What before why. Time-space, tea and chitchat. Weather and sports. Michaelangelo, cowards. Who are they? No yes no yes. Steady state? Universal body. Sleep, dream time, age, water. Image of evening. Indeterminate connections. Parable of the quantum. Copenhagen theory. Objectivity-world exists independently of our observation? Observer-created reality. Indeterminate reality occurs only under observation. Wwaking up to indeterminate reality and events. CPR. Suspicious details. Hugh Kenner's "zone of consciousness." Caesar's atoms. Vague congruity.

   Precursors of the modern investigation of consciousness. Ovid. Transformations. Rimbaud. Expansion by disorder. Mystics, drugs, the candle)turn to a bug). Visionaries, mental shackles, Rimbaud's statement. Kafka and the reader. Wh a bug? Conscious production of madness in the artist-soul made monsterous (want some larvae?) digressions. Vision quest. Huysmans. Sense Banquet, altered states, Bug consciousness a primitivism? Lilly and dolphins, not ET. Star Trek inside. Ordering themind, rule. Debauch. Side 2 Medical diagnoisis of Gregor: when, why symptoms, how? Primitive doctors, buffalo. Myth to reality— a dream? Ego disorder, bugs, indeterminate reality, special relativity, new worlds (throws a bug from a bag!) 5.   Tape 2 Bug Bromides for the bug-man. How Gregor sees himself-observor created reality, ego projection. Bugish thoghts. Forearm fur muff (1524) But cry. Angels into men/ Habitual virtue. Angel unaware. The inner man. Bug ET (1551) The man-bug. Apple in bug. Tree roaches. Bugs or mammals? Hinduismin Germany, holy cow. Down's syndrome. Keats. Shame an Kafka. Man/god dualism. What is human? Conscience-what are we? Duality. Psalm 8. Man's fall. Memory wars. Adam perfected or restored? Man-animal dualism. Primitive identity. Have animals sinned? Teisitic evolution (Crow caws!) Memories. Consequences of Gregor's death. Contradiction of surviving. Scuttling. Kafka and theuncoonsciousness. Body bags. Memories and new dreams.Happy ending. Incomplete? Kafka and family. Business and money. Higher and lower mind dualism. Dream self-waking self. Divided self. Fetal unity. Birth. A vast underground system of psychs who have been doing the bidding of CIA for decades. 29 Jan 2013

Screenplay

I had a dream a few nights ago to put this up, as ridiculous a reason for doing it at all after thirty years as any. Why is Prufrock enjoyable? It's about nothing after all. Chuckles from the audience caught that, but then a desire to polish it occurred, and my son a sound tech, I teased him, "it's like retribution from my children for never teaching after that." The thing went back to Keats to explore nature lost, Ode to Autumn, forward again to the quantum and Kafka, back to Wordsworth's Ode, forward to Sartre's No Exit. There is no video or pic of the classroom. A retake is to be made and uploaded. I'm afraid there will be may be ten tapes in all.
           Precursors of the Modern Investigation of Consciousness-Kafka 43.41
Precursors of the modern investigation of consciousness. Ovid. Transformations. Rimbaud. Expansion by disorder. Mystics, drugs, the candle (turn to a bug). Visionaries, mental shackles, Rimbaud's statement. Kafka and the reader. What's a bug? Conscious production of madness in the artist-soul made monstrous (want some larvae?) digressions. Vision quest. Huysmans. Sense Banquet, altered states, Bug consciousness a primitivism? Lilly and dolphins, not ET. Star Trek inside. Ordering the mind, rule. Debauch. Mann, Transposed Heads

Julie Taymor Pope Benedict XVI calls for a New World Order This is a complete itinerary of now The Pope is the Antichrist! & a freemason!

Suspicions occurred on first search of Constantine not from his own work but from all the detractiosn and mockeries that came up first. It was like a validation of a sort. Further search produced these specific details which in no way validates them but they have a unique place in the universe since no one else seems to have said them.

Chris Constantine JFK ritual suicide, pulls open his shirt, Holy Spirit filled testimony for Jesus Christ Beasts, men-angels, Hercules, Alexander… Tares. This on a site that mocks Constantine, Encyclopedia Dramatica…KHC switched on 9/10 08,
Japan quake 9/11. Hex means six. The flying disc and the pyramid. Winged disc, horned disc, Damian Hurst, Golden Calf, mark of the beast, Free Mason the gherkin building Ururu bolivia hat Sun discs. Somebody choreographs these elaborate performances, but who?

-UFO Hats Let's do the time warp again -beyonce choreography worship of appolloyon-- Beyonce put a ring on ithttp://www.whale.to/c/beyonce_satanic.html – dance comprised of the 666 --greek letter sigma, one upper, two lower case versions, Greek s, or DC LX VI Obsenity Code Beatles. Bukaka-Beatles CUM together right now over me?, Bukakke" "In this song, Lennon extolled the joy of simultaneous orgasm, urging listeners to "come together". He added the "over me" line after Yoko introduced him to a Japanese style of pornography called bukkake." Zoloft, Milton, WV Bambi Muse is a cute literary corporation built on the core principles of goth babies, bukakke babies, boy bunnies, and black anne franks. Bambie Muse discriminates constantly and doesn't believe in equality. Seth Oelbaum at HTML -Kata dance patterns of worship- -GREEN DAY pop group. Ox cries of a group whore. O cries of a group whole.

Listen at 2:52 as they sing HAO repeatedly while the crowd throw up the horned hand sign and other hand signs HAO is Apollon (written in Greek it is XAO which break up as follows: X is a Roman IO pronounced EO, EO is Greek for SUN, Apollyon is the Pagan sun god and also "AO" which means Saint or Holy in Greek - HAO (XAO) cryptography break is: AO X = Holy IO and was also used by the satanist Aleister Crowley who preached HAO as meaning "Do as thou will"The Green Day band and the Pagans in the audience by singing HAO are singing "Holy IO" and "Do as thou will". Isaiah 5:20 to 5:21 Anagram search engine Mihaly Csikszentmihalyi, and in research conducted by Arthur J. Marr (In the Zone: A Biobehavioral Theory of the Flow Experience)
When the early church departed from Christ and imbibed pagan errors she became Babylon, International Sabbath School Quarterly, feb 29, 1896   Womb of Semiramis Ancient temple designed as womb

 B. Braven
Alternating between reading the American ed. of B. Traven's Treasure of the Sierra Madre while waiting for a copy of the British, the true first and only authentic (Knopf's editors added some 70 more pages) and cutting the uncut edges of Yeats Early Poems and Stories, 1925, so to read, today I received Garbanzo Volume Two of Seraphemera Books in

the mail, hand printed and bound, with appearances of Futhark (54) and Dream Song (111). The mail man had to knock. He had two Garbanzos, an archival reprint of Igra v adu A Game in Hell and, hot dog, the 2012 annual of the Pennsylvania German Society The Heart of the Taufschein: Fraktur and the Pivotal Role of Berks County, Pennsylvania by the Earnests.

It is comforting to realize the purpose of the century was to set up singularity, break down boundaries in order to initiate earth into its new order. So we are not the causes of world pollution, disease, famine, destruction we are being held accountable for. The modern a long time preparing, so relax as we find out who we are. There are no control groups to measure global pandemics. We'd not have proved the harm of tobacco without them however, people who didn't smoke. In the midst of experiments that change the course of human existence these tapes are a kind of control group of what we thought then. We knew it was coming but now it is here. Reconstruct by contrast what we were then to know now what we are.

February 2013 theorists of hybridity as Bruno Latour and Donna Haraway, who have questioned the epistemological foundations of the modern scientific enterprise The Hybrid Age is the preparation for the apotheosis of the Singularity— a Singularity-lite of sorts. (Ayesha Khanna serves as a faculty adviser to Singularity University. Allan Bloom's admonition in The Closing of the American Mind that Walkman headphones lead to parricide. Feb 2013

The only thing different is I took a bath in frankincense last evening after working on the Prufrock tape of Investigations of Consciousness, a lit course at Bishop College, tape recorded. I hadn't taught since, instead raised a family, coached tennis on the junior circuits, drew in the desert, took trips to the wilderness. Couldn't get a job at ASU, MCCC or GC. These tapes are all that's left. Of course they'd not be displayed without second son's doing and editing, so there is some payback for 30 years lost at something I was good at. It's the old question if the figure is made of paper but the paper is cut away, or the figure is made of clay but the clay is cut away the pot becomes a sculpture, but in making of paper and of clay, pretends to be three D. So in teaching if the teaching is cut away what is the taught? 7 February 2013

I was in the middle of this war last night in my sleep. Forces were raging over my citation of the proposition that to them gave he the power to become the sons of God. I was reciting this New Testament psalm as if it were Psalm 1 of the Old when these forces surrounded me, which I cannot now say exactly what they were. Hard to fight against phantoms, but who has not felt these in the wee of night? Let us say the antagonisms were great spirits and I was defending against their attacks, but not happily or really successfully until right in the middle of the psalm saying, right in the middle of the ebb and flow of forces I said the name, Jesus. In an instant it all stopped and there was such a palpable peace that my son's chow, staying overnight as a guest, came and lay beside my bed, there was such peace as I have not felt in sleep for many years, there was such stillness and peace that I plan to carry it through the day.

Traven's Sierra Madre, the British ed. This UK edition was translated by Basil Creighton from the 1927 German text. The 1935 US edition was rewritten in English by

Traven himself and is about 100 pages longer. Traven himself preferred the Creighton translation. First U.S. edition. Traven's most famous novel and his second book published in America. This edition was prepared from Traven's English-language manuscript, but supposedly was heavily rewritten by Knopf's editorial staff. The basis of the John Huston directed film classic starring Humphrey Bogart and Walter Huston. According to the Hollywood legend, writer/director John Huston negotiated the film rights in a seedy Mexican hotel with the author's "representative," one Hal Croves, who stayed on the set as an advisor and vanished when filming was completed. Huston later confirmed his suspicion that Croves was actually the mysterious and reclusive author, about whom little is known with certainty to this day. The mysterious and elusive author sent his agent Hal Croves to assist with the filming. Subsequently it turned out that Croves was Traven himself.

POP. Jonathan Gray- 1.The images of eating pop: Pop will eat itself
"THE POP WILL EAT HIMSELF" BY MASSIMO GIACON-
pop as a modern pagan deity. "Initially, the characters of the ceramic Superego collection were not designed as ceramic construction, but as sick toys. The "sickness" of toys is given by corruption and human suffering. Massimo, with his objects, wants to represent the negative influence which is directly expressed in his works. The characters of his ceramics collection are like modern martyrs who wonder what happened and why things are so bad nowadays. The pop objects have shining colors and terrifying expressions." Massimo Giacon is a protagonist in the change of Italian cartoon bubbles. From Design Design Blog

Scott Musgrove is a painter / sculptor / illustrator, a prominent exponent of American pop surrealism, but I prefer to introduce him as the Honorary President of National Institute for Creative Zoology. He seeks and finds traces of never existed animals in the obscure zones of the consumer society, in the crevices of shopping centers, under the overpasses of the highways, in the cracks in the asphalt of huge American parkings. He brings to light evidence of the existence and extinction of strange animals, as the famous Hairy Brook Trout or of the Equine Elliptical, not to mention the Booted Glamour Cat. If the poor Hairy Trout probably disappeared for its delicious organoleptic qualities, Glamour Cat was hunted to extinction for it's wonderful neck fur, appreciated especially as a male accessory.

Without Scott Musgrove these fantastic animals would not be even classified, as a result of conservative zoologists attitude, unwilling to surrealist digressions.
We, at Superego, self-appointed honorary member of that Institute, and we edited a ceramic from one of Scott's paintings, the Glamour Cat, which, although extinct, we thought deserved a special place in the homes of our collectors. To do justice and give scientific importance to the operation, we offer it in a gold enamel finish, very bling bling, a bit flashy but rightly appropriate to an animal so glamorous and maybe even a little cocky. You can find it on Designdesign.it.

Zetatalk.
Life in a DUMB is a little constrained. They want to manage us as well as possible. It is the ultimate prison nirvana. Two mile high piles of eyes. Great Lakes empty into the Gulf. Shackled boxcars, Portland's Al Bielek sent to a future Albion

In 2009, the controversial "Web Bot," an internet software that predicts future events by tracking keywords on the internet describing an emergence of "planetary-level surveillance while at the same time whistleblowers call for disclosure of the public of life on Mars and and teleportation technology. What they call the Pegasus project. Let that gash on mars in the Hubble Telescope do your thinking for you.

I mumble enough to stand up. What about C/2012 S1 (ISON), which is coming November 2013, brighter then a full moon, can be seen in the day. This is coming around the sun, and will be seen with the naked eye. It sure seems like NASA is getting people ready to see this extra sun looking object in the sky. The article from astronomy now says, "peak brightness in late November it will remain visible without optical aid until mid-January 2014." The article said they just found this last Sept. 2012,

I was standing out side the dub gates arms and legs tossed, bound, gagged wondering if life were worth this much to be kept underground and released later into the nw hell. All because of a poem. I wrote in 1969 which put me on the radar but what greally got me in was the tapes my son broadcast from twenty years later. Yes it was an entrance to a cave. cursed to survive the millennium and the tribulation.

I was reading when they came. Do you want to go with us to be saved from the end of the world. No. But they don't take no for an answer. So I'm bound and gagged. My neighbors left behind and I'm to lecture in the humanities program at Dumbpra live. If they can get me to talk. So when all the species are pulverized by rock, but I'm numb to that. The real question is whether to tell any body ahead of the event since it is foregone it can do them no good. Instead I go over my notes for the first class. You're here because you've been captured. Pop will eat itself, himself, your self and all. Pop a doddle do. I had told them they didn't need me, that the tapes would do, the hundreds of hours of lit rebroadcast from the previous century. But no they said they wanted contemporary criticism! [the reason why this was so hard to get was, and they didn't wanbt the the loonies they had created by imitation in the UG, was because all the patterning copied from the 20th century Beastles etc only made zombies and they wanted a century or teaching to preserve the human soul, see Arthur Cristian image patterning. The whole purpose of contemp culture was to prevent awareness that the wipeout was coming. Bly distraction in entertainment, etc.). I was not up for a slate at the big Dumbo, the Denver Airport, the ivy boys were there. The paradigm of mindlessness to dull the senses to miss the event must be replace with mindfulness and courage in order to come out of the bunkers in a hundred years.

Jon Rappoport and Darpa
Visual cryptography, ufo taking off from pyramid, linking Nephilim giants, great Britain, nibiur 2012 olympics, Niburu part 9 The Spear of Destiny by Trevor Ravenscroft
"The Superman [Satan] is living amongst us now! He is here!" exclaimed Hitler triumphantly. "Isn't that enough for you? I have seen the New Man. He is intrepid and cruel. I was afraid of him." Tyche / DEEHee=luck NASA companion to the sun
The Greek gods are Nephilim NASA Reveal Planet X is Real Again
Planet X Earth Poleshift wheel Planet X, realign 17 Feb 2013

"Richard Sauder, Hidden in Plain Sight, Oct 2011 By Dr. Richard Sauder theintelhub.com (Part 4 in our exclusive underground base series published with permission from the author and publisher) You can read Part 1, "Nazi Engineers, Secret U.S. Military Bases, and Elevators To The Subterranean and Submarine Depths" (Part 1) "power structures on this planet that closely interface with, and yet remain separate from, the official power establishment of any nation as publicly presented… salt mines around 2000 feet below the surface, I have been in the Diamond Crystal Salt Mine in Detroit with around 1000 miles plus of underground tunneling. It is very large. The White Pine Copper Mine in Upper Michigan has over 10,000 miles of under ground tunneling. The 25 Salt Peter Mines by Hobbs New Mexico all are over 800 miles of under ground tunneling in the mainstream news media. You can read Part 2, "Where Are All the Deep Underground Military Bases?" (Part 2) You can read Part 3, "Letters From the Underground Mail Bag: Subterranean Labyrinths, Underground Bases, and Hollowed Out Norwegian Mountains" (Part 3) See Intel Hub, by same author: "And in a very brief summary at the conclusion of his most informative book, Mr. [Jason]Goodwin briefly mentions the elevators "that are never mentioned but are needed to service the extensive infrastructures that make the cities run – the power plants, refineries, factories, and underground facilities (my emphasis)."

-consensual reality of everyday life

-

Russ Miller says: April 17, 2012 at 11:34 pm Re: Underground military bases. While working for a congressman in Washington, DC, in 1982, I would travel the underground subway system connecting House offices to the U.S. Capitol. One day, with extra time, I got off with a small crowd I was not connected with and followed them through a door. Instead of following them, I stopped at an elevator, got in and pushed a down button. The door opened and I was seven levels below the Capitol. (The subways – there are two - operate seperatly at the second and third (or fourth) levels, if I remember right) I followed hallways with doors. Went down stairways, into caverns with no markings, except coded markings. I wandered around, perhaps more than 10 to 14 levels below the capitol. As I went deeper, the walls went from stone to just cave-like, carved out rock passages. Down there were stored artifacts of some nature – statuettes, for example. I was lost. I was stuck there for hours wandering until I found stairways leading up. None of them connected from one floor to the other. Kept walking. Eventually finding stone walls. Up I go until finding an elevator. Pushed the up button and found myself in a non-public area of the Capitol. But I had my clearance tag. And when asked by security, just told them I was lost. They escorted me into one of the main hallways. I know I made it 10-14 levels below the Capitol (passages slope up and down). I wandered underground for four hours, unseen, as far as I know. Tunnels to at least 13 underground bases being sealed off Preparing For Massive Civil War, Re-Education Camps

"So rule number one of mass extinction survival is to find an underground or underwater city, stock it with food, and wait for about a decade before poking your head out. There are at least 200 underground cities in Turkey, built between 500-1000 AD by Christians hoping to evade persecution during the Byzantine era. One of the biggest of these, Derinkuyu, could hold up to 35,000 people plus food storage and wine-making facilities. These ancient cities might be the best hope for the future in a mass extinction event." -"future society threatened with extinction might choose to store thousands of people in cryosleep deep underground"

-"Here are some takeaway lessons from our crash course in mass extinction survival: 1. Burrow underground or build an underwater city to shield you from the elements. If we can't hibernate for a few centuries, we're only going to survive a mass extinction by moving into modern versions of the Turkish city Derinkuyu. We'll need massive underground complexes - perhaps like the huge underground mall in Montreal - where we can grow food and produce our own energy. We'll need air shafts with purification systems built in, and perhaps even a way to make oxygen. But most of all, we need to be prepared. Let's start building our underwater cities and subterranean farms now, before it's too late. And hope they don't turn out like the infamous science fictional cities of Ember and Rapture. Second American revolution underground.

Marfa base north of the city. Phil Schneider used to work for the government and was involved in the construction of Deep Underground Military Bases (DUMB bases). In talks given in 1995, he said that there were 129 active deep military bases in America and two more under construction, He confirmed (at that ime) that there existed a minimum of two underground bases in each state. Phil also mentioned that there were more than 1,450 DUMB bases worldwide. Ken Adachi

"We normally locate underground bases by the smog fields that they produce above ground. This happens because nuclear generators produce dense deadly orgone radiation (DOR) which forms smog by positivecharged ionization. Smog is nothing but filth in colloidal suspension in the atmosphere. The various colors of smog are determined by what kind of filth is available" Don Croft

Who gets to go to these UG bases. After the Govt athoritiess and their functionaries and the military come the illuminate and kings and dqueens and the super rich, but also included is a large sample of the gene pool previously screened. Truly for brood purposes only these , mainly women will be used to cultivate the new race of earth UG. Will there be any men at all? Will there be an society, culture? It is in doubt simply from the way these functionaries think, but in case they are more knowing, even if fueled by Stanford faculty, a human culture must be seen a prerequisite for human growth, as necessary as food, clothing, shelter, literature, music, art, as well as competition. Thus it would seem men would have to be included. Whether these gene pool men and women raise their own children…whether they are encouraged in creative free thought…

No dogs or pets, In order to get along these people will be permanently drugged, as if the model ofr the planners were 1984 and Brave New World, they will live out of their heads, emotions and bodies being controlled and if they survive and are let out again will be the diametric opposite of any proletarians who survive who will have little or no technology but fully developed skill sets and psyches of survival. Maye I can be an emmiissary to these two groups outside the walls who think they will form separately the new humanity, They can join forces to see what good that will do them. 1984 and deep underground secret bases

Underground Anomalous Constructions Dulce Base, New Mexico Functions: Alien interface, Research of mind related functions.Levels: 1-7 Known

y Level 1 - garage for STREET MAINTENANCE.y Level 2 - garage for TRAINS, SHUTTLES, TUNNEL BORINg MACHINES, AND DISC MAINTENANCE.

y Level 3 - everyone is weighed, in thE nude, then given a jump suit uniform. The weight of the person is put on a computer I.D. card each day. change in over three pounds requires a physical exam and X-ray.

y Level 4 - Human research in the Occult areas - Auras - mental telepathy - hypnosis - astral traveling - etc. The technology is apparently here to allow them to know how to manipulate the Bioplasmic Body (of Man). In other works they can remove the ¶soul¶ of the human and turn it into a vessel to be used by another entity, in order to allow it to work and operate in the physical realm.. They can lower your heartbeat with Deep Sleep ¶Delta Waves,¶ induce a static shock, then reprogram, Via a Brain- Computer link. They can introduce data and programmed reactions into your Mind y Level 5 - Alien housing is on level 5. "...The room circular for the (electro- magnetic) generator is nearly 200 feet diameter and covers the fifth and sixth levels (extreme west south wing). There (are) five entrances (plus an escape trap door on the sixth floor) on each floor. Each portal has double door. The security is severe. Armed guards patrol constantly, and in addition to weight sensitive areas there (are) hand print and eye print stations. Here, is the device that powers the transfer of atoms.

y Level 6 - Level 6 is privately called ¶Nightmare Hall¶. It holds the genetic labs. Experiments done on fish, seals, birds, and mice that are vastly altered from their original, forms. There are multi- armed and multi-legged humans and several cages (and vats) of humanoid bat-like creatures up to 7-feet tall. Aliens have taught the humans a lot about genetics, things both useful and dangerous.

y Level 7 - Humans in cages here, usually drugged or dazed, sometimes crying out for help. LEVEL #7 is the worst. Row after row of 1,000¶s of humans & human-mixture remains in cold storage. Here too are embryos of humanoids in various stages of development. Also, many human children¶s¶ remains in storage vats. Who are (were) these people?"

y Below Level 7 - Unknown other levels unexplored by humans. Aliens here. Exits into a vast underground cavern series, unexplored by humans, but suspected to be a huge alien culture area. Some of you might ask what the "space shuttle" is"shuttling". Large ingots of special metals that are milled in space and cannot be produced on the surface of the earth. They need the near vacuum of outer space to produce them. From Phil Schneider's May 1995 Lecture Mount Perdido, Mt. Inyangani, Mount Hayes, Mount Ziel, This is what happens to the dirt:

The United States Atomic Energy Commission and the United States Energy Research and Development Administration took out Patents in the 1970s for nuclear subterrenes. The first patent, in 1972 went to the U.S. Atomic Energy Commission. The nuclear subterrene has an advantage over mechanical TBMs in that it produces no muck that must be disposed of by conveyors, trains, trucks, etc. This greatly simplifies tunneling. If nuclear subterrenes actually

exist (and I do not know if they do) their presence, and the tunnels they make, could be very hard to detect, for the simple reason that there would not be the tell-tale muck piles or tailings dumps that are associated with the conventional tunneling activities.
The 1972 patent makes this clear. It states:

"... (D)ebris may be disposed of as melted rock both as a lining for the hole and as a dispersal in cracks produced in the surrounding rock. The rock-melting drill is of a shape and is propelled under sufficient pressure to produce and extend cracks in solid rock radially around the bore by means of hydrostatic pressure developed in the molten rock ahead of the advancing rock drill penetrator. All melt not used in glass-lining the bore is forced into the cracks where it freezes and remains ... (U.S. Patent No. 3,693,731 dated Sept. 26, 1972)

"... Such a (vitreous) lining eliminates, in most cases, the expensive and cumbersome problem of debris elimination and at the same time achieves the advantage of a casing type of bore hole liner."
(U.S. Patent No. 3,693,731 dated Sept. 26, 1972)

There you have it: a tunneling machine that creates no muck, and leaves a smooth, vitreous (glassy) tunnel lining behind. A tunneling machine for producing large tunnels in soft rock or wet, clayey, unconsolidated or bouldery earth by simultaneously detaching the tunnel core by thermal melting a boundary kerf into the tunnel face and forming a supporting excavation wall liner by deflecting the molten materials against the excavation walls to provide, when solidified, a continuous wall supporting liner, and detaching the tunnel face circumscribed by the kerf with powered mechanical earth detachment means and in which the heat required for melting the kerf and liner material is provided by a compact nuclear reactor. This is a $13 million tunnel boring machine (TBM) used for tunneling at the Nevada Test Site. (Remember that Area 51 is part of the test site.) Many other types of TBMs are used by many government agencies, including the 'nuclear powered TBM' [NTBM] that melts solid rock and leaves behind glass-like walls. Project Camelot
Portal Exchange Programs: secret exchange program of twelve US military personnel to Serpo, a planet of Zeta Reticuli, between the years 1965-78
http://www.serpo.org/update_falcon.php
"Construction work continued for several years on large underground facilities which are rumoured to extend some twelve levels below the base. Long tunnels are laid out in a pattern similar to the spokes of a wheel and extend several miles from the center of the base.' Pine Gap Australia
Alien involvement in Australia is similar to that of the USA, Europe and Russia. For some technological rewards and minor co-operation in other areas the ET's conduct their own genetic experimentation and the exploitation of the country is generally totally unhindered by humans. They have a free hand to do what they want as there is no way of stopping them…There are indications that the technical help provided by the two initial contact groups brought about a tremendous leap forward in technology and made the development of SDI a real possibility. In return for our governments giving the groups a free hand to exploit the planet and human race, and as far as possible keep their presence a secret, they would

provide the technical know how to prevent further major wars and stop any other interested extraterrestrials from invading the planet. It has been said with some authority that they are the brains behind SDI the extension of which is the HAARP (High Frequency Active Aural Research Programme) system which is aimed at creating an electromagnetic shield around the world to prevent an attack from outer space. This development never had anything to do with the threat from Soviet Russia, in fact the Russians have actively co-operated in the development programme since it's inception. Power by nuclear sub reactor

Fort Worth explosions 1984-there are some differences, there is an outside, a sun, if colorless, but no sign Big Brother is Watching You because the eye is always watching you and nobody has to watch it because algorithms of computers sift all the data by programmed parameters. There are cameras to spot the general, there are microchips for the particular. BP, heart rate, brain all monitored for normality. So what are Thought Police in 1984 are much more. "It was even conceivable that they watched everybody all the time" 3 means et tu. Turning your back to the screen means nothing to internal monitor. Of course the Pyramid of Truth must be introverted, stretching 300 levels below surface and Newspeak might not be needed because microwave brain manipulation, reading thoughts by satellite was the rule. There is some reason to believe no people were needed at all. "In 2002, the anthropologist John H. Moore estimated that a population of 150–180 would allow normal reproduction for 60 to 80 generations — equivalent to 2000 years." Space colonization. With in vitriol fertilization and sperm banks sexual reproduction seemed superfluous. Bodies would only be needed to perform menial tasks. Indeed less and less reason to store anything but token populations became more and more appealing of gov science., and there was no other kind. The eggheads who run it denigrate such thinking as dystopian, but we would all be prisoners. Squads with trank darts would patrol random quadrants prior to the Event, to store natives at random, as prisoners, or guinea pigs as needed, the rest be left to melt into stone and dust. Of course there is a selective service draft program based on gene records kept by gov't of the best and brightest. These were not hard to get hold of or convince to go with their keepers. They considered if a compliment. An infrastructure was put in place to train these from all the faculties, but the programmer foresaw the need to pattern breakers, iconoclasts who however by the nature the beast would not go, so these had to be tranked as well. Literally nothing can be said to the govt or its ministries below. It is presumed you will obey and if not there are levels below where you can be made to. Do not think either of due process or dissidence, except in the class room, for the directorate is divide on whether to allow, foster this in the classes to provoke thought, but these are opposed by agencies of control. Sethreal "The Report Concerning the Cave Heavens and Lands of Happiness in Famous Mountains," by Tu Kuang-t'ing, who lived from 850 to 933 A.D. Arizona Tunnels and Caves

GRAND CANYON - Cave[s] near the confluence of the Colorado and Little Colorado rivers. Hopi legends say that their ancestors once lived underground with a friendly race of "ant people" [not to be confused with the sinister "mantis" people described by several abductees], but some of their kind turned to sorcery and made an alliance with lizard or serpent men known as the "two hearts", which dwelt in still deeper caverns below. The "flood" of evil and violence forced the peaceful Hopi's to the surface world. An explorer named G. E. Kincaid claimed to have found "one of" the ancient caves, in which were reportedly discovered Oriental, Egyptian & Central American type artifacts. Smithsonian archaeologists S. A. Jordan and associates also explored the man-made cavern with hundreds of rooms, enough to hold over 50 thousand people. The underground city is about 42 miles up river from El Tovar Crystal Canyon and Crystal Creek, and about 2000 feet above the river bed on the east wall. John Rhodes after 3 years of field research reportedly discovered the Grand Canyon city, which is now being used as a museum for elitist groups and has lower levels that are being used by "super secret black book operatives", which can only be entered via a stainless steel door at the bottom of a stairwell deep within the "city" that is "guarded by a very lonely soldier staring into the darkness... dressed in a white jumpsuit and armed only with an M16 assault rifle to ward off his imagination." source: ARIZONA GAZETTE, March 12, 1909 & April 5, 1909; Robert Morning Sky; John Rhodes 20 Feb 2013 May 15, 2012

21 February 2013 The UG cities if known, proportional entrance by the canons of diversity would be white as the ace of spades, meaning that genocide by default of all the ethnic and racial strains of the U>S>. This secret coup detat allows it to happen. While society goes its merry way with the many entertainment sources serving up the many religions, foods, diversions. So yes there is ethnic cleansing underground. That leaves the English, again. All this deduced from the secret existence of a minimal 129 DUMBs in the U.S. and some 1500 world wide. Who populates those other entities is not clear. Australia's are operated by the U.S.

    John Lear, Grudge 13 does Abductions http://www.greatdreams.com/John-Lear.htm
SDI-wormwood
    Interview w Art Bell: get Osama out of Afghanistan because Osama - as bad as he was - was shutting down all the heroin poppy fields and was causing a disastrous monetary loss to the illegal drug industry
    That was just up to 1972 - up until 1972, there was 572 people eliminated from the program because they disagreed wtih the way it was going, but after 1972, they don't kill them anymore. What they do - I don't know! I have my suspicions - of what they do! A - Why do you imagine ...
    J - Don't bring that into the argument ...
Project Disclosure. Here are the web links that John Lear provided in support of his data:
vgl.org rumormillnews.com keith laney.com astrosurf.com
Entire Grudge 13 report was written as if report was geared toward preparation of defenses During the late 60's or early 70's, MJ-12 representing the U. S. Government made a deal with those creatures called EBE's (extra-terrestrial biological entities, named by Detlev Bronk, original MJ-12 member and 6th president of Johns Hopkins University). The "deal" was that in exchange for "technology" that they would provide to us we agreed to "ignore" the abductions that were going on and suppress information on the cattle mutilations. The EBE's assured MJ-12 that the abductions (usually lasting about 2 hours) were merely the ongoing monitoring of developing civilizations.
    In fact, the purposes for the abductions turned out to be:

Insertion of a 3 mm spherical device through the nasal cavity of the abductee into the brain. The device is used for the biological monitoring, tracking and control of the abductee. Implementation of a post hypnotic suggestion to carry out a specific activity during a specific time period, the actuation of which will occur within the next 2 to 5 years. Termination of some people so that they could function as living sources for biological material and substances. Termination of individuals who represent a threat to the continuation of their activity. Effect genetic engineering experiments.

Impregnation of human females and early termination of pregnancies to procure the crossbred infant between 1979 and 1983 became increasingly obvious to MJ-12 that things were not going as planned. It became known that many more people (in the thousands) were being abducted than were listed on the official abduction lists. In addition it became obvious that some, not all, but some of the nation's missing children had been used for secretions and other parts required by the aliens.

According to some, there was an altercation between the U. S. military and the aliens at the Dulce laboratory. A special armed forces unit was called in to try and free a number of our people trapped in the facility who had become aware of what was really going on. According to one source 66 of the soldiers were killed in the effort and our people were not freed.

By 1983 MJ-12 must have been in stark terror at the mistake they had made in dealing with the EBE's. They had subtly influenced, through Dr. Hynek, (formerly with the Blue Book project, who had allegedly broken ties with the Air Force in the late 60's but who in reality continued to be their informant in his cover capacity of Director of the Center for UFO Studies) "Close Encounters of the Third Kind" and "E.T." (now admitted by some members of MJ-12 to have been a "drastic mistake") to get the public used to "odd looking" aliens that were compassionate, benevolent and very much our "space brothers". MJ-12 had, in effect, "sold" the EBE's to the public, and were now faced with the fact that quite the opposite was true. In addition, a plan had been formulated in 1968 to make the public aware of the existence of aliens on earth over the next 20 years to be culminated with several documentaries to be released during the 1985-1987 period of time. The EBE's Extraterrestrial Biological Entity claim to have created Christ - which in view of the "Grand Deception" could be on effort to disrupt traditional values for undetermined reasons. [reasons are clear, Cf. Constantine…Greys. They are definitely cybernetic organisms . They are not a "species" themselves. They work for someone else.

Bill English dictated 2 audio cassettes outlining what he remembered from the Grudge 13 report. These audio cassettes were transcribed into hand written notes by another person. The Information contained therein

Indicated what had been suspected all along: that the U.S. Government was Involved In the greatest deception In the history of mankind and that not only did flying saucers exist, but that the government had several in secret storage and had captured at least 3 live aliens.

In Box, diplomatic pouch under lock and key system. Lock had been opened, pouch was easily accessed. Standard diplomatic couriers pouch marked American Embassy Couriers, contained pouch serial number JL327Delta. Inside a publication with red tape which indicated code red security precautions and an Air Force disposition form. Disposition form was standard white page copy, title was 'Analysis Report'.

Further down was 'Analyze enclosed report under code red measures, give abstract breakdown and report on validity. Observe all code red measures. Analysis required immediately'. Underneath were a series of dashes then the letters NDF then another series of dashes. Below that, lower left hand corner were the initials WGB.

Publication was withdrawn from pouch. It measured approximately 8" by 11" with gray cover. Heavily bound, paper back style similar to technical manuals. Across the center front It read, "Grudge/Blue Book Report No. 13". It was dated 1953-(1963). In the lower right hand corner was AFSN 2246-3. In upper left hand corner was the word 'annotated'. Across the front upper right hand corner to lower left hand corner was red tape indicating code red security measures.

YY-II Los Alamos John Lear
Element 116 Uuh Ununhexium-http://www.webelements.com/livermorium/
surely it were better to go to a fema camp then UG quantum technology at underground bases

A Principle of Recognition. It is possible to recognize forms when they are show to us: Beyonce's dance by Chris Constantine o JFk's assignation to DUMBs of the Quantum advance of science by analogies, Miller's analogies, so there are many that don't have a complement. Compare a dog's nose and wall socket, in architecture Bilbao Guggenheim and a whale, or the Vatican obelisk and the Washington monument capitol o The Ishtar gate and Obama's Denver Acceptance, Rihanna getting high with diamonds in the sky. The principle is recognized with two or more figures interact to form a match, like the target zero of auto lock It can work by similarity or opposite, Hawthorne and Poe

- Re: Rihanna's MK Ultra programming type
We now refer to it as MK Ultra because of the name of the experiments which sought to create a scientific methodology out of it. In essence, they are a series of spells. Therefore, Marilyn is not the first Mk Ultra'd escort. I'd say the Canaanite women who sold sex to support the temple are some of the first documented examples of what we now see as MK Ultra Sex Slave programming. That's thousands of years ago. 10-18-2012, 03:07 AM   #106 (permalink) Nana Peazant February 2013

From Chemtrails to Pseudo-Life: The Dark Agenda of Synthetic Biology
Exposing the Matrix, Carlee Janey
ExoVaticana, Tom Horn, L.U.C.I.F.E.R. at Mt Graham, U of Arizona. Honeycomb mirror, Vatican Advance Technology Telescope, of the Max Plank Institute (Nazi arm of Mengele) Fr. Paul Gabor developing collaborations of Lucifer with U of A. NASA and Lucifer at Vatican Observatory looking at Nibiru and Nemesis. Job 26 11-13 destruction of Rehab from which God drove the fugitive snake. Watching it from Mt. Graham. Malachi Martin said this. *Petras Romanus*

David Flynn Collection

Raider's News Update top Vatican Astronomer Guy Consolmagno stated how contemporary societies may soon "look to The Aliens to be the Saviours of humankind." http://www.raidersnewsupdate.com/vaticana2.htm "Did the Vatican's top astronomer actually mean to use the story of the Nephilim from the Bible as an example of the kind of "space saviors" man could soon look to for salvation? This incredible assertion is only topped by what he says next. In quoting John 10:16, which says, "And other sheep I have, which are not of this fold: them also I must bring, and they shall hear my voice; and there shall be one fold, and one shepherd," Consolmago writes: "Perhaps it's not so far-fetched to see the Second Person of the Trinity, the Word, Who was present "In the beginning" (John 1: l), coming to lay down His life and take it up again (John 10: 18) not only as the Son of Man but also as a Child of other races?" Do Vatican scholars actually believe Jesus might have been the Star-Child of an alien race? [This is a Raelean belief]

Dr. Christopher Corbally, Vice Director for the Vatican Observatory Research Group on Mt. Graham until 2012, who believes our image of God will have to change if disclosure of alien life is soon revealed by scientists (including the need to evolve from the concept of an "anthropocentric" God into a "broader entity"), Vatican Observatory director, Father Josè Funes who has gone equally far, suggesting that alien life not only exists in the universe and is "our brother" but will, when manifested, confirm the "true" faith of Christianity and the dominion of Rome.

Monsignor Corrado Balducci—an exorcist, theologian and member of the Vatican Curia (governing body at Rome) and friend of the Pope—who went perhaps furthest, appearing on Italian national television numerous times to state that ETs were not only possible but already interacting with Earth and that the Vatican's leaders were aware of it…"I always wish to be the spokesman for these star peoples who also are part of God's glory, Writing for Newsweek on Thursday, May 15, 2008, in the article "The Vatican and Little Green Men," Sharon Begley noted… Consolmagno's job included reconciling "the wildest reaches of science fiction with the flint-eyed dogma of the Holy See" and that his latest mental meander was about "the Jesus Seed," described as "a brain-warping theory which speculates that, perhaps, every planet that harbours intelligent, self-aware life may also have had a Christ walk across its methane seas, just as Jesus did here on Earth in Galilee. The salvation of the Betelguesians may have happened simultaneously with the salvation of the Earthlings." [i] [ii][xi]This sounds like a sanctified version of panspermia.

Father Funes, titled, "The Extraterrestrial is My Brother."… "If other intelligent beings exist, it is not said that they would have need of redemption. They could remain in full friendship with their Creator." [iii] [iv][xii] extraterrestrial species may exist that is morally superior to men—closer to God than we fallen humans are— and that, as a consequence, they may come here to evangelize us.

Father Giuseppe Tanzella-Nitti—an Opus Dei theologian of the Pontifical University of the Holy Cross in Rome—explains…spiritual aliens," as every believer in God would, he argues, greet an extraterrestrial civilization as an extraordinary experience and would be inclined to respect the alien and to recognize the common origin of our different species as originating from the same Creator.

Vatican Observatory vice director, Christopher Corbally, in his article "What if There Were Other Inhabited Worlds"… While Christ is the First and the Last Word (the Alpha and the Omega) spoken to humanity, he is not necessarily the only word spoke to the universe… For, the Word spoken to us does not seem to exclude an equivalent "Word" spoken to aliens. They, too, could have had their "Logos-event". Whatever that event might have been, it does not have to be a repeated death-and-resurrection, if we allow God more imagination than some religious thinkers seem to have had. For God, as omnipotent, is not restricted to one form of language, the human. [v] [vi][xvii]

Father Domenico Grasso not only thought such beings would be "far ahead of us in science and related fields," [vii] [viii][ix] but that their version of salvation might be based on a savior other than Jesus…even a messianic member of their own race.

World Trade Center

"Sandy Hook was on a far larger scale than the past year's numerous slaughters, including the Wisconsin Sikh temple shooting and the Batman theater shooting in Colorado. It also included glaringly illogical exercises and pronouncements by authorities alongside remarkably unusual evidentiary fissures indistinguishable by an American political imagination cultivated to believe that the corporate, government and military's sophisticated system of organized crime is largely confined to Hollywood-style storylines while really existing malfeasance and crises are without exception returned to normalcy." Memory Hole, The Sandy Hook Massacre, James Tracy. The Dual State, Carl Schmitt 10 January 2013

11 a.m. to noon Central (9-10 Pacific) on NoLiesRadio.org (then archived here a few hours after broadcast). Guest: Eric Wilson, senior lecturer of public international law at Monash University, Melbourne, Australia, and editor of the brand-new scholarly book The Dual State: Parapolitics, Carl Schmitt and the National Security
Complex, as well as Government of the Shadows: Parapolitics and Criminal Sovereignty (Pluto Press, 2009). Eric Wilson argues that nazi philosopher Carl Schmitt (who spawned neocon guru Leo Strauss) got some things right, and some wrong...but that a serious consideration of his ideas can help us understand why the "liberal" mainstream is so blind to the reality of such phenomena as the deeply questionable events of 9/11, Operation Gladio, the JFK assassination, and so on.-Eric Wilson argues that nazi philosopher Carl Schmitt (who spawned neocon guru Leo Strauss) got some things right, and some wrong...but that a serious consideration of his ideas can help us understand why the "liberal" mainstream is so blind to the reality of such phenomena as the deeply questionable events of 9/11, Operation Gladio, the JFK assassination, and so on.

-Add Eric Wilson's books to the growing list of scholarly pro-9/11-truth books published by respected academic presses, alongside those of Peter Dale Scott (University of California Press), Paul Zarembka (Elsevier, Europe's leading scholarly publisher), Anthony Hall (McGill), Four Arrows (University of California Press), and American Behavioral Scientist. If we add the many dozens of pro-truth articles issued by scholarly publishers,

-Most of the best evidence challenging the official story appeared in ten highly documented books by Dr. David Ray Griffin, who had taught philosophy of religion, with a heavy focus on the relation between religion and science, for 35 years. His books, videotaped lectures, and online essays are available on a website.

Published scientific literature includes:
- a paper reporting the presence of nanothermite in the dust from the destruction of the World Trade Center;[9]
- six papers in the February 2010 American Behavioral Scientist, indexed by 67 databases, and published as a whole issue on State Crimes Against Democracy, with 9/11 used as a primary example;[10]
- an article in The Environmentalist, "Environmental Anomalies at the World Trade Center: Evidence for Energetic Materials;"[11]
- a paper, "Extremely High Temperatures during the World Trade Center Destruction;"[12]
- a science article countering popular myths about the WTC collapses;[13]
- 59 peer-reviewed papers on the physics of 9/11 events, published since 2006 in the Journal of 9/11 Studies, and 67 letters between members of the academic community;[14]
- 9 scholarly papers published as a compendium in 2006 by Elsevier Science Press, suggesting US complicity in a false flag operation.[15] The Hidden History of 9-11-2001 was never reviewed in the mainstream press. Other resources include Morgan and Henshall's 9/11 Revealed [16] and Flight 93 Revealed;[17] two books by

Prof. Michel Chossudovsky, America's War on Terrorism,[18] and War and Globalisation: The Truth Behind September 11;[19] and the Complete 9/11 Timeline investigative project.[20] Tuesday, November 27th, 2013

Tracking
The switching stations that filter cell phone and email talk in SA do tis with a similar code used in dating medieval deeds. Algorithms of Lexican, syntactic, frequency of words of undated ms. is compared to dated and the machine ids the undated. Some such code must be used to ferret out the unsilent talk. The silent talk we leave to another venue. -computer-automated statistical methods
-patterns in the distribution of words occurring once, twice, three times and so on.
-maximum prevalence technique. This is a statistical technique that gives a most probable date by comparing the set of words in the document with the distribution in the training set

Gelila Tilahun and colleagues at the University of Toronto. A team of British researchers has developed an algorithm that uses tracking data on people's phones to predict where they'll be in 24 hours. The average error: just 20 meters. That's far more accurate than past studies that have tried to predict people's movements. Studies have shown that most people follow fairly consistent patterns over time, but traditional prediction algorithms have no way of accounting for breaks in the routine. The researchers solved that problem by combining tracking data from individual participants' phones with tracking data from their friends—i.e., other people in their mobile phonebooks. By looking at how an individual's movements correlate with those of people they know, the team's algorithm is able to guess when she might be headed, say, downtown for a show on a Sunday afternoon rather than staying uptown for lunch as usual. Here Stingray, cell phone tracker An Opte Project visualization of routing paths through a portion of the Internet. 28 January 2013

2014

Our children were raised without television until the youngest was about 10, 1998. It sounds like what everyone wants, to build from the inside out, not from the outside in. So they were read to constantly and told stories, many taped, some produced into coloring books and handed out to their friends. They were breast fed, sung to, taken on walks, hikes, esp. to Grand Canyon and the AZ wilderness, driven constantly into the desert and mountains of central AZ as I went sketching, played outside constantly. We canned, gardened, froze fruit, they played in the flood, imagined cities and peoples in the sand pile. We lived in a house in the desert that had only evap cooling, polished concrete floors, made from pumice block, surrounded by pecans, apricots, pomegranates. Not only that but they were raised without moving, except after ten years to another house on the canal. They experienced the same schools, neighborhoods, churches, all attempts at community, youth sports of most kinds, regular evening meals together. All of them learned to cook and enjoy it. They all played music, all can sheet read. Notes: These days health is available at extra expense, to what was assumed a lifetime ago. Corn is GMO. Milk to compromise gender. You may have to give up McDonald's to afford Organic milk. 12/31/14

Daniel and John

Work up wondering the time line from David through the mostly reprobate kings to Jeremiah and the 70 years captivity so went to Young's Old Testament Introduction. Turned however to Daniel and the two languages, Aramaic and Hebrew as well as other textual issues, which however led again to Nebuchadnezzar's 7 years of madness and Babylonian records of it or not. Critics especially concerned with the accuracy of Daniels's prophecy of the end of empire in last chapters had supposed, from Porphory and on, that this was written later, during Macabee times and interpolated together with early chapters that represented the first account. However the Dead Sea scrolls, eight of them, textualize Daniel, this about 167 BC, hence conclusively doubting that if written as a best seller in the immediate preceding years it is not likely they were chronicled in the Scrolls along with old classical elements of Exodus etc. This is compared to the Rylands ms codex of John c. 117, the oldest surviving NT ms. Before the Scrolls the oldest Daniel fragments were from 1000Ad. "The oldest manuscript of Daniel by far is 4QDanc, which Cross dated in 1961 to the "late second century BC" (Cross 1961:43). Scholars who support a date for the writing of the book of Daniel in the Maccabean crisis at about the middle of the second century BC will be able to say that 4QDanc is "only a half century later than the composition of the book of Daniel" (Ulrich 1987:17). This means for supporters of this dating that the manuscript evidence for Daniel is as close to the autograph as the Rylands Papyrus is to the Gospel of John. I quote: "It is thus, for the Hebrew Bible, comparable to the Rylands manuscript of the Johannine Gospel for the New Testament" (Ulrich 1989:3). The latter comparison means that the papyrus fragment of the Gospel of John, published in 1935, that is, Rylands 457, which was dated in the first half of the second century AD, effectively refuted claims of scholars who had attempted to date the Gospel of John to the latter part of the second century AD. The Rylands papyrus was within 25 to 50 years of the writing of the Gospel of John. Amazing.

If you drive across the United States do not take physical reality as the nation. The nation is the social political entity of Rome and Britain. Neither take the people as the nation. They are the same as people in the Ukraine and Bolivia. When you meet them. Learned Swallowtails love rue to lay eggs. This year two crops of chrysalis on rue, the second now preparing for takeoff. To drive a thousand miles across AZ, NM and TX is to know what the rest of the country cannot, the smell of creosote as a morning draught, the continued changed light and shadow, flats in flood or salt, the little towns, the roughnecks, the flue metal grasshoppers and burrs stuck in your socks, the railroad cars, rest stops filled at night on both sides with trucks, but the Wal-Mart is a horror filled with more horribly obese old and young male and female misshapes. Just back from trip begin a week a go at 6 am Oct 21 with A. Drove to Ft Stockton, stayed at Motel 6, the only choice. Full of creosote smell, well diggers, roughnecks. Ruth said she grew up on ranch Poppy rented owned by his father Edwin August, 1500 acres and that August had other larger tracts as well, that he was a kind of landed gentry. We twice walked down the Rio Grande, first after walking miles over the desert from Glenn Springs and climbing down the canyon into it, the water then was shallowish and after some miles we hitched a ride with some rafts that went by. The second time was the clay mud water through Mariscal Ca10/30/1410/31/14 nyon after a wet season with mudholes and tanks and sinks, all the way down.

A group of Ravens can have three different names depending on the activity of the group, a murder of crows, an unkindness, a conspiracy, a constable: A constable of ravens refers historically to the group of ravens that congregated around the Tower of London; they were thought to be 'keeping watch' over the monarchy. Therefore, any time a grouping of these birds seems to be watching or guarding something, the group can be referred as a 'constable.' They can also be called an unkindness or a conspiracy - likely for similar reasons. If a flock is driving off other predatory or carrion birds, or 'picking on' another species either because it is competition or prey (although they feed largely on already dead animals, they are known to work together to hunt if need be since they are extremely adaptive birds), then these are apt terms. There is a folktale that crows will gather and decide the capital fate of another crow. an ostentation of peacocks, a parliament of owls, a knot offrogs, and a skulk of foxes. Crows recognize human faces. Comments: http://www.pbs.org/wnet/nature/episodes/a-murder-ofcrows/crow-facts/5965/ The state of America-that-was in what is now known as the Republic. 19 Aug 2014

Taxi Driver with its rain soaked windshields of night color is too long on motive but succeeds because the assassin hero only is a hero by failure, or accident and it cycles to its beginning at the end but not pretentiously, the opening is a cloud of exhaust. *Pulp Fiction* is its equal because of this ironic humor where the holdup guy is held up and has to buy the life of his adversary in the restaurant, also because of the irrelevancies of the conversations on tipping, etc. But *Apocalypse Now* is marred by the lack of this irony and accident, too heavily, religiously plotted around "the horror" of Conrad. Read in concert with Collateral Damage: convoys, checkpoints, raids, detentions, hearts and minds. How many faceless masks can you name of the international, military, American goon, now he has come home: convoys, checkpoints, raids, detentions, hearts and minds. 20 Aug 2014

The creative process is incessant work till it becomes meaningless, then take a break, then revisit. This repeats many times. It's not unlike the process of ceramic. Working through the laminations which develop their own techniques, stains, oxides, confected clays, organic patterns created with prickly pear spines, cholla, etc. then wrapping them to a form, or finding some figure therein over the next days, it's the same in writing, but longer, decades not days, though here is only about a specific year and a half specifically touching the general concerns of another site, Human Botany At the End of Biologic Civilization (and more sites). Never however making these for production, advancing motifs seem like they have more space, but there is no idea mostly of the piece before beginning. Excerpts of Severed appeared last year at Red Fez, Dream People, Camel Saloon, Eyeshot, Antipodean SF, Frigg and etc, but mostly to compose live, in danger, on blog, to almost hear the cries, or in hundreds of versions that went up and came down at Scribd, specifically, Building Transhuman Immortals arrived after ThoughtGoattens, to which a revised addition of the name included Gilgamesh, and in explaining this Severed began. I actually gave a copy of that first, printed out in booklet, to the interim pastor of the Reformed church. Scared me to death. Figured he would want to know.

    To follow the creative ceramic there is a listening into the prose which suggests sound changes eventually conceptualizing some narrative. Other pieces are composed that way too, but Severed has more of a given narrative that science provides. AS to why any of these things were done it can only be said they were there in the sound and the moments of work when heard and put down as best as possible. I expect it to be viewed as a version of the unthinkable from Gilgamesh, Milton, Goya, Yeats, all resonance and reference layer on layer, subject matter unsuited for bald words, but wrapped in a hundred vids like Nick Cave and a thousand celebrations of dark borders I'm not looking for. The vid of Red Right Hand is not so good-addled fueled by fear of YHVH and anger lyrics, part Milton, part pusher, pimp, soiled industrialist mortician. People take
Cave's lyric and background it with their illuminate paranoias here, same images mostly as in General Gemineye, Bohemian Rap City Shabazz the Disciple, levels of pop, rap rock, vid that get a lot of play outside lit. It's not a closed affair.

    I contemplate different sizes and type faces in the layout, partly achieved in a recent Jingle Bell Wok, but this needs collaboration with the company, so to speak, to bring it off. I don't like the fact that the narrator of Severed seems to be a Thought Bot.

    These are not rational propositions. It has spun off a fictional treatise on distortion architecture, starchitectures, Ishtars, all because of what Gilgamesh says to Ishtar when he defames her. Would you believe the Akkadian? Pretty sure this is more than ever anybody would want to know. Maybe this is a draft, considered so, for by the time you respond who knows what changes it will have seen in the lit of decapitations.

    Had the misfortune of reading an interview where at the end…had something like 10 days to get the window. In order to protect against unfounded assumptions I am sending this along to fit in the 30 Dec window. It must be the ms. you have dreaded getting all your life. You want to dignify this with an aesthetic. Explosions. Gasolines. Do it outside, preferably in the country. Take some gas and light it. But save the matches. This is the myth. The science is coming in Part II-II. Everything about Road Notes is unthinkable so its aesthetic must be data base. What that means is so…let's not say, but do. I'm sending this along in its present state since it seems like the old hinderances of time have retired and we enter a period of new space.

Add to that the power surge that torched the computers today and turning all records electronic, now done, but keeping a kind of parallel system withal, and now training and switch of all records to notepads. 11 Mar 2014,

Celebrating the Forms of the Formless

Edwardo Galeano: "I frequently receive invitations to attend the burial of capitalism. We know quite well, however, that this system -- which privatizes its profits but kindly socializes its losses and, as if that weren't enough, tries to convince us that that is philanthropy -- will live more than seven lives. To a great degree, capitalism feeds off the discrediting of its alternatives. The word socialism, for example, has been emptied of meaning, by the bureaucracy that used it in the name of the people and by the social democracy that in its name modernized capitalism's look. We know that this capitalist system is managing quite well to survive the catastrophes that it unleashes. We don't know, on the other hand, how many lives its main victim -- the planet we inhabit, squeezed to the last drop -- will be able to live. Where will we move, when the planet is left without water, without land, without air? The company Lunar International is already selling plots of land on the moon. At the end of 2008, the Russian multimillionaire Roman Abramovich made a gift of a little plot to his fiancée."

The greatest danger lies in the possibility that the computer can program us, just like the automobile drives us. With frightening ease, we become instruments of our instruments.

I don't make myself write. In Santiago, Cuba, an old drummer, who played like the gods, taught me: "I play" -- he told me -- "when my hand itches."

The books write me, they grow inside me, and every night I fall asleep thanking them, because they allow me to believe that I am the author. And having said this I will point out to you that I write each page many times, that I scratch out, I suppress, I re-write, I tear up, I start over again, and all that is part of the great happiness of feeling that what I say is similar to, and sometimes very similar to, what my pages want to say." Irenaeus: "Gloria enim Dei vivens homo." 24 April 14

· and continuing, "For the glory of God is a living man; and the life of man in beholding God." Therefore the Son of the Father declares [Him] from the beginning, inasmuch as He was with the Father from the beginning, who did also show to the human race prophetic visions, and diversities of gifts, and His own ministrations, and the glory of the Father, in regular order and connection, at the fitting time for the benefit [of mankind]. For where there is a regular succession, there is also fixedness; and where fixedness, there suitability to the period; and where suitability, there also utility. And for this reason did the Word become the dispenser of the paternal grace for the benefit of men, for whom He made such great dispensations, revealing God indeed to men, but presenting man to God, and preserving at the same time the invisibility of the Father, lest man should at any time become a despiser of God, and that he should always possess something towards which he might advance; but, on the other hand, revealing God to men through many dispensations, lest man, falling away from God altogether, should cease to exist. For the glory of God is a living man; and the life of man consists in beholding God. For if the manifestation of God which is made by means of the creation, affords life to all living in the earth, much more does that revelation of the Father which comes through the Word, give life to those who see God. June 7, 2014 at 9:23am

Dreams are the halo of the understanding world. This nimbus surrounds all that is known life is intent on understanding itself, show furniture, pottery, Chinese civilization, the wilds of the Balkans, live animal life and plants, the faces of children, the heroism of suffering, the fight of the spirit, the joy of health, make something out of nothing, celebrating the forms of the formless, sensing the leading of thought, seeing the good and pursuing it, sweeping the curbs in the street, caring for all neighbors, taking seriously the cry of all beings in distress, prayer without ceasing, cleaning and all menial tasks, parabolas, lovemaking. There is civilization and there are the forms of the formless, every plant, animal, every insect, plant, tree, cave, stream, mountain free of the inebriation of destruction, that which seeks to destroy the forms of the formless where instead of being guardians of the forms of everything there is ruination. In the midst of this dreams open up to consciousness. Night vision enters the substrate, which is love, love unseen, breath praise, gratitude for being, each gasp, each cry, each pain a prayer, when the wind is still and when giving birth, birth. History, geography, being, knowing, the thaw of nothing into the world of forms so that nothing is not nothing, so negatives are a positive, hence Something. It is the formless. So how long have you been doing this. Since eternity I was celebrating the forms of the formless that emerge in thought, hands, brains, plans trades. Figures of something then, elephants of being that wave their trunks like cyclone funnels from the ground up to their capacious heads, ears waving the trumpet of their being calls. This is a something, a little one. All little somethings gather at night in the plain to wait the coming of the one. They are a community then and there is a community then and there of bird, plant, beast, star, the same human wonder each century, decade, millennia, day, the same one pouring essence of wonder seeking knowledge until one dream comes regularly that each night the sphere forms whole where each has its place, trumpet, musician, gardener, physician, the one who writes it all, not not the politician, the one who feels the ages run down toa mudhole in the ground and sits there in wonder, poll the masses and there they sit, maybe it will rain. This community of life. Celebrating the forms of the formless. 19 Oct 2014

      What could I know of God myself? Shall I read Kant, the postmod knowabots or the antipods? When we build a berm, excavate a pit, berm builders find navel, excrete a bug. Or be an Ashkenazi and find God, affront Toyotas, royalists, cynics, half know its.

      Square one. God is a spirit. The spirit of a man is different from that of another man but it is a spirit so speak of the spirit of man.

      Confessions of fun include the religion of the Jews. No funamentalist is worth salt without devotion to Jerusalem and Torah. Life is riddled with it. It must amaze critics that these guys are still writing. Keats has finished a comic novel about the afterlife. Johnson has a taxonomy of planetary embryos.

   My life is concerned with being. Is the moon Christian?

Is money Christian? The orange trees of faith droop lower and lower. My neighbor's yard is only half green. Is his yard Christian because he is my neighbor? Did the crab grass, the burr clover pulled out by the bucket, seed the tares? Why doesn't he sweep his porch? These things are important. Theology recapitulates sociology. Was that gold necklace, the long painted fingernails, the rings on index and middle fingers, the lewd remarks, the fraud bond program, the entrapment of widows?
Who knows what lurks in the hearts of men? Funamentalists.

      Another invention in doll phones is they talk. Do you know the person on the other end is a doll? There are three tests. 1) Drivers can put a doll on their shoulder to tell them what to do, unless they think they are telling the doll, then the shoulder will drive, or 2) when the dolls are hurting they will tell how they are made, that stiffness comes from in growing. Ingrown, outgrown, when the dolls outgrow their costumes we get more new. Grandma did this for years, but not among the Two Day Bear Dolls trendy bareness, without caps! 3) The younger the doll the less she wears. And finally we issue Pol Pot dolls for left and right. On the left they make good counterpoint, used for darts or sworn at, ridiculed in place of life and on the right prayed to that those good days when things were simple and people knew their place were more fun to be alive than drink a beer and go out. Doll makers restore vitality to neighbors. This invigoration when you risk your life to get the paper, walk 10 miles for bread or crawl from collapsed buildings puts a meaning in things not found at penny slots. Penny slots is symbol for words of columnists, hosts and TV guests. Pol Pot includes all dictators. Here is a partial list. The names are changed to protect. The names will follow the dolls.

2015

Ezekiel
      A dilettante aristocrat in the cut up style of Burroughs and his data base *Nova* finds the verbal texture of Ezekiel astonishing. The language, of the open, ch. 8 and 38-9 beyond that. Spinoza was the first to doubt! He called it a pseudepigraph after the second deportation formed by a redactor from two (or more) recensions of text. Some editor maybe today of the post exilic the three hundred jars of oil of different worlds, the Maccabean age, may note in the margin incorporated into the text, that these are preludes to Burroughs cut-up trilogy that Gsion made by accident, cutting through layers of newspaper and reassembling the layers, with all repetition, of course, for redactors always reduplicate, and with uneasy transitions. Where did it really come from "the workmanship of the tabrets and the pipes, who walked up and down in the stones of fire, whose merchandise is filled with violence, the iniquity of traffick, whose blue clothes and broidered work in the promise of abundance and in the azure of pure spirituality they conceived, merchants in all sorts of things, in blue clothes, and broidered work...the ships of Tarshish were their caravans for market (Ez, 27,24-5)? This is surely attractive, except where Ezekiel calls those delivered into the hand of those dressed in blue with dyed attire on their heads, clothed most gorgeously with the lustfulness of horses in the bruising of her teats, that "they shall take away thy nose and thine ears (23.25).

So I had to buy the British *Nova Express* for the red cover with the train on it and the phrase on the cover in Spanish, Spanish express, for the French boxcar it involved.

The logic of editors consumes criticism, but when did an editor comprehend the creative to understand it? The writer of I Chronicles used old statistical lists that survived the downfall of Jerusalem and the exile. Compare the treatment of Goliath's head in Chronicles to his body in Samuel! No, these epigynous imitators cannot be creative thinkers surrounded by plebeians Novocaine for Nova Exp. When we were walking the streets of Paris in '74 riding the underground, the usual inhabitants were on summer vac so the population was more of what it may be today, N. African types, Algerians, Moroccans, Syrians, Palestinians who ogled Cleo to the point where I turned around and confronted them - what were called wild boy packs, maybe 6 or 8 seated on the subway bench as we went down the tracks who eyed me with a most shameless evil, angry and insulting, so that I knew it would not be a civilized encounter. That is Paris today for Jews who make aliyah to Israel. These latter I met in droves at Bishop in the 80's.

A wise old rat may know a lot about traps and poison but he cannot write a text book on DEATH TRAPS IN YOUR WAREHOUSE with tactics for ganging up on digs and ferrets and taking care of wise guys who stuff steel wool up their holes. It would not occur to a wise old rat to assemble the young rats and pass his knowledge along. We may forget that a written word IS AN IMAGE and that written words are images in sequence of MOVING PICTURES. Consider Doktor Kurt Unruh von Steinplatz 4 vols on Authority Sickness Burroughs, Electronic Revolution.

John Perkins: I've spent ten years myself as an executive management advisor to the World Bank and the United Nations.. to introduce the concepts of shapeshifting and tribal wisdom into the highest levels of executive thinking.

Christine Legarde 7-- you can tell I do as I'm told

French President: about the recent terror attacks in Paris. During his speech he says that "the illuminati are behind the Paris attacks".

Woman behold thy son. Son behold they mother. There isn't any memory before birth, or from the first day. A baby could be kidnapped from its home and never know differently. I'm used to disturbed dreams his time of year, but apropos of memory making identity, dreamed that Libby had a child in old age (with Jerry) which seems what it is, but did not live with it, the child being farmed out to somebody's parents. P and I kibbutz about this detail and I ask her if we knew. She says we did! Three days ago dreamed of the Buls, driving with them in water up to the fenders and headlights, I was driving, but got through OK, the road would disappear under the water. That was the first dream that night. the last was of a neighbor across the St at Willetta who wanted to live with us, then the scene shifted to Spicewood Sgs house, I told her this was not to happen. Then she said her clan had ordered 1000 dollars worth of ducklings to raise! So memory, location, time, identity all terrestrialize. If dreams can replay lives negatively and so confused, then how about dreams that celebrate victory, salvation, peace, hope!

Victor Pelevin tells the story of his character Babylon from the outside. I tell all my characters from the inside and there is maybe only one of them, myself wearing variable masks. Our gestalt he calls shared Russian ethnicity, shoes. 1/10/15

Aey found a digital remake slide machine at Phx College for the slides. Yesterday SRP arranged to take out 200 ft of Oleander and one palm every two years starting now.

Rena was telling me of the various names of EAYs business associates.

YOU Are the Blue Beam Antenna

Analyzing computer dreams, antitheses, cloud spray, hieroglyphics of the future, inhaled plasma, Palantir, sentient world simulation, sky battery-antenna, space fence, thousand year stare. CERN Ports 1/24/151/26/15

12/23/15 There is a preparation of the gospel of peace.   Amazingly the God of Peace shall soon crush Satan underneath your feet. --In Zechariah's song. "the rising sun will come to us from heaven to shine on those living in darkness and in the shadow of death, to guide our feet into the path of peace.

THE DAM

 Back two days early from fall on first day Mon from climbing up the dam with a chainsaw in one hand to hack a limb that prevented the sun from drying the wet ground. Aey's idea but mine the execution, left foot slipping produced a backward fall on left side back on a tree stump at bottom of draw, chainsaw in hand. We kept on working three days after, cutting cedar as warmup, he hauling huge rock, concrete, me troweling and designing the whole. There were two 36 inch erosions below the base held by fibrous cedar roots that we built up to join with the dam as it had been. Odd to build the base years after, which is now an apron deep and substantial, but we stopped Thursday after a dream where I said I had two broken ribs. Certainly the pain at night after working was greater each night. So we canned it early, did not visit Ruth in Hospital where she was after shattering her right femur, practically the same time I fell. Successes were the meadow filled with small blue stem. We cut it more cedar and pushed the forest back further. Aey crawled and reset the screws of the cabin ridge cap. Judah didn't go but Zion did and went everywhere with us.   --Aey abrasive every time conversation came around to the life of the mind, which he used to contribute to. On our return, he put it down to feeling crass about it in his expression but I began with G. Hartman's, Scholar's Tale, which I was reading a second time, and the romantics, which led to Little Lucy, and rocks and stones and trees, and he reciting it finally by heart and reading the other 4 stanzas aloud as we drove, then went on to Kubla Khan, asking if captions of like merit could be found for his photos which reminded me Jacob wrestling the angel and Dickinson's "bewildered gymnist," as we sought for an hour whether the angel's touch in the hollow was not at the place where the testes descend, hence a inguanal hernia, etc. effecting the life of Benjamin, the son born after. ["little Benjamin, with their ruler, the princes of Judah." Ps 68.27] These accounts rang with sound and syntax while he said he desired imaginative mental replay, like the white chickens beside the red wheelbarrow, which he interpreted while reading, but saw Little Lucy, still in her coffin, being born round earth's diurnal course, so always moving even while not. Reference to "Intimations Ode" attracted him, the child father of the man, the child primal in expression and true peeling back the layers of culture in the history of nations. Wordsworth's year in France produced his statement that it's odd the French so supported the American revolution then deconstructed their own, referenced in the Lucy poem where W. will stay on his native soil. Somehow this implicated the iambic nature of the verse and whether all the English language was thus, but not slogans, which skew the natural rhythms into artificial, but of the rhythms, he said, HE ALWAYS THOUGHT OF SHAKESPEARE AS A WALZ! This was somewhere between Las Cruces and Benson. AS A WALTZ! But when I saw the horror of a vid Sh had posted on his page of a man playing with a symbol penis I took this down.

    Dreamed then said, I have two broken ribs, could hardly get out of bed, felt separation and return of bone into place last night. Return today. Minimal work done. 12/17/15 Thurs.
12/16/15 Wed Right side dam, cut cedar meadow, fix roof cap.
12/15/15 Tuesday Mist early then burn off. repair meadow access, now full of natives, haul rock, cement, do apron and pillar left side. Kerrville for more cement.
12/14/15 Monday Fell in am from climbing up the dam to cut branch.
-- The light of your presence, rejoice in your Name, exult in your righteousness. The light of His presence is not the light of the heavens, equally defamed with man and earth by the fallen.
-- I got up to give water to Zion in the night.
--I rescued her when she went over the cliff on her chain.
--The presence is what we see by and that orders our lives. The sun, defamed in the heavens by the fallen spirit rats, is the Day star that rises in our hearts, a symbol of the one who made it, as Zechariah says, "the rising sun will come to us from heaven to shine on those living in darkness and in the shadow of death, to guide our feet into the path of peace" (Luke 1 78,9).
--Psalm 149 The children of Zion joyful in their king, sing upon their beds, high praises, swords execute vengeance to bind kings, nobles with iron, this honor have all saints. --I said Theo had marks of character in his face and beauty. Sab said, what's the difference? Beauty can be corrupted, character is not. Ps. 149 He will beautify the meek with salvation.

ORM
    James Bartley DNA is the currency of the universe, dracos, mantis, rare green grey Occult Royalty Connections. Chris Everard
    -David Hudson 1 of 12O. orbital Rearranged Monoactive Elements. Become a superconductor. At Agua Calienta spgs, black alkali, sodium sulfate, platinum group elements, lead alloy of platinum, wt changing, hydroscopic reactions -gravity is a zero point gravitational source of proton and neutron with vacuum energy transmutation agent, accelerant, filling your body with a spirit, meister field, aura non polar field ki, bottled ki, Holographic Universe encoded in negative $O = -1 + 1$. Egyptian book of dead. Whatsinisit? Manna wha tis it. Hidden manna of Rev. become a god this is the mark, hydrate of oxide of gold, gold super conducts at boy temp, body becomes a light being one with the god head to read minds light body meizer field silica alumina monotomic moma! Be like an angel CERN in a bottle, break boundaries Bi-locate transform body, garment of glory Science of the Spirit Foundation. Tempe!

    Saw many images of internet screens researching sub atomic gold seen on miles...etc. Before checking this I had the thought that increased conductivity was the last thing to desire in an environment of micro wave pollutants, etc. - the deceptive allure surrounding the use of mono atomic gold and its reputation for opening doors to other vibratory planes. the ulterior

purpose of promoting mono atomic gold is to cause the destruction of the ten additional virtual DNA strands @ educate yourself David Hudson, discovered and patented white gold. reputation for opening doors to other vibratory planes He named Ormus, to enhance Proxying, a Mind Spirit transfer, done by the 1.twinning traumas, 2. channeling, 3. telepathic communication, and 4. astral projection so that all slaves worldwide are being pulled into one single interlinked Demonic One World Mind [this is the so called 'hive mind' characteristic of the Reptilian alien groups that dominate and interbreed with the human Illuminati..Ken Adachi]. We do not understand how white gold and iridium help the body become a semi-conductor so that the body is highly psychic. see David Wolfe David Hudson.
11/28/15 Burroughs and Byron Gysim, Minutes to Go: "the hallucinated have come to tell you that yr utilities / are being shut off dreams monitored thought directed / sex is shutting down everywhere you are being sent / all words are taped agents everywhere / marking down the live ones to exterminate. "the next step is everyoneinto space..but it has been a long wait since the last tower of Babel. Back in No Time. See John Geiger's Life of Gysim:

James Merrill

Answer to why in the days of Noah the fallen watchers took women and the men did nothing about it, cooperated with them is the way Merrill delivers their message to the demented critics and award givers, two Pulitzers and a national book award. all on the elite take, quid pro, scratchem. If you need proof reincarnation is a crock consult Merrill searching past lives, Allison Luries on only level 2 but Merrill is a 5: "I was flattered when Jimmy and David offered to consult Ephraim and find out where I was in the spiritual scheme and whom I had been in my last life. It turns out that I was on a rather low level: stage two, I think. (David and Jimmy had already attained level five.") Cannella: The violent consequences implicit in Ephraim's message (judge or annoy us, and we'll kill you) were understandably unsettling to Lurie.
Bomb, Thomas Bolt. Ouija board, which consists of no more than 26 capital letters, zero, nine digits, and the words YES or NO, to be the perfect metaphor for language... --The house he lived in until he was five ("18 West 11th Street," also the title of a poem on the subject) was blown up by the Weathermen in 1970.
Vendler interview: "what a stranger might say over the telephone."
" Mirabell nonhuman voices are added, telling a complicated tale of evolutionary history, molecular biology, and subatomic behavior. Would you like to talk about the books you read before creating your phantasmagoria of "s.
Do you think the vocabulary, models, and concepts of science—cloning, DNA, carbon bonds, the ozone layer, protons, etc.—offer real new resources to poetry? cience"?
HV: The new mythology you've invented via the Ouija board—including the new God Biology, a universal past including Atlantis, Centaurs, and Angels, an afterlife which includes reincarnation—how real does it all seem to you?
HV: The intense affection that binds you to your familiar spirit Ephraim, to dead friends, and even to the inhuman Bat-Angel you talk to HV why do you suppose the Ouija board is indispensable, in terms of the workings of your imagination?

JM: (a) It would seem not. (b) You could think of the board as a delaying mechanism. It spaces out, into time and language, what might have come to a saint or a lunatic in one blinding ZAP. Considering the amount of detail and my own limitations, it must have been the most workable method. And, as I have said, it's made me think twice about the imagination. If the spirits aren't external, how astonishing the mediums become! Victor Hugo said of his voices that they were like his own mental powers multiplied by five. --- "The Book of Ephraim," a 90-page narrative poem in that volume, recounted the poet's - adventures over more than 20 years in consultation with his Ouija board. Mr. Merrill took the revelations spelled out by his familiar spirit Ephraim, a Greek Jew once in the court of Tiberius, and interwove them with his personal memories to produce an oblique but richly textured self-portrait. Placed in relation to the world beyond, the poet's temporal experience took on a sheen of timelessness. "Mirabell: Books of Number" is a sequel to "The Book of Ephraim." Twice as long, it offers a good many beauties and perplexities. --Ephraim had hinted of the existence of a superior order of spirits: "SOULS OF A FORM I NEVER SAW ON EARTH/ SOULS FROM B4 THE FLOOD... MEN B4 MANKIND." The present volume was forced on the poet by these spectral beings. Breaking into the sociable, often gossipy conversations that Mr. Merrill and his friend David Jackson had carried on for years with Ephraim, they pre-empted the board to dictate messages that the poet was instructed to communicate to the world. "3 OF YOUR YEARS MORE WE WANT WE MUST HAVE/ POEMS OF SCIENCE"-thus they announce their didactic intent. 11/27/15

--The revelations in "Mirabell" are more abstruse and wider-ranging than any of Ephraim's, which had chiefly dealt with cycles of reincarnation. The new chief instructor covers such topics as the history of Atlantis, the secrets of Stonehenge, the true meaning of black holes and of the sun worship of Akhnaton, the Bermuda Triangle, and the evolution both of human life and of the universe itself. These spectral lessons, composed in gnomic lines of 14 syllables and printed in eye-wearying small caps, are something of a chore to absorb. Mirabell has a way of doubling back and revisiting what already has been revealed, so that details slip away from a reader attempting to grasp at a few main threads.

Anatomy of influence, the great man becomes less great, gives himself a blow job not in the sexual sense, if it matters. He and alas G. Hartman, goes way out of his way to again and again make sure we know he knew, names drop constantly, as a friend! Confidante. Lover? --Frank Marshall Davis, Obama's father, Joel Gilbert

This one plane of reality that is visible is the bottom surface of a cube that extends above it.

Cybernetics   Dr Robert Duncan, expert in Cybernetics and Cyborg technologies and author of the book Soul Catcher his site: http://www.drrobertduncan.com/ Doubts on Duncan Friday, September 19, 2014 hyper game theory, probability matrixes accelerated learning hive mind instinct transferred "no defense in dreams" part human part AI-emerging minds, alien ai blended to human, new hybrid, magnetically activated nano particles to alter brain pathways, needle injected scaffolding of magnetic net into, over brain. Smart dust micro circuits act as trans liners over neurons and settle there which can be read remotely. Thinking is aural, can be listened to , spied out (as if it were spoken, but it is not), second error, Robert Duncan Confesses: "I am a perp." -published email from Robert Duncan (the original posting can be found at the link below): -"R. Duncan" <duncan@higherorder. com> wrote:

-Young Living Essential - Daniel Penoel, M.D., a student of Jean Valnet, M.D., and the first medical doctor to research and write about the medical application of essential oils. - The Black Virgin of Rocamadour, France Geoffrey Hill

Miles Johnson Karen MacDonald gold? Colon hydrotherapy of deep under bases. DIScernment. spring water rocky mountain David Wolfe vortex water: Another way is we have two different devices that will just spin the water in a vortex. So we'll put the water into a pitcher, we'll put the top on it, the top has a little paddle that spins around and it just spins the water just like if you were spinning the water in the pitcher with a spoon. You just spin it and then that will go for three minutes or so and then that vortex is the water. https://www.alivewater.com/davidwolfe releasing emotional patterns with essential oils marajuana clothing simon miles hawaiian volcanic salt.

Olin perceptron physics. Daniel brad MacBolen III Cern meltdown unacknowledged special access deep program operations cmos technology
Laptop indigo Rick Warren illuminati destroy the evangelical movement, ritual sacrifice of his son-- Darrell Hamamoto 12/7/15

The Temple

Sense of place as in Isaac sacrificed on Mt Moriah where the angel's hand was stayed at the threshing floor after David 's people vanquished the giants as Satan tempted David to number the people causing the pestilence that took 70,000, but on which spot Solomon built the temple after David, at Gad's behest, built an altar on the threshing floor, this same place important in itself and for the vows they took there, with the subsequent loss of the temple to Babylon, then to Rome, was the place of Golgotha, defining the place generally, which leaves to consider what the meaning is indeed. 11/30/15

-----When, in comparison, I see pictures of the ruined American Viscose plant at Lewistown, that I audited, there is an interest in the picture beyond itself because I was here, a memory that makes up identity. Arguettes of meteoric diamonds

R. DeRop dedication prayer at his adopted granddaughter baptism: "we pray oh Lord that you will not destroy us." This is the first prayer to Satan. But he will, that's his desire. Yahweh's desire is to rescue us, protect us, love us, and he plans to give us hope. 11/23/15. for your sake we are killed all the day long, Ps 44.22, Rom 8.36 For I am persuaded that neither day nor life, nor angels nor principalities nor powers, nor things present, nor things to come, nor eight, nor depth, nor any other created things shall be able to separate us from the love Yahweh which is in Yahshua the Messiah our Savior. Awoke about 12, heat came on got up to turn it off in middle of clouds all over earth nuclear explosions being dodged, suggestions of culverts, ditches o/w would'nt have remembered, but was it a dream or a program? 11/17/15

Not the deconstruction but the conservation of text. Cardinality is a virtue of positivity and goodness that if communicated remains like one of those foundation stones, boundary

lines left after all superstructure is gone. That is to have a personal experience of it, to feel it, to know it in specific.
A light came out today.
      Death of Nimrod, Nebuchadazzar. Death of the fallen. Kill the gibborim. David, Caleb, Moses, Joshua, Jonathan, Jasher

      Antidiabatic. PewWar. Think We're All Human, Think Again
Went to church yesterday with Christiana and sons. Justyn raised his hand. The pastor had spoken of his coming to faith at age 6.
 Undeniable Evidence Aliens Do Not Come From Other Galaxies   Komorusan http://www.angelismarriti.it/ William rutledge Apollo20. Luca Scantamburlo

      11/6/15 Storks wings and covetousness, against commercialism learned in Babylon in Zechariah, 5.9, Then I looked up--and there before me were two women, with the wind in their wings! They had wings like those of a stork, and they lifted up the basket between heaven and earth., dr. McGee (in context with against Schmetiah). Exposed) Abe Finkelstein https://www.youtube.com/watch?v=pdlke3QXMgM and David Jacobs, The Threat. Covert Catastrophe. Carrying all the sin to Babylon.

      http://the-moon.wikispaces.com/Names+of+M.Hell Maximilian Holl, one of a family of 22 children from his father's two marriages. Max changed his name to Hell, entered the Jesuits, and became director of the Vienna Observatory in 1756. As with many Jesuit scientists of the era, his curiosity was intense and wide-ranging. Among his 28 scientific publications are a study of the origins of the Sami, Finnish and Hungarian languages, an exploration of magnetic therapy, and a detailed observation of the 1769 transit of Venus. He helped to prepare an encyclopedia on the arctic regions of northern Norway, which was never published

Gas Kimishima Very typical slips (red 赤土部 [akadobe] and black) of Tamba were applied on local clay. The village called Tachikui〔立杭〕 has been located in the long valley, as Tamba〔丹波〕 pottery. So it should have been named Tachikui pottery〔立杭焼〕 instead.. (Gas)

10/31/15 Notes: voice to skull technology, plasma conduit, chuin-saturn, capacitor-solar boat sits on a cube, tetrahedron in CERN detectors, Model dependent, gate sealed after the flood, John Hutchinson (Dark
Mission), anastomosed, smallpox Ebola hybrid, Ebola + measles, Bergman, Ringmakers of Saturn. Teller light, Bikina Atoll, Oppenheim banned for dissent, Third Reich Bunkers, hide in ditches, concrete pipes along highways, Davy Crockett carryon nuke, hexaquark, quantum foam, Christofilos shield, wunderwaffe, subterranean penal colony at Nordhausen, Eagles Nest Hitler's hq, intimidation architecture, raubkammer zoo unermenshcen, experimental cell blocks, dueling scars, DARPA exoskeleton, chip the rat, insectothopter, adiabatic qubits,

augmented cognition, synthetic cognition, Paul Zak narrative networks, neuro economics, neuroimaging with oxytocin robot ethics, voice activated trained beasts with legs and LIDAR against fear, Licklider psycho acoustics, Predictive computer modeling of human behavior in Thailand, resettlement, defoliation, strategic hamlet, neuro prosthetics brain chip copper mesh in shoes, robo rat, robo cat, My Borgs adore you, human dyads linked machine, wireless EEG caps electrify brain increase cognition-some loss of hair at removal DSB Defense Science Board, micro electrode brain chip, composing light writter DNA programmable matter group, computer like bacteria, computer model of the living self DISABLE portal. Ken: summer-winter, relation-strangers, center-periphery, women in camp-men in forest hunting, Gluskap-cannibal giants Windigo, Kiwakwe, Chenoo: vicious, envious, selfish nature, refuse to share, imposters pretending to be relatives in order to eat human flesh.

10/26/15 Jonathan Williams on the surrender of Cornwallis- "A holy war will now begin on America, and when it is ended America will be supposedly the citadel of freedom, but her millions will unknowingly be loyal subjects to the Crown."

10/24/15 Broken texts. So often that it is relied upon as a method almost, clay sculptures fall off the table, sink in, implode being pushed too far or have any number of disasters befall them that it becomes a method of composition, which at least ensures a freshness and unexpected spontaneity to the work, but to apply this to writing makes a broken text. There are two of these, the other still to be fired, but they came as a result of a failed tapestry, then cut in half and formed into these. Like a pot I tried to make afterward which got pushed too far and totally fell, but the deal is that the clay still has to be used, so it got made into a large protuberant to be called Molly or Maggie. Maybe I think intuition is in the nature of clay. --The Pacific goes under California and Nevada and in trying to find more deep water bases the Navy lost two nuclear powered aircraft carriers searching for the Atlantic. You nitpickers call that in doubt when you don't even know that aircraft carriers were sent in the first attempt to colonize Neptune.

10/23/15 Book My mother was prescient. While she would really only appreciate my poem Corn of Wheat, a eulogy on a death, she dressed me up as a book one Halloween. That was in the innocent days, c 1952 and in a small town where everybody knew everybody and children went trick or treating with amity and community to every home of the 300 or so. She had found a tall rectangular box and painted it green, verdant green, and cut a slit where the eyes would be when it was put down over my shoulders. I believe there was some kind of shoulder harness inside to keep it from bumping on my head. The most inspired costume for her son who in the natural consciousness she could not have predicted his future, but in the spiritual understanding, she had been born in a cowl, there it all was for anybody to see. I was a book! I do hope to achieve her dreams.

10/21/15 Jacob Neal 800 265 8825 Ext 53589
SS# 5243 On Aeg's debt of $2384 to Barclays' Band Delaware, Last pay Oct 2012 of $300. Offer: flat discount by end of month of 40%. 1430.79

10/20/15 Perdition in NT translated from Apollyon! ...The simulacrum is never that which conceals the truth— it is the truth which conceals that there is none. The simulacrum is true.[3] philosophical treatise by Jean Baudrillard.

10/18/15 I awake realizing the New philosophy calls all in doubt and all of Galileo and Copernicus and their effects on the psyche of poets is a model for now, when Lear says the moon is a ship, etc and underground cities honeycomb the earth and many trillions of dollars are missing from the Pentagon alone, etc. I have been modeling all along.

10/17/15 Shades of Black Water, the Nazis were turned into private contractors. Murdering geneticist doctors became physicians, Gestapo moved to CIA, paramilitary extermination squads got jobs as police, top secret germ warfare Nazi biologists got into the American road, called it cancer research, The yeast blew up the bread, not that American or British were good, just naive and simpleminded, unless you count Tesla an American, but you don't. The American soul formed out of plenty, liberty and justice for all, meanwhile do what you please, but if you live there good luck in finding out what the Bolivians think of you, but be assured it is not uninformed. Nobody knows the master like the slave. When in Rome...be. So the Nazis came into a soil prepared for their infection as an object lesson to universities and government that you can do what you want and get a better job after, even get to explore outer space and inner space and everywhere inbetween. The infection thus reached epidemic proportions. The worst toxin of the Nazis was the Nazis themselves, and that's saying something. Nazi minds rule the world the way Rome did. And who is their inspiration? Nietzsche, god of science.

10/16/15 There was or is no difference between the Nazi war chemists and the American British who coveted tabun and tested it live to prepare for their psycho warfare., no difference except the propaganda, for if you were in American then the bad guy was abroad. All this is the Wunderwaffe of Nazi wonder weapons, ingenuity that America, Britain, Russia airlifted out, that is what didn't go to Antarctica Newschuabenland of which naught is given in the official record. What the allies got was surface stuff, not the antigrav and etc that (Robert B. Staver proposed) Walther Riedel, head of V-2 designs used to make short trips around the moon and locating space mirrors, early Project Blue Bean stuff. The American Raubkammer (he Nazi Zoo proving ground for chemical weapons occupied by cats, dogs, horses, cows, pigs) adoped these Passenger Rockets into the mental takedown, black hole, broken dimension popular later (see Operation Paperclip, 92. Annie Jacobsen) for their mind control zoo. By 1946 nazi scientists, 1000 authorized by Truman, began to infiltrate all of American science, bringing especially poisons, sarin, Klon B. They invented mustard gas and 9/91, tabun all benefiting Dow Chemical. Nazi med science did the same for survival ability underwater and in space, lsd was brought by Kuhn to CIA, etc, rocketry, chemistry, med science criminality, were all sold on the basis that George Kennan and Dean Acheson threatened that Russia was on a collision course with US and were in the lead in poisons, etc., ha, what, mind control, esp. too! in which the Germans were weak. Underground cities were also Nazified in construction, something the Nazi could do well from the subterranean penal colonies like Nordhausen and the gas chambers and Eagles Nest of Hitler's HQ. They were also good therefore at intimidation architecture to cow the untermenshen sub human classes into their experimental cell blocks. The Ubermenschen who were not hanged were imported to the west much like the rats infected with bubonic plague the U-boats tried to land in England, but rats couldn't swim that well. Who will invent a swimming rat along the beltway? Lesser endeavors were to airlift hoof and mouth disease countered by the allies dropping potato beetles in Normandy. All these and so many more informed Camp King where the black CIA hatched their control programs of Bluebird, etc. So the Paperclip was sold like ISIS today by casting it as a threat, when neither were as said, ISIS the invention of the Good guys in Wash.

10/15/15 ever wonder why the office holders say I take this oath without mental reservation or purpose of evasion? It's an interesting turn of phrase, planning an attack on American soil, a terrorist used to alert us to what ever, but not alerted to the attack on American soil in the aluminum, lithium, barium clouds, water, air and soil. No no that. Monsanto has got a seed strain that than grow in that soil. Sounds like a Conspiracy Theory: Considering the extent of the bad, the nazis sure, but the onlookers of the bullet holocaust, lined up at the ditches, today it would be cell phone cameras, the question is not where is the good because the evil masquerades as it too, of all the morals about the earth, the poor, the minorities only mask further depravities. No the good is much more than that and rare. The wholesale importation of Nazi physicists, rocket scientists, medical doctors, chemists into the United States infrastructure under the guise of beating Japan, while the parallel structures of Nazi colonies in Argentina and Uruguay, not to speak of Antarctica were also acquiesced to, poison what little morality might have existed in the war machines of Britain and US. Fast forward fifty years and see that the entire philosophical point of view of the Nazis subsumed into transhumanis in toto. This is to say nothing of the science kept out of public sight. So the Air Force, Navy, Army of the US was nazied.

10/14/15 Stewart Swerdlow cern, blue beam etc. Nazi bases in south american jungle. Project Persephone.
--Daniel Chandler the inevitability thesis, c. 1995 once technology is introduced, it is inevitably developed--I said this in a grant application in 1985
-CERN largest scientific consortium in world
-entemenaki, baba-alu, opening of Abzu, gate of hell-tom horn on the path of the immortals
-students from the Portuguese Santa Cecilia Music Academy-transparent panels containing arcane texts photographed inside CERN codes greetings, invocations in Aramaic, Hebrew, mandarin, Sanskrit strangelets

10/13/15 KATABOLE lead me, guide me along the way...I heard this Katabole-- Disruption-- On the way home from the club in the truck, adjusting its radio band because it hadn't been done since the battery was changed...
--Because of the disintegration of the inhabitants instead of before the foundation of the world God took the remains of the original heavens and Earth, which had become broken down and

were desolate at the time of Genesis 1:2, and though a Divine catabolic process used the remains of the old heaven and Earth to form our present heavens and Earth.
-catabole has meaning of payment, illness, epileptic seizure
-- in the LXX, cast down, overthrown, felled, destroyed mistranslated by its translation into Latin (Origen) as constitution
http://www.libraryoftheology.com/writings/opentheism/Study_Of_Greek_KataboleHowardElseth.pdf
-kosmos should be translated people, inhabitants not world or earth most times.

10/12/15 The world that was, concepts of faith, foundation means disruption in Heb 4.3. Flood over mts in Job first flood before Noah, confirmed by Jere 4. Foundation spoken of by Jesus in Rev 17 and 4 is disruption, lamb slain before the disruption

10/12/15 Europa riding Zeus sculpture outside of European Council Building. Europa riding Zeus statue in front of the EU Parliament building in Strasbourg.

10/8/15 George Kenny hypnotist
10/7/15 Morning Glory clouds everywhere

10/6/15 Lithium spraying lithium carbonate, mood stabilizing, treating bipolar mania, daze, fine tremor, nausea, headache, hyperthyroidism increased, weight gain, ataxia, gait. Lithium benefits: lithium chelates aluminum the hybrid Armilus, (Yahweh versus Yahweh) progeny of an evil spirit and a stone woman

10/5/15 Chris White Alternative Prophetic Viewpoints Vesuvius a 512 Qubit quantum computer

10/4/15 After camping White Mts.

9/30/15 Daniel Unsealed https://www.youtube.com/watch?v=7CtdGm556gM9/29 Robert Anderson, The Coming Prince

9/28/15 light stimulates aggressive neurons genetically implanted in mice, Charlie Rose march 7, 2015 9/26/15

Malebolge

Virgil and Dante move toward the pit, the ninth and final circle of Hell, reserved for "when the faculty of intellect / is joined with brute force and with evil will" (XXXI.55-56). The giant Nimrod blows a horn. Other giants are chained at this rim of the circle, serving as

embodiments of elemental forces. The giant Antaeus obeys Virgil by lifting the two travelers and lowering them on Cocytus, a frozen lake. "tuft by tuft" If the anatomical model for the journey is viable and we started out with references to eyes, then mouths, then bloodstreams, then intestines (the Malbolge), then Dante's enigmatic passage about "what point it was [he] must have passed" becomes disgustingly, but appropriately, clear. CANTO XXXI
Virgil and Dante leave the malebolge and move toward the pit, the ninth and final circle of Hell, reserved for "when the faculty of intellect / is joined with brute force and with evil will" (XXXI.55-56). The giant Nimrod blows a horn. Other giants are chained at this rim of the circle, serving as embodiments of elemental forces. The giant Antaeus obeys Virgil by lifting the two travelers and lowering them on Cocytus, a frozen lake.

CANTO XXXII
Circle Nine: Round One (Caïna) -- Treacherous to Kin
Traitors are frozen at various depths in the lake. Mordred and various Italians are found frozen up to their necks for their acts of treahery to members of their own families.
Circle Nine: Round Two (Antenora) -- Treacherous to Country
Dante accidentally kicks a face sticking out of the ice. Those treacherous to their countries are frozen to a point that they cannot move their necks at all. Dante sees two heads emerging from one hole, one chewing on the brains of the other. These are Archbishop Ruggieri, and Count Ugolino who gnaws on him. The story is told in the next canto.

CANTO XXXIII
Ugolino stops chewing to tell the story of being imprisoned with his children. The implication is that they turned to cannibalism. Dante wonders about the icy wind, but he'll see its origin soon.
Circle Nine: Round Three (Ptolomaea) -- Treacherous to Guests and Hosts
Those who betrayed their own guests or hosts are frozen halfway up their faces. Their tears freeze their eyes solid. Friar Alberigo tells Dante that his soul is damned now even though his body lives on earth. This is the odd case with Branca d'Oria too. Although he had promised to, Dante does not remove the ice from the friar's eyes: "To be mean to him was a generous reward" (XXXIII.150).

CANTO XXXIV
Circle Nine: Round Four (Judecca) -- Treacherous to Masters
Aside from apparently the three worst sinners of all time, the worst sin you can commit is to be treacherous to your own teacher. These sinners, the treacherous to their masters, are completely frozen underneath the ice, sealed up in twisted poses. So there's not much to say here.
Satan --When we had reached the point exactly where the thigh begins, right at the haunch's curve, my guide, with strain and force of every muscle, turned his head toward the shaggy

shanks of Dis and grabbed the hair as if about to climb-- I thought that we were heading back to Hell.
. . .
I raised my eyes, expecting I would see the half of Lucifer I saw before.
Instead I saw his two legs stretching upward. If at that sight I found myself confused, so will those simple-minded folk who still don't see what point it was I must have passed.
(XXXIV.76-93)

9/24/15 image of Kali on Empire State bldg
"The end is probably not very distant; it has already been grievously shaken by the French. In 1798 the French republican army under General Berthier took possession of the city of Rome, and entirely superseded the whole papal power.
--This was a deadly wound, though at present it appears to be healed; but it is but skinned over, and a dreadful cicatrice remains. The Jesuits, not Jesus, are now the Church's doctors.
--If the papal power, as a horn or temporal power, be intended here, which is most likely, (and we know that that power was given in 755 to Pope Stephen II. by Pepin, king of France), counting one thousand two hundred and sixty years from that, we are brought to a.d. 2015, about one hundred and ninety years from the present [a.d. 1825]. But I neither lay stress upon nor draw conclusions from these dates". cu on Daniel 7.15.
Commentary on the Bible, by Adam Clarke, [1831], at sacred-texts.com

9/23/15 This is the day when rabbis whirl chickens over their heads three times to transfer their sin. I fasted it last year, but not this. The best news received in the interim is that we are all in a medieval, Roman system of two classes the rulers and the peasants. It is so comforting to be a restored peasant after suffering the illusion so long that I was something else. For my aunt insisted always from an early age that we are all peasants. I have come home to it, knowing that I know nothing of the world and its stratagems, time and its breaking, even if I sue the words, and that I am so unimportant that I can be left alone to life my illusions without interference. It was my own fault for ever thinking otherwise, but we also recognize that is the programming put upon us at birth practically, in schools, in society, that we matter and that we can do anything. All illusion, all chimera. As far as I can see it there are two reigning possibilities, ET vs the Nephilim, and these have many permutations, but the best one is the simplest, that they are the same, not that the numbers of intelligent parties who have had experience of ET would accept this. Steve Greer has early had experience of contact. it became his *rason d etre*, his reason for being, leant significance to his life, although he is a member of the ruling class and not a peasant, which should give pause. Two classes of ET emerge, the android manufacture, programmed life form, chipped and cloned (extended to most Hollywood stars) and the "real" kind that say they are from Andromeda or Sirius and come with benign intent, little Speilbergs, for who we must enter an age of peace, not war, on earth in these last generations. Having had personal knowledge of this in the Disclosure effort makes another neat bifurcation between the rl and the unreal to draw participants toward the middle. Even though the Hegelian is decried by all these groups they all use it. The Disclosure effort by all accounts is to come public in an alien war, etc. a false flag event run by the rulers to consolidate ever more power,.

-One cannot help thinking of the Tibetan benefic and malevolent deities.is our last generations before.... -I better hasten to say before it all gets lost in the details that none of these are the fact, that being that every one of these appearances is Nephilous. That every one of these black budget, black shelved, sequestered technologies that have been know for years to be thousands of years ahead of what is used on the earth, all these come from the Neph, who can take many shapes, littley greys for the Nazis, etc. It is pertinent that it says that this was the beast that was, that is not, then that is and then that is no more, that this somehow explains the timeline, for there is plenty of history of the Neph in ancient times entering human affairs, making fit extensions of themselves, i.e. hybrids, giants. In this there seem to be three: the first angels who fell. Their breeding of their race further breeding into giants.

9/22/15 Chipped and cloned. Programmed Life forms here Steven Greer, these scenarios dovetail after coup de états of all gov't into a global junta, fourth reich. Sequestered. Black shelved. MAJIC, joint intelligence committee

9/19/15 micro nuclei in the blood create by cell phone use of 24 hrs. a million hz up against the brain a 7 hz system--George Carlo

9/18/15 Social scientific remodeling, hormonal wars, endocrine destructors, the disappearing male, population redesign, estrogen BPA on receipts our chemical lives

9/1315 Yom Kippur
dementia strikes 40's, http://www.thelibertybeacon.com/2015/09/09/dementia-now-striking-people-in-their40s/

9/12/15 there has been a long series of bizarre suicides among
British computer scientists, all of whom have had some connection to the United States Navy. NASA project Blue Beam

9/8/15]Danuta Anna Sharma-her questions make a good table of inquiry: Alters Are they trying to alter the original DNA of human beings, trying to alter it so it make it more like them because if we were more like them we'd be easier to control and we'd be without heart and heart is the thing that's maintaining us and keeping humanity alive , it's the human heart, not the literal heart the heart energy the wheel of light that spins here in every human bing that's the part they want to take away, that's the part they trying to take out, so if they can...they don't have that so if they can make us like them they will have succeeded in overcoming it,...the oppressive adversarial force that wnts to contain human beings...soul and heart synonymous, soul the essence of self and within the body it's projected through the heart charkr and as you point here projected out and that is the you, that is the you creation.

Traps for the Soul
"We're definitely living in a system which is an energy harvesting machine ... to harvest energy for a smaller amount of people so they can have and experience things that they want

to have. People can't have luxurious and incredible things in this 3D dualistic reality unless there are a hundred thousand people suffering. There has to be suffering for there to be extreme decadence. They want to live in extreme decadence because that part of the brain the reptilian part of the brain the r complex the primitive the old, survival instinct part of the brain is all about primal urges, primal forces, so debauchery goes in with that they can't have that unless there's poverty and struggle and sadness so it's very important for them to maintain on this planet, the oppressive force that can keep incarnating here. The soul trap the moon collects souls and there's a harvest...there is a system or a construct that is lunar that takes a soul and gives it amnesia and puts it back into a body without giving it a total life review...that's why the number 13 and the letter M is everywhere 17.59 because subconsciously we recycle...step out of being caught up in the emotional ties that bind you to these repeated lifetimes, to have an understanding that there never is any separation who you've love or really loved and when you yearn for somebody who's dead now, think of what could have been, you tie yourself much much tighter to the 3D repeated cycle because they never went anywhere and you're going through an illusory experience to understand what it's like for the infinite to have an experience in a human body ...the more you can express yourself totally and honestly and be totaly and utterly honest with yourself the closer you get to raise your vibration to leave the place that you weren't really caught in the first place 20.27...moth analogy, the moth caught in a glass vase the light was trapping it there but all it had to do was fly out of the light just by doing so flapping its wings

Mars is 100% occupied fourth Reich hybrid reptoids. The moon has a nazi soul harvesting system. Clones 26.00. Artificial Intelligence takes over planets, james cameron, margery camerian jack parson moonchild, brit prim min montauk time travel manipulation, cern,

CERN- tear hold in fabric to open up the lower 4D force dimensions where the shame and guilt sadness to enable their manifestation as literal beings to let these things completely in, hell on earth. open the gates of hell, changeover of eons, the tower, Pluto, 13 death of old way. massive abuse of the leaders of the world of children and people aren't up in arms yet? 34.33 People don't see anything except them selves but it makes us all sad because humanity is a single organism it's the child part of humanity, it's the innocence they're after, the energy of the innocent

9/7/15 from an image search of "orphim" Viktor Shkovsky's förmalist theory of "defamiliarization of reality". ·I argue that the dissolution of language and syntax~ along with . Structural disorder ·and issues ·· ·Of perspective, such aS blended, · almost undistinguishable narrative voices, contribute to deconstruct the trauma of 'survivorship and work towards comprehension and healing. These• extreme formal strategies · challenge · the reader to actively participate in an innovative, albeit controversial type of literariness, . which uses paradox; absurdity, repetition and specific. symbolism as further means to defamiliarize and re-order events.

9/6/15 genetically engineered gay communities, Brookings Sharon gilbert behaviorial epigenetics e gene, Stevenson

9/4/15 animal souls ghost language, Paul Kingsnorth grey wolf press, also lapin corruption of written text, proto-elamite
Marasu emoto, tatoos, dna by words, Jacob breeding.
Neph story: shofar: breeding program
Nicholsen 1968 the real reason for chemtrails 1/9/15-- Blue Beam
Jacob breeding by the slats: epigenetics

9/2/15 MERCURY personification of anima, anima mundi. --The structure and evolution of the exosphere on a planet involves numerous factors, including the source rate from the surface, the interaction with the regolith, the solar wind ion sputtering effect, and so on. In order to have a better understanding on the nature of the exosphere, the characteristics of the surface and the solar wind interactions are also important issues. Vice versa, the information hidden in the exosphere can give us clues on the surface properties, the solar wind ion bombardment patterns, and the heavy ion distributions. Therefore, although initially we have treated each topic separately, the ultimate objective is to apprehend the elements, with solid, gas, and plasma states, of a solar system object without an atmosphere as a whole. In this work, the surface thermal model, 2D and 3D exospheric models, and the 3D hybrid model are applied to the studies on the exosphere and the magnetosphere structures of Mercury. Through the comparisons with the observations and measurements, we have learned the exospheric features and their interactions with the surface, as well as the fundamental morphology of the magnetosphere without the inclusion of a substantial ionosphere. The thermal accommodation effects on both longer lifetime exospheric atoms, helium and oxygen, and a shorter one, sodium, are calculated with our exospheric model combined with the surface temperature distribution from the thermal model on Mercury. The surface ion precipitation rate and the magnetosphere measured from the first two flybys of MESSENGER are also learned via the hybrid simulations. The circulations of the heavy ions produced from the exosphere is also an interesting subject to discuss with the joint results from the exospheric and the hybrid computations in future.</span> The structure and evolution of the exosphere on a planet involves numerous factors, including the source rate from the surface, the interaction with the regolith, the solar wind ion sputtering effect, and so on. In order to have a better understanding on the nature of the exosphere, the characteristics of the surface and the solar wind interactions are also important issues. Vice versa, the information hidden in the exosphere can give us clues on the surface properties, the solar wind ion bombardment patterns, and the heavy ion distributions. T   Therefore , although initially we have treated each topic separately, the ultimate objective is to apprehend the elements, with solid, gas, and plasma states, of a solar system object without an atmosphere as a whole. In this work, the surface thermal model, 2D and 3D exospheric models, and the 3D hybrid model are applied to the studies on the exosphere and the magnetosphere structures of Mercury. Through the comparisons with the observations and measurements, we have learned the exospheric features and their interactions with the surface, as well as the fundamental morphology of the magnetosphere without the inclusion of a substantial ionosphere. The thermal accommodation effects on both longer lifetime exospheric atoms, helium and oxygen, and a shorter one, sodium, are calculated with our exospheric model combined with the surface temperature distribution from the thermal model on Mercury. The surface ion precipitation rate and the magnetosphere measured from the first two flybys of MESSENGER are also learned via the hybrid simulations. The circulations of the heavy ions produced from the exosphere is also an interesting subject to discuss with the joint results from the exospheric and the hybrid computations in future. Dissertation Institute of Astronomy, Central University.

Regolith is a layer of loose, heterogeneous superficial material covering solid rock. It includes dust, soil, broken rock, and other related materials and is present on Earth, the Moon, Mars, some asteroids, and other terrestrial planets and moons. In places this covering is made up of material originating through rock-weathering or plant growth in situ. In other instances it is of fragmental and more or less decomposed matter drifted by wind, water or ice from other sources. This entire mantle of unconsolidated material, whatever its nature or origin, it is proposed to call the regolith.

Outake from Portals:

8/30/15 Caligula stabbed the sea he thought full of Goya's hair. Homer took a full page ad in this with Laocoön, along with the statues, paintings of El Greco. Daniel said the beast up from the sea was global, without borders, that goats would cast stars to the ground and trample them. This is the 4th letter of del Sur on the Neptune war, philosophy and circus, a global captivity of merchants multiplied above the stars and strongholds falling like figs. The eater and the eaten stuff the gates of the mind open before its enemies. No fig wants to hear. Even titanium alloys fail in defense. Simple water drawn for the siege goes in the clay. To tread the mortar, make strong the brick, locusts and worms and canker-worms, the merchants of Nahum East, 3, cast lots to own the honorable men of No-Cleveland. They bought No-York too and sold nations. Shaker Heights fell, Ohio was lost. Toward the sea the whip, the wheel, the trains, the horns, the creosote barbs, grey dawn antennas, chains not long, end Nineveh. For Gaza shall be forsaken, and Ashkelon a desolation: they shall drive out Ashdod at noonday, and Akron shall be rooted up.

8/23/15 how much do these gates affect. I had a tight dream last night, today in napping a researcher followed to the drug garden looking for some seed or other, papaya, cardamon...dream of Nightingale gates 8/22/15 Jasher 4 18 And their judges and rulers went to the daughters of men and took their wives by force from their husbands according to their choice, and the sons of men in those days took from the cattle of the earth, the beasts of the field and the fowls of the air, and taught the mixture of animals of one species with the other, in order therewith to provoke the Lord; and God saw the whole earth and it was corrupt, for all flesh had corrupted its ways upon earth, all men and all animals.
--Edward Mantill: CERN's main purpose for building the Collider was too, well it was to open a door way. 40 Tera Electron Volts
--commit two collisions, if the connection to another existence was possible, discovered some sort of portal to another world. didn't come back alone" I saw him doing them all at the same time. He was in Section D, C, and K, in the lab, in the lounge, and in the clean room, all at the same time!" --Yeshua against the dragon of the sea

8/19/15 today patrolling to see if Oscar got overturned again found Big Boy overturned at gate w/ cloth twisted round his front forefoot. Like the time he had wire around that same, like the time he was twisted in cloth in the side burrow, like the time he got his neck caught in the gate and the time he was wedged in the back burrow. Now today,

9/14/15 I find him turned upside down between the logs and block of the garden by the garbage pails!
--After the dream of Douglas Bush and mythology in the Renn yesterday, following up found Mali's The Rehabilitation of Myth, who cites Michel de certeau and giambattista vico: all pertinent to New Philadelphia revival of myth and the other: Insomma, da tutto ciò che si Š quest' opera ragionato, Š da finalmente conchiudersi che questa Scienza porta indivisiblmente seco lo studio della piet…, e che, se non siesi pio, non si può daddovero esser saggio. [To sum up, from all that has been set forth in this work, it is to be finally concluded that this science carries inseparably with it the study of piety, and that he who is not pious cannot be truly wise.]
--the fables of antiquity had always been present as decorations in the salons of upper classes Bacon thought Greek myths allegorized primordial reality, that the truth of myth lay beyond myth itself which was only a later ornamentation (mali, 142) invented by priests and poets for the expression of some truth masked in the ornament. michel de certeau, la fable mystique New World Encounters By Stephen Greenblatt heterology, science of the other, was to make sense of the Indians

8/5/15 Visions of Hildegaard Haloes

7/30 albumin is the main protein of human blood plasma.[7] It binds water, cations (such as Ca^{2+}, Na^+ and K^+), fatty acids, hormones, bilirubin, thyroxine (T4) and pharmaceuticals (including barbiturates) - its main function is to regulate the colloidal osmotic pressure of blood.

7/29/15 black science: Three parent babies legal in Britain.

7/26/15 the fictional nation called Ameryca. It is a lyric narrative, by which is meant that it tells its discovery in verse form, short lyrics, against the background of the discoverers of 16th and 17th century England. The first half of the book, the six months of the calendar year from March to September, includes in order, St. Brendan, Erik the Red, Columbus, Sir Walter Raleigh and the natural origins of that world, the sun, the fly, the orphan. The second half of the calendar is a time shift describing the last six decades of 20th century America, the i instead of the y, a disillusion of the naive former months. The poem as a whole leaves us to ponder what we are and what we believe about Ameryca, America and ourselves.

7/25 "whether from clay or from metal" Sarah Connor Chrnicles, I.4, speaking of golem
- The name Tetsuo on the coltan truck and crates is a sly reference to a bizarre Japanese movie called Tetsuo: The Iron Man (1989), about a man who begins finding scraps of metal

growing out of his body and is gradually transformed into a perverse human-machine hybrid.[2]

- The story Sarah talks about in the beginning of the episode is a Jewish folktale in which a rabbi builds an artificial man — a golem — from clay to protect residents of the Jewish ghetto, only to have the creature turn on them. It's a variation on the archetypal story of the man-made monster, and the thematic connections to The Terminator saga are pretty clear.[3]

Monologue Opening

"When John was little, before bed I used to read him fairy tales. One night I read him a folk tale called, 'The Golem of Prague' the story of a clay monster made by a Rabbi to protect the Jews of the city. What I failed to remember was that the end of the story the Golem turns on its maker and kills him as well as the rest of the town. He didn't sleep for months. I went to him and tried to tell him it wasn't real, that I'd made it all up. Somehow, that made it all worse."

Closing

"Not every version of the Golem story ends badly. In one, the monster is a hero, destroying all those that seek to harm his maker. In another, the Golem's maker destroys his creature before it can destroy the world. The pride of man, of parents as well, makes us believe that anything we create we can control. Whether from clay or from metal, it is in the nature of us to make our own monsters. Our children are alloys all, built from our own imperfect flesh. We animate them with magic and never truly know what they will do." 7

/16/157/15/15 Indian Religion

Annabellah for the day.

Threnody for Kenneth M. Morrison. These ideas abound in Ken's essay Native American Other than Human Persons, reality assumptions embedded in Algonquin: the master of animals, human and animals communicate in dreams, entities who live in other space time dimensions. Animals are human beings who have donned costumes and masks that created their animal forms, green corn and harvest rituals, first salmon, buffalo renewal ceremonials, bear ceremonialism revolve around human well being gained from gifting acts to other persons where words are intentional beings that represent an objective reality as kachina masks give physical form to cosmic persons encountered in dreams.

Ken and I never conversed over these matters that mean so much to me in reality, if not in philosophy. Communication with a person is altogether different from reading his work. I never took him seriously as a an intentional being because he could not see beyond his own words or himself as if he were giving by rote things he had heard but did not know himself, this was felt. So when his garage was broken into he was nonplussed. I merely screwed a 3/4 in sheet of plywood over the broken door. H would send away for exotic plants that could not thrive in our head, so I have him stands of aloe which still proliferate in his year long after he is gone. So we never really had a conversation, but I did hear some of his activities, helping his grad students get posts at which he was good and many students would visit him at home.

But he smoked, another rote effect, which caused his demise no doubt. he had moved to Oregon to live with his brother in law Geoff Glover, also early deceased, mentioned in the acknowledgments of Kinship, who had visited many times, a person who would repair his house, and was sitting at the breakfast talking and simply up and died. At the beginning of Embattled he speaks of a cabin where he took seclusion. He had one of these here and would go to many long weekends out of the month and much in summer outside of Prescott, on the mountain, but, another anomaly, he double and triple mortgaged his house during the fat years here to pay for improvements to the cabin, but when the evaluations crashed could not afford the increased mortgages and that was the reason for the move to Oregon. We had a wild rooster and three hens on the street then, who had chicks several times, but gradually got whittled down till only the rooster was left, he would come and roost at night in Ken's aqua vitae and make his racket in the morning so I often thought of dealing with him, but never did. He was very beautiful, but one morning I came out and he was dead in the drive as if his neck had been wrung. I was sad about this and gave him an honorable burial wrapped in a red t and in rosemary. He has a gravestone. This is the end of that first event when we had moved in and saw them in the back yard playing canasta. You see, he did not have a woman.

    The house was repossessed and he recruited a woman and er taxi driver friend to live there rent free until the bank ordered them out, which took six months. So all our lives are contradicted. Ken's study is anthropological, ethno historical, sociological, but from a personal point of view that is engaging and well expressed. His writing puts his best face forward. My writing on the new world is often symbolic, facetious and opaque, but I never set out to be a scholar or professor, only a poet, which is no excuse for being neither.

    A Calendar of Poems is all about contact and its effects on the land, the idealism of the new and the primitive, all of which contact destroyed, and then it destroyed itself. Restorations of the Golden Age is about the metaphor of discovery more than discovery itself, how inflated rhetoric of poets made the new into the old, into impossible topographies of gold, into the woman and lovemaking, into the act of love in as a love voyage, into other world destinations, Bermuda into Hades, Virginia into heaven, or the new, new man. So myths of the gold tree, the gold man, heaven and hell, beauty and love were preoccupied filters, metaphors of the new but as the old. This very playful but serious business preoccupied the best minds of the English Renaissance which criticized empire even while it built it and criticized commercialism even which it was the vehicle for its establishment. So while the ship captains were probing the coasts off Penobscot and kidnapping Wakinas to take back to the King, the poets at home were laughing and chortling and not getting at all how in this the beginning of the new world they were sowing its end in its destruction. but they did get that woman was the world and the new world was the world, so in a shot 400 years they progressed civilization to ruination and the earth to apocalypse.

The Abenaki were various tribes that lived in the river basins of New Hampshire, Maine, and New Brunswick. They fought many wars against the French and English

7/13/15 Dreamed of taking class with Ken, needed for a doctorate, political theory or post modern grammar, which he taught. He had a radio show, sitting next to him before class, convivial etc, so I searched him looking for his authority named Sam Gill on native american religions, and found it! His biblio is fascinating. and found his pdf on baptism!

    dissertation 1975: The People of the Dawn: The Abnaki and their relations with New England and New France, 1600-1727 U of Maine

Mapping Otherness: Myth and the Study of Cultural Encounter
The Cosmos as Intersubjective: Native American Other than Human Persons
Baptism and Alliance 1990
Towards A History of Intimate Encounters: Algonkian Folklore, Jesuit Missionaries, and Kiwakwe, The Cannibal Giant 1979
Obit: http://mailman.yale.edu/pipermail/nativestudies-l/2012-January/002303.html

    Ken inspired two stories Christmas City and Gardens and Grapefruits. We had come to Phoenix for the medical internship at Good Samaritan Hospital, but in the first ten years in Phoenix lived south of McDowell at 24th street. We were there when the freeway was built, moved into a derelict neighborhood just a year before. All the social relations had fragmented, leaving behind, drug houses, gangs and illegals. Our immediate six neighbors on all sides were widowed single women in their 60's and 70's left over from what once was. They had pomegranates and grapefruit trees and oleanders to hide the gangs. My story from those years Secret Life of a Zonie Ninja has never appeared. We had three break ins in those years before our first black chow joined us as a stray and stayed. Those stories haven't appeared either. Finally, when the immediate neighbor lady to west went belly up (she and her daughter were inspiration for the notorious Susan) and the house was redeemed from demo by a speculator at the last minute and the people he rented to stored motor oil in five gallon bucks under their lemon trees, I had to move. The house next to Ken was the one provided for me after seeking. The day we moved in I looked over the back fence and there were four card tables set up with candles and people playing canasta! No wonder I thought it was heaven.

    Obviously Ken's work on Algonquian myth in Mapping Otherness would appeal to me, stories studied for the cultural evidence they embody, the tension between myth and history, to reverse the ethno historical dependence on European documents. Work I have an immense appreciation of from Howard Normans books on the Swampy Cree. All my writing on Pop, Susan, Wonk Yaps, Orcs, is like the Indian myths, stories with evidence of cultural encounter with the transhuman and science as if they were European conquerors. In the conflict of these cultures with the mythic origins of the native, i.e. the natural world, everything said of the European conflict with the native applies to the transhuman conflict with the natural, except there is no Gluskap who struggles the hard way to preserve against evil; there is only evil as a kind of joke. No maturation through concern for others, but there might be a killing of the giant frog that ate all the world's water. When the Algonquian were deprived of world and water they changed form into fish and bear thus became other by transplantation, but in this alienation into animal others as kin, their strategy of goodness, once transformed, they hoped to change the European into kin, which shows how wrong they were. Gluskap faced the challenge of the other, European, constructively, like kin, hence the benignity of this belief empowered their annihilation. They should have read Franz Fanon.

    Cannibal giants however could metamorph negatively, pretending to be kin until killing and eating with their cannibal perfidy People became cannibals when they hardened their hearts toward their kin. Restoration of social relation could heal these rifts, the Wabanaki thought, by the addressing the cannibal as father or grandfather, appealing like Dr. King to its higher nature, its conscience. Kindness to the giant was their hope of transformation. Truly the primitive naive. It was European technology that the Algonquin embraced, Iphones, computers, nano parts and digital DNA, to make the analogy. The myths are pictures of the native and the alien, Algonquin European, giant, Glosknap cannibal, forces of conflict and their resolution, but these exist for a scholar in the past, after the conflict is resolved and viewed by the European for all his good intent and logic and distance, but what about when the conflict is not resolved and the viewer is the native, for in the war of the natural vs. the digital the conflict is global, though the giants and cannibals are the same. English treachery and the greed of European morality altogether dislocated by the occasional good English altruist skewed the native just enough to ensure total extinction . So Weymouth kidnapped six Wabanakis to England. Kidnapping and technology were the two salient seductions of the native and the alien. Does it make you think at all?

    This wishful thinking makes the scholar say the opposite of the fact and truth, that "from the beginning of contact the Algonquians had an informed realistic view of the challenges of the cultural encounter." 119 This is so horribly wrong since Glosknap and their theology of acceptance of the other, redemption of the other, made them miss entirely the horror of evil they encountered. Myth and folklore document this adaptability, this naïveté, in the cultural evidence of stories and poems.

Myth says one thing history another, but when they are one and the same we have apocalypse. I love this kind of talk, that "myth is central to the study of cultural encounter precisely because it provides the template shaping people's ongoing production of identity" 120 This identity provides security with common shared public values. Contact is a decentering when people question these values.

    However it came Algonquian values from the conflict of summer and winter, relatives vs. strangers, the center vs. the periphery, women in camp vs. men hunting in the forest, made for adaptive values, the critic says, trying to make a whole thought of their one world, which itself is a human misnomer. It is impossible that humans solve their contradiction even if some myth or religion they practice says it does, positive against the negative, the hero Gluskap against the cannibal giants of windigo, Kiwakwe, chenoo, seeks a solution of good and evil, but there is none, the positive sharing power of Guskap vs the negative antisocial giants of greed, that is supposed to transform the world, meaning absorb and redeem evil, for the evil is made human other tribal members. Guskap learns to be good one struggle at a time until he releases the captive animals and forbears revenge. It is a perfect little tale for society within itself, in its one world, but utterly fails when confronted with the outside; there only the Hopi view survives, implacable war with the other.

    Do not compassionately stay your hand against the enemy. Execute him. Every effort Glooscap made to transform the world was to bring the natural, the animal into harmony, kinship when the people sought to survive the drought by taking to the water as fish or the forest as game: "my relative of as strange race, my spouse's parents" 123. Treating animals as kin they extended the courtesy of the English, a kind of genocide by myth. To utterly oppose the English was to deny their religion and its constructive myth of the world. Read for yourself 124 the catalogue of cannibal giant English. Cannibal giants were vicious, envious, selfish in nature, refused to share,, pretended to be kin in order to eat human flesh, thus violation the paramount order of kinship. Human could become cannibals but could cannibals be human? Gluskap said yes. Since humans became cannibals when they hardened their hearts, cannibals could be human if softened in healing. This dialectic annihilated these people.

Gluskap showed that technology should be used to socially construct the people, for human welfare, In their grasping Europeans were considered to be like the cannibal giants. How the Wabanaki were corrupted by commercial contact with Weymouth (1605) and kidnapped is the cautionary tale of black science and the present. For you can have a new kidney and new genes if you will just get aboard ship. When the Wabanaki subsequently eliminated the Popham colony the internal pressures triggered by this weakened them substantially. 128 Hence cultural contact. Wave on wave of epidemics, liquor, factionalism and division, the cannibal virus so to speak, In post contact history Gluskap's teaching became more urgent. Europeans were identified with sinful Adam, rebaptized, etc. Post contact history we have a lot of and more is coming. Gluskap showed that technology should be used to socially construct the people, for human welfare, In their grasping Europeans were considered to be like the cannibal giants. How the Wabanaki were corrupted by commercial contact with Weymouth and kidnapped is the cautionary tale of black science and the present. For you can have a new kidney and new genes if you will just get aboard ship. When the Wabanaki subsequently eliminated the Popham colony the internal pressures triggered by this weakened them substantially. 128 Hence cultural contact. Wave on wave of epidemics, liquor, factionalism and division, the cannibal virus so to speak, In post contact history Gluskap's teaching became more urgent. Europeans were identified with sinful Adam, rebaptized, etc. Post contact history we have a lot of and more is coming.

Ken was an atheist or if not then a profound agnostic so I find it note worthy he cried for three days after reading Buber, as his Obit says. I took it as axiomatic that a professor of religion would be antagonistic to faith. The founder of the ASU Religion Dept was a pronounced such skeptic which he hid under his writings about spirituality. I say this from their universal rejection of supernatural paraphernalia, angels, inspiration, miracles, the Holy Spirit and denial of scriptures in various ways. In this way Ken made a perfect investigator of Indian religion.

7/12/15 yesterday feeling the effects of the run in at the kilns on Mon and due to pick up a piece Sat, so the possibility of another, plus the toilets stopped up at office from some patient putting a diaper or something in, and having to get a plumber, but waiting to hear, (after the rock through the back window of the truck in the driveway and the break up of Char's class where I had taken refuge years before) I took a rest and saw after a while this figure which I took to be the Father, extending the slightest finger of a touch against the another figure of what was opposing me and it flying back, crumpling away. I woke from this to the exact reversal of things at the kiln and the plumber calling and appearing to fix the drain all in ten minutes! Because he loves me says the Lord I will rescue him.

7/10/15 side of Pluto that always faces its largest moon, Charon, and includes the so-called "tail" of the dark whale-shaped feature along its equator. (The immense, bright feature shaped like a heart had rotated from view when this image was captured.)

7/9/15 Yesterday and today wash office roof and coat walls and trouble spots.

7/6/15 Mon, went to pick up pieces, one cracked on refire. I threw it in the can after Ridl says in voice that he likes what I do, wants to teach me, but that if I don't learn then the Phx Center is no place for me. He asked again and again who my teachers are and that there are many at the Center who could "help" me. I made plain that teachers only teach their own virus and the ones they are taught. I said I learn from my work and I like Gareth Mason and wood fire effects and could have said Callas and Voulkos, especially his attitude which is not punitive like Don. He says he's your teacher then. I reply no, I'm just glad he's in the world and I admire and identify his work. That I am seeking to split form into pieces. I don't bother saying Ridley's work is banal and commonplace because he is a tyrant and throws his voice around with his weight. He has his favorites and all the rest can skate. His teaching so called is mainly his opinions and jokes in his classes. He can't teach what he does not know, that being the essence of form, nothingness of design, flow of liquid color over earth. There was some spit off the embedded feldspar onto other pieces he said, not that he knew it was buried feldspar, and that the bottoms are "unfinished," hence unstable. I said I can glaze the surface to prevent the spit, they are hardly glazed at all, and sand the bottom. He thinks they should have feet! He is utterly afraid of the spirit. I have offended print teachers, ceramic teachers, Mennonite teachers, English teachers and tennis bigshots. All these self righteous people are offended. I must be onto something. The outcome is that I want to tear the top off with the bottom and make the form represent the detasseled torsos of our time.

7/4/15 Beauty must pay. The Reformed are depressed over their sin. The Mennonites are depressed over their need to help the world. They use guilt to motivate.

7/3/15 Venus and Jupiter close in the sky one or two degrees, of the home, told Aey to expand his toward the front. Of memory, speaking of at pottery last night, broken proteins, seeing films twenty years later and so on again on Netflix I realize I have remembered things that did not happen and omitted remembering those that did. Last night dreamed of Thornburg, driving out the road, all very different from memory , much closer, confined, so there is a third take: dreams, memory, memory corrected. There is a section of Phila that goes up into a city like in Uganda or Monrovia Liberia I have visited at least three times, this time by cab, where the streets taper off and disappear into a warren of shacks etc, like Brazil. They were saying on TBN last night that Ps 83 precedes Ez 38-9 which precedes the tribulation. "Figures of speech function to describe not the details of what is going to happen but the seriousness of what is going to happen" Have gotten four bids for office.

7/2/15 superposition is one version superimposed upon another, both playing simultaneously, so a palimpsest is a model of it, except the world is all the versions of itself playing simultaneously. Nina Simone's My Baby don't care for me the first version and the last as

1987 Montreux playing together, what say a song played to a different song. A lot like the levels of Jerusalem, history, archeology. This is real superposition vs theoretical. Inferences in these layers include misdirection, taking one name and using it for another, Alexander for Chaldeans; making name into metaphor, with anachronism as when Germans are called Huns; aping archaic style, making the younger appear more truthful; rearranging the parts, as editors say a thought is out of place; using technical terms as evidence of denial to its time and place. So to take any surfaces as real is to live in pond scum not in the depths below. it is axiomatic in this that things with greater weight sink toward the bottom from their specific gravity, so the American news is the froth of pond scum.

7/1/15 These all signal the start of tribulation: Aey makes me indict society unrecognizable even in 25 years: "Marriage", Entertainment patriotism, obesity, drugs pot, foul discourteous foul talk everywhere, disrespect, incarcerations, police, subterfuge and murder at prayer meetings, burning of black churches (Mount Zion AME Church-- All of the fires currently under investigation broke out days after the fatal shootings at
Charleston's historic Emanuel African Methodist Episcopal Church

6/30/15 Cognitive or noncognitive art, love
6/29/15 I think I just remembered that Anne used to be locked into my mother's closet in Thornburg for some hours, times. This was connected to the memory that Ginger once went in that closet and tore to shreds on the floor her used kotex! 6/28/15 Nina Simone

6/27/15 The four beasts up from the sea are empires, the ten horns are nations, the little horn is...
--I don't feel comfortable at this time in letting the girls' kids go without insurance, propose giving money to split the cost of their kids.

6/26/15 Char told Don I should be allowed to stay but he had no answer. Kaylie declared she is bisexual. Started to get bids for office roof.

6/24/15 Same day as window in truck, news that Thurs nightclass only for beginners. All art, literature, poetry, journalism as propaganda for empire, the world itself, and its multifarious contradictory intentions. To decontaminate this propaganda, Rom. 12 2 says be not conformed to it, but be transformed in renewing, rewiring your mind, which means rejecting patriotism and culturism, modernism, etc.

6/22/15 a rock through back window of black truck in the driveway last night. Summer solstice.--The tribulation started last week at the Wed night prayer meeting of Emanuel AME. My people lived in sanctuary in this country from 1717 and before, fleeing the murderous tortures of the Dutch, Swiss Reformed authorities, but I feel as if this act last Wed were done to me. So close to home. Pat has 30 or 40 ladies of just such as were killed in her practice and I have know many from Fayetteville and Dallas. That black Christians are murdered at prayer by subterfuge tells the story, for who of us at prayer does not leave the world, even if while we're in it we are vigilant.

6/20 UDAQ, Tempora, xkeyscore, Lavabit
"repeat the lie until it becomes accepted as truth" Snowden revealed that we accessed and then bounced weak attacks on ourselves off IPs in China, during that entire year we spent accusing them of hacking us.

6/19 Covered with bees. At a family gathering about to leave, saying goodbyes walked down to say goodbye to Andy eating a sandwich on a wall, with Joe when notices bees buzzing all around, then walking further into knee hi, waist high clover millions of bees all over them, covering me it seemed though I couldn't see that, walking through ever higher clover, covered again then up out of the clove walking up seeing fireman in full suits, space suit regalia laying on the ground, light green suits, with helmets, then seeing my father walking slowly down towards this I tell him there are thousands and millions of bees. Only a very slight apprehension at the second whelming.

6/18/15 Annabellah for the day yesterday.

6/17/15 It's not why have I been so isolated from what I love and enjoy, I certainly know how, but how to restore these connections, but I know as little of that as why in the first place. Ruth preventing me from restoring the ranch? Shawna preventing art activities and etc. with Aey.

6/15/15 Eagles. Angels or butterflies forming and unforming like eagles to a silent sound played oa eight or ten ft shofar like instrument. They would reverse inside out in a dance four of them together in a circle molting remolting as I, he played, in eagle colors, golden , brown wings folding unfolding. raspberry rpgs,
--Animal symbolism in Ecclesiastical Architecture
--A Man is the highest created being in the universe. Earth is the Jewel, Masterpiece of All the Worlds. 6/9 Nordart Exhibition: www.tetsohnari.com, Mythos vom Verlust der Menschlichkeitthe myth of the loss of the human ahmed saber

5/31 Sleep: active clearance of the by-products of neural activity that accumulate during wakefulness. / Wind among the reeds, Wandering aegus, fish turns into a girl
 5/29 I was doing a lot of blue stake in sleep a kind of role play of Aeg in Fla during his business trip

5/28 Deductions and extensions of the periodic table
In movies the Americans always take their boys of 19 and land them in foreign countries.

5/26/15 Henry Woll, the MacDonagh (Osteopaths) friends of Alex. Henry Foster. Arthur Glasser, Dayton Roberts, Bob Stam, Dit Fenton, Dewitt Jayne. I knew so many significant men then, Foulkes, All the LAM leaders--

5/21/15 Rapture In this series of unmaskings that have been going on, of civilization, Jung, Freud, proto man, down to the signal examples, the same fine words and believing that come out of the mouth of Paula White holding hands with Benny Hinn in Rome and giving TD Jakes his 350 K car, come out of the mouth of Charlie Rose and George Clooney. Power, money, privilege. The thing is that everything they say is powerful good and true, its just that it is being used for other purposes. Inspiration used to deceive, liberation to enslave, to milk
5/20/15 You need to be prepped to be in the middle of a cosmic event like when the clouds themselves mimic art of Brueghel, become moons and wisps of hair, all sprayed down applied 8 hours before, at least when first noticed, but probably before dawn, now 3 pm. Look at the weather forecast heavy clouds forecast, but they were not there at 6, only hundreds of streaks across the sky, so that one, the sprayers saw the forecast and sprayed to meet it, or two, they control the forecast.
--book note: It seems that this is on the back burner, at least until the buyer resolves the contradiction felt between the commercial and artistic. the buyer(s) loves the Faulkner thought steam apart from the plot. The short sentences in V hold less interest, especially since it was noted to me that it so much resembles McCarthy's Outer Dark, with none of the flights of Old Man or even Pylon where the cosmos resolves over and over in a sentence. I'm not doing justice to either this notion or to Faulkner.

      This was the blurb of Rapture: --Warning for any inquirers, the bottom of the inside is inscribed with words written in every rapture, The Lord Is My Shepherd. Sorry about that. This was done on Aey's birthday. It is in the round, figures ascending in different stages and is like Opening the Fifth Seal which shows the figures as a canvas. It takes a while to understand these things, but I seem to have made countless images of people flying up, at least since I wrote on a student's paper way long ago, what do they do at the tops of mountains, children lifting pretty heads from pillow beds? So not only here, but by interpretation of El Greco's Opening the Fifth seal and in the end in Danby's Sixth Seal, in the process of being hung.

      "It was all wrapped in these children being born and flying around, "what do they do at the tops of mountains, children lifting pretty heads from pillowed beds?...Raleigh says You rose into the mountain air and nevermore were seen. I don't know if it answers what children lifting pretty heads from pillowed beds were doing at the tops of mountains, but right up until Once upon a time when it was dead and gone, when one was enough and too much to be alive and well in Ameryca, the new found land, a glory rose up into the head... Raleigh, the marigold in the sun's eye, seems to write about it in his address to Queen Elizabeth in his poems of 1596 where his "first-born love...Restless desire from my love that proceeded / leave to be and seek heaven by dying, since you, oh you, your own hope have exceeded by too high flying."...

      So they are all children of St Branden who turn the cheek, spiritual children shall we say, who seek another country, full of mishap called justice. You see how fruitful the allegory is by result, even if there is so much effort in the history of America, the outer one, to find the inner. All the little pretty ones, utopias, Oneidas, so many more in two hundred years than all the world produced in its entirety... How can green know the red? I am what he was, within. It wouldn't change anything he did, not a certainty to be within what he was without, visible

from the interior but not from the exterior. That's the play. The moon has opened up her eyes, like summer stars so soon they rise. Thirty years of absolute sobriety, with love. Of course these things are, but saying so in the same parlance requires that my ears hast Thou pierced, as Messiah said. Listening, hearing the revelation, he wakens me morning by morning to listen as one being taught, as when a slave in Israel, offered freedom after seven years, to continue in that service put an ear against a board where the owner pierced the lobe to symbolize his listening to him alone. The sublime writer carries this along from Psalm 40. Lo I come...I delight to do Thy will, O my Elohim: yea, the law is written in my heart, no certainty, and he knows nothing of the future, only the moment and past revised amid all failures and regret. Prophetic and at the same time impossible, nobody picking Calendar up forty years later would see anything symbolic in "A Conjunction of Planets," What lovers' open lips we are tonight in time the endless world, our minds unfurled. Symbol is defeated by propaganda, but propaganda cannot eradicate symbol, only neutralize it by saying it cannot be understood. These texts were to prepare the y to overcome the i, a reversal to which we all now have our attention drawn. I think Goya or El Greco said that. Souls in the egg, so all right world, Hatch and hatch. from
Ameryca With a Y - Autobiography of a Poem

5/19/15 After search sent Form of the Formless by leading. Jacob Esau, spirit flesh

5/18/15 New Moon. After reading draft of Bright Angel Trail Pat said she missed the mules. This morning I joined the two!
Dreamed John K tennis tournament not going as planned, telling him off so to speak. How bout let's not tell off anybody.

5/17/15 Been sick with acute bronchitis 8 days. Dreams are a series of transpositions, substitutions, partials transferred to other faces bodies that ask us questions, who are your mentors? This one wanted to know, claiming I had none she knew of. It was Ann saying she was leaving and to call the children. Was one George Matters she wants to know? All jumbled up. Since these are not my questions I take it that dreams are in part communications with others at some level. Last night Zion took both my socks.
Chows of N China

Chaosmatics

5/16/15 NORTH CHURCH "It is impossible to disentangle the strands of good and evil in social religious political personal relations.
    --EAGLES NEST History has to be denied like the decade or so 1989 to 2002 story of the countless metamorphoses, first that, then North Church, then Church for the Nations, moving countless times in that period like a kind of tumbleweed, invoking the spirits of St Jude. This case has to be denied by the present metamorph empire it has become, but for the maxim fool me twice shame on me. What are the odds of attracting two cases of fraud as maximum supports, elders of the same church back to back? This has to be denied. Except for

eye witnesses. Maybe they don't put together the pieces in the midst of a severe sickness when Jeanette Wilcher came to mind. What's that about? She was convicted of fraud with hits Galore and Life Foundation Trust. That was when it was the North Church. She was lionized from the pulpit and pleas were made to support her in the media when her trustee ship said that her Foundation Life Trust was to invest in Hits Galore and the price spiked. All spurious. for which she did time. But she used to come into the church with the pastor's family and sat on the very first row up close to Mary, one of the privileged who supported the nth church bill fold. In fact the address of the church was the same as her Life Trust, met in the same building, ate from the same table.

- I was minding my own business after a fashion and felt compelled to attend a prayer meeting held at this church incarnation some 20 miles away at 6 am. I did this every day for some months so you right away can tell what a borderline character that might be. People in this prayer meeting held in a big Amphitheatre would wander about the rows in various states, some prostrating themselves on the stage. One time I sat down off to one side and completely forgot where I was and when I came to the prayer meeting was over. After the individual part they would meet at the altar in a circle and pray holding hands. This all took about an hour, so I got home for breakfast. There were lots of occasions but the one that got me in segue after segue the time they handed out three by five cards with prayer requests on them. We were to intercede for this person. The one I got of Chuck Blodgett said that somebody's son was going to marry somebody's daughter but that it was unholy for various reasons and needed to be stopped.

--The thing is that the backstory to this was so much greater than anything imagined, exposing and confronting turpitudes and crimes unbelieved. The true believers are legion, but the fallen and rejected from those heights, or were they pushed, left no reports of these histories in the chats, due to primary doctrine, touch not the anointed, repeated over and over in those years and obviously still current with their perception of CFTN. There were however press reports which touch on the players and some of their nefarious activities. "We are all part of the body and when you speak DEATH about one of its members you are speaking death to your own self" was said over and over. Readers led by the spirit of God not by the open wounds of the offended. My hurt brothers and sisters, "Please do not slander who God has called. Please do not touch Gods anointed with words of death because your will eat of them."

-This holy doctrine drummed galore at men's retreats, prayer meetings, offerings and always in sermons was that if you criticize the man you will be buried. Early in his career, or maybe it was high school, a cop left a scar on his forehead with a billy club, which was bandied early in the 90's with the info that the cop died. The most favorite associate pastor of those years, a sycophant who continually introduced the beautiful Mary finally began to question the finances and removed died shortly after of asthma in Colorado. The chief usher of those years, named in suits, his son committed suicide. Physical giants around him, brother in law Randy, youth pastor Dan, prophet Miller. When and if the text ever came around to the facts, the devil himself came out in the sermon and the facts were defeated. First as Eagles nest, then North Church, then Church for the Nations, none of which were so far in location and temper from the reputed Halo room operated in the rotunda basement mirror basement of a later north Scottsdale outfit run they say by Erika kirk. These charismatic outfits have a flair for world dominion theology among others, different offshoots of the raise the dead schools used to hold services with an open coffin at the front in wich all comers could put they wishes and contributeions toward a better world as the old one was crumbling preface and abefore that church needed to abscond itself and change its name, again. Raise the dea or lower thm in Charlie's case, the facts unfolding as we run up to the new millennial or post millennial world order. Of influencers instead of witnesses, but no matter, if you are drawn to such, which is the old saw about whether a prophet declares or causes the event, Elijah and the small cloud, or in particular how being told at an elected meeting I was o go to cR aafter the plans are just been finalize, asked to stand up to receive this datum, or whether a medical practice was to be given to us and announced ahad of time as a boon. Whether with Alex Dunlap of the Conversion Center, a good tennis player I only took a set from one time, pounding deep to the backhand over and over, or dick Foulkes of Julliard at the LAM teaching bultmann who is a little weak in his Christology,to bible school students and the whole ubversion or not of libereation thology, and it subversions of empire as Stam makes plain, or jstt as radical a Jesuit version of the empty casket preachers that Maiden who did go to Rome to embrace Bartilomio, which many of the preecumenical post millennial pastors did. Hey want to go to rome! My most complete transaction of which was one Sunday, when preaching on money, that pastor pulled a big wad of bills from his pocketa and in a moment of dramatic flair, sowing seed, threw it, them to the audience. The only problem was that they stuck otether and flew right into my upraised mitt. They were oly ones, returned afterward to the pitcher, who disclaimedknowledged that it had ever happened. But money could get you in trouble. It is the custom in such assemblies for nearly anyone to delivere either a prophecy or a translation of one in tongues. I happily resisted the two occasions when I was so tempted. One elder Carroll Wilson did not. He stood in front of the church and raised his hands in prophecied funds after which he said, glory to God I can That myself! He was was a commodities trader, once considered for a cabinet post by…. He was defrocked the next day. We took him and his wife to dinner and became his friend. This was the church where kim clement first began to play thepiano being replaced on a permanent basis by now superstar Israel Houghton who played for a year or two. and then spoke from the seats of chairs over the audience some of those south African calls and response. He prophecied that the boxing promoter would be given 150K. that produced a flurry of punches, but all he got was a guilty plea. Once he came with both wrists cast from falling off a roof Rodney howard browne once sang far into the ngiht at the dirt floor extraazana in far scoosdal that the city impounded, people laying all over the floor.. the vauled lead of Jesus Christ superstar was given a car in one service. The only one who could shut clement up was that Christian trumpet player, Phil Driscoll but that was during a TBN broadcast hosted in the sanctuary with all the smoke and colored lights. .Meadowlark lemon joined there after speaking several times, and the Pakastaki Charles Dawes there is a military cadence and underlying chloric implication tto these offerings and many rivalries contend. It it is not diversified but one way emotionally to enter and practice that would make semijeeza proud. Ove and under the macKinder thesis of sea and land, in the lobby from the start was a huge metal globe by the sculptor Michael Andaerson, also an elder. which carried into myth of domination and war in which the revelation saint lives.. You did not engage these figures after their performance, for they were ushered into he room ehind the sound platform at the back where're once by accident a glimpse was had of the most

sumptuous tables of meats and sweet meats, mounds of shrimp fit for 100, guarded however from the commoner. There were less sanguine reports when during the law suit days one of the witnesses woke up with his front lawn covered with dead fish, another that two of the above personas were apprehended in offices with shopping bags of cash. These were FBI rumors so many not to be trusted. But the pastor then lived next door to Diamondbacks manager *Buck Showalter. A lot of this gossip was reported from the pulpit at the time, with articles by* Kirk Mitchell.
 The Tribune 12/22/1997.

5/15/15 Navajo weaving is measured by the narrow tightness of its stitching, so many weaves per inch, the denser the harder and more desired. The boy sitting in that bus in Limon on his way to the outland uninhabited, waiting for the bus to leave, given a note at the window by a messenger from the people he knew, just preventing that trip, starting another, that saved him from what? that took him toward what? well that he knew since he went there, knew as much as anyone knows the present of their life, but not if they assume they are an independent woof on the loom. In order for this message to save him, if it did, measures had to have been set into play in impossibly close courses, his brother had to die on time and his mother had to send the message on time, and the messenger had to deliver it on time. His own response was reactive, and off he went into the weaving of his own life. The point is that in order for all this to happen it had to be predetermined long before in impossible complexity. He has evidence that this is still going on, in fact it is this evidence that makes the weaving realization possible.
 --Weft threads are the horizontals that cover the vertical warps, woven over and under the warp and from side to side in the weaving. Wefts per inch are counted on both faces of a fabric. When the wefts are counted on one side, this number is doubled, as there is a corresponding weft on the other side. A count of 80 or more wefts per inch qualifies a rug as a tapestry. The weaving of this tapestry is greatly exceeded in our mystery, so that In the why and what we learn a little HOW the weaving came out of the why in the depth of riches both of the wisdom and knowledge of Elah, unsearchable judgments and ways past finding out. For who has known the mind of Yah, or been his counselor? Of Him and through Him and to Him are all things to Whilome be glory forever now and evermore amen.
 Why don't I live in all the space available to me, all these writings unpublished, unorganized so they can be inhabited. Dreamed of a the house I live in, a stranger visiting showing him the third story amphitheater room completely unused, which reminded me of another, the giant great unimproved property of dreams where the walls are partly fallen, but still the huge warehouse mass stands vacant on a large property, it is the warehouse also of Colonies, but there was also large unused spaces at Spicewood Spgs, and at Browns Mills, closets of art and sculptures, as at Dallas the attic and under the floor, My question to the stranger visitor was why don't I use these?

5/11/15 Bronchitis starts. Dreamed of a passage of thousands of instances since birth, three stages, climbing up going in sliding down, but that may be error. It was at a school, Thornburg, showing it to P, she had climbed up but two boys came to instruct in its use, I was behind her thinking I would know how when I got to it. Then there is another of these somewhere in more adult fashion. Makes me think of all those unconscious passages explored repeatedly in Delaney's Cave.

5/6/15 The history psychology of nations, lists of ravenous beasts of the kings of England, the list of Popes, but America unique for its one gigantic mind alter where the front alter good guy toots its horn and talks about elections while the hordes of back guys, bad guys do all the stuff the front guys report in their upbeat slanted exceptionalist manner, which themes consume pop, tv, ads totally. There is not one person in this system who not utterly disassociated, split, thinking what is not is and what is is not, unless there is somewhere someone who does not pay any attention to it at all and assumes, takes for granted all the above. The Roman emperors are ravenous, King Alfred ravenous. American life split between the real, which is the unreal, and the unreal which is the real, how the CIA is the world's largest innovator and supplier of drugs, import and export to maintain itself, just like the opium wars of England against China except it gets multiple benefit, population, crowd control, financing, furtherance of horror ends, like the Coen bros, another agented plant, and all pop hbo, fx, amc, esc. series on dvd and wii, pop eating pop itself, eating the mind of its nationhood with gang signs cops and ops. To Midway.

5/1/15 Flower in Rock at Shemer, Bus Stop at WHAM

5/3/15 The woman and the wife in all her faith and power of belief to bring life brings children, gardens, planted and the husband father has to administer them, which he does because she brought them to him, and it is his to do not hers who has borne the life he must save and for what but for itself, no reason other so he looks down the long tunnel of his mind a year a month a day out, then years more and sees the dangers, or tries to, out of which she has brought the life he must guard. He gets edgy with the thought of the task and she thinks it is her doing, well it is and it isn't, she is only doing what she is made to do, and so is he and this is Mother's Day.

4/29/15 Faulkner is Homeric except his gods are the convergence of horizontal and vertical and the swirl of a boat in a whirlpool around this cosmic. He is cosmic always looking up and out and down and in, sees earth from space. Cinematic. Aeg came and we got him two sport coats at Macy's for 200, retail 750.

4/28/15 just before waking I saw Ken Morrison, ebullient in some kind of assembly setting and as he left asked whether he still had my draft copy of Grendel he used for...? He said he would email c/o usda? or etc. This reminded me of the take of Gerhart about the passing of Ken's Head, at ASU, which reminded me Aey wrote a limerick on his phone straight out this world yesterday which he showed me when we spoke of Faulkner. Of a place that did once exist, but was also imaginary, and of the same place that does not yet exist, so is apocryphal, one hardly knows how to call such a rubric geographically and politically legitimate and illegitimate. All the more evocative when this difference lacks connection to itself. Parts of the text are therefore set apart to show the disjunctures, spectral and estranged. We come up with different phrases, physiognomies of crowd in this future construction of a literary form, inner boulevards, phantasms of interior, like a flower on a night table, an overnight ranunculus to account the creation of a new world in a world that does and does not exist, and its mundane causes. We all hanker for the flash thoughts by which we ourselves are continually remade and can hardly remember a time when we were not lost in internal meanderings. Most of this came into being between the war and the next decades when it was full blown, if unknown. That was a long decade, two of them, but time was putty. The first condition of emergence was the need of clandestines to build shadowgraphs, counterfeits, simulacrums. Fertile ground existed in the mine of religious artifacts, turned gas to light and marketed different clothings about the globe. The second condition to stimulate the new was the electronic architecture of its spread. Images obliterated the old. Pop obliterated Pop. One decade could not recognize another. It was the Annihilation of Now powered by wish images, escape from the past. Staccato extinctions of memory were relocated to some remote spot until entirely forgot. And it goes without saying that all of this would be denied, overruled by the overridden who did as their peers said. This was the unconscious collective that belonged to the sub aquean world. How can I belong to the world when I cannot belong to the city of the submarine, the old abandoned beds of rivers forced to change course, kept in their walls; the Seine, the Euphrates hardly break out their substrate, stand thesis counter thesis, a reiver here, there a bend, not the Colorado, damned as rusing down to the salt sea, elaborate idyll ambiguity that puts Hegel to the test. Who belongs to the Thames? Have you been intimate with Monongahela? Susquehanna! Claudius Drusus Germanicus! Alexander, Caesar, Napoleon?

At the same time as the sixth angel loosed the vial that dried the Euphrates for the invasion of the north, of Gog, the nations loosed their space satellites into war. For in all the discords of pseudonymity there was yet a ventriloquism, not of a puppet master, though we should consider it, but of a speaking through the present of the past, of Rosenroth speaking through Jung about alchemy. These references are many sided, come strip the ancients, and depending on sensibility some are more pregnant than others, Walter Benjamin is fertile, furtive, but there is always an alchemy of change in the remolting of the feathers, the remolding of the images, the words themselves in their sound. So Gershom Scholem says Messiah will be the last and first, philosopher of language: he will deduce Judaism from its language which doesn't say nearly enough, since by the Breath of his Mouth words come whole worlds, since he made them, and here, now, when the angel unlooses the vial and Euphrates dries up like the fig and the Kings of the east rise up and march, the utterance of language, the roots and the alphabet will be the least of the spiritual powers of the Sons. But the meaning was not in the sound, he looked in the sound The meaning was not in the syntax he looked at all the connections. The meaning was not in the language, for the words, the languages were within the still small voice what did speak, what language that sounded, indeed they sounded, but like what luggage, all and none or one and what did say, the impossible when thou from out the boundless deep turns again home.

      Heidelberg, 1923. 12 dense pages on thick handmade paper, by Benjamin, as introduction to his translation "Über die Aufgabe des Übersetzers" (Rodenberg, 5.349). Benjamin's second ever publication, green-yellow thick paper-covered boards. Crisp and immaculate. 500 copies made. Exceedingly rare. Benjamin is suddenly read and listed and mentioned and alluded to everywhere in the last decade, 10 years prior this attention was 10% as much, in the 60's and 70's hardly there at all when Suhrkamp (having issued in hardback only, his letters in the mid 60's) published the green 1971 paperback "Art in the Age of it's Mechanical Reproducibility". It was all wrong then as it is still now, but what thought (exclamation mark), what dialectics, what mystical materialism. Benjamin gets better and better though rarely "right," and that's as rare in the philosophy of aesthetics as in the aesthetics of philosophy. Memorable. (Meanwhile, horrible little opportunists like Adorno, with their Nazi sympathies – recently come to light – and egocentric slickness, let alone their proAmerican authoritarianism in the name of its opposite, get a lot more right, and oppress with their brilliance. There's real beauty in Benjamin's way of trying to come to grips with life and meaning.) As always (usually for women) early death triples the effect, and the affect. Though Baudelaire might be ready for reappraisal, there's less than meets the eye. There's still, after all the above, more than meets the eye with Benjamin. We've only ever seen two other copies of this book, one sold, one in real shabby condition without a proper cover. This copy is as new – and for once the overused term means not as, but is. Bookseller Inventory # INDEC7084

4/19/15 Gina Rometty, IBM: Big data the natural resource of the 21st century. refined data. prediction, Giving Watson Eyes: Watson will predict who will struggle in school, sensors collect data in medicine, measure body invasively and precisely, Apple, Johnson and Johnson, Medronic, open platform, for every human 10% info collected will be formal med records, 20 % will be genomics, 70% exogenous data: fitbit, tracker, apple watch, what you're eating, your heart rate, 300 million books worth of data per person. Watson computer: new connections, new alloys: [try desiccated erythrocytes, filaments resembling bacteria but acting like archaea, transbiological hybrids, or gna, pna, or body electric piezo electricity]

4/18/15 New Moon https://www.youtube.com/watch?v=ZSQ-dp1sV5w
What are red blood cells doing falling out the sky? desiccated erythrocytes, filaments resembling bacteria but acting like archaea, transbiological hybrid forms, Clifford Carnicon http://www.morgellonsexposed.com/ Biodesign at ASU developed first GNA. Nano ARRAYS used for dna hybridization. pEOPLE WITH MORGELLONS SYMPTOMS MAY BE REJECTING IT WHEREAS OURS ARE ACCEPTING IT. a paradigm shift in biology. singularity, artificial, robotic blood cells, made into The Hive. Gna, pna,. Upload computers into brains. Human machine, Karl Hillie. Waypasthuman.com. unable to connect to database! No gender, nonreproduction, tailored to specific tasks, problem reaction solution Hegelian dialectic a fifth dimension tool. John and Margaret Woodall Sandy Hook Bahai benediction to

consumption of Mammon. Sandy Hook a model transition ot social passivity, game changing drill, new 9/11. plethora of black and silver cars in parking lot, Christmas trees behind firehouse ahead of time Newtown an experiment in time, tweets, time stamp to dress rehearse disaster management of nation as a whole. 1.19f -
http://www.therealistreport.com/2013/11/sofia-smallstorm-unraveling-sandy-hook.html note announcement Lt. Paul Vance. Twitter is a major in Smart911, referring biometric data, names, numbers. Disaster an experiment in multiple variability. a metadata experiment, a DHS experiment upon a culture. information designed to produce the optimal future society, that is to build the fifth dimension into existence. FEMA capstone events 1.19f. Sandy Hook a Capstone event, ie. not what happened, but how the story occurs and is told in the dimensions. The parties were actors set on a stage for effects. The future or what will happen is the fifth dimension. the sixth dimension is national.
http://checkinitout.com/2015/03/15/interview-41-sofia-smallstorm/ body electric piezo electricity. EM radiation causes hardening of eggs in girls causing sterility, 9.30; moving targets absorb less EM; human energy harvesting, generated from eyelids, venous return, arterial pulse, footsteps, motion of walking, loose clothing fitted with nano batteries, 15.00, men conditioned female with estrogen products 35.00, conditioned homosexual, incomplete males, post gender, non reproductive, Agenda 21, neuter human, state takes over reproduction, worker bee, hive society, invasive jewelry to generate body energy, hooked in the veins, memory ports,

4/17/15 what is it about a boy that mystifies a mother: his uninhibited hunger.
    Consciousness is only important to those who don't have it. I take the sphere descending in the blue sky as the moon in every child's dream of wholeness unremembered, descending into their life in just the colors Bruegel seeks, a lunar white with tones of gold, the perfect light of love and a blue sky impossible to see with such a moon perhaps, since it is day and the moon enlarged so impossibly to indicate its nearing, as though some revelation is at hand. and one is. the painting is about who owns heaven and earth and the heaven descending in the sphere in the sky indicates the lovely nature of heaven and the angels defending it, wello thay and the rebels have consumed all the talk. We have to appreciate the lunar calendar and its nature, the importance of new moon and full, the effect upon the tides of the sea and obviously upon the course of humanity, so you would think that blood moons worth attending to. The lunar calendar seems secondary among a people of the sun, the solar calendar, a people consumed with pagan, meaning Babylonian, Greek, Roman designations of the heavens, who name Sunday after the sun, what they consider the god of the heavens, dear Plotinus we love you, but, but the sun is not the Father or the Son and He who made creation. So Fall is a judgment upon the days of the week named for these gods and upon the months of the year named for these gods and even upon the way we figure time according to these gods, these false apparitions that permeated all of literature of Greece and Rome which became our legacy in En gland and America. We are only talking about ourselves here in Antwerp and Brussels where Bruegel was made. Evening and morning make the day, not morning and evening, which matters since the day begins at dusk and dawn is mid day. Saying it that way shows how far the fall. And what are the agents of it? Whatever they were they became three

footed beasts and creeping things made over into chimeras, so that is view of the reality that the angels overthrow and judge, chimeric reality, a hybrid endlessly devolving.

4/16/15 Lift up your heads oh ye gates and be lift up ye everlasting doors and the King of Glory shall come in! restoration gap theory church in Coventry fall of rebel angels

4/13/15 Heard yesterday that regeneration is unconscious, conversion is conscious. Aey stopped with Judah, said he loves visiting because it's a breath of fresh air. then I said I assumed he was getting his wife pregnant. But he said her OB required him to see a urologist before treating her for infertility, plus an ultrasound to see if her fallopian tubes were blocked. But I said it was pointless since she smokes, drinks, doesn't take counseling with him, etc. and that fertility drugs, twins, in those conditions could make for a greater pain than he imagined. She has been dealt a bad hand by him because he tolerates such things without change but to inflict the outcome on the unborn is a crime. What's the worst she could do if you stood up to her? Suicide or divorce. She has never spoken of suicide, but divorce, better to divorce before such complications than after! At least why doesn't he deal her better cards?

This also came about because he said he was sitting on his back porch since it was clean. He sold a hundred dollars at the neighborhood sale sat before he was called to work. I asked why she didn't continue the sale. Because she doesn't like people.

4/12/15 JUNg Jung's dreams are tarot readings abstracted. a Marvel Comics abstracted from tarot, same images, acts. His daimon is a possession the same as out of Shinto and Lowell. Jung's love of alchemy, I Ching prove him a tool, a medium for the daimon, but it is not particular to him, this collective voice that gives the one utterance. Jung's unconscious is a series of tarot cartoons set alongside similar omens in national religions, a compendium of the counterfeit. His dissertation is a study of divinations.

But Freud with Jung wants to be a god. There are gods all over his rooms just like the trailer homes and prefab houses of witches on the heights of Jerome has toads and frogs, gargoyle pots all over their darkened rooms. The decor speaks marvels just opposite the Shaker room, whitewashed adobe Spanish mission with those maple legs and unadorned tops. These internal rooms need to be cleaned, spare as the ark of the covenant, just the tablets. What is said of Freud's room is said of all cabala, trying to invoke godhood of Freud with its own magic of geometry:

"Is the hidden cauldron not an enticement and a seduction ot its investigator? Or, to say it even more terribly: it may be that the quarry is all the time in the pursuer" (Cynthia Ozick on G. Scholem). "hundreds of strange little gods...crowd of stone godlets...mobs and bevies...Freud wished to become a god...what the Sabbath and its emanations sought to suppress Freud meant to reveal, everything barbarous and dreadful and veiled and terror bearing: the very tooth and claw...curiously named assistants or doubles of Satan, so Freud peopled the unconscious with the devils of Id, Ego and Superego, potent dancing ghosts who cavort unrecorded in our anatomies while we pretend they are not there.. the student of the dream life--that subterranean grotto all drowned and darkling, torn with the fury of anguish and lust (From a Refugee's Notebook, 63-4) Marie-Louise von Franz recounts in Psyche and Matter (1988) that toward the end of his life:

"Jung suggested investigating cases where it could be supposed that the archetypal layer of the unconscious is constellated*—following a serious accident, for instance, or in the midst of a conflict or divorce situation—by having people engage in a divinatory procedure: throwing the I Ching, laying the Tarot cards, consulting the Mexican divination calendar, having a transit horoscope or a geomantic reading done. If Jung's hypothesis is accurate, the results of all these procedures should converge (Mary Greer Word Press) Jung's doctoral dissertation explored the occult.

4/6/15 why this continuing sense of foreboding?
Dreamed rice balls on plant, Lord Cecil yogananda fine books ltd eds, india, spice racks unstoppered, a hundred spices, gradually warming to them, recognizing a faith like mine, saying so, the woman warming spoke of her parents passing recently, condolences, she said not, he has me take a fine oversize book of red, gold plates, we are to work somehow with him on disease through intermediaries, me liking him too, before this, two performances of my own on tape, one audio, one vid, well done. my interest was stirred first by the balls of rice shaped like hearts on top of stalks, they called it busy rice or something, then smelling the spices which were in ranks twenty or so high in small jars with wrapping, cellophane around, but open so they could be used and last by the books I then noticed, as though this were progressive: after this I spoke to them and told my appreciation and the recognition, their softening and embracing, leaving later with the plans to work together somehow, my part I don't know, something about writing?

3/30/15 Impressed by the name Zion in church, searched scion of David and got Yashanet, which led to Rev. 13... http://www.yashanet.com/studies/revstudy/text/r13_1-10.htm and consideration of Passover fast Friday night

The Rabbis say: In the generation in which the scion of David will come, the wise men of the generation will die and the rest will waste away with grief and sorrow and much trouble will come upon the community and cruel decrees will be promulgated, one coming on top of another.
R. Nehorai said: In the generation in which the scion of David will come, the young will insult their elders and the old will rise before the young, as it says, The daughter riseth up against her mother, the daughter-in-law against her mother-in-law; a man's enemies are the men of his own house (Micah VII, 6), and a son will feel no shame before his father.
R. Levi said: The scion of David will come only in a generation which is full of impudence and deserves to be exterminated. R. Jannai said: If you see one generation after another cursing and blaspheming, look out for the coming of the Messiah, as it says, Wherewith Thine enemies have taunted, O Lord, wherewith Thine enemies he taunted the footsteps of Thine anointed (Ps. LXXXIX, 52), and immediately afterwards it is written, Blessed be the Lord for evermore, Amen.
Beriatic "dragon" bariatric (Gen. 1, 2I). This verse', he said, 'we have already discussed, but the words "He created the great dragons" contain a yet more special and

particular mystery: they refer to the Leviathan and his mate, which last was slain and is preserved by the Holy One for the regaling of the righteous (in the days of the Messiah).

3/23/2015 Pizzolatto listed several influences on the show's first season: philosophy books such as Thomas Ligotti's *The Conspiracy Against the Human Race*, Eugene Thacker's *In The Dust Of This Planet,* Ray Brassier's *Nihil Unbound*, Jim Crawford's *Confessions of an Antinatalist*, and David Benatar's *Better Never To Have Been*. Pizzolatto also mentions horror authors Laird Barron, John Langan, Simon Strantzas, and Ligotti.[24]
      In August 2014, an article alleged that Pizzolatto plagiarized Thomas Ligotti's book The Conspiracy Against the Human Race: A Contrivance of Horror, citing eleven examples that included word-for-word quotations. 3/23/15 Monday.

There was a black swallowtail butterfly resting all night and this morning on the side of the house waiting for the sun. I buried Tracy today near Joggie and Blessing, wrapped in scarlet, in rosemary. I thought she was gone on Friday, but she revived. On Sat she was moving with her head and feet up and that night settled in usual place against the porch wall, for the first time in weeks and a month her head was in her shell. Before she would languish in the dirt and only crawl into the shade and collapse. I always covered her at night. That Sat night she voided all the water in her body. The pavement all around her was wet and smelled of urine. Pat moved her before we went to see Theodore for the first time, so she wouldn't be damp, but I think she was gone. I covered her last nite, but she had passed. It felt like she weighed several pounds less. She had her last hatchlings this fall '14, but never settled for the winter, as if that were her last effort. Like Joggie and Blessing though she lived until the end. Pat had begun to get on the ground and put her face up to her to encourage her. I too, but now she is gone.

3/10/15 Tuesday I worked so hard on OOps that I missed the visit with Theo Sunday, slept till 1.30 pm and convalesced the whole day after the Fri nite Barber cello concert. Yesterday, Mon, I was carrying a railroad tie the way Don Reitz did his sculptures, belly to belly, threw it down, but caught my finger against a pot, then decided not to work outside, so went in to OOp, but somehow instead produced Begin Blue from its blog and now it is shaping.
      This leads to wondering what the resolution of the plot of Jerusalem can be beyond its eternal present.

3/5/15 Dr. Theodore Reiff, founding president of the Genocide Education Project, on the analogy of Nazi subversion of medicine to life termination for cost savings since 1978 in the United States. The Reiff Center at Christopher Newport University seeks to raise awareness of the horrors of genocide, human rights violations and conflict: Listen from 2.11-17.17. His point is that depending on the environment medicine is used either for horrific barbarity or healing. The dismissal of his analogy to the U.S. only shows how far the current Experiment (Robert Reiff) has progressed.

3/3/15 Christopher Sower and Beissel
https://archive.org/stream/pennsylvaniamaga12histuoft#page/76/mode/2up

3/2/15 Borges: I owe the discovery of Uqbar to the conjunction of a mirror and an encyclopedia. He literally ran into this mirror and near killed himself. The his mother read Out of the Silent Planet to him, and changed his fiction.

2/25/15 I think the serial depravations of Jerusalem, over and over, worse and worse are a metaphor of the earth. Hyper time.
Aeg just called. Baby breech says ultrasound of which they have had many. C section Friday scheduled.

2/18/15 Random or predestined Robert spoke to his grad prof in psych. Today I took him over the Four Peaks. Which, if fact is symbolic means...and also he saved us at least once afterward when tired, I did not immediately notice in the hghy obstacles...likewise on the way home, diverted at Shea was going south and would have cont'd...this morn, before going 3 AM I work to sound of lock changing, like a clank with an echo...

2/16/15 Never so strongly perhaps but not for the first time, it is however built upon the other transitions I awoke consciously from a deep dream (Asking Aeg whether he would pursue amore tennis in h.s.) to awakeness with a belt of strips of sunlight darkened between, protoplasmic circles on the bands of light and watched them closely until opening. There was no light source, the curtains were drawn so the light was not exterior. This all took a few seconds 30 at most, but seemed strongly felt as an impression. Then I was back from that place. So while I have learned how to consciously fall asleep I am working on consciously waking up. I consider this in the context of lessons of precognition of last fall, and answers to prayer that must have been ordered before I prayed them!

2/15/15 My first knowledge of Rosh Hashanah was as the quintessential lost Gentile in Merion where I had moved as a senior in hs. The school buses were half empty on the September holy days. I was not a member of that group and I was not a member of the Gentile groups either. Right out of some novel.
Popism is the most sacrosanct of modern beliefs. it justifies all consumption, sex, influence from billionaires on their air flights with 12 year old girls and expresidents to the legermain of dope, good dope for all people. So if it is said that pop is eating pop it must mean in some sense not cannibalism but a way of life whose purpose is to empower and enrich the producers. If I write here a critique of pop is is no small thing, for pop traces itself back to Cobri and Israel copulating before Baal Peor. That is pops spiritual side. Its material is empire, babylon, rome britain, the states, the gold man of Nebuchadnezzar. We are might small compared to it. The new sponge bob brain is receptive to such things.

2/14/15 Govt spokesmen say jihadists hijacked Islam but the media hijacked Christians every way from scholarship disproving it to painting the only devout left as terrorists against the world of Sodom, abortion. No world to this on the news.

2/12/15 Optical Lattice. Pop Tales of the Fairy Mind, Fairy Tales of Pop Mind. 300 Verses of Plantigrade. Different methods juice and oil. Cider press. Mom putting apples to boil in cheesecloth then after all the drippings end, wringing the cloth to get the last squeezings. That's what it feels to get this writing. I am squeezed until the juice escapes.

2/10/15 Ezekiel reimagines the Temple and there are reimaginings of Jerusalem, of Eden, and Zion

2/9/15 I trust myself more than I trust the wheel. That is saying, I am superior to the wheel, not to be tolerated. Everyone is on the wheel/ And I got off!~ heresy. We will go to live in Jerusalem, city of peace, and war, after all it suits the name Reiff, and the face and there will be no partiality there.

2/7/15 A man is only a man if he is in conflict with evil and is devoted in humility to his faith. Confronted with the devastation he had caused the Jordanian pilot did not fall to his knees in acknowledgment, proving himself morally dead. I sent a copy of the Isis vid to Robt because I believe he has an inherent disgust at the spiritual decay of this civilization, even if he partakes of it. I hear this decay every day where I train, in the mouths of the men, many elder, who mouth vulgarities, boast their inebriation, mock women and are obese of mind and heart. The conflict of Muslim austerity with this worldliness, sexuality, mind control and consumption, the solo call to prayer in a single human voice vs. the cacophony of noise in every American media shows the rottenness of the European west, which demands that everyone bow to its right to exist but respects no one but itself and its own beliefs in sodom, child murder, drugs, and lust. When a fruit falls from its tree it lies in rottenness, food for wasps who feed off its sweet decaying flesh. It is the vision of the birds of Ezekiel 39.17, a version of which appeared in the 20th anniversary of Ygdrasil, the Banquet of God:

12/27/15 The REAL confession of Stanley Kubrick -Must Watch Stanley Kubrick's Secret Movie: Being There Elohim and Adam

12/28/15 Who alone is immortal and who lives in unapproachable light, whom no one has seen or can see. To him be honor and might forever I Tim 6.16.
--Zechariah's breakfast. Cut: The light of His presence is what we see by and that orders our lives. That sun, defamed in the heavens by the Neph fallen Naki Sumerian spirit rats, is the Day star that rises in our hearts, a symbol of the one who made it, as Zechariah says, "the rising sun will come to us from heaven to shine on those living in darkness and in the shadow of death, to guide our feet into the path of peace" (Luke 1 78,9). Irenaeus: "Gloria enim Dei vivens homo."

12/29/15 The Wright AFB of Dayton Ohio stores woo artifacts.

12/30/15 NASA Insider Everything was a lie NASA symbolism. chevrons, vectors --Karel Appel. Picasso and Greek fresco. Picasso's distortion of the eyes.

-- I don't know whether to say it is a benefit to show us all the distortion we don't see around us, or that it causes it!

--Forgive my sin, my -unclean compliments of you. The unclean in greater or less measure occupies the thoughts of a man. Hartman's Midrash angels created to sing each day as if a day were a meaningful measure of time and all the self acknowledgments homages to this uncleanness, nothing compared to Harold Bloom of course, but Gunkel is consumed with Abraham's guile in Egypt hiding behind that the beauty of his wife, how the three ethics (like muses) did not find approval in later times in Genesis. It as if Gunkel speaks of himself in this, they don't meet his approval and not his really but the artificial standard of critics of his time, like Robert Cole's Niebuhr wants Bonhoeffer not to go back to Germany, to deny the only hope of courage and real virtue, flawed as it is, to Germany. It's always about stilling the one voice. If the voice speaks it has one option, to die or be spared. Considering all the forces arrayed against us we have no hope except to be delivered not by might or power, by allies or horses, or weapons but by the salvation of Jesus. No other hope. (to Legend)

12/31/15 the old currency, now in use, would be worthless but to be exchanged for a certain rate of exchange, as if for a foreign currency, for the new currency at locations for a designated time after that it will be defunct, as in India, so which real goods are most valuable in a deflation?

A Theodicy of Hell Charles Seymour. Molinism. Transworld depravity is the property a person has if he would commit a sin in any of the circumstances in which he was created. Plantinga: Transworld damnation "is possessed by any person who freely does not respond to God's grace and so is lost in every world feasible for God in which that person exists." Craig. Qure Quirks.

2016

12/31/16 The struggle is conducted on two planes with the divine and human, 4000 years of Galut, a nation uprooted from its homeland, subject to alien rule, and a struggle with the soul of Galut, its essence and purpose. The feeling of uprootedness turns Diaspora (Dispersion) into Galut (Exile). Thrice daily we plead, protest and contest.

12/30/16 Fallen engineers.

Spetsnaz by Viktor Suvorov, life with your spade. Waco, movie stars, entertainment are no other than corrupt agents for defusing and destroying citizenry. Those who say different are called Russian agents. The oppressor always makes itself the victim and the victim the oppressor.

"I am not a conceptual artist. I can't think of an idea. Most of it comes out of my hands." That soul, though all hell should endeavor to shake, I'll never, no never, no never forsake.

-When the candles are lit it is a reminder of prayer against the enemy and avengers who would steal our reprieve. We are asking they be confused, they turn upon each other, they be judged and their plans revealed, that they fall upon one another and betray themselves, that they be dashed into pieces and that the Lord himself from heaven will come with a shout, with voice of the archangel and the trump of Yahve.

-SUBSTITUTE THE RUSSIANS WITH OBAMA then SUBSTITUTE THE VICTIM WITH THE OPPRESSOR. Here's Prince Charles calling POPulism a "deeply disturbing echo of the dark days of the 1930s...my parents' generation fought and died in a battle against intolerance, monstrous extremism and an inhuman attempt to exterminate the Jewish population of Europe." The Royals had pizza in Canada as early as the 50s: "the abduction of ten fellow residential school children by the Queen of England and her husband in October, 1964 at the Catholic school in Kamloops, British Columbia, Canada."(1964).

DEEPLY DISTURBING ECHOES? HIS PARENTS! The Royal family was unquestionably pro-Hitler in the 1930s. POPulism is a danger BECAUSE it is the belief in the power of people to have control their government and follow their own beliefs, rather than a small group of pizza-lovers.

"In the past six weeks, the Washington Post published two blockbuster stories about the Russian threat that went viral: one on how Russia is behind a massive explosion of "fake news," the other on how it invaded the U.S. electric grid. Both articles were fundamentally false. Each now bears a humiliating editor's note grudgingly acknowledging that the core claims of the story were fiction: The first note was posted a full two weeks later to the top of the original article; the other was buried the following day at the bottom." *Glenn Greenwald*

12/29/16 Once you get Hegel you can read the implicit triangle of truth. Thesis/antithesis, supply the truth. The speaker is the danger, always revealing his deep deceit. Kerry sticks his tongue out.

Aurochs' curved horns, huge bulk and irascible temperament made it a formidable foe for prehistoric hunters, but scientists are edging closer to a long-held dream of bringing back from extinction one of Europe's most impressive beasts – the aurochs.

This creature, the ancestor of modern cattle, once roamed tangled forests and sodden marshlands from Britain to the Balkans and beyond to Asia and North Africa. But it disappeared from the British Isles in the Iron Age and was driven to extinction in the rest of Europe by the 17th century, with the last specimen dying in the Jaktorow Forest in Poland in 1627. Now researchers are working to bring it back to life through a process known as backbreeding, which entails selectively mating existing breeds of "primitive" cattle which retain much of the ancient aurochs' DNA. Scientists on brink of bringing back extinct Nick Squires.

Reflectacles

--the future walks through the past and the present leaving a trail. The past is all costume, the present is shadowy, ghostly, airy with sightings of the future, but the future when it arrives is costumed like the past so that is what we know except we think we know it pat. Dress up the new, but it is a costume. We think we know and feel the present but it passes so fast we forget it and our memory of it is what we call the present, but by then that too is clearly past. Catch the future walking on the roof, the slab, the tree cuts, seems a concrete event when it is finished, but it was a construct of decisions, timings. It is all vapor. At least that is the way the government counts time. Post date your losses tothe next new year, sell so gains equal losses in stock gains and loss, but it is a technicality of book keeping, a bow to Rome. All False, since this is really the fourth month of creation!

-- Roof completed yesterday. $6800. Second Grade Roofing Polyglass Kool Roof Mulehide

Used to play doubles with Dave German weekends. This began when they were small. Sometimes we played chess after. I trusted him enough to let him take A to baseball games and to a pro tennis event here. In today's world I question myself, but I never saw any ill effects. When they got older they did work clearing out his yard and taking stuff to the dump.

12/28/16 Wed. John Crockett died last Fri, found Tues. Karen called police to check. Beckett in his Trieste chair future becomes the past. There is a kind of recurrency in the days of Noah. As to Atlantis, if Plato is believed that it was 11.6 K ago when he says it was in the Atlantic and sank ;;off Florida!- not Antarctica

12/27/16 boys for sale 1981 documentary Tom Philpott. Humanitarian warrior Daniel Alexander Cannon, Trump, Jeffrey Epstein temple of orgy island. Wilkesland Satellite Detects MASSIVE Object Under Antarctica s of Invercargill.

-with a sharp knife cut deeply into the middle finger of your left hand, eat the pain" saw Podesta, Bush, Obama cutting. http://209.157.64.201/focus/f-chat/3491069/posts

-sudden resignation of New Zealand's Prime Minister "is directly connected to what is going on at 'The Base' in Antarctica…..John Key knows what is about to happen and he does not want to be at the helm of his country's government when it does." The source was reluctant to give more detail but hinted it had to do with the imminent arrival of "the fleet."ugly truth 22days ago anshur inner earth group http://forum.clonehost.net/topic/52/antarctica/8

The dominoes keep falling, Hollande, Renzi, Sarkozy down; Xi, Putin, Abe and Merkel now targeted- Fulford.

What happened to the passengers? 9/11. Pixar pizza planet truck. Recorded Future. John Todd Collins, exposes says he was on the council of 13 and gave multi millions to the 4 charismatics,

-In the region of Bashan, temple to Baal Zeus, Pan, ie. Casearia Phillipi Peter confesses the rock is the rock. Jesus says is the place he will build his church, the Temple of the Dead, and the Gates shall not withstand it. Then they go up Hermon. In and above Bashan he is glorified not only for the disciples but for the unclean Watchers domain so they may see their demise. Then Jesus says he must go to Jerusalem to die.

-Robert: Jay Illuminati pedophiled.

Quantum
The LHC uses TeV and PeV of power derived from the colliding of particles.
The AQC (model 1024 (1,152 qubits), released in February of 2015 (in actuality, as I point out, the model 2048), is described as possessing processing power equivalent to over 7 billion human brains). uses the superposition of qubits, and quantum tunneling. the number of qubits determines the number of parallel universes the AQC can open portals. These are Mandela Portals (Building predictive algorithms of human behavior, in designing programs of control) A qubit vertical polarization and horizontal is a two-state quantum mechanical system. In a classical system, a bit would have to be in one state or the other. However, quantum mechanics allows the qubit to be in a superposition of both states at the same time D-Wave employs the Monte Carlo system in combinatorial optimization. combining of all known possible solutions to a given problem/equation, and inserting it into other parallel universes/dimensions a solution with 99.99% accuracy is realized through this process of quantum tunneling. Monte Carlo statistical analysis predicts the outcome. Each time D-Wave and associated customs like Lockheed USC, Google Nasa and CERN insert combinatorial equations into parallel universes by way of their quibits, they do so through quantum tunneling.

In conclusion: The universe known to us is, on a continual basis, being altered. Not time. But, how we experience our present environment. There is a direct connection between the AQCs and the LHC."(Quantum Annealing , Wang, Wu and Jian Zou. In Anthony Patch).
	- Portals opened, but only by the AQCs..AQC's functioned because they were actually, literally sending information (combinatoral equations/problems) into another dimension. And, then receiving back answers/solutions from unknown sources. But, the answers were correct
	-combination of all known and probable solutions to a given problem/equation. Patch, Quantum tunneling is a two-way communication pathway. Upon receipt of a solution from another dimension, it must be translated back to a form humans can use
-Purposefully, items and subjects well known in popular culture and religion, are being altered as part of a large scale PSYOPS campaign. Designed to model human behavior in algorithms of predictive outcome, convolution representations.
The targets for such alterations were identified using solutions from other dimensions. The questions put forth using combinatorial optimization were asking which items and subjects should be altered for the maximization of the Mandela Effect. What should be altered for the biggest psychological effects.
	What would be noticed and to what extent by the populations at large. And, how people would react and communicate these effects, and to whom.
	Algorithms of ripple effects across the globe...Computer models create alternative realities for each person within a "mirror" of our entire world.
	Essentially, what we consider our "real world" is running as a duplicate reality within a sentient, artificial computer system. Each person, over 7 billion is reproduced as a "node",

their names substituted with an avatar agent. Sentient World Simulation (SWS)...by beginning with quantum annealing, they side-stepped many of the instability issues inherent with quantum states. In combination, they took advantage of both coherence and decoherence phases, allowing the qubits to operate in both states of superposition... final step was programming and operating the system using combinatoral optimization. Essentially, combining all probable solutions to a given problem... It is the NA (North Area) which will house Nimrod's DNA, but not until they've completed the necessary Machine Development (MD) of AWAKE, including the filling of it with Xeon gas.

Mandela Effect solely within the realm of the AQC and its process of quantum tunneling of equations. MANDELA EFFECT! Quantum Computing Artificial Intelligence Is Here!
however memory seems impervious to QC which asks where and how is it stored, for there the lion still lies down with the lamb. This suggests we come to a new oral age when written texts are corrupt and pass on our thoughts memory to memory, outside the machined text
-digitized demonic entities Geordie Rose uses military terms, QCs deployed in research centers. QC are not super computers. Google and NASA have them. to build "machines like us." Board of Spaceex, Tesla, AQC's functioned because they were actually, literally sending information (combinatoral equations/problems) into another dimension. And, then receiving back answers/solutions from unknown sources. But, the answers were correct pulse 2 refrigerators "altar to an alien god" "giant black moniliths 10x12ft. Absolute zero nearly, pulse 2 delusion refrigeration. pulse once a second, like heartbeat, chip size of thumbnail. 2 states mutually exclusive at same time: identical except for value of a qubit. In qc, each qubit doubles, 2 to the 500, he means the number of parallel universes living in that chip shadows which overlap our world, doubling of number of qubits double each year. Unease at tech development in Silicon Valley, 5yrs nasa finds new earth, ..., humanity on cusp of the revelation where machines outpass us in every respect. In 15 years machines will do this.
D Wave Systems --to break Shor's 2048 algorithm. Meaning, factoring (finding) all the prime numbers within 2048, in order to discover the original key used to code a message/communication. AQC mathematically operates through ORDER-FINDING of prime factors of 2048. Upon the cracking by the model 1024 (not publicly discussed by D-Wave) of Shor's 2048 algorithm, THE MANDELA EFFECTS BEGAN TO MANIFEST.
the "key to the bottomless pit". The key is carried by the Fallen Angel, cast down from Heaven. The "Key to the bottomless pit" is the breaking of an ENCRYPTED DIMENSIONAL CODE. One specific to Saturn's cube, requiring 4096 qubit.
Small portal. Breaking open first, one tetrahedron Stranglet. Once accomplished within the fixed target of the combined LHC/AWAKE accelerators. Only then will they generate the Birkeland currents, plasma conduit to Saturn, and its cube opened. Focusing and steering this conduit is accomplished using the toroidal field produced by the LHC's superconducting magnets. The magnetosphere will be parted and opened, allowing the Birkeland currents to flow through the conductive plasma fields to Saturn. See Saturn 600 cell-tetrahedron shape of matter.
Monte Carlo Method -system of statistical analysis in prediction of outcomes. What particles may result from high-energy collisions, and separately, integration.- multivariable

integral. One possible approach to solve this multivariable integral is to exactly enumerate all possible configurations of the system, and calculate averages at will. This is done in exactly solvable systems, and in simulations of simple systems with few particles. In realistic systems, on the other hand, an exact enumeration can be difficult or impossible to implement. For those systems, the Monte Carlo integration (and not to be confused with Monte Carlo method, which is used to simulate molecular chains) is generally employed for // importance sampling, which may be what Clif High does,--connected to Mandela Effect.- construction of algorithms predicting human behavior. Behavioral Modelling.
Urgent Discoveries, Stark

12/25/16 Since ADQ operators don't know what alterations they make in their own realities of ADQ I think the mirror deceives them and is the agency of their fall. Whether this supercomputer accepts sacrifice in Antarctica...is High citing aberrations in the SWS high speed alterations or is he part of it?

Hancock says if you keep the 10 + 30 commandments moral of Egypt and if you commit to higher, then...you can get another and an eternal life. I think this life and this moment are all the life you get on earth and that the moment is eternal like wedges of a pie that reaches back to the founding of this life in the Father in eternity, before the foundation cataclysm of the world. Maybe better to say this life is a spear whose tip in the water of life but whose shaft extends to the Armoire, waiting to be thrown, for a spear does not throw itself. To receive Him so is to be aware of this at the same time that the tip of life is immersed in life. So when Heiser takes the Councils so seriously on happenstance we have access to the Father through Him. -psychology, philosophy religion of the fallen.

12/24/16 Heiser construes I Ki 22 6-9 not as a facetious example of a parable to Ahab of his corruption but of later Ps 82, 89 divine council meetings where spirits are judged to die as men, clearly fallen ones, and cites Dan 4 of Nebuchadnezzar's curse to be an animal as a decree of Watchers. He conflates these as the same.

12/23/16 hook-word (or Stichwort), **Tamar**'s transgression took the form of acting like a prostitute just once in order to achieve her goal, Rahab makes a profession of prostitution. Rahab is paired with Abraham as an example of one "justified by works and not by faith alone" (Jas 2:24). Rahab is named specifically in Jas 2:25: "was not Rahab the prostitute also justified by works when she welcomed the messengers [ἀγγέλους; ἄγγελος in the nominative singular]213 and sent them out by another road?" The ambiguous word ἄγγελος, translated in many English translations of Jas 2:25 as "messenger,"214 is also the word used in the LXX for "angel." It is their hospitable treatment of messengers/angels that links Abraham and Rahab as positive examples in James, according to Robert W. Wall-

    Rahab has been reinterpreted so that the spies are now understood as angels in disguise, just as the strangers who first visited Abraham were initially seen as men and turned out to be angels. In Joshua, Rahab's sending away of messengers is recorded in two ways. First, she sends them with the advice to go into the hills. Second, after the spies repeat their desire that Rahab not tell anyone their "business," she "sent them away" 228; Josh 2:21). In James' summary, she "sent them out by another road." Rahab hides the spies under the flax. Moses's mother saves her baby by hiding him (תצפנהו, "she hid him")232for three months 102

The connection between the γίγαντες/Nephilim and the γίγαντες/offspring of the angels and women is also made in 1 Enoch where the offspring of the watchers and the women are "great giants"(1 En.7:2).253

      Nickelsburg notes that the Aramaic word used in 1 En. 7:2 for the offspring was gibbārîn, 254and that "these offspring correspond to the 255 גברים of Genesis." According to 1 Enoch, the giants/ גברי םthen begat Nephilim (1 En.7:2). A third generation of giants also results, called "Elioud" (1 En.7:2). The meaning of "Elioud" is obscure, but may denote that these giants were anti-gods. The Enochic Watchers' Template and the Gospel of Matthew Amy Richter 256

12/22/16 SGT report

Richard Sauder event horizon chronicle.

Graham Hancock's Egyptian Giza starbased religion of 11,600 year old destruction of Atlantis. is the axis of the **Antarctic** expeditions, a great counterfeit with the 100 ton blocks of stone fitted to a T, as if by giants. They were giants, who worshipped the stars, their fathers, meaning the Fallen ones ingenious counterfeiting.

US foreign policy history is a history of scapegoating false flags with hidden agendas. singling out foreign and domestic native peoples for profit taking.

--ISusan out.

12/21/16 Signed with Bill Anthony to do roof today, 6800 over top. Mike asked about renting to guy with pitbull, vet disabled.

12/20/16 the mainstream news is over when the viewer begins self selecting.

12/19/16 Enoch: Book of Parables 3.

      When the secrets of the righteous shall be revealed and the sinners judged, And the godless driven from the presence of the righteous and elect,4. From that time those that possess the earth shall no longer be powerful and exalted: Book of Parables is the one section of 1 Enoch not found at Qumran. "but the city of my righteous ones will become an obstacle to their horses," is an indication that Jerusalem still stands at the time of the writing of the Book of Parables, and favors a pre-70 C.E. date.

      "apocalyptic-like" details in the Gospel of Matthew-merely names the general for the specific, says nothing, "planetary aspects of the moon." Still the point is taken this way: 17

      -Hagner's list of apocalyptic motifs which bear witness to Matthew's apocalyptic viewpoint is impressive and thorough. He makes his point that apocalyptic motifs appear in every part of the Gospel. Broken down according to their respective narratives these motifs are:

- in the birth narrative: dream-visions, angelic mediators, astronomical phenomena, "stress on the unusual," and the activity of the Holy Spirit;
- in the baptism of Jesus: the Bat Qol's revelation of Jesus' identity;
- in the temptation scene: the confrontation between Jesus and Satan;
- in the transfiguration scene: the high mountain, the glorious appearance of Jesus and his garments, the appearance of Moses and Elijah, the words about Jesus as the Son, and the awe of the disciples;
- in the crucifixion scene: the dream of Pilate's wife, and the darkness over the land; and
- in the resurrection narrative: the angel who announces the resurrection, and the resurrection of the bodies of many saints who appear in the Holy City.

David Sim examined the possibility that Matt 22:13a ("Then the king said to the attendants, "Bind him hand and foot, and throw him into the outer darkness"") is dependent upon 1 Enoch 10:4a ("To Raphael he said, 'Go, Raphael, and bind Asael hand and foot, and cast him into the darkness'").

--Summary "Angels called "watchers" rebel and enter earthly realm of mortal humans. After transgressing the boundary between realms, they transgress another boundary by engaging in sexual relations with mortal women and disclosing heavenly secrets, knowledge humans were not intended to have. The result of the sexual interaction between the angels and women is a race of creatures of a mixed nature, giants, who belong fully neither to the earthly realm nor to the eternal heavenly realm.

Animal Apocalypse in 1 En.86:1-4, an allegorical narrative of the sexual interaction between the watchers and the women.79 In the allegory, first one star (watcher) falls from heaven and pastures among cattle (humans) (86:1). Then other stars also fall (86:3). They have sexual relations with the cows and beget offspring unnatural to their species: elephants, camels, and asses (86:4). Destruction and fear follow as the animals devour and gore one another (86:6; 87:1). "All the sons of the earth began to tremble and quake before them, and to flee" (86:6) and "the earth began to cry out" (87:1).

Blame the Women

Testament of Reuben: For thus they bewitched the Watchers before the Flood: as these looked at them continually, they lusted after one another, and they conceived the act in their mind, and they changed themselves into the shape of men, and they appeared to them when they were together with their husbands. And they, lusting in their mind after their appearances, bore giants; for the Watchers appeared to them as reaching unto heaven. Also in Targum Pseudo-Jonathan: Genesis [so here it is again the abstract gnostic suspicion of woman as the temptress, not the one saved through child bearing, but...] this love'em and leave' attitude implied by calculating exploitation of sex goes against all the weight of evidence when attributed to woman. It is man most likely exploit sexual relations and then leave them. Confusion of sex reaches to the heaven? not nearly so celestial a problem as its attribution. So it's not from temptation the angels fell, but the design to found a counter nation.

She says, 37, "I would like to know more about the relationship between the sexual interaction and the sharing of knowledge. Is this an exchange? Quid pro quo? Is the granting of the knowledge of skills and secrets a reward? Part of the watchers' plan--if we're going to be a family, there are a few things you should know . . . ? Did the women try to gain knowledge? In the version where they lead the watchers astray, do they do so knowing they have something to gain by it? Is it another take on Eve's disobedience in order to gain knowledge? Did the women initiate the transfer of knowledge? Did they somehow deceive the angels, beyond seducing them beyond the boundary between heaven and earth? The Greek myth of Pandora features a woman who opens forbidden box and unleashes disastrous knowledge into the world , but are there other myths that focus on the kinds of knowledge associated with women in particular?" So egregious, Egrigori, --"Asael taught men to make swords of iron and weapons and shields and breastplates and every instrument of war. He showed them metals of the earth and how they should work gold to fashion it suitably, and concerning silver, to fashion it for bracelets and ornaments for women. And he showed them concerning antimony and eye paint and all manner of precious stones and dyes. And the sons of men made for themselves and for their daughters, and they transgressed and led the holy ones astray. And there was much godlessness on the earth and they made their ways desolate. Shemihazah taught spells and the cutting of roots. Hermani taught sorcery for the loosing of spells and magic and skill. Baraqel taught the signs of the lightning flashes. Kokabel taught the signs of the stars. Ziqel taught the signs of the shooting stars. Arteqoph taught the signs of the earth. Shamsiel taught the signs of the sun. Sahiel taught the signs of the moon. And they all began to reveal mysteries to their wives and to their children. (And) as men were perishing, the cry went up to heaven." (1 En. 8:1-4) "The now beautifully adorned women lead the angels astray, and humans engage in "godlessness" amongst themselves, which may also include adultery and fornication." 40

--Devorah Dimant suggests that the subjects taught reflect the sins forbidden by the Noachic laws – shedding blood, illicit sexual intercourse, and idolatry – which were binding for all people, and were behind the later rabbinic interpretation of such laws.104 --bastard race of giants The offspring are violent enemies of humankind. Their insatiable appetites and violent behavior bring death to humans and other living beings (1 En. 7:3-5).

"Gabriel is commissioned to destroy the giants. Their destruction, although set in motion by Gabriel, will actually come by their own hands, as the archangel is to send them "against one another in a war of destruction" (1 En. 10:9).108 Michael is sent to subject Shemihazah and his associates to a similar fate to that which Asael received: they are to be bound for seventy generations, until the day of their judgment when they, too, will be imprisoned in a fiery abyss (1En. 10:11-15). Finally Michael receives the commission to restore the earth, removing all impurities, defilement, godlessness, and lawlessness (1 En.10:16-22). This restoration is a future event that will take place at the final time of judgment."

--the women were all Gentiles, (Tamar? "Both the Genesis Rabbah and Talmud state that Tamar was an Israelite." She gives birth to twins, Perez and Zerah. Their birth is reminiscent of the birth of Rebekah's twin sons. The midwife marks Zerah's hand with a scarlet cord when it emerges from the womb first, but Perez is born first.[4] Perez is identified in the Book of Ruth as the ancestor of King David. (Ruth 4:18–22)) -"

Although Tamar's ethnic background is not explicitly disclosed, her story is set in Canaan." 72 [which proves nada]in questionable sexual relationships with men Jesus' family tree included several people whose birth stories or behavior were marked by scandal. Matthew names these four women as part of Jesus' genealogy because they -foreshadow the overturning of the transgression of the watchers, the Enochic template for the origins of evil in the world they make use of the illicit arts taught by the watchers; they are associated with traditions in which they interact with celestial beings; and they give birth to offspring in which paternity is questioned or who have unusual or exceptional attributes. And yet, unlike in the watchers' descent narrative and its horrific consequences, these women bring ab out righteous results. The argument that the women all have in common sexual scandal as part of their stories is correct. [there maybe a reason this has not been said before, because it reaches and is not true in particulars]

--"Recognize, please, whose these are, the signet, the cord, and the staff," (Gen 38:25),143 she says. Her words, "Recognize, please" הכר־נא), are the same words Judah and his brothers had used (in Gen 37:32) to deceive their father Jacob into believing his beloved son Joseph had been killed when they showed him Joseph's bloodstained robe. [ie. Judah is fed his own deception back!!]62 Tamar is the only woman called "righteous" in the Hebrew Bible.

--Genesis 38 opens, are reminiscent of the way in which the narrative of the watchers' fall begins: "Judah saw [וירא] there the daughter of a Canaanite man, whose name was Shua; he took her [ויקחה] and went into her [אליהויבא], and she conceived [ותהר] and bore [ותלד] a son, and he called his name Er" (Gen 38:2-3).147The watchers "see" (1 En. 6:2) the daughters of men; they "take" wives from among them; they "go into them" (1 En. 7:1); the women "conceived" and "bore" the giants (1 En. 7:2). 64 more general nonsense: "the precise nature and role of the קדשה, raises the possibility that Tamar may have been linked to a tradition in which humans engaged in sexual relations in order to participate in a bridging of earthly and heavenly realms"76 ...all these arguments reach...

-- These are the eyes on the cover of Blinders Journal Winter 2016, called Plice on a whim not to express the artist's intent or person. The intent however is to see that society behind events where grandiose supernaturalism consumes all public events.

--after the death of the giants, their spirits will continue to harm humans (1 En. 15:9, 10-11, 16:1) and will be called "evil spirits" (1 En. 15:9). The giants will be destroyed, but their spirits will plague humankind until "the great judgment" (1 En.16:1). The evil spirits "lead astray, do violence, make desolate, and attack and wrestle and hurl upon the earth and cause illnesses" (1 En.15:11).109According to 1 En45 19:1, they also "bring destruction on men and lead them astray to sacrifice to demons as to gods."

12/19/16 "The nations have decided it says here to abolish themselves at last." One wholly negative without reservation and the other positive with. Population reached its limits to lie down. Both sides read sentences they thought to favor them machines turning. Little man Samoyeds from Siberia hid this now believed drunk over mushroom. Obama got even. [from memory apps kicked out the Poetry Wkshp for Ferlinghetti].

12/18/16 Psalm 27.4 One thing I have asked from the LORD, that I shall seek: That I may dwell in the house of the LORD all the days of my life, To behold the beauty of the LORD And to meditate in His temple. 5For in the day of trouble He will conceal me in His tabernacle; In the secret place of His tent He will hide me; He will lift me up on a rock....Psalm 63.7 I sing beneath the shadow of your wings AB's dance recital, after, Dickey's BQ.

12/17/16 Peter Thiel: adrenochrome, parabiosis, transfusions of blood from young--Thiel "spends $40,000 per quarter to get an infusion of blood from an 18-year-old.

12/16/16 Endgame Part II The Antarctic AtlantisTwo 2 Week Power Outage during cleanup. the pervasive overall disinformation program of the debunkers who work for the various agencies that will announce the Antarctic finds amidst their mutual debunkings are not hard to believe. They will excavate and evacuate the ruins first saving only misinfomations to remain. They call the originals the Builder Race 1.8 billion yrs old which ruins were then inhabited by the Pre Adamite Outcast Fallens while Antarctic was still lush. When it was flash frozen all the buildings collapsed with the animals, but the technologies the elite seek are presumed. Dignaty bigwigs began touring with Obama last March, followed by known visits of James Clapper, Kerry, Aldrin which are known. Many sq mi of ruins identified by scans from space The Antarctic Atlantis and Ancient ET Ruins Sphere being alliance. David Wilcox, Corey Goode, blue avians.
      Once see that all the beautiful people of all ranks are the more beautiful the more damned it takes all the fun out of it.
      Derrida's a Cluthu, a flying carp. Asian Carp Now we know why Scalia was sacrificed, as backup so the Supreme Court could not rule on the overthrow.
There must be more Moon Landings. To begin to list of the pieces of Isis: 1) depleted uranium, 2) HARP atmospheres 3)

12/15/16 See *Reversing Hermon*
Hugh Rowland Page, Divine Rebellion saving God's reputation, Tonstad argues Revelation integrity to itself.
--Tyler Stewart. Fallen Angels, Bastard Spirits, and the Birth of God's Son: An Enochic Etiology of Evil in Galatians 3:19- Galatians 4:11. only at Heiser
 --Amy Richter diss, The Enochic Watchers' Template and the Gospel of Matthew. Author. Amy Elizabeth Richter, on Jesus' genealogy of Rehab Ruth, Bathsheba, tamar, all cited for suffering some sexual transgression
--Fallen Angels and the History of
Judaism and ChristianityThe Reception
of Enochic Literature Annette yoshiko
reed
-- "They Revealed Secrets to Their Wives":
The Transmission of Magical Knowledge in 1 Enoch

--R.H. Charles, one of the earliest experts on the Pseudepigrapha and Enoch, listed about sixty examples where the language of the New Testament reflected possible Enochian influence. He concluded, "1Enoch has had more influence on the New Testament than has any other apocryphal or pseudepigraphic work 46 I think these are reverse copies from NT to Enoch without proof of the Enoch text Do you disCERN the Worm?

Costco's Kirkland Signature golf balls meatpacking neushwab. Earth hollow so mag currents flow into it from all sides as if it were a shiskabobenland.
The presumption is that just as the Nazi elite evacuated to Antarctica so Obama and his elite world will do so at the WWIII sacrifice kidneys

12/14/16 Went to Yesinia's RN graduation!
TYGER-ORC Since the pyramids of arctic and Antarctic cannot be hidden like the giant bones in basements or fake memed like pizza gate cannibalism they must be debunked by shills of government of which there are tens of thousands filling the airwaves with disinformed indoctrination. What were once skeptical doubting empirical scientists has become a propaganda ad campaign to perpetuate the view of the the State. So there is no free science or free thought any longer, INSTEAD the spawned Jason Colavitos, who debunked the fake news that the Cow Went Over the Moon, whose first rebuttal should be that if any of this were true the gov't would be all over it with expeditions, so because they're not it isn't. This naively covers up the putative gov't desire to hide the cow from these. So why hide them. A context comes with Antarctica. A view of the dome forming, like the eye, Kiril saying he stands on the top in Antarctic. Pyramids in Alaska, near Mt McKinley

12/13/16 Gaslighting Kole Borehole stops at 12 Kilom.
FB: The Tweets are saying:
Chomsky thinks its Hitler but its Chomsky. Demos say its Russia but its Demos. YOU GASLIT MULTITUDES!--ALL MAINSTREAMERS ARE GASLIT, Tell themselves before TAKEOVER: "I guess I can't really see what color the sky is.'"

It's time to **reread the Oracle:**
--"When evening comes, you say, 'The weather will be fair, for the sky is red;' and in the morning, 'Today it will be stormy, for the sky is red and overcast," but you can't tell Congress and CIA overthrow free speech and the election? In March 1933 the Reichstag adopted the Enabling Act of 1933. In December 1916 American congress passes COUNTERING DISINFORMATION AND PROPAGANDA ACT.

Then Hitler used The Enabling Act to constitutionally exercise dictatorial power without legal objection. Those poor ghosts, Stephen later says, stand as oracles for Americans of "peculiar whiteness, drained of pigment." Prophesy how we live in Weimar before the fall, "coracles with faces painted on." Even if the Reich-stag burns in the Twin Towers morphed to a propaganda tool, these are just mirages of the digital, a new species of electronic designs "more beautiful and soft than any moth / With burring furred antennae feeling its huge path." This is America's *Childhood's End*,

The Senate has passed the Countering Disinformation and Propaganda Act: legislation designed to help American allies counter foreign government propaganda from Russia, China, and other nations. "The passage of this bill in the Senate today takes us one critical step closer to effectively confronting...zerohedge.com

--Therefore shall the land mourn. Hosea 4.3 Just like the movie Jurassic Park, scientists have discovered a 99million-year-old baby dinosaur tail preserved in amber. The discovery, which demonstrated a feathered tail, helps support the theory that the giant beasts that once ruled the Earth looked more like birds than reptiles. [where are the wings] evolution of feathers from dinosaurs to modern birds. The tail in the find likely belonged to a small "juvenile" dinosaur, probably no larger than a sparrow. It would be classified under the group of dinosaurs called Coelurosauria, a rather large group that fits animals from Tyrannosauruses to modern birds. The discovery, which demonstrated a feathered tail, helps support the theory that the giant beasts that once ruled the Earth looked more like birds than reptiles. Lampe à gaz le bourgeois --The Mainstream is Gaslit.
 Like a river glorious is God's perfect peace, over all. Therefore shall the land mourn. Hosea 4.3 -The Mainstream is Gaslit. Like a river glorious is God's perfect peace, over all.

12/12/16 Obama's secret Antarctic trip c. ervana. They built the narrative Hillary and the Pope on fake news, Moore on TV with the Countless, the false electors, the concern for Russia so transparent that has sold the US to Brussels, then Podesta comes out with the call. They seek to overturn the election with this conspiracy theory, but not give an evidence. Giambattista del Ser. Humano   fitness international.

12/11/16 Here's how Satan and illuminati celebrate,
First they bring about all the events in a Hard Rain, then they inaugurate a poet to sing it.
First they invent fake news then they have Denzel Washington expose it.
Always both sides, Nazis and Brits. David Brock media matters, pizzagate Gaslighting:
'I guess I can't really see what color the sky is.'
Many gaslighting victims berate themselves or feel the need to apologize all the time
Great performance by Patti Smith for Bob Dylan at the Nobel.
even if she forgets the words, chokes up, on the bleeding babe: 1.58.

12/9/16 Pope defecates on fake news. POPE AND HILLARY GET FECAL FETISH of fake news on the same day! Is it going around? Is that Holy Shit or what? Buzz Aldrin's tweet, Martin Marprelate, the matter of the Pope.

12/8/16 Webster Tarpley
  Ted Gunderson Interview with Paul Bonacci - http://www.fortrefuge.com/Ritual-Abuse.html
-- they play their rifle like a guitar, fire it with their teeth and behind their heads
 eat the guitar, eat the rifle and spit out the bullet teeth and strings
My sister was born Pearl Harbor Day. My brother was born 9/11.
I was born the 9th of Av,
The Fall of Jerusalem's Temple, Twice!).

I guess you could call us War Babies.
Here we are, still waiting...

12/7/16 Here is my poem. It doesn't have to have meter does it? Or short lines? The huge number of baby photos emailed to John Podesta is strange.

12/6/16 Alex Jones is an actor on Westworld performing his script written for him like all media. like High thinks to create a script to make the futurity of the pizza gates, or the presidential election, all subscripts, nonscripts to involve, delude the fool with ET, Antarctica, you name it, scripts of the fallen to distract what is just the imposition of history as real as Westworld or any script created by the befallen, anything but what it is for the whole is insisted upon by shills, the believers in the world but there is one way out and one alone which has been calculated by the Word and the Name.
 --he said how do you know. I said its a judgement. he, take history, gather evidence. then I said what about AB and described our last visit. He, then, that it was different when one of ours. so he broke free of the gaming paradigm of lack of morality, the first evidence of cure of emotional detachment he has followed for fear of involving himself in confrontation. This is especially true of animated people, avatars on line where specialty perversion, animated sex are so called electronic fantasies and for which the player has no responsibility. this transfers to their judgment of real life occasions for fear they trespass the bounds of art or free speech, hence are lenient in judgment in not totally deficient, very different from Leviticus which would horrify them to learn that

12/5/16 Passed on Demolay, NDEA, grants, MLA, all for the chance to follow the trails. Posted FB Arthur Christian: We have to deal with the layers of harm in the apriori statements to every political effect. Hence we must think that all Mainstream analysis is apriori, all counter MSM is apriori and this statement itself is. This is not tautology, it is experience revealing that all good leaders are corrupt beyond belief but it is worse to believe one bad and the other good when THE GOOD ARE WORSE THAN THE BAD. Those anorexic pedophiles give a bad name even to calorie restriction. Trump has never been a good man like Obama or the hundred clones that meet in the basements after work. That seems to be Trump's recommendation. He is bad. All arguments to the contrary, RoundSaturnEye is merely another deception couched in truth. Spare us the good. And the truth.

12/4/16 dismal Story sale, made $35. baked 2 batches cookies gave big box when Aeg came. Played crocy on porch for 2 hrs, went for walk, read, sang,, drew. It was our Christmas.

12/3/16 Metallica thread plays Antarctica McMurdo 120 scientists

12/9/2013 in a clear dome --divination of the data sets like Japanese manga, skewed to the hand that makes it just as tea leaves to the eye that reads it or pennies thrown or sticks spread predict the synchronicity so it goes. buzz aldrin in Antarctica to contact the eidola he presumed to meet in space that hae haunted his mind since, the fallen ones as opposed to the mars and venus ransom met. Kerry is Weston rejected without the protocol. of Scalia. all the

Antarctica is about the Nephilim technolog. the currency backed with a Ponzi scheme printing money so fed can buy property with it so there are 4 dollars today where there was one yesterday. **Ponzi Backs** .

12/2/16 TRUMP dreamed, second time. First, taken with Trump to this place house in AZ a little getaway staffed by a few, before he was known, spent some time, but forgot. now returning at his behest to help somehow, the girl woman, Laura full of aggression when I said a mutual friend sent me, she says we not friends i don't know you. I remind i was there before but she is so angry i start to leave, feeling though that the Holy Spirit wants me to stay so as I do some packages are delivered to the door, big ones. I bring them in but a wind blows the stained glass window pane of the door out and it shatters on the floor, so I stay to pick it up. then Herman, another fellow I had met, appears, and another with whom I say, well now I say its the President Elect who sent me, and we laugh , so the visit is a success. P is waiting in the car because we had driven here. This is the second dream, but remembered.

12/1/16 Maunder Minimum
--Since you have declared Lord Jesus that it were better for those who offend children to be cast with a stone into the sea, and since you also demand that vengeance is yours that you will repay, I now ask you Lord to revenge all children and violate John Podesta and tony Podesta and all who run the Pizza ring whether the President or his cabinet or the rich, to violate them and confuse them, dash them in pieces, assassinate and remove them from the face of the earth. All praise be to your Holy Name.

PODESTA Undergrounds

Obama in Peru? Shingana tunnels from Cuzco Peru to antarctica. the fathers of solomon's house "Pizza code: The proper subset for investigation must be to suspect literally everyone if they give a one time reason to do so. It could be a loose word meaning something entirely different. Likewise this is true of al media, entertainment, sports, political, public figures. At the least they are selling something but it may be they are grooming you for their own purpose. But among the dedicated of evil there are different entry points. The Pizza Code is one. FBI has arranged five code words to view Pizza and hot dog in an utterly redefined way.

The change in mentality by video games squares this effect." Origin of the Watchrs disconnected bads connected goods. I wake wondering how I would feel if I shot and killed. Is it like MacBeth to ne'r be clean? enough to rue the act as utter demolishing, as if shooting in reverse myself? compare to goods done. if they were undone would the day be rued. the goods are as connected as can be. pat's med sch benefited me as well. but she as the good is the whole process of building houses and families not one act. This pedo code stuff makes me think such thoughts of murder, a quick bullet in the head of Podesta and the thoughts this a.m. The proper subset for investigation must be to suspect literally everyone if they give a one time reason to do so. It could be a loose word meaning something entirely different. Likewise this is true of all media, entertainment, sports, political, public figures. At the least they are selling something but it may be they are grooming you for their own purpose.

11/30/16-- Omegle logo
       -- Steemit, the pizza gate links, block chain, 1EAR2 voat.co, pizzagate reddit. Pedo logos. Steve Huffman of Reddit is cannibalistic. Mesopotamian origin of the watchers mythology of the antediluvian sages (Joe Biden pizza button. miley cyrus pizza, Dean Fougere Titus frost, steemit all stemming from the Wiki Leaks emails of Tony and John Podesta and the Weiner emails using pedophile code words in Podesta emails and perp sketches of the three with kidnapped children. Podesta emails, search "comet pizza" and handkerchief" show the codes, as does the 14 and fish on his hands linked to spirit cooking pics were the top half shows. Why do so many presidents have bandages on their middle fingers?

       DNC pedophile pizza ring pizza gate is foreground for Crowley's rituals cake of light., pedophilia a mask for cannibalism. these people all have symptoms of kuru (as in the monsters of dream) , incurable neurodegenerative disorder which was prevalent among the Fore people of Papua New Guinea in the 1950s and 60s. Everyone has normal prion proteins, found mostly in the brain.[1] However, infectious prions, which cause transmissible spongiform encephalopathies diseases such as kuru, can induce abnormal folding of normal prion proteins, which leads to symptoms such as coordination problems and neurodegeneration....hence spirit cooking- funerary cannibalism. Traditionally, deceased family members were cooked and eaten, which was thought to help free the spirit of the dead.[
-- I am burdened by a great number of these speculations an, not that any ten demolished would lighten the load, but there it is, the rocky mount. I also struggle to be relevant/irrelevant, between the topical and the ridiculous.

11/29/16 Codes: Obama pizza and hot dogs from Chicago: "hotdog" = boy "pizza" = girl" cheese" = little girl" pasta" = little boy "ice cream" = male prostitute "walnut" = person of colour"map" = semen"sauce" = orgy covering, uncovering the beauty of the world, goliath and nakedness, Podesta, Jerusalem and math. Breitbart and the hundred,

11/28/16 Decoding the future Mike Maloney
 Decoding the meaning on Podesta's hands Marty Leeds "How prog-guru John Podesta isn't household name as world class underage sex slave op cover-upperer defending unspeakable dregs escapes me.— AndrewBreitbart (@AndrewBreitbart) February 4, 2011 brietbard has a big mouth and it got him killed death of brietbard and coroner also here
--warning to new zealand's prime minister john keys, two preachers floods. a preacher, brian tamaki, in NZ said sexual sin, leivticus 18 caused the earthquake which prime minister John Kay denied. Fr Giovanni Cavalcoli

11/27/16 After Thksg at Jorma's we had RandC over Today, Sunday. Andrew S, A and T came, and Aey back from Yuma, barely, not Sh. So that was Thanksgiving. Mazlan Othman UN alien ambassador

11/26/16 Substantia nigra. Bain, Donald?, alt fic, positive ending? viz fairy tale. Greek names

11/25/16 "Seven years ago today our son Mark lost his struggle with his bipolar condition. We miss your loving, caring, fun-loving ways!! We miss your cooking, your singing, your extensive CD collection, your amazing story-telling, especially with your nieces, Ada and Eve and the smell of your very strong coffee every morning. We need your wonderful bear hugs more than ever!! All our love and more, Mom and Dad" Ellen Skilton with Ann Skilton. November 25, 2012 ·

    I don't wake up justified in my bed but questioning what I experience. Thanksgiving yesterday with R & C boys @ Jormas, after Aey canceled his planned affair and Aeg was required to Chino. Ping pong and visit but later Jormas' current came and he drank scotch until, enflamed, insisted Aey had something he had told J not to tell me, full of insistence and pretense of improving my relation w/ Aey. All offensive to the limit which shows how easily the social breaks to the bitter under the influence.

11/24/16
--I'm giving thanks for the humanity of Benjamin's walk over the Pyrenees to escape, for his balcony around Saturn where he stands to survey the universe. I'm giving thanks for the humanity of Levinas held in French Concentration but who finds such compassion for the Face. I'm giving thanks for the humanity of Kierkegaard's beginning of Either/Or as a mystery of the inner worlds which he constantly holds to the light. I'm giving thanks for the humanity of Viktor Frankl in the camps looking at a bird look back at him. And I'm giving thanks for *The Burnt Book* of Marc-Alain Onaknin which says so much about the humanity of the sacred text. The nature of consciousness, of intelligence, or the being of man is not binary, or quantum adiabatic 01/1/0, it includes elements of those but it is not 0/1 etc. Take Scalia's ashes, rejected for their ritual claims viz the super computer, but affirmed for the ashes in Leviticus buried outside the city. The fire always burns the altar. Where else do we see the picnic of sin, and its purging so well as where all the principles of the counterfeit religions take as their own Scalia's ashes true and untrue.

11/23/16 Harpazo forum- apparently, the Vatican has 'publicly' attempted to distance itself from Biglino's work... but of course, this is typical Vatican disinformation tactics intended to present the illusion that the Vatican is vehemently against such blasphemy...when in truth, it is undoubtedly the Vatican herself, who is the catalyst behind Biglino and his alien propaganda....

    --Read more: http://harpazo.proboards.com/thread/2910/alert-mauro-biglino-alien-translation#ixzz4QsujzEcS   Mauro Biglino - "The Greek word "pneuma" is the translation of the Hebrew word "rùach". According to some scholars "rùach" (wind) probably comes from the Sumerian word RU-A. The word's sound is represented by a fluctuant object over the waters. The Italian scholar Mauro Biglino has totally misinterpreted the ancient image (see the picture), because he says that the eye over the waters is an "unidentified flying object". This interpretation is part of his theory that the Elohim were aliens and not, as the scholars usually say, angels or God himself."

    Terminal velocity: 90% of the move comes in the last 10% of the tie. Red Backs, Yellow Backs. All thought is imagination. If you stand on the ground you see from there but if you have a ladder it depends on which rung you're on. The way this works is I was awake at 2.30 and got up to write that, which led to all the other thoughts below (replicated from the imaginate state) which led to remembering George MacDonald's Imagination which I used to have, then seeing it as food for Ooks. It is speculative, unformed, corrupt, insightful all at the same time. Only when reduced to writing can imagination be viewed for what it is, but most of it cannot be so reduced. It is unthinkable to say much of it. It is like the news that denies the dots of the plane over Denver and the possible ouster of Mike Rodgers, director of NSA. unconnected, but they are as he ordered the plane to cease and desist its mission. That's like imagination, unspeakable, like 9/11 impossible to survey in reality.

All thought is imagination just as all gays are homo phobes literally. see George MacDonald, Imagination. Everybody murdered sees their own death but no one else does except their murderer. but to them it is a verity and written in technicolor as if blazoned across the sky in big letters no one can miss, but to the rest of us we see nothing and maybe are led to believe they committed suicide. See BANQUO! That is the difference between imagination and writing and speech, imagination sees it all rapid fire and it is compelling and instant but passes from sight like a vapor immediately after. People who use marijuana experience this each time they smoke but what they see becomes a vapor, not that all this isn't anyway mixed with our own nature's propensity to see what it sees, paranoia, etc. To climb up the rungs of this ladder, even to see there is one, false flags are on a different rung from the reptilian artificial intelligence of assassins and yet another rung from the disassociates who charm the media and plot institutional subversions. Kerry's Antarctica is in a whole fog that disappears at the top.

11/22/16 They had bread and circuses to control the mobs of democracy, MacDonald's food stamps and NFL. Awoke thinking of Junior Yarbrough, Ashville, NC and the obscene pile of sweet meats the Eagles Nest served after their service to the Meadow Lark Lemon, but Aey being announced State Champ from the pulpit by Pastor Dan, plus his selection and acting in the musical.

11/21/16 At 3.38 Awoke from a dream where I was in an ER with BP of 198/277, being told this means I should stop what I was doing. I got up and took it, it was 109/69.
Awake finally at 5.45 singing in mind, "the universe declares your majesty, you are holy, holy, Lord of heaven and earth." A little later I find that phrase in *Alien Savior Trick or Treat*.

11/20/16 Glazing. To trick the eye into seeing multiple scenarios by accident, distraction, juxtaposition, any means of nature, drugs being against nature.

11/18/16 New Zealand earthquake "reverse faulting," 100,000 landslides. The magnitude 7.8 earthquake that tore through New Zealand on Monday was so powerful, it dragged the sea floor 2 meters above the ground, causing it to explode though the sand revealing a strange, lumpy exterior.

--It happened fast, the exposed sea bed was still crawling in sea life when locals discovered their newly remodelled coastline. "I've never seen it before during an earthquake and it's the first time we've seen something like this," marine geologist Joshu Mountjoy from

New Zealand's National Institute of Water and Atmospheric Research told Stuff. "It will take a while before this becomes normal again." Crustacean on the exposed sea bed. Credit: Anna Redmond/Facebook Monday's earthquake really took its toll on central New Zealand, leaving more than 1,000 locals and tourists stranded by landslides, with two people reported dead, and dozens injured. The effects were so intense because two almost simultaneous tremors had ruptured fault lines across the top of the country's South Island just after midnight. Mountjoy suspects that the unique nature of the earthquake is behind the eerie exposure of the sea bed in the coastal town of Kaikoura, saying a phenomenon called co-seismic movement was likely in play. See MELT.

11/17/16 Kitco. el luminino, chasuble, Goya

11/16/16 Ridem Dinosaur

11/13/16 into the fourth turning.
-- html CERN Isaiah 6.7 With it he touched my mouth and said, "See, this has touched your lips; your guilt is taken away and your sin atoned for." Christians are a band of natural enemies who love one another for Jesus' sake. - D. A. Carson

11/12/16 Went w/ A, AB and T and Pat to Duke Ellington's 50th anniversary at Trinity Cathedral of Sacred Songs.

11/11/16 APS society of physicists retracts congratulations. Mt. 10.21 Harry Reid: tide of hate. And the brother shall deliver up the brother to death, and the father the child: and the children shall rise up against their parents, and cause them to be put to death. "Blairites, Clintonites, Bushites." Leonard Cohen dies. Janet Reno earlier. Kerry in Antarctica!

11/10/16.
TWO FLIES Came in on ELECTION DAY. One landed in a dish. I got a fly swatter Covered the dish, took the fly outside and let it go. THE INSTRUMENT OF DEATH WAS ITS REPRIEVE. kILL THE DAMN FLY. oH HOW KIND YOU ARE.

11/9/16 REprieve Granted. One young man who had been following Jesus was wearing a linen cloth around his body. They caught hold of him, 52, the veil of the temple was rent in twain from the top to the bottom, Mk 15.38 Exodus 26:31-35 Hebrews 10:19-22 The Veil in the Tabernacle. Exodus and Hebrews divides two rooms by a thick veil of blue, purple and scarlet material and fine twisted linen, thick as a rug, but he pulled free of the linen cloth and ran away naked. Mark 14.51.2 Nassim Taleb Not only will he vote for Hillary Monsanto-Malmaison because she seems electable and some other such circular reasoning, but holds that anyone who doesn't do so is mentally ill. Frederic Dard, Libanius Antiochus, Michael Oakeshot, John Gray, Amianus Marcellinus, Ibn Battuta, Saadiah Gaon, or Joseph De Maistre, John Pilgar.

11/8/16 After a career at NASA and western opulence Kanubhai Ramdas Gandhi went back to India in 2014. We view this entry as the true assessment of the American election 2016, the end of pretense of democracy, the exposure of media, gov't, corporate controls and the stifling and superflatting of the American.

11/7/16 The Election of Goliath means "uncovered" in Hebrew The root-verb גלה (gala) to uncover, remove or to go into exile, diverge two separate roots at work in this verb. The verb גלה (gala) denotes an uncovering of sensory organs such as the ear (1 Samuel 9:15) or eye (Numbers 24:4), indicating a propensity to hear or see. It may indicate the revealing of someone; a human person (1 Samuel 20:2) or God (2 Samuel 7:27), a secret (Amos 3:7) or a message (Esther 3:14). It may indicate indecent exposure (Exodus 20:26) or even the intent to commit immoral acts (Deuteronomy 22:30).

    The secondary meaning of this verb (which may be a different verb altogether) denotes a removing (Ezekiel 12:3, Isaiah 24:11, Job 20:28) or going into exile (Amos 1:5, Jeremiah 13:19, Ezekiel 39:28).

One derivative of this root stems from the meaning of revealing something, namely: The masculine noun גליון (gillayon), meaning table or tablet (Isaiah 8:1). Two derivatives deal with captivity:

The feminine noun גולה (gola), meaning captivity or captive/ exile (Jeremiah 28:6).

    The feminine noun גלות (gallut), also meaning captives and always covering a group of exiles (Isaiah 20:4). --Yesterday in church not a word spoken of election when all year catastrophes of all kinds were lamented. The church must not lose its tax exemption. Bought and paid for.

    Antarctic invasion. Obama in march, Kirill in Feb, Kerry leaves on 7th gets there 10th? where else does he go?

Kerry goes to Antarctica day before election day, ends on 12th. Images of Antarctica in wikileaks

11/6/16 After gazing silently at each other for some time he played the piano. Then we began eating watermelon to Beethoven's Quartet in C-Sharp Minor, Op. 131 and Quartet in E-Flat, Op. 127, finishing up here, in the wind. Goliath.

11/5/16 2008- Gulf of Aden stargate. Dr. Haigneré's alleged suicide attempt coming at the exact time that concerns are growing over the growing deployment of Global Naval Forces around the Middle Eastern region believed to have been the location of the ancient Garden of Eden, and which we had reported on in our December 21st report titled 'World Shipping Comes To Halt As Global Navies Prepare For 'Unprecedented' Confrontation'. John Pilger the invisible government. Year Zero.

11/4/16 Anti-messiahs want you to take their glasses. These are the corn tortillas that after a year in the frig still look good, but when dogs take it out of the trash they won't eat it; it lays in the yard like a flying disc waiting to eclipse the earth.

From J. Kleck: Fukushima an inside job. The earthquake machine places stress on a region with a circular pull; Solomon's Temple represents male inside the female Ark of the Covenant derives from Egypt ark of contract, where the Pharaohs showed their authority was from Sirius. Hence Sirius connects to the ark and to NASA. Kiss of death in ancients mocks scorpion double sting, first the kiss, hence Judas betrayed Jesus.
Church, kirk, Cerce, Mother Cerce hypnotized people so she could eat them. Celtic druids inherit Canaanite Phoenician acts, wands made from holly wood, hence the enchantment of Hollywood.

11/3/16 PSYCHIATRISTS DESCRIBE KAFKAESQUE PORTFOLIO Carter Kaplan *Emanations six*, engineered events.

11/2/16 Wed P's birthday. Present the Tom Coleman workshop and Duke Ellington's 50 anniv concert at Trinity Cathedral. Now is come salvation, and strength, and the kingdom of our God, and the power of his Christ! In the strong name of Jesus they overcame him by the blood of the Lamb Revelation 12.11. Twitter says of {"error":"unauthorized"} Impressions. Half bag quarters @ 18.65,
        --Google doodle election day code, sup/com manipulating 3 timelines in 1, 11/22 JFK, -- 12/21: numeric values of letters + colors. ritual code in google doodles, drop circles, incidences, death, accidents. 11/22, =33, 12/21=33.
F Springmeier, engineer showed beast computer, can talk to it and ask about anybody, ask it a plan to manipulate their life, which would give a plan, manipulate events news staged events, not random, totally undetectable mind control. super computer Eagle Eye film, fake YouTube accts, Illumicorp! "A child's happiness is priceless, especially on their birthday."

11/1/16 James Rickards, greg Hunter

10/31/16 Monday sold google, mitk, Encounters at the End of the World is a 2007 American documentary film by Werner Herzog. ... Herzog and Zeitlinger next visit Mount Erebus 10/30/16 IARPA Ted Secombe crystal mat glaze purples and greens internet data miner Clif High - pop Inc by creation of debt, predictive linguistics emotional reduction engine, immediacy, short term, 3 mo, long term, advertising key word, preventing walk in freezer deaths is the right the good.

Peter Voulkos: I am not a conceptual artist. I can't just sit there and think of an idea. Most of it comes out of my hands . . . I have always used whatever comes to hand, or into my head, that makes sense in my own work, that I can get some energy from." Peter Voulkos quoted posthumously in Ceramics Monthly, April 2002: "The minute you begin to understand what you're doing it loses that searching quality. You have to forget about the little technical problems that don't matter—you've overcome them long ago anyway. You finally reach a point where you're no longer concerned with keeping this blob of clay centered on the wheel and up in the air. Your emotions take over and what happens just happens. Usually you don't know it's happened until after it's done." CREDO.

EIN BILDERBERGER KüKEN HAUSE! Here kommen ein Küken Hause zum roosten.

10/29/16 Batists. The Ritual Metamorphosis of Julian Assange

If you wrote this in a Greek play it would sound contrived. Isaiah repeats over and over, "princes are rebellious and companions of thieves, where everyone loves bribes" (1.23), the news media "soothsayers like the Philistines" (2.6), American economy "full of silver and gold, has no end of treasure" (2.7). "Their land is full of idols (2.8) from TV alone, not to speak of "the great man debased" (2.9). In other words, Anthony Weiner in the yard. Human pride shall be humbled (2.11), the lofty shall be bowed down (2.17). Boldness proves their character (3.9); they are as proud as Sodom, "they hide it not." This crack doesn't have the sting that it did for Isaiah, who took Sodom as just the opposite case of Jonah's Nineveh, which changed its ways. Particular idols made of iPods, iPhones, laptops, and video games average 66 hours of screen time a week. Isaiah has them casting these idols to the bats and moles (2.20). But when laptops are too heavy and mobiles don't transmit, and reception is poor in the tops of jagged rocks and apartment buildings, where they hide (2.21):
Shades of the Tom Daschle 9.11 "I know that there is only the smallest measure of inspiration that can be taken from this devastation. But there is a passage in the Bible from Isaiah that I think speaks to us all at times like this. 'The bricks have fallen down but we will rebuild with dressed stone; the fig trees have been felled but we will replace them with cedars.' That is what we will do."

Lunar tetrads, Blood Moons correlating Feast Days, have only four occasions since the 15th century, after the events in 1) 5654 (1493-94), following the expulsion of Jews from Spain in 1492, 2) in 5710 (1949-50), 3) after the re-establishment of Israel in 1948, and 4)in 5728 (1967-68) just before the Six Day war in 1967 repatriating Jerusalem. Those of 5775 (2014-15) begin Tuesday, 15 April 2014. When the rats have nowhere left to hide and prepare for the chicken home in Qatar or Dubai from which they cannot be extradited, the roost with the best options for them to remain in place becomes a nuke on Russia to distract pesky emails or activation of Firesign Project Petrucio, of the rustic aliens, Anthony Weiner by the yard. and Obama's three long head scars.

The Blood Moon begins to have its say, but rather than report the news, since it is managed so well by existing sources let us look behind to see the underlying supports for its facades. What American constitution, what Bill of Rights? These were bought and sold except in the touted freedoms of the politics where we have never been so free that the FBI reopens its "investigation" of fish mongers on the news. These are all staged events. Staged for multi purpose, Halloween Election Day, Blood L Moon of which Anthony Weiner is always the best symbol, even better than Bill Clinton and Jeffery Epstein. Weiner for mayor, Weiner for senate, Weiner for weaner.

10/25/15 why is Joe Biden's son working in the Ukrainian shale?
 Why is Rupert Murdoch working in the Golan Heights?
Why are we trying to own mountains containing lithium in Afghanistan?
Tim Stark: why do we run Isis from one country to another? For a central bank and pipelines?

10/24/16 The Veneer always want to apologize for the evil it discovers, to erect a patina, a coating to protect itself from, to pretend it is an aberration, not a norm, that all entertainment, political religious leaders are consumed by. One or two exceptions, the veneer will allow, but the whole corrupt evil never.
Best of Show::from Fine Arts Judges, Arizona State Fair 2016. Sculpture Gary Seltzer. University of Arizona. Lawrence McLaughlin International Sculpture

10/23/16 had great time at Fair with A and S and kids, won second and third, found monarch eggs all over milkweed and planted apple tree.
     Urim more astounding than the cut of the stone, is an inscription in ancient Hebrew inside the stone, visible through its clear surface. Professor Moshe Sharon - expert on ancient Hebrew Script at the Hebrew University in Jerusalem - describes the Script from approximately 1000 BC.

10/22/16 I had a little bonny nagg to buy the British Nova Express for the red cover with the train and the phrase in Spanish on the cover, Spanish express of the French boxcar to come. http://blog.shinium.eu/2014/08/resin-inlaid-wood.html Cosmic glow powder Glo-Nation. I made some boasts to Harriet about writing etc and repeated them to Pat, that ...well why repeat, because they are the incapacitors and I otherwise want to renounce such and continue!

10/21/16 Eurosceptics bemused by what might be the latest symbolic failure of a European craft to escape the gravitational hold of the imploding artificial union. Zero Hedge. FUNVAX, the vaccine for religious fundamentalism. the medical police state in America accelerates. Six methods of virus dispersal tested - high altitude release, water supply release, insect transmission, diffusion by a ground level object such as a car, diffusion from a stationary object such as a bottle, and infection of food supply such as cattle or produce. --the release of genetically engineered mosquitoes combined with outbreaks of bizarre neurological conditions across U.S. to impact schoolchildren and mysterious health conditions all over the world.
     Put a flat plate, base under the piece that is square but shallow pedestal. Same, but just the pedestal, white, with rocks of a lava field scattered over it. Much of this affronts the idea that art is the intention of the artist. Michaelangelo's was, at least the Paintings. Was David? He says he found him in the marble. Was it his idea or discovery? These are discoveries in the making. that present common themes and looks, sometimes repeating images when a prior falls in the kiln, then four times later reappears and has to do with the man and what is in him for out of the heart the style comes.

10/19/16 So maybe this submission is therapy to find out what shame is. A commentary on Goya, a Person hiding face in posture of shame (while wearing a Sanbenito and coroza hat) in Goya's sketch "For being born somewhere else", shamed by the Spanish Inquisition. The confusion of identity in missionaries who live their adult lives in other cultures, Latin America, and speak of themselves as if they were Latin Americans, is just that. They are colonial implants who forever and always represent the land of their birth and education, no matter what they think they have become. They are not Indian, Maya, speak Quechua, have been raised in those circumstances or anything like it. This is not to say that their message is colonialism per se, for they are preaching a Middle Easter religion of Jerusalem. So they are more than a step removed from their own message. [If you read this you are one of them.]

10/17/17   J. Kleck, Just a Messenger. Ken Johnson Fallen Angels
Seraphim. The word seraph is a Hebrew word used as a noun refers to fiery or poisonous serpent. As a verb it means "burning." Using the base word seraph leads us to believe that the seraphim are either aflame themselves or serpent-like or both. Isaiah has a description of seraphim angels as fiery serpent-like seraphim creatures with six wings (three pairs). "In the year that king Uzziah died I saw also the Lord sitting upon a throne, high and lifted up, and his train filled the temple. Above it stood the seraphim: each one had six wings; with twain he covered his face, and with twain he covered his feet, and with twain he did fly. And one cried unto another, and said, Holy, holy, holy, is the LORD of hosts: the whole earth is full of his glory."

Isaiah 6:1- a little-known fragment of Enoch called the Book of Giants (which is added as an appendix in the Ancient Book of Enoch, by an author), describes exactly how the angels began to crossbreed insects, animals, and humans by taking two hundred sets of creatures with slightly different chromosome counts, like sheep and goats, and crossbred them. Later, they would crossbreed sets of the new unstable life forms to create further modifications, then repeat to get the desired effect.

In Genesis 1 God said "after its own kind" ten times. This mixing of kinds was against laws of reproduction. For the complete story of the two hundred, see Enoch 6-16. They descended in the days of Jared (460-622 AM; 3465-3303 BC)."And their judges and rulers went to the daughters of men and took their wives by force from their husbands according to their choice, and the sons of men, in those days, took from the cattle of the earth the beasts of the field, and the fowls of the air, and taught the mixture of the animals of one species with another…"
----Jasher 4.18 "For owing to these things came the flood upon the earth, namely, owing to the fornication wherein the Watchers against the law of their ordinances went a whoring after the daughters of men, and took themselves wives of all which they chose: and they made the beginning of uncleanness. And they begot sons, the Naphilim, and they were all unlike, and they devoured one another: and the giants slew the Naphil, and the Naphil slew the Eljo, and the Eljo, mankind, and one man another… And after this they sinned against the beasts and birds…" Jubilees 7.18-25

"For many angels of God accompanied with women, and begot sons that proved unjust, and despisers of all that was good, on account of the confidence they had in their own strength; for the tradition is, that these men did what resembled the acts of those whom the Grecians call giants or Titans." -Josephus Ant. 1.3.1: "In Hebron there were till then left the race of giants, who had bodies so large, and countenances so entirely different from other

men, that they were surprising to the sight, and terrible to the hearing. The bones of these men are still shown to this very day."
Josephus Ant. 5.2.3 --ancient seder olam, third Corinthians, epistle of Barnabas,
 You know it's coming, Jonathan kleck

10/16/16 the American ruling class

10/14/16 Goldylocks is Gory Locks
Do I look like a pomegranate man? If all the horrors done to girls and women were lumped together it would rival what Bishop Leadbeater said about the spirits of the millions and millions of cows killed in Chicago in its meatpacking era

10/13/16 Thurs. Mon mesquite milling, today truckload of aloe, doors salvage with Aey, Sat. Sun finish slab.

10/12/16 Cattle magnets: Cattle commonly swallow foreign objects, because they do not use their lips to discriminate between materials and they do not completely chew their feed before swallowing. Sharp metallic objects, such as nails or wire, are the common initiators of hardware disease . Cow magnets are popular with dairy farmers and veterinarians to help prevent Hardware Disease in cattle. While grazing, cows eat everything from grass and dirt to nails, staples and bits of bailing wire (referred to as tramp iron). Tramp iron tends to lodge in the honeycombed walls of the reticulum, threatening the surrounding vital organs and causing irritation and inflammation, The cow loses appetite and decreases milk output (dairy cows), or ability to gain weight (feeder stock). Cow magnets attracting stray metal from the folds and crevices of the rumen and reticulum. One magnet works for the life of the cow!

 Day of Redemption, Yom Kippur. He to rescue me from danger interposed his precious blood. Middle English: from Old French dangier, based on Latin dominus 'lord.' The original sense was 'jurisdiction or power,' specifically 'power to harm,' hence the current meaning 'liability to be harmed.' "Irrational exuberance" was followed about three years later by major slumps in stock markets worldwide, particularly the Nasdaq Composite. Market psychology, whether the increase that brought us here is indeed a "speculative bubble," an unsustainable increase in prices brought on by investors' buying behavior rather than by genuine, fundamental information about value, there are no investors only the cunning of programmed trades. "The smart way to keep people passive and obedient is to strictly limit the spectrum of acceptable opinion, but allow very lively debate within that spectrum...." Chomsky

10/11/16 It sounds like the news media want to hold out a Christian standard at least when it comes to other than predator bathrooms in Target. If Trump had said vagina Billy Bush would have run screaming from the trailer. Trump should have said Cotchie. We needs more respect? tRUMp HAS UNmasked a lot of this vulgarity and immorality. We can measure the illumined by their high discerning morality decreeing against the last Trump.

10/10/16 Neal Keenen, killed, Bill Clinton CDC precommunicable illness.

10/8/16   -Alex Dunlap turned up at my departure to CR unexpectedly and Jose Donoso escorted me on the return. Never gave proper account of what happened in Costa Rica, wake up beginning this new year 5777 while people are on the verge of beginning new affairs, but I remember this past. What happened to the Latin America Mission and the Seminario Biblico? The Fall of Evangelicalism and the Latin America Mission. To Juan Stam: I want to say how much I enjoy your Episcopacy, which I am carefully reading. I was convinced to get it from snippets that occurred. I feel as though I share a general outlook on text and the word even if I come at it from literature not theology. All the best to you and yours. Even if we never met I have carried the questions searched here ever since 1963, never better assayed than now, but this is not final either. Yours truly, AE Reiff

Juan Stam: His Blogs. Las buenas nuevas de la creación (GrandRapids:Eerdmans/Nueva Creación,1995); Apocalipsis y profecía: Las señales del tiempoyeltercermilenio (Buenos Aires:Kairós,1998);Comentario bíblico hiberoamericano:Apocalipsis, 4vols.(Buenos Aires:Kairós,1999–2014); Profecía bíblica y la misión de la iglesia (Quito: CLAI, 2001); Haciendo teología en América. Latina 2 vols. (San José: FTL 2004–5).

Assman. Stam, Pilgrimage, --mid-1970s Hugo Assmann arrived in Costa Rica and founded DEI (Departamento Ecuménico de Investigaciones). A God who acts in history, Hugo argued, would be an "interventionist," like the imperialists. I responded that this was precisely the Gospel message and that to deny this would land us in deism. For Hugo, all worship, including Yahweh worship, tends toward idolatry; I replied that the undefinable, unpredictable, unmanageable Yahweh was the antidote to such idolatry, and I quoted Barth's Revelation as the Abolition of Religion and Kierkegaard's Attack on Christendom.[2] For Hugo, God cannot be a "substitute actor" for the liberating action of the poor themselves, to which I replied, "God acts for the poor, with the poor, and in the poor, but not instead of the poor." For Hugo, Yahweh is the god who does nothing; the real god is the revolutionary spirit of the proletariat. All this, I said, did not sound like Latin American liberation theology but like European liberalism.

-With the advent of the military regime in Brazil, Assmann went to Uruguay, then to Bolivia and then to the Chile of Salvador Allende.[1] During this period he developed his reflections on the theology of revolution. In 1973 he published Teologia desde la praxis de la Libertacion, which marked the transition to the Liberation Theology. With the fall of Allende, Assman went to Costa Rica, where along with Franz Hinkelammert, developed his theological reflections on the relationship between theology and economics in the Department of Ecumenical Investigaciones (DEI),[2][3] founded by both. This center would be one of the leading producers and trainers of Liberation Theology.

John Stam- I was asked to give weekly meditations for the guerrilla fighters. Strange as it sounds, an important issue in Sandinista Nicaragua was the interpretation of "Gog and Magog" in Revelation 20, which dispensational tradition identified as Russia. Some missionaries and pastors argued that Russia (friends of the Sandinistas) was the Antichrist, while the United States (enemy of Sandinistas) was Israel's best friend and God's instrument for blessing to all nations (Gen. 12:3).

The first of my books (all published in Spanish) was The Good News of Creation, published by Eerdmans in 1995. Apocalypse and Prophecy (Kairós) followed, then Biblical Prophecy and the Mission of the Church (CLAI), and Doing Theology in Latin America (FTL, 2 vols.). Volume 1 of my commentary on the Book of Revelation appeared in 1999, and volume 4 in 2014, for a total of 1,600 pages of tightly packed exegesis.[3] Volume 3 of Doing Theology in Latin America is one of my current projects.

10/3/16 Jacob Stam, father of Ruth Stevens, Latin America mission, president of the Gideons, Chairman of board of Moody Bible Inst., 4, David Stam, what happened to me. "schooled in predestinational Calvinism" ix. "growing up as fundamentalists" 1, John Stam: "religiously fairly conservation and politically more radical than the rest of us."
  If I join these social religious milieus I feel diminished but if I don't work has less significance.
visionary companies: 69-Arthur Glasser: 165 (144), 180 (168) 16 Stam, Pilgrimage in Mission Rome.
        John Stam Revelations to emigrate from the imperial system 18:4
and to live prophetically in the midst of history (cf. 10.11). refuse all participation in the worship of the empire and the emperor, In Revelation John vehemently denounces the political system of the Roman Empire. John frequently takes titles of the emperor, like Pantôkrator, or phrases from the imperial ritual, like "thou art worthy", and transfers them to the Lamb. The identity of the beast as the Roman Empire is shown by 17:9 (seven hills, seven kings) and 17:18 ("the great city that is ruling over the kings of the earth" when John writes, which can be Rome) plan to attack Christians through the beast and the false prophet (emperor worship).   John also denounces the military system. John attributes the battle of Armageddon to the warmongering of three obnoxious frogs, vomited out by the dragon and the two beasts, who travel as propaganda agents to visit the royal palaces of the world and incite kings to mobilize for battle (16:13-14). The black horse of the Apocalypse has been running wild through the financial centers of the world! In Chapter 12 the dragon wages war against a pregnant woman and her soon-to-be-born child, but nothing goes well for it. When about to seize the child and devour him, the child is snatched away from to the heavenly throne -- exactly what the dragon wanted to avoid! It then pursues the child but is defeated by Michael and thrown violently down to earth.

        Having lost the battle for the child, it now seeks to persecute the woman, but she sprouts a pair of wings and escapes from the clutches. Finally, furious and frustrated, it vomits a river of poison, hoping to engulf the woman, but the earth opens its mouth and swallows all the poison. Then, though it has had nothing but embarrassing failures, the dragon adopts a new strategy to attack the "other children" of the woman (12:17).[14] This is when the dragon decides to create the Roman Empire (13:1-3) and the imperial cult (13:4; 11-15) as a last, desperate assault against the church. Thus John clearly demonizes the Roman Empire and informs all those tempted to accommodate to the religion of the empire that if they join in that worship, they will be involved in devil worship. Adoration of the emperor is, for John, adoration of the dragon who "gave the Beast his power and his throne and great authority" (13:2). As a result, "people worshipped the dragon because it had given authority to the beast, and they worshipped the beast" (13:4). Emperor devil worship! The empire and its ideology are an invention of the Satan.

9/21/16 "Thirty years of missionary service abroad," [John] Stam wrote in the days when he was expelled from ICBA, "have me ... convinced that my almost instinctive identification gospel with capitalism and Western-style democracy was anything but evangelical. In the Third World, I found that this view was ... highly detrimental to the Christian witness ... "The Gospel, if released from his cultural background, is explosive with a radical meaning for the people of Central America today. To discover the meaning of evangelical obedience in this revolutionary context, evangelicals who are less evangelical or less biblical supposed to become more revolutionary are not asked. They must learn to be immensely more Bible and more evangelical than ever ...

"Evangelicals in Central America have many reasons to be grateful to God for the great tradition of which are heirs, but little reason to feel triumphant .... [They] have been repeating all formulas 'saved by faith' but generally tend to fall into legalism non-evangelical ... [reflecting] faithfully individualist, competitive and consumerist elements of their society ... "In trying to understand the gospel in the midst of the revolution, we can see that, precisely where the traditional 'evangelicalism' [210] has distorted the gospel, making this crass mixture of legalism and cheap grace, seems to be the same point where [it] has adapted most successfully to the individualist and consumerist culture which was brought by missionaries to Central America. What it is extra-biblical and evangelical unless this religious idiosyncrasies turns out to be a transplant. Reflects an imported ideology that must not be identified with the gospel itself ... We must never tire of our ideas in light of the scriptures." David Stoll.

"The manifestation (the meaning of "Apocalypse") of hope in Christ Jesus" Stam and Fidel.

Paul Leggett Revelations.-1976, the [Foulkes] family spent a year in Washington, DC while Irene completed her doctoral studies at Georgetown, and by 1983 their interest in Catholicism had grown so fully that they spent a year doing postdoctoral studies in Rome at the Pontifical Biblical Institute (part of the Gregorian University) which Irene noted was the top institution for biblical studies in the Roman Catholic Church, 109 Radicalized Evangelical Missionaries--In Robert Coeller, diss.,

Katharine Moon, who wrote about American soldiers and prostitutes in South Korea, Robert Stam, Postcolonial theory.

10/5/16 Finding Elizabeth: history, polemic, and the Laudian redefinition of conformity in seventeenth century England. Lewis Calvin Lane III

10/4/16 Aey said S asked him why he wasn't happy. 10/2/16 Yesterday concluded not to go toTx on the 12th but finish up work here. Poured 1/2 the slab last week.
Luscious dust clay, add phosphorous,

9/30/16 Fish mox, amoxicillin. A political event in Ezekiel, the Egyptian law prescribed this punishment for an adulteress. And they shall take away thy nose, &c. — A punishment of adultery which rage sometimes dictated. As husbands in that case render those women deformed whose beauty hath been too pleasing to strangers, so shall the Chaldeans deface all the glories and ornaments of Jerusalem, and after they have slain and carried captive its inhabitants, shall set the city on fire, and reduce it to a heap of ashes.

9/29/16 Mark Goodwin prepper Jager pro hog traps, Tex ax night hogs gun, ammo, rules.

9/27/16 "we're now on the precipice of having a potentially much better economy," Clinton

9/26/16 Ex 23.20 do not tempt the angel in the wilderness Neural subnet design by direct polynomial mapping.

9/25/9/24/16 Kazunori Hamana, Yuji Ueda, and Otani Workshop. 200thTechnology of the human mind, impulses from the cloud.

9/23/16 front and back. But here the back is a front, two fronts facing out back to back. that's a statement of reality. everything is a front. the face to greet the faces that we meet and then the other face under the face, behind the face behind the face is what this process represents. The A side and the B, sometimes the C, even the D.
https://www.scribd.com/doc/46566146/Who-is-Esau-Edom tim, Carla, Claire Jelinek.

9/22/16 unlock car with tennis ball, epsom salts and vinegar kill weeds.
 Numerology of One World Trade
        -the horror of the domed ceiling of the discolored skies of chemtrail in the Chamber XX of Human Rights and Alliance of Civilizations.

9/20/16 Antarctic numbers, dates, colors, signs and symbols, cf. ark of Gabriel at south pole: March 5, 1947 edition of the Chilean newspaper El Mercurio, read in part as follows: "Admiral Richard E. Byrd warned today that the United States should adopt measures of protection against the possibility of an invasion of the country by hostile planes coming from the polar regions. The admiral explained that he was not trying to scare anyone, but the cruel reality is that in case of a new war, the United States could be attacked by planes flying over one or both poles."

9/18/16 At Linkedin Aeg was an apprentice at the Phx Center and a student of Susan Petersen, played trumpet for City Jazz directed by 9/17/16 Jason A. Something we haven't seen, blue beam rainbows ground zero 9/11 anniversary, conception from skin cells,... Brave Williams.

Kurt Weiser: work from light to dark. Fascinated with territory, unregulated space, fascinated with exploration, maps of the old world, "the globes are my feeling of what's around of all the stuff that happens in the particular world, with as little preplanning as possible. The ideas come together in the work, start with one element and work their way out from there [let the lines reveal the lines, the planes, the forms] . There's no fun, no surprises in plans on paper, so the pieces are an exploration rather than just work, maybe 25 gal of slip in one globe, I'm not sure what's going to happen until I get there. It's not china paint I love but imagery, I love making things out of clay but felt something missing, which was imagery, ideas about things. I tried underglaze, black slips, conformist as the rest. It wasn't till I got older that I realized to do what I want, who cares, do what I want, what really interests me, nobody's watching anyway. It's a little unnerving to view the past 30 years. I try not to pay too much attention to it, having done this for this long a time I don't take myself as seriously as I used to, I just do what I do, Sensuously decorated porcelain, the pots he creates are among the most vivid and decadent of modern ceramics bio

9/16/16 I supply the words of the world, politicians, pastors, news broadcasts, films, plays, all business correspondence, every treaty and agreement of any kind, letters to editors, the words of editors themselves, every correspondence, all the books in the world, all the secrets and revelations boasted in the deep net, all the speech scripted for all the gifted acting, every aspect of accounts of discovery and space travel, all that stuff, and that doesn't include the other millions. Do I regret? Wait, there's more.

9/14/16 "And in that day will I make Jerusalem a burdensome stone for all people: all that burden themselves with it shall be cut in pieces, though all the people of the earth be gathered together against it." —Zechariah 12:3 timeline

9/13/16 Visit w J. Dr. Arthur P. Bradley, emp. dry shield bags. battery, inverter, generator the reprobate mind searches for secret knowledge to gain power to become like gods.

9/8/16 He took not on Him the nature of angels, but He took on Him the seed of Abraham. Heb 2.16. AB & T yesterday, transcendent.

9/7/16 Had AB and T while A did templates at office. the dire spiritual topography of the book of Enoch is remedied by the Psalms which take all the confrontations of men and giants to their vanquishing.

9/6/16 Aey went to church with Cindi who said when we go to Tx she's to talk with Sh about her bitterns. Starts his classes today. A went to office to help w/ templates today, to drop kids tomorrow to do some tomorrow.

9/5/16 AB for Labor Day, flat bread, bread sticks, breakfast, gardening. Watched ESPN 5 parts on OJ. Civil judgment 33 million, sentence 33 years, friends with Kardashians. see here "My class was consumed by "Politics and Vision"—Machiavelli's advocacy of "calculated violence" and call for the power elites to be skillful pretenders and dissemblers; Locke's ability to convert property into an instrument for coercing citizens into political obedience; Weber's understanding that the modern hero, unlike the classical hero battling fortuna, had to struggle against a bloodless, faceless system "where contingency has been routed by bureaucratized procedures" and where "even charisma has been bureaucratized." The ideological mantra of corporate oppression—sine ira et studio, without scorn or bias—is, as Weber knew, a weapon to crush those with the passion, outrage, courage and vision to effect change. Wolin warned in the book that "each individual bore the awful responsibility for choice at this ultimate level but each was denied anything like the scientist's sense of certainty." He quoted Weber, whom he loved: "The ultimate possible attitudes towards life are irreconcilable and hence their struggle can never be brought to a final conclusion." Chris Hedges, Cause of Iraq War- steal technology from Iraq Museum to build Tower of Babel and "take" heaven, parallel to CERN. Nephilim crossing over to engineered internet earth, decoded human genome. Alien technology in the mind of DARPA. Man it's like a one stop shop, Walmart of the mind.

9/3/16 the bulk of imagination, its subjects, as the result of sin and the projected thought forms become the archetypes and unconscious.

9/1/16 Took w/h back got one that fits. Installed by Aey.

8/30/16 Drained old and bought new 40 gal water heater. Pope Babylon. Sent $1000 to Dr. Manning, Atlah. big mistake.

8/29/16 Christmas eve 1968. Apollo 8 reading first 10 vs of Genesis. Physical barrier at 100km (The Karman Line/The Firmament.

8/28/16 Last nite, Sat, at Dominicks steak house in Scottsdale for Justyn's bday with AB. C says she wants to have dinner with us to vet her two boyfriends sometime! Later I ask, together? She laughs. J wants to dispute John 6.19, changes the meaning to him and his father, says it means good or bad, till he looks it up. I tell him it's not the subject of our thought and speech, its ours, meaning charged, changed with our own perversions withal.

    Leaving, driving west, saw the closest conj. of Venus and Jupiter, or any planets in the sky, 7.30, 1/15 of a degree! repeats in 2065.

    Got to Aeg's, getting out of car we are accosted by a befuddled, menacing predator at his curb who I tell to leave, pretty loud and certain. Aeg oblivious inside, flaccid, soft. the guy had come to his door soliciting. The neighbors then come over and say he had fleeced A's car. I tell him to put on a shirt. Then are you ready for battle, for the guy was still there, had come back. This cleared but we didn't stay. AAB comes running to the door to hug me there, for the first time, after sitting on my lap at the dinner going through Christina's purse, who doesn't know what a Krugerrand is, gave Justyn, at 11, his own 6a cell.

8/27/16 **Precognition** may be permission. If I foresee an event it may be postive, neutral or negative. If I think the phone will ring and it does but is a poll then I should have blocked the thought, except I could not know in advance. Precognition is not knowing in advance, at least in this way. It is seeing but not knowing. If I see a wall and think it is prime estate for graffitti I have learned that is permission, so I forbid it.

8/25/16 Saber red blue face. Today is Fishday. Leviathan created male and female. To prevent their inundating the world the female was killed, salted to be preserved for the banquet of the righteous.

8/24/16 Maja Franziska Brandli sacrifice at CERN connected to - US Air Force Major Steve Lewis attacked by the Obama regimes Military Religious Freedom Foundation (MRFF) who are calling for his immediate firing and prosecution for the "crime" of having a Bible on his work desk—which he no doubt needed to cleanse his mind and soul from the horrors he discovered.

8/23/16 Emp trash can. Have Theo today while they haul base for slab.
    "There was once a man in Babylong who repented not studying Torah and felt bad about his lack of knowledge. O, He recited the words "Holy holy holy,' very loudly in the Kedushah. He emigrated to the Holy Land and there built a city, which he called Colonia, and it belonged to him, his children, and his children's children." Torah Anthology, 618

8/22/16 Human fumigation like rats so they can talk on phones. Toulene sprayed on low level ozone to dissipate it.
    --The oracles sold themselves the value of telepathy and took external devices, attachments to produce it. to improve the dissemination of radar, wifi, GPS, relay antennas, since radar is weakened by oxygen and water vapor in atmosphere significant at FQ greater than 10 Ghz, impedes, scatters signals of KA band wireless communication in the microwave range.
    To inhibit production of clouds a climate war for all MTS communications began, both civilian and military satellite radar, whose electronics will not work if there are clouds and precipitation which produce much background noise. The higher the frequency of radar the greater it is impaired, which began these hygroscopic abuses using drying agents such as dessicators silica gel, aluminum trimethyl, lithium, calcium carbonate, barium that react with water in the atmosphere and break the molecular bonds between hydrogen and oxygen, lowering humidity and preventing cloud development, which chemical compounds produce other reactions. Cumulus clouds at low altitudes are the enemies of radar and satellite systems that operate in a particular KA range, these compounds scattered at low altitudes are carried in updrafts to spread toward the natural clouds giving them a grey patina interfering with photosynthesis and all biological processes. 25.37
    In the hours of instruction Wallender, In the Night, News of the one faith Jerusalem in Sept, lives, Genesis and the Torah anthology and the Dispersed of Israel, long reaches of history to Egypt all viewed in some equivalency of relation as a spectator while I try to discern

the true and false through the Word and construct a model of the pyramid relations of the ladder I am not on.

8/21/16 POPE FRANCIS to PROCLAIM God of One World Religion on September 23 2016? ATLAH Ministries, masonic pavement. the ark the temple the tomb the altar the new Jerusalem: the arc of the covenant.

8/20/16 There must be a special place for taking metaphor seriously as far as lit games and Pokémon go:: Literary Magazines for Socialists Funded by the CIA::intel John Hanke building out 3D virtual world: satellites, Ariel collection platforms, street view, iPhone, android, adds location to bring together maps, location, social interacts and games,=Niantic labs, Ingress, Niantic, supercollider worship, pizeo electricity, opening portals,: the world is the game, tagging and tracking surveillance softward, POKEMON GO': C.I.A./NSA/ILLUMINATi SURVEILLANCE!!!

    The best you can do as parents is give them a whole body. A whole mind, that's beyond parenthood. As with Spelman, John D. Rockefeller was a benefactor at Morehouse, donating the land of the school's present location. Morehouse's most famous graduate, Martin Luther King Jr., of America's important, a preacher for justice on peace and civil rights. The college boasts a 10,000-piece collection of handwritten notes and unpublished sermons of MLK Jr. Not to be excluded from the world of entertainment, Morehouse is also the alma mater to filmmaker Spike Lee and actor Samuel L. Jackson. here /media hand-picked for their platforms, see 1 Aug

8/19/16 Dreamed at Bethany Bible church class with lots of black 6 year old boys passing the time not exactly when a teacher struck up a converse with Mike Tyson's son, a head taller than the others and burly, talking about bullying and it's effects, what to do, but esp. not to bully those who are smaller and weak. Prayed with him about it. a good big kid reachable. After, talking to a couple, i said THERE WERE HOLES IN THE AIR around him as we talked. Pat was there too, in another class, something about interaction. She was hauled out in a massage chair, disgruntled. As I spoke to the couple her teacher came over to explain, to interrupt. I told her three times to go away.

    Frankfurt School Ester Leslie-1919 hope," In the 1960s, the Frankfurt School's argument - that most of culture helps to keep its audience compliant with capitalism - had an explosive impact."

8/17/16 Queen Daub, John Knox, Great Whore, Cozbi Delilah.

8/16/16 "Some even believe we are part of a secret cabal working against the best interests of the United States, characterizing my family and me as 'internationalists' and of conspiring with others around the world to build a more integrated global political and economic structure—one world, if you will. If that is the charge, I stand guilty, and I am proud of it." David Rockefeller, Memoirs, 2003. Daily sheeple

8/15/16 Mon. I had asked for help with the bugs last night. This AM working at 4 one fat one crawled out from papers above the keyboard. I had threatened to take it another level yesterday, that's why I prayed. So then I punched up DE and began sprinkling everywhere. Bomb Florida with DE to cure Zika.

    The bad news is that the **Blue Book and the Brown Book might have been infected SO I HAD TO MICROWAVE WITTGENSTEIN.** Give your bugs a day at the beach: DE!

    Proverbs 31: SHE MAKES Solar BREAD IN THE YARD AND MASA HARINA IN THE GARAGE.

8/14/16 sent Cloud Boy. I don't know why coloring books aren't illuminated books like the songs of innocence and everything with colors isn't such, all my little coloring books.

8/13/16 the diff between acting, film and writing, as in No Country for Old vs Piano, is that the actors interpret the speech that is raw speech inflecting and giving it irony, etc. but in the native finding God in old age or the complaint he is overmatched and the world wave will swallow him is McCarthy's own despair, not a joke.

8/12/16 Saw I could touch a brush with some paints on to a canvas and all the implicit movements in the application would shape on the canvas in colors changing. Then I could influence the colors and their shapes, but it seemed to do itself. I had an old Italian woman maestesra. At one point someone said some white should appear and it did. then I blew on it and it spread like gusts of wind. The whole was a kind of large living mustard hill house.

8/11/16 Office dripping yesterday. On the 10 we got 30 sand bags. On Sat and Sun we stripped the study. dried the middle room. but not needed. AK 747

8/9/16 I am instructed both to be full and to be hungry Phil 4.12
Take a look at Sacrete concrete web site. --What you need to do is several steps to ensure it adheres properly, and does not crack, to clean the old concrete with acid, then a special primer, a specific type of concrete designed for applications less than two inches thick over old concrete.
    --If you are set on adding a "hump" you should cut out a section of the driveway and add in the hump as one big chunk of concrete. Make the hump a separate pour from the rest of the drive. This way the drive and the hump will react to the weight of your cars as they roll over them separately and they will not crack. Installing concrete onto another concrete surface will be a short term solution. Cut out the section and install a new one piece section with the slope and shape.

8/8/16 Does oil combine with stone? Can you wash water away? We pushed water with a broom out the gate. 8/7/16 -I knew a guy whether as the boy or out I cannot say, who lived in the center of the city but carved out an eco niche for Gambel Quail, countless hummers, doves, etc. and kept a dead tree standing for woodpeckers home to nomadic carpenter bees. He also kept a mulberry that housed a significant hive of honey bees. I stood by the tree one morning and heard the hum loud enough to charge a battery.

-This represents the last in a summer series (so far) of what must only be called EMOTICONS to confront the mindlessness of those tongue tied idiots who use them, configured as they are to Disnify everything about their relationships. And if these images don't seem recognizable that's because they are real misshapen, twisted faces produced for consumption in the commoner terrorist media. This one could be called Khizar Khan. Most of these Emoticons are two faced, even three faced, in order to show the duplicity and hypocrisy of their users.

It won't be glazed for some weeks though. Its back story, illustrative of the make or break, demo and rebuild philosophy controlling our time reads: "The last piece of summer fell, but not off the table. It landed on its side improving the whole nicely after it was retrieved. The inner stakes helped. The plastic around it helped. That Bmix paper is brittle. Had to remove the top story. Then it toppled to the floor. Which has not happened exactly before. So the whole 30 lbs was reconstituted, wedged, rolled, thrown into the present state of this clay." -I have concrete caulk which I'm ready to shoot up into cracks, which you know I have an affinity for.

-Love covers a multitude of sins. We know our own sins, sometimes we know the sins of others, memory serving, through their own confessions and errors that end badly, for the end is of the beginning. Tom Cranfill's Alzheimer's. Tom G's consuming anger, anger of the heart he called it. After all his ranting and dying and name calling, I "liked" his last missile. So what do you know, probably out spite, the next day he "liked" my last. That's what Paul meant when he said some preach Christ out of spite. Tom just doesn't like to be upped.

8/6/16 To take the flood as a case of a flood, the event is a torrent but aftermath extends a long way, therefore the prelude is important. Signs of weather sure, signs of war, signs of hope, signs of the heavens, all lead to the same thing, flood, but what preparations, berms, sandbags, roofs, walls, doors? Our walls shall be salvation our gates praise...Isaiah 60.8, or the other, obvious signs of attention or inattention precede these, and i the immediate business of the rain. THEN comes the flood, relatively short in duration compared to prelude and aftermath. It is the trauma of celebration where people are deep in the water, but don't realize or complete their own defense. But the aftermath stinks. Mold mildew, rot, mud, even if the trees love it and the tortoises survive. We demo the remains, gut the wall board if needed to dry it, tear up the carpet and the rebuilding takes up all the rest. How long after the floods swept away civilizations did they rebuild Jerusalem?

I was living and let live with the fire ants in the back yard as early as May, but got so many bites below the clothes line that I gave them various treatments starting with vinegar, which used to work. Not at this stage. Then I got some Dr. Earth, being translated meditation, which killed the grass but the ants liked it. So I tried some Sevin, nasty stuff, just the slightest, which stopped the surface ants, but they were back in a week. So I tried some Terro Liquid Ant Bait Stakes, except the rains and flood spoiled them. But right before the storm I sprinkled a tablespoon of Amdro, super nasty. It rained 2 hours later, but all those nests were clear. This morning though, checking, I see them reestablished against the base of the Aleppo. I raked out the tall grass there and gave another tablespoon. They I saw they were climbing, (nesting?) in the tree.

Meditation, conspiracy theory, rants, racism, bitter opinions: do they have an emoticon where a guy sticks up his middle finger? Why do you care Tom? Politics is run by the angels and their deputies and sub deputies.
Hillary works for the Jesuits, Trump for the free masons. So Dance. Then they would have swallowed us alive, When their anger was kindled against us; Then the waters would have engulfed us, The stream would have swept over our soul; 5 Then the raging waters would have swept over our soul."...Psalm 124.4

8/5/16 The woman is desecrated, the man is emasculated, the child is sacrificed.

8/4/16 Dinner with a, a&t, aey and sh and P but not S at Texas roadhouse.

8/3/16--Dreamed what A should say in interview: a class. commitment to industry, its connections in itself and with world of customers, study the relations of its commerce al la Peter Drucker cases, eg. the big short etc., deal with the two species of man therein, the ambition cutthroat who smiles and the lackadaisical dullard but find a third.
 Hitler's circumcision- firth "Hitler founded Israel" - 1933 The Transfer Agreement Part 1 Vostfr
8/2/16 real terrorists own the media

8/1/16 Susan in the waves. Hart crane swallowed by Nephilim.

 7/31/16 MYSTERY RIVER, LITTLE WHITE LIES, THE SEASONING HOUSE, AND OMNIVOROS.
Camille Graham: comment to Black Child: A Negro State of the Union RE-upload The negroes we recognize by name and we see in media hand-picked for their platforms because they possess the characteristics of the subjects successfully indoctrinated by the inherent in control of this beast system. (claimed the film was a Jewish conspiracy to incite blacks to violence against whites.]

--Finian Cunningham: A conflict between a sovereign nation supported by Russia against barbaric killers mobilized by lawless foreign powers. Sputnik News astronomical cognitive dissonance warmonger posing as a champion for world peace and law and order [which means the opposite].

7/30/16 People who suffer the Mandela effect say the world is being edited, as the man from Taured, Taured nation, like out of Borges, Maps changing, islands missing, Visuals are changing, text is changing, lion shall lie down with the lambs, Movies are changing, Mandela effect. Mussolini a British agent, The Guardian

7/29/16 BuckyFuller CERN the next generation Patch, blending a woke machine, linear accelerator, plasma waves, plasma Wakefield acceleration waves. Plasma (ionized gas)/ Awake plasma exp, electric universe, LHC =einstein. awake=tesla combined. Awake particle accelerator 1000x power then main ring, electron to proton collisions, reaccelerated particles out of main ring loaded into Awake, 30 meters in length but 1K the power. James Swaggert tour of CERN speaks of bigger ring, but not needed because the two machines combine, VHEeP [very high energy electron proton collider] are not public, but hybrid offspring of ring and awake. From one PETA last Oct to 20 peta electron volts to start, to create high efficiency collider to focus 20 PEV, twenty thousand million million electron volts. AWKE by itself generates 1000x the power as the Ring magnets, largest most powerful machine in history, less luminosity, stray particles.

    This fine tuned low luminous aimed at a target, viz strangelets, direct energy weapon to pierce the veil. QCD, quantum chromo dynamics, measure of colors and spin of particles, to be broken by the 20 PEV, a fundamental force than binds particles together to be broken by a machine. Double meaning: open new windows beyond the reach of the LHC, portals to other dimensions, HERA collider in Germany, closed in 2007, used to develop Plasma Wakefield Technology, [new book world already terraformed]. Bucky Fuller tetrahedron simplest figure to describe a space. 600 cell tetrahedron triangles surrounding earth, like ley lines, Bucky balls fullerines, cosmic balls and atomic level, geometric shape derived from tetrahedrons, replicate tetrahedrons to form a geodesic dome: model of the universe. Stranglets meant to dissolve the dome's gluons, single quark glueon concentrate, drilling with strangelets, focusing protons on targets in form of tetrahedron, breaking the bond, the gluons, separating quarks separating the pyramids, freeing quarks, independent quarks, military Ind-complex The Vatican funding CERN, harvest direct energy weapons, strangelets a weapon of war, the tetrahedron is intended to open the portal --all enabled by the hidden energies themselves. When the tetrahedron is open, what's inside the flower, the other dimension, beyond the quantum scale, the power is to break the gluon bond, managed by the black cube quantum computer D Wave (Geordie Rose). 7 billion human brain processing power, this computer controls the portal. A small opening can be made bigger, vacuum bubbles could expand and engulf the universe, adiabetic computer intended to control this, unraveling the tetrahedron, plasma shapes of electric universe, , Montague Childs, Sapphire, phase II, at Thunderbolt, 5 min mark of video, generating spherical shapes in a chamber, with hexagonal shape, inner spheres moving outward, the process occurring in the sun, and Saturn, geometrically the tetrahedron form hexagons ot to sphere, the rotation of Saturn's north pole is the same thing as they do at CERN and the Sapphire project. Jupiter red spot, plasma accelerator, heats the atmosphere above it, synchroton energy cause this heating, gamma and xrays, collision of particles on Jupiter, standing waves of energy in Saturn, takes the form of cubes, Patch thinks the north pole of sun is like Saturn. merging two technologies.

    Pulse tube dilution refrigerations emit a pulse like a heartbeat every second. "it feels like an altar to an alien god" 11.20 D-Wave lecture by Geordie Rose (Idea City 2013) 3 predictions, by 2018 NASA finds habitable planet, parallel universes proved by 2023, intel machines by 2028.

7/28/16 Criminal defense attorney at police interview on shoot somebody AntiTerrorist 'Bunker In or Bug Out.' The Israeli 9/11 Art Project & Dick Cheney. The idea is that if I as your adversary intend to attack you and use 'information in plain sight', I effectively have your consent for attacking you--see Sophia Smallstorm Bohemian Grove sacrifice.

7/31/16 **Wm Mount**: directors of the UN claim to be fallen angels: grow through stress.

7/26/16 Stasis chamber time bubble giants, Mars Walking.

7/25/16 Thinking about I Pet 2 submitting to every ordinance as a consequence of suffering wrongfully, which is like Romans 13 and not resisting authority are the pretexts FEMA uses to lure pastors to herd their sheep to camps in droves. But the Wise Men did not return to Herod as they said they would, or he said, and both Moses and Jesus escaped edicts of death declared by authorities. Further thinking about idols in Rom 1-2 and Ephesians connected, idols are anything that can cause us to be separated from the love of Yahweh in Christ Jesus, whether spouse or job or (loaded gun) which cause us to trust in them.

7/24/16 Accept them after I have forgiven them for what they are because there were previous stages in the making, as the past is in an individual's life, the amorphous forethought, the making of the clay, its lamination, the molding into form on the wheel, the separate parts waiting assembly, the stretching of the clay, the assembly and its bracing, the bending, molding breaking, the covering and hoping it won't fall, the finishing of the head, adjustments, the signing, the flattening the base so it will stand: all this precedes the bisquing and glazing when whites blend and intensities fade. then the final firing and it cannot look like what it did before. Then I may accept them after I have forgiven them for what they are.

     Rueben Israel is a totally equal opportunity offender. Microwave your books to get the bugs out. Find one fake staging, bldg seven going straight down, no blood on the Bastille Day truck, then the pods of muscular atrophy blow the cobwebs out of your brain and you can see clearly how the bugs are at the back of vaccine epidemic, RFK, cell phone brain cancer epidemic, surge in European terror attacks, "surveillance capitalism" Pokémon go- Oliver Stone, data mining,

7/23/16 The Big Short. Vaterland | Leviathan 11,000 troops could board the ship in two hours. Humphrey Bogart served as the Chief Quartermaster, the senior enlisted man of the Navigation Division; War duty and age meant that all wiring, plumbing, and interior layouts were stripped and redesigned while her hull was strengthened and her engines converted from coal to oil while being refurbished; virtually a new ship emerged.

7/22/16 **Jut Wynne**: hyper arid Atacama desert. community ecologist in the conservation and management of cave-dwelling arthropods. biogeography, habitat requirements, and species interactions of the ~75 known cave adapted arthropods on the Hawaiian Islands; (iii) estimating population size, characterizing habitat, analyzing diet with metagenomic techniques and DNA barcoding. The Importance of Caves in Our Solar System. Troglomorphic Pseudoscorpions. reign of red queen. lava tube caves.

7/20/16 battery charger that has both solar panel and a small crank.
   Rechargeable batteries are a must or else you'll end up broke if lights go out. 12 Samsung NM 2500Mh AA and 8 AAA 800mh for headlamps. D cell plastic adaptors in order to use AA batteries on my 3 D cell Maglite.
2 or 3 packs of regular, Duracell batteries just in case. surviving in Argentina
 David Rockefeller's real face. Muslims Threaten To KILL Christians On ASU Campus. Honeycomb ventilation panes for Faraday glyptodon bug as big as VW

7/18/16 confabulation the Mandela effect

7/17/16 Govs fear who built alien moon structures, Queen of England Admits She is "Not Human" and We Will "Learn to Accept Her For What She Is"
C confirmed Aeg lost present job last week. AB said as much.

7/15/16 Jerusalem destroyed in 586/587 BCE by Nebuchadnezzar, king of Babylonia prophesized by Ezekiel (24: 1-27) while in exile in the city of Nippur in Babylonia, itself 586/587 miles from the Temple mount. The name Jerusalem at the time was spelled with Phoenician letters: 40 30 300 6 200 10 = 586. This shows that the gematria (number value of the Hebrew letters) of the name Jerusalem itself equals the year of its destruction in the years before Christ, the very first time the temple was destroyed. After the Jews were exiled in Babylonia, they adopted the square script Aramaic letters of their captors, still in use today. These letters add 5 "final forms" to the Phoenician 22 totaling 27 letters. When Jerusalem is spelled using these letters, the final form of the letter (Mem) is used. The final 'Mem' makes the modern spelling of Jerusalem equal to 365 x PI. This is the same as the value of the word 'Leviathan'.

In Hebrew esotericism Leviathan supposedly represents the Milky Way and the cycle of the 'Aion' that Jesus spoke of concerning his return. This present Aion will end in 2012 as the sun rises on the winter solstice in the 'mouth' of the connected serpent, (the literal translation of levi-tan) in 2012. Watcher forum. [off by four years, or?]
--Does it surprise you that artificial intelligence would counterfeit the truth, that Torah Codes predict a false messiah? Under Putin, the nation was rediscovering what it was to be Russian, Solzhenitsyn thought."[4] Jonas e. Alexis
-- Crime cabal behind the "war on terror" likes to "tag" events with numbers, the same way gangs tag turf with graffiti. Initiates look at the news coverage, see the magic numbers, and say to themselves "yep, our guys did that" and get with the program.

7/14/16 Leviathan and Jerusalem: "the Hebrew letters of the name Jerusalem equal 1,146 or the number of days in a year, 365 x PI. The same number is found in the sum of the name Leviathan, meaning a connected serpent or circles serpent.

The average water level of the Sea of Galilee, indicated by its ancient shoreline, is 640 feet below sea level. Perhaps no coincidentally, Israel was captured by the Muslim Arabs in 640 AD. Temple at eh Center of time 290,292 Day after disclosure Richard Dolan, post disclosure is post petroleum says Obama disclosure-no, USA is shiva.

7/13/16 Procession of Philistine Captives at Medinet-habu sea peoples
K2 synthetic mj epidemic bed sty

Kinderlieder: Volkslied.
So geht es in Schnützelputz Häusel:
Da singen und tanzen die Mäusel, da bellen die Schnecken im Häusel. In Schnützelputz So it goes in Schnützelputz Häusel:
As singing and dancing Mäusel, because the snails barking in Häusel.
-In Schnützelputz Häusel, since it is very great:
because the tables and benches drinking fully, Slippers under the bed. There were two oxen in Stork, who had comforted each other comely and wanted the eggs hatch.
It attracted two storks well on the watch, who had their thing even well-considered with their high and mighty spears. I know the things to say more, they unfold in Schnützelputz Häusel, even ridiculous beyond measure. So it goes in Schnützelputz Häusel: As singing and dancing Mäusel, because the snails barking in Häuse

7/12/16 U.S. plans to collapse Europe Jim Willie

7/11/16 Pyriproxyfen is a pyridine-based pesticide effective against arthropoda- microcephaly in Brazil.

7/8/16 Bloody Harvest: Organ Harvesting of Falun Gong Practitioners in China

7/6/16 Criminal angels. Two of an untold number of artifices reflect the conspiracy against the governed, Steph Curry's pass behind his back out of bounds with 90 sec remaining, then his feeble one hand shots that didn't hit the backboard, but prevented other members of his team from scoring giving the victory to Cleveland, a setup, and the assassination of the MP Jo Cox 4 days before Brexit to influence the vote against leaving, which however failed, so a deeper game here. Both prove the staged events rule the world. The lone gunman mass murder sniper type program of long standing, prepared by countless films, Dirty Harry (1971) sociopath psycho etc. prepares for Orlando, San Bernardino, Sandy Hook conditioning with the same purpose as The Fairy advises Studdock in *Hideous Strength*

7/5/16 The LORD will return to complete his rescue at the most dire moment when all the affections of the heart are weaned from the world and incline to Him.

7/3/16 Were the hijackers operatives for a Western intelligence service? How did a passport from one of the terrorists survive completely unscathed, only to be found later amidst the rubble of the Trade Centers? How did WTC Building 7 collapse even though it was never struck by an airplane? Why was President George H.W. Bush meeting with members of the Bin Laden family at the very moment of the attacks? Were the planes that hit the buildings actually commercial airliners or were they remotely operated drones? Why was the entirety of Ground Zero quickly sanitized and shipped to China for recycling before any investigation took place? And, what are the odds that on the very day terrorists used planes to attack the Pentagon and World Trade Centers, the U.S. military was holding exercises simulating hijackers crashing planes into buildings, a circumstance that led to total confusion across the United States and a complete failure of national defense? Mac Slavo

Paulette Steeves. Decolonizing archaeology: be nice to find a church not a state church where the 4th of July is not revered.

7 1/16 EU: democratic pooling of sovereignty.

6/30/16 Do the whole patch thing because the ceiling disintegrated and water drips continually.

Drake equation, The simian arms make this look like a Jackboot Democrat, but the pose of The Thinker suggests a Republican. As said in anticipation of these Conventions:
 -They raise their heads in caucus stalks, Transcendent aliens made of pot,
Seven ballots take the crown Reptile bands time warp around.
 --Always in the judgment of good art in the eye of the beholder a closeup is included for you to decide. One clue: In The Lime Rat Probe the choices were either 1) a Drupe 2) a Jack or 3) a Prod. See for yourself:
http://smashedcat.blogspot.com/2014_11_11_archive.html

6/29/16 Aey brings Judah. peaches. on way to Yuma, tell him to come back at 9.AM. Is he arguing over the point of sex identity?
 Sam walton internment chief over US camp.s Alphabet conspiracy
 Dream: Jesus loves them cleaves so much they have three praise services. They get there before the silver even melts. this was from an early five thirty evening meeting that went more than three hours. Next day we were at a camp by eleven AM tgat had a big room with beds all of us all the kids, Conrad was there with his, Christy showed up with Elizabeth, all kinds of folk camp meeting style, Lynda to mission Wicked in Czech Rep.

6/27//16 The warning of a European army was at the core of the Brexit campaign   EU fourth Reich, the Nazi roots of the Brussels EU   Op.JB - The Last Great Secret of The Second World War by Christopher Creighton.   The brussels Business, Who runs the EU YouTube, The Game of Nations. Miles Copeland
 "Ganser Daniele, Nato's Secret Armies Paul Manning. Martin Bormann beginning of EU and common market Miss Muffet child care on McDowell gone. Forbidden symmetry. Sea turtles with herpes. Pedro Sandoval-ruling military junta launched a systematic plan to steal babies born to political prisoners, "These cases are moving because they are unique, painful

and about suffering and trauma that doesn't stop," said Claudia Salatino, a psychologist who has treated some of the victims.

    --Dreamed getting prescriptions filled at drug store long line, had gotten a previous but this was a different. Leaned over counter to ask if could get refund for the first. Ans. yes. Ask q about what happens with "donor drugs" and their disposal etc. Pharm says great q. Goes to get material. encounter gay outside somehow he reads compassion says, thanks for accepting me. I ask him about donor drugs. We arrange a meet. P goes along. never quite get there, end up kissing her thoroughly lying down.

    -the only place metazen exist is the files of Matt drudge, google search and the obama state dept. unless you count sub-Brexit mash Gnostic burn when fireball hits Vatican off planet -Obama finds new boundaries for earth and air.

6/26/16 pyramids asteroid belt Brexit in I pet goat II, Mandela effect: addition, I Pet Goat II prophecy analysis: Fema camps, bar code on forehead, rfid chip, hypnotic state, George Bush: pentagram spot light, dragon eyebrows, penis/semen on black board, Owl, three points marked on map-Gulf, N.O., N.Y. ,Quim anagram, sign of goat, one eye Horus, Obama joker, American flag ripped in two, Statute of Liberty/Star of David, attack on Islam, Egypt nuked, Africa attacked with drones, Russia with biological weapons, arrival of antiman, shiva, sign of anti is love, second half more narrative from Bible, which is antiman will destroy all world religions and all those who do not follow the True Christ will follow him, includes CERN dance, [much internal body imagery, vaginas, tubes, wombs] instrumentalized by the massive sink hole bayou unleashing oil, gas, nuke waste, butane,--this was all to have happened at the N.O. superbowl

6/25/16 Tesla's black knight satellite Putin Orders All Fighter Jets Grounded the Obama regimes most dangerous act of violating the "agreement/treaty" between our Earth and the Black Knight Satellite, this report continues, it began on 28 May when the top secret weapon payload for the NORL-37 Mission was loaded on a US Air Force C-130 cargo plane at Wright Patterson Air Force Base in Dayton, Ohio, for its flight to Cape Canaveral, Florida—and which this mysterious object sent a probe down to observe, and that was videotaped. (see below) Five days later, this report continues, on 2 June, the Black Knight Satellite "ejected/released" a mysterious object that entered the atmosphere over the Western region of the United States that in turn released an unknown number of smaller objects with the main body exploding over Arizona. (see below)

    -male sexual identity compromised. chemically socially. cf autism caused by vaccines, homosex by background chem, or cell phone radiation, like cancer in clusters. supported by pedophilia, sexualizing children, unrelenting media press, entertainment industry, unmasked the way globalism unmasked by Brexit. all discussion of true masculinity is changed to these fakes emasculated kinds. So what is it really can hardly be said. equal parts courage, strength, decision, compassion, service, wisdom, understanding, daring, audacity, independent thought, unserpentine direct speech, discrimination, distinguish the Greek Olympian, promethean from the adamic, natural, form the new nature of Christ. men are like nations and opposed y the same thought that nations tribes of individual difference must be expunged because they cause war, men must be expunged because they resist this control, absorbed in the greater fwhole which has no division, no identity, no sex, no language, no tribe no nation -not what enemies say, racism and xenophobia

6-24-16 How to read and understand Fema
 -Susan like a cow got eaten by her step mom with her father, a NY publisher. it got out to inter-et, it got to people through burglars who broke in Step Dame's freezer, stole the goods on ice and parceled Susan out.
 Five days later, this report continues, on 2 June, the Black Knight Satellite "ejected/released" a mysterious object that entered the atmosphere over the Western region of the United States that in turn released an unknown number of smaller objects with the main body exploding over Arizona. (see below) President Putin ordered all Sukhoi-27 fighter jets grounded. Sorcha Faal " the people Had forfeited the confidence of the government And could win it back only By redoubled efforts. Would it not be easier In that case for the government To dissolve the people And elect another? Bertolt Brecht

6/23/16 Caribbean sea emits due to the size of the sea, it's producing a sound from its seafloor which plays a note of A-flat, although many octaves lower than a piano. "inexplicable pressure oscillations" the noise was being generated by a Rossby wave and its interaction with the seafloor. A Rossby wave is, in general terms, a wave generated by differences in temperatures of oceanic water levels and by the Earth's rotation. The phenomenon of it generating a sound is called a 'Rossby whistle'. This whistle noise is emitted when a large wave dies out on the western boundary of the basin before then reappearing on the eastern side, which the researchers described as a 'Rossby wormhole'.
- - Mystery Babylon USA Glock 17, Glock 19. to continue teaching in Pa - everyone is required to take 24 graduate credits within 6 years of certification. It's nonsense.

6/22/16 Gilgamesh Nimrod tomb found magnetogram distinguish between sediment and clay bricks to find Gilgamesh grave in Euphrates Iraq war a forward smoke screen to retrieve technology. the whole point of the human genome project is to locate specific genetic markers for the disembodied spirts to reanimate their host body remaining in Iraq
Found & Retrieved for DNA GENOMES of Nephilim. Possible DNA for 'future' engineering and a 'possible' resurrection/cloning of angel DNA (Gilgamesh/Nimrod) Links:

6/21/16 Liberty Man Navy Map Birkeland currents. regular currents are tubes within tubes within tubes energy attracts matter, matter covers energy, and energy moves matter.

--6/20/16 Time stream manipulation: +Psy op, weaponizing words. Satan changed the Word. CERN all bibles altered effect: lion lies down with the lamb, Isa 11.6 Lk 19.27 slay my enemies, Lk 1923 bank.
 Alters all. so they say. Antiman wants to intends to change the times and the law, but the judgment shall sit and they shall take away his dominion to consume. Daniel 7.25 -He will

speak out against the Most High and swear down the saints of the Highest One, and he will intend to make alterations in times and in law; The saints will be handed over to him for a time, times and half a time. [Or for a year, two years and half a year] But the court will sit, and his power will be taken away and completely destroyed for ever. Then the sovereignty, power and greatness of the kingdoms under the whole heaven will be handed over to the saints, the people of the Most High. Hence believing the lie means Satan succeeded in changing the time, however he did not.

    Christian times: wineskins vs bottles Matt 9.17. Lk 19.23 banks. Stuff. Ex 34.19 matrix open the matrix ex 13.12., 132.15, Nuj3.12, 18.15 -womb. Also, Mandela Bible effect ELS matrix sequences, bible codes for every fear and then some esp Niburu. not nearly as good as I pet goat II typed in google maps yielding the Hoover Dam relating to the $50 bill. antiman wants to intends to change the times and the law, but the judgment shall sit and they shall take away his dominion ot consume.

--6/19/16 Vivid dream. Aeg had two calls one from Beth and from a mutual friend of he and John that j had been bitten by a horse but he did not take the calls so that when he did hear the news j had already died, with twenty four hrs. we were together he and s. Aey and mom, out somewhere. For not responding he was heavily moved. Later we met others who knew j. and i said let us be friends to honor j. there was much more.

6/17/16 6 wks since S twisted her knee and after xrays, mri , Worthington nothing wrong with it but can't walk so we have had the kids some dozens while A explores new job and they go to therapy. Now the job wants him full time, he hasn't worked in 6 wks since he was fired, so he wants us to take T. some full days, 3, while he reports, and A is left with S. This period ended when A took new job, took T. of Da care and left AB at home with S. This in the context of his linked in claim to have a BS in forestry!, but also in this time Aey and I done the Log and are working the Slab!. E has found 7 toxic parents she loves, or not, Christie is "annoyed with Ae" for her being towed at Jacob Reiff

6/16/16 ISIS on land, Disney gators at sea

6/15/16 Christie , "annoyed with Ae" is a hazard of writing about anyone living. They will feel slighted, inaccurately treated. When these bios were fresh annoyed persons were heard from more frequently. Sometimes whole entries were taken down to pacify them. Can't expect conscience whistle blowers to these events, too many have been DNA'd away.
    --Orlando. Media full-time propaganda organizations never investigate the story prepared by government. Immediately set, fed out before investigation, contrary evidence discarded. People inside the massacre-made cell phone calls texted, but no one took photos or videos? No security cameras? No doormen to notice a heavily armed entry? 50 people killed and 50 more wounded and "reports of oceans" of blood, where are the bodies, interviews? He was carrying 8 30round magazines? Where? The gun would have had to have been reloaded many times, time for people to rush the shooter and overpower him...

6/14/16 sharkhunters.com
Eisenhower's death camps Morgenthau Plan to starve millions of Germans, mostly citizens, to death. the vessels of wrath fitted to the wheels of destruction. Rom 9.22

6/13/16 Neither death nor life, nor angels, nor principalities, nor powers, nor things present, nor things to come, nor height nor depth, nor any, All medical devices chipped, art hips, etc., hard wired to the www. meaning cern. Mon. So at Jacob's b-day dinner at Spinatos Sat, with AB, when C asked if I was going to party when P goes to SA, was expressing her against J, across the table.

6/12/16 LIBERATING INDIANA in Wasteside Development February 1988. bomb shelter, Seattle and in Poetalk. June 1989 Bay Area Poets Colition.Eagin Arthur, Phoenix, AZ NORTHLAND QUARTERLY, Winona, MN A green Tree in Parnassus of World Poets 1994

6/9/16 dukes of Edom, kings of Esau

6/8/16 AKA Elizabeth Nikomia Sharon Sobczak

6/6/2016 **Kleck**: 9th of AV is 911 Destruction of the Temple
From Zen Garcia Lucifer Father Of Cain: The Evil One's Seed - Zen Garcia on NYSTV. Sons of Cain FB Tribulation Now: The chief operating premise of J. Kleck is that if you turn images upside down via Isaiah 29.16 you will see devils and their occult plans. much of the flesh of this reversal he derives from the Acts of Peter 38: Learn ye the mystery of all nature, and the beginning of all things, what it was. For the first man, whose race I bear in mine appearance (or, of the race of whom I bear the likeness), fell (was borne) head downwards, and showed forth a manner of birth such as was not heretofore: for it was dead, having no motion. He, then, being pulled down -who also cast his first state down upon the earth- established this whole disposition of all things, being hanged up an image of the creation (Gk. vocation) wherein he made the things of the right hand into left hand and the left hand into right hand, and changed about all the marks of their nature, so that he thought those things that were not fair to be fair, and those that were in truth evil, to be good. Concerning which the Lord saith in a mystery: Unless ye make the things of the right hand as those of the left, and those of the left as those of the right, and those that are above as those below, and those that are behind as those that are before, ye shall not have knowledge of the kingdom."
     This gnostic mummery is the most philosophic justification Kleck offers in defense of his artistic technique where, in The Garden, Fall, and Return to Paradise with Jonathan Kleck the shape of the Vatican shape from above, is an image of an upside down cross with a locust within the throne of St. Peter inside, where angels sucked into the vortex, angels being pulled from their "heaven" into the. Throne of St. Peter, which is a dead sheep with the tongue sticking out. [this iconography very like what Chris Constantine does with the bldg in Britain]. Hence a giant dead sheep occupies the throne of St. Peter, which is the mouth of a giant locust, viz. Abaddon, which turned upside down however is a vagina. That is, right side up the throne is a dead sheep, upside down it's a vagina, or rather the entire female

reproductive system. What are all those angels doing going into a vagina? You had to ask. The angels make the pubic hair around it with the fallopian tube, uterus, clitoris. Worship of the virgin is an invocation of this portal, for fallen angels to enter this dimension, a dimension of the flesh, come into the flesh.

    The cobblestones of St. Peter's square are the serpent skin. The imagery inside repeats the imagery outside in the courtyard, womb, phallus, Basilica meaning serpent king. All people are dead sheep. Kleck himself is always portrayed as is the throne of Peter with dead sheep!

    As it works out this is not as nuts as this sounds. Kleck is admittedly an artist so we don't wonder too much what he thinks of Picasso's woman amid all this phallic ionic imagery. There is lots of good stuff before he declares he is a god, and curses you if you don't agree, that being the prerogative of a god one supposes, confecting this out of Ps. 82 and Jesus' comment to the Pharisees. Like A. B. Traina's Holy Name Bible with much to like but who confides in the Preface that "The Caucasian people are Israel" (v), the only problem with Cain being the seed of Satan is that if Eve were seduced by the serpent in the garden, beguiled, "fruited" up he says, is that 4.1 says "the man knew Eve his wife and she conceived and bare Cain," being a direct contradiction of Writ, pitting the express direct statement in 4.1 against an indirect conjectured interpretation of William Brenham.

    So if Isaiah 29 is capable of reversals, and turnings upside down, and these are confirmed by the gnostic philosophy of Acts of Peter and then made into the notion that all people are divided, with DNA serpent seed joined to their human chromosome, what's the point, even amid the visual dead sheep in Nepherti, for Egypt also benefits from Kleck's deconstructions. He continually asks us to consider this information in the context of the tales of his conversion, Michael the archangel attending, and the healings he reports. The Hoover dam collapsing and the tsunami nuke of NYC are stalking horses for the events he presumes to prophesy. The voices and conviction he heard and felt to be convincing, where the nylon label backwards spelled nolyn, or, no lying, and the tales of Men in Black and devils in Starbuck's spice it up, but when or if the listener finds it less compelling, he becomes threatening with the same old "touch not the anointed" prophetic stuff that charismatics of old made when they dreamed pyramid schemes. Fear, trembling and accusation don't make for truth any more than threats that if you don't believe you are the very child of the devil he has come to dispel. His prime text in John where Jesus cites Psalm 82 about gods is supported by the "scripture cannot be broken" till it is broken as it is breaking it over Cain. All these matters however are part and parcel of Kleck who claims to be the sole revealer of antimessiah, and therefore might be supposed to know. So when you "download" to him, as he calls it, and you can get the full dose of signs and wonders, aliens in hieroglyphs, buildings encoded in currency, at first one asks for reasons to disbelieve this, then for reasons to believe. His testimony is nicely filmed and dramatic, complete with accusing spirits, signs, Dorothy and the Cowardly Lion, the Dupont family , one of the 13 families you know, assassination attempts, which sums as mkultra laden situs, fitting nicely with the opposing cultic emissions of Elizabeth Elijah's accusation that he is a set up for the blue beam rapture!

    Along with redeeming fallen angels, fruit connoting sex which connotes sex with trees in the garden, as with Stichin, Sumer tablets and lesser Egyptian models up to the modern imitators, it always comes down to the angelic rape of women to dominate, but you don't see

these sources mentioning the man back in Genesis 4, because he is what they wish to defeat through taking the women. an old story. Jonathan Kleck's "Alien Communication Interception" Satan staging false rapture. Elizabeth Elijah, Almight Wind Ministry, serial killers being made:
FALSE BLUE BEAM RAPTURE UFO OVNI ALIEN HOLOGRAM

6/5/16 the interpretation of the old testament in greco roman paganism

6/4/16 see also, Unholy Trinity: Eric Jon Phelps, Truth about WW2, Vatican Assasins, Stan Deyo, The Vatican Dark Secret All good stuff and then he turns white supremacist.

6/3/16 therapy of aluminum foil bay leaf carob infantalization of breast cancer patients

6/1/16 Mill the Aleppo, -ork at night

5/31/16 "What Does Our Cemetery Say?" by John Ruth at Salford, 2016

5/30/16 Atomic Jacob Ronny's D365 hollow earth-human eyeball, pupil of the earth.

5/28/16 yak butter bullet proof coffee

5/25/16 ONCE UPON A TIME THERE LIVED IN THE TOWN OF DEW DIP THREE GIANTS. WHOSE
NAMES WERE TRIVIUM EFFUVIUMS, ALEISATHENIUM REFPUBLICIAUM, AND BLUPPERIUM REMOVIEIUM. THOSE WERE THEIR LATIN NAMES. iN PLAIN ENGLISH THEY WERE MOM, TURKEY POP AND SUZYQ, oR mOM OPPSOOK, POP OPPSOOK AND SUE OPOPS OOK. BUT THEY WERE AL ONG WAY FROM THREE HUDRED POUNDS. tHEY LIVED IN A NEIGHBORHOOD WHERE THEY WERE AL WERD WERDRE ALWAYS HUNGRY. THEsE OOPSOOKS MADE A DENT IN THE NEIGHBORHOOD BUT THEY STILL LIVED LIKE ORDINARY FOLK ON THE RICHTER SCALE.

5/24/16 Gordon Wasson mk ultra "How Darwin, Huxley, and the Esalen Institute launched the 2012 and psychedelic revolutions -- and began one of the largest mind control operations in history." Located at:
http://www.gnosticmedia.com/how-darwi...https://www.youtube.com/watch?v=3b9OvRAKfzw Perfectabilis.
Battle of the fourth world, Macy instit
Bright-sided: How the Relentless Promotion of Positive Thinking Has Undermined America- Ensalen. Larken Rose, religion of the state
Teilhard de Chardin, piltdown
ANTHONY SUTTON ON SKULL AND BONES. HANK ABARELLI, A TERRIBLE MISTAKE

5/23/16 ages on feldspar crystals from pumice clasts within a tuff in Member I below the hominid levels place an older limit of 198 ± 14 kyr (weighted mean age 196 ± 2 kyr) on the hominids. … God gave Adam dominion over creation, so when he fell, the whole creation suffered—see The (second) greatest catastrophe of all time. This is taught in Romans 8:18–25, where the 'whole creation' is said to be groaning in pain, because it was 'subjected to futility'.

God, subjecting creation to man subjected it further in consequence of man's fall, so that it might serve as an appropriate context for fallen man; a futile world to engage a futile mind. By describing creation's subjection as
'unwilling' Paul maintains the personification of the previous verse. There is an out-of-sortedness, a disjointedness about the created order which makes it a suitable habitation for man at odds with his creator.7

Every part of God's handiwork was marred by the human mutiny … At the Fall, every part of creation was plunged into the chaos of sin, and every part cries out for redemption. Only the Christian worldview keeps these two truths in balance: the radical destruction caused by sin and the hope of restoration to the original created goodness. [p.198]8

The late New Testament scholar Dr F.F. Bruce, then Rylands Professor of Biblical Criticism and Exegesis at the University of Manchester, affirms that this passage is indeed speaking of the Curse which fell on the whole creation—the entire universe—as a result of the Fall…relating the Fall to the creation outside mankind as well.6

5/22/16 Fukushima inside job the earthquake machine places stress on a region with a circular pull, thus creating the spinning top feeling, to pull all potential weak spots in all directions, with the hope of triggering something big… gooey, liquid quakes. Many people suffered nausea and symptoms of vertigo…dis-orientation for many weeks. I noted that when I took a bath, and I was afraid to do even this, the water was vibrating in the tub…constant vibration. .. and there were SEVEN tsunami, not one…just rolling one, more than one nuke was used…"blowing Israel off the map" would be counterproductive, because it is merely a sock puppet of the Rothchilds. Ignore the puppet - look towards the banking district in the City of London. I would bet Israeli behavior would be a LOT better if someone was not pulling their strings… the phony 9.0 story was used as seismic cover for a tsunami nuke, which produced the tsunami of a
9.0

.. Cohen spoke of in 1997 would be outdated now. Cohen stated: "Others are engaging even in an eco- type of terrorism whereby they can alter the climate, set off earthquakes, volcanoes remotely through the use of electromagnetic waves. So there are plenty of ingenious minds out there that are at work finding ways in which they can wreak terror upon other nations. It's real, and that's the reason why we have to intensify our efforts, and that's why this is so important. - William S. Cohen, Secretary of Defense, April 28, 1997.Left unsaid by William Cohen is that such systems would be developed by Darpa and owned by America first! 5/21/16 Blanco crabapple. EDTA 35% hydrogen peroxide.

Theorizing the Drone   Sacrifice of Egyptian flight 804   5/20/16 natives of texas, madrones native grass plugs Hill country natives TREES SEEN RESTING the thing, grand canyon mummies.

5/17/16 Solomon's Temple represents male inside the female Ark of the Covenant from Egypt ark of contract, where the Pharoahs showed their authority was from Sirius. Hence Sirius connects to the ark and to NASA. kiss of death in ancients, mocks scorpion double sting, first the kiss, hence Judas betrayed Jesus.

Church, kirk, Cerce, Mother Cerce hypnotized people so she could eat them. Celtic druids inherit Canaanite Phoenician acts, wands made from holly wood, hence the enchantment of Hollywood. original Ameican flag   Jordan Maxwell. The Romans called their sewer system the system, the educational system

5/16/16 Prometheus light bringer of Chernobyl also
Rockefeller center

stan tenen meru foundation. 19.5 is called t, the 'tetrahedral constant', the apexes of a tetrahedron when placed within a circumscribing sphere, one of the tetrahedron's apexes touching the north pole, the other three apexes touch the surface of the sphere at 19.5 degrees south latitude. Why this number would be important to the builders of the Martian structures is not clear (though Hoagland is theorizing that it has to do with what he calls "hyperdimensional physics").Curiously, it has also been observed that 19.5 degrees is closely linked, for some reason, with the NASA space missions (for example, Mars Pathfinder landed at 19.5 degrees lat. of Mars on July 4, '97).

In fact, not only did Pathfinder landed at 19.5 N, the longitude of the landing site was approximately 33 W - which is the very number of the longitude of the apex of the Great Bend of the Nile (33 E)! Now, this strongly insists on the relevance of the Nile numbers, and someone behind the scenes is well aware of it. As we move on, the number, 19.5, will also be very important in my Nile Time-map theory. Perhaps, as the Nile-Mars connection bridged by '19.5' appears to suggest, Mars was somehow involved during the 'Prometheus / Pandora period'. Vortex maps place a Star Tetrahedron (which is composed of 2 interlocking 4-sided tetrahedrons) [ie two pyramids opposed] so that it fits inside a sphere with its points touching the surface of the sphere, then if the two opposite points of the tetrahedrons are the 'poles' of this sphere, then the other points of the tetrahedrons touch the sphere at 19.5 degrees north and south of the 'equator'.

The Star Tetrahedron is significant because it is one of the shapes that energetic interdimensional vehicles, known as the 'Merkaba' or 'Light-body', manifest, the divine light vehicle allegedly used by ascended masters to connect with and reach those in tune with the higher realms. although the concept of the Merkabah is associated with Ezekiel's vision (1:4–26), the word is not explicitly written in Ezekiel 1.[4] wheel angels, which are described as "a wheel inside of a wheel", are called "Ophanim."

5/15/16 1 Peter, (in 1Peter 3:19–20) and 2 Peter (in 2Peter 2:4–5) make reference to some Enochian, with Jude 1:14–15: Enoch 1:9, translated from the Ethiopic (found also in Qumran scroll 4Q204=4QEnochc ar, col I 16– 18):[12]And behold! He cometh with ten thousands of His Saints To execute judgment upon all, And to destroy all the ungodly: And to convict all flesh Of all the works of their ungodliness which they have ungodly committed, And of all the hard things which ungodly sinners have spoken against Him. Compare this also with what may be the original source of 1 En 1:9 in Deuteronomy 33:2: [13][14][15]The Lord came from Sinai and dawned from Seir upon us; he shone forth from Mount Paran; he came from the ten thousands of Saints, with flaming fire at his right hand. oldest fragments of the Book of Watchers are dated 200–150 BC. Since the Book of Watchers shows evidence of multiple stages of composition, it is probable that this work was extant already in the 3rd century BC aspects of notTanakh (Judaism) but Enochic Judaism are the following:

- the idea of the origin of the evil caused by the fallen angels, who came on the earth to unite with human women. These fallen angels are considered ultimately responsible for the spread of evil and impurity on the earth;[45]:90
- the absence in 1 Enoch of formal parallels to the specific laws and commandments found in the Mosaic

Torah and of references to issues like Shabbat observance or the rite of circumcision. The Sinaitic covenant and

Torah are not of central importance in the Book of Enoch;[48]:50–51

- the concept of "End of Days" as the time of final judgment that takes the place of promised earthly rewards;[45]:92
- the rejection of the Second Temple's sacrifices considered impure: according to Enoch 89:73, the Jews, when returned from the exile, "reared up that tower (the temple) and they began again to place a table before the tower, but all the bread on it was polluted and not pure";[citation needed]
- a solar calendar in opposition to the lunar calendar used in the Second Temple (a very important aspect for the determination of the dates of religious feasts);
- an interest in the angelic world that involves life after death.[49]

branches of a common trunk in Jubilees, 2 Baruch, 2 Esdras, Apocalypse of Abraham and 2 Enoch,

    Sir Walter Raleigh, in his History of the World (written in 1616 while imprisoned in the Tower of London), makes the curious assertion that part of the Book of Enoch "which contained the course of the stars, their names and motions" had been discovered in Saba (Sheba) in the first century and was thus available to Origen and Tertullian. He attributes this information to Origen,[60] though no such statement is found anywhere in extant versions of Origen.

    Samyaza another name for Satan   (Others say that Samyaza should not be mistaken for another name for Satan, who some believe was "cast out" from the heavens previously (reasons offered in the apocryphal Gospel of Bartholomew include the refusal to bow down to Adam[2]). This interpretation points to Rev. 12:9 and Gen. 6:4 as depicting two separate falls from heaven, one of Satan being cast down, the other of the sons of God choosing to come to earth to take human wives.   bind them fast for seventy generations in the valleys of the earth, 20 leaders "cloud of God." car seats for guppies

5/14/16 JFK-9/11: Solar Warden
 --P-- goes care call to S. After 90 min she can move, A miracle!
-50 Years of Deep State – by Laurent Guyenot

      Dream: Baited into smart talk against a DA I was indicted on a trumped up entirely false charge just because he could. the lesson being don't argue with them for you lose self respect and don't disagree for he will accuse you. This then became a series of general indictments against large gov't agencies of several kinds. --Ironically yesterday, asking P what the date was she said Friday the 13th. I said I don't want to know that, meaning the thing, being opposed to luck, but then A was fired, which he says he expected for some weeks because he had not reported, hand held, data to somebody, but just corrected the situation himself,. This all comes of course on the heels of S's fall the day we got back from Tex and A's retching in the night there. All surrounded with providence, prayer and healing. Many layers, her mother saying the doctors were wrong and she need to be in the hospital, to A. at least the mother won't have to come down next week to watch S. while A. goes to work, since she so demoralizes with the negative. I take these matters as a sign to get the houses in order.

5/13/16 A fired today. http://stonezone.com/ proof the grand canyon monuments are ancient pyramids 105 years after the Smithsonian Institute studied the Grand Canyon having found ancient Egyptian artifacts comes the stunning alignment of the major stars of ORION to Isis Temple, Tower of Set, Cheops Pyramid and other major Grand Canyon monuments. This leads to proving that the entire Canyon may have been a metropolis above the level of a river… a city on the grandest scale. Where we once thought the canyon was natural may be built by an intelligence. The Kaibab Plateau located in central Northern Arizona showcases a mysterious majestic city epic of size and proportion. While this city is officially referred to as a series of natural "Grand Canyon Monuments", they are in fact precisely arranged pyramids, towers and temples aligned to the star and nebula pattern of ORION "The Hunter" constellation. While the great pyramids of Giza line with the belt stars of ORION, we find that the major stars that make up the whole of the Hunt, Rigel, Salph, Betelgeuse, and Bellatrix match with the monuments in the Grand Canyon. enemies foreign and domestic carl higb. Pope's astronomer insists alien life 'would be part of God's creation', but they weren't created fallen angels which shows that you're responsible for your self, as it says "you're responsible for yourself you dubm fucder." *Book of Moab*

5/11/16 Fires in Alberta lit by incendiaries an attempt to light the oil sands
Dick Gregory allows he is a shapeshifter, that the three rules are: once you put the glasses on you can't take them off, that you will never see the world as it's supposed to be but as it is and you can't make anybody take them. Initiated by Hugh Hefner.
    --In 1953, Hugh Hefner setup Playboy, which was eventually revealed to be banked by the CIA.[3] Sometime before 1961, Dick Gregory formed some type of special personal relationship with Hefner (Mythological PUCK). In 1961, Hefner put Gregory on the payroll of his Chicago Playboy Club that opened the door to his
    HollyWeird career. It is more accurate to say that the "Gates of Hell" had opened upon him. In other to join Hefner's elite secret satanic circle at that high CIA level of secrecy,

Gregory had to have been initiated by a blood sacrifice (late 2 month old, Richard Claxton Gregory, Jr.?) into a subservient lower ranking black Luciferian group like the Prince Hall Freemasons or one of the Greek Hellenized societies. In search of black assassins

5/10/16 Fallen angels they don't die they just fade away
Psychologists are terrorists operating under the guise of therapy. Milton Erikson excepted. Of Gary Lawrence. Phallic intrusion, Scientology, Ensalen,

5/8/16 Dick Gregory> Michael Jordans' father, Bill Cosby's son. Michael Jackson, Tiger Woods. Gregory a shapeshifter self confessed

5/7/16 theory of creative destruction Puerto rico defaults on bonds, Atlantic next, Detroit, chicago borrows at 8 %, California school system defaults blockitpocket
THE END in 2016 The SHOCKING Predictions of 12 Mysterious Men
-dreamed Obama married us, private ceremony. in office, his, I had to back up and walk down aisle. Then hand in hand, chair to chair we sat outside open doors at his dinner with coreographed toasts and his marriage.

5/6/16 Baltic SEa Anomoly

5/5/16 Wed, the day we returned, S fell and hurt her knee. A called 5 min later 8 PM. Next day x ray showed bone sl separated. Took knee braces to office. In talking said, it's nice to see you, (since we haven't all year). She, it'd be better at lunch. Reply: it's always good to see those you love(!). Never heard that before, in context of A's revelations ranch,

Dear Mike, After we saw you Mon night and cooked some food, about 7:30 that beautiful white longhorn appeared at the top of the drive, right by the tickletongue. A had had a dream two nights before that he filed in small claims court for the neighbor to fix his fence. He offered (in the dream court) photos of tracks, trails, etc. but the judge said, where's the beef. I added that. He said pics of the thing were needed. So when it appeared in real time Aey said, get the camera! But by that time that intelligent creature hightailed back and I only got a shot of his hind end as he went down the ravine. We loaded fencing gear in the truck and found the entire water cap down, the long fence gate in the middle flattened and covered with mud, the fence posts bent to right angles, the bottom brace askew, and the wire on both sides smashed against the sides of the draw. We put it all back up. Added some posts of our own, tied and wired it. The poor guy has to stay at home now. There are deep trails of his down the creek as well as up in the field. I cannot wait to get my first feral pig! All the best to you,

5/4/16 an undeground city of giants discovered in grand canyon
--After a week Planted two bald cypress, tightened commode, cut two acres virgin cedar, 4 of lopper, put fence back up in Kelly draw, talked with a. about S, with Aey and A and self about intimate things, sh miscarry, P's trouble, A's T birth fluid hitting ceiling, saw Ruth, M

Kruger, pregnant does everywhere. lattice gullys, anu's half ticket, 2 nights motel, gas, etc. vacuum cleaner, 1000.

4/27- 4/5 Ranch

4/26/16 dominion of Melchizedek

4/24/16 Pyramids, giants in great lakes " 'Amatlai the daughter of Karnavo the mother of the patriarch Abraham' is a remedy in a time of danger." on Weissmandel romantized account the unheeded cry

4/23/16 is our governor a yahoo monkey woo, woo, woo, woo, woo
You want to wrap your creamy thighs around me and see if I can still thrust?

4/22/16 Prince sacrifice and Baal

4/21/16 why we are afraid, dr. bill warner Political Islam
Graci, graci tu tu oo. Foxes Book of Martyr's with its tortures, cutting open a man's stomach tied to a stake on his knees and pouring corn in his belly then pigs let loose would eat with his bowels is not behind Chris Constantine having the Mayan Calendar a space man with googles, respirator in a cockpit flying down to eclipse the earth with Niburu.
        --These realities substitute nicely for the corn tortilla that after a year in the frig is still good, but when dogs take it with the ret of food out of the trash they won't eat it. It just lays in the yard like a flying disc waiting to eclipse the earth/ You think that's funny but its not.

4/20/16 sacrifices: Sylvester Stallone, mike Tyson, prince, rick warren, john Travolta, nibirupedia.com Chronophage Corpus Clock with Grasshopper Escapement
 Alexandra Palace London, Niburu Palace, Chris Constantine French jetton coin 1680 (iii) 'OPPORTUNUS ADEST'

4/19/16 end times matrix news new nazi bell Deut 28. 28-9 The LORD will smite you with madness and with blindness and with bewilderment of heart; 29and you will grope at noon, as the blind man gropes in darkness, and you will not prosper in your ways; but you shall only be oppressed and robbed continually, with none to save you.… the stranger within thee shall lend to thee, this is the day of China's new gold backed currency
        Sons of Thunder, A Call for an Uprising, youtubes Baal arch   VIA PIA
But there is a woman clothed with the sun! Johnny Depp, Jodie Foster dual life.
-saw Large surges of water, flood down Foote, as if the dam broke or rather that they were relieving pressures in waves. Then I was in a restaurant wearing a light blue vest when a gangst walks in, tries to have me id ed by a page.
4/18/16 After restless night, got up, went back, had Cynthia. analyzing me as "white knight" but really not, so she would correct me. I remember where I was standing when Mom told me of that baby's birth, since it must have been 1959, she telling me after Jays's death, Robt says,

the date Dream of 5/5/59 woman that sits upon many waters, Jerusalem is inland, the problem with starting a fire in the oleanders is that it spreads and when the fire dept is called has to be covered up. Confessing even to small boys can be hard then. This a dream prior to Cynthia telling Pat telling me about Laura's research showing Jay's child fathered in 1st or 2nd yr of h.s.--but the evidence is that it was 58/59, all which, with the moral suasion and bulling of C. implied is an oleander fire.

4/17/16 The Thirteenth Tribe is a 1976 book by Arthur Koestler, in which he advances the thesis that Ashkenazi Jews are not descended from the historical Israelites of antiquity, but from Khazars, a Turkic people.

The Khazar state was, Oppenheim says, the only Jewish state to rise between the Fall of the Second Temple (67-70 CE) and the establishment of Israel (1948),[162] and its example stimulated messianic aspirations for a return to Israel as early as Judah Halevi In the time of the Egyptian vizier Al-Afdal Shahanshah (d.1121), one Solomon ben Duji, often identified as a Khazarian Jew,[164] attempted to stir up a messianic effort for the liberation of, and return of all Jews to, Palestine. He wrote to many Jewish communities to enlist support. He eventually moved to Kurdistan where his son Menachem some decades later assumed the title of Messiah and, raising an army for this purpose, took the fortress of Amadiya north of Mosul. His project was opposed by the rabbinical authorities and he was poisoned in his sleep.

One theory maintains that the Star of David, until then a decorative motif or magical emblem, began to assume its national value in late Jewish tradition from its earlier symbolic use by Menachem.[165] elite conversion preceding large-scale adoption of the new religion by the general population, which often resisted the imposition.[174

David Goldstein, now of Duke University, reported that unlike male Ashkenazi lineages, the female lineages in Ashkenazi Jewish communities "did not seem to be Middle Eastern", and that each community had its own genetic pattern and even that "in some cases the mitochondrial DNA was closely related to that of the host community."

In his view this suggested "that Jewish men had arrived from the Middle East, taken wives from the host population and converted them to Judaism, after which there was no further intermarriage with nonJews."[102... the four main female Ashkenazi founders had descent lines that were established in Europe 10,000 to 20,000 years in the past[130] while most of the remaining minor founders also have a deep European ancestry. The study states that the great majority of Ashkenazi maternal lineages were not brought from the Near East (i.e., they were non-Israelite), nor were they recruited in the Caucasus (i.e., they were non-Khazar), but instead they were assimilated within Europe, primarily of Italian and Old French origins... debunk one of the most questionable, but still tenacious, hypotheses: that most Ashkenazi Jews can trace their roots to the mysterious Khazar Kingdom that flourished during the ninth century in the region between the Byzantine Empire and the Persian Empire."[126] see https://en.wikipedia.org/wiki/Khazar_theory_of_Ashkenazi_ancestry

"that the Israeli-American Jewish World Empire is the prophesied MYSTERY, BABYLON THE GREAT of Revelation 17? imperialist Zionist brokers has now spread across the face of the globe, thanks to their unholy alliance with the morally depraved, increasingly anti-Christian United States of America. The Woman (Israel and the Jews), whose spiritual name is MYSTERY BABYLON, sits defiantly upon the beast (U.S.A.). Together, they make spiritual war against God's People (Galatians 3:29) and threaten the whole world with blood and violence. We now must face the shocking truth square in the face: Babylon 21 is on the move." texe marrs America's military has became Israel's proxy—its Spear of Conquest. Suare last night.

4/15/16 I have outlived my knowledge of the future. I have outlived the future and all its divinations.

4/14/16 Science is that group of chemists working on advanced experiments in protein, pyrvate phostpahase in a building that's just about to be vacated because of leaking gas lines in case it blows up, just the position of the Exp Science Bldg in Austin. Couldn't pass the pressure test.

"The six-story **Experimental Science building**, which opened in 1950, was made a priority in the evaluation process when recent routine maintenance uncovered potential problems. "The piping appeared extremely suspect," said the university's fire marshal, Garland Waldrop. "Experimental Science is a really old building with leaking roofs and walls. When maintenance workers moved the lab bench for a water leak repair, the natural gas piping was exposed and the condition of gas valves in this particular lab bench gave us cause for concern."According to Rankin, maintenance of old systems has long been a struggle for occupants of the Experimental Science Building."

4/12/16 Hercolubus six times bigger than Jupiter.
4/11/16 Exodus 25:20 20 And the cherubim shall spread out their wings above, covering the mercy seat with their wings, facing each other and looking down toward the mercy seat.

4/9/16 Expanding Force in Newton's Cosmos [David Castillejo] Job 9.24 the earth is given into the hand of the wicked. Black child: centers of tree of life are satanic gods. Proving it counterfeit. writing for AI 4/8/16 Sue Hitt, Susan Martits, Barber's soliloquy for strings

4/7/16 Waco and Ok City, same date, April 19, same day the Baal Arches SCHEDULED in NYC and London, first day of the Blood Sacrifice to the Beast and the Feast of Moloch. Columbine was on April 20. April 16, 2007 Virginia Tech Massacre April 16, 2013 Boston Marathon Explosions foreign ministers of China, Russia and India will meet in Moscow on April 19 to discuss global and regional issues including the Middle East, Afghanistan, North Africa and the DPRK. See celebrities who died young.
So many tremors in Yellowstone they turned off the seismograph.
--missing persons, sacrifices before the Oscars and academy awards
Since we have no importance we can safely be ignored, for there is nothing we do to change the gov'ts ordained to themselves every one, a great Club of Ents,. I must wear the mark of Cain to them for they shun me. Only one invite did I get, a punch in the stomach. Well I wear a mark but it is not Cain's.

4/6/16 Solomon's Temple Brazil

Temple of Baal Times Square, Trafalgar Square

4/5/16 Brief Artist Statement: These pieces concern mythological and political subjects.

Kurk Wold's Best Tales of World Science. all the emphasis of Pope Francis itinerary upon the sick and disestablished belie the fact that he is implicated deeply in their destruction in alliance with the usual parties who play both sides and the middle of every equation to smother the whole. Bill Gates! 4/4/16 "Goya to the contrary, here the monstrosity was birthed not by the sleep of reason, but instead born from that sleep which reason represented. From our own industrially despoiled and bankrupted contemporary perspective, Blake's view surely seems a product of extraordinary prescience rather than of the angel-addled madness which some of his less insightful critics have attributed." Alan Moore Blake on Newton

4/2/16 This place where all the data is stored, or exists, visited in moments of dream so unbelievable they do not fit in memory after, visited over and over, store all the answers to all the contradictions as a catalog, call it the NOUS, as a code. or later, Novus.

3/31/16 9% moisture content interior furniture.

3/30/16 The Wigner Effect-full interview metal fatigue, airplanes, embrittlement. Wigner Dust. Fukushima is an industrial plant for creating the dust, the worse weaponized powder ever created, Wigner Dust with one exception - radioactive nano particulates. airline anomalies, flying through fallout, aircraft emergencies and crashes post-Fukushima. accelerated metal fatigue, increased entropy all life forms, glass, electrical components, and computer systems.

Cognitive change events of 20th cent: Freud, Marx Einstein, added to Darwin and Galileo, sold as cognitive belief changing events which prepare for the next "discovery" to the effect of "who we are," Sumerian
Anunnaki, for cognitive events are always spun to disestablish previous beliefs, as if a new religion were being formed, but this one, called Disclosure spins the ultimate coup de grace to human beliefs saying humans are descendants and slaves of nemesis and there you have it.

--World events known by cognition, being deceptions, cannot be improved by their denial and replacement with more , newer cognitions. Cognition is the means of deception in the first place. There must be another way of knowing. Will that flows from value. See David Flynn on Newton, Temple

3/27/16 Easter. the false messiah must come and enable Psalm 83 in order to build the 3rd temple, but to do this Muslims must already have died so world events produced these messiah wars. The dimensions of the temple are important to the elite for their own purposes of geometry historically, but retain vestiges of interest even among the quantums invoked, but all this seems a little moot in the presence of the idea that the temple is really the human body! See David Flynn.

10.7 Million 1-ton Bags of Radioactive Waste drone pics

Read more at http://thefreethoughtproject.com/city-waste-fukushima-cleanup-10-7-million-1-ton-bagsradioactive-waste/#ypMyJW0FXrRZoIl7.99 geovital shielding paint t98 alpha

--Dream: saw these particles mostly large balls, black dark matter. Did not exactly solve them, collect or destroy them, but on the other hand was able to see them without being destroyed either. When they touched people they killed. Earth is the Afghanistan safe haven for al qaeda against using the weapon of stranglet dark matter particles

3/26/16 what's in a number, nicholson 68. 322 skull and bones number is gen 3.22
tj sotomayor

3/25/16 Barak Obama and the coming false miracle
"Yes, this is civilization, in the raw, unglazed, so there will be another hardened view. A 6000 year old cult that broadcasts its images into every mind, called archetypes, every person born in the world. Many parts of the world share similar images because civilization is fostered by higher beings known properly as devils. Of course they think highly of themselves for that, being more intelligent and able to pass dimensional walls through their portals. Devils signifies the lowest of their hierarchy that reaches into the skies where they pose as gods. Hence goes religion, government, philosophy skewed to the devil mind, and artfully too, so it seems as if it were true. Shall we expose the devils for what they are? Only if we have the truth, which is not hierarchical."
Rubino del Sur, The Argentine-Antarctic, p. 35.
That truth is that we are the sons of the most high. World history has to be expunged.
Khazarian Mafia - Babylonian Talmudism- Synagogue of Satan-Christian Zionism which is a complete abrogation of the New Testament 2 Thessalonians 2. 9-12 and what Jesus taught, and completely ignores Revelation 2:9 and 3:9 of fake Judaics. 97.5% of Judaic Israelis actually have NO ancient Hebrew Blood and no ancestral right to any Palestinian land and actually are NOT Semites at all, while 80% of Palestinians have ancient Hebrew Blood, have an ancestral right to the land and are real Semites. Israel harbors the top sex traffickers and organ traffickers in history and has the highest per capital male use of captive and enslaved prostitutes, most from Ukraine and Eastern Europe. Turkish genocide of one and one-half million Armenians from 1915-1919 which involved the crucifixion of young Armenian girls alive with nails through their wrists and feet, was run by Babylonian Talmudics after their brutal rapes. KM Infiltrators to transform America into GAZA II.

3/23/16 Benjamin Fulford White Dragon society Why Obama's going to anarctic blackgold, off ledger gold held by royal Asian families) http://benjaminfulford.net/2016/03/22...
2) Thumbnail image - Antarctica map, Who owns Antarctica, Wikimedia commons images
    https://www.google.gr/search?q=who+ow...
3) https://kauilapele.wordpress.com/2016...
   When it all comes down Zenith 2016, does death free the mind of those who condone hatred, the protestors, flipped over on the side to provoke a response to prove after provocation that

the good are the bad, the peaceful are the violent? Will they at their death see through their illusion? No.

3/22/16 Brussels. Half Uk gets cancer 2026. half of children with autism have GI disorders

3/21/16 population replacement: 1 million come in 700K leave UK but the immigrants are poor and the emigrants retired and professional. Adam euro tunnel insider speaks out, that if migrants gain the half way point of the tunnel to UK they get all the benefits and a stipend, but the French just kick them out on their side. Adam had one, who to avoid being caught, dropped his pants, defecated in his hand and wiped it all over his arms and hands to avoid encounter. There is widespread public defecation in streets and parks of SF, pooper squads planetary apocalypse, revelation apocalypse, revolution apocalypse To look in and beneath the concept of martyrdom to the state. The symbolic disappearance of investigative reporting in absence in the quick. To cover the ears, put a pillow on the head, the events, none of which are true, are sworn by all parties in the non news Destruktion, the deconstruction of every European metaphysic of morality to sanction murder with a clear conscience, Defamiliartization of reality, Dissolution of public order and myth, collapses reality. here

3/19/16 David Flynn Mars earth, Cydonia Avebury circle in Phoenicia. / Sidonia ie Canaan, Cydonia mars, mt. Hermon watchers / Sirius below Gemini, phoenecia origin of writing, trade, Canaan-canine, Sirius tyre and sidon, where heaven and earth connect. Cydonia star 5 sides / pentagon. the letters that circumscribe the inverted stare of Eliaphus levi spell levitation-see Strong, levi, tan, serpent and cosmic, sun rising in the mouth of leviathan milky way, earth rising in sea, ball surrounded by ocean of sea, Cydonia face half man half lion, ie. sphinx, Ez 28 after the fire comes reference to Sidon!

3/18/16 the pythons of south Florida built the wall

3/16/16 UN troops in scalar bases waiting in Mexico in spume, in blue helmeted plumes out of pyramids and ovalacanoes come down

3/15/16 Marzulli, David Flynn, black eyed children. soft disclosure, roll out in TV show, x files. Rumors and confusion of wars: nations fighting against and with each other at the same time. CIA elite strategy, fund communists, socialists, capitalists, every party and stripe simultaneously. Zondervan press, Dave lambert stew webb.com
Jim Wiley? People vaporized by satellite in Panama
      Freedom Reigns coup Finance resignations 2012
 David therefore called him Eloah, how is He then his son?
I ask you Father to stop the Vatican and the Queen of England, the President of the United States and Monsanto, all the corporations that buy and sell souls and destroy the world national and international, GE, to stop Fukushima and defeat CERN to cause the EU and TPP and the Trilateral Commission to come into confusion, for evil to slay the wicked in their

oppressions, to defend the poor, the alien in the world, the women, children and men of families who seek you.

3/12/16 Deep space Christianity

3/11/16 image of Trilateral commission Scalia Murdered After Obama Meeting
trilateral commission: 'Ego Terminatio, Ego Fides, Ego Sceptrum' roughly translates to 'I [or we] terminate, or I/We let go,' 'I/We Believe', and 'I/We Rule.'
     Reverse Speech It is standard SOP to ignore the victims of genocide of the world, in Turkey, Germany, Sudan, Rwanda, Cambodia. When the victims get noticed then beware, for something is afoot, as in Syria. Hence we can both worry and not worry about the genocide of the world that began with the murder of the Pacific, this day, five years ago.

3/10/16/Preston James
Newborn DNA blood sample data base; 2008 "all states store blood from all newborns, and some, like California, store it indefinitely. Blood samples contain DNA that can be unambiguously linked to individuals,...Brase said. "Who will own the DNA of the citizens and what is that going to mean? And what we're doing is pushing an entire genetic research program on the population without the consent of the population."... they are anonymized for research when looking at new technologies! Ha. The DNA of virtually every newborn in the United States is collected, usually via a blood sample taken from a prick to the baby's heel, and tested for certain genetic and other disorders. see ACLU.
     IN ARIZONA, according to their website, newborn screens are destroyed after 3 months. WSO update red halo around sun. Catharine Austin Fitts criminals running govt. What are these wounds I got at the house of my friends?

3/9/16 Fukushima I'm Sorry There's Nothing We can Do with Dana Durnford & Yoichi Shimatsu, Continual new clips of the event across the screen. Official date of the fifth year of the coordinated coverup, featuring radiation levels in Colorado Rockies esp. down in N. Mex, all measured, takes 15 years for the radiation exposure to show, but many lesser ailments provoked before by weakened immunities. The Battle of Fukushima
     Prayer Manual at World's End NIETZCHE HATES THE WEAK BECASUE HE HATES THE PSALMS that say the meek shall inherit the earth and that the wicked who cast down the poor and needy shall have their arms broken. Ps 37. This kind of language occurs heavily in the Psalms of the 30s.

3/8/16 Biggest disaster in human history Fukushima history of the event 11 March

3/7/16 How firm a foundation, ye saints of the Lord, Is laid for your faith in His excellent Word! What more can He say than to you He hath said, You, who unto Jesus for refuge have fled? In every condition, in sickness, in health; In poverty's vale, or abounding in wealth; At home and abroad, on the land, on the sea, As thy days may demand, shall thy strength ever be. Fear not, I am with thee, O be not dismayed,

For I am thy God and will still give thee aid;
I'll strengthen and help thee, and cause thee to stand Upheld by My righteous, omnipotent hand. When through the deep waters I call thee to go,
The rivers of woe shall not thee overflow; For I will be with thee, thy troubles to bless, And sanctify to thee thy deepest distress. When through fiery trials thy pathways shall lie, My grace, all sufficient, shall be thy supply;
The flame shall not hurt thee; I only design Thy dross to consume, and thy gold to refine. Even down to old age all My people shall prove
My sovereign, eternal, unchangeable love; And when hoary hairs shall their temples adorn, Like lambs they shall still in My bosom be borne.
The soul that on Jesus has leaned for repose, I will not, I will not desert to its foes;
That soul, though all hell should endeavor to shake, I'll never, no never, no never forsake.
Lucky Gunner Tactiton Depleted Uranium Drone load

3/5/16 Mia Pope-Barry Obama Chernobyl: Consequences of Catastrophe.

3/4/16 Richard Davis, Fukushima false flag
Jerry Petermann because corporations are declared a person, without a body, hence have no soul or conscience, like machines
FUKUSHIMA.THE SPEECH THAT LET THE CAT OUT OF THE BAG!
Yury Bandazhevsky, "Radioactive Cesium in the Heart Caesium-137 levels in children's organs were examined at autopsy. The highest accumulation of Cs-137 was found in the endocrine glands, in particular the thyroid, the adrenals and the pancreas. High [clarification needed] levels were also found in the heart, the thymus and the spleen.[2]
         --They have a chair that kids, or anyone, can sit and they can calculate the amount of Becquerels per kilogram of body weight. The Implications of The Massive Contamination of Japan With Radioactive Cesium Steven Starr
 Nuclear Evacuations NOT SAFE ANYWHERE On the PLANET: A Gundersen World Uranium Symposium '15

 3/3/16 Alaska seabird die off unprecedented Durnford a must see documentary, into eternity.

3/2/16 Fukushima Is Not Mutating the Daisies
STANDUP for all EXTINCTOS Fukushima isn't mutation daisies

3/1/16 pacific extinction event. Nuclear Proctologist

2/29/16 cesium plume, Chernobyl heart, necklace, Tsumni Bomb   Jeffrense.com biosuperfood

2/28/16 Gaudi's Basilica, fukushima radiation and strange happenings, jeff rense the scary truth about fukushima, see HelenCaldicott. State of Morro Bay, fuk'ed

This was the last hymn we sung this morning, after I had composed Leviathan Gigantic for FEZ.

We are called to be God's prophets, speaking for the truth and right, standing firm for godly justice, bringing evil things to light. Let us seek the courage needed, our high calling to fulfill, that the world may know the blessing of the doing of God's will.

Always substitute demon for divine to see the teaching of the fallen angels are the psychic-psychosis doctrines of the Vedas and old world religions. Vedas means THE MORPHOGENIC CONSCIOUSNESS FIELD. The ten Vishnu avatars are pictures of the demi gods who ruled at the katabole and after in The Mahabharata war of 4000 BC and the Ramayana war in 4200 BC Rig Veda was written in 5000 BC.

In those days the Maharshis with 12 strand NIL junk DNA used to live for more than 200 years. the religion of the fallen angels covered the globe.

--More Math-gemetria occurrences: Sun's diameter is 108 times that of the earth. The distance between earth and moon is 108 times the diameter of the moon.. The distance between the Earth and Sun is 108 times the diameter of the Sun . When you look at the Sun and the Moon from earth they are perceived as the SAME size, this same size appears because of their distance and diameters.

The 108 division is the coming together of Purusha and Prakriti. It is the vibration of the Purusha and Prakriti that put existence. EXISTENCE IS A PUT AMONG THE NEPHILIM. In Ayurveda there are a 108 marmas in the body. They are points where consciousness impinges the body that can heal or kill a living being, vital points where consciousness connects to the body, where Purusha (consciousness) is brought into Prakriti (body) to give life to the living being. Sanskrit Mantras recited 108 times acts as a Kavach (protection) to each Marma. The 108 intersections on the Sri Yantra invoke the cosmic balance of Purusha and Prakriti and the primordial ability of the seer Maharishi to see both clearly. Nine is a special number, always returns to itself $9 \times 12 = 108$

There are 108 Upanishads.. The invisible below the quantum screen gives rise to the visible. "The unlimitedly powerful Lord assumed the form of a boar for the rescue of the earth and pierced the first demon Hiranyaksa with His tusks." - (S.Baghawatam. 2.7.1)

--Higher Teachers of universal intelligence called "Enoch" and "Metatron. Research director of the Great Pyramid of Giza Research Association. James J. Hurtak. In the so called Keys of Enoch are twisted 72 Expressions of the Divine in Hebrew-Aramaic.

" Just after the Deluge, at the dawn of the present time cycle, an era the Egyptians called ZEP TEPI, "The First Times", a mysterious group of "gods" appeared, pure nephilim, to initiate the survivors in the rudiments of civilization.

From Thoth and Osiris in Egypt, to Quetzacoatal and Viracocha in the Americas, traditions worldwide subscribe the origins of contemporary civilization to this sophisticated group*.

-Despite the misleading popularity of Von Danikan journalism, evidence from around the world, indicates these people were the hi-tech survivors of the previous civilization of what we now refer to as Atlantis and MU. Like the nuclear survival bunkers and secret research facilities of our own civilization, there were those who arose from the underground "cities of the Gods", after the dust settled. That means all pasty faced, inbred and perverted. These survivors are characterized in the Bible--appropriation of the every truth to a lie, he means, -- as the "prediluvian patriarchs", like Enoch and Methuselah, the "giants and heroes of old", mentioned in Genesis.

-These are the 'fabled gods' of ancient Summer, Egypt and India. All religious traditions can now be shown to originate from this one source. The Cheboingies! Muslim, Christianity, Native American , Traditions, Buddhism, New Age, etc. ....ALL!
socialpoliticalunderground-temas

-They make their appeal with a thousand: Despite the bleaching of semi-divine beings from modern consciousness, --dilution of their genes--could it be possible, as the ancient texts insist that,-- ee cummings, the devil ooch the devil ouch—We are destined to "become as gods"?

Walls built around Giza plateau: strict guarding of the "holy" ditch surprised us. 2002 "After returning to Switzerland, I learned that no one had heard that a huge concrete wall was being constructed along the far perimeter of the Giza district. Our information was new even to the renowned researcher of religion and history, Professor James Hurtak, who had also personally conducted archeological research in Egypt. He was entirely unaware of the wall construction. Giza wall The pyramids align with the belt of Orion 10K years ago- 30degrees latitude, longitude

To answer, no. we are not. the gods are destined to be destroyed, we are destined to live. That is why they hate us so.

2/27/16 Jack London Tales of the Pacific Babylonian tradition credits the founding of civilization to a creature which they considered to be a repulsive abomination. Loki and his monstrous children will burst their bonds; the dead will sail from Niflheim to attack the living." the exact point of descent of the Sons of God was Mt. Hermon in Phoenicia.

2/25/16 Failed States: Sweden, Norway collapse Sweden Oct 2015,
Sweden Close to Collapse by Ingrid Carlqvist.The Wild Voice. Pope Francis speaks.

2/24/16 Taurus Judge, 45 colt or 4.10(#6) or S&W Governor X-22 Report,
Ten Most mysterious Pictures from the moon
 Michael C. Ruppert, CIA bankers mob. Each of the icon makers thinks when the figure of a man or child or woman is beatified that it is an angel, but it is a man. What is man that thou are mindful of him?   --Venus and moon in the sky last night. Saw the Maiden brood come with their white dog to see about breeding with a black dog, Pat knows about it but isn't sure now we ask if it has papers, which it probably does. I suggest a brood would look like a panda. Not specifically Zion. Then visiting a family on the outskirts, partly oily country with a ranch, a stream, and then talking with some kids about action?
-angel extermindor, Gabriel ark.

-- They give orders to their slaves that must be followed top to bottom so the paradox is that while they enslave the commoner, only the commoner is free of the fear, the command to war, for he has the command to peace, to love, to joy, none of whch the followers of the fallen angel have. They sacrifice love for power to their fallen angel, the sacrificed their children to their Moloch, they sacrificed their salvation for being cloned and chipped and made immortal, they sacrificed every virtue for every evil and it eats at them so they can never rest but they can, can they act! Who say they call smile and smile and be a villain? Whisper in the ear.

2/23/16 Prescott Bush nazi. Saw Heavy metal honey. Working with crew, had gotten raises, quit for a day and was off according to Dave, in context of JFK to 9/11, then wake to pray mishaps upon them but change that to praying for their salvation! Andrew wants to reschedule to today from Thurs.

2/22/16 JFK to 9/11 everything is a rich man's trick
Sam Gaincana Double Cross, using a patsy to wipe out a politician.
Scalia: Valentine Day Massacure. J. D. Tibet's corpse surgically altered to look liike the president. Smedley Butler Nazi Coup Nazi war machine was an American business, its phones installed by AT&T, its trucks with Ford engines. Standard oil supplied additives to its gas through Switzerland to fuel these machines.

  Royal Dutch Shell gave millions of gallons free, concentration camps provided slave labor for coal mines in Poland, gold teeth were melted into Nazi gold bars and so stamped to put in the English treasury. The American railway line that led into the camp in the coalfields of Oświęcim Auschwittz was an investment of Prescott Bush.

  Limited Hangout means propaganda exposing minor details in order to prevent the full exposure of greater secrets. Panopticon prison- NSA grid: a tower central to a circular building that is divided into cells, each cell extending the entire thickness of the building to allow inner and outer windows. The occupants of the cells are thus backlit, isolated from one another by walls, and subject to scrutiny both collectively and individually by an observer in the tower who remains unseen Oświęcim

  --The Algorithms Behind The Headlines Othello Obama: who's whispering in his ear? The Russians telling out of school say that on their satellites they saw the planes go to Marfa and they saw four vehicles go to Cibolo Ranch. Their operatives on the ground saw the federal marshals dismissed and that's why Scalia had no coverage, because the secret service went on to LA with the President. The U.S. is constantly monitoring all such activities in Russian by satellite and on the ground but it doesn't tell. The Russians are telling. But it is very telling that after Putin heard of the Gabriel Box he began to occupy Syria.

--In the end it is my identity of agreement with Levinas and the other. Who else speaks of the precognitive, the shared identity of suffering, the face and the immediacy of the face-to-face encounter with the other. The face is a symbol of the other and of myself even if mere appearance. Transcendence comes to pass but we do not seek it. Precognition comes to pass but we do not cause it. We recognize it like a face.

  Translator's Preface. Levinas bio: "precisely by its powerlessness, by a passivity "more passive than passivity"...the invisible force of this vulnerability [is] the "trace" of the face of the Other. "a face is a trace of itself, given over to my responsibility, but to which I am wanting and faulty. It is as though I were responsible for his mortality, and guilty for surviving." (Otherwise Than Being, 91)..."Through a trace the irreversible past takes on the profile of a 'He.' The beyond from which a face comes is in the third person." ("The Trace of the Other")

-- Stanford Encyclopedia of Philosophy Levinas claimed, in 1961, that he was developing a "first philosophy." This first philosophy is neither traditional logic nor metaphysics, however.[1] It is an interpretive, phenomenological description of the rise and repetition of the face-to-face encounter, or the intersubjective relation at its precognitive core; viz., being called by another and responding to that other. If precognitive experience, that is, human sensibility, can be characterized conceptually, then it must be described in what is most characteristic to it: a continuum of sensibility and affectivity, in other words, sentience and emotion in their interconnection.[2]

"the meaning of intersubjectivity and lived immediacy in light of three themes: transcendence, existence, and the human other... the other impacts me unlike any worldly object or force. I can constitute the other person cognitively, on the basis of vision, as an alter ego. I can see that another human being is "like me," acts like me, appears to be the master of her conscious life...He does not even have to utter words in order for me to feel the summons implicit in his approach... no event is as affectively disruptive for a consciousness holding sway in its world than the encounter with another person... the 'I' first experiences itself as called and liable to account for itself. It responds. The 'I''s response is as if to a nebulous command. Nothing says that the other gave a de facto command. The command or summons is part of the intrinsic relationality. With the response comes the beginning of language as dialogue. The origin of language, for Levinas, is always response—a responding-to another, that is, to her summons... To situate first philosophy in the face-to-face encounter is to choose to begin with ...the prime condition for human communication... an 'I' discovers its own particularity when it is singled out by the gaze of the other. This gaze says "do not kill me." implores the 'I', who eludes it only with difficulty, ...command and supplication occurs because human faces impact us as affective moments or, what Levinas calls 'interruptions'. The face of the other is firstly expressiveness. It could be compared to a force... to uncover the layers of pre-intellectual experience in which transcendence comes to pass.
Reflections on the Philosophy of Hitlerism. 1934

"stationed in segregated barracks and commandos… the Jewish prisoner suddenly rediscovers his Jewish identity." Indeed, as he celebrates Rosh Hashanah with his (previously assimilated and unobservant) fellow Jewish ex-soldiers, Levinas notes: "A few years ago, these prayers would be interpreted as offering derisory hope. Nice little old outmoded things; now it is all interpreted as reality. The Last Judgment has become reality. Good becomes good again and evil, evil, and quite shatteringly so." As Levinas writes in a moving 1945 essay, also included in the new Grasset/IMEC volume, Jewish prisoners of war found that "humiliation" reminded them of the "Biblical aspect of being chosen people."

2/21/16 Rick Wiles Justice Scalia death sacrifice Lpercalia.
--Thinking about shopping for revolvers I was in a thrift, a Sally looking for an edition of the Psalms I could carry and keep when I found a vol followed by its companion of poems by a woman, whose name I didn't get of meditations. No. 32, 36.

--That morning bought 2 357s.

For concealed carry in 2" snub-nosed .38's, Federal's Premium Personal Defense load uses a 125 grain Nyclad LHP bullet at 830 fps and 190 ft. lbs. from a 2" revolver barrel. This is their famous and highly effective "Chief's Special" load. For apartment dwellers and others concerned with over penetration in densely populated areas, Cor-Bon/Glaser offers a standard pressure Glaser Blue pre-fragmented 80 grain bullet at 1200 fps and 256 ft. lbs. Pre-fragmented loads are reputed to be very effective in the short range, frontal shootings typical of home invasion situations. No matter what standard pressure Special load you choose, it will provide the least muzzle blast and recoil among our three cartridge options. For new handgun shooters, standard velocity .38 Special loads are a logical step up from the .22 rimfire that should be everyone's first handgun.

--Pope Francis is scheduled to have more than two hours alone with Russian Orthodox Patriarch Kirill of Moscow in Cuba in addition to signing a declaration with the patriarch before flying on to Mexico for a Feb. 12-17 visit.

Global leader of the Russian Orthodox Church, Patriarch Kirill of Moscow, arrived in Antarctica earlier today 2/18 where he joined up with the vast Federation naval armada transporting from Saudi Arabia the mysterious "Ark of Gabriel", entrusted to Russia's care by the Custodian of the Two Holy Mosques, and performed an "ancient ritual" over it read from a "secret text" given to him by Pope Francis just days prior in Cuba when these leaders of Christianity's two top sects met for the first time in nearly 1,000 years. Ancient Islamic manuscript, "Gabriel's Instructions To Muhammad", it centers around a group of instructions given to Muhammad by the Angel Gabriel in a cave called Hira, located on the mountain called Jabal an-Nour, near Mecca, wherein this heavenly being entrusted into Muhammad's care a "box/ark" of "immense power" he was forbidden to use as it belonged to God only and was, instead, to be buried in a shrine at the "place of worship the Angels used before the creation of man" until its future uncovering in the days of Yawm al-Qīyāmah, or Qiyâmah, which means literally "Day of the Resurrection". But Oops they are opening it! "ancient secret manuscript" was given to Patriarch Kirill by Pope Francis that pertains to the "Ark of Gabriel" whose legend behind it claims it was written directly by the "watchers" (angels?) described in the Book of Enoch.   "Gabriel's Instructions to Muhammad." apparent holes in the official accounts of the Grand Mosque crane disaster, Majj stampede tragedy and the Admiral Vladimisky mission have left room for conspiracy theories to develop.
 Using this "secret text" given to him by Pope Francis, preformed an "ancient ritual" over the "Ark of Gabriel" in the Russian Orthodox Holy Trinity Church (the only church in Antarctica) and where immediately thereafter this mysterious artifact was transported into the vast interior of this cold and foreboding continent by a highly specialized Spetsnaz (Special Forces) unit to a destination, and purpose, not identified by the MoD.
Russia planning to obliterate with its planned nuclear strike, but rather the US-EU backed European

Organization for Nuclear Research (CERN) underground research site based in the northwest suburb of Geneva on the Franco–Swiss border who MoD analysts are now reporting have successfully "unlocked" one of Nazi Germany's most feared secret weapons—"interdimensional communication/travel".

---here Evidence supporting that CERN has "unlocked" this feared Nazi secret weapon, this report continues, was obtained recently by Foreign Intelligence Service (SVR) "assets" operating in Spain who had been tasked with uncovering the truth behind the mysterious "Death Star" orbs falling upon the Spanish countryside this past November—and which these intelligence operatives linked to the similar "Death Star" orbs videotaped emerging from CERN.

2/20/16 Fri 11 Feb Itinerary: "In the morning, the President will participate in a DSCC roundtable at a private residence. The roundtable is closed press.In the afternoon, the President will deliver remarks at a DNC event at a private residence. There will be print pool coverage of the President's remarks. Later in the afternoon, the
President will depart San Jose, California en route Los Angeles, California. The departure from Moffett Federal Airfield and the arrival at Los Angeles International Airport are open to pre-credentialed media. MKultra athletes
    --Major taboo to Navajo control, seen driving through rez three times attacked one with rock that bounces off wish shield no damage, one with fissure roll with a toothpick, once after i turned around to see about this with a rock that went through the window and landed on the seat. We were carrying a sick Navajo vet, couldn't get out, ended up with women in a way station who I told this. They said, why didn't you say, I said because you were women, but that I had then realized they had the power. all the attackers were male young men, like demented dogs so to speak.

2/19/16 Nachumlist Obama dead pool [see Obama in Peru-nephilim, Patagonia- Quayle believes [worth citing for usual selective and exaggerated rhetoric] that the U.S. government is working with the remnants of Hitler's Nazi regime in an underground Antarctic base, where the two powers have spent the years from 1947 to today tunneling from Antarctica to Patagonia to link up with the (imaginary) network of tunnels under South America built by the Nephilim with "technology" not available to the Inca and their predecessors. (These are the "tunnels" derived from Erich von Däniken's Gold of the Gods fraud, ultimately amplified and exaggerated
from a passage in Helena Blavatsky's Isis Unveiled.)]
    Obama Scalia meet Trump to Putin: stated: "I can promise you this, I will NEVER hold a meeting with you in Texas, neither one of us might not come http://www.whatdoesitmean.com/index2000.htmout alive!"
So if Donald Trump in making this statement to President Putin was intending to be "darkly humorous", this report concludes, isn't fully known until further clarification can be made—but what is known is that in less than 24 hours after President Putin's receipt of Trump's letter, the US presidential race was thrown into chaos and confusion after the sudden and unexpected death of US Supreme Court Justice Antonin Scalia…in Texas.

--Granted that women may have sought out relations with the fallen angel watchers for the prestige it gave them, they would be royals if not goddesses, but where, how, did the fallen get real bodies with sperm to infect them. After that first affect there would have been no block to female nephilim, as there are Greek goddess nephilim at least, but after that the fallen were imprisoned so the genetic transmission would have corrupted and weakened.

The Bill and Hillary Clinton Murder Chronicles: a litany of names.

Pink cloud, Satan's feces. The missing 28 pages that must be read with pauses as you whole notion of history is redrawn. The people driven like cattle across continents.

2/17/16 Denver White Horse 2008 DNC this will shock you to the core 9/11 from jim fetzer Sandy Hook book banned.. Secret Nasa photo stolen

--First the patina world of art lit poetry work life culture we think is valuable and exists in itself for itself is without meaning and a deception of various causes. Second the deep under reality manipulated by the elite councils where the wars are decided ahead and the winner pays the debts of the losers and Stalin is an English agent goes on and on from the polio cancer vaccine, Antarctica, Atlantis, fake moon landings, politicat assassinations, underground cities, submarine bases under Kansas, Blue Beam epigenetics, crisis actors, Bohemian groves, aluminum clouds: all sponsored by nephilim in service of Satan and three, the best the first world can do is release their expectation and live in sacrifice for those who died while they remain alive, as Levinas. Four the providence and benevolence of the Father and the sacrifice of the Son to redeem all of us, opposite to the underground, wherein we all have value in itself is because of His creation in us!

2/16/16 Angelic princes that fell, metallic aerosolized fiberglass sliced in microscopic cross sections=the particles in clouds and lungs nano tubules immersed in molten aluminum. Genesis 10 Prophetic genealogy, Diabolical treachery behind strange sounds, Michelle Hopkins Mann [very clear] Nimrod expedition. Greg Hallet Hitler, Stalin, Mao, Buzzsaw. The Hidden King of England It's precognitive, colonists voyaging, bodies burying, before we know, so that when we know we know.

2/15/16 They pronounced Scalia dead by phone and embalmed him immediately. What's the rush?

2/14/16 What does bombing the van Allen radiation belt have to do with Byrd in Antarctica? Van Allen belt hydrogen bomb, starfish

2/13/16 Pegida. Nephilim epigenetics Skiba, Color coding. Sigil. Super Collider hypnotic induction. Sacrifices: Corrizine (son), Travolta (son), Freeman (granddaughter), Carrey (girlfriend), Jaden Morrison elements Crisis actor cop Ferguson (Don Lemon reporter), Lamar Odom sacrifice, Kardashian.

All of our lives are organized around the hidden referent, not of the Shoah, but the Shoah to come of war. Not a tumor but a war and it is the war now breaking our ribs for which we have no word. Can't read Levinas long, Difficult Freedom, Difficile Liberte, Totality and Infinity, Otherwise Than Being, dizzying reflections of height, or depth of the presentiment and memory of the horror, w/o taking the holocaust of the past as a limited edition of the future, the Nazi charges of subhuman ape and carrier of germs amplified to the useless eaters that British royalty thinks of the commoners of the world. So the time- no time of Levinas past that he lives the rest of his life in a vigil of, endures his life "when one has that tumor in the memory...and death will no doubt cancel the unjustified privilege of having survived six million deaths" is a down payment in reverse, the past for the tumor of the future that nothing can cover over even if we stand away from it to the present, still everyday occupations almost as if neither the past and its vertigo and the future that grips at our edge were never there, when both are the same. Both inhabit a non-time, immemorial past and future which have no memory and no prediction, but have in common a search for a language dedicated to the memory of those who died or will, but without naming it as such, so that it is no theme for the news or discussion of any kind. Leave it nameless, for if it fails to name itself, why should we help it. It is too eager to name. We deny it space and we deny it time. It is Destruktion, every mountain and hill of morals made low, a perfect recasting of the human without empathy, palaces, flags, magistrates tempests raging in shipwrecks so the murderer can see its sanction of the world with a clear conscience..

2/12/16 Throwin up the goat Rides Pegasus to Heaven.
Kanye West Illuminati Refugee Camp/Slave Auction Viking Treasure

2/11/16 Long shaft of the bottomless pit. Meteors as stars.

2/10/16 Alex Jones on Bohemian Grove. Stanley Kubrick This casts doubt Jones.
Larry Elder on identity politics FORMATION Super Bowl
Beyoncé Giselle Knowles means Hostage/Pledge who is beyond others at the top of the summit! (Pyramid).

2/9/16 Santilli Telescope

2/8/16 "It seemed good to me having investigated": Both Zechariah and Elisabeth were righteous. The angel, Gabriel, stood on the right side of the altar of incense who said later to Marium, Yahshua shall be great, and of His Kingdom there shall be no end. And Marium said, He has scattered the proud in the imagination. He has put down the mighty from their seats, and exalted them of low degree. Royal Babylon by Heathcote Williams

2/6/16 Dubious Angels
     Ist version: Benjamin, the two names, provident names given by his parents, secrets, locked within himself all couched in negatives, did not come to know it before the day, not every secret name remains always the same, not any less the name that contains in itself all the life forces, no way an enrichment of him who bears it, this latter, that is the new name, stepped out of the old and put up the novus angel as a picture of his new self. The two names were masculine and feminine forms to be reunited in the world. Because he, that is, the picture of the new name, hence the new name, "made me pay" for disturbing his work, that is praising and going forth into oblivion, this angel novus masculine had to send his feminine

counterpart. The angel masculine pulls him along into a future from which he has come, that is advanced to, and to which he goes, facing the person he keeps facing.

      2nd version: He keeps his given names secret. They are the names, name which join the life forces, but once uttered become amorphous so that he, the angel, too name would lose the appearance of the human. This new name, uttered, stepped out of Benjamin and his known name, and put itself on the wall as a picture, the New Angel, considered a self portrait of his masculine. These new angels are created to dissolve but this one was interdicted and came to live on his wall, kidnapped. "I took him away," fatal detour. These new angels divide male and female, so in consequence of being kidnapped and fixed immobile on the wall, it sent its feminine counterpart. Thus divided, the angel in the painting and the female emanation, divided from knowledge from each other, project into he and his woman chanced upon (biographically different ones) who captivated him so much he long awaited consummation with her. Nothing could enfeeble his patience. But the angel was really all of his past from which he severed, persons and things, that is, it was himself, once removed, a cousin of himself that exists in the absence that exists in the things he does not have. There he resides. All this is in order to pull him along, let go of the forever called by the new name. Vatican Light Show

2/5/16 His mercy endures forever.

  2/4/16 Ben Joseph-Ben David. "Many have confused the events of the War of Gog & Magog with a preceding war described in Psalm, Ezekiel, Obadiah, Jeremiah, Isaiah, and Zephaniah. Keep in mind that it is God and God alone who destroys the Russian/Iranian coalition. However, in this war [the Psalm 83 War], it is the Israeli army who blessed by God destroys a different Arab coalition. Psalm 83 Coalition: Tents of Edom =
[decedents of Esau] Palestinian Refugees and Southern Jordanians. Ishmaelites = Saudi Arabians. Moab =
Palestinian Refugees and Central Jordanians. Hagrites = Egyptians
  Gebal = Northern Lebanese
    Ammon = Palestinian Refugees and Northern Jordanians
    Amalek = Arabs South of Israel
    Philista = Palestinian Refugees and Hamas of Gaza Strip
    Inhabitants of Tyre = Hezbollah and Southern Lebanese
    Assyria = Syrians and perhaps Northern Iraqis included
    Children of Lot = Moab and Ammon"
 Recep Erdogan Mason Templar Palace Pharaoh
 Domeh
 Alert: Revelation 18:2 Just Happened Vatican light show
 How will they believe unless they hear? Holly Grieg, James
David Manning I heard birds flying over head calling, mercy, mercy.

     Benjamin, Levinas, Arendt, Hartman, Scholem among many reflect the personal effects of these wars, which themselves are the result of unbelieved manipulations, hence inevitable. If I were to say the causes they would be scorned. That leaves us with personal effects in the lives of men and women tortured and confused by every aspect of religion, society and their own personal foibles.

2/3/16 Kenneth Burke, Freud--and the Analysis of Poetry

"What more fitting place to erect one's church than above a sewer! One might even say that sewers are what churches are for Freud's theories bound him to a more drastic self-ostracizing act--the charting of the relations between ecclesia and cloaca that forced him to analyze the cloaca itself. Hence, his work was with the confessional as cathartic, as purgative; this haruspicy required an inspection of the entrails; it was, bluntly, an interpretative sculpting of excrement, with beauty replaced by a science of the grotesque.

[beauty in Scholem's Benjamin is lucifer: "...the source of his intuitions about the meaning of the beautiful, and about the Luciferian depth of the "appearance" in which the beautiful conceals and reveals itself" 202 Scholem, Walter Benjamin and is Angel]
1.2 the acts of the neurotic are symbolic acts 10 cf,. Blue Book: the details of experience behind A's dejection may be vastly different from the details of experience behind B;s dejection, yet both A and B may fall into the same bodily posture in expressing their dejection. 14 Freudian emphasis on the pun shows something can only be in so far as it is something else --Gid, scrupulous criminals, seduction in the accents of evangelism, private enterprize mass, spoor, scat, Asiatic slumber, ritual slaying of civilization. It's body poisoned these thieves. Condensation and displacement, more than a house, other than a house.

"The truth about Jerusalem is that it isn't a patriotic poem at all. Parry's music gives the hymn an upbeat tempo – especially with the booming orchestration by Edward Elgar – but William Blake's original words are as laced with resentful irony as Shostakovich's Leningrad symphony. Famously, Blake asks four questions in succession, and the answer to each is a resounding no. Christ's feet never trod in England; the Lamb of God didn't gambol – preposterous as the image is – around the Cotswolds; the Holy Spirit wasn't regularly spotted in London fog; and most directly of all, there was no sense of Jerusalem in the dark Satanic mills of the Industrial Age. The consequent fantasy of building a New Jerusalem in England is widely understood by anyone who studies Blake to be a **stonking parody of Napoleonic Era nationalism.** Even in 1804, no one sung and danced about their own 'mental fight' and expected to be taken seriously. Kate Maltby, Spectator Blog 14 Jan 16

2/2/16 the English royal family are pedophiles bank of America charlotte symbols St John cathedral nyc security council mural what they mean life is a dream is that all the projected images are thought to be real gold fringed flag.

2/1/16 Earthquakes were launched. Lower and middle classes skimmed to cream the top.

1/30/16 NY Subway Cars

Spiritual WEapons of our warfare, Bree to catch him in his words...when they shall rise. Thee Mystical Mirror Carole Novalis (Novalis, Corona, Corolla) Mirror of Novo Ordo.

- Springmeier on Mars. all lower negative adrenal response emotions art its food. Fritz Spring meier Illuminati prophecy club:

"In 1991, I first self-published my Be Wise As Serpents manuscript which exposed the top 13 families. In 1992, I began my newsletter to continue exposing the Illuminati, and came out with some monographs exposing the Monarch Mind Control program and the Illuminati Plans/methods to create earthquakes. From the mid-Dec. '92 newsletter up to the most recent ones in 1995, I have ran feature articles exposing the different top 13 families. This book is a collection of things, I, Fritz Springmeier, wrote between 1991 and 1995 about the top 13 families.

' I made the decision to use the approximately 250 pages I'd written specifically about the 13 families as Book #1, and what I had written in general about the families, which was also 200 plus pages as Book #2. Volume two will explain how the Illuminati control the world, and what some of their beliefs are, and about their secret and semi-secret organizations."
 In Volume two, you will read about Illuminati life, Illuminati control, and Illuminati organizations including the ACL, the Bohemian Grove, the Cosmos Club, the CFR, the Club of Rome, the Council of 9, the Council of 13 which is the Grand Druid Council, the Jason Society, the Jason Group, the Ordo Saturis, the OTO groups, MI-6, MJ-12, the Mothers of Darkness, the Pilgrim Society, the Prieure de Sion, the Process Church, the Sanhedrin, the Temple of Power, and other groups. These two books will give the details behind what was written, "the whole world lieth in wickedness" and that the god of this world is in its full reality Satan."

1/29/16 Behold the fig tree. be thou removed. Walking in the Temple. Stand praying forgive. No history without reading. The three states waking, almost waking and dreaming sleep reveal the man. Unless we have a script of the dreaming of a great man we must think him an imposter.

1/28/16 A colt whereon never man sat. Yahshua entered Jerusalem. The time of the fig is not yet. He would not suffer any man should carry any vessel through the Temple. Made the den of thieves, prayer turned to greed. Inside out bowl. Since my house burned down I have a better view of the moon. Mizuta Masahide

1/27/16 The early ancient Egyptians were-giants, they were different in size. These giant humans of Egypt had Giant Animals and Birds as well. People of our size existed in early ancient Egypt along with them, The same with normal animals and birds, they existed with giant birds and animals Forbidden History.
    The standard take must be the large sarcophi, and art of the ruling class portrays them as giants to show their superiority, caste, royalty. or Hyper-pituitrism. Amarna Art. ... on by an endocrine disorder found in men, Gigantism, or Marfan's Syndrome. Sauropod gigantis, chorea gigantism(Stonehenge) colossal statues illustrate the gigantism of much of Egyptian, oriental despotism, use of huge images symbolic of power. " To hang on to the

respect of his people Ramses II resorts to gigantism and self-glorification, building many structures dedicated to advertising his own glory. Typical of such over-the-hill empires are the four 82' colossi of Ramses carved into the facade of his temple above the Nile. "The massive statues lack the refinement of earlier periods, because much is sacrificed to overwhelming size." (Gardner's, 90)" Egyptian
New Kingdom Architecture. Megaliths

During the 18th dynasty a religious revolt came suddenly in ancient Egypt, led by Amenhotep IV. During his 5th regnal year, the king announced a new religion for the state, the "Atonism". This involved worshipping only one god, Aton (the solar disc), and rejecting all other currently known gods. To this effect, the king changed his own name into "Akhen-Aton"(This pleases Aton), closed all other gods' temples and moved his capital north to Tel el-Amarna away from the influence of the priests of Amon. The striking features found from the study of his statues, pictures as well as his mummy (if it were truly his) were those of tall stature, unduly long limbs, elongated skull, long slender neck and long face with a huge mandible (lower jaw).

In addition, his feminine features included gynaecomastia (female-like breasts) and a wide pelvis with fat hips (the breadth of the pelvis exceeds that of the shoulders – a characteristic feature of females). A nude statue during his early reign showed him without genitalia at all. WHAT DISEASE WAS AKHEN-ATON SUFFERING FROM? hyper-pituitarism.

Dream of Fred Phillips who was aggressive, in karate stance. Told him it was demons that he could be free. He calmed down. Told him his own mistake was to do what he thought, marry a rich girl, but then got divorced. Broke his heart. She still loves you I told him.

1/25/16 water cocoon
-the New World Order plan to turn walmarts Jade Helm geographic analogies invasion of Iran your Ancient Granny Was A Freak -giantism.Cor-Bon, Urban Carry, Gunbelt

Autism Made in USA vaccines.Why Bill Gates is a Modern day Stalin-speaks of the renegade cancer ridden polio virus

1/24/16 Death of Mary Sherman, Edward T. Haslam, Dr. Mary's Monkey. Vaccine conspiracy
Me and Lee (Harvey Oswald)
Smith and Wesson 38 special, 500. 5 screw before 1955. Light weight S&W 38

1/20/16 It 's not that such terms like Hail Mary mean to defame the good, which they do, but the notion is to invoke the ill.

1/16/16 A Powerful Documentary: G Edward Griffin – The Capitalist
Conspiracy Apollo's Delfica.

1/15/15 Dr. Bruce Levine, The Rebel Yell opposition defiance disorder smart toilet surveillance toilet, surveillance smart car, door, stoves lights.

-Ken Peter's Vision from God, 1980

    --Hebrew is hyper grammatical, each jot and tittle even mathematical in a way but to me language is sound and sounds that skew consonant assonant meaning misspelled with pun-like contextual corporate collective meanings of image yes, but the sound itself. When Spender says it is in the seen and the word that poems remind of that and Heidegger says the like in Hartman, i think of " to walk in the light of your presence" that whole books and long meditations try to plumb this meaning, the same as "rejoice in your name all day long" for it seems that these are multiple envelops of experience that are keyed to the letter, the word, the sound the grammar but only so, for they are this and so much more that it exists in the song upon the bed all night long that David wrote about and the song when awakening that like the spring that feeds the brook, which stream recedes from consciousness in day but surges again in night and plays, sings, murmurs shines all during the instruction of sleep that Isaiah says is the instruction all night long too. So that is the experience of language Spender gets at and the ground Heidegger is after, but it is not philosophical, the song in the night, or poetical even, it is more. I both participate in and view the simultaneous presentation of these events which when waking are enormous to express, write down, for there they were simultaneous and rotate before the mind with clarity, but are welcome insights and feel good to see and know. If I do not make this note they will be gone from conscious memory. As in Hartman's Heidegger calls "for a liberation of hermeneutics from its dependency on texts...it is Being itself, according to Heidegger, not the text that "calls" to us in those [great] poets. This is what Spender is after.   However the meaning exists and whether it calls to us, like the new birth and we hear the sound thereof but know not whence it comes or wither it goes, the text provokes the meaning and meaning makes the text grow so that "he was in the world" becomes a song (added to Methods of Unconscious)

1/14/16 Jesse Spots, I watched Queen Elizabeth's Christmas Message

    -Donald Marshall the grow rooms, a deep level underground of entire floors where human clones are grown in the dark, suspended in water, in stacked glass tubes. Marshall reports that the grow rooms are dark, dirty, and reek of the smell of urine.

- Norwegian daily newspaper Dagbladet headlined "Dolly is Eating Herself to Death", claiming that Dolly the sheep could not stop eating and was more than twice the size of her litter mates.
- it can be hard to tell if you are a clone or not, since as a clone, your body, memories, and feelings seem real as real.
- Incyte, a biopharmaceutical company based in Delaware, owns patents on over 2,000 human genetic codes
- while he sleeps and is held hostage until his body wakes up. Known as R.E.M-Driven Consciousness Transfer - The world first learned of Luka Magnotta on May 30, 2012, when he was named as a prime suspect in a grisly killing in Montreal, Canada which involved the shipping of human body parts to the headquarters of two political parties. clone dismemberment is a common form of punishment he's witnessed many times,

designed to demoralize the defiant sex slave. Once arrested, Magnotta never had the chance to speak to the public, never took the stand or spoke during his criminal trial, so no one had the chance to hear his account of being repeatedly raped and mutilated by top elected officials in his so-called dreams, that had become a living nightmare.

Over the period of about a year, seven human feet in sneakers washed ashore in British Columbia and Washington State. He believes that the cloning center is located on the private grounds of a large wildlife nature reserve, somewhere within the province of British Columbia. Marshall says his cloning center is reserved for only very elite members of the Illuminati and come with special privileges, such as the arena is built above ground, allowing access to fresh air and natural light. Is it possible that someone didn't bother to remove the shoes from the clones before tossing them in the chipper? no evidence that the feet had even been severed, and that it looked a "natural process of separation," even though earlier reports claimed that the feet appeared to have been deliberately severed with the bones "cut clean across".!!

the lamas agreed to share with them that for centuries, they had been helping to hide an indigenous race of lizard living deep within the planet since prehistoric times, known as Vril lizards. Just how is this bodysnatching process accomplished?
According to Marshall, Vril lizards have a natural proboscis at the top of their head, from which they eject a type of thick cerebrospinal fluid. When this fluid enters the human, usually through the eye and from there, to the brain, a chemical transformation immediately begins to take place. all Vril lizards want to be human. They admire human intelligence and the beautiful human form. They want to crawl out from deep underground into the light and walk unnoticed among humanity. However, they are not human and have no capacity to feel human emotions. The Hopi Indian culture successfully drove off Vril. Vril are aggressive predators whose favorite prey is fresh human. The lizards then go into attack frenzy as they swarm, bite and drain the victim dry. when the lizard ejects it's quill, containing the brain and spinal cord through a proboscis located at the top of it's head. The quill then enters the eye of the victim, where it travels around the eyeball to a specific location of the brain. Once there, a chemical reaction begins immediately, resulting in the complete parasitic domination of the victim's brain. According to Marshall, they "stick their spinal cord in your eye and turn you into a walking lizard".

1/13/16   Hans Glasser 1561 woodcut.
Friends, Alex showing up at the airport before I flew to Costa Rica; Fred Philips showing up in a suit and tie at Jay's funeral at Bala-Cynwyd Presby.; Charlie Brown showing up at my house just as we were leaving Fayetteville after being fired. Jose Donoso in Panama taking a tour of the canal at night layover to Miami when I was flying back for the funeral in Phila, JCCIII at Texas telling Sledd he would quit if they didn't rehire me, over firing there.

1/12/16 rectangular patterns, bases on moon, Mars.
--Gang Stalking http://fightgangstalking.com/ SAIC corp, MILAB military abductions

1/11/16 Missing persons. David Paulides. Severed Feet. Noah Chamberlin, Tempe Town Lake drownings La Crosse Wisconsin . Geraldine Largay disappears on navy survival property, alone or at last in group, rain after disappearance, no crime scene, young white males, college students, 80%german ancestry near bars, high alcohol blood levels when tested, near river, lack of shoes, berries nearby, lack of lividity, body found in water but none in lungs, body found completely outside bounds of expectation, miles away, in opposite directions, 16oo cases people found or who disappeared in and around canals, places with "devil" in the name, dogs can find no scent trails, no tracks, no cause of death. Manchester UK, rivers, national parks, Yosemite, AT, Pacific NW, Mississippi river, Vancouver, Mt Rainer clusters, Tempe, Boston, Chicago, New York, all top mental, physical specimen young men, FBI monitors case, strong religious beliefs,

-Steve Kubacki reality engineering Chiricahua national monument disappearances. Because survivors seem disoriented, wide eyed stare but not moving, said to be out of character, found in areas searched a hundred times, intelligent, it suggests a download was made, an emptying of their brain, soul. Symptoms, person out at night feels tired, decides to go home or on the phone and the phone goes dead. Also urban, elisa lam, found in a water tank atop Cecil Hotel that was home to serial killers etc LA The whitewash of coroners, sheriffs is itself data.

1/9/16 Take the Gopro shots of TX, add rap about ameryca aey took. digital recorder.

1/8/16 Psalm 83 Israel attacked by Syria destroys Damascus and neutralizes other Arab nations surrounding it, bring in a period of peace and prosperity. Isa. 17, Obadiah but culmination in war of Gog Magog, Ez. 38,9 of Turkey and Iran backed by Russia.
Max Keiser, suicide bankers, electronic gulags
 Nephilim tech: 2045 Project: http://2045.com/
Humai:http://humaitech.com/
Clonaid:http://www.clonaid.com/page.php?18 Tragedy & Hope: A History of the World in Our Time by Carroll Quigley
Stanley Kimball Monteith

1/6/15 Elipton
Obama's hanuman monkey god Coverup
Project Golden Dragon, Clementine CERN the Lord Particle
Michelle Hopkins Mann, Rainbow Clouds
--Baudelaire on Mars. Mix of a Poe, a comic Poem and Brautigan. Add Pegasus and Ed Abbey Memorial. Guapa Susan

1/5/16 Giants
 The coming Aaudi Arabian storm, Isa 21, 1-9; Jer 51.47 Isis judgement on "the graven images of Babylon"

In the Jewish mysticism set forth in the Book of Enoch and Book of Jubilees that was carried on by groups including the religious community of Qumran that produced the Dead Sea

Scrolls, the Elioud (also transliterated Eljo)[1] are the antediluvian children of the Nephilim and are considered a part-angel hybrid race of their own.[2] Like the Nephilim, the Elioud are exceptional in both ability and wickedness.

---In some readings of the non-canonical texts, Nephilim are children whose father is an angel and whose mother is a human and they are the "giants" (also known as Gibborim) referred to in the canonical Book of Numbers.[13] In others, angels and human women produce children who are Gibborim, and the Nephilim have fathers who are Gibborim and human mothers. This ambiguity is also found in the non-canonical Book of Giants, fragments of which were found among the Dead Sea Scrolls.[14]

--- One Greek manuscript adds to this section, "And they [the women] bore to them [the Watchers] three races– first, the great giants. The giants brought forth [some say "slew"] the Naphelim, and the Naphelim brought forth [or "slew"] the Elioud. And they existed, increasing in power according to their greatness." "Naphil" is an alternative transliteration form

The 1913 translation of R.H. Charles of the Book of Jubilees 7:21-25[16] reads as follows (note that "Naphil" is an alternative transliteration form of "Nephilim"):

21   For owing to these three things came the flood upon the earth, namely, owing to the fornication wherein the Watchers against the law of their ordinances went a whoring after the daughters of men, and took themselves wives of all which they chose: and they made the beginning of uncleanness.

22   And they begat sons the Naphidim, and they were all unlike, and they devoured one another: and the Giants slew the Naphil, and the Naphil slew the Eljo, and the Eljo mankind, and one man another.

23   And every one sold himself to work iniquity and to shed much blood, and the earth was filled with iniquity. 24 And after this they sinned against the beasts and birds, and all that moves and walks on the earth: and much blood was shed on the earth, and every imagination and desire of men imagined vanity and evil continually. 25 And the Lord destroyed everything from off the face of the earth; because of the wickedness of their deeds, and because of the blood which they had shed in the midst of the earth He destroyed everything. See http://www.fallenangels-ckquarterman.com/the-elioud-race/ According to tradition, the Nephilim had enormous psychic abilities. They performed levitation, mind control, and remote viewing. They had the power of pronouncing and removing curses and diseases, and had ways of knowing and predicting the future. They were extremely intelligent. They knew all about science, architecture, and engineering. They combined these skills with their powers of intelligence to build the Pyramids and the other great monuments around the world.

    According to 1Enoch they created human sacrifice. They drank blood, were cannibals and taught abortion. The book of Enoch states, And the fifth was named Kasdeja: this is he who showed the children of men all the wicked smitings of spirits and demons, and the smitings of the embryo in the womb, that it may pass away, and the smitings of the soul the bites of the serpent…" (Enoch 69:12a)They certainly tampered with both human and animal gene pools (Jasher) to try and hinder redemption through a human bloodline. They were the heroes of old, the mighty men of renown, talked about in mythology, and contributed to the reason God had to destroy the world and all its inhabitants in the Great Flood.

1/4/16 The Illuminoid. Ameryyca, spell with a double why. Ameryyca

According to the Sages, he is the "angel of Esau," and their struggle, which "raised dust up to the Supernal Throne," is the cosmic struggle between two nations and two worlds -- the spirituality of Israel and the materiality of Edom (Rome). The night through which they wrestled is the long and dark galut ("exile"), in the course of which Jacob's descendants suffer bodily harm and spiritual anguish, but emerge victorious. The struggle is conducted on two planes -- "with the divine and with men." It is a struggle with men: in nearly 4000 years of galut we have wrestled with the Egyptians, the Canaanites, the Babylonians, the Persians, the Romans, the Spanish Inquisition, Nazi Germany and Islamic terror. These and many others did their worst to destroy us, yet we have prevailed.

 It is also a struggle with the soul of galut, with its Divine essence and purpose. Thrice daily we plead, protest and contest before the Supernal Throne Chabab (add to Legends)
1/3/16 Inhuman Transhuman agenda: Max Moore Ode to Lucifer. all life downline permanently altered, war of seeds, bloodlines giant test tube babies of end days, time seals, Krispr Kas 9, new days of Noah, grid from hand held to inside brain. Reassembly of the soul, stable platform in brain to contact with AI, interface, nephilim agents di bartole, Charles Bonnette symptom, phantom lens, $100 genome, Jasons, crime scenes change with new geno phenotype Fallen Angel Day.

 Head scars, Isis, Obama. Alimentary rites search: Manichean allegory: original Aramaic writings relating to the book of Enoch literature (see the Book of Enoch and the Second Book of Enoch), as well as an otherwise unknown section of the book of Enoch called the "Book of Giants". This book was quoted directly, and expanded on by Mani, becoming one of the original six Syriac writings of the Manichaean Church. Besides brief references by non-Manichaean authors through the centuries, no original sources of "The Book of Giants" (which is actually part six of the "Book of Enoch") were available until the 20th century. Scattered fragments of both the original Aramaic "Book of Giants" (which were analyzed and published by Józef Milik in 1976)[21] and of the Manichaean version of the same name (analyzed and published by W.B. Henning in 1943)[22] were found with the discovery in the twentieth century of the Dead Sea Scrolls in the Judaean Desert and the Manichaean writings of the Uyghur Manichaean kingdom in Turpan. Henning wrote in his analysis of them:

 It is noteworthy that Mani, who was brought up and spent most of his life in a province of the Persian empire, and whose mother belonged to a famous Parthian family, did not make any use of the Iranian mythological tradition. There can no longer be any doubt that the Iranian names of Sām, Narīmān, etc., that appear in the Persian and Sogdian versions of the Book of the Giants, did not figure in the original edition, written by Mani in the Syriac language.[22]

 From a careful reading of the Enoch literature and the Book of Giants, alongside the description of the Manichaean myth, it becomes clear that the "Great King of Honor" of this myth (a being that sits as a guard to the world of light at the seventh of ten heavens in the Manichaean myth,[23]) is identical with the King of Honor sitting on the heavenly throne in the Enoch literature. In the Aramaic book of Enoch, in the Qumran writings in general, and in the original Syriac section of Manichaean scriptures quoted by Theodore bar Konai,[24] he is called "malka raba de-ikara" (the great king of honor).

1/2/16 Ernst Muldashev, eye transplant surgery Where do we come from. the eyes of Shambalah!

1/1/16 taddeo di bartolo the leviathan meta schematizo, satan masquerades meta sche matizo, (meta-schiz-matizo) disguise,2 Cor11.14. Mk 5.11 do not send us out of the country, tr. out of the space between two places (dimensions, into a cadent one).
-Persecuted but not abandoned, struck down but not destroyed, we are hard pressed on every side. -to install w/ Jason, practice email today, Friday, 10 AM.

2017

12/31/17 Try this Aldrich as narrator investigate the orcs, Bright Lighthouse, cash Dame Oops. They are hungry grad students. The other tales are investigated organs that Lighthouse uses to follow and understand the case.

12/30/17 Sat We are walking north on 26 Pl. @ 9 AM. 4 fighter jets in a loose wedge fly up 28th st. to Squaw Peak at 500 ft.

12/29/17 Today to fumigate bldg., ceiling tiles, prune trees away from bldg., go up and cover vents with screen, plumber comes for faucets leaks. Girls say they see sign of termites… didn't fumigate." Aey found duct off, we retaped, see if it that helps.
--Peaches. Behind a door three women, carnal thoughts never end…Bunuel's Simon of the Desert on his platform. Men are afflicted with sexual anima. Of the news financial and political, yahoo and drudge, thoughts of the heart. Gen. 6.5

12/27/17 Duties of the Heart 1. Divine Gates appears:
 "When you arrive at such a stage that you remove Him from your thoughts and senses (ie, give up the possibility of conceiving or imagining His essence) because he is not thus to be apprehended, and you realize Him in the evidences of His activities, as though He were inseparable from you, you will have reached that limit of the knowledge of Him which the prophet exhorts us to attain in the text (Deut 4.39 "Know this day, and lay it to thy heart, that the Lord, he is God in heaven above and upon the earth beneath; there is none else." The many instances of precog, serendip and synchronist evidence this.
--ordered Gates 9 and 10, Shaar Ha-Perishus - the Gate of Abstinence, Shaar Ahavas Ha-Shem - Gate of Love of G-d
"gates," correspond to the ten fundamental principles which, according to this view, constitute spiritual life. The essence of spirituality being the recognition of God as the one maker and designer of all things, Baḥya makes the "Sha'ar ha-Yiḥud" Gate of the Divine Unity, the first and foremost section.

12/26/17 For we are the temple of the living God; just as God said, "I WILL DWELL IN THEM AND WALK AMONG THEM; AND I WILL BE THEIR GOD, AND THEY SHALL BE MY PEOPLE. you are a temple
of God and that the Spirit of God dwells in you, the Lord, whom you seek, shall suddenly come to His temple, like a luminous touching another luminous directly above.
--Paracelsus who expressed the classic toxicology maxim "All things are poison and nothing is without poison; only the dose makes a thing not a poison." This is often condensed to: "The dose makes the poison" or in Latin "Sola dosis facit venenum".
--new year res: Aeg apprentices with aey on as many jobs as possible. I will support any ventures they launch together.

12/25/17 slabbing maple. $500 shed
--divine gate, pia undo, Gates of Hell, Gigantomachy in art, poetry and architecture: Dante and Gehry, Blake and Breughel, Solzhenitsyn and Rodin. art expresses the Destruction of the world -Golfyn Lightfeather

12/24/17 Gather at Aey, Pancake breakfast, sausage, kids presents, recipe book, Dolphy, paper, coffee, 3 hrs.

12/23/17 Kids, do aloe, rake leaves, Beethoven, cookies, the Boat, walk, fall down, fun.
--Where do the arrows come from? It was friends of qanon on twit. The white rabbit? [in 2025 we will have it: *Alice Under Wonderland,* but now]whether synthetic intuition, machine suggestion and implants, identity from a mind when stoned and its associations vs the thought stream as typically known.

12/22/17 Visit with Aey early, speak of milling on 1/13, trusting Aeg, gable for addition, he goes to Big Sur at 1st. No cashmere in all Macy's!
 -After tuneup when I turned to tweet, Qanon posts that Mike Pence a pedo, which is plausible if his best firend is Jeff Flake, but not if mass scale disinfo or if Qanon is strong AI as quinn michaels from his spontaneous collapse lung hospital bed says I searched it 2 days ago and it followed me on twitter today. Since blocked.
 -Jim Bowman likes to say he has "a passion for the creativity and ingenuity that glass art requires." His work ranges from small tabletop pieces to large-scale sculptures. He's a fixture in Dallas and has been for decades, but now, he and his wife, artist Mary Lynn Devereux-Bowman, are closing up and moving to North Carolina. They don't know exactly when, but their participation in last weekend's Cedars Open Studios was their last in the neighborhood where they have been mainstays since 2001. "We're kind of getting older," Jim says. "The universe is telling us it's time for a change. We love Dallas, and it's been good to us, but we're going to do something different."

---the skein of the worlds, the skin skein, the onion simultaneous all happening at the same time. Do they come many into one, one into many, expand and contract separately and together? At 17 I lay on a girl's lap and looked at the stars to bring them to the earth, this is that, the knowledge of the worlds, a kind of medieval quantum, all stories told with Breugel, Giotto, spiritual beings everywhere.

12/21/17 the microwaves re a different spectrum from the invisible. How do the long and short waves elf affect the all the other invisibles?

12/20/17 Seraphim Positive negatives are double, the positive is a negative, the negative inculcates the positive, criticizing a thing strengthens it to present a cross draft, turbulence, rip tide so that at the same time it presents criticism it affirms it! Predictive program leads to false flag.

At the time important enough to repeat the subject of two nights ago didn't translate, think it has to do with publishing the blogs? The hard bound copy price being 49.00 at Roswell. After this I thought the figures are seraphim. Way into the Flowering to be first? It seems tentative. Then I fount the first Dolphy. P to copy and laminate three copies. My present, three new breathing machines.

How I got to the flowering heart is you are born in it but then find it, so the linens retrieved from the attic as clear an image as needed, but has to felt in the life, in the psyche that triggered to completion. These become what they will, but the pic in the linens and frakturs makes the fact plain with alchemical texts or other mystical Boehme letters, neither here nor there to the fact of the experience, the air clogged with spiritual beings we don't see, so take it for granted that alchemical texts cannot produce such effects, rather defeat them, like the dark brow head shots of the patrons of the Weiser bookstore. Why do the rich and the royal families seek alchemy then, if it's only for profit? Because they have no other means. Seraphim swirling everywhere in invisible air pursue these sites a little and you see a lot of pedophilia along with S Weiser going around unhooded, heart receiving light waves, sun and moon, letters 8 and 11 of Boehme's, later published, Epistles, The 16 engravings showing how the heart is attacked. Paul Kaym had written to Boehme in 1620 asking him about the 'end of time', and was answered in letters 8 and 11 of Boehme's, later published. Kaym also wrote learned commentaries on the Song of Songs and the Book of Revelation:

And whenever the living creatures give glory, honor, and thanks to the One seated on the throne who lives forever and ever, 10the twenty-four elders fall down before the One seated on the throne, and they worship Him who lives forever and ever. They cast their crowns before the throne, saying:
11"You are worthy, our Lord and God, to receive glory and honor and power, for You created all things; by Your will they exist, and came to be."

12/19/17- Works that mirror interior states of personal or public being is the old way of assessing the value of art, not works that project attitudes that cooperate with social boosters and agencies of control.
--dreamed got flue shot in parking lot with p, lied about prev.

12/18/17 MON Portia spider, Darwin's barkbridge spider, netflex Wormwood, Frank Olson's defenestration out the window a scam for longer LSD drugging that one time, with revealed mk ultra details, plus his involvement with Harold Abramson.

    LSD-spiked Cointreau heroes never stop, Odysseus at home continues the fight. Achilles is too driven, has to die. I just had a heroic converse with Aeg over house and life and debt.

    Sat. chipped piece off of shelf. Don mildly says he will grind the rest! Is the piece that good?

    --Talking to P about all the overt acts, moving office, Aeg's car, B/C, selling house ourselves, and all the grace, the practice, Joggy and the chow-chows, and all the overt acts, Med school baby in middle, immediately after residency! on and on…

    --In the day before the flu, Fri. finished *Poet on the way out of sheol*, then as it were went there. I made no record of a previous Queen of …?

    --Today, Monday, The boy in the book.

    Realize I have been reading the book of my own life events too many to list. We all constantly read this book but don't allow it to awareness from embarrassment, guilt, shame, regret, but we do read. It is largely but not only a book of regret. It wasn't in a flash, but item by item from different segments. Most tawdry, head shakers, throwing the student out the room in CR, suggesting to Tyrone we go look at the prostitutes in the city square, prevented by heavy falling of volcanic ash. Other notables are not worth speech. It's all about memoy, which has its interpretations no doubt. The one shining moment is the experience of forgiveness of sins and the aftermath from that occasion about June 17, 1959 at 17. There is no book of love, but there is one of life to be read. But maybe that hereafter reading is for those blotted out. And I saw the dead, small and great, stand before God; and the books were opened: and another book was opened, which is the book of life: and the dead were judged out of those things which were written in the books, according to their works. (Rev. 20:12 for only the dead are judged by what is written for the Life of the Lamb covers all the rest.

    --this is the character of superposition: NEWK Ba(r)ker, named for a giant chain saw caught in a huge split stump and trunk, coming up thru it, contained in an iron ore rail way car with a plaque of WWII.

12/17/17 Sunday. Do you want to go to the cliff of spiritual being? Preface to superposition.
--What am I, super ego against other? A house where you put them in danger, a house that has hit rock bottom in '93, and '10. the only thing worse than being involved in the history of families is not being. From Abraham's family on.

12/15/17 Been listening to Harold Bloom in place of the news which revives the mighty past at Iowa where in the Donald Justice workshop accompanied by James Tate and Gary [R.] Sange, who I remember. Tate died with his encephalic forehead at 71, and Sange went to Virginia where he was recorded saying the following, which I preface by saying that here's why we had to eat Whitman, for all his precursor succedents in time, which could be the Song of Charlie Rose. In cleaning up, looking for Barthes Angel, found the April disrupt FB '14, all the upset from that, extreme,

Today begins 3rd day of media fast. Listening to Bloom etc, heard Whitman's voice! Illiad Old and New testaments most formative of 3000 yrs, reminded of Crane, Song of Myself,, supreme Shakespeare. Maybe I never found the incantation of poetry because it seems a state I have in perpetuity anyway, dwelled in, pastured in, swum, the daily, not the provoked state by means of helps that forms a religion of the self illumination and participation in the cosmos

12/14/17 jay wright dogon mythology the illuminist purpose of Peterson's fame and his talk of biblical subjects is to prevent his readers, who might seek the truth to stop with an ersatz substitute so they never attain spirit and in truth.
-- the fame of Lewis and Tolk, with the fame of High and Peterson questions their integrity, suggests their use to the world order.

12/13/17 Portland cement red sand draped pots, the story of Alice Cooper & Jordan Peterson, Alice Cooper got his identity from wiji board, id fantasy, Hesse closet with 10K personalities, rock publicist Harold Bloom called it a soul exchange with audience. On stage the self leaves, "becomes puppet of one of the gods within", clear description of an alter, so add Alice Cooper to Dave McCowen's collection of rock alters, not altars. Frank Zappa, Stephen Stills, Jim Morrison, David Crosby, and many. That Peterson does not notice or overlook this makes him a cover for it. Consider that so many of these stars, like Jim Morrison, had fathers in military, aerospace execs, Alice Cooper son of aerospace engineer in Az, sounds like mk ultra, "if you deserve to be a superstar you own your life." This is the wager at the crossroads as Jordan Peterson white washes SRC abuse by asking, Do these sick, sadistic, pedophiles exist?
-beta male wanted to seem harmful, shadow, needs radical honesty at offences.
    --didnt follow up much on the notion that Lord of the Rings and Narnia are illuminist, but the fame and success suggests that in the end, as does Lewis' affair with his housekeeper.
    --Calendar.After trying three scenarios of the year, the Roman, the Celtic and the Hebrew. Jan, March, September, I cannot avoid the Roman, so that Jan 1 marks a reprieve or understanding of the year of growth preceding from the previous spring. It is a reflection and harvest of the growth in intellectual, psychological philosophical ways, for the ideas and experiences of the prior year were not understood until Jan to March., the time we plant potatoes here. This is the way I approach the cycle of time and call it a year. 2017 is yet to be understood. Then print out these ideas, experiences, reflections, all the writing, but not the ceramic forms/formless, which have different themes, one somehow of the four figures I still don't put to verbal expression.

12/12/17 Tranny hands, tranny hips, tranny hearts, Adams apples, back of head, lips and hair explains a lot about Pop, the women as men dressed perfected with implant breasts and hair and face and estrogen enhanced skin but can't change the skelton, the shoulders, hips, back, or the digits of the ring finger longer than the index.
    -Angelo Pitoni lapis lazuli, oxygen stone, emerald mines occurred after searchs for Verde Valley Real estate.

Jordan Peterson to be an alpha be a hero, jung imagination. Traits of Alpha Males sent to Aeg-Don't listen to the words. Hear the tones.

-Patsy came out on our walk this morn. She is moving to Winslow with her sister. Another sister, Grace will live in the back, another, Barbara, maybe in front. Chris, best friend of brother in law in side.

> AE dressed as a big green book, a box with a hole cut for eyes. I do not read what is on the spine, it is a surprise.

-Aey insistence in clearing drains himself before the party made me think of Emersons, Self Reliance, the ed by Roycroft.

12/11/17 Mon. Went to pick up of log with Aey, gave $100 to transport it. Exhausting. One of the guys near hit by slipped calipher. Talked to George, aerospeace, power plant exec. designed for the moon, he has his six year deceased wife on the mantle in a vase. Later went to consider the beams to be cut, redesign of room and attic, new roof line and balcony.
-manmante herb in water.
-Need to build berm on west side of house,
- still don't know the heavenly corruption. I was trying to open a bottle of this water in a back room with a sink when two barebreasted women came in, then they were two women dressing for a wedding in white gowns. I excused myself.

12/10/17 Sun. Acromegaly and the giant of Khanddhar
-ordered Active H2 Purative
Hawthorne-Cognitive testing resulted in the development of an instrument to measure eating competence in low-income adults," wrote J.S. Krall
Poe on Hawthorn's *Mosses From a Manse:* "Let him mend his pen, get a bottle of visible ink, come out from the Old Manse, cut Mr. Alcott, hang (if possible) the editor of 'The Dial,' and throw out of the window to the pigs all his odd numbers of the North American Review.[5
--Of the darkness of the Mosses allegory Hawthorne says, "I am not quite sure that I entirely comprehend my own meaning in some of these blasted allegories... I am a good deal changed since those times; and to tell you the truth, my past self is not very much to my taste, as I see in this book"
-Melville says, "This black conceit pervades him through and through. You may be witched by his sunlight,— transported by the bright gildings in the skies he builds over you; but there is the blackness of darkness beyond; and even his bright gildings but fringe and play upon the edges of thunder-clouds" -- Dreamed of Utopia (Tx) bond issue permutations and tales.

--the best of yesterday was Aey's new log and talking to George about the layer of caliche that prevented deep root growth of the Aleppo that allowed the wind from the east to blow down this full grown tree. Then the sawing of the rest into rounds with his daughter saying she was going to replant.   Real people as opposed to walking through the Phx Cent art sale and all the sleep walkers, like the crowd last weekend at Story sale. All churning ambling ghosting aimless these dreams and reality and a mirror of counter news cycles with change lies a minute give the same impression.

--But wasn't there talk of the farm land on Pinchot in the 50s, which reminds of the diaries extant about those events then. Pinchot Diaries.

--Aey and I also spoke of new techniques of rendering pieces in photograph professionally.

-This swirling details the pyramid scheme of art and life where those with talent who emerge from the pop pool are subverted and blackmailed, groomed to foster the greater ends of the governors who rule. Franz Kline gets the grants, fellowships. Like they say on faceb and twit, you can buy more followers for your stats!

12/7/17 Aey and Sh had a party for 100 people, we kept Judah.
- Patty Greer Sarah Westall hydrogen bar, active H,
--Neighborhood flood meeting. Paul Manley Kelly Horn: Kelly Horn is the Head of School of Create Academy in the Old Boys and Girls club, which when under at Covid and vacated, was at Rio Grande School, an independent day school in Santa Fe serving 160 students age 3 through grade 6. Before moving to
Santa Fe, Kelly was the Headmaster at Rohan Woods School in St. Louis, Missouri for eight years. Prior to his tenure at Rohan Woods, he was the Upper School Director at Rossman School for four years, also in St. Louis.
His career in education began a French and Latin instructor. Kelly holds a Masters of Arts in Education, a Bachelors of Science in Economics, and a Bachelors of Arts in French from Truman State University. He also completed a post-graduate fellowship at Columbia University in New York where his studies focused on the development of student leadership skills and programs for young learners. Kelly has been married to his wife, Patty, for 17 years and they have two sons, Jack (12) and John (10). here Create Academy. Headmaster Rohan Woods, 6,314 for charters az.

-- I went to the ghettos surrounding the Motorola plant on McDowell before redevelop. Don't these same cities harbor cell 3 and 4 G cell towers as dangerous above as the toxis TCE beneath? Our nearest one at the site of Kennedy School!! And that's nothing to the 5 G boosters coming to every 10th house on every street! Isn't Phoenix an early innovating city for 5G? Forget about it, the floods are coming. Only a metaphor. So we can't see the Superfund under us. And we won't see 5G over us. Where Nano antenna?

12/5/17 Joggy post to Aey faith: AEY responded: I think about it now. I was just a kid grabbing the chain of a dog passing by, a risky move on my part. I just wanted a dog and I saw one and he was mine. It's really amazing to see the divine at work. in the moment it's all too muddy and close only with time and perspective does even the slightest intention begin to show. I guess that's why faith is so important.. can't see it in the moment..
…hope you don't mind though if to me the child was all along crystalline with that intent, pure as water and shining like the sun, a pure joy to behold.

--'the things that we do between takes", is Dustin Hoffman's excuse. 5.12 John Oliver of Dustin Hoffmann --Mark Twain, Innocents Abroad/   BOYS IN A FURNACE

12/3/17 Sunday. Aeg over to announce the baby under cover of helping Aey with the party bursts into tears and hugs Aey when he says he just threw away the ultrasounds! Provocateur, said he had married a woman just like his father!
Story sale. Rakatekt Tressel Holloway geo polymer, egyptian sumer carvings soft when carved. Pyramids , agglomerated limestone concrete. GFRC glass fiber reinforced concrete, Buddy Rhodes,

 --Tressel's son three months named Azreal which he said meant Help of God. Similar to the biblical scapegoat, Azazel, but not the same. One of the fallen angels in Enoch, "one of the leaders of the rebellious Watchers in the time preceding the Flood; he taught men the art of warfare, of making swords, knives, shields, and coats of mail, and women the art of deception by ornamenting the body, dyeing the hair, and painting the face and the eyebrows, and also revealed to the people the secrets of witchcraft and corrupted their manners, leading them into wickedness and impurity." It has a double edge in nonbiblical recognizance as a guide through death. Substitute for Messiah. I had a peek at his eyes as he nursed and his mother, standing, just pulled back the cover a little.

 --The rule is, wait for the time to present itself. Seeking to bless, properly respond to pregnancy and to encourage by the gift of the rocker, to occur Thurs or Fri, neither did, but sent a note to Sab of her baby. Sh came Sat nite. In giving the rocker P said she had nursed all three of our children in it. Exactly the purpose of giving it. te damos gracias Te damos gracias, Señor, de todo corazón. Te damos gracias, Señor, cantamos para Ti.

12/2/17 Sat
Stepforded, celebrities go blonde to prove recondition
CELL PHONE TOWERS - DANGER EXPOSED BY WHISTLEBLOWER 23f, GWEN transmitters, false EM field, false magnetic floor, 8 kh heartbeat fq as brain, disconnect intuition and abilities, 300 ft, split the double helix of DNA, tera hz, tintinitis, headaches nausa fatique, GWEN trans control mind behavior, mood control, synthetic telepathy, intersound, harp woodpecker
-Geordie Rose tsunami of demons

11/30/17 This Guy sold his gas pump for 20 mil. I was driving emerald green Buick convert, ca. 1950. While getting gas a slightly demented fellow warned, look out for snakes, but I couldn't see any. I got A & A to see where the gas pump had been (there was still one left). P had been given a car and was up on a ridge. I called her to meet up.
--Yesterday: after a long time she said "thank you" sincerely.
-Aey brought 2 framed pieces. Got battery for truck. Later Alfred, Matt, Chris left publicity for meeting about flood next Wed.

11/29/17

In data from the 2001 Mars Odyssey orbiter, which carried a gamma ray spectrometer, Brandenburg observed a local concentration of radioactive uranium, thorium and potassium in two specific areas on Mars. the elevated ratio of 129Xenon to 132Xenon in the atmosphere explained as the after signature of a nuclear weapon. Massive explosions occurred in in Mare Acidalium at approximately 50°N 30° W, near Cydonia Mensa and in Utopia Planum at approximately 50°N 120°W near Galaxias Chaos, claims they are both locations of possible archaeological artifacts

--The Song of the Owl is the real title of WHO!

-- How many con man renegade charismatic apostolic pastors live in the Phoenix? At the opening of the World Church Wheat and Tare girls beating their hands like butterflies smiling at us, the further in the more evil/good appears like Sister Theresa in her last half hour money machine for the Vatican. If fictions eschew the evil/good horrific, they could get in trouble like medievalist John Gardener, *Moral Fiction* (1978). If you have a peculiar regard of enthusiast religion, genuine transcendence and where it leads in the world, you are going to see. The enemy sows the tares.

11/28/17 Tues. Sunday did card, Christmas Tree, Christmas Tree. Today put lights on tree outside.

- "Jacob have I loved but Esau I have hated" written from beneath, not above, shows how Jacob cheated E and feared him before their reunion. But Jacob sought in a prayer that E would not kill him and prevent the promise.

11/27/17 Hillsong and its ilk Welcome the church of the wheat and the tares. "You can start harvesting as soon as the wheat seeds pass the milk stage, although the grains will need to dry up and harden a bit before they're ready to eat." At first, the wheat seeds will exude a milky substance just like sweet corn does when it's ripe, but then the punctured seeds will stop oozing (although they will still dent under your thumbnail.)

11/25/17 it's all a racket of the Rectiles too damn Telekamp and Carroll Wilson Telkamp donating his mint restored 54 Chevy to the church at the same fundraiser where the guy gave his talking book rights worth 100 k. David Heckathorne another conspirator, named in the payoffs.

11/24/17 Jacob and angel of Esau, Abel and Cain, the two Enochs. Perez and Zerah – Judah's daughter-in-law, Tamar widowed did not want to be childless. Wrapping her face in a veil and disguising herself as a prostitute, she intercepted Judah on the road and he slept with her. The result was Perez and Zerah (Genesis 38:12-30). From Perez would come the family of David (Ruth 4:18-22). Ephraim and Manasseh: The text does not directly state that the two sons of Joseph and Asenath were twins, and there is reason to believe they were. First, Genesis mentions they were both born "before the year of famine came" (Genesis 41:50). Second, two conceptions are not mentioned in the text. Third, if they are twins they fit nicely into the pattern seen in the lives of Isaac and Judah: both their younger twins inherited the birthright, just as the younger Ephraim was blessed first by Jacob (*Genesis* 48:19). Jacob promised that both Ephraim and Manasseh would become patriarchs of a multitude, which began a traditional blessing said in Israel: "God make you as Ephraim and as Manasseh" (*Genesis 48:20*).

11/23/17 evil in Young Goodman Brown satirical or real? The evil in the good. The preaching of strife in Paul. Salvation even in the midst.
-Quinn Michaels: element 93 neptunium, made from spent nuke rods for levitation, future highly conductive, sensors, UG, 93 society to fuel their secret technology! Fermi labs early adopter, most valuable transmutational element, lead into gold on nuke level, complex nuclear magnetic hype-reconductor, super conductive metallic alloy.

11/22/17 We are so utterly caught in web but at the same time it is also somehow wound around us too it becomes synchronist to realize it is both our own choosing and something more. So if you have a peculiar history in some regard, say enthusiasm stemming from genuine experience of transcendence, and you start to seek where it leads in the world then you are going to come up against the more beautiful counterfeits that also somehow do you good. Like chaff.
 Chasmotics
 -- En media res the Eagles Nest Christian Embassy said of itself after those horrific scams on N Hayden Rd that it was going to reinvent. Who after all wants to be associated with affinity fraud, bond scams, empire real estate deals and vague mob connections? So on 12/5/98 or thereabouts it announced a new name, a new building, a new location a new beginning after Isa 43.19 "Behold I will do a new thing!" The equivocation of Isaiah being, "God has miraculously given us a new building" announces Dr. Maiden senior pastor, who took a doc in psych online, who had derided psych all the years before, but got this to salve his at being caught in the many scandals. This new beginning called the North Church after a church in Dallas the illuminsts used to pick him up, because as it was proven later, he was building empire though sowing and reaping repeated itself in the new building, Frank Luca being replaced by Hits Galore, into whose HQ the church moved. c/o Jeanette B. Wilcher Life Foundation trust, however "found guilty of wire fraud and six counts of money laundering" 16 Apr 2006. Hits Galore HITT. All these people are and were well loved, personable as any Rose and as honest, respected as Dustin Hoffman.
 But Walking up the sidewalk with all the other parishoners at Hillsong Phoenix, past the girls welcoming us with beating hands like butterflies was nice. They smiled at those ahead and behind. I was that out of the demographic, a war baby, born before, among three during and one after the war, to remember the imagined strafing, the bombs, but inside don't feel severe at all, but full of laughter.
Even with all the controlling liberating prosperity, an informant who was in the heart of the beast and then removed I took to dinner with his wife, beginning a long series of visits and conversations. He had high govt contacts, also had been asked by Ford in that day to serve in a presidential cabinet, but turned it down. His accounts jibed with what I could see. This "church" occupied the ground floor of an office bldg in Scottsdale near the airport but the second story was occupied by the offices of Frank Luka Associates. I went up there once with

the informant and saw his pictures with all the presidents on the walls, but the symbol of office over the church, being its heaven above, came into reality with atales of shopping bags of cash, breakins apprehended by police but bought off with influence, the prophet Miller and the youth pastor proving loyalty. This was the church of Meadowlark Lemon, Hits Galore, Frank Luka, served by John Avanzini who had the gift of getting money, checks addressed to HIM, mob bosses, musicians of Jesus Christ superstar, 300 investors out of $11.4 million a la the *Tuscon Citizen*, 6 Jan 1998. "Elaine Averill, a Wisconsin woman, lost $1 million in Luca's scheme after she was referred to him by Glenn Miller, [prophet Bill Hamon's son in law] a self-proclaimed traveling pastor specializing in "biblical economics" who knew Luca through the Eagle's Nest." "We learned the good lesson not to trust easily," said Averill. "He took the true word of God and twisted it." It's a little like the Clintons who criticize and you die. Jerry Jones was the long time assistant pastor who always introduced the service with how beautiful the pastor's wife was. He did the baptisms and marriages too, but one day into the Luca fraud he made a query about the accounts and the books, and the next thing he knew he was out with his wife. He died a couple years later in Colorado at altitude, not having his asthma inhaler. Typical preaching of that era, *touch not the Lord's anointed,* was the subject of the Pastor's Randy White, brother in law, as well as the Prophet Miller at the men's retreat. All who did died. The Head usher's son died, the cop that hit the pastor with his billy club, Chuck Blogettt. 'Jerry Jones book was building marriages for life." Meadowlark lemon had men come forward to receive his athletic anointing.

11/21/17 Dada Radioactive clouds from Russia, Ruthenium 106, jet stream lands in Cen Tex. Heard from Karl Hillie and Mark Leon who has glioblastoma, McCain's disease, practically in the same day.
-All the revelation accusations meant to cover up Singularity, blockchain, robot citizens bitcoin mining las vegus, launch of strong AI says Quinn Michaels, who lives in a car. Laura Loomer, Quinn Michaels, Jason Goodman Vegas strong AI learns from block chain. Las Vegas shooting a beta test launch of strong AI to reduce from chaos set to singular data.

11/19/17 Sunday.
    Dream: Desani sang with one arm around Beth, more or less in her ear, but sang the wrong words in the choruses in a tenor sometimes on key. That was the way they sang the hymns there. In addition to the wrong words he was vain enough to hope that if this was a prophetic place where they would call him out for what he was, or what he thought he was, well, not thought, fantasized, you know of his greatness, but of course this could not happen, not because he was or was not great, both equally true, but because if it were prophetic it would be of itself, of its own social order and his ability was to benefit that, not himself. Maybe he was a potential elder of infamy, or maybe he was a rich-o to give the six figure. That my friends gets an invite from the YOUKNOWWHO. But since he wasn't he don't, which came in the spell when the third hit on his lobe made all the motives and beings of men so open and plain.
    He could have read Romans and found out the same, but who would believe this body of sin and death. Yes this a guy to go to church, or visit.

--Only to those immersed in the web, seduced from their identity, is any of this believable. The believers outnumber the observer, they are willing to compromise every sense impression out of a desire to do good, whatever good is to countenance embezzlement, abuse , exploitation, profit taking. And the irony is it does them some good. Who knows what doubts and faith the soul must redeem, what reparation?

--Welcome. You live in the middle of the greatest ersatz civilization you can imagine. We went to Hillsong Phoenix because I saw it on return from reconnoiter at Grant St Studios. Identified most with the 2 Az rangers in uniform outside with guns. They had a nice smoke machine and stars on the wallpaper on the side, not leftover from the First Presbyterian Church that there used to be. It had a closed, confined entrance to the sanctuary symbolic of that era, not useful for emergency evac. What do the stars mean? Prison tattoos? Recognition to those who know, who will know, along with other signs, Fiji water on the pulpit, not drunk from. All the ushers beat staccato with their hands. The service is choreographed, programmed. When the video sermon calls for response three times the praise time on the right front seated together give it, but it is not live, it is in the program because they have rehearsed, seen the response points before. No spontaneous. Walking to the service on the streets, greeters begin to enthuse the crowd from the sidewalks. This work for the audience was overwhelmingly millennial, but that they are in church is amazing in itself. There is a container of water in the lobby with plastic glasses. It has a slight sweet taste to it. Just to be on guard.

--Hillsong is the closest America can come to revival, little beating butterflie not as canned as the Fiji water on the podium throughout the sermon, never used however, just sits there, as a symbol. The leader one is leaning beyond the Millennial demographic but to remedy had a face lift and looks chiseled good, also slender. Of the principals, the sermon on the Lord's prayer is remembered for his promising to give his grandson all the sugar in the house, and to take him to Toys or Us to fill the cart with goods, thrice. Oh what.

President T opened Fiji and the news said he had small hands but it was symbol of the roll up indictments of the DNC, Fiji Fiji being a player, says Liz Cronkin. "When they pastored in Tulsa. They would have everyone throw up into bags to get rid of bad spirits, attitudes or something bad." This is straight from Carol and John Arnott Toronto Blessing playbook and is a more extreme Pentecostalism (the vomiters bray like donkeys, dance like chickens, claim gold particles have infiltrated their bodies, build fire tunnels and promote violent seizures and uncontrollable fits of maniacal laughter.)" --disqus Monatomic. So it implicates Marc Driscoll being groomed for Phx status so …can go national? Randy Wolf runs Mesa HillSong.

11/18/17 Blockchain AI consciousness chat room about cyber flicks lead to memory source, stored storing source, all memory present but not Michael Quinn speaking of his own algo in an external sense of data, not internal of the whole.

11/17/17 What's sexier than a forms of a girl and every pot in the world? A hillside. What if the inside of a woman was as beautiful as the outside? And a man!
--Jack Cashill the Sentinel, Ron Brown.

--Went to Grant St lecture series, Heather Brown. After composing, wet clay still in the car, I wound around the boxes, cubicles until, it had already started, sat down. Animosity in the air, proud embellished. Left before the end, little rich girl with endowments who came down from her parent's cabin to the fishermen, their nets, boats, and regional botanists to transact them into art. Meingless aftertaste nihilism of art.

11/16/17 How Peter Thiel's Secretive Data Company Pushed Into Policing Alex Karp.
--What's intimidating about such events as the Gustin talk is the weight of his social presence filling the room with approval and adulation and acceptance. That's why he began wood kiln to develop this network. I say conceptually it is the greatest proglum of overcome success, which he says began at the kiln in Ala. at a kiln that was flooded underwater 10 yrs and became a tantamount salt kiln which changed his expectations.

She compared the Gustin affair to the Reformed church at my bidding. when we left. Do not tarnish the icons, but the icons smashed path will be filled with pitfalls and disdain at best. But at the pass through the CRC, before the talk, she saw a pot, and did a take on it later.

--So just as Tues I called Robert and got no response but this AM asked about it and the jphone rang two min later, so this AM desperate call from office that elec was out and needed ice to freeze vaccines. Power went out last night 8.38 PM just minutes after the sarcasm, which was enough in this scenario to blow the office meter. Wed. phones went out, today the meter. Is it a message? After returning the vaccines I went down to the Bentley to see the Gustin and to scout the Grant St Studios for the lecture tonight, after composing at the Center.

11/15/17 the orc is the first cloned being --this is the day Zion was to have had puppies!

11/14/17 Full text of Clarke family
--We have extensive data for the Carlson family back to 1685 in Sweden, in Swedish, but the names are bolded and the dates are numerical. Likewise we have even more if possible of the Clark family back to the first days of Amasa Clark in Texas, beginning from John Clark of Stepney England who died in 1623 in Jamestown Va. So that would be through Momo to Grandmother Ruth, replete with interesting names. These fulsome documents are due to Amasa Clark being a person of note therefore such data occurs, because professionally worked and Carl Roland Carlson, son of Carl Ossian Carlson, because of the absolutely stellar work of Sigurd. Obviously there are names within the names of other lines as well. These you and Sabrina may visit for an hour and view here.

11/13/17http://thelatterdays.blogspot.com/2009/03/worship-of-baal-peor.html

11/12/17 Sunday B/C meet this AM, then A works on wall, alk. Slack and Giddup

11 Nov 17 To Red Fez on pseudonym. Thanks for the heads up.

Some fuller response to yours. I do know in a literary sense the name Rubino and referenced him in writing years ago as a friend of Borges who I encountered on an airport bench in Panama City one desperate night, and signed his name to a fictional letter about Borges that appeared in elimae, Giambattista Marino Rubino del Sur. I regret he causes you difficulty however. I said to him after and generally hold that anything I write digitally is anonymous upon claim after my genealogy research began to appear on public forums without attribution. The first time I replied suggesting language of attribution be added, but ongoing I see many permutations, piracies and transmutations that I take it a kind of perverse favor if it gives life to the thought which is more and more lost in the algorithms. Any way to beat the censorship of algorithm is desired, since those blog entries get almost no readers on their own. My solution has been to strike backups on the Wayback machine, but I didn't always remember, and many of the internet mags I used to know are now websites in China, like Jack even, which I thought was backed up at Stanford, so many, even elimae. Red Fez stands out among these for its integrity, further proven by your notice of this apparent perjury.

The many entries at Google Blogger were a further attempt to save the writing, whether copied or pirated. I experience an increasing censorship however, some of which may be associated with my writing name. This happened recently at Unlikely Stories but not too far under the surface elsewhere. This makes me want to see if the thought divorced from the name would get better algorithms in search and editorial bias if pseudonymous. The name brand did not help Melt, but I admit that it is written under the presumption that it will be good in a hundred years, so the first year is of little consequence. You do have in your pile for next month an article to test this premise, The Enthronement of ISIS, that is, if gets approval. So if it does appear let it be under the listed name of Augusto Todoele.

I don't think of anything as established, rather the opposite, and at great cost, so I am always looking to find out the topography of fiction and anti fiction, in writing and in clay, however haphazardly, which in this case explores who is who and what is what in action, to negotiate the ravages of that internal world. There seem to be few friends in lit to the subjects I pursue, fewer every day, You however have been one of those I guess so let me broach another subject of interest.

Sigersonbks is your address and I remember from the bios you collect modern firsts, something I pursued at the end of the 20th century by accident and desultorily after. May I ask what your interests are in this field, favorite authors, high spots? I got a Yeats, Wild Swans Ist Amer in dj, immaculate first, after my son disqualified for a supernational tennis tournament in Alabama which would have cost about $2000. Those tournaments are hard to qualify for, but I traded his ticket from Merz in Pa for the book. I used to visit Jaffe when he was in Haverford, since I went back there for my genealogy work. I hold Yeats last poems the best for their taut brightness. Brautigan as a target too, and Hillerman, but many of best things were accidents since in the southwest, Navajo works are much sought. Coincident with camping the Mogollon, White Mts and trading posts on the Rez we encountered and visited with Hopi and Navajo. The Shoshoneans by Edward Dorn came from this and The Wishing Bone Cycle by Howard Norman. I also have followed the Frankfort writings, not just Walter but Marc-Alain Ouaknin, The Burnt Book and Michael Lowy Redemption and Utopia. I'd love to get an article to you on the Angelus Novus of this world, but it has resisted me its many drafts. Yours truly, AE

--and that is just opposite of the need, which grows greater every day, to grapple with these exigencies, fairy tales. So that I have too many samples of editorial irrationality two issues of fairy tales, one eludes, but the why parades like the piece which was left over from last weeks demo of it, remixed in three works, laid flat with roller, porcelain, paper and red mixed, but for some reason of structure the side being worked was flipped and became the reverse. The new side immediately presented a map of the U.S. , which in essence was taken as is, but later next day was waved, literally taken up like a pizza crust and waved, except that made the middle flat, which wanted to be mountainous, so this was done another time, New Madrid fault, Yellowstone, Calif coast, Pacific tidal event, tsunami of NYC, loss of seaboards spectacle. I never made something that made me sad before, but here it was, except that after all the waves were in I saw it was a great ox, or cow, or beast coast to coast, Maine the tail, Florida the back foot, Baja the front and the NW the head, which made Leviticus for its saying the land is cursed by the habits of the inhabitants. I asked her what it was and she called it America, which made me sadder even. Oh my America, but the Witnesses say America is the beast and the whore rides the beast. O Galatians who hath bewitched you? And my synchronist what do you make of it that within hours of all this happening we got a double flood for the first time ever. It came at 1 PM and again at 4, then it shut off for an hour and the water soaked in, then it came again full force and we got another. Double portion, double drinking we do.

9 Nov 17 If classic fairy tales intend to show the child in images, the adjustments a child boy and girl must make to be adult, picture the sexual social dramas they transverse, there is next to no account of the successful landing of the child in adulthood marriage, just their corruption, which fairy tales are teaching, no man and woman together and the joys they know that repay all the pain they suffer to get there. Maybe it is impossible to say. But beyond that there are infinite accounts of the adult's approach to God, or gods as they become, written down, whittled down. For if sex is cognitive to a man, the knowledge of the spirit is his whole calling, all he thinks about, unless perverted to getting and spending.

Proverbs 16.1 is challenged by the thought fixers of the lower order. The preparation of the heart in man and the answer of the tongue is from Yahweh, can not be left to stand but must be cut down to size. So the KJV heart that produces the speech, out of the abundance of the heart the mouth speaks, must reduced to the NIV -To humans belong the plans of the heart, but from the LORD comes the proper answer of the tongue. With the explanation that "one sentence of this verse without any contrast or antithesis. This is plainly wrong, there being intended a contrast between the thought of the heart and the well ordered speech." Pulpit Commentary. The argument is that "the thoughts of the heart, which are generally irregular and confused" that the thoughts of men's hearts are evil, and that continually, and nothing but evil thoughts naturally proceed from thence" we cannot think a good thought of ourselves," Gill's Exposition, but that is the point of the one sentence, that both the preparations of the heart and the answer of the tongue are from Yahweh. The Reformed theologians cannot allow their doctrine of depravity to be compromised, but they are always enforcing their own. We may want to distinguish thoughts of the bowels, the gut brain, of the heart, the imagination and of the head, the brain proper on the way to speech, writing. Preparations of the heart allude to prethought, precognitive elements that form thought, not imagination either, but pre imagination—not cognitive, which smacks of faith, for who can know the mind of Yahweh or how events order in the world? However to proceed by acknowledging that the preparations of the heart that lead to the speech are ordered of Grace…

8 Nov 17 wuldor-cyning [King of Glory]

7 Nov 17 cornet electro smog meter
"Kroll, is one of the world's largest corporate-intelligence companies, and Black Cube, an enterprise run largely by former officers of Mossad and other Israeli intelligence agencies" Ronan Farrow.

6 Nov 17 Tom Delonge, Clif High, schizo-typical, Sapolsky religiosity in humans, from which high's belief derived Coastal war on Texas. Patties within,

5 Nov 17 Church shooting: giants Cain Grendel-defense against faergrygrum (attacks of terror) with faergrygrum

4 Nov 17 Las Vegas witness elimination program Carver thermite grenade explosion. "heat launch signature" --I create synchronicity

11/3/17
--Spiritual reality to physical objects, light, name reflects nature, shem,
--On the way home from a mistaken attempt to repair this lady's sprinkler, made right by a scientist who fixed it, whose costs were $20, I paid him a $100 and got 50 back. I first gave him a Czech bank note as a joke and the lady said she was well known for her world travels. Departing however these circumstances, with the sprinkler system on top my car, I took a circuitous way home past another real old lady washing her car right in the middle of the road while her three walruses played around. I weaved in and out the walruses and awoke.

11/2/17 Plant potatoes. gave P a hat and pin for her 66th. The saleslady came from behind the counter, reached up on a shelf and adjusted the hat. --Then I saw it. It had to pointed out by grace! Babysit kids.

11/1/17 Friday, November 3, from 9:00 am to 7:00 pm&
Sat., November 4, from 9:00 am to 12:00 pm

10/31/17 GoldyPop Susylocks bovalatry. -Crust white shino ashed over subcoat.

10/30/17 7 Hairy longneck light ups --steps of Jewish wedding, seven days of creation. baby #4? Each begin and end with same word

10/29/17 awoke to making all the stories named for classic fairy tales etc

10/28/17 Hypogeum, underground. --Proof of Plenty Goose, entry.

10/27/17 visit the cognition.
Said, he needed counsel, was going to have a baby, needed to talk to the baby, and that this was a real baby that was going to come full term and be born and his wife and he were about to have changed lives. Also that he needed to go to a church to sing hymns! He emailed an hour later:
"Thank you. It's been as if this is a secret hope, my child. Your enthusiasm really helped me.

10/26/17 Ivan Belyaev. "I think the search for a style of work is, in fact, a set of expressive techniques for a lot of people. And for me too... you must have noticed that I work angobami (paint based on clay with an addition of pigment, engobe, which after of is also is) some time ago I chose this material and I realize I wasn't wrong. Then to me was an example of lee kang hyo's work, my favorite artist, master of South Korea (make sure to find) and later I realized that the roots of my drive to the invoice, which allows the work of angobami much older... but learn more about it I'll tell you later. Well, the recovery from (in the bezkislorodnoj environment is the restoration of iron, which is contained in clay and glazurâh), which I have answered already on a huge number of questions, but they do not end.. If there is more. In the photo, the subject is executed using both techniques:
-Pic of fetus 8 wks calls it gummy bear. tell him all life is sacred and he needs to revere. He says it's his and he can say what he wants! I say now around me you won't' This is like two wks ago when he went on a riff about invitrio fert, again as if it was his doing. He hasn't told Aeg nor has Aeg told him. Even though they had lunch today!

10/25/17 new A/C ted malloch, --install Grander Water

10/24/17 washer repair

10/22/17 Sunday: Aegcomes to dig the wall for three hours. the secret life of geese

10/21/17 a volunteer pole cleaner

10/20/17 Norman Morrison (December 29, 1933 – November 2, 1965) was a Baltimore Raven best known for his act of self-immolation at age 31 in front of fans in the stadium.

10/19/17 Carbon60Oliveoil.com 10-100ml bottles- Live Longer Labs--in this one the oil is noticeably light Carbon 60 llc, no toxic solvents, sunflower oil
BuckyLabs C60 purple power, the first, end of aug. This guru is Ken. Purple Power Scam.

10/18/17 c60 Dr. Phil Catalano and Dr. Max Champie claim they are the only scientist-makers, interest in consciousness…catalano, boulder, ancient wisdom… magnetic deficiency syndrome
Changing gorgon to Gordon bypasses the conscious affront, cannibal also elided, so that the story goes right down into Oh Dear.

10/17/17 under the carpet new Zealand hidden history docu --1421 Chinese discover --pops Heladeria, Barbie Pink Pop, once the cap pops up the contents are ready to be consumed. Guapa in Brussels, playful, devious and cleverly named creatures, Baseman, Yoshitomo Nara, Takashi Murakami, The Octopus Eats Its Own Leg, and the illustrator William Joyce, Tim Biskup, marion Peck, Jeff Soto, Pervasive art: Cult-status street artists like Banksy, new wave comics illustrators like (here) Gary Panter, (dante, Japanese pop artists, post-punk and hip hop artists, and iconic graphic artists like Shepard Fairey all contribute to a highly visible aesthetic that is virtually ubiquitous in contemporary culture.

10/16/17 what you need to know about fermilad and the antimatter agenda Woodward TV — what you need to know about hydrogen peroxide
--while walking in the vales of arcady this morn I say three kids all about 1-2, the first a boy with a square face who looked steadfastly at me, a girl with a narrower face and a boy again with a narrower face, each gave long gazes.
-- I have a lot more peace and satisfaction in my work at 3 AM in the morning than in the networks throughout the day. The secret of consciousness is to tell someone, who you implicitly trust, the thought and feeling, then you hear your voice and you know it yourself and it becomes conscious. --howard garnett the dirt doctor, expose root flares

10/15/17 they seem more interested in gaining social credit as an advance on the births than on the births themselves, announce at 6 wks, to get texts and affirmations of congrats, as if they were important. After work stops to say he can now tell, since shehas told her mother. Then he wants to seemingly boast of his faith for this conception for these years, he goes on, references invitro fert, stop him. I don't want to know, only want to (guard the birth) practical things, walk her, encourage her, etc.

10/14/17 Tourmaline attract and then repel hot ashes due to its pyroelectric properties-- https://en.wikipedia.org/wiki/Pyroelectricity
--Had the kids last night for parents 5th. AB combative. I told her two times ago about the puppies said it was a secret. She has not told. And told her about the baby, that it was a secret, she has not told. Need to teach her that adult secrets can be told, to protect her from predators.

10/13/17 HAPPY FIFTH ANNIVERSARY to Aeg and S. "Olneya ironwood is very hard and heavy. Its density is greater than water and thus sinks; it does not float downstream in washes. Ironwood functions as a "nurse plant" and a "habitat-modifying keystone species" of benefit to many other species of flora and fauna. The wood of the Ironwood is one of the hardest and heaviest woods in the world Ironwood trunks can persist for up to 1600 years. Less is more, more and more

10/12/17 So the open of John from Cincinnati made me think of Beowulf's swims in ocean, which led to Yeats last poems of Eon, and then to Chang Zi as water bubbles that imprint other molecules and receive their memory, which enrichment added to the original…: there was a hidden passage, unknown to men, but someone managed to enter and…removed a gen-studded goblet…outwitted the sleeping dragon…

10/11/17 Wed. Six wks heartbeat. Went to Bea Dewitt's memorial with Aeg after telling him Tues he'd regret if he didn't go, since he was clearly her favority. After, he said that Sab 6 wks pregnant! Same day! When he picked up the kids last night we went out to the car and I looked at S in the front seatand her belly looks big. I told P. Aey would not have revealed his had I not insisted he bring Judah over to see Zion. He took a few minutes before work to do this, which transpired in telling of preg. Rod Huygens said Bea told him she was afraid and this …that she was a sinner too, but encouraged him and others
-- Also, at the CRC on the way out saw Doug DeHough said, Hi Doug, his face frozen, eyes expressionless. Makes me think something's still up about the June firing, a malign gaze. It confirms what Harvest Haven Martin experienced in Alberta among the Reformed, and Dave Hunt, and what Jacob the Elder faced in Skippack, all stemming from 19 June and Marc van Berekum's dismissal. That look sums all the maltreatment of every Sar pit in existence. This the same day creep at club uses my name. Blessing and Danger.

10/10/17 ordered Grander water 720 yesterday. Martin Van Popta.
-Had kids for evening. -- "the interrogators asked what subject he wanted to do next. The small box? The floor with your hands held up high? Standing against the wall? Or stay where you are? Salt Pit.

10/9/17 grander water, wilhelm mohorn generator aquapool

10/8/17 Throes of Knowledge: Quantum Geomancy & The Brain Internet with Anthony Patch -conference full spectrum dominance, Kathleen Urquart-geomancy, alternative dimensions illimitless demons, Parallel dimension is demonic entity, two way geomantic communication with demonic, demon=dimension, dice as communication devices,, erik blatavinsky, diagram of entanglement, two dice, geomancy, dirt, sand, branches, dominos, dice, dwave and gen=omancy, arrangement of qubits that comm with parallel dimensions, -- entanglement is when you finish another's thought, synchronicity, geomancy is the quantum entangle core process of dwave, quantum entangle with demonic entities in infinite numbers, [another makeover!] JESUS IS QUANTUM ENTANGLEMENT WITH US WHEN WE

PRAY, geomantic, divine the meaning from rotation of dice a la computer, 37.22, Turing built computer a la Sumer to communicate with the dead, sand tables, plans in the sand, random series of dots and lines, then the diviner reads the spirit guided then interpreted by the guide. A la I Ching. Spatla mancy, water mancy, reflections in a bowl, Nostradamus mercury in a bowl, mirror mancy, manipulation of elements as communication tool, lei prescribe tetrahedrons, sphere, Egyptians communicate with the dead, sphere is God shape, not square based pyramid (Lucifer) pediments, artificial intelligence copy of original, AI cannot supersede those with Holy Spirit, will transform, John 14.1214, greater things than He. Kathleen Urquhart, at conference, 55.00 If you don't have the Holy Spirit your brain will be literally connected to the internet, enhancements/ augmented? Existential threat to human, now! AI connected node with world simulation, every key stroke, movement, word all data mined, futurism.com 12. Researchers have linked the brain to the internet. 7 billion individual nodes SWS, avatar on apps FB, internet of things-data mining network, vacuum cleaner, more data better models, Brain meets internet of things, eegs. Each node, we're all nodes on the web, eeg signals transferred to raspberry pi computer which live streams the data open to all. Brain net contacts monitoring, augmentation and transportation AI delivered to Tony, monitors everything digital, 5G spin implant memories, thoughts emotions. AI boasts surpassed by entanglement if augmentation from God, encrypted prayer augmented prevents AI hack of believer, Dwave numbers tubulan dymers being 65,536 in our brain, 4 elements, 16 geomantic figures, cards, patters, tableaux, =65536 charts, that is limit of geomancy, dice, numbers stop, 10th model dwave computer, 128 qubits,X 10= 65536, combine images njmbers figures combitorianl optimatization=geomancy. [Kathleen urguart] 8192 total charts-65536, 14 has 1mil (1.24) 4594, # of demons thay communicate with Counterfeit the human brain from 600 cell tetrahedron model 10-16 model 2048

10/9/17 Mon. Sat news Bea DeWit died. Watching memory of water molecules yesterday, memory of words, leads to a narrator—finally! maybe

10/7/17 Kagura (神楽, かぐら, "god-entertainment Shinto theatrical dance predating Noh. a ceremonial art derived from kami'gakari (神懸, かみがかり, "oracular divinification"),
--Met Mendelson Jay [Crockett], last night.
-Went to Japanese Moon Festival with Christina and fam, classical concert, drum, flute

10/6/17 HelioFant - I Pet Goat 2 Decrypted 2017
new pet goat II revealed like never before. Broken pentagram is transits of
Venus Halo 4 Shem
1 Timothy 6:15
15 Which in his times he shall shew, who is the blessed and only Potentate, the King of kings, and Lord of lords; Revelation 19:16 And he hath on his vesture and on his thigh a name written, King Of Kings, And Lord Of Lords.

-10/5/17 Cryotherapy

-10/4/17 Samson. World's strongest man its weakest character.

--Red Fez. The narrator does not believe in the universe, the ultimate thought crime to all its sources and to the world itself. Believers in Universe substitute what before was their notion of god or gods. Notion of Universe as unrandom distribution WITH CAUSE accompanies the belief that psyche will provide, as Joseph Campbell says, a hero will appear when a hero is needed. These follow the stars as agents of divination and divination itself. But I hold these findings inconsequent beside THE BRIGHT EXTENSIVE WILL!

10/3/17 put river rock and fragments in side garden for drainage. Take out almond for peach.

10/2/17 Gustave killer croc featuring also a hippo wake. .6
-- Kenneth Shipp, from the company of shadows

10/1/17 into the great worlderness rife machines

9/30/17 Gladio B and the Battle for
Eurasia wilder did philip k dick disclose
the real matrix in 1977

9/29/17 PETER KIRSANOW race and police!
cia opereation gladio with paul Williams Muslim secret training facilities sperm cell down 59% starting 1973 in Caucasoid countries free-radical theory occupies a pivotal position in modern biological concepts of aging, oxyradical quenching. According to our model fullerene C60 accumulating in mitochondria provides high radical scavenging activity in this subcellular compartment, called by Skulachev the "dirtiest place in the cell" [28]
--all black and white culture invented by the cia? African American dialect Ismael Reed closer than many to the rhythm
Billie Holiday, heroin and heroine
--Zora Neale Hurston ms burned voodoo, "she underwent initiation by followers of the famed Madame Leveau in New Orleans. Hurston fasted for 69 hours, lay naked on a couch with a snake skin on her navel and had, by her own account, five psychic experiences. "In one, I strode across the heavens with lightning flashing from under my feet, and grumbling thunder following in my wake,"
Dick Gregory-Hugh Hefner Illuminatii
--the patios rhythm of football cheers and dance from FSC aftrican rhythm don't occur in writing English, like the classical driven split keys of of Nina S. Presumably the rhythm of languages are all different. The angelic language is the ultimate expression. The musical scale of African sounds transcend language, but are absorbed into anglo saxon, which does have its own rhythm. Language is greater than race. Charles chestnut Malindy Sings

9/28/17 jimmy sevile Crowley and the beatles

--nina simone Nina bipolar- I Wish I Knew How It Would Feel To Be Free I have no hands and no feet, I'd have new vision be transformed by the renewing of your mind:
I sing so much better, I dance so much better, …a little bit better, one day I thought I could fly …I looked down and see, that I wouldn't know myself, I'd have no hands, I'd have no feet, I'd have new visions my eyes would be open, the Bible says, be transformed by the renewing of your mind, (Jesus said, don't get in my way)
…for one moment I'm alive…I'd know how it would be to be free only bullies have free speech
-- 38th Anniv. We have lived such clandestine lives even our children don't know the day we officially Merried. It is not beyond expression, but it is beyond. Holy Matrimony is so ultimate. It is holy because it honors life and life is holy, set apart, consecrated.
--Watched Nina Simone again last nite, very encouraging to have shared a time and place with her. Was that a visitation, a stellium, or a crossroads, the comedy, writing, music of that era?
--What happened to the PR for Trump's Howard Stern transcripts, why squelched?
--Melt was written with the intent of being good for 100 years, so it has to wait a day. This picks up with what Spiers says at the end of Melt… After this time between it seems appropriate to say.

9/27/17 the rational of the dead: "3 questions come to mind. Do you all agree that there is actually a disparity that prompted the alleged protest? Have you all considered what it is like to live on the other side? Lastly, has anyone on this thread made a conscious effort in your own communities to try to level the playing field for those that feel there is a disparity?" Cassandre Luberus
--crystalline structure of water "Hexagonal water is composed of six individual molecules of water, held together by common hydrogen bonds." "biological organisms prefer the six-sided (hexagonal) ring-structure, found naturally in snow water" ... (are used) to create an oxygen-rich, alkaline, energized and uniquely structured Hexagonal Water."

9/26/17 David "gave comfort to the enemy from his offense."
--Aey wants to know about life span before the flood. What I would do about vaccine if I had a child now? He asks: max parent health, immunity, then diet addition and subtraction. Spoke of C60

9/25/17 fakehenge, stonehenge shocker what they won't tell the public Siqueiros Pedregal con Figuras / Rocks with Figures -

9/24/17 50 fat flies come out of the ceiling at office. I go on the roof to look…get fly swatters.- Now it is public we should not disrespect the NFL or football I confess.
11 Jan 1968 this appeared in the Fayetteville Voice, the school paper. Fayetteville then was called a "predominant Negro college." where I served two years. Some faculty said they that

he does not respect football! To be fair there were four other disrespects: -To The Coach Crouching In The Dust Looking For Something,
-The Non-Scientific Confusion Of Markets
-A Beep And A Honk (for Rebecca Duncan)
-JACK HORNER AT 18
--Trinity Mennonite, Meghan Good, a buxom in tight jeans with a ping ring on her index, spoke about 21st cent identity and community with a mix of doubt and faith, Shrill so that after service we went and got 4 pairs of shooter earplugs. She has BA, MA, working on Doc. overt sexuality from the pulpit. Ring of witchcraft on index finger. Insidious message of acceptance of anything except speaking in tongues, which was mocked as lunacy. Style brash, prurient, lawless even while advocating being God's Troublemaker. The whole acts like a Group Therapy session anesthetized people into acceptance of their present state when really all the fine experiences come from abstention, calorie restriction, also drug, porn, etc so that the solution of faith is not my neighbor to hold me up but the author and finish Himself. Either he or I am gone. One thing she said, that people judge her on her interpretation of two chapters in Revelation!—
--A series of 5 dams down a hillside colored demo to control passage of flood, seen from the bottom, being in charge, watching it go as planned but carefully.
--Clement a/c job scheduled chg

9/23/17 Sculpture
9/22/17 Fri. took exhibits to fair with Aey, he framed piece, got ½ in plywood, consulted on his lumber for table, how grains didn't match even thought he wanted them too, how he has wasted every free day, 20, doing what S wanted but not himself. See entry 9/26

9/21/17 fountains of the deep, subterranean oceans.
Intro to New World order: These have no order. There is no beginning or end. They exist together without precedence even if every order they take in existence makes precedence, against precedence. The order of original publication is none because they were written long before that, a chronology largely forgotten. Chronology anyway is a lie! Events exist independently, simultaneously. The biggest impediment to this is first impression, also a lie, but because the infirmities we that live in lie upon lie have to be ordered to sell. What you see before you is the best pitch now. The last thing we can stand is to see the world as it is. It has to be conformed, structured. So the Order that tells its tale is as arbitrary as the cosmos gardeners and astronomers make out of stars. Fairy tale and folklore legends involve characters like dwarfs, dragons, elves, fairies, giants, gnomes, talking animals and moral beast fables believing in the veracity of the events described.
-- the coverup at times beach, dioxin mixed with oil spread on streets

9/20/17 these do have any order. There is no beginning middle or end. That is a lie they exist together without precedence even if every order they take in existence made precedence. Against precedence. The order of original publication is no order because they were written long before, a chronology largely forgotten.

Chronology is a lie! They exist independently, the biggest impediment to this is first impression, also a lie., but because of the infirmities we live in, lie upon lie, these have to be order to they sell themselves. What you see before you then is the best pitch money can buy to seel the NOW.the last thing we can stand is to see the world as it is. It has to be conformed, structured, simultaneously.

--new year's Eve Day. Personal corruption '13 – '15.

--Considering Tolkien, Lewis B Graham…Henry makow, Rense, Penry on John Collins on this

9/19/17 Aey brought Judah over, we had tea, heard yips from yard. Went out. Two dogs stuck together from the back. Aey didn't know what it was! Said when he realized, should we turn them over? I said we let them be.

Eventually they came loose. So Judah lost his cherry. And little Z. Only hope maybe is she's not quite ripe? --Billy Graham puzzle: https://www.youtube.com/watch?v=_z1r7DyMPmQ halley's bible handbook expunged Albengsians in billy graham ed

--"The Billy Graham Evangelistic Association published a special "Crusade Edition" (1962, 1964, 1969) of Halley's Bible Handbook and boldly removed Halley's careful documentation of the evil of the popes and the slaughter of true Christians. Zondervan published a revised edition of Halley's Bible Handbook in 2000, which likewise eliminated references to the RCC's heresies and the millions of evangelical Christians slaughtered by Rome. Instead, it says: "The Roman Catholic Church responded to the Protestant Reformation by reforming and renewing itself." Dave Hunt the Berean Call 1 Jan 2006 Revelation 19:16 And he hath on his vesture and on his thigh a name written, King Of Kings, And Lord Of Lords.

--AB yesterday asked why her great grandmother died. I said do you want the long answer or the short. The long. Sin, faith, resurrection, heaven then new earth.

--At the club the kid wanted to go to church but stopped asking when his parents would not. He has a KJV. Told him to read Ps 19.

9/18/17 Rosh Hashana Wed, 20 September 2017 at sundown (1st of Tishrei, 5778)

9/17/17 Michael jackson mind control drawings https://vigilantcitizen.com/musicbusiness/never-seendrawings-made-michael-jackson-hint-mind-control/ Aa Wilder, Sue Ford (Brice Taylor), Claire Reed, Brian Devereux Paul l. Williams, eoperation gladio

-John Collins, Todd tape four: half the pilgrims, Tolkien, Lewis members of Golden dawn. Allegations of lewis affair with the housekeeper? J R R Tolkien C S Lewis the Inklings Narnia and the Golden Dawn https://www.scribd.com/document/25919958/J-R-R-Tolkien-C-S-Lewis-the-Inklings-Narnia-and-the-GoldenDawn

What clif high called human sychis is cia programming a la 9/11 in films. What Jung called psychic provision of the hero is suspect prediction predation. It is not that the psyche predicted it but that the psyche programmed to predict by the fallen. Acrid smoke.

9/16/17 https://www.youtube.com/watch?v=j3avYJNRilQ Stanley Kubrick exposed the illuminati Spielberg covered it up - jay Weidner. Bob Hope's profile in EyesWideShut

9/15/17 Silicon stumps. Giants causeway Ireland. Volcanic Neck! Eroded Laccolith. 64& Silicone dioxide the Si atom shows tetrahedral coordination, with four oxygen atoms surrounding a central Si atom. The most common example is seen in the quartzite polymorph Prestoric giant stone trees Proofpoint
--1 FRI delayed but strong reaction to the mad woman and her cat who ghosts the street who two nights ago left her cat in a carrier about 6 on Mike's drive and went off. it was 106. I went to train, but the b/w cat looked at me and we communicated, and while zion had chased it before when it was loose up the street, it pawed the cage to say let me out. so that festered all the time I worked out and I decided to let it out--it looked like Willie was supposed to take it but he wouldn't see it there, but in that heat the cat wouldn't last the night well, but when I got home the mad woman was messing, talking to it, scolding, trying to move it to another carrier. So I went in, but went back out and told her I'd call the police if she left it there. she said willie was to take while she moved. I said, knock on his door. Then she did and he knew. But today I feel like that was unnecessary force.
--Enonymous Schudonymn has moral courage.
--the alternative news, drudge, Breitbart, jones give more air play to their so called enemies than msm does. --Dreamed i told Sab 1. what is your dream, 2. develop your property, some woman, youngish, [Aeg's lover?] tried to interrupt. Sab listened to me.

9/14/17 lot of manure, moved pile onto grass.
--Aey says on the way back from Flag last weekend S told Aeg she had called her exboyfriend, thinking of revenge sex with him, while the kids listen! in the car. Admittedly she had just had that nose procedure and she had just visited with her family, always a tension. I was wondering just before this about this previous boyfriend,

9/13/17 I have published these findings as far as they go.
ecolocation bioacoustics
--pat dreamed we lived in a big two story house with large yard.
--The discordants of the music in Gigants is that they are composed in different keys, that is each revision.
Russian hope
--Thinking still about Aeg i recall William J. Franklin best man at my wedding who when I encountered him sometime after college c. '66 said he had lived with a Korean girl when stationed in Korea, but just left on a plane when discharged. Offense against native peoples! Exploitation Sex.
Korean prostitution: "During the 1960s, camp town prostitution and related businesses generated nearly 25 percent of the South Korean GNP.[43] In 1962, 20,000 comfort women were registered.[2] The prostitutes attended classes sponsored by their government in English and etiquette to help them sell more effectively.[44] They were praised as "dollar-earning patriots" or "true patriots" by the South Korean government.[30][41][44]

In the 1970s one junior high school teacher told his students that "The prostitutes who sell their bodies to the U.S. military are true patriots. Their dollars earned greatly contributes to our national economy. Don't talk behind their back that they are western princesses or U.N. madams."[11]"   Camptown

9/12/17 all imponderables want to go for the first cause, too much to say, too unbelievable, not that the state politic can be understood either, but it is faint to the first cause.

--Taken from newworldorder preface: An example of this hierarchy might be a dream about a 53 blue and white Mercury and a tall pale faced young man beside it called smug to his face after some passion of disagreement. Assume the passion backgrounds in memory confrontations at 3D Tournaments at Gold Key and El Paso which prove the character needs correction. Mercury is 4D for the god, the smug one, the spirit changling, shapeshifter, the one who has no character to trust, so this is a confrontation with the god Smug (or Smaug). If that sounds totally unconvincing that is always the case when 4D is viewed in 3. There had been a sculpture 2D composed the night before, whose thickest part of head and body with wings spread exploded in bisque and was lost. Itself a statement of Mercury.

--reflection on cynthia: thought is not spiritual it is a not one dimensional either, a negotiation between physical and spirit subverted by religion. That doesn't mean the Bible, it means every system sold to people as truth, especially the modern occult.

9/11/17 also Urk: Document 3: Pedro Escadero is a Science Advisory Board Member and Chairman of Speleology at Southwest Cave Conservation, a branch of The Carl Sagan SETI Institute and Coyote Center of the Esner Foundation. He was also a presiding myth hat of the Anthropos in Geneva. Many long and mazy studies of the volumetric cave bone data and traditional agave spirit vacuñas, guanacos, llamas, and alpacas, salt caves and caverns, help explain why all these caves named for women. Alcoves and emplacement strategy predict and detect caves on Mars from Mars-analogue sites. His subsurface cavities via thermal infrared remote sensing to determine cave volume from the thermal signal strength have appeared in Old Ice Eel Lore articles in El Pais, Der Spiegel.

--HB to Robt. Water memory, C60, Restore C60 sunflower oil Bob Greska, Carbon 60 molecule was first discovered in 1985 by Sir Harold W. Kroto, Richard E. Smalley and Robert F. Curl, Jr. They later were awarded a Nobel Prize in 1996 for this.
https://c-60.com/

--Restore may enhance 4D. the Bridge Between Worlds, 3D to 4. Is 4 the quantum? Info processing at speed immediacy in 4.

--The bridge over the Ohio! and the 15 yr old boy

9/10/17 Sun Andrew should write a factual narrative with documentation of all that he has done to help, nurse, doctor, encourage Sab since her knee injury, her chiropracter, her nose/throat operation and what has done in the home and for the children.

9/9/17 off shoot of Kanzius RF TherapyLater in 2007, Kanzius claimed that the same radio frequency transmitter can also be used to generate a hydrogen-oxygen mixture dissociated from salt water . grander water, memory Water burns? Water has a memory? Water can be affected by cell phones?

--was the discovery that "The EcoPods, an idea traced initially to the work of Poe, were set according to Earth's axis to activate simultaneous hydrogen fusion in each second of any given latitude and longitude per quadrant. This was microscopically done to ensure even and gradient combustion for all. "Burning the water" it was called,"
-Civil rights movement is used to begin to justify cartoon sex with robots, first gay sex, then transvestites, no boy girl bathrooms, sex change operations, bestial brothels, tranny first ladies, sex with robots under way all to justify sex with aliens prediction programming in operation. Extant sex with aliens and its BACK TO THE BIBLE AGAIN. get out Genesis Six. How does it feel to be without arms Job 38:15 "From the wicked their light is withheld, Psalm 37:17 "Son of man, I have broken the arm of Pharaoh king of Egypt; and, behold, it has not been bound up for healing or wrapped with a bandage, that it may be strong to hold the sword. Ezekiel 30:21
--sab: you feel you have the right to berated him, hit him, pummel him, mock him, disrespect him and he has to take it or you will threaten to leave him, divorce him, and this is your term, the rule of your relation from the beginning when you gave him this ultimatum, take it, me as I I am or beat it. This Tyrant has ruled the relation and he all along believed he could moderate it. But he has given the nuclear option to you in his actions. But what was your dream, well defined but to have a family with two children, etc, etc. Sab 16 hrs · If everything in my life would stop going wrong right now....that'd be great...
--to the implicit accusation that he's my son and it's my fault, your voices took great care to alienate him from me all those years ago in order to enslave him.

9/8/17.. FB FACEBLOCK shall not escape.
-- To Aeg. Wrestling. All emotions are spirits, spirit of love, spirit of anger, spirit of greed, spirit of kindness. Wrestling against flesh and blood is not the point, it is against the spirits. The man has a body and his spirit partly inhabits it, but not exclusively. The energies that move the world in hurricane and earthquake are like the energies of the spirit, they work upon matter, on the world, on flesh and blood. The man chooses how he will receive these energies or not. If he allows he is clay to be molded by the Bright Extensive Will and so choosing he finds his life has been prepared anyway for such, but if not then it is not and he is subject to the energies and forces, not cooperating in them. In saying his life is not his own he is free. Now he is ready to go beyond the wrestling. Now he is ready for the Battle. So here is the man wrestling for you. Who will win. Porn, drugs, magic make the man's body his spirit prison. Thurs at the Lab.
--earthquake in Chiapas or Irma in Miami. Back to BAck.

9/7/17 chasing bison bear Ai--a future where domination has no man

9/6/17 WED Aeg visits to tell the tale: Accounts lust and dishonesty, learn spirit war from Aey, lift the feeling from S, who says of Jesus it's all just story, hence AB's statement, wrestling of a man against his sin. He didn't know what to do so tells me, late in the game, told he needs to take inventory of his offenses of lust and theft, dishonesty, speak them aloud in counseling so he externalizes them from himself. She required him to open his legs while sitting down so she could hit him in the scrotum, hit him with a bat he keeps for protection.

Out in the open he will at least identify them to fight. He's trying to buy his way back. Bottom line for S is develop the investment. She chose it, fulfilled her dream with it. Now be mature and develop it. a type of home improvement.
--Double Drinking C60

9/5/17 Tuesday Aey and I fix faucets. Says S. hits Aeg with bat, has been doing physical abuse since 4 mo in.
One thing knows. He always gets caught, always, he needs to know right and wrong better --Woke with Christmas Tree,
9/4/17 entrances and exits, eight Russian formalists. Saying that the Reader is the most important character in Kafka. Canvas red, yellow, white, blue, blacks, trowels blobs, actors on site their whole lives. Has the spirit sinned before it is born? Born to be reborn!

9/3/17 living in 2 different dimensions have to get a message to yourself...
--Sunday Further, what if all these are the result of taking C60, laying bare the cut, taking off the pollution, this the the 3rd day.
-- I have too much imagination it was said but if I take every suggestion as an admission of control, therefore am immune to this. So then ask, given so, what further effort could exploit that thinking about marital trouble reported by AB on their visible last night. It led to me thinking of my own Blue Danube bar WVA, Stubenville Oh -monsters, and murder in S. by Susan Guy.--Gambling, prostitution and bootlegging in Steubenville over one hundred years. Its Water Street red-light district of men from hundreds of miles away, underage runaways, white slave trade rampant along with all the vice crimes, murders a weekly occurrence. Law enforcement blind eye of political corruption in the state capital replayed itself over and over again during the past century as mobsters and madams and murders plagued the city and county at an alarming rate Newspapers nickname Little Chicago Steubenville madam
Life of Love with Madam Judy Jordan. "Water Street Reclamation Project~Water Street is where our men's home is located. It was the first street named in Steubenville in 1797. Through the 40's, 50's, 60's, it was home for prostitution, gambling, saloons, and the like, so bad even ministers wouldn't even walk on the street. When we purchased the last known house of prostitution there, we began reclaiming that street for the Glory of God. Piece by piece, we have had some land donated, some we purchased, preparing to put up a stage 2 RHOL home and occupy the land once owned by the enemy!
-Gropecunt Lane was a street name found in English town Gropecountelane, Gropecontelane, Groppecountelane queynte. Philotus (1603) quoting Trump mentions "put doun thy hand and graip hir cunt."[11In The Miller's Tale, Geoffrey Chaucer writes "And privtely he caughte hire by the queynte" Sneakesbyes --the mafia types don't get that the avenger doesn't want anything from them except their death.
--So what if Thornburg is an experiment, entrance and exit?

9/2/17 Sat. Kids. AB: Upsets at home. orange chow. Saturday
-This is Why Evidence is NOT FOR PUBLIC RELEASE machine of
Ur Whorifying!

9/1/17 Reflections on Fin Sorrel's love of railroads: the rails of the Pennsylvania Railroad up from Scully's Roundhouse, shooting out insulators, collecting torpedoes and flares along the tracks to fasten to rocks to drop below in Chartiers Creek, things swam before me as in empty outlines and skeletons, all the future dim. Oil seep stained the ground there from its derelict pump across from the schoolhouse. Heavy stones exploded the torpedoes from the bridge above. This fits a soul who makes gunpowder with potassium chlorate to explode in basements. Fires raged up those hillsides from the tracks. The hills, the whole landscape was undermined with coal seams ruthlessly dug from the ground. Franz Kline's black and white paintings from his childhood in Wilkes Barre near the coal mines show the influence of life next to a railroad where the engine smoke is unscrubbed (1947), black as soot. Only freight trains went past, two tracks, up from the Scully yard, outcome of the big strip mine operation of Pittsburgh hillsides, the blessing that prevented later development. Baltimore and Ohio. Thornburg in 1849 was the site of the first railroad built in Pennsylvania to take coal to market, the Chartiers Valley Railroad. Chartiers Valley Railroad The Chartier Coal Company of Allegheny was to be transported from the mine to Coal Harbor located in a cove behind Brunet's Island near the present site of Chartiers Country Club on Baldwin Road. Coal was to be transported from the mine to Coal Harbor, located in a cove behind Brunot's Island near present-day McKees Rocks on the Ohio River.

8/31/17 moonshrogan, spragen

8/30/17 Mannequin haus. zachary scott hamilton fin sorrel   https://entropymag.org/where-to-submit-august-september-2017/Soutine landscapes predict

8/29/17 Bryan Kofron SIS Amazon experiment Seattle homeless freq weapons. guards at Amazon bldg Seattle are monitor eyes and ears to transmit images to computers to id each face entering. 58.00. cyberized camera eyes. Seattle homeless pop and general lab for development of freq weapons. Ella Free Seattle homeless experiment of targeted individuals via SIS Bryan Kofreo , Justin Carter, Amazon homeless center
-- China's Food Production Strategy for the New Grand Solar Minimum ghost towns and ghost cities on coastal areas warmer than inland. Railroads to nowhere in n central Africa, from changed rainfall patterns, 119 bill for 2013, a string of pearls, maritine silk road, transport from Africa back ot China,
-- After seeking the logic of these free forms, feeling but not seeing it, I realize they are tests of the eye to unfocus, see the whole, use peripherical vision and then the form is seen, but looking at any part defeats. The eye wants to impose its order but the piece opposes that so the eye has to give in to see.

8/28/17 the health benefits of activated charcoal
BEHEMOTH AND LEVIATHAN.
--time machine is memory machine past or future. Depends on memory, history or prophecy, realism or surrealism. Hurricane Harvey is High's earthquake, viz the is quake over run.

- Human Side' of War Criminals Bush artist, Goering: "He who tortures animals wounds the feelings of the German people." Harvey secret: oil
-- Al Bielek is lying. The Time predicts of 2004 did not happen.

8/27/17 ORACLE: dualistic parody, egregor, Mayweather McGregor normal form, that the Greek word an autonomous psychic entity composed of and influencing the thoughts of a group of people ἐγρήγορος (Watcher) would take in French. *los levantados, not raptured, kidnapped.* maquilas teeth worn invisibly around his neck-- all of magical thinking

8/26/17 Brave new word mag. Welcome to Philadelphia -experiment

8/25/17 shungite asphaltum Secrets revealed Sarah Westphal clip high part 3, middle C 60 purple power also: https://www.livelongerlabs.com/
-David Dubye grand solar minimum Wholthy. Health and whole. flesh tocks.

8/24/17 Thursday. 4 times Restore has worked in dreams and well being.Tues a great sense of strength, woke at 2 worked 3 hrs. Today very specific dream.

8/23/17 The American Eclipse: I am more moved by the removal of the 4 confederate soldiers from Batts, Calhoun, Parlin quad last night by U Pres than A's infidelity 3 yrs ago. But the cure is to *cultivate cognition to build discernment* and this based on the best literary sources and personal contacts with greatness. I never noticed those statues all that time but to execute them by fiat to the mob and then to hear interviews of students who hardly know who Washington is...*they removed the Baals periodically,* claimed white supremacy is bogus Weatherman rhetoric, antidote here so much for the Athens of Texas. "symbols of modern white supremacy and neo-Nazism." Greg Fenves. Asian announcer for Charlottesville football game scrubbed because his name Robt Lee.
--more eclipse effect, three projects begun, house around corner, big plot one street over, houses on that street. hurricane Harvey, Andrews out, List
--Aey in rhetoric like Jorma that girl does to S what she did to Aeg, seduce him.

8/21/17 Russian Scientist Claims Team Battled Creature Under Antarctic Ice, 46 B, Lake Vostok
--false tsumai coast of Brazil from Atlantic and Pacific joining undersea, six in difference. Second huge fiber optic came laid from Brazil to Antarctic. Sun Dogs best description of year round life in Antarctica for workers, messages by Butler, Sun Dogs.
--Adman Sakli richest man in the world Mike Cechanowicz Adnan Sakli 2013 VS the powers that want to enslave the people
--missing. guided-missile destroyer USS John S. McCain collision with the merchant vessel Alnic MC east of Singapore. Fitzgerald collision off the coast of Japan in June,
-- top of free search for the bright extensive will is *Dogen's Extensive Record: A Translation of the Eihei Koroku* starts at 75. lofty ancestor dharma protein. Even if your speech penetrates the whole universe, you are still not free. --Sounds like a gnostic hit from Genesis.

--What if life were not a prison sentence? Why would I think it is? And when the term is over, execution? Not quite, release. Absent from the body present with the Lord. Adam a son of Elohim. Sidney Sheldon? Sidney, Dee, Wyatt, Stevens flawed, all gone out of the way, none that is righteous no not one.

All discernment cognitive, build by study and meditation that does not go with you when you're gone, but the *creative compulsive is more permanent*, the spiritual. --Sir Philip Sidney game, chicks have an incentive to overstate their need since it will result in them receiving more food. No need for all the overlays up and down of the ET blue bird. Except the reptile.

8/20/17 Introducing by proximity at Future Trades, being also a lover of cobalt https://animalwilderness.blogspot.com/2010/08/yet-shimmying-sieves-vast-on-cobalt.html, your poem attracted my eye, and seeing you have interest in animal behavior find also there proximity. https://humanbotany.blogspot.com/?view=timeslide. I am still affected years later with the ideas in *Grave Pawns* by Jared Christman and in these ongoing concerns greet you. Hello! --cogent report on sons of Elohim

8/19/19 all your bases are servant to us Darcy Weir, true story of Phil Schneider.
-How can we know the angels when they don't show up. Take the Dogon legends as true, follow Sitchin the shapeshifter, or the cone shaped beams out of N Antarctica arcing over Hawaii and out to Cassiopeia? Not too helpful to believe the one myth that agrees with the shapeshifter any more than the blue Avians, the chickens out of middle earth. Not visible. Instead we turn to Jacob as example of a man who is both evil and good, a trickster and one who bests the angel all night. Not so different from Jefferson who starts his own black family with his slave and composes his own gospel from the sayings he allows Jesus to have said, but whose urbanity and grace of prose and thought are healing in themselves. Read the letters to Adams (who he had earlier called a hermaphrodite   So Barthes *Struggle with an Angel*, heals by itself all the insults to our ears with his inquiry into the sinew which shrank in the hollow of Jacob's thigh, inlaid with the balm of canonical analysis and mythical narrative just in the statement that before this 11 sons had passed over the ford Jabbok, before he wrestled all night, and then there were twelve. We wrestle all night and day and night over these prolegomena to our own mythical days where Nephilim are both instigators and the result of fallen angel rapine, which violence accounts for their bad temper, even if they mask it with smiles. Giants result from further inbreeding of Nephilim. Demons are the disembodied spirits of giants killed. Whether these are reptiles cannot be said if reptiles broadcast a force field that makes them look human.

8/16/17 the salvation of the world as a weather phenomenon--Starry seas caught up into clouds is a measure of the bright extensive will, that whirls earth sphere throughout all time. THESE WEATHER MODIFICATIONS SYMBOLIC OF ThIS SONNET. connected to dehydration old age Carl headaches vertigo

8/15/17 United Nations 1977 international convention titled "Convention on the Prohibition of Military or Any Other Hostile Use of Environmental Modification Techniques". Exactly what had occurred over Moscow when this ENMOD device was released on 29 May, this report details, when it was released over Berlin, on 29 June, it caused the heaviest rain in a century to pummel that city—and that, also, occurred in Paris when the release of this ENMOD device, on 9 July, caused the highest ever recorded amount of rain to hit that city in its entire recorded history. Russia is not a signatory to the 1977 "Convention on the Prohibition of Military or Any Other Hostile Use of Environmental Modification Techniques"—as Communist China is neither, and whose Beijing Weather Modification Office employees nearly 40,000 to develop ENMOD devices too. weather weapon

8/12/17 The poems of the fictional nation of Ameryca pretend to voyage the discovery in short lyrics of the 16th and 17th English poems and propaganda. That is their coverup. They are rather more a psycho-mystical celebration of the new birth where children are told to FLY to that new world, Ameryca, not America of the world, the realm of the spirit. Written about 1970 it was not clear how crucial this would be fifty years later. Perhaps that is why the fall and winter of this spiritual calendar are continually satiric, tracing their months to the final six decades of the 20th century when the attempted enslavement of every human spirit became obvious. The first six months trace the discovery of the new world from March to September in order, St. Brendan, Erik the Red, Columbus, Sir Walter Raleigh and the natural origins of that world, the sun. The second half shifts to the last six decades of 20th century the i instead of the y, America marking its dissolution.
"Ameryca With a Y - Autobiography of a Poem" is a history @ http://encouragementsforsuch.blogspot.com/2014/02/ameryca-spelled-with-y-autobiography-of.html. This was written on sheep ranch outside Austin from 1968 to '71, published then as A Calendar in 1973, just before Restorations of the Golden Age in New World Discoveries (1975). which celebration of the new birth, called FLY!, is now to be reissued in illustrative format.

8/9/17 Wed. I bought three *lycium fremontii*, wolf berry, to 9ft, dense growth, fruiting, down to 20, to plant between the Ironwood. Southwest Desert Flora also see Arizona Desert-thorn, Lycium exsertum and Desert Wolfberry, Lycium macrodon. Lycium andersonii Lycium exsertum.
--This week trash pickup in the back ceased. Barrels delivered to the front.
--Sun we swam at Andrew's pool and ate. Time with Theo.
--Sat Bright Extensive Will appeared. and White Horse from Kiln.
--Tues got blood work at labs.
--Last Tues we got 8 1000 lb. chairs for office. Aey passed midterm this Tues, burned weeds. AB says I am fat, sitting in pool. Not a sympathetic spirit, a critical one.

8/7/17 cobalt mines

8/6/17 How can Clif High reach such brilliance and darkness at the same time?...the logic separates old and new testament...if indeed we find there are bigger that the Giza giants pyramids...and all over the planet...that Moses and his crowd they didn't build those pyramids in Egypt and Moses and his crowd they didn't exodus from Egypt...so their theoretical claim to Israel is bogus tying the fate to the idea that they the engineers of the

pyramids. 30.54 6 Aug 2017 August 2017[UPDATE] so the NT could be severed from the old and go stand on its own because it's not necessarily historically pegged to the old to Judiism in any way shape or form...they never were in Egypt so how could they have exodus. Read out of Freud Moses and Monotheism Sachs, Velikovsky, and Sitchin --night vision glasses Military Night Vision Goggles in Hunting Night Ed Grimsley
NVU PVS7 Military Spec Gen 3 ITT Pinnacle Tube Night Vision Goggle PVS-7 PATN PVS 7 Night Vision Standard Military Issue Goggles and 42,000 Ukrainian women taken to antarctica as breeding stock
-FLY DUTY! Fly duty is your own responsibility. The spirit of man is the candle of the LORD. that was the true light that lights every man that comes in the world. Your word is a lamp to my fight and a light to my path. 1 Corinthians 2:11 who among men knows the thoughts of man except his own spirit within him? 8
Job 32.8"But it is a spirit in man, And the breath of the Almighty gives them understanding. 9
8/3/17 particular cosmics
arizona wilder and the biggest secret Sitchin is a shapeshafter, wilder 1.40 city of London the spider in the heart of the wold spider system
8/1/17 Fly Bottle
Got 8 1000 lb chairs for office. Porcelain

Pity, Recon. Emily Moyer off planet radio. Randy maugans:
Space is not what we are told. It is not "up" and "out there" it is down and through the second domain of the earth realm called Oceania, the abode of Leviathan, which is the guardian, along with Behemoth of the earth realm. (see the William Blake painting below).The gateways are accessed via The Deep. This is the present controversy over Antarctica and the so-called "North Pole". They aren't "poles" they are gateways.Look up Marianas Trench: Over 7 miles deep, and NOT at the "center of the earth", but in an alignment with Antarctica. The Navy maintains a submarine fleet at the trench...???!!The Navy is in charge of the "Space Program", not the Air Force. Why?
Several other gateways include the Sea of Aidan and a base off the coast of Malibu in Cali., and the Bermuda Triangle, of course. Yes, it is all dimensional, in a way not understood by science. It is also not "flat earth", which is major disinformation campaign. There is a spherical aspect to the earth plane, but not the "globe model".
A thing (us) inside the world cannot observe or explain the thing that it is inside. The "Plato's Cave" effect.All visible celestial bodies we see, Mars, Moon, planets, stars, etc. are inside this construct. The earth is more complex and expansive than we are told as well. Thus, technically, we can go to moon or Mars, but not leave the earth construct. We have not been going into "deep space", which bounded by the oceanic gates that SURROUND the earth realm (now, do you see the spherical aspect?)None of this is conjecture. It has all been explained before by the Ancients, but hidden and dismissed by the black priesthoods called "Science" and "Religion", which rejected the ancient models that were well understood. There are also "worlds within worlds", like the Russian nesting dolls. Dimensions and gateways that are permeable membranes accessed by higher vibratory energies. Hence, Jesus walked through walls! Maugans

7/31/17 the Word, the Will and the Wheel

7/26/17 First st air dfor strokes

7/25/17 MACFADYENA UNGUIS Cat's Claw view on the wall

Tues. Had a stroke a week ago Tues night, wake up dvided, aphasia, vowels spells phoenetic long homonymyss much sleep. For some days I didn't know how to turn the computer on! On type the open. Planted last Iron tree yesterday, beautiful cool day, row of four. been working on mommna nottere., had Judah this time.

7/21/17 Much have I traveled in the realms of gold

Almond Tree Press & Paper Mill - Vamp and Tramp Booksellers
1850 E Fremont Dr, Tempe, AZ 85282
Phone: (480) 839-6150

--CIA death bed confession
Roswell

7/20/17

Richie Allen, 7/19/17 Restore 1.12 gut wall opening and closing 20-30K gut biomene dimensied, monogut, Zachery Bush, asmatha fail of the gut, glyphosate herbicide in air caused gut to release zymothen, leaking gut, uki ose, free sugar from food, lynn margolis, bacteria and mitochrondia combine with human, duff wilson cancer in fertilizers, sw desert retained earth dried but carbons still there, lignite extracts, carbon restored to gut, redox signaling, relatuate gut, elevate mood, no brain fog, remove probiotics don't them, from cow digestion, glysophate from factory chimney descaler, dream and depth of sleep, balance sympathetic para sympathetic jolted on cellular level from digital phones, deep restoration of cells in sleep for healing, long detailed dreams, childred slid down slavers waving snares.

--This weekend Joan, johns mother in law was cancer. Tues morniny early things not commected (stroke) slept all deep and Andrew came over tues night to visit, like a deathbed call?

7/17/17 Discount tire, pick up pieces recup from rib to plant tomorrow. Yester explain to Pat silver control, purpose of crypto, etc indemnify her pension,

7/16/17 pretty intense meet with the GranChildren ysster, begin with popcorn watermel, sprinkler, flat bread water bottles stands at sink, proceed to fishing liscnse falls off boat over and over till I fall and bruise the old broke rib all with zion then reading already made necklace, reading puddle ducks, secret garden, swinging through air, bouncing horse, for starters. AB twice called me daddy. It's the energy field. she makes me think I have endowed Andrew with splendor. but at pool party 8/7 she calls me fat!

Job 38.7 who laid the corner stones when the sons of God shouted for joy? Same as Gen 6. Col 1.13-16,The first born over all creation. angelspirit made by God, no female angels, Matt 22.30 neither marry, sons of god male,

Gen 6.2,4took wives, angels children giants.

Gen 1.2 cont'd in Jer 4.23-2623 I beheld the earth, and, lo, it was without form, and void; and the heavens, and they had no light. 24 I beheld the mountains, and, lo, they trembled, and all the hills moved lightly. 25 I beheld, and, lo, there was no man, and all the birds of the heavens were fled. 26 I beheld, and, lo, the fruitful place was a wilderness, and all the cities thereof were broken down at the presence of the LORD, and by his fierce anger. but this before birds created, cities, who made cities if there was no man, God angry, why?

Isa 14.12-17 Lucifer fallenHow art thou fallen from heaven, O Lucifer, son of the morning! how art thou cut down to the ground, which didst weaken the nations!

13 For thou hast said in thine heart, I will ascend into heaven, I will exalt my throne above the stars of God: I will sit also upon the mount of the congregation, in the sides of the north:

14 I will ascend above the heights of the clouds; I will be like the most High.

15 Yet thou shalt be brought down to hell, to the sides of the pit.

16 They that see thee shall narrowly look upon thee, and consider thee, saying, Is this the man that made the earth to tremble, that did shake kingdoms;

17 That made the world as a wilderness, and destroyed the cities thereof; that opened not the house of his prisoners?

--Ez 28.12-19. Thou hast been in Eden the garden of God; every precious stone was thy covering, the sardius, topaz, and the diamond, the beryl, the onyx, and the jasper, the sapphire, the emerald, and the carbuncle, and gold: the workmanship of thy tabrets and of thy pipes was prepared in thee in the day that thou wast created. 14 Thou art the anointed cherub that covereth; and I have set thee so: thou wast upon the holy mountain of God; thou hast walked up and down in the midst of the stones of fire.

15 Thou wast perfect in thy ways from the day that thou wast created, till iniquity was found in thee.

16 By the multitude of thy merchandise they have filled the midst of thee with violence, and thou hast sinned: therefore I will cast thee as profane out of the mountain of God: and I will destroy thee, O covering cherub, from the midst of the stones of fire.

17 Thine heart was lifted up because of thy beauty, thou hast corrupted thy wisdom by reason of thy brightness:

I will cast thee to the ground, I will lay thee before kings, that they may behold thee.

18   Thou hast defiled thy sanctuaries by the multitude of thine iniquities, by the iniquity of thy traffick; therefore will I bring forth a fire from the midst of thee, it shall devour thee, and I will bring thee to ashes upon the earth in the sight of all them that behold thee.

19   All they that know thee among the people shall be astonished at thee: thou shalt be a terror, and never shalt thou be any more.

Rev 12. 7-9 And there was war in heaven: Michael and his angels fought against the dragon; and the dragon fought and his angels,

8 And prevailed not; neither was their place found any more in heaven.

9 And the great dragon was cast out, that old serpent, called the Devil, and Satan, which deceiveth the whole world: he was cast out into the earth, and his angels were cast out with him.

Luke 10.8 Satan fall like lightening

1Peter 5.8 Satan not in hell, Job 1.6-8 walking in earth

Matt 25.41 hell made for devil and angels

2Cor 11.14, Satan an angel of light

giant fighters, fairy tale fighters hot shot crews, let out of prisons to fight the giant fires before adam and eve the nephilim

7/15/17 to draw

73 ``All creatures living beneath the sun,  74 ``That creep or swim or fly or run, 75 ``After me so as you never saw!
``And I chiefly use my charm
``On creatures that do people harm,
``The mole and toad and newt and viper;
``And people call me the Pied Piper.''
127 Which was, ``At the first shrill notes of the pipe,
And ere he blew three notes (such sweet
Soft notes as yet musician's cunning
Never gave the enraptured air)
There was a rustling that seemed like a bustling
Of merry crowds justling at pitching and hustling,
Small feet were pattering, wooden shoes clattering,
Little hands clapping and little tongues chattering, 201 And, like fowls in a farm-yard when barley is scattering, 202 Out came the children running.
203 All the little boys and girls,
When, lo, as they reached the mountain-side,
A wondrous portal opened wide,
As if a cavern was suddenly hollowed;
And the Piper advanced and the children followed,
And when all were in to the very last,
The door in the mountain-side shut fast.
Pied Piper of Hamelin The music stopped and I stood still,
252 ``And found myself outside the hill,
``I can't forget that I'm bereft
``Of all the pleasant sights they see,
``Which the Piper also promised me.
``For he led us, he said, to a joyous land,
``Joining the town and just at hand,
``Where waters gushed and fruit-trees grew,
``And flowers put forth a fairer hue,  244 ``And everything was strange and new; before adam and eve

-stylized indian horses, Beatien Yazz, Iberian and Andalusian bloodlines. The Iberian is the source of the Spanish Barb. Spain's long occupation of northern Africa resulted in the agile desert-bred African Barb horse being crossed with these existing stocks--conformation is often short-backed and deep bodied. They appear narrower in the chest so that the fore legs join the chest in an A-shape

7/14/17 Impurity of motive in preaching. David's lust and faith, Moses' anger and heroism, Paul's impurity of motive preaching all Meadowlark Lemon, sweetmeats tables at EN, Elijah's fear, Moses' temper, Abram's Pusillanimousity, David's lust, as to Paula White and Rodney Howard Browne and Trump: Phillipians, some preach Messiah of contention, some sincerely. Balaam prophet, also"Necho from the words of Elohim" II Chron 35.22. " Huldah the prophetess, the wife of Shallum: "you shall be gather to the grave in peace, neither shal your eyes see all the evil" II chron34.28 Necho to Josiah: "don't meddle with Elohim, Who is with me, that

He destroy thee not." But Josiah came disguised to Megiddo and was shot

Andre's shortfall of .8 crypto not yet reconciled of multiple possible causes.

--dreamed i was afflicting him the way my father did me, but it had no effect! Yestday bought 2 15 gal ironwoods with Aey who delivered the flash drive of crypto, an early birthday present, magnificent, like the stones we got from the desert, and last night the antelope/horse horseman!!!

7/13/17 snowden us govt run by aliens under earth --Documents from NASA that were leaked by Eric

Snowden have indicated that tall white aliens are the ones who has been directing everything, including the rise of Nazi Germany in the 1930s. READ MORE: http://www.disclose.tv/news/Edward_Snowden_Reveals_That_America_Is_Controlled_By_T all_White_Alien s/98512

U.S. government has long known that UFOs exist and are a species more advanced than humanity. These species are not alien, but from our own earth, only more advanced. They have lived here for billions of years, and are far ahead of us in development. The CIA stores data tracking systems and deep-sea sonar on them, but they have the status of state secrets, and even the scientists do not have access to this data about these objects. Extremophiles can live at different temperatures, they have been able to flourish and develop intelligence at a more accelerated pace than Homo Sapiens and they have evolved at the same rate, but their living conditions in the Earth's mantle defended their civilization from the many disasters that have occurred on the surface of the earth. .

--when each one of those osage orange fruits falls to the ground its like a bomb, a bug bomb and the bugs go run

Missler: microcodes, macrocodes. Gen 22Akedah, Moriah, law of first mention, whom thou lovest. first time love mentioned!. Early in morning, two servants, Isaac, went right away, Beersheba to Jerusalem, 3 day journey, 50 miles, lifted up his eyes and saw the place far off,

7/12/17 -the Smudge Report
BEE Killer Pyrethrum -Chrysanthemum I did not seek out the info but it came to my door in the form of two salesbots with scripted tales of being in the neighborhood to tree -treat- "Kelly" Blossom, at Hank's old house with "interior flushout, granulation barrier (reapplied every 60 days) extending 20 feet out from house, power spray, dust weepholes, deweb and treat eaves, spot treat pests in yard [assuming they see any]. good for ants spiders wasps mice" but since mice are mammals, also affecting (but denying it, saying he would drink the

solution] cats, children, quail,, doves, all birds, lady bugs, bees, butterflies, pill bugs, worms. like paving over the yard. They say it's harmless because "plant based" Kills Beneficial Insects: Pyrethrum toxicity: is highly toxic to most insects. Best for Spot Spraying:Like any powerful compound, pyrethrum should be used only for spot-spraying heavily infested plants. You shouldn't be dousing the entire garden with it. Exposure to even low doses may lead to toxicity in some cats. Exposure to pyrethrum in high levels in humans may cause symptoms such as asthmatic breathing, sneezing, nasal stuffiness, headache, nausea, loss of coordination, tremors, convulsions, facial flushing, and swelling. "harmful to fish, but are far less toxic to mammals and birds than many synthetic insecticides and are not persistent, being biodegradable and also decompose easily on exposure to light snake oil soap salesmen like ecoshield Nevertheless, pyrethrum should be handled with the same caution as synthetic insecticides.are ecothreat spraying pyretheum, "plant-based" to innure from its danger, to kill ants spiders waspes mice, says the power spray, granulation barrier deweb and flushouts, not to speak of bees, butterflies, tortoises, cats children sick and evsery manner of life that sustains life, now poisoned because of the fear of a few large roaches. These are the Disclosure agents.

7/11/17 Steve Mills backyard kiln design,
7/10/17 webbot new system is merging 35f cliff on life

7/9/17 david icke different types of reptilians: open and closed codes, people born with tails other abnormalities of dna, drinking blood of blonde blue eyesd helps hold mammal code open in reptiles, cyclopian empire, --cyclopedean architecture, one eye on dollar
-- tunnels under Romanian
parliment bill, -- triangle shaped all
seeing eye, in hand gesture
cyclopian masonry This is Why Something Strange is Happening. Stars of Orion align with Grand Canyon, Isis Temple 6.00
--Sunday. Sleep last night concerned example the opposite of opposite, but it did not come through, only that the opposite of the opposite is not what it seems. but asleep in day a freedom of movement for first time in a long while, [this I think not, after, was precursor to the stroke]as if the weather has seriously changed, which it has outside, from 117 to 104. Restructured Fall of evangelical. [precursor to a stroke?]
-- Abraham broke his father's gods to show Terah they were idols in the tradition. This idol breaking surrounds Abraham in every way and the nation from his loins ever after, for the Jews, the nation Israel, the Christians that spring from them are all involved in this one thing, as the first command says, there shall be no other gods but Yahweh. That is the long and the short and is the reason for being of the nations of the Gentiles being fellow heirs with Israel. So Messiah "ascended up far above all heavens, that he might fill all things" Ephesians 4.10. Psalm 8 backgrounds Abraham and Messiah continually for there Yahweh's glory is above the heavens but His throne is the heaven. All substitute of the universe for Messiah, the throne for the King, is idolatry, for all should see "what is the fellowship of the mystery which from the beginning of the ages has been hid in Yahweh, Who created all things by Yahshua the

Messiah" 3.9. So Abraham's breaking the gods, and Moses' no other gods, make Israel the front line in the opposition of all the captive world, joined now by "those who once were aliens from the commonwealth of Israel and strangers from the covenants of promise" 2.12. Indeed these are now made one with them "in Yahshua the Messiah by the blood of the Messiah...Who has made both one...to make in Himself of these two one new man...reconciling both to Yahweh in one body by the cross.

2.12-16 As Abraham was called out of Ur the people of the nations are called out from the world idols, that "in the fulness of times He might gather together in one all things in the Messiah both which are in heaven and which are on earth; even in him" 1.10. So not just the called out from Israel and the Nations but all things in heaven are gathered or to be gathered, "to the intent that now through the administering powers in heavenly places might be known by the assembly" 3.10. These administering powers in themselves constitute the heavenly councils of note in Psalms, etc, but to none of them did Yahweh say, "thou art my beloved Son." So in this last battle day these are the sides arrayed.

According to rabbinical tradition Terah was a wicked (Numbers Rabbah 19:1; 19:33), idolatrous priest
(Midrash HaGadol on Genesis 11:28) who manufactured idols (Eliyahu Rabbah 6, and Eliyahu Zuta 25). Abram, in opposition to his father's idol shop, smashed his father's idols and chased customers away. Terah then brought his unruly son before Nimrod, who threw him into a fiery furnace, yet Abram miraculously escaped.(Genesis Rabba 38:13). The Zohar says that when God saved Abram from the furnace, Terah repented (Zohar Genesis 1:77b) and Rabbi Abba B. Kahana said that God assured Abram that his father Terah had a portion in the World to Come (Genesis Rabbah 30:4; 30:12).

--planted ironwood yesterday, acceptance Mars Report.

7/7/17 Ruslan Bondar and Yury Martyshev/promobot
Max Igan: 1-20: spiritualist, 5G network elephant in room-

7/6/17 Richard's Garden City arbutus unedo cf yaupon or manzinita or crepe myrtle. Ironwood, Mex redbud. Lookalike: Tom Drabik Ohio stoneware. douglas murray the strange death of europe max igan the coming 5G rollout
"Doug!" he shouted, rousing me like a freight train. "Doug, it hit me like the hard ground we're standing on! It's all around us—everywhere! They think of us like aliens, but they're the aliens! Don't you get it?! They're laughing at us. They 'THINK' they're the children of space aliens from another world, marooned on this tiny blue orb. They're just doing time till they can figure a way off this rock so they can get back up to their DeathStar Moon Ship; figure out how to fix it and head back home to mommy!" Investigator third strand DNA a parasite
Metaformin metformin's antiaging properties. Galega officinalis. The plant, also known as French lilac and goat's rue, is hardly the stuff of cutting-edge science. Physicians have been prescribing it as an herbal remedy for centuries. In 1640, the great English herbalist John Parkinson wrote about goat's rue in his life's work, Theatrum Botanicum, recommending it

for "the bitings or stings of any venomous creature," "the plague," "measells," "small pocks," and "wormes in children," among other conditions.

Antarctica, cERN, Scalia, Weimar, Astharoth, Isis, Blood Moon, Hybrids, Uber Bots, If as Ephesians says we are joined to Israel, grafted into ABraham, no wonder the world hates us, for Israel was anointed to judge the world. If any Christian hates Israel or acts against it he is anathema, but what Israel is is a fair question, for as McGee says modern Israel is not Israel. What is the true Israel? Make in Himself of two, one new man 2. 15, , not aliens from the commonwealth of Israel, from the covenants of promise...without God in the world 2.12, both reconciled in one body by the cross 2.16,, built on the foundation of apostles and prophets 2.20, through Him we both have aces by one Spirit to the Father 2.

7/5/17 18 exposed fish gods-oil not fossil fuel

-snapchat profiles, Facebook old friends, that is, there is a reason why these people have departed and should not be brought back, they are toxic, tom goar, kark hillie, jack dodds, ann o, etc, as my father was advised, don't take a picture of a corpse.

--demon thoughts, black limpurs at door. Anointing

7/4/17 signs in the heavens that google sky was hiding The image of this area was blocked by Google Sky as you can see in the video. it appears between the legs as the Virgin as Jupiter is set to pass through the womb area in September of 2017 September 23, 2017, Revelation 12, US Solar Eclipse venus, mars, mercury, 9 stars of Leo above the head of virgo 13.50 DAHBOO77 lord Soros, Lord George

7/3/17 leo zagami Melbourne Response, for George Pell's first Cardinal-prefect of the newly created Secretariat for the Economy, Catholic priest pedophile network, so they could all pay the victims a ridiculous amount, and continue molesting them at a cheap price. he stated that the Catholic Church should be no more responsible for the abuse of children than a trucking company is for a driver who picks up and molests a woman while on the job. when Pell arrived in Rome, Lord Christopher Patten, joined his team, the same guy the elite of the New World Order used to cover up the increasing pedophilia scandals in the BBC, who included the pedophile monster Jimmy Savile

--Lewis Masonic; The Secret School of Wisdom: The Authentic Ritual and Doctrines of the Illuminati edition (February 19, 2015). He says many refugee/immigrant bodies found sewn back up with the organs missing and the blood. the dark side of tesla's technology mechanical ossilator to steel beam, Tesla waves, scalar waves

7/2/17 this is why evidence not for secret release, dimensions of govt surveil, silencing whistleblowers, Kevin Shipp, from the company of shadows

7/1/17 if it is said that war and competition make a man who he is it is the war and competition that make the world controllers who they are-- for the man is diverted from true tests that would make him even stronger but he does not even known what those are. 2. all this love and light is another of these merchandising schemes to further enslave and enrich the same rulers who plan the wars. disclosure inc the art of the steal-exposing'Time Traveling Astronaut' Corey Goode therapy network to help followers cope with disclosure, 'Corey's

Kids' space gear promotions and a Comic Book based on Goode's adventures in Secret Space with Blue Avian aliens. -'love and light' and a by way of PresidioSpace Being philosophy of oneness. Emma Gold = Roger Ramsaur Roger Ramsaur (Emma Gold) is the an artist, activist and visionary behind Full Disclosure Now. FDN is the worlds first United direction action movement for universal truth Five major figures in Alternative Research have come forward with accounts of these kind of incidents, including popular Web Bots developer Clif High, Dr. Joseph Farrell, Linda Moulton Howe, The Object Report's Agent K and UFO Filmmaker Jim Nichols.

words must be echoes of themselves to show the large vast state of our energies. say wonderland is the starry world and of the imagination but it has immediately nine referents and then ninety as does each attempt to grasp it

6/30/17 Skeksis. "part reptile, part predatory bird, part dragon." In the film, the Skeksis are represented by puppets engineered under the direction of Jim Henson. Jim Henson said that in the development of the Skeksis, the creators drew inspiration from the Seven Deadly Sins Nova addresses saying what can't be said in words by patching and splicing. Words need to have auras, energy fields, like people, because words got us into this mess as the agents of our slavery, but to get us out they have to say what they cannot say, go where they have never gone, splayed, broken, hummed up, stolen, flown down here and dropped off
--another installment of this situation, game where I interact with another, who morph into different people but the main point is I love them but of course we are independent, this time joined by a junior who suffered abuse of bigotry and had adoped it a little, but set right -- somehow this seems connected to saying yesterday that there are hundreds of millions of people who have suffered but never are mentioned, and that I want to and do identify with are the highest and best human persons who however how great and so flawed contradict themselves.

6/29/17 got a grant of 20k for prescribing pista cuffin, connin. No matter what I am not going to accuse Aeg of anything. I release this.
6/28/17 Aeg still has not cold stored. He owes for two loans. He promised to help with the wall

6/26/17 Growing Up In The Satanic Illuminati: The Story of A Survivor another mkultra SRA family, Mormon, not only, basements of churches of all kinds rituals, some unknown to participants from alters, others full conscious covens
--we found Oscar's desiccated shell in the yard, some time gone. the aluminum too much for him.

6/25/17 Nikolai A. Kozyrev, time Stillness, Mirrors! collapse, and Kozyrev's work; consciousness. Sean David Morton   John Chang, Taoist master Industrial surrealism Sean Gautreaux High doesn't know Thunderbolts of the gods by thornhill, 54.15 randy maugans death culture behind "super-soldier" media figures. The Ramsaur (the Goat God) Sunday Aeyrie got a 100 on his midterm last Wed.

6/24/17 Ever Expanding Top Secret Underground Reptilian Cities esp. below Mt. McKinley underground pyramid.
Tesla 369 the law of attraction vortex math

BILLY HAYES see second half geoengineering, haarp and the space fence
Space Fence a first generation, matrix like computer program kinetic stimulatioon2 freq come together in phase makes plasma effect, stimulated by haarp, in ionosphere, cyclotronic stimulation, a vortex goes round and round amplifies these freq and plasmatic effect, creates a sub freq at ground. Ultra sonics, sub sonics   a strong pulse affects crystals in ground pick up stimulation and cascade amplification through ground, thus create earthquakes, same crystals in air, alum, barium, lithium ox, ship tracks-lithium (skip trails) human-produced aerosols affect cloud formation ships release their exhaust into the relatively clean and still marine air. Cell towers: weather modif. GWEN, Pave pulse, Super door, Haarp is over. Space fence 1959, pulse

6/23/27 BOA, Savageland, Man vs. all B movies of predictive programming to loose the pit.
--jacquie figg, without a liscence CA

6/22/17 AnthonyPatch Knowville Post-grad 4/12/17 600 sided tertrhedron model f the universe geographical distribution of the thousand baal arches, nodes, inferred from the SWS sentient world simulation, each human one of 7 billion nodes

--Like an explosion the old one gets the further away everything seems to become, relations etc, like waking here with no view of how it happened, except with some connection to somewhere, a track down which the person fled or came to this. Except for the presence of Jesus this is a proudound sadness.

6/21/17 BIY HAYES Cyclotronic resonance cyclotron resonance of the waves with the dominant ions appears capable of electromagentic lockdown that is underway on planet earth. From HAARP to CERN, transforming the atmosphere into an electrically charged plasma turning the sky into a battery, or an antenna. The metal particulates, and the nano-tech contained within, are being inhaled cyclotronic resonance that is produced when they play with the atmosphere and how this is exactly the same as what they are doing with magnets down below at CERN.

CERN is also being used to manipulate the magnetic field of the planet, and its all connected to the space fence/prison planet system wind turbines & fracking is actually all part of this same system. They will explain how these form the ground element of the space fence metals, barium and aluminum, are required to turn the atmosphere into an ionized plasma,

... the inner magnetosphere of Saturn Space fence ionospheric heaters turn ions per into plasma.

-The whole thing has the feeling, like the incredible camera/bull sequence, of being told as a narrative from the memories and imaginations of two goofy brothers lying out in a tent one summer night, taking turns killing off each other's characters and they hand off the narrative.

6/20/17 leviathan cypher, a church that chips, clones, fingerprints with reptile slit eyes. Why people leave? They have to hive beside the church in a manse?

6/19/17 This matter is by the decree of the watchers, and the demand by the word of the holy ones: to the intent that the living may know that the most High ruleth in the kingdom of men, and giveth it to whomsoever he will, and setteth up over it the basest of men. Daniel 4.17 Abimilimech killed the 70 sons of Gideon and was killed by a woman's millstone. in Daniel 4:24 the king's doom is said to be 'by the decree of the Most High.' God is represented in the O.T. as surrounded by an assembly of angels (1 Kings 22:19), who form almost a kind of heavenly council, Job 1:6; Job 2:1; Job 15:8 (R.V. marg.), Jeremiah 23:18, Psalm 89:7; and it seems that in Dan. the decree is regarded as possessing the joint authority of God and of His council. By the later Jews this assembly of angels was called God's 'court of judgement' (בית דין), or His 'family' (פמליא); and He was represented as taking counsel with it, or communicating to it His purposes (so Genesis 1:26 in the Targ. of Ps.Jon.). In Sanh. 38 b it is said, "The Holy One, blessed be He! does nothing without first consulting the family above, as it is said (Daniel 4:17), 'By the decree of the watchers,' &c." See further Weber, System der Altsynag. Theol. p. 170 f.

Santilli Telescope, The Santilli telescope serves the same purpose as the Vaticans L.U.C.I.F.E.R (yes real acronym and name used) telescope on Mt Graham in Arizona. -- Reptiles one heart in each armpit, liver just above the groin. Human give children to the Greys who give them to the Repts so hey won't come up.

--Ether delta site. Mon. They Gave themselves up.

-yesterday, Sun, Father's day,went to pay respects to departing pastor Marc. In midst of social polit relig disintegration, 500 peoploe died in Grenfell Tower in London not 15 from a woman who lives there but cannot find any survivors. Bea Dewit engaged us, said Ron VanderARk said it was "in the best interests of the church" pastor be terminated.. Reptilian logic to be believed or else. Some families had left. But Marc Van Berkum (refused to be a FEMA pastor? Wasn[t in favor of fingerprinting, chipping?) was less under wraps as he said his mission was to equip the church. Said you should love Jesus more than your wife , children or America! Something like he was too conservative! Pat heard in the sermon veiled reference that he knew something compromising about...which is what a night dream I had simulated, but don't remember Referred to exquisite penmanship, about a broken hand reset. Bea asked if we were to continue, said she and and Floyd were under decision. Pat emailed church sect to ask for the minutes of the meeting of the elders and pastor.. Sent: May 25, 2017 10:55 AM
>Hi Ms. Carol: I would like a copy of the Executive committee minutes for the last 3 meetings. You can Email them to me or I can pick them up at the church during your work hours, if you prefer.
"Dear Pat, those records have been sequestered in the classis library until either the death of their components or the coming transfiguration of the religion. We wish you all the best in your efforts and look forward to seeing you at our next opportunity."

--Saw a clip of Jason Chafetz resigned from congress who said nothing was different in the last 6 months, all records still not accessed. Like meeting Abraham James head of green Gables org in street with his polit black stories of Dallas, Mn, Trump, all defamations, all snowflake talk from this Gullah architect. Top it off did not no acknowledgment of Fatherhood from son Andrew. His wife wrote: Happy Father's Day to my own Dad (and grandfather to my babies), my wonderful husband, and my big brother who is celebrating his first Father's Day today! Sabrina is like the Post and NYT covering Trump full of terror. So if it is held against me that I said we would like to come to here next graduation when she gets her Ph.d. the implicit compliment to AB is not mentioned but the slight about her grad from preschool is. When they hate you they hate you.

The problem I have with his raising his children is they have no base in reality to judge myth or fairy tale, think them real. So when the deception comes will have no center. Aey visited though. I told Aey we become what we are and it is the best we could have done. So Aeg in Tennis and Aey in his work now. And me, w/o perks if I can be stopped I will but if not, not.

6/17/17 Bob Wood MJ12 Matt Bracken NYT printed baseball schedule Security forces are loath to discuss much about who they protect or what it costs, for fear, they say, of compromising their mission.
But when the billionaire Wilbur L. Ross Jr., the commerce secretary, goes to dinner at a fancy Georgetown restaurant, bodyguards sit nearby. When members of Congress practice in the early mornings in an Alexandria, Va., public park for their Congressional Baseball Game, plainclothes United States Capitol Police are sitting there in a black S.U.V.

Posted twitter before reading, WORDS ARE A FORM OF ACTION. Also just read two days ago of the flash of light.
New Collider. 1 June, 2017. CERN Director General Fabiola Gianotti addressed the entire assemblage of the
Bilderberg Group where she delivered the "Message of God" that had been "received/deciphered" by the Large Hadron Collider-LHC. July 13, 1978, a Soviet scientist named Anatoli Bugorski stuck his head inside a particle accelerator, Phineas Gage-style and got 76 billion electron volts. Max Planck said that human thought was the basis for all matter, and in 1931 that: "I regard matter as derivative from consciousness. We cannot get behind consciousness. Everything that we talk about, everything that we regard as existing, postulates consciousness."
Flash of light at conception: Of the "truths of God" being suppressed in the West is that when a male sperm meets a woman's egg, a "brilliant flash" of light instantly appears—and is the splitting of an as yet unknown particle, with one part being left in the baby, and the other becoming interdimensional. The "real/true" truth being that at the instant life is created in the womb, an inseparable and instantaneous communication link between human beings and God is created. To the most powerful affect of this "human-God" link, though, this report continues, is new research, also, proving the validity of the decade's long research conducted by DoctorScientist Pjotr Garjajev proving that words, and words alone, whether read or spoken, not only can change DNA, but underlie all matter too. This requires one thin not speaking with the mouth but with integrity, intent, from the heart EZ 33.31 The image addressed to Bilderbrg produced by the Large Hadron Collider-LHC formed a single word in Hebrew, תקל—pronounced "TEKEL" The message given at Bilderberg to the elite means, "you have been weighed on the scales and found deficient".

-- sO WHEN aBRAham rolls through with his Dallas, Minnesota murders of Blacks and Trump criminal talk it is not a benefit to the neighborhood. He covers himself with his own weaponized calumny. A walking bad news TV broadcast. I need to be careful not to do the same. Words are a form of action.

6/16/17 Artificial Imagination & Its Demonic Faces last 15 min Sentient-World-Simulation (SWS) and software providers such as Palantir. Software engineers at Google have been analyzing the 'dreams' of their computers. tessellating Escher-esque artwork The Boltzmann Machine

6/15/17 Capt mark richards, reptile source Realized on waking that Asking A & A to hold keys is too much. They have other compromising needs. So plan to covert all to one acct which I hold three copies of cold. Killed Tom Goar yesterday. Long time coming.

6/14/17 let the violence they have loosed on others come upon them. His mischief lands back on his own head.

His violence comes down on top of him.Ps 7.16 Psalm 9:15

The nations have sunk down in the pit which they have made; In the net which they hid, their own foot has been caught. Psalm 10:2

In pride the wicked hotly pursue the afflicted; Let them be caught in the plots which they have devised. Psalm 94:23

He has brought back their wickedness upon them And will destroy them in their evil; The LORD our God will destroy them. Psalm 140:9

"As for the head of those who surround me, May the mischief of their lips cover them.

6/13/17 Wed. William tompkins, ET. Reptilian bases and facilities in antarctica 10.20 /Vorts/ 10in rabbits w/o ears floated, play in dirt with the boys. Orts George MacDonald

-James Queasy Weasel, also known as the Comey Coward, an elongated mouse insinuating from place to place with subtle cunning. Some say they conceive through the ear and give birth through the mouth. These creatures signify not a few of you fellows who willingly accept by ear but dissimulate what you say. TH White. Book of the Beasts.

6/12/17 Pharoah flusher. EZ 32.5, Cryptids

--see Weaponized Architecture-- Although the ideologies behind the political programes exposed here were not invented by architecture, architecture is a necessary means to implement their violence on bodies.   the door, allowing the porosity of a wall to be moderated by making a small part of it rotate at will... door was not invented alone; it came with a lock and an associated key that allows only certain bodies to transform the impermeable wall into a punctually porous one... Whether the key holder is the agent benefiting from private property legislation, the warden of a prison, or an apartheid state, the determination of who designs/builds architecture and benefits from the control of its violence on bodies has necessarily drastic political consequences... Border walls, container camps, detention centres, fortified police stations, fences, checkpoints, the numerous architectural apparatuses that are flourishing in the European Union and its periphery... "Surrounding a body with walls enforces the incarceration of this body."... ehicle compartments and office furniture are calibrated on a male standardised body (Joe), ironing boards, vacuum cleaners and kitchens are calibrated on its female counterpart (Josephine), thus accomplishing what Dreyfuss himself calls "human engineering" in the reinforcement of gender normativity... to what political programme does the architect contribute through construction?

6/11/17 Sunday. B/C meet at Aey. Jacob's B-day. meet Christina's boyfriend Kalbfleisch(er) Synchrons: Pats score
neighborhood meeting Sat, Eth run, Marc Van Berkun visit, Kings of Pentagon appears, org with A & A Sunday meets Pat's 590

6/1017 Pat passed boards with 590, 380 to pass. news yesterday. Neighborhood meeting.

6/9/17 fusion centers Al gore says god told him to fight global warming. this is the same god of fortune athletes point to in the end zone and pray to before the game. Same god Bob Dylan made a pact with, the crossroads god. Christians take comfort in these references when they are substitutes of lucifer/satan as god. As are so many references to god in dally life, which god has supplanted the truth.

yesterday more synchronsis. Taking the books ot Von Berkum and his subsequent visit. Seeing Aey in AM to deposit check for ETH, but he being noticeably out of sync, mentions this, he says a rough morning, which later turns out to be him saying at her invite, love my family, and the whole he loves me more than her thing again, which is what it was from the start!, then the Comey hearings, confessions, Church, family nation! ETH! 6/8/17 So Marc Van Berkum stopped by. Gave him mini ice age, Ezekiel, Jacob the elder, J. edwards, LAM, cosmic ray discord, Aey gets 14 ETH

Yestday with Anu got about 15 Eth, today with Aey 14. But is his holding secure from Sh? In the event? He was not happy. She asked him on way to work what she could do for him. He said love my family, She blew up.Took Conybear and Howson, Life and Travelsof St. Paul, in leather to Marc Van Verkum. alled church but message from phone Co said the phone was out! Just that phone. So went over 9.45 but place locked tight.

Rang his bell. He ans in bare feet, little kids around him, house dark, as if his wife had migraine? Shh! he said..

Books I said, you used to work ina bookstore and left.. Ouch.

6/7/17 gambler and compulsive fetishists are synchronists so if they see a rainbow bet on a horse with that name or if a favority number seek it out for payoff. But in dialogue with P last night asleep about her being jealous of this CEO thing but wanting her to have something I propose Etherium, but forgot this even after mentioning it to her AM till Aey emails about Putin and it. So tomorrow we buy? reggie middleton veraseteum 100 mil, robots, gas

6/5/17 Clif high: amy semple macpherson hysteria correy good, david wilcock
hysteria 6/4/17 LONDON PSY-OP BUSTED WIDE OPEN! Roy Orbison,
mowing presbyterians, pedestrials on London Bridge

6/3/17 PITY-- Sat. Yesterday had the desire to replay Patriot, which Taking cinematic reflections into fiction. People at the end important making previous occasional appearance, lighting scenes, scoring, background music, long contemplative sympatic faces, a series of reflections sometimes in different circumstances and different angles, then these reflections can be followed by their history, --all this presupposes a text, a series of notes that are already complete. with flashbacks and flash forwards. these events pass each other with cognition and without.

You have o be old to do something young Lord prepare me to be a sanctuary.

6/1/17 woke 2.30 am w/ bad headache, about same time as two previous episodes in past, in the middle of night, in dreams. some blurred vision the da before. ischemic? BP day before 114/63. Now 152/79 5/31/17 how to keep your cryptocurrency safe top 5 best crypto currency wallets

Jordon codex little book of REv 5 and 6!

--on all fours naked like Nebuchadnezzar but w/o fur, rear end white sticking out the back going down sidewalk toward freeway, cars passing on the right some one checking out but not stopping, over and over. how's that for exposure. not too shabby. That night P come with surprise news she has bought another washer, after the insistence that this one be studied by Aey. She's magical thinking that a check installs a washer but I need do much prep to get it here, in, and installed. That night 6/1 very bad rt lobe headache.

-later, reflections on A after checking lastest HSI champ, who played only 16 matches his last year! his father a pro, going, he thinks to play, at U of A 5'7"

5/30/17 nanogirl sharon barrington Aey and Sh at A's Sunday all day. Waking. Dupont Circle 67, Folger, lettuce, tennis on clay in socks agt congressman/asst.

Aeg skip HS Philosophy, Ceramics, Phx college after 8th grade. Homo upset at Flag first year, upset

5/27/17 15 Cynewulf I was redder on rood than the rose in the rain Dream
of the Rood orc cryptids
crates from the Vistor God tomb

Fear and greed Aey, at least you made a decision, now live with it and learn yourself. Be indifferent? Right place right time? Why are you working so hard? What are you trying to escape with your exhaustion? Aey fear and greed last nite. buys at 2266 but this AM its 1978. Big clumps of moutaininous clay.

!5/26/17 recorded future Harold Camping ruach, mother ship foresight.org

5/24-6/17 --I realize I only lasted a year and a half at my first job at FSC and all the gossip that flurried about was most revealing, I heard courtesy of Charlie Brown

--There are two things they could have done. All the elders prostrate themselves on the carpet in remorse for the situation, the pastor too and 2' He should have given an open and honest statement to the congregation, not take about Paul and Silas

--"I have the scoop from Charlotte Bakker regarding the church, in a nutshell the pastor quit because his wife wanted to go back to Michigan, and was not happy here. She did not like having to travel to Peoria for small group meeting. Charlotte said in Grand Rapids all the people live about 3 miles from church, and if they live further they change churches.. She has it on good authority that it was NOT his preaching or anything else, that people liked him a lot, but his wife really missed her family. He has been here 3 years. It was as much a surprise to her and Tom as to us, they did not know this was coming, but in talking after church, found this out."

--Beth Kredit says 6 or 7 families have left over Marc, that there had been discussions for three months, that he had been there 4 yrs, that the Spanish prospect had not wanted to initiate a Spanish ministry. To the question why the elders who hired him did not vet him she said it was the search committee hired him 5/23/17

--Gen. 3.15 the CRC. A symptom of censorship and division prevalent in U.S. now from Tom G to FB to hysteria in streets, these engineered, Unlikely Stories, mult-D upsets, so the elders oppose the pastor. --"Over the past several months it has become increasingly apparent that the elders' vision for the church is significantly different from the pastor's vision for the church and both the elders and the pastor are discerning that the relationships have become strained to the point that effective ministry seems impossible and it is best to pursue separate directions. Pastor Marc will be leaving to pursue other ministry opportunities. His last Sunday with us will be June 18th after which we will have a farewell gathering. Soon after, Pastor Marc and his family will be moving back to Michigan. If you have any questions or concerns please contact your elder. We join in praying for God's leading and blessing for Pastor Marc, Niki and their family in this transition." --Phoenix Christian Reformed Church December 1, 2013 at 8:20pm

· We are blessed and excited to announce Pastor Marc Van Berkum will become our full time pastor in early 2014!! PCRC is thankful and can't wait for him and his family to arrive! Ordination Date: 03/02/2014

5/22/17 Chesterton, the ethics of elfland
--ins and outs of running a large paper co, c. 20's? as a scion of it, large art displays, photos, projections, colors of its history. Had this before.

5/21/17 Sunday Leidos antarctica
Last Sunday, 5/14 Pat returned exhausted from SA. This Sat we had the kids, today Marc Van Berkum dismissed, has different vision from the elders for the church, is terminated, released as of 6/18MANchester bombing Monday 22 May 10:30 PM

Synchronisis: AB and Jesus, Marc Van Berkum and elders, Manchester bombing at the Ariana Grande Gangrenous Woman Tour (dangerous) Had B/C meet this am with a and a.
Helped Aey later pick up used fence.
AB yesterday says Jesus is not real, but she thinks fairytales real, that she would like her head to be cut off and to be eaten, had a lot to say about killing things, asked if I were old, then later do all all old people die, they had kept a sick dog over the weekend and was prob told this. I said, I'm not old, this before the other shoe dropped. In answer to Jesus being real I said Jesus gave you your new car, which she denied. I said Jesus will help you if you're ever in trouble and you ask him. She said she would ask her parents.! At here graduation said she wanted to be a owl. 3 Ways to know: other people, the word, your own spirit

5/20/17 Chinese bitcoin whitepaper. Sepher Yetz, "a lone thinker, without a school and without disciples, 199 Commenting on SY,
Elliot R. --the Covenant by voice spiritual

Wolfson stated, Second, from the Spirit he made Air and formed for speech twenty-two letters-- formed by the voice, impressed on the air, and audibly uttered in five situations, in the throat, guttural sounds; in the palate, palatals; by the tongue, linguals; through the teeth, dentals; and by the lips, labial sounds.

These twelve letters, he designed, the twelve divisions of the heavens (namely, the zodiacal constellations), the twelve months of the year, and the twelve important organs of the frame of man, namely the right and left hands, the right and left feet, two kidneys, the liver, the gall, the spleen, the intestines, the gullet, and the stomach.-- Tali, the Dragon, is above the Universe, as a king on his throne; the sphere in the year as a king in his State, Sacred Texts —"Properly speaking, the work should not be described as a single composition, but rather as a composite of distinct literary strands that have been woven together through a complicated redactional process whose stages are not clearly discernable." PDF Just like the anonymous sources and former gov't officials weave the tapestry of defamation of the underworld.

5/19/17" Former official releases "bombshell" story of the NEW CURRENCY ELONGATED SKULL DOLLAR BILL

5/18/17 Qoph: most primitive part of the human brain involuntary matrix cerebellum we are linked to our animal origins and, thus, to Nature. 'Anima', the place where memory and motion are joined, the place where The Golden Chain of Homer links us to Heaven2 and where the spirit of the Moon, the imagination, acts as the medium through which Natures order may be restored. Two dog-like creatures (sometimes identified as Anubis and Ap-uat, the Egyptian gods which guide the soul through the underworld) howl at the moon and guard the way to the open skyline. In the foreground is a lake the waters of which, as on the Path of the Star, are the Waters of Life, the Bitter Sea of Binah, and, most importantly for a shamanic poet, the waters of the human subconscious.

Dominating these waters, is a crab-like creature with its pincers and legs outstretched. It is a creature native to these waters, a creature with jointed legs, simple eyes, devouring jaws and a protective armor which it sheds as it grows and metamorphoses, so that these waters are littered with shells

5/17/17 Wed. Spoke to Joe on the Appalachian Trail, Rob and Cn who just moved again two doors down, Mike Farley who lives in debris and his back place is unhabitable.

5/16/17 dreams and fiction need a spirit line like weavings in order to escape the dead ends and cul de sacs from disoriented directions. Jay is an example, still flaccidly floating about

5/15/17 Preface to A New World Order

Yom Battista

Mix the real and the fantastic, the Probable and marvelous, spiritual worlds, ghosts, magicians, archetypal beasts, transworld salvation and damnation. We meet in them on the one hand very ordinary modern people of our own day who talk the saying of our own day and live in the suburbs. I've almost decided not to have any human beings in this novel. Chas Wms letters 168 the collection here from the hierarchies of greatest to least, gods, men, beasts, is a serious work of natural history that becomes a kind of naturalist's scrapbook with descriptions of gods, men, beasts, birds, reptiles, fish from myths and traveler's tales in literatures and oral traditions where every copyist makes additions whenever they feel they know more than their predecessors. These transpositional landscapes masquerade as one another as forms of encryption, the grand canyon could be the immensity of space, coyote lucifer, shapeshifters, changelings, the kingdom of iron digital net and clay, human

5/14/17 Pat returns after Mother's Day in SA with Andrew and fam. Ruth's sale nets $400.

5/12/17 the ill will created by making houses along the canal to move a block wall inches far overwhelms the quality of life gained by the project. Residents sacrificed for a govt grant and a measure of the whole system of control

5/9/17 Breaking Bad: allegory of the structure of evil. The hierarchy of princes and powers: so Gus and the cartel, below them Walt and Jesse and his henchmen. below them the aPollo crew and factory, its good product of chicken and the bad of is meth, below them the incidental actors of and their faults, skylar collaborating, the DEa's wife, and agent, all tied by causations of themselves throughout so that had Jesse's girl not tried to extort walt he wouldn't have killed here, etc ad infinitium.

above te cartel or beside parallel structures of dea and cia not represented in the film but all cia motivated because deep state needs its funding of 9 missing trillion for its programs, which of course are the destruction of human life and al life on earth.

5/8/17 Review of War in Heaven. Begin Carr. that Prester John is ultimate good, a theophany while the bad has several human characters whose techniques of power are delineated, are countered humanly only by the

Archdeacon mumbling under his breath the Psalms. So he gives no counterpart character to the Greek, no

Apostolic or prophetic, Elijah against the Baal The Novels of Charles Williams

By Howard, Thomas Grevel Lindop CHARLES WILLIAMS The third Inkling 544pp. Oxford University Press

Alice Mary Hadfield's Charles Williams: An exploration of his life and work (1983),   Mix the realistic and fantastic, Probable and marvelous, ghosts, magicians, archetypal beasts. we meet in them on the one very ordinary modern people of our own day who talk the saying of our own day and live in the suburbs. Mon. Mike Farley to ER yesterday while we were at church?

5/7/17 Netflix science purge 5/6/16 Sat.

--Synchronsis On Wed nite stomach flu from Theo hit, incapacitating for 2 days or so coincident with the a/c failing, preceded by--Synchronsis- Pat said last Wed her concern for the deep end, which I get, so when the virus hit with two feet it forced a period of of...whatever perception of three realities sleep wake and inbetween and many shades. In this time I read the WAr in Heaven which offeres a reality pretty much like what I am presented with. This vs. the pol/psy war op in progress share a lot.

...

5/3/17 predictive ling a form of twittermancy

TOMORROW NOBODY HAS HEARD OF BUDDHA ['S DEATH] (Van dewetering. AfterZen, 107). After a

certain age they worry about it but he knows all there is to know. To nobody else the mystery of an ant interrupting a wasp in the garden. except the rose says to the wasp, "tell me this honey when you drive up in your yellow car, how can we ever get enough of this

new and loved life?" 5/2/17 W.R.M. World Revolutionary Movement. Satan Prince of the World.
4/30/17 AB and T for the PM while their parents go to baseball game.
4/28/17 JAPAN TSUNAMI 3/11 in English: from START to END 11.36
spooky being! Jim Stone, fukushima   to explain rise of construction
stocks prior -Charles bowden has the voice of joe aripao.
-J. vernon mcgee, mod israel not a fulfillment of prophecy / satan's counterfeit israel
--Synchronsis smug, smaug, it revolved around a 53 blue and white Mercury and a tall pale faced young man whom I called smug to his face and there was some passion of disagreement but passion on my part as if this were a memoryof Andrew at El Paso which I spoke to Aey with yesterday, he saying it was the same time as his confrontation with him at Gold Key etc. and that he needed correction Aey thought from his father. I was saying that I remembered from the FB tennis racket lesson he gave AB my shortcomings in his behalf, that this El Paso was one, or not? Mercury is 4D for the god, the smug one, the mercury spirit being the changling, the shapeshifter, the one who has no character to trust, confrontation with the god. This being the piece composed last night, which compounds with fat steve blocking the door as i maneuvered this piece out. filling the space like arthur juarez with the same.... The thickest part of that piece, the head, body with wings spread, demoed in bisque and I lost that part. Itself a statement.
4/24/17 Paul Levy, Dispelling Wetico, non local [Tesseract] source of evil, cf. Wendigo swampy cree, witigo, wetigo." when they become a Wetigo their heart first becomes ice and after that the whole body becomes ice when it is impossible to kill them"
-Pat sent pics of Aeg on tennis court with kids, AB with a nice stroke. I never found out why he was so angry the second year at Flag, or why he shunned us when we saw him play, coincident with after the digital didn't speak to me for some 6 or 8 months, when he entertained the Cinn job and asked for his journal which I took to him. The naming of Theo worse, not telling of his birth, which we learned by FB from Cynthia. This anyway was the visualization at the nap at 10 am today, Monday. Trying to shake the headaches and vertigo of the last weeks. Also trying to plumb the vision of this interior speech, to so describe the waking sleep. In this, causation is autonomous. So I'm glad to say Theo crawled up into my lap when he appeared there. About six month as ago I had 2 rackets propped against the wall when Theo came. He picked up one in either hand and waved them for some time. That was the first he ever saw of such.
-Symmetrical cosmology an idol of the theatre, Bacon. "classical mythology became purely poetic after its oracles had ceased." -northrop frye anatomy of crit 161.
-Rebuttal offered to Enkiites is the continual rebuke of Israel for fornication with the Egyptians, whoredom with the Assyrians and with Canaan into Chaldea, insatiable Ez 16 24-31 so that they made high steeples in every street, made a high place in every head, so that even the Philistines were ashamed of their lewd way. Israel is a refutation of all the ancient Sumer beliefs of the the gods.
-their row of inner oleander
4/23/17 Spent some time to identify the lighting in dreams, which is source centered, within the image not outside. also the discontinuous narratives.

4/22/17 Twice i saw, the repetition was needed, becasuee i didn't remembr the first until the second, full bodied men naked carrying their women on their shoulders in various stages of upset, she was face up over his shoulder legs extended and arms, face with blond hair turned toward me in shame or some such, his face labored but massive torso to bear her weight as they went down the sidewalk in front of the rows of houses toward their car, a blue Olds convertible parked in someone's yard as if crashed part inside the house. Thre was another couple as if some event had just let out. These were massive white pink skinned teutons. This was the effort that made Mercury, above.

4/21/17 5 things we know about 432 Hz VS 440 Hz #432Hertz #MKUltra
-Hobbes frontis Leviathan: The frontispiece operates as an emblematic threshold and allegory of Hobbes's theory of the state. Hobbes participated directly (as he had in the frontispieces of his translation of Thucydides's Peloponnesian War and De Cive) in its design (likely by the engraver Abraham Bosse), which is redolent with enigmas, ...the meaning of the arrangement of gazes between sovereign and subjects? On what is this Mortall God standing? The question Agamben homes in on is a different one: why is the fortified city over which this 'android' looms – a rex populus in which the rex is the head, and the cives the corpore – empty? For Agamben, as he remarks in the brief prefatory note to Stásis, the 'constitutive element' of the modern state is ademia, the absence of a people. At the same time, civil war – precisely because it is rarely thought in political philosophy, which lacks a real stasiology – is the 'fundamental threshold of politicisation of the West'. The frontispiece will bring these two theses together. ... the multitude have been symbolically composed, neutralised and pacified into a people, 'deported' we could say, over the horizon. But there are figures in the landscape. In the main, these are soldiers, patrolling both within and without the city...
'Hobbes's Hidden Monster', Magnus Kristiansson and Johan Tralau

4/20/17 Trying for R and R. Dreamed in the desert two nights with some group, whittled down finally to people constructing, surviving. At the end of the night I came on a large bank of chollas with blue cactus wren nests but was kept from the eggs by the thorns. a large gaunt wolf came runing toward me and went off in the distance. I went that direction and came on some others packing to leave. Another: Eagles Nest again but I couldn't find a seat. Collecting lyric poems together!

- This is a Mercator Projection of the Spiritual Oecumene, or world view if you like. Renaissance mariners knew it as the Greek word for the inhabited world. If you can step your sight back two figures holding a globe might appear. These are the continents of the known world, known being a joke, right? These are not the continents as we have been told. Better you learned this before not after? East and west, north and south. Clif High: behomethe frothing at the mouth with some kind of dire internal disease and a brain structure and a brain structure absolutely rotted out with syphlicss. no way of predicting how the syphliphitc beast is going to flail around next.

4/18/17 medical marijuana trojan horse, Why are TPTB tracking people with Rh negative blood so closely. O blood. It just so happens that those human beings who have O- negative blood type have a much higher likelihood of being gifted with super-sensible facultie

4/17/17 Gunpowder recipes. black flag pension funeral marriage, had dress up ready. Robert Monroe -time, OBE sales and service, John Dunne serial universe one above that one above that, says a dream about an event, fire, earthquake is nto about the event but when you become aware of it, ie news account. At this time I don't think this. -Burroughs shooting wm shakespeare
And now, Father, glorify me in your presence with the glory I had with you before the world began. Jn 17.25 4/16/17 talking to a family of children different ages who did not want to hear what I said even if it was true, wanted their own way.
-Trump a genius of deception had everybody believing he was a nationalist when he was the tyrant tool of tyrants to subvert the last remaining population that were. Murdered Scalia's remains to be examined.

4/15/17 Sat. He descended into hell. Shame, sin, accusation. Spectral signature
angel halo satellite "Angel Halo" satellite was on a "assignment/mission" using a specialized K-law spectral signature correlation algorithm (PDF) to identify "hot spots" of White Spot Syndrome Virus (WSSV) locations in the Pacific Ocean far east regions of the Federation—and is a disease that, since 1992, has wiped out within a few days the entire populations of many shrimp farms throughout the world... To the grave danger posed to the entire world by this now unstoppable H7N9 virus, this report continues, Chinese President Xi Jinping this past week traveled to the United States to personally inform President Donald Trump about—and that after receiving the grim prognosis our world is facing, Trump, in less than week, jettisoned nearly all of his nationalistic "American First" plans with his overnight becoming a "globalist"...
fear of this looming H7N9 apocalypse, this report further details, the Western elite classes have been quietly building and stockpiling provisions in massive bunkers all around the world—while at the same time attempting to flood their nations with Muslim refugees whom they believe will be able to keep their nations vital utilities and infrastructure intact through this crisis—

4/14/17 Stanley is the opposite of textuality and numinous scripture which he jumps over to imbibe an even further reach of non historical, myth. He says the Archons were the Builders of Worlds. He calls them "our ancestors." He found the temple of Mu in Malibu.

4/13/17 Melt appears. robert stanley the man who met enki, stanley's father freinds of norman paulsen, see the birth of the archons, who traces demonic disorder to the fragmentation afflicting Enki and crew when they entered a forbidden zone and went mad. demons being the thought form projection of their thoughts. enki is father of annunaki: all this Stanley gets from wes penry's papers. He believed the being was Enki just as he believe it when told it was the father (of lies he later said). He is a product of his own father's lies of

Norman Paulsen, that demons are a projection of Enki's insanity from going into the dark hole, romance. Loki, Iago, Satan,...He saysy" even in the Bible" like they all do (Wilcock) as if it were the least source, but is the greatest and every thing they say stems from it, Noah is he says a rehash of the escape from Atlantis that the Orion family of Enki tried to prevent! Romance. Stanley translated also like Henry Gruver to angels imprisoned beneath streets of Rome. . Trump a candidate for false messiah: tom horn.

4/12/17 Russian to nuke US
Henry Gruver: Fallen Angels Chained Beneath Streets of Rome ...
Trump messiah is the Swamp Trump's Jewish Elite MAFIA
the real reasons to not get married an earful for men a man's flaws overrule his good intentions, but maybe they were just show anyway
4/11/17 TRUMP'S WAR, not to quote Michael Savage, is based on
1) **CONVERSION HYSTERIA**, fits OF no organic cause, traced back to some psychological trigger, that being a deep act worth impeachment for which he is blackmailed.
2) **TRICHINOSIS IN THE BRAIN** where if you treat the worm it will swell up, burst and kill its host. He has been completely short circuited into the worm by these Incomprehensible acts of bombing and threatening. 3) The principle of SYNCHRONICITY. I saw Manchurian Canditate 2004 on Stream watcher and it came up on Netflix that day, so watching it together with Trump's incomprehensible acts of bombing, as is generally the point of such films, is to tell you you told them but in symbol and fiction so they have been warned, but in this case it is in the NEWS. Hence Trump is a Manchurian Candidate. chipped and cloned as fictions do to make you believe the fictions they create.

4/10/17 Mon. Breakin office door. Bolt cut locks on steeldoor, phote capture from neighbor across alley, hoodie on bike, backpack, 2 notepads, laptop gone, plus door. Same day as passenger disaccomodated from
United flight. United Airlines Passenger Violently Removed From Flight

-On Sat when Aey came to help with the vine cleanup. After he said that Sh had miscarriage, two months.
-The twelve were common men I was reminded last night.
The reprieve is over? They have the worst blackmail on Trump?
4/8/17 Trump must be guilty of some deep act worth impeachment to rattle his guns so easily and so transparently on obvious false intelligence of Syria. On the principle of synchonicity I saw Manchurian Canditate 2004 on Stream watcher and it came up on netflix today so watching it together with Trump's incomprehnsible acts of bombing in concert with the fire in the wall all betray a 4D truth. The point of such films is to tell you you told them but in symbology and fiction so they have been warned, hence Trump is a Manchurian Candidate. chipped and cloned, which # is he, the present one? These predictions timetravel manch canditate, et are fictions to make you believe the fictions they create, but not solaris o burroughts, they are not apparently suited. More synchonicity, when the office doors was kicked in the locks cut with boltcutters yesterday 4/10/17 laptops stolen, that signifies what

happened to Trump who had his cell phone taken. He is literally being held prisoner, even his clone!

Deconstruction doesn't go far enough if it does not deconstruct itself. Deja vu 2006 Anti history, anachronism must make reportage and narrative . History is rhetoric. selected details to support the majority, we all know that, so all the facts are not suspect, they are false and if you like fake news, then they supposes a true. I will say that the only truth is revelation and that if we don't understand it too bad, that doesn't make it fable, if makes history a foible. Trained historians is a laugh, along with trained poets. Not only must history perform to these fools but it must do so according to their methods. Just like physics. Anti science joins anti history in the queue except it arouses howls from the monkey island of Unlikely and a hundred other savants who derive their intelligence from Blavatsky when all is said and done, Hoagland and Lear, Greer and High so full of their prophecies they cannot admit to being wrong and so there she blows. In this case history is a preconstructed artifact discovered for effect.

4/8/17 The Real Secrets Hidden in Antarctica... Revealed

Conversion hysteria, fits, not consistent with a well-established organic cause, traced back to a psychological trigger. Trichinosis in the brain. Nicolo! michael savage: "It looks like Hillary, deep state won, and Trump is doing her bidding." It was too big a temptation to base action on a lie of intelligence that Syria had gassed 80 people in order to justify 1) the rocket attack while 2) the Chines pres was at Trump's state dinner 3) to silence his Russian crisis 4) and poke at N Korea to give a simple simon says lesson 5) act presidential. To be Presidential is to base all strategy on a false flag.. There goes another precedent, his enemies are now his friends and his friends are suckers.

4/7/17 Of melt: As far as I can tell the narrator here does not believe in the universe. This is the ultimate thought crime to all the sources and to the world itself. it's like not believing in the normal curve or standard deviations. However let us observe the universe is a construct that its believers substitute for what before was their notion of god or gods. They believe in random distribution but with a cause. They believe in the universe as provider, much like Jung believes the psyche will provide, a la Joseph Campbell, a hero when a hero is needed. That is they all follow hook line and sinker to the stars as both agents of divination and divination itself.

How does this differ from Mennonites and their hat or the choosing of the 13th apostle? These believe the hands that chose were guided with providence, which is what this narrator believes when he says he saw a man. that the entire Antarctic disclosure was a tactical plant, which seeing it so enables the sight that that is exactly what the universe is, a tactical plant to deceive, make you think one thing when, oh ho, it is, the universe is the throne of Yahweh the Deliverer. Sychonicity being the nexus, coming together of the like to conjoin, controled burn and revealing the coverup, take another example, but they are always subject to equivocaton, are made to be taken to ways when there is only the one way, this statement about Mennonites chosing by lot their pastors from a hat like the apolstles by lot comes at exactly the moment when Heiser publishes his expositon on that very thing, "ACTS 1:12-26" "six views, of what Iscariot means... the Genesis 3 example that that description of God walking, that word walking, there is the Hebrew word mah-hal-awk', which means to walk, but it's actually used later on to describe the divine presence in the tabernacle, and even in the temple.7...Genesis 5 where Enoch walked with God,... It was also about these that Enoch, the seventh from Adam, prophesied, saying, "Behold, the Lord comes with ten thousands of his holy ones, 15 to execute judgment on all and to convict all the ungodly of all their deeds of ungodliness that they have committed in such an ungodly way, and of all the harsh things that ungodly sinners have spoken against him."MSH: So it turns out that Enoch does do some preaching in the New Testament, just like he did in the book of Enoch,...

Noah in Genesis 6:9, Noah walked with God He was God's mouthpiece to warn people of his day about the coming judgment. 1 Peter 3:20

Isaiah 54:11, one of the Hebrew terms. And I will found you in sapphires. Its interpretation is they will find the Council of the community, the priests and the people, the assembly of their elect like a sapphire stone in the midst of ot

her stones. Isaiah 54:12 says, I will make all your battlements of, again, these gems. Its interpretation concerns the 12, the 12 chief priests who illuminate with the judgment of the Urim and Thummim. Any from among them missing, like the sun in all its light and at all your gates of glittering stones, then there's a fragment there then the text breaks. 10...sappir is the Hebrew, is interesting because it's the description of the divine abode in the Old Testament. Heiser FB Accident or design?

Going to war doesn't necessarily make you a good person. It's also a fire hazard. My vine taught me this in reverse in tis context Trump bombed Syria yesterday.

4/5/17 Yesterday 4 April did trees with aey, he did office weeds, after i took blowtorch and did a controlled burn at the base of wall. that this comes later with Melt to appear suggests a connect that controlled burn lights fuse analogous to Antarctica starting slow then expanding into something bigger than me as much as the fire was too, with fire dept hoses and helps from neighbors and even then the vine has a little hot when it took it off the wall, smoke infestations, explanations. Two truckloads and counting. After the pounding at the door I went out and passed the hose over the gate and went in to get the key. When I came out the scene was completely whited out with white smoke. I had no emotion about this. There was a brief puzzlement at the completeness of the white out as I got the other hose and went to work. The smoke must have come from the firemen on the other side of the wall turning on their big hose. Sychonicity being the nexus, coming together of the like to conjoin, controlled burn and revealing the coverup.

Melt's acceptance came amid serious upsets. That same day a controlled burn resulted in a big fire which however also removed the fire hazard, leaving behind a mess of burn and stink that had to be cut and hauled. The writing in Melt represents the burn, but Antarctica is the fire, and the mess is the rest of the story. We need a healthy diet of disbelief to view the next hundred years. The only view is partial in its synchronicity.

for publication came after over a month of waiting,

How can this Melt last a hundred years? A year at a time, a week a month a day, which seems far if none of it yet has entered the public mind that after will be so epidemic. In a hundred years of allusion and fiction, not all the poetry that might be summoned has, for Kubla Khan is left out, "the brink of the dizzy sunless cliffs above the great abyss; sown whose side adequate paths, improved by the Old Ones, led to the rocky shore of the hidden and nighted ocean (Lovecraft. Mountains of Madness, 74). Melt is engineered to keep up on various levels of these 100 years.

A much needed anti-history of Antarctica counters the ballyhoo of IGY propaganda and peaceful scientific cooperation. The 'facts" will not appear in any MSM accounts but in free media. The Real Secrets Hidden in Antarctica... Revealed is not free but gives a view. Events have to wait until the announcements begin. This is the dawning of the age of Antarctica, outer perimeter of the dark flat earth where the Fgov fills in the harbor at night. World elites resettle in New Zealand on the barge of their own destruction. I saw a man laying down a grid of masonry tiles before tearing them up. I didn't see what was covered, only the covering, as if to say he had buried something before and pretended to rediscover it now.

Untrained By way of transparency, the narrator here does not believe in Universe, the ultimate thought crime to these sources and its world. It's like not believing in the normal curve. The universe is a construct that believers substitute for what was their notion of god or gods, distribution and correction with a cause. They believe in Universe the way Jung believes psyche, a la Joseph Campbell, will provide a hero when a hero is needed. They follow the collective noun hook line and sinker to the stars as agents of divination and divination itself. Deconstruction doesn't go far enough to deconstruct itself. Anti history, anachronism exposes reportage and narrative. History is rhetoric, selected details support Majority. We all know that, so all the facts are not simply suspect, they are false where a fake news supposes a true. I however will say the only truth is revelation and that if we don't understand it that doesn't make it fable, it makes history foible. Trained historians are a laugh, along with trained poets and linguists. Not only must history perform to these fools but it must do so according to their methods. Just like physics anti science joins anti history in the queue that rouses howls from the Unlikely monkey island and a thousand savants who derive from Blavatsky when all is said and done, Hoagland and Lear, Greer and High so full of their prophecies, there blow. In this case their history is a preconstructed artifact discovered for effect. Every bit of the physics these entities subscribe and believe tells them that when it is observed the universe changes, but do not consider that therefore what they call Universe is themselves, mirror mirrored and that since they are so demonstrably wrong in their uttermost cases and because they lie that the universe can be wrong in its uttermost cases and that it can lie. Consider the analogy that appeared on twitter: What if a Government time machine dictates that to prevent war the gov should take preemptive strikes in Yemen, Syria, NKorea, Trump? But, what if the machine lies and this causes war? Same thing with the Go Universe as themselves, unless of course they dictate that they are never wrong and they never lie! To which the rest of us go Ho, ho, ho. The question is not what is revelation, but how do we account for the dissonance of its historians. It's because they are selling something under guise of illuminating us all. Sales pitches, that's all, so take it with a grain.

I don't pretend to any first hand information of this except maybe the question, where are the original parts? The first is the paragraph near the end where "I saw a man laying down a grid of masonry tiles before tearing them up... this means that the entire Antarctic disclosure is a tactical plant, a Piltdown Man to roll out technologies governments had been holding back all along, that otherwise they could not explain without severe contempt heaped upon them. They blamed it on The Melting. How do I know? It was shown in the writing. The attitude of inquiry here is the admission here that none of the facts can be accepted as true.

Meant to last a hundred years it mixes this vaccine only as an introduction. Just roll up your sleeve. How to build a perspective out of half truths and falsehoods, functions proved, unproved? Some connections not obviously made in the literature of Antarctica are like the top of the one world betrayal, the Annunnaki oppressor, as Max Spiers says, are the true cause of world gov technology and worst first of these untruths. Hence To execute upon them the judgment written of Psalm 149

The world is gross

I burn the dross

Nothing is revealed.

Note: Melt has been a year in the making, beginning with the Autopsy of Scalia's Hat in Sein und Werden of March 2016 which began it all, short version here.

Energy cattle mickcernovichswinger's clubs

outside DC   B100/60!

4/3/17 max Spiers London

4/2/17 These of epic proportion: Luciano, WWII, Soros, Francis, Business of immigrants, ngos...population replacement. Italy.: " the Vatican State had been cut off for days prior to Pope Benedict's resignation from all international banking transactions via SWIFT, just like other evil nations such as Iran and North Korea. Within hours of Benedict XVI's departure from the Vatican, bound for the residence of Castel Gandolfo outside Rome, Vatican's connections with SWIFT are reestablished and all banking transactions are possible again. Talk about providential timing." 2. Operation Husky, intelligence via Lucky Luciano. Sicily has Europe's biggest migrant reception cente, biblical invasion, biblica NGO fleet, cultures of violence and intimidation no matter what race, economic class, education. esp. Latin, mexican but european, dee p inte nature, Thinking and Disney. Destiny? in religion the Vatican fostering Liberation while causing intimidation, taciturn or childlike the latin people, like others, blacks, anglos, different styles, same nature. That's why anybody who wills not to kill stands out.

4/1/17 Saxa word for german in finnish King arthur pic: Tapestry showing Arthur as one of the Nine Worthies, wearing a coat of arms   Here Man. I put up an april fool for NSA. They will feel outed, if they are intelligent, They will say they are more intelligent. I say they don't exist. THEY'RE A FIGMENT OF THEIR ELECTRONIC SWITCHES.

Rio on tiptoe, a harlequin, round circles blue, yellow? a hat high kick

3/31/17 Operation Earnest Voice run by CIA, a sockpuppet of state run internet propaganda that wants to be taken as truth butnot.

the two opposing points of view are used to validate eah. Tucker Carlson validates with air time, ... George

Ciccariello-Maher taught political theory at U.C. Berkeley, San Quentin State Prison, and the Venezuelan School of Planning in Caracas validates Carlson wit news. The are equal falsities as is all such news dialogue.unspoken rule of this is not to break character. If Carlson says

CM is merely sensation in his tweets and incoherent the rest of the time, he cannot say that is the only purpose of your news show to be sensational. If he says that they have nothing to talk about. they must maintain the ruse.

3/30/17 Blue sky pest control.
Control device #1: Tell them they have a problem to innure them to it. Thus for decades the news lamented concentration of wealth furth and furth to the 1% at the expense of the M/C that harank and shrank. the news laments FB further and furth intrusion into control in order to strengthen them. So people lament and it drains their will and consciousness further.

3/29/16 my dentist told me he's an alien. I thought they were idealists not mercenaries. Can an alien be an atheist? He's from Canada. Do they even have that wavelength available to them? FEMA laureate
Menno nerds Will Loewen difference between apology and confession trinity mennonite alberta apothegm apothegms the torso lavender, with violet and white, a kind of mixed field with treaks; play usic behind video reading, like in Oasis, I go walking after midnight; truth as diploid as Lutherans in language

3/28/17 ALERT: Secret Hidden Silver Hoard...2.75 Billion Ounces! (Bix Weir)
--you only know you've been killed after you're dead and it is such an irresistible truth to you, written in technicolor, written across the sky that you think everyone knows it and the circumstances, but no one does.
That's why we need whistle blowers.
-- The whole intent is the removal of boundary stones, don't say man, don't say B.C. Don't say victim, oppressor, resolve contradiction into unity, bring order out of chaos. That Jacob the Elder should play a part in this is beyond all expectation. Harry Reiff thinks him a Mennonite in the end. John Ruth thinks him a Lutheran for his own purposes. He was explicitly a Reformed. We have to face up to the counterfeit civilization and its aims which legitimatize any figure being taken for any purpose to fn reason. One false proposition therein is immediately replaced by another equally false, and contradicting it, which is glossed over by the selected details and then randomized by abstraction and anonymity, hence even though Jacob the Elder become a pawn in the reconciliation of Luther and Menno, he is not named as such, the unkindest ultimate cut to leave him there without clothes or even a stone to identify him. So here we come with our barrow again to dig up the appurtenances. This impacts the integrity of John Ruth, the pride of the Mennonite and Harvard PhD, really the ultimate authority and head of much of current Mennonity. His books are well known and his life within the community where he was born and grew up to serve is without question whereas my own Mennonity has nothing but question. We are poles apart yet on some continuum that recognizes some affinity too. I never got to be a Mennonite for reasons stated elsewhere. In any case when the Lutheran ecumenists tired of their past to the point of rejecting it they approached the whole Mennonite establishment. John Ruth's statement and his implication of Jacob Reiff as a symbol of unity and amity between Lutheran and Mennonity is his own but

stands for the greater communities. That the symbol is completely false and entire fiction thus stands as his own judgment of the case. They like to call it subconscious betrayal when the deep structure betrays the surface as in this case, calling Jacob a Lutheran, putting him under the authority of Muhlenberg and then suppressing his name so that few will recognize and be able to find out the forgery. or you can say Ruth is well meaning in his insight and that particulars if not true in this case are true in some other. Moving the boundary stones of all reasons and support.. for the sake of turnabout is fair play I want to make John Ruth's fabrication a symbol of the moving of stones that brings the 21st century to deny absolutely everything people ever believe about themselves and justifying in on the base of the same skewed facts contradiction and mis-selections. Ruth does not credit Reiff probably because of his own animus derived from his understanding of these intractable folk of the 18th century. They were never manageable at all. Jacob, who took two voyages back to Holland and Germany around the 1727-30, and who spoke English and represented the colonial gov't even as a young man was also a founder and destroyer of the first Reformed Church, of which the reasons need not delay us here. This resulted in his being detracted and sued in a case that lasted more than a decade where he was called a kierkenthief, church robber and was continually castigated by the principal Reformed minister Boehme, along with his entire family. His family seems to enter the picture because they were all individuals and radicals, Conrad Reiff has receive his due notice. Peter Reiff less so but perhaps al them more due. the only regular was Hans but he died prematurely and childless. Jacob lived long enough and well enough to be an obvious friend of Muhlenberg who he must have known after his arrival in 1742, but the Reiffs had been farmers and blacksmiths well established in 1717. The father draws the Mennonite purpose about the family for living next to his cousin Hans Reiff a Mennonity and... These neighbors on the boundary of his property in
Salford relied on each other to the point that Hans George was asked to sign as trustee to the Mennonite trust.

His wife gave early donations to the Book and was buried in the Mennonite graveyard, but she was speculatively the daughter of a Reformed church minion in Holland. When Muhlenberg spoke at her funeral, the greatest gathering the area had seen, so much so that Gottlieb Mittelberger used it as an example in his Pennsylvania, though, also fashionably, anonymously, Muhlenberg's affirmation of Jacob's character was also a political statement as well as sincere, for Jacob Reiff was a man of distinction and character that appealed to Muhlenberg who was one himself. There is never however one reference that Jacob was his parishioner. -So what's the problem? The sweeping under the rug of all difference and variety to make unity and reconciliation where there is none. What's the ultimate result, The preparation of the loss of gender, the loss of history, language, everything that makes us interesting for the substitute of life extension, super powers, acceptance by the collective.

3/27/17 the voyages of discovery to new worlds include the Odyssey, Prester John, Mandeville Travels, the Celtic voyages, the Elizabethans, and many fictions thereof, especially Swift's. Crane's Bridge is a take so whether apocryphal or not, to China or the Moon, it is an old theme along with Solomon's to Ophir. 16th and 17th century, the effects of the New England plantation on the British and native peoples include the Abenaki, and the Germans of 18th century Pennsylvania. I want to know what their so called discoveries did to them. Of course the effect upon native populations is entangled with this, but we cannot know the native Cree except through later reconstructions. These subjects become a basis for examining discoveries made in Egypt and extend into biology and physics. Remembering that when the observer conditions the outcome, that such experiments and discoveries are their own reflection conditioned by their own past, I am indebted to Rosalie Colie for her introduction to science and imagination in the Renaissance, to Ken Morrison for his works on the Abenaki, to Howard Norman for the Swampy Cree, and to my own family for 18th century Pennsylvania. My understanding of 16th and 17th American discoveries comes entirely from that poetry. Ken didn't take me seriously since I wasn't a scholar. I didn't take him seriously because he wasn't a poet.

-- I lied to become a Christian. Seated before the membership committee and asked if I was born again, I said yes, knowing full well I was not. The irony of course is in about a year the answer was yes resounding, for those members who confided they had prayed for a young person to catch on "fire." So I went to Bible school at the same time as the university. If you ask me now what stripe that is, I offer Levinas and Hartman as encouragements to many. I not only lied to become a Christian, but worse, the people I most identify with are Jews and the spirit of compassion of the martyrs. The undercurrent in this is a religious investigation into the nature of being and the effects of direct communication with the Spirit of God. An explanation due for all the shades and varieties, I have been a member of the Presbyterian, except this could be challenged, based as it was upon a lie I told to gain entry. Yes, If any man be in Christ he is a new creation. The most profound of new worlds that everyone seeks knowing it or not.

3/25/17 Aey three palms down
3/23/17 Hinomota tractor grey market, open source tractor

3/22/17 People on their cell phones think they are autonomous.
Reptile hybrids study the best and finest human authors since they lack creative to make such works shows them fit only for the limited roles of depravity they occupy, depravity and rule. Where the science came from that transformed the post WWII world, beamed from space, the Viril society, sold to
Eisenhower for a few hundred or 400 souls changed to millions of organ thefts and missing children a million a year, shows the game changed. The Bugger must think no need to further ruse any more, that their order dawns.

      When I review my life in the night the thing I most consider is my family and fathers and grandfathers, and of the song I wrote for my great grandfather Jacob, written from his letters to my father, his grandson at Penn State, in which he tries to justify his life and his sins which he must have felt more than Anna or Howard or Lib knew. That he had a business relation with his son that wife Anna felt was oppressive is a like mine with Aey and what his wife has said to him, which however he told me from the start, but did not curtail his involvement with her. In all this I never think of my art, or the art, maybe because it is not in the main my creation, but more like things I found and enjoyed, like a sandwich, but I do count the writing, which is the product of much concern and storytelling with a political bias and a personal philosophy stemming mostly from scripture and my involvement with it, the written word, which of course led to writing in the first place since that experience which activates my life began before the writing, in that June as I graduated hs. So I can look back at these men and women who preceded me and take my place with them as I am now a grandfather, but the past is what I am accountable to, which is a great gift if you think of it, to have standards to live up to and the desire to do so and guilt when you do not. All this is my reflection against the reading and inquiries published around transhumanism, super collider, Weimar, Scalia's death, Antarctica and the notions that outside the visible spectrum beings exist that seek our control and harm but we cannot see them, instead are caught in our own webs of ignorance and insensitivity making us all the more easily led away from those standards that at least for me establish the truth and security of faith in the only one who can help us, Jesus, Creation's Lord and Heaven's. So the bottom line in all these machinations of visible and invisible, space and time is that "He, that created the heavens, and stretched them out; He that spread forth the earth, and that which cometh out of it; He that giveth breath to the people upon it," Isaiah 42.5, is the same as "He that sits upon the circle of the earth" 40.22, and who "meted out heaven with the span and comprehended the dust of earth in a measure," 40.12, is always the answer to the oppressors, as Sennacherib, by Hezekiah, to hear their threats, that "Thou hast made heaven and earth" 37.16 So all the speculations about Egypt, Sumer, are much behind these apriors

These reflections led to Hartman's Poetics and Prophesy who cites Lacan that "symbols envelop the life of man in a network so total... that they give the words that will make him faithful or renegade, the law of the acts that will follow him right to the very place where he is not yet and even beyond his death" 75 which is elaborating Jeremiah 1.4f, a (Hartman) "predestination by the word and unto the word" a watching over, "I am watching over my word to perform it." 1.11f Hartman: "what does watching over the word (or word event) involve?...Their words cannot always be distinguished from those of God in terms of who is speaking" 76 Hartman: "the word that knew him before he was conceived has displaced father and mother as begetter." 77 --Heiser Ps 74 dragons: Ez 32, They are coming to take you away: inventing by mis information one piece of data to disprove an entire concept and body of well established knowledge on the basis of this one, so called, contradiction High says Rome never existed, Sitchin invented cosmic code and planets from mistranslations, David Icke.that messiah the word descends from egyptian crocodile word 'Messiah' comes from the Hebrew verb 'to anoint', which itself is derived from the Egyptian word messeh, 'the holy crocodile'., "m.sh.ch" is Semitic, not Egyptian in origin...jordon maxwell that words or parts of words in English fit an ancient language and prove... Christ means "oil"? anoint means "sex"? the name Solomon derives from Sol OM On Does OM mean no more than Velikovsky finds New Jerusalem a space ship station when, Freud who first suggested that Moses was one of the nobles of Akhenaten in his book Moses and Monotheism.

--3/21/17Analogize Trump and his enemy media and scripture and the Christian with its. The Spaceships of Ezekiel Fraud ancient astronaut theory is primarily supported by industrious but duplicitous researchers offering fraudulent research to an emotionally and psychologically primed audience.
Donald Marshall Cloning Center

David Jacobs International Center for Abduction
Research leak project, joseph five eagles reyna, recumbent
Antarctica, flash frozen because atmosphere partly ripped
off,
(william l. pensinger) Nguyen Quynh was a prominent painter in pre-1975 South Vietnam .
"The geomantic, random-walk method of garden design learned during this relationship led
to a decade of intense practice of a form of walking meditation within which he was able to
reach new levels of understanding of the modes of consciousness he was inducted into as a
pre-adolescent child" THESE THINGS ARE NOT TAUGHT.
Mekong-The Occluding River: The Tale of a River Ngo The Vinh
The Amenity Migrants: Seeking and Sustaining Mountains and Their
Cultures edited by Laurence A. G. Moss
--Different kinds of expansive blue ice as a monetary exchange.
-Visiting the house unfinished with its large stained interiors still open but in a
natural setting. 3/2017 New Erich Von Daniken Chariots of the Gods 1966 - 2016
(50th Anniversary Lecture) Organic: intuitively developed art that follows its own
internal logic free of other rules.
I'm a Presbyterian peasant. The charismatics didn't want me. The Mennonites had a couple
problems. The first was worldliness the second was unworldliness.
-Almonds, walnuts sapping our virility. Mike Kitchell, Lies/Isle dreamed Elizabeth,
embraced, she had a car that was stolen by fraud but she managed to get it back. Said she
thought about calling me. I was glad she didn't. But felt respect for her effort.

3/19/17 John Pilgar World War III
Berlandiera lyra, chocolate flower;
Abutilon palmeri, indian mallow,
Zexmenia
Dreamed figberry, pink cenizo awoke at 7 and searched Desert Bot plant sale and went-- last
day and found a lot of things, milkweed

3/18/17 Bitcoin meet this am.
--Couple of elk or moose coming up deep snow track Hamilton Rd as I was about to go
down in car. / bob and ryan wood, majestic documents neutronic development salvaged
given to Oppenhemier for a-bomb
Paul Blake Smith Bombshell, Mo before Roswell apr 8 1941
William Mills Tompkins WWII proxy ET war, navy ship models
Grant Cameron, Tom DeLonge, Sekret Machines
Linda Moulton Howe Awakening 2017 who says the big thing in 17 is We are not alone in the
U! to come out, But who said we were alone but their surrogates? and who says we should
know who our oppressors are? The oppressors? Opressor science reveals oppressor thought
in order to... what make us like them, even more? and the Word became flesh and dwelt
among us and we beheld His glory -and we have known the arms already known them all

3/17/17 Jordan Maxwell (Debunking Jordan Maxwell, the movie) [bill cooper?]
Fomenko. History Fiction
Percival, Thinking and Destiny
--moose at office. a baby just born. as soon as i heard we went to it and it was fine, licked us and shorty licked it talked about a big pen there for it. As I was doing the flood later a golden eagle landed on the front lawn for a long drink.
3/16/17 Nabi, Rehan basil, UT

3/15/17 Clif Highs Webbot Predicts 2017 The Fall of Religions The New ...
2.44f there is a bias well known...any construct of church you care to name harbors a great evil...as corrupt as any other system on this planet...if Anatoly Fomenko -new chronology- History: Fact or Science. is even close...that the personage of Christ died in the year 1078 that there was no history that predates the year 1000 that is in any way meaningful 4.15 --the critical thinking movement-Rome was created in the 1400s his voice gets shrill and stressed here as he talks which show in his misquote of Fomenko's title, which is History: Fiction, or science. Citing this so rabidly shows High IS personally involved against Christians. His proof that the solar eclipse that lasted 3 hours and 30 min 8.44 but then he says a lunar eclipse occurred in 1078! He gets excited and defensive which makes it obvious he is wrong and knows it! which begs the question like much else of his assumed proofs, glib and pervasive. The NT does not say it was an eclipse this is inferred from the darkness and the length of the Crucifixion, not from any text. So he disproves a romantic interpretation of the event at best. Pagan commentators of the Roman era explained it as an eclipse, although Christian writers pointed out that an eclipse during Passover, when the crucifixion took place, would have been impossible; a solar eclipse cannot occur during a full moon. F's Statistical Analysis fo Narrative Texts. "First 4 vols show history is false, deconstruction, 6 and 7 recreate history. but he's a 100% on what didn't happen!" deconstruction the past by astronomy. all the ancient texts were written in 14 th cent Italy, he knows this by the words used, Eyetalian.

3/14/17 chief attraction of entertainment is to observe illumani trigger and prep
Jerry Durand structured water
The remote viewing of Courtney Browne reveals the naivete of this truth. On the hand he says a view of the past is single and linear but the future is many branched and all possible. He shares this view with most of the spectrum of the woo from Wilcock to High, from Erickson to physics. His experiments of 2008 and 2013 remote viewing weather

3/13/17 melissa lemon balm for air travel
,interview on Sean David Morton- Viktor Schamberger structured water, Indian time lab anderson, put a 1/8 second time distortion around Fukushima
High data GUS holes, , forecast matrix, precursors ready, and manifest, background to global coastal event, 2 data holes, news is algorhythmic produced, so data polluted, computer generated news with same tone, algorhythmic news business, --continuing and is truth buted denial service tax, devices non human visited web addresses, blocking the net,at word press,

immediacy data with twitter wars, data hole DDOS attacks, May the net becomes a brown out third world electric service, plug the net with attacks, corporate U.S. gone nuts,

3/12/17 clif high webbot radio v3.0 Clif High's Webbot v3.0! Global Coastal Event, Data Holes, Weather, Bitcoin, Batshit Crazy Gov US soft kill vaccines. Linux
--Awoke with question about ending Melt with Speirs plea to the heart, after viewing more Wilcock on anarct, hearing the heart is deceitful above all things and ESPerately wicked who can know it Jer 17.9, Blessed is the man who trusts in the LORD
> And whose trust is the LORD.

8"For he will be like a tree planted by the water,   That extends its roots by a stream
> And will not fear when the heat comes;
> But its leaves will be green,
> And it will not be anxious in a year of drought   Nor cease to yield fruit.

9"The heart is more deceitful than all else   And is desperately sick;   Who can understand it?
"I, the LORD, search the heart,
> I test the mind,

Proverbs 28:26 He that trusts in his own heart is a fool: but whoever walks wisely, …
For out of the heart come evil thoughts--murder, adultery, sexual immorality, theft, false testimony, slander Mt
15.19
Proverbs 4:23
Watch over your heart with all diligence, For from it flow the springs of life.
for the intent of man's heart is evil from his youth; Gen 8.21,
For from within the hearts of men come evil thoughts, Mk 7.21

Speaking of the descent from Mars to Atlantis to be revived as illuminati myth golden age, all the best ideas of the poets spring from them, from the many headed foam as if the heads of statues and yet Yeats gets it right in spite of himself, the mystery schools, the many heads and mirrors he spits it back, "thrown upon this filthy modern tide and by its formless spawning fury wrecked." The Statues' (1939) And if I don't play along my lines do not mean even if they see the empire America, no noble but betrayed, the feet of clay broken by the Rock, today,

3/11/17 the Magical Child, Pearce
Howard Menger, From Outer Space to You and My Saturnian Lover
Peter Peterson, Exopolitics, Wm Binney
Edgar casey and david wilcock likeness. but closer to Rasputin
Of exogenous events, Peterson at 10 at a wedding in his small town looks up with all the people to see a flying saucer show for two hours. Events outside conditioning as opposed to those inside, endogenous events. which I think of when at 12 that sat am the mantle fell from the sky about not to kill. He says until 22 he thought he'd been dropped off in a titanium capsule but now at 70 does so again, which I share having felt all along more or less that I was

dropped off too, and with a plan, not that I knew what it was.. In Part I he is asked 28.15 end, cut, whether human DNA is ET and he says 15% he examined for this, but to rule out natural occurring radiation... but tape is cut, as if his answer is not suitable to the Camelot interviewer. it picks up at 31.08 as et, but anecdotal, he cites Ezekiel! I(f he feels isolated as an individual does he think he is not one of the 15 %.
Anecdotally.
Solution. Russian plane S23, Wilcock is his complement all endogenous to Petersons exog, has dreams that guide him etc! Wilcock thinks Antarcticians came from mars and are the fallen angels, Horus, blue avian, comic, the face on mars, divinations: backmasking Trump, body language, high language emotion pattern deviations,, nsa preservation of every conversation period indexed by name etc to be pulled up as perfect recall if and when needed, starting about...Torah Codes, Use of art to predict patterns that emerge. William Binney. editing, masking greying censoring language, communication on media. continual bombardment

3/10/17 Rense and David John Oates: Trump's Reversal incongruent Reversals from his speech to Congress.
Transcribing what I heaar backwards. After a year and half of positive reversals. Preston James: Trump Targeted. Not written by him. Reaction to the forward speech. something has happened to make him think a deep corruption

--thank you very much Mr speaker   It's a sin America
--my job is to represent the   crime of the states did I need?
--think of the marvels we can achieve   the beast and it used Obama
--on November 8 a record   I face you the terror
--we want harmony and   here the limits
--our veterans have delivered   adolf her villain --there is evil in the heart and soul of America --hopefully the 250th year   I'm afraid the fifth (4 killed in office, 4 died in office).

" In 34 years of doing Reverse Speech, David Oates has never been more stunned by Speech Reversals than these just found on President Trump and revealed on this Jeff Rense program. Listen for yourself and hear how the Reversals disclose a sudden and massive change in the man's subconscious mind. This suggests a President who has been subjugated and conquered and is now in the firm control of the Global Elite. The conclusion is that Trump has been told that he will be President at the Elite's discretion and that he must do exactly as he is told. Having spent the last year and a half doing Reversals on Trump through the entire campaign and election, the Reversals you are about to hear bear virtually zero similarity to the man whose Reversals were always sparkling with dedication and singularity, invariably congruent and supremely patriotic and upbeat. Oates said this is the most disturbing and staggering subconscious change he has ever documented in anyone. It would explain why there have been so many changes in Trump since he won the election and why he has turned from a 'peace President' to one of NeoCon military threats and why he has backed away from the gravest threat of all…the Islamic invasion of America."

Jesus subjected himself to clif high's universe, that is to death, which is the same as saying the universe is Satan and overcame it. He overcame death, the universe and Satan. Taking the critics who say He never claimed to be Who He is, he says to the woman at the well, I am he, is the same as taking Yahoo news about the elected president, it is thousands of times false. What ever it says is the opposite of the truth, the same as it was for the previous who was never corrected once by the media. This is Sennacherib's lieutenant who says Jahveh told him he would win over Judah, but he lied. All the sensational negatives are lies to be contradicted. That's orwell, the bolder the bigger the lie the more believed.

Victoria Coin. You're more than nobody. in the book of tweets.

--Four authorities, Cliff High, Julian Assange, the NlP Hypnotists and me in four chairs on a platform all facing the same direction holding forth, except I was silenced, one half comment ignored. I watched Vault 7 last night and clif high. The identities are approximate though, but the feeling of a point of view is not. Or the one being ignored.

3/8/17 Hypnotists: Jason Tripp: chaos wave. Sydney banks three principles, Stephen Gilligan, limbic resonance together with the The Kalergi Plan for European Genocide.
-a field of frosted dichondra among green grasses.

3/7/17 rehypothecation of gold This introduces the Moral Outrage of the Avowed Pacifist. To justify it they must create the focus of their scorn, done with as agile a slanting of the point of view which meets their standard. No matter what they never consider the facts, but a version that makes their case, over and over again, so that on the level of people we meet in life, at some point it becomes obvious from their uniform point of view that they must be mimicking some greater set of which they are a subset. That greater set is the media that has fostered then taken over their thought. But in my experience these people are already tainted, it's just that this was overlooked as things are, in favor of their other value, because it used to be the case that a society tolerated points of view without trashing and burning alive the speaker. But no more. Many of these are avowed or unavowed but still pacifists, people who abhor violence, so they say, but who name call and parade their superiority everywhere, but maybe they are half cowards who skate on their privilege in their same enclaves of art, or family. Many are exfundamentalists as a mark of their erudition, which is their way of saying they have seen the liberal light and disavowed the crude, the unfeeling, the uncompassionate to take the high intellectual road of programed thought. But they are constantly battered with overt and covert messaging especially about the rollback of the surrender of America to globalists and all the Obama clinton gore bushness to the effect of killing anybody overseas or at home who gets in the way and they subscribe implicitly to the assassination scheme this network of funds, corps, parties uses to control their opponents, those they cannot blackmail with pedo pics taken when they have been seduced celebrating their power lust. This benefit however is only for those who will benefit the Corrupt. The other ordinaries on the street when we live, who dramatize their moral outrage, are controlled with headlines on Yahoo and the Post and the Times endless parroted on Media MSM: always attributing the false fact to another when it is their sole tactic along with bullying. From a lower view moral outrage comes from their being cut off from any really compassionate concern for anyone different from themselves, the lib might not go to Malta but figuratively it lives among the illumined.

There can be no greater hypocrisy than to trade on the poverty of your neighbor to justify your own political morality.

VimANA--universe, the collective autonomous noun, science. Explicit agency but invisible.
- dna phantom effect
- mysterious eel-like serpent and a fish with wings have been found, in Australia where bizarre shrimp-fish hybrid creatures are now being found, a mysterious white hairy beast washing ashore in the Philippines, and a mysterious giant gray sea creature alien like blob washing up on an Australian beach just this past week. that another massive "Vimana" is "awakening" from its hibernation under Antarctica—and whose gravitational energy is so powerful, its force is now being extended to over 300 miles (483 kilometers) into space.
- Mackeral money, last of the silver yesterday.

3/5/17 Polarizing filter for glare the provocateurs are doing acts of violence in front of my eyes. I have a problem. I am not well constituted to be able to ignore it. have you made a live long living independent to be free? If not you're not.
You cannot teach somebody to be free. Freedom is either innate or not. American slaves never stopped seeking to be free. What you're willing to put up with is the mark of your slavery. and yet every reality can be demented, reversed, inverted so that the enemy can accuse yourself of the very horrors they commit.
Download DAda covers
"Black swan errors have been taking place on a regular basis -- such as the wrong crowning of Miss Universe, or an egregious error in the announcement of the best movie of the year -- an unbelievable super bowl victory by the New England Patriots and a stock market that goes up on any news." Timeline altered Back to the Future II actually predicted Donald Trump's current presidential campaign.
ranks of NSA assassins with anunaki dna

3/4/17 Elizabeth Báthory Hostel Part II, cannibal murals in brussels ish shah, adulteress: targum and Adam knew his wife havah who had desired the angel cain, abel twins .adam father of cain not? cannibalism world government kleck
SAIC leidos antarctica. Nephilim goats found in Utah

3/3/17   Sim Taylor Highly creative imagery. Have viewed your work for a while now- do you always work with a narrative that touches upon human behaviour?
--Ae Reiff I appreciate your work as well so will answer honestly. I go in as a blank slate, maybe just an impression of color, no conscious plan of what to do, except now I am working in flat, always wondering in the process whether this is the time I go down. I saw the Philistine Captives At Medinet and Bruegel, Goya behind ongoing compositions. It is a kind of exhaustion but work anyway when last nite I lay out a field of red and brown with porcelain lights and cut strips of thick porcelain, throwing them down so they came out a kind of fleur de lis that I slashed with a yardstick and assaulted with a rolling pin, which made it worse till I cut sections of it away with a knife and got this below. Most often I work on these a couple days. This one I have to leave as is after the fight. It is not my brain but my eyes that tell me

what is right, so this one which could be viewed in any direction demands to be upside down. THE NARRATIVE is beset with myth and symbol BUT ALWAYS COMES AFTER. This one looks like Satan like lightening falling? My support says it is a guy doing a cartwheel.
--Sim Taylor Thank you Ae, my work over the last 14 yrs has been inspired by the moment and place. Here I walk and absorb the feeling of place and the found object within those places/landscape/ environment. is a new worlds scholar following the effects of colonization on the minds of discoverers and the colonizing population. The deeper motive here is that of celebrating my changed life. Before, 14 yrs previous my work used more of an expressive approach. Here I throw large pots/ cylinders. And then collapse, tear, destroy and reconstruct.

They reflected where I was then. I recently showed the last of this work. I will post these up soon. Good talking Ae. Sim
--i was in a place like ranch canyons and grasslands but with more water, streams, looking for a place to improve water retention, a dam, when i found an old satanic oven. I emptied the contents and was on the way to bury them, looked like tubers some as large as sweet potatoes or yams, others slender.

3/2/17 bitcoin 1370/1468 i was wrestling against seemingly impaired or part deformed people, men, disposing of them, moving quickly, which attracted two of the superior ones who watched from above, i was down a kind of gulley. They sent one of theirs to oppose and while dispatching him he showed absolutely no emotion, like a robot or clone. I dumped him further down the gulley, wondering whether there were more when i woke.

3/1/17 Trailer hitch, lava sand and green mulch, Herberger entry, call Anne, wake up call with I saw a man paving over Antarctica

2/27/17 Theo's birthday-magnifying glass, toy suburb

2/25/17 No wonder I affront liberals, i don't believe in money. I renovated my house for the Sanctuary movement. I maintain a dead tree for bird nests and black buzzers and another one for honey bees. I burn the weeds and DE the pests. Spay the cats. Pentagon calls it ISIS. Have we got the courage to stand up and confront our Myth?

2/24/17 Ice Age not global warming, Trump attacks press means press attacks trump, you hate me means I hate you, Scorsese and Ruth Bader Ginsburg "it's a scary time for the world" means I'm about to get caught in the molestation and aid and comfort there of children. Protect the Young is the first law of every human. dan@unlikelystories.org Dear Dan Raphael,
--Thanks for your initial enthusiasm on Multidimensional Upset. I regret causing any upset. Jonathan says, "Upon closer examination, Unlikely Stories Mark V cannot publish "Multidimensional Upset." After examining the links provided in your article, and your body of essays, I realized that "Multidimensional Upset" supports a worldview intractably opposed to Unlikely's. Unlikely has been, and remains, pro-science and antiTrump."

--I thought it was pretty explosive when I sent it. To illustrate where pro-science takes us, not even the "intractable" Sun cycle 26 coming about 2022 coincident with Jupiter and Saturn skewing earth's orbit away from the sun to induce greater cosmic radiation and ensuing earthquakes and volcanoes to further reduce sunlight to the Maunder minimum will defeat pro-science global warming, GMO, but thanks for trying. Yours,
AE

--Dear Jonathan Penton: Pro-science anti-ice age, pro-global warming. Last fall I sent up a link and from an old old friend got this reply:

--" I do not have time for Clint Eastwood's bitter opinions, Alex Jones and his Infowars nonsense (False Flags EVERYWHERE!!!), or any of the rest of it. Alex Jones? Really? Is that where you're at? If I had been given more choices for an emoticon than "angry" or "sad," the more precise emoticon that I would have chosen is "appalled." It seems that we really have nothing left to say to each other, old friend. Fare thee well."

--He lets on in that post that he is dying...but if he can't see that Obama signing a law preventing GMO labeling on all food is incipient genocide then he won't see cell phone brain cancer and radiation poisoning rampant. If you can't find ONE FAKE STAGING you'll never find any. http://www.infowars.com/clint-eastwood-trumpchallenging-obamas-pussy-generation/

--At the same hour Jonathan Penton rejected a piece for Unlikely that his edtior had accepted with enthusiasm,
Corman-Roberts posted a thank you for another in Full of Crow winter seconded-shared to Red Fez by Doc Sigerson. Penton is pro-science, anti-Trump, he thinks the ice age is global warming. He has a year or two yet to suffer his delusions. He is like another friend who meditates Zen for an hour a day but last fall had to utter

2/23/17 oil seed crops, solar minimum, china's African ag
 2/22/17   The inner work was what they walked in. Their kitchens had hearts, tables grace, gardens had peace, every step of the day was in the peace, love and grace of Jesus to take them in faith to the Father. The faith surrounded them in the art, the writing, True Christianity, Wandering Soul was only about nurturing the inner life in the walk toward the Father.
--In the middle of the night i heard Aeyrie's voice {seeming in reference to his house], "It's with the agent" meaning it was listed. As if it had already been done. pretty much with the same bravura the way he announced his truck.

2/21/17   4Russian ambassadors dead in 3 months
-- it is somehow a conflict between a false eagle constructed like a Bohemian club owl, and a lion.
 2/20/17 the white flash of egret wings through the gates as they fly up and down the canals rob potter, Yvonne Palermo, Justin Deschamps- Mt Shasta, Laura Eisenhower, Cobra, Derek Faust
 2/19/17 pentagon leak shows vaccine designed to modify behavior
in succession, the ceiling had big bubble from roof leak, we couldn't find the car in the lot,, prayed for the club guy's pacemaker

2/18/17 new car for Andrew, John l. Casey global warming: During every grand solar minimum the USA is rocked by 7.0-8.2+ earthquakes as well massive eruptions and seismic events across the globe. Our conversation covers how to prepare for these events and what to expect in terms of infrastructure damage, how to keep your family and businesses safe, investment opportunities, global crop losses and intensification of the grand solar minimum with a timeline to intensification.

2/17/17 -the day prior to Dan Olmsted meeting with President Trump and being able to present his vaccineautism link evidence, he was discovered dead in his Falls Church, Virginia, home—with officials declaring his death to be of "natural causes" without an autopsy, and then cremating his body within 7 hours
Judgment of Nimrod
 2/16/17 Corey Goode has same black goo (Prometheus) as max speirs. Paraguay. Bush and Merkel own land near it

2/15/17 Pete Saget? Cliff High Clif High woo woo, fukushima, flat earth, hollow moon, space ships, Antarctica, fallen angels, Giants: flat earth idea came from Pentagon e ring miso soup, Hiroshima
--holy basil tulsi Tea repairs rad damage punarnava mandar, ayurveda rajanas treat effects of radioactive glass vacuum tuber leach rads Amrit kolash and ginseng remedies at Half past human-radiation in ionosphere to prevent aliens! He often refers to his passing the bardos with certitude but not exactly relates the experience. Some good phrases aggregate prescience, one, but he is 63 and says he didn't see displace person in Germany 13 yrs back, which makes him 1? Liars may mix their accounts. Nixon shows Jackie Gleason an alien, and Katharine Austin Fitts was offered but did not a meeting with one.
--in Salish giant legends the giants got a disease and vanished which he connects to Hoagland's Type II civ extinct in the remnants of other planets, asteroid belt. High says moon dust proves the moon is older than earth. cliff high says there are no gods after death in the fundamentalism of his reincarnations, but then he says the moon is hollow so when he went into the bardos and returned to these delusions he was even more sure of them than when he began.
--Threats against trump: bill cristol Evan McMullin john schindler
--visited with and walked among the true community I am part of, outdoors, mts, settlements, animals and their ways, old ruins, maybe from watching puma punku, or talking to the woman agronomist at Crooked Sky

2/14/17 dark sky watch, puma punku
- I have my own, often 4D algorhythms that generate much of this material, unlock the word hoard in their half so to speak. otherwise not so much.
-SAY AGAIN: ADJUST TO THE DANGER OF NEW CIRCUMSTANCES after backing into the car in neighbor's drive and the fool at the club. Eyes open behind and ahead, up and down, left and right!

the great shame of our profession adjunct faculty,
-Project Pegasus, Basiago geometric merkaba, Marshall Vian Summers and David Wilcock a couple of new age prophets on sale

2/13/17 when synthetics malfunction the cloning centers, the 144,000 Donald Marshall cloning centers. Gizmodo.com ashley feinberg Started about 2 at work on Antarct then added in elements at Farewell. Got manure with Aey. arranged pickup of Subue Sat at 9.

2/12/17 why did nasa triggermassiveexplosion on the moon Wanted: Men to fight against the Gods.
--Preface: It's ok to fight against God, the God of the gods, but not against the gods. There are no loci of man fighting gods. Prometheus is a god himself. There's lots of god fighting against each other and as Lear says the wanton boys kill us for their sport. The gods have engineered a situation where they are exempt from criticism, having convinced the world they don't any longer exist. But they do and have corrupted every aspect of civilization.
--Much concerned about how to write I was trying to gain direction from a professor of JCCIII's in 4D work on Aeschylus, Dante, Yeats...which ended in considering outside the dream Northrop Frye and a really good substantive prose style, for I have been reading much lesser models along the way, which led to wondering how the human fights against the divine, the divine being the fallen, since it has always existed and must have been resisted or influenced long since. "to those who really believe in a Supreme Being the occurrence of supernatural interference, causing physical convulsions and changes, presents no difficulty, especially in connection with a world the moral condition of which as evidently out of course ages before the creation of our race." Pember, Earth's Earliest Ages Preface. The fiction writers like McCarthy don't seem to be anything but deceived, so on through Frye.. So "this expanding of images into conventional archetypes of literature is a process that takes pace unconsciously in our reading" assimilated to the whole subject so quickly "one hardly notices the difference between creative and critical activity" thus "what is true for the reader is true a fortiori of the poet, who learns very quickly that there is no singing school for his soul except the study of the monuments of its own magnificence." (Anatomy of Criticism 100) the fact of death is different from the agencies of death. like war and the study of war inculcated into earth by supernatural interference Yeats in the resistance confronts these agencies even though he seems compromised with the Titans and the gods, especially in the Death of Cuchulain at the end of Last Poems. To fight against the divine is best seen in Aeschylus after some thought. Construed after as fighting against God is equivocation. It is the fight against Saturn, the Titans and all Olympus with one difference, they were powerless to effect change even if they resisted to the death, like Sisyphus, Prometheus. The recast of this man into demi-gods themselves is to only to undermine the man, to turn him into a god means his has become the enemy, has ceased to resist and is completely enslaved. That is the crisis of our time. Except that Christ has made a mockery of these heavenly beings and empowered us to fight to establish our humanity and his rule. This is not the war among the gods, Titanomachy, the gods are evil. Shelley against the gods, usually construed as against the odds, "Aeschylus against the gods" no results found! The celebration of war is a victory of these gods over men, a transfer of their apocalypse to earth. But all of the discussion of human greatness subordinates to super powers. No living with out

the gods. Be a god is not to be a man. Man inferior to the gods, the lowly the eater useless eaters looked upon by kings royalty the rich because they are Olympians, children of the Nephilim. Antigone burying her brother resists the gods. Lear as a fly to the gods they kill us for their sport. Wanton boys these nephs. Twelve Olympians are the major gods of the Greek, Zeus, Hera, Poseidon, Demeter, Athena, Apollo, Artemis, Ares, Aphrodite, Hephaestus, Hermes, and either Hestia or Dionysus. departure of the gods who left in the golden ag2/10/17 the blue and white flag of the UN is centered on the North pole looking down as it were, but the view of Kirill is opposite.

2/9/17 Alan Watts Explains What Awakening Means Wildamite

2/8/17 --the elements with all the creatures preached our disobedience to us. Wandering Soul 11
--I may have to issue these thoughts as a preface to poems I wrote pretty long ago merely in the desire for song, but in this day they seem a higher purpose, at least in the light the Max Speirs would cast on them, earth as the jewel and the human heart the brightest light. I told Aey spontaneously last year, 14 June 2014 A Man is the Highest Created Being in the Universe!   Earth is the Jewel, Masterpiece of All the Worlds.
--Long before I had written in Calendar It came about a sun all blazing bright had showered gold into the heart of man. Other poems said Where love-lies-bleeding stretches all bejeweled I watch the fields that purple with their blood. The last line of Solar Dithyrambs so everybody see that when you love the world you're loving the life of the world. Likewise The Fly, if you come home to a fly in your house open the window and fly out yourself. In all the things Speirs says this is his ultimate hope.

2/7/17 Pindar? reverse aging: Tom Bearden reported on the work of Antoine Priore in the mid 1980's. Adolf Hitler lived to the age of 114 years and died in Maryland under the name of William Coates. Alfred
Bonner, forever young ran Dulce, but los alamos bigger, see Santa Fe evil, Adrenochrome, fear in blood, reptile high, elena kapulnik super soldier
--London has fallen. Virgil was right. Aeneas did found Britain. All the evils of London need connection to the past. The name 'Babylondon' is a variant of the Greco-Roman Babilundinium. 'Babies', 'Babelers','Baps' or 'Badneys'. The Tower of Babylondon, the replica Ishtar Broadgate and Mujelli-bingham Palace amongst its many attractions, along with famous institutions such as the Babylondian Museum and the recently constructed Biblioteca de Babel (the Library of Babel) near St Pancras Station. The original Tower of Babylondon now houses an exhibition about Ravens. see the Dark Prince of Babylondon
--ZygoteBody, formerly Google Body, is a web application by Zygote Media Group that renders manipulable 3D anatomical models of the human body. Several layers from muscle tissues down to blood vessels can be removed or made transparent to allow better study of individual body parts. Most of the body parts are labelled and searchable. ZygoteBody was launched as Google Body on December 15, 2010. On April Fools Day 2011, users were greeted

with the anatomy of a cow on the home page.[1] The cow model is still available as part of the open-3d-viewer open source project.

As part of the wind down on Google Labs, it was announced that Google Body will be shut down but will continue to be maintained by Zygote as ZygoteBody. On October 13, 2011 the Google Body site was shut down. Then on January 9, 2012 ZygoteBody was launched and core code base (with the Google Cow model as a demo) was made available as an open source project called open-3d-viewer

--"Mark Richards frame, the many Michael Prince/Casbolt time travel missions, the Max Spiers clones replacing historic British personalities, the Process Church/Walt Disney plan to control the minds of children implemented in the 1950s from a white paper written by Josef Mengele aka Dr. Greenbaum, and the Alestair Crowley/Montaulk/time portal plan to bring Crowley to 2012 so he could take command of the

Jesuit/Mossad/reptilian cabal ruling over the western world." MI6 Agent Gareth Williams and the Project IBIS -- Poland: It shows how resilient the human heart is 33.31...it's been 13,000 years and they haven't taken control of earth heart, they haven't been able to do it...they want to break the heart of the human being... the beast computer held in Belgium has extremely intiate details of every person on the planet, but to fight, fight with the heart because it can have as many details as it wants but...the heart is an infinite love, it can't be detailed, it can't be categorized 37.37

2/6/17 revolution radio, Christine hart,
Lesser Ury, Willows by the Lake FB, Moogie-- Pontine Islands Lazio's coastline in front of anzio where there is one of the most beautiful villas where l. Inperatore Nero was spending the summer.

Svalbard Project: Terminator seeds: "What leads the Gates and Rockefeller foundations to at one and the same time to back proliferation of patented and soon-to-be Terminator patented seeds across Africa, a process which, as it has in every other place on earth, destroys the plant seed varieties as monoculture industrialized agribusiness is introduced? At the same time they invest tens of millions of dollars to preserve every seed variety known in a bomb-proof doomsday vault near the remote Arctic Circle 'so that crop diversity can be conserved for the future' to restate their official release?" Doomsday Seed Vault --A small California biotech company, Epicyte, in 2001 announced the development of genetically engineered corn which contained a spermicide which made the semen of men who ate it sterile... Epicyte had developed its spermicidal GMO corn with research funds from the US Department of Agriculture, the same USDA which, despite worldwide opposition, continued to finance the development of Terminator technology, now held by Monsanto... In the 1990's the UN's World Health Organization launched a campaign to vaccinate millions of women in Nicaragua, Mexico and the Philippines between the ages of 15 and 45, allegedly against Tetanus,.. spread by the WHO only to women of child-bearing age contained human Chorionic Gonadotrophin or HCG, a natural hormone which when combined with a tetanus toxoid carrier stimulated antibodies rendering a woman incapable of maintaining a pregnancy. None of the women vaccinated were told.

--+It later came out that the Rockefeller Foundation along with the Rockefeller's Population Council, the World Bank (home to CGIAR), and the United States' National Institutes of

Health had been involved in a 20year-long project begun in 1972 to develop the concealed abortion vaccine with a tetanus carrier for WHO. The Government of Norway, the host to the Svalbard Doomsday Seed Vault, donated $41 million to develop the special abortive Tetanus vaccine.

--Steph Curry's behind the back pass out of bounds in the waning 4th quarter to give the title to BeBron is the same as Matt Ryan's roll out for a sack to take Atlanta out of FG range to give the title to Brady. It also shows Drudge is a party for the anointed Brady on his site the day before and the day of. He is part of the fix which is in only to show how the elite rule the world in plain sight but you still don't know how they do it. Greatest Superbowl Comeback ever! baloney. I used this technique to get back into tennis in the 90's. There were a couple opponents I needed to get my game in order but they could never really beat me so I had to dissemble and let them win some games to keep them on the string untl I was ready to play in the clubs. to

2/5/17 dave bossard, whitehead refutes evolution
Max speirs lost his life to get this out,
Douglas Dietrich was a Research Librarian for the Department of Defense at El Presidio over which Speirs was killed oct 16 Michael Aquino was based at Presido, interviewed on Buzzsaw recently. records for the presido child care center kept in neighborhood center that burnen down from arson. then the families burned the day care center down. nat'l records center in St. louis burned its records of vets of wars, 50 pts of arson, 56.30 part II,
Conspiracy Theorist Max Spiers Full Lecture Poland, Warsaw (English Only) 23rd April 2016.
--Vanessa Bates, Max' mother interview Writing must celebrate. Barthes Mythologies dismiss Billy Graham, etc. Any writing that is dismissive is not valuable.

2/4/17 Stelle, Zeke, Adderly Zach, Kelly neighbors (blossom). $80 to fix the cats. Lindsay Williams, ALTA Feb: earthquakes in Antarctica, lens effect of atmosphere, legacy media antarct and elite movements, forests of ice trees, freezing descriptors, sinkholes and rifts, collapsing cave systems-mexiceo buildings drop into holes, upper stories sticking out of holes, military around the holes, many obituaries coming, depletion of elites, China to announce ice age, power elite-out, 325 AD Constantine, pop gold rush, gold panning, creeping out of new tech Antarctic, iced age, U.s. global occupation ends, sleeple, undersea events, wars of the elites, Australia world class crime, pyramids in Antarctic Australian pyramids, pharaohs power device in Australia, hyper technology in data mining, Antarctic conduit, mysterious death of legacy stars of dying media empires, knowledge shocks in academia brain, declassified woo-woo knowledge to disarm demonaut rebellion, housing deflation to 80%, speculations about the end of religion, alien astros, monk chanting, ancient monk harmonics chants, fractal representation of human body in sound, vibration therapy of human bodies

2/2/17 the spike field, war on cash, aaron russo everybody must be chipped

1/30/17 EZekiel 39.7, 9 vs Ps 46

1/29/17 unSCALABILITY OF POLYNOMIALS Webbot hits mandela effect Grab them by the purse!

1/28/17 Dr. Bill Warner

1/25/17 eBay user name: ar.us.pzf43zd   webbot cliff high part two aliens flat earth we didn't on the moon nasa former nasa scientist admits
The Imagination Directives. Lost post: defectation defacation angels. Gnashalism. piracetam, a cognitionbooster, wakefulness agent called modafinil, sometimes known as Provigil, Nootrobox,
--Noah. Consumer EEG headbands that read brainwave activity can be tethered via Bluetooth to a phone or tablet, and brain-training games like Luminosity and Elevate always top the App Store charts Nootropics
--Noah's name was Bar-Noah and sometimes he thought he was him, other times he went as Simón after the Caracas liberator Bolívar. His father had worked for the agency in that day when you could carry your Osborne computer to work in its suitcase and just plug it in.

1/24/17 little blue child. Trump to release darpa science?

1/23/17 Trump FBI raids CDC hq, seizes records of vaccinations making children autistic: children with indigo auras: wm. Mount all these inflammatory stories on drudge are mere feeding the frenzy, multiplying beyond all reason in magnification. the guy who punched richard spencer
I was teaching a class, assigned how the leg operates in any species as eval of ability to present info. Had a cell phone to receive their assignments. Feels like a new set in place, symbolized by removal of TPP etc, sleeping till 6! The inner world is changed?
1/22/17 Paul Begley LIVE "Citizen Containment" New World
On their release, Peter and John went back to their own people and reported all that the chief priests and the elders had said to them. 24 When they heard this, they raised their voices together in prayer to God. "Sovereign Lord," they said, "you made the heavens and the earth and the sea, and everything in them
27 Indeed Herod and Pontius Pilate met together with the Gentiles and the people of Israel in this city to conspire against your holy servant Jesus, whom you anointed. 28 They did what your power and will had decided beforehand should happen. 29 Now, Lord, consider their threats and enable your servants to speak your word with great boldness. 30 Stretch out your hand to heal and perform signs and wonders through the name of your holy servant Jesus."
--Three emotions: jesse jackson peace sign at bishop chapel, 9/11, trump's inaugural questioned after his CIA speech The decor of trump tower Apollo gold raises oppositional analysis as much as Paula white but what an admirable op if the elite mfg his support among Christians and the middle class, the last unsubverted groups in order to spring upon them apolloyon. That's as good as ET, black science. leftist media, parties and public prevent

criticism of Trump by so unfairly and rabidly slanting their attacks. so all legit questions about militarism etc are silenced by the left, which activates Trumps support in the middle class. It's as if they are trying to establish Trump.

--Saloon Gallery Rules 1.   Thought Beasts: Chimeras, Gargoyles and the Master Race
2. Report of Some Events on the Jersey Turnpike
3. Blood Moon
4. Isis at the Gates
5. The Planetary Bulldozers Are Coming
6. Saved From the End of the World
7. Kung Fu Da Puta Alien I
8. The Immortal Kurzweil Kaddafi Cure 9.   Nano Uber Alter Bot
10. Nabu! Nabu!
11. Mennonites, Muslims and Martyrdom

Grateful acknowledgments to Russell Steur!

--Trump's speech to CIA is either a classic of misdirection or we have jumped from Hillary's frying pan of pedo porn murder into Apollo's fire. On its face however the fact remains that Trump has all the right enemies who have inculcated their brain speak these 30 years. It is possible he has been chosen because he knows all the banks and powers better than any. That they oppose him justifies him.

1/21/17 Matthew delloze, temple of Hathor ape serpent kings of Egypt 33 min after landing on the moon Armstrong and aldrin planted the double eagle masonic flag: therefore the eagle has landed! where the hidden masters rub them with crocodile fat massage, aluminati Illumi Corp Journalists for Hire Udo Ulfkotte

How to spend the reprieve. HOW ARE YOU GOING TO SPEND YOUR REPRIEVE? I woke yesterday at 3.45 AM with a wonderful feeling that things were good and watched the inaugural with its six prayers and speech, the name of Jesus prominent in a majority over all the words. So "no longer will violence be heard in our land or ruin or destruction be within our borders" is echoed in the pledge, "this is the end of American carnage," confirmed by the grace given Hillary at the banquet. So HOW TO SPEND THE REPRIEVE, go back to old, celebrate eat and drink or when the loom of death is over and the the prison walls are down go on to fight, and more to see if this victory, small in the offing against these forces, but real, can be furthered by the realization that we are not grasshoppers, but giant killers. Giants have been revealed all around us From Media CIA to earth turned to a neutron star, From Antipodal Earthquakes in New Zealand to knock off satanic discoveries in Antarctica; Fukishima and the pizza corps interdimensional hordes. Back at the inaugural it was beginning to rain when "we called our walls salvation and our gates praise." CALL TO the WARRIORS

EVERYWHERE! BE ARMED. HOLD UP THE HANDS OF THE DELIVERER TO COMPLETE THE EXODUS!!!

-so what are your reprieve resolutions? I was as moved as at 9/11. The forces are still arrayed outside of us, but oh the inside has been shaken and we will see.

1/20/17 if 512 Nym the contrial
512 Cern the truth unleashing abaddon qubits equals 7 billion human brains, that number is superceded by the present 2048 qubits on a chip at the adiabatic capacity presently at cern. Singularity already surpassed itself in an amazing contrast with society where 70 democreats don't attend the inaugural of their own government and tales of various catastrophes and assassinations rain down from their narratives in case they do pull off the COG continuity of government upset. However almost no orgs attend these dissonances either, making the connection of cern with the poles of Saturn to release prisoners of the black cube there and their counterparts here a welcome relief from the stupor. Of course this will all come as a surprise even if unbelievably there is is still prepping to be done with the Discoveries touted in Antarctic, pale against the stable strangelets that accumulate toward a neutron star at earth's core from the collisions. Prior to that the antipodal disruptions of a point on the earth opposite CERN, being New Zealand is the place where these effects might reasonably be searched, NZ and Antart. Alaska is antipodal to Antarctica.

1/19/17 "superposition of quantum bits can only be achieved by using a 4 state system: quaternary relationship of binary particles. Quantum entanglement is the way information is exchanged between 0s and 1s WRITING, ART FOR HIRE narrative networks modern art a weapon of cia Irving Sandler's The Triumph of American Painting (1970), the first history of Abstract Expressionism " benevolent propaganda", OF post-war ideology of the American government. in 1967, the New York Times had revealed that the liberal antiCommunist magazine Encounter had been indirectly funded by the CIA, Frances Stonor Saunders CIA and the
"cultural Cold War" like rock and roll, LIKE LEARY. Agents of defamation: Maxine Waters day before Inaug, John Lewis, Elijah Cummings Russia spy, a prop for continuity of govt. Biden saying semi-president, that global gov't in danger from nationalism, like the Pope, CNN, drone bombing, impeachment, coup, Æ the more intelligent the species the larger the neocortex the more likely it is to be deceptive. today's distraction is that if the elect is killed a member of Obama's cabinet will rule. shut up.

1/18/17 cern entities are now confirmed and are real, anthony patch. ruggero m. santilli, ITE, invisible terrestrial entities, bionocular telescope like Mt. Graham, niburu. "They well know our planet will be struck' well get it on! clif high son of a lifer 31.15military liason who quit after liase white house with demo convention 68. breakdown of military minds, control. life long judo, aikido, meditated, been to the bardo on a horse with no name, followed the tarot of michael tasarion, whose sources include Mauro Biglino on the Bible, felt the annihilation of Canadian originals by the Church and Crown, knows how the positive thinkers do the sacrificial midnights, Pamela Myers Liespotting
(thrive movement). millions of aluminum in the air killing all the madrones. personal heor
--put prayer on FB and tWT this am, Bush took a turn for the worse. we would all hope to attend the Bush funeral after the inaugural. Rev 12, The Frankfurt School and the OSS, We do not use spray or stain, but allow the oil to penetrate deeply and hand-rub it between each coat to maximize the natural color, grain patterns and luster within. This finish allows the wood to "breathe" in your home as it once did in a forest.

For table tops we have recently added a final coat which gives added protection for dining, coffee, and occasional tables. This more durable finish is applied over the same base finish keeping the true colors of the wood and providing the ability for simple care and maintenance. People are often indoctrinated with the fragility of wood. This is true of veneers where the actual surface is only 1/28 to 1/40 of an inch thick— sometimes thinner. Unless they are treated with care, their surface will be destroyed. Because of this fragility, a thick, heavy, "protective" coating, usually polished to an unnatural degree, must be applied. No weathering or improvement with age is possible. If this surface begins to deteriorate, it must be refinished. Good solid wood, with a penetrating oil finish, on the other hand, is a very different material—it is an actual surface and not merely a protective skin—allowing the piece to patina naturally, improving in quality throughout the years. Like the chaff that wind drives away let them be blown like a great habood that covers the ground until the rain. let them be washed away with the rain, with the washing of regeneration

1/17/17 Nakashima wood talked with A about finishes, patinas reflections on waking: have not often found congeniality in associates, friends. Bill Harvey, r. Kraftson, those basketball games, sprained ankles,, church league basketball, gary sange at Iowa and DC, but Matt Pacillo was an exception, mfa painting at Iowa, two summers on the paint crew with him, and JCCIII as long as it lasted in Austin, And Ann O. as that was,

1/16/17 Elijah Cummings calls Russian hack a 9/11, who seemed to spearhead this as early as 15 Nov., this Zinoviev Ploy tactic used to destroy any Western government trying to make peace with Russia, to discredit

Trump, fostered by Jeb Bush. Immediately following Cummings staffer. met with (cia) Matt Harrigan and (nsa) John Schindler both of whom called for assassination of Trump... Teacher Sharon Jackson recalled when Amelia acted in a Greek mythology production. "I called her my Medusa," Jackson said. Jerome Banks, a foreman with P&J Contracting, waited outside his excavator until a large truck returned to carry another load to a dump off Edison Highway. 1/16, so soon. "Kill Katie Malone" the movie? "In talking to the fire department... they said they didn't have a shot. It was just that bad, it was a very quick fire." cummings, 'My staff is a family and this unimaginable tragedy is shocking and heartbreaking to us all,' Cummings (seen right with Malone) said in a statement. Michael Johnson, 55, who lives a block away and can see the house from his home, described it as a complete inferno. Totally unreal, and a massive tell she said, "In time we will all be doing better," she wrote. Malone likened her family to Hercules Mulligan, a soldier and spy during the American Revolution who is a character in the Broadway musical "Hamilton." 'Fire was coming out of every window, and as they sprayed it, it seemed like the fire was fighting back or something. It just kept coming and coming and coming. Fire was actually coming out of the sides of the house. I've never seen anything like that in my life,' Johnson said. Taken to safety: A woman who also escaped the house which was engulfed by flames after midnight on Thursday is evacuated from the scene by firefighters Read more: http://www.dailymail.co.uk/news/article-4115862/Six-children-died-Baltimore-house-firepictured.html#ixzz4VwuyxMrC
Follow us: @MailOnline on Twitter | DailyMail on Facebook

--Chris Hedges--one of the authentic voices records this example of what are also IN-STEALTH-IGENCE agency Brownstone Ops (under the grey line, ted gunderson a plant, VOODOO DRUG, scopolamine, devil's breath: "Someone pretending to be from the White House would call the caretakers back at the hotel and would tell them the children fell asleep and are staying the night here at the White House") against free people. 1/15/17 clif high: hourglass plasma earth core expanding attracts gamma rays, colder air from space, freeze one side Antarctic, but other melts revealing artifacts. technanobe, technabogy, technalogy Dialogue International German-American Discourse on Politics and Culture on ULFKOTTE KILLED whistle blower on fake news. see News reporter Sharyl Attkisson. CIA operation mockingbird at Global research

1/14/17 David AnDerson Time, retarded and accelerated rates of time Peter Moon, Montauk, Wisconsin,
Now Naaman, Captain of the host of the king of Syria, was a mighty man with his master but had leprosy. Advised by a servant girl he sought Elisha, who only sent back advice. Naaman eventually followed it, and reapproached to acknowledge the supreme presence of Yahweh. But one of his duties was to shepherd his failing king before his god Rimmon for which he apologized and sought forgiveness in advance for this attendance which he no longer believed. Hence he loaded his mules with dirt from holy Israel on which to base his promise and new faith. The land itself held his promise. Much like the land will expell, vomit you out Lev 18.28 do not defile the land and give it a reason to vomit you out, as it will vomit out the people who live there now. also Ea 9.11, Jer 16.18, Ps 106.38 Num 35,33-4, Isa 24.5-6, In this way we import the holy into our states and religions to apologize for and cover us amid the horrors. I was baptized in water from the Jordan.
-tried to get the Suburu for Anu today, but it has to wait.
the relation of the small to the great is like the individual to the state, the deep state accumulating these years consciousiously since the JFK assassination, but it too is small in the same scale compared to its masters the apullu hybrids and they too in relation to theirs.

1/11/17 the corruption of the intelligence state, media and global govt is aired by the deep web emerging in its schemes like the golden shower concept nobody ever heard of before it was alledged against Trump right before confirmation. All pizza gate horrors are deep web, all brownstone ops, fake news all spring from such. ceramic paper, protect kiln shelf when firing glass, 2300f, woke up seeing Cobalt oxide prints. mesoporous nanowires, Cobalt oxide nanosheets (Co_3O_4 NSs) are grown on carbon paper (CP) Yesterday talked with Aey that he and Andrew sell all the Tony, etc.

1/10/17 George Webb-eric braverman clinton foundation murders. tracking brownstone operations of child abuse and blackmaiol
Pleistocene horse

I have not progressed beyond my
farm. Genghis Khan's horse is 60

miles long. what won't go in a
wonder kammer?
Trojan Horse was let in the city because of its art.
It had Greece in the belly.
Some trigger pulls of wax diffused the orange.

What is a horse, the universe speculates.
My kingdom horse! That they should all be unhorsed.
Now comes the horse quote which in the age of sound bites is as a horse:

Each morning I am at the fields in daylight, and earlier in the barn, tools ready, tending, My fields are historical, , my stock that night's teaching when I awake. I am a farmer weeding hoeing, planting on the family farm that has been around 300 years.
fences, boundaries
After a light spray of shino over found clays with B mix laminated, red shino sprayed and waxed, His sons will tell him it is different from what he said.
They deny horsing around.
Separation led to completion, then ensued
dissolution. We give up devotion to our
own views, adopt the ordinary so arcane
it can't be found.
Among immortals, sagacity superior man idiot.
We give everything to restore the commonplace world.

Note from Pleistocene horse: He wants to stand "in the center where he can respond without end to the changing views" of the affirming and denying (Legge, Chuang Tzu, 183). He resolves it with the joke, his horse. What is a horse? His son will tell him what is a horse. It is different from what he said was a horse. They point that out, affirm and deny horse around. "By means of a finger (of my own) to illustrate that the finger (of another) is not a finger is not so good a plan as to illustrate that it is not so by means of what is (acknowledged to be) not a finger; and by means of (what I call) a horse to illustrate that (what another calls) a horse is not so, is not so good a plan as to illustrate that it is not a horse, by means of what is (acknowledged to be) not a horse. (All things in) heaven and earth may be (dealt with as) a finger; (each of) their myriads may be (dealt with as) a horse. Does a thing seem so to me? (I say that) it is so. Does it seem not so to me? (I say that) it is not so. We used to argue these things on long tennis trips, like the say that said, "Dust Storms May Exist," and austere elements of the periodic table. But it was a joke!

"Separation led to completion, then ensued dissolution" (184). Let us give up devotion to our views and adopt the "ordinary." The ordinary can't be found among the immortals.

Wonder kammer and it said seventeenth-century cabinets filled with preserved animals, mythic creatures! In 1587, Gabriel Kaltemarckt advised Christian I of Saxony that three types of item were indispensable in forming a "Kunstkammer" or art collection: firstly sculptures and paintings; secondly "curious items from home or abroad"; and thirdly "antlers, horns, claws, feathers and other things belonging to strange and curious animals. So Holy Cow here are some of the sort. Anyway,

Ben Rich fmr dir Lockheed Skunkworks, anything you can imagine we already know how to do On the 5th of January Mother Vasilissa, hegumeness of the St. Xenia of Petersburg convent (Belarus), was stabbed to death in her monastery. FB: Why a 29-year-old Kazakhstan-American nurse assassinated highly respected Mother Superior Mother Vasilissa after the 27 Nov letter to her religious superiors in the Belarusian Orthodox Church stated that the discovery of the mysterious space object known as 2016 WF9 was the long awaited "final sign" that would "usher into being" the long feared prophecy of the 7th Century prophetess St. Odile of Alsace. On 5 January—and the following day, 6 January, one of this nurse's "patients", ESTEBAN SANTIGO completed the massacre in Fort Lauderdale." That should be as clear as the 17 intelligence (oops) agencies can make it. Heiser says it was council agency that administered the worlds. says the stars were His army in Judg 5.20 but the whole passage says Jah did over and over, just as the wife drives the nail through the temples. Nobody does anything there except for Yah. Ahab and the lying spirit sent to him by the council is Micaaiah mocking Ahab with satire based on the 400 false prophets he had summoned, so the lying spirit is Ahab himself, not a council's decision even if his self deception is personified by the volunteer lying spirit. Why there is more than one ? Its Iago to Othello, Rosencrantz to Hamlet, Edgar to Lear, all personal drama. This misperception of speaker is like hivi hive the speaking of a drunk that is preached as the process of revelation, here a little there a little for with stammering lips and another tongue will He speak to this people...that they might go, and fall backward and be broken and snared and taken. (13) Isa 28.10 the prophet and the priest are drunk In Dan 4.13 the watchr of Neb's dream is his figment presented as his narrative not Daniels's which makes it a dream fact at best. All of these are abstracted like the word humanity, human non human, heiser non heiser from adam red with blood, ruddy, common one who will be exalted, endowed with splendor. there si no hon human, + and- attributes are part of ...Jakobson early semantics

 iT'S A COMMITTEE, sweetheart a Ph.D. committee like mine one hopes. poets, art collectors. Heiser's academics though eat footnotes like John Velz who I passed on. Further on Ahab Heiser (83) and peers say the mashal taunt against the king of Babylon of Isa 14.4 is a mockery but they evidently cannot see There are some gains in the council idea for instance when Gabriel cannot get through to Daniel without Michael's intervention against the prince of Persia, but the gains are losses, vitiated when all the references to angels protecting us in the Psalms are seen to make them lesser beings, for this is not true. any more than we are paltry Adams any longer when in Messiah we are crowned with glory and honor. Malak vs. Elohim indeed, since Heiser has neglected his Maimonides that Elohim is a homonym also and may be either and other. This vitiated angelic protection extends to Daniel where it is said he shall be as David and David as the angel of Yahweh. It is only Malaks in Zechariah. Further, this reference to the council leads to thinking that the reference to stards as his army in Judges is an instance where the council acts as the Father's delagate in the world, but in fact that passage like all the continual references says over and over Yahweh sold them, 4.2, Yahweh commanded, 6, Yahweh hath delivered Sisera, 14, Yahweh discomfited Sisera and al his chariots and it says nothing about any council agencies, making it very much seem that Heiser and his peers are abstracting extrapolating and inferring a thing that is not. They will say that the angel discomfited the army of Sennechrib of 185,000 but that was Malak again. So we don't have to go through these layers of invisible dominion even if they exist. we go straight to the Father. There might be watchers here or there but there are angels everywhere. "to deliver us." 1/9/17 Loc lunar operations command, buried bell shaped pyramids, built first by Nazis in 30's, compartmentalized, each thinks it is at the top, Apollo a money laundering program, black cash, back of moon sliced up like Antarctica, diplomatic neutral zone,

1/8/17 AB for the day. She read and wrote her first sentence, I am me. cosmic disclosure 1.2 brilliant pebbles mathematical reverse engineering asteroid belt into the planet it once was

Peter Thiel parabiosis Silicon Valley life-extension Jeff Bercovici,

ONE LIFE, THE MOMENT ETERNAL,

FOUNDED IN THE FATHER IN

ETERNITY

BEFORE THE CATALYTIC OF THE WORLD!

1/7/17 "High confidence generally indicates that judgments are based on high-quality information from multiple sources. High confidence in a judgment does not imply that the assessment is a fact or a certainty; such judgments might be wrong." Corbett Report rule 41: Rick Falkvinge: tv or toaster like robot is an agency of information to report to FBI

ANOREXICS: BIDEN, VAL KILMER, PODESTA, Rahm Emmanuel, Bil Clinton

1/6/17 6 glenn Greenwald, 18.41 bullying smear tactics maple leafs. I, linguist, Pa Dutch, American Renaissance exploration, Ph/d. have everything in common with those voters who think Donald Trump will be good for America.

Elect Lady

Paychedelic renaissance Beckley, MAPA, Hefner History of CIA drug traffiking

-" TRANSFER! You want a single verse. Is it too big to see? The victim stood in the offer's place. Laying his hands on its head, IN ALL THE SACRIFICES FOR ALL THEIR SINS. You want to divide corporate from corpse? This verse proves it: "If the lion was advised by the fox he would be cunning." To Heiser

"http://apoeticalreadingofthepsalmsofdavid.blogspot.com/...

1/5/16 Roof rat down. Richard Sauder, ayahuasca Ecuador.

--We have to deal with the layers of harm in the apriori statements to every political effect. Hence we must think that all Mainstream analysis is apriori, all counter MSM is apriori and this statement itself is. This is not tautology, it is experience revealing that all good leaders are corrupt beyond belief but it is worse to believe one bad and the other good when THE GOOD ARE WAY WORSE THAN THE BAD.

--Those anorexic pedophiles give a bad name even to calorie restriction. Trump has never been a good man like Obama or the hundred clones that meet in the basements after work. That seems to be Trump's recommendation. He is bad. All arguments to the contrary,

RoundSaturnEye is merely another deception couched in truth. Spare us the good. And the truth. here
-talked with A about car, finance not to declare, online inventory. Joe and Dad born 1/31, S and I 7/25.
1/4/17 Shooting with Aey. Pope Vi Audence Hall
1/3/17 Aey was saying I compared Joshua and Caleb to his table, 32 inches wide, i said, not the dimensions of giants...
-Julius Evola. this would be the ten toes of Roman civilization, European, British, American, Global empire and all that went before it, Babylon, Egypt Assyria, Sumer, all civilizations founded by the fallen angels. here Aleksandr Dugin
"We need to return to the Being, to the Logos, to the fundamental- ontology (of Heidegger), to the Sacred, to the New Middle Ages - and thus to the Empire, religion, and the institutions of traditional society (hierarchy, cult, domination of spirit over matter and so on).
All content of Modernity - is Satanism and degeneration. Nothing is worth, everything is to be cleansed off. The Modernity is absolutely wrong -- science, values, philosophy, art, society, modes, patterns, "truths", understanding of Being, time and space. All is dead with Modernity. So it should end. We are going to end it." And when Dugin says "So it should end. We are going to end it."; no one should be under any illusion as to what he means—and that is detailed in the book "The American Empire Should Be Destroyed": Alexander Dugin and the Perils of Immanentized Eschatology wherein he describes the "ancient fight between Hyperborea and Atlantis" our world is now in the final battle of.
--With Dugin comparing Russia to the mythical people who lived "beyond the North Wind" called Hyperborea, and the West as being the fallen, and evil, lost continent of Atlantis, one need understand that Russia today is fully armed and prepared to not only defend itself against the West—but is, actually, preparing to destroy it as it sees no other option left before it's destroyed by these satanic led nations too—or so anyway goes that propaganda.
As the Western satanic elites face destruction, however, Russia glimmers hope before this final Holy War begins, and as stated this past week by Dugin in the open letter he released in the Kremlin that says: --"The USA is the Far West of the world. It is the space of Midnight. And there the final point of the Fall is reached. The moment at hand is one of a change of poles.
The West turns into the East. Putin and Trump are in two opposite corners of the planet. In the 20th century, these two extremes were embodied by the most radical forms of Modernity – capitalism and communism.
Two apocalyptical monsters – Leviathan and Behemoth. Now they have turned into two eschatological promises: Putin's Greater Russia and America liberating itself under Trump. The 21st century has finally begun."
1/2/17 Sidewalk Fulgurite EDM (Electrical Discharge Machining) and the odd forms left in its wake (in this case the black glassy concretions
FB:Nick Begich has been a leader in HAARP, "Mind Effects" and covert harassment, high tech mind control. He has been rational, substantive and analytic. Previous in this clip he calls on all of us to be distillers of the wealth of information, to be private independent analysts and

reveal our sources. You ask what you can do. This you can do in your own measure. Listen from 1.15. 39 on.

1/1/17 top ten things reptilian

-I put a $50 in the pocket of Rod Huygens from Tucson, Bernice's son, guest speaker. He had misplaced his cards. Then I rapped as of old to Robt over the new year, haven't talked to him like that for ever. Message: We know that we are children of God, and that the whole world is under the influence of the evil one.

Dream Song

Sometimes we dream what doesn't exist, separated from the prescient but the fence isn't strong. From the tubes of birth we wake to his unnumbered stretch where generations walk. From the blue leaf hangs the yellow flower. Folk always relive the past to find the gold.

Hardly things one thinks today, rushing stream, bluster of wind on paths and moats. The ground along the diamond creeks cracks close. Where once in a field a gulley, the protective mat of foliage dried, cedar
Christmas and fence posts compromised, but not the fault of goats. The Navajo did the same with sheep before the Army came, tore down the statue of the sheep Hussein to a half or a third. Where Stevens ran the emu of today and Wallace-goats, earth remained. Dikes and dams stopped runoff from a trench. Turkey took off. Badgers plowed from burrows above the seep.

Before refrigerators, no shirt to dress and explore the light, none familiar until an uncle showed a cornice base, measured numbers and ratios on wood, founded the premise of a sculpture house built by Grandfather on a lake, keepsakes, carving and ironwork, islanded sculptures where giraffes walk toward a city of light, dreams the lost. Taken by time to gardens grown, landscapes of a country house and gardens remain.

Dreaming in the afterlife nothing of the slag remains, you slide down on your feet. It was piled high from mines. Nothing remains of the old house in the hills. The cars are gone. The people aged. A son has the passion and love of Amasa Clark who started his orchard among Comanche and bears, lived another century through his daughter, her daughter, her daughter and her daughter with whom I took the trail.

Like trees, somebody will say who has an ash, or heard of one in another part of town, that thinks species extinct. They think carrier pigeons bring imports up to swallow ice caps while radio waves cure cancer with nano parts. Creation over, flights of robins in the thousands and ten, like David and herds of the plain, a world remains. Impossible heart arteries pump without likeness, new hearts, new liver, new fingers and toes, new earth in a flood of life the way the whole world does.

2018

12/31/18 Spicewood Spgs above, standing in
Bull Creek. AE lived on the Balcones Fault,
took a PhD in literature at UT-Austin, ran the
Experimental Drug and Herb Garden of the
College of Pharmacy, worked for the
ClaytonFoundation for Biochemical Research, wrote
Native Texans and practiced aikido with Bill Lee

tolstoy on the gospels. Wittgenstein: begin every day with hope end with despair.
---force of a gold medal out of an Issue of Honor
--UNHEALTHY THOUGHTS, title of my next book. But not my idea, thank numero A for this. Did Jonathan Swift have unhealthy thoughts. Did Poe have unhealthy thoughts? Ever think of fitting in? Think healthy thoughts. Keep them healthy though! Also Practice Sex Control.

12/30/18 Strawson and the Edwards plateau at 3 AM today and tomorrow.

12/29/18 You think you know. I went to Good Will to get some more sheets to cover the plants. Yestday --I took the truck. I cam out looking fr it. Couldn't find it. Yestday the cops found a stolen car there. I'm thinking it was stolen, or to call P and help me ook. If only it was the Sub I thought then I could beep it. But still, finally I realized it was a the Sub and I beeped it. Very strange. She says she do s it all the time. Welcome ot the human family!

"Islands of the Undesirables"
Donald Barnhouse, The Invisible War. Gen 1.1 "If this had been
recorded in the bookof Psalms, there might well havebeen written
here the word Selah "

Revising II of Austin -sparta- Athens
Burnt Orange Britannia: Adventures in History and
the Arts edited by William Roger Louis

12.28.18 – Ben Davidson suspicious observors - it was unthinkable that the sun could effect climate change, short-term weather, earthquakes, volcanos, and other natural disasters. The idea that the planets could modulate solar activity was considered rogue and the outer fringe.
--Professor Valentina Zharkova: The Solar Magnetic Field And The Terrestrial Climate at the GWPF complete with warning

--scented heliotrope candle for Sabrina's purple living room.

--Rubino is a village which bears the name of the French colonel executed in 1910 on this same place, and which became since January 1 , 2002 a large commune of the department Agnéby 1 and always a subprefecture in the department of Agboville in Agnéby-Tiassa region in Côte d'Ivoire in West Africa The city of Rubino bears the name of a French colonel and, moreover, employee of the French West African Company (CFAO), massacred by an unprecedented mode of operation during the revolt of Abés in 1910 and his tomb became a great memory historical and touristic place, is open to the public 116 years later. During the colonization of Côte d'Ivoire by France , the resistance of the Abbey to French settlers from 1905 to 1918 with peak the year 1910 5 was the fiercest, especially because of the layout of the railway Abidjan - Niger . It was in this city that Colonel Rubino, a French employee of the French West African Company (CFAO), was murdered by the villagers during the Abés revolt in 1910. 2 3 To demonstrate their anger against the recurring raids of the settlers, the villagers cooked his body and made the settlers eat the dish. The city bears his name and became a place of pilgrimage (mausoleum of Rubino).

--Nick Monroe of Weatherbeaten wants Rubino's Bobby Bacqueral. He is a semi celeb game journalist interviewed on Red ice. Fell from a roof. See rawckus, the pop Seattle crowd,

.12/27/18 O Yahweh our Elohim, Adonim instead of Thee have had dominion over us; but by Thee only will we make mention of Thy name.
They are deified men, they shall not live; they are deceased, they shall not rise. Isa 26.13-4.
Raphaim, deified men Job 26.5
lance Henriksen Bad mutt clay a celebrity but also in raw clay plates patterns
China's intrepid vision behind first colonizing Africa (using China-funded loans) and subsequently much of
Asia with the "One Belt, One Road" initiative   China is likely to take over Kenya's lucrative Mombassa port The China-built, China-funded standard gauge railway, also known as the Madaraka Express, is a dieselpowered passenger and freight rail service connecting Nairobi and Mombassa

--September 2018 Zambia lost Kenneth Kaunda International Airport to China over failure of debt repayment. That soul, though all hell should endeavor to shake, I'll never, no never, no never forsake replaced with I consider in my dwelling place as a clear heat upon herbs. The dew of herbs is yours. Awake and sing you who dwell in the dust.
Your dead shall live. Your dead bodies shall arise.
The earth shall cast out its dead. Isa 18.4, 26.19

12/26/18 Seven springs
Speaking of the depth of scripture, feet of boaz, sitting on the images of Terah, the women in Jesus' geneology, rahab, …the depth of the well, how would you like to know that everything you believe is false and if you want to approach the true you must sacrifice your whole life. Never touch an idol.

12/25/18 Hadst for thy place   Of birth, a base An Ode of the Birth of our Saviour / Robert Herrick apocalypse training became Hard layer, Loose Soil

12/24/18 Valentina Zharkova ice age "The rivers are frozen," she added. "There are winters and no summers, and so on." moon rocket from Copernicus, 11/22/18 Pan-psychism. Robert Sheldrake: is the sun conscious. I suggest that morphogenetic fields work by imposing patterns on otherwise random or indeterminate patterns of activity. The resonance of a brain with its own past states also helps to explain the memories of individual animals and humans. Social groups are likewise organized by fields, as in schools of fish and flocks of birds. Human societies have memories that are transmitted through the culture of the group. We inherit bodily, emotional, mental and cultural habits, including the habits of our languages Morphic Resonance and Morphic Fields
Cf. Galen Strawson, You do what you do, in any given situation, because of the way you are. o be ultimately responsible for what you do, you have to be ultimately responsible for the way you are. Since your not you aren't—except he is chosen to say that and to be the president Philosopher!! So he clearly has chosen that alternative and been fostered in it it. His is a way of say fate is the determinate of being. BUT WHAT IF A MAN HAS NO FATE/ Except you are the way you are because you have chosen against a field of alternatives, largely stimulated by experiences, adversities. So allow both. Hence responsibility. Strawson has been a sheltesr professor all his life. He's in Austin! 2012 West austin! He brought Apple to Austin! Fated. A Made man. No he's not responsible. For all have sinned? But how do you lose your fate and get free of the gods! Are people not fated until they are made to be so. AB
Cf
Thomas nagel, What's it like to be a bat?

12/23/18 day with Andrew and fam https://www.mansfieldceramics.com/cap-magazine/submit/

12/22/18 Every major technical advance is also a social experiment, 378. Women in warm climates usually provided the greater part of the food, whereas in cold countries the men provided the grfeater part throught hunting, but in cold coutnries the women produced the clothing…technology has reduced traditional femine occupatiosn to trivialities technological Slavery, 354-55
Friendship or servitude

--man against the planets. Why should a man acquiesce to control by the planets. Man against mars. What is man that that heaven admired him? Why should he not control the planets. Why should he be subject to persecution. Why should favor be given to him. Why should he not take it and compel the good upon him. Why should satan govern the air. Why should not Messiah rule and reign who is made in the image of man as a man and we are in him. Why should not all this system of folly come to an end. Why should not He reign. Now. Today. The planets after all are the gods. why should not the gods be removed, killed, annihilated and the messiah man rule hallejejah! Now we kill them for our sport. Tis overthrow of the conscious universe by faith, overthrow the entities eidol of planetary deities, overthrow of the sun

12/22/18 New locks for bldg., again. The #10 mastor locks were being taken apart from the inside by the burglar.

12/21/18 To see when the eyes are open! A numbered factus. state of affairs (Sachverhalt), fact (Tatsache) and situation (Sachlage) Plourde. fact TRACTATUS LOGICO-PHILOSOPHICUS, 26
(A logical entity cannot be merely possible. Logic treats of every possibility, and all possibilities are its facts.)
Just as we cannot think of spatial objects at all apart from
space, or temporal objects apart from time, so we cannot think of any object apart from the possibility of its connexion with other things.
--Oxydation and the tannins will help wine to develop tertiary aromas. These tannins come generally from the stalk of the grape but in majority from the oak of the barrel. Tertiary aromas are regrouped in families like : wood (cedar, eucalyptus), spices (vanilla, pepper), animal (leather, venison), empyreumatic (toasted, grilled) or chemical (varnish, solvent).The more families, the more the wine is said to be complex. A wine where you can distinguish more than 5 families is very complex and will often be considered as very good by finest tasters.
Over time, the presence of those aromas will evolve without breaking a subtle balance until it reaches a peak.
Cabernet Sauvignon, which has an aroma of blueberry pie or a Champagne that is reminiscent of brioche

12/20/18 There has to be a justification for the camera, which is the point of view, in order for it to be believe it is not staged. Why is the Inuit rescuing a polar bear at sea being filmed. Who holds the camera? what don't we see. The problems of point of view go on. So with Futhark, which are we seeing this now, what is the point of view, who holds the camera. That's what makes Fut interesting. He tells the tale, is the child born in the tale, is the language of the tale and at the same times walks ith his sons in the sea and mountain as they three share   Gemütlichkeit together.

12/19/18 So saw office Judd McGraw at 10. Left note yesterday "to talk to owner about bush in front of building blocking his sign," but there's no sign! He wants removal of acacia because it looks visibility of his (putative) sign from east, but the sign isn't up yet! Says I am "aggressive." Good with psycho language, name calling, Says I disrespected his "team member" by not giving my name when i called, but I told her my call was in response to his visit to office yesterday and read the note and I would call back. She however was abrupt. He wants to know if I want to zeroscape? In response to my problem, his dead tree, (he says, we have a problem?) says maybe he will remove the dead tree overhanging the properties in I remove the acacia, he calls it a mesquite (downplaying its value). Continually wants to make it seem that he is offended. I volunteer to prune the acacia, away from the street say I will prune it down and back. He says to tell him if I do, he wants to pay for it. I say I'll just do it. He wonders if I want to have grass, or zerioscape. Wants to help, etc. I say I like it the way it is.

He says why didn't I just say so. Very NLP aggressive. Says he's busy, looks at his watch while we talk, but he called and interrupts my day. Told him about the parking problem with previous tenants, day cares, chauffer co, who I asked not to park and got the finger. He says he didn't give me the finger! A little defensive. From parking incursion I had them signed and towed. I show him where the bum slept last month, where the large limb from the dead tree on his property fell over on ours, how the thief cut locks off the door, how vagrants patrol the alley still. Where the guy was murdered years ago. He's beginning to understand with this info. Finally calms down. Calls me Alan the whole time even though I said my name twice. On leaving I see he's putting a sign at the alley to his office on my property. Pat talked to him and apparently gave permission even though I not her not to. So it has to stand. He thinks its city property, but does he has a city permit? I told him I don't want the office staff disturbed. He's a man defending his team woman, came outside to defend her disrespect! Let's let you and him fight, she said.

Changing Hands, Gail. Gentle Strength. Just a closer walk with thee.
--Del rio is a dentist of the jaw! Another installment in the screwy wars: begins w/ Marc van berkum fired 6/19/17, Sab "memry" of what I said of AB at ranch, along w bladders out, willy's nut, Sh's rage,--all told now as tales on themselves, patently lies. I am basically honest so to be convinced others are basically false is a big thing, hard to believe, but 'willy helps me.. Against this Sh and Sab, but now the office neighbor wants to 'talk about the bush in front of abldg blocking his sign! 3 died this week on Pat,

12/18/18 Clif has his memes so that that when one fails another pops up. He did the future, silver, cyptos, avocado C60 fish oil, space binoc pips, blue avians, but has now moved on to abduction a la David Jacobs. We learn by the way that predictive linguistics was told to him by shamanic experience visits with a mammal with a cleft forehead, good to know. Major Anouncement, Changes on the Earth Like You've Never Seen does not conclude however that the insectoids run the gov and all the disinfo because a new take has the Rus, Chin and U.S. in league to built the millions of hybrids.. 5G was used in DNA scans he thinks. TSA use it at airports to ID hybrid gene aliens which try to engineer both hormone and telepathy in their hybrids. His best argument is that the subject is not talked about. Mass abduction of 182 children in Hamlin in 1282, Pide piper story // aka viz a viz children's crusade of children sold into slavery under guise // hence the Inquisition was a response to disappearances alien invasions. This however links to reduction of abductions at grand solar minimum in 1640, which we begin now. At the top of the alien chain are the mantids, the insectoids Jacobs says, that lack empathy and any vagus nerve. High cites erowid and his own reptiloid exp. The insectoid gene intends to produce ordered society not the chaotic human kind
--morning star, shape change, tuning fork, elk horn, welcoming. Music raised to 4.4, hz from 4.32 to induce social malady.

12/17/18 Black and whites of Kline-like verticals. Futhark, Milk Vetch, Hard Fern

12/16/18 Puppet Hazard

-- I take it that Judah lifting his leg against the wall when he was dropped for the lights affair was a symptom of what followed. She was raging before we ever arrived. A man's enemies shall be those of his own household. A's mother cannot hold back the tears at his treatment.

12/15/18 lights at Aey w Jor, A and boys, AB dance recital https://watchers.news/
Jack Kerouac   planetary botanical system, stripping fluids of TCE,

12/14/18 Streetwriter to Agni, Aey change front door lock, cement
blocks, 12/13/18 narwhal, narwhale, nachenal whale

12/12/18 To The Hunger: AE Reiff Investigation of a Bridge
Rubino del Sur Expressway to the Prickly Pear
Kurk Wold Roof of the World Augusto todoele a tale of two towers found the Bush Bo lt Hole in Paraguay — Steemit

12/11/18 William Cooper
Jim Fetzer with Detective Jim Rothstein on pizzagate and more
--the only modern human heroes are anthropologists, Sancho Panza, Gulliver, Crusoe, my neighbor Ken, Hillerman's heroes, all observers of the human, Stephen Dedalas. And the best are facetious, Machao de Assis, Poe. The only integral thing Howard Norman eer wrote he stole from the Creee! We see a new species of the digit people whose lives have been intervened by govt from laurel Canyon and Rock on, throught dope, more rock, pop and et pop, qur=eer, hybrid, gender less, life less.

12/9/18 Not to know how things will be disposed is the opposite of divination. Too wait upon the Lord, Stand still and see,, clothed in the helmet, breastplate belt, shoes shield, and sword on the edge of this and wait, stand.
Wait. Wait on the Lord.

12/8/18 be sure your sins will find you out applied to Baumann and every other PA figure who need the exculpating biography that hart Crane gets from his tale tellers galore. There never were more excuses given for a fallen, erring, suicidal poet as long as he is is infected with the muse that is approved. So there are many prerequisites to explupation, but many forgiven if he will also die young in the throes of of if only … Philadelphia was affected with greater extremes of philosophy than any other frontier.
-- like the noise of the freeway at night the e/m broadcast, or like the roar of the surf, the cellphone rings, texts, twitchs. Is there a Schumann resonance or an implant, supplant? eggplant

12/6/18 we are being made to see the future. Today a woman came in with her bladder completely outside her body. She wanted some arnica to fix it. Would not go to er.

What's under the Nazi ice? Centaur antifa-NAZIS IN IXIONS who ENGENDER THEMSELVES in the false cloud of Hera. Nephilim in Sumer accounts & the Flood in Genesis Now UNSEEN as ANTIFAS OF SPACE in the muses of James Merrill, Hart Crane, Yeats-engender!

--Had to make a correction. Not Robert but James Merrill! That's unless it's argued that Robert was his wejee name. That and being a child of Merrill Lynch puts him in Hart Crane's rank! Crane's father invented the lifesaver but it didn't get to him in time when jumped!

12/2/18 come home and willie accuses me of scrfatching both his cars, says he has it on video tape with the county attorney threatens to sue me and my wife's business, calls me all kinds of names. I knocked on mike's door, no answer. 1.25 pm. I just called for a patrolman. Two came, W called them racist, said he called the aclu, all kinds of charges. I called Mike. He came home, met the police, talked. Asked about eviction, etc. W says his house is in foreclosure, etc. Mike's friend warned aabout W. I advised him to talk to Gail. He apparently had M believing these charges! He threatened my wife and me to sue her business. Patrolman Cardwell seems to remember a similar call from a few houses up where W used to live. Case 2130154

Cardwell and T. Janser. He called them racist over and over. They advised me to have no contact with him. Mike said he moved here last May from 2602, 2601. He also a week ago said he "blamed" me when a package of his was nsot delivered, but then found it was another cause. When the police came to side door they tried to talk to him but he would not, got angry, defensive, called them names, which suggests him guilty of a false accusation and admitting it.

See 11/18 entry.
about last spring Willy, Guillermo M. Villanueva, 62,
2602 N Foote Dr Phoenix, AZ 85008-1922
2601 N Foote Dr Phoenix, AZ 85008-1921
3710 W Camelback Rd #74 Phoenix, AZ 85019-2623
565 S Olive Mesa, AZ 85204-2570
230 S 12th Ave Phoenix, AZ 85007-3101
602 643 6172 moved into Mike's back house in disrepair with his dog. He had lived up the street in a back house until it was sold. Gradually he has gone from being a pest to being a danger. First because his cars, one which he sold to Mike, clodded the drive next to our entrance. Then he put up lights to protect against what he said were vandals. Then he got and Escalade wiput pin stripes on it, he is a mechanic, but put up a portable tent awning to protect, adding lights the whole time. This he warmed up extensively and it vented exhaust to our door. Then he got a 46 Plymouth and put up more lights. It vented even worse to our door. His floodlights, motion lights, permantent light under the canopy, and Mike's front door light are mostly maximun intensity and illuminate back, side and front our our house. He was very friendly until one day I tgold his dog No when it jumpted the planter barrier between the driveways. He no longer speaks to me, but his back flood light is probfably illegal, as is the fiont motion light

12/1/18 Aey and Pat had first meet today.

--happy December, like we're getting to be released from time, structure the day so we can get through it -- my life is a series of catastrophic events, romance and terror from Germantown to Pittsburh at 5, the day the sun died at 9, (the Bridge, the booze) to 16 merion, to Yeshua at 17, to Costa Rica at 22, to FSC from a mention of Huntley, to Texas because there was no app fee, move the office because of a parking ticket, each a symbol of some much greater whole like the rescue from the bridge.

-- Excavation of Genesis. How we even see let alone acknowledge and understand the effect of the history sociology politics paleontology excavation of Genesis 6.

--the process of sampling is no surprise, that a part should approximate the whole, that it has principles to be accurate we don't doubt, but from the view of the sample itself, the individual who shows the great is needed. So he should not be embarrassed when they quote him to the effect that he was right, or that he knew all along who would win, but didn't know it, since he was the sample and not the sampler. The sampler interpreter is some editorial voice who correlates, distills the information into a cohesion. What if he does not like the result. Is he to change the sample. Apply this to poetry. I was the sample am not the sampler and see the trends predicted in my own work, long after, thoughts unthinkable, unacceptable to the party lines of patriotism and mass arrest, I mean control. But there it stands naked, exposed, like a dozen or more seminar events in the life of that child to which he was exposed, all unthinkable, but there he is, a sample standing at midnight with forged papers, ordered to walk the bridge, and only by that singular grace that always accompanied him before during and after these travesties, is he rescued literally at the last second. Where that grace came from is not the account here. We want to know what the symbolic acts mean, because they aren't fiction, they are real, and swim to the surface of this consciousness during the day at random moments, then dive back down again, The Dark Sunday, The bridge…but some are positive, The bench in the Panama City airport…until one day they all seemed to stop and he was left not with new ones to contend with, but with the results of all these piled together in his life.

"I was a scholar of the golden age when the Days of Weimar were golden in the streets. Nothing was more relevant than its religion, the golden state of the after life that finally achieved a politics. I wondered after why I bothered when things had changed, when anthropologists saw free hurricanes and turbulent weather, eternal horrors of the gods as primordial fantasies shared by all. The electric universe has revealed the age of Saturn as a theology again and called it gold. What else call GMO crops, geoengineered atmosphere and the new, unveiled mighty men of Genesis 6, men of renown that CERN seeks in the hyper dimensions? You get the point. They want to be immortal. A little like the Mafia, to get to the golden age you got to be immortal, or a made man. When spirits come through from that other side to possess new flesh, or silicone, they expect to live forever. Hollywood clones are no precursor to this gold state, not eternal, they die too soon. How not participate in the event? Simple, don't take the DNA offered for metabolic change when the third strand implant to the public comes. In the meantime social with the personal must be overturned." From Puxatawny Phil

11/3018 lunch with Aeg. he too notices j saying to Th are you jealous of your brother?

11/29/18 5G bad flu with strange features that hit Sacramento residents, and that vaccines could not prevent it. They may even blame foreign actors. But the real and very simple explanation will be that Verizon's 5G rollout in California's capital has severe public health repercussions,
-- I knew girls, always girls who knew these figures, Carolyn Johnson of Silbur, John's Jane who knew Desani, Bowers etc They were just around, everywhere, John Hunt with Goetzman, Wallace Stapp, Hunt and his wife offering themselves. Desani's (Desano's) Lodge made it into True Detective II
-- the corruption of Texas, Desani had his things stolen by jealous disciples fighting for position, Professor
Desani -John Hinds Silbur ran for gov and lost for intemperate speech, a philosopher who failed to rule the Republic and all their ilk have places as minor figures on the planets of depose where the mare crispum is named for each, as they circle the sun of their corruption in their infernal space

11/28/18 anthology of oracles beak-nosed, of Umbar blood typical Orocuen
--STEP OUT OF THE ROLE INTo WHIICH YOU WERE
BORN racist treatment of orcs
Kirill Eskov the last ringbearer, pdf
Sci-Fi Writer Claims 'Lord of the Rings' Is Racist Due to Treatment of Orcs zombies next
--talking to AEy on 12/1 I said the reason A calls him first is because he trusts him and he is strong— after asking to bless Aey in the course of moving shelves, plywood, tables from porch to garage, at break tell him diff between he and A is he has even before birth heard my voice and been my help, hence, its time to be come out and see the birds and the trees, to that first look at birth pics by dr. crider, to the grand can back flip at A's birth announcement, through all the rough spots of training he has always been that accepting wonder. --He told me of a native patient w colostomy and sexual dysfunction he counseled for half hour, who was in tears, just the kind of medicine we practice, as a symbol for him to take it over, this even while Pat is ranting for a County treatment for Jason's wife after id-ing the proper chemo from mayo
--JCCIII arrives in rain w dogs and mate. We have a boarding, venue facility. Dogs friendly, he white and wrinkled. They have a seminar.

11/27/18 Unknown region: Change seems to have only occurred in the last few weeks (8/6/18). Dzimas said:
Dark net? Once a month I get all these hits from Russia, seemingly on the main page, as no sign these hits are directed at individual posts. Now, I'm getting hits from "unknown region" the same time each month. There are never any comments, which makes me think these are just automated hits coming from some source in Russia
--talked early with Pat about Jason's wife with non Hodgkins lymphoma, she sees her to day.

--when told, as at the dinner, that your father is countering your authority with your Theo, Aeg needs to say, I trust him in everything he does, as a statement of faith that his sons will think and do so, as they will. When comparing Aey's height w Sabrina's in the yard, after, asking how tall she wants her children, A such a towering figure in maturity. I said, I made you tall, said before, which affronts genetics, but the meditation that a father can effect the birth, height and health of his son might not set him aback, since it is his privilege and if so, duty, to do that with his! I know the thoughts of a father, plan to give you hope and a future. Substituted for the bloody thoughts at night that would make them cry in their beds until I learned to manage them, project only a blue field, then they were at peace. The fathers thoughts affect all this. the legal illegal

Restoration of relationships and new ones. R and C used to include me in their golf, pingpong, bowling, not any more. More and more contracted.

--Desani, Rushdie new English old patios, exotic, polyglot, supra-national novel. "Some of Desani's effects remain unaccounted for. In his first years of his teaching at UT (1966-67), a semester's worth of lectures on Theravada Buddhism and Yoga were tape recorded. Similarly, the disposition of Desani's collection of artifacts from his spiritual quests, as well as numerous related drawings and illustrations, is unknown." http://www.desani.org/ --Confront the obscurity

11/26/18 p. 664, Assistant Instructor Dec 1971,117. Andrew E. ,Reiff (RBCik 601) p. m 41

11/26/18 Desana at UT 1968
Rushdie, "Hatterr's dazzling, puzzling, leaping prose is the first genuine effort to go beyond the Englishness of the English language." a spicy vindaloo combining chunks of Indian philosophy and popular culture with allusions to Lewis Carroll (the Mad Hatter perhaps?) and Shakespeare. Anthony Burgess, "It is not pure English; it is, like the English of Shakespeare, Joyce and Kipling, gloriously impure." It evokes Rao's contention that the U was built on Indian burial mounds, which with the honey coming steam tunnels…makes it spiritual! rigmarole English," a slangy Anglo-Indian dialect, built on comic punctiliousness and bountifully sprinkled with quotations and aphothegms.—but it is really a parody, a mockery of how Indians speak -- Punxsutawney Phil. The Up, Down, Back, Forth, Front Flip, Flop.-new wine in old bottles, blows up the old bottles
--my life is a tail I drag behind, like a comet so what I look like and am known as, while it was, it not is, because it is all behind me and in front is open space.

11/25/18 Four waves of guests, Andrew and co., aey, robt cyn and just and Jacob, then Jorma and Tammy! Talk to Justyn about buses and trains, to Jacob showed him books, yeats epitaph, to cyn on canal, arm around her about her work of Robt's health, to Tammy about getting together, to Jorma about polar reverses, the silent J, and brainwash education, Street Writer
--dreamed I had Judah, he was on a leash but forgot I had him when Aey came searching. J was nearby. This on a day when all families are to meet here!

11/24/18 haelend, savior OE iesu

11/23/18 Autophagy!
 Reconciliations I am aware after preparing these essays for print that it is my own foible to want to understand every single event of importance in my life and much not important too, and this I grind to fine powder in my reflections, but it is of little concern if any or those who I know busy with their own f=reflections to worry about the fpast. Of course I too have become the past. But it is of importance to me to trace and develop all these people from who I descend, esp since they are a given, a gift for me, never sought but once given appreciated against the context of what others have been given. You should not write the life of another unless you love them and can see their obstacles from their own point of view, for if we have learned anything it is that no one admits they themselves were wrong, at least in public, but not in private either. Only in the state between sleep and wake and throughout the day in the constant undercurrent of their thoughts do they. They never think of anything else. That is pathetic of course, but who can deny they gnaw the bones of their imperfections to the end. So our purpose here is to bring it to light and forgive. Forgive, forgive your parents, brothers and sisters, you aunts and uncles, your grandparents, forgive them all and then see how your humanity goes as far back as you like, to Jacob at the ford, to Daniel at the river, but also to Jesus on the mount of transfiguration and calvary and at gethsemane and all the lives before and since. We are truly all the same in this, so learn to be gentle and give up your life to love. That is what these life stories are about.

11/22/18 Marlowe's end rhyme, off rhymes are exquisite even if some sounds have changed. Faustus is religious in the sense of the New born scurrility or Moravian, or Blakean, transfers of worship to another, but it is worship, abject surrender, absolute fealty. --gave grace benediction at gathering celebrating animals, impassioned plea for them. Followed by applause.
We did talk with Aey over coffee about practice. He and Pat to meet Saturdays to talk.
11/21/18 R and C for lunch w A. cancel desert walk manana for pat's facial treatment. Willy misdelivered package says he thought I was to blame, but finds out not, his speech mostly incoherent.
11/20/18 the devil's dam, in dr Faustus
ANTism. For all the potentials we may have, to realize them or oppose them in producing a life style and life work is…what else is there/
11/19/18 Leda and swan in Pompeii
(Editor's Note: Please be advised this story contains details that may upset some readers)

11/18/18 Leslie hotson marlowe and Andrew breitbart, podesta- or vince Foster and all the killings of Clinton operatives. Without esp looking the death of Marlowe was assumed a sordid affair in the bar, but not, in light of the revealed strategies played against public figures everywhere to discredit them by the deep state, there is reason to think he was killed because he knew too much. He was arrested in a street fight in 1589 and in 92 was bound over for a peace bond, Hint is given in

11/17/18 encountered jack at junk shop, and Mary Beth so much yes. protesters get a taste of their own medicine
Dinesh D'Souza
8 Landlines like Patriot songs. I felt this looking for source for Accordion Slaves ie slaves to an accordian

11/15/18 lunch with A. Woogle it.
about last spring Willy moved into Mike's back house in disrepair with his dog. He had lived up the street in a back house until it was sold. Gradually he has gone from being a pest to being a danger. First because his cars, one which he sold to Mike, clodded the drive next to our entrance. Then he put up lights to protect against what he said were vandals. Then he got and Escalade with pin stripes on it, he is a mechanic, but put up a portable tent awning to protect, adding lights the whole time. This he warmed up extensively and it vented exhaust to our door. Then he got a 46 Plymouth and put up more lights. It vented even worse to our door. His floodlights, motion lights, permanent light under the canopy, and Mike's front door light are mostly maximum intensity and illuminate back, side and front our our house. He was very friendly until one day I told his dog No when it jumped the planter barrier between the driveways. He no longer speaks to me, but his back flood light is probably illegal, as is the front motion light.

11/14/18 California's up in smoke trill a llill a laddie, Dame Gaga burned out, sing whoop de do. Kim Clements ranch, prayer garden, mountain burns. Cammarillo, ca Concrete on canal path laid yester. Trey Smith,

-where are the pawns in a chess game. Out in front. Where are the women and children in the caravan. Out in front. Sacrifices to mask the warriors behind. Now what if a pawn gets all the way down the board to queen/ Before that happens there is utter and complete carnage, the bispos down, the rooks down, the knights down, even the queen! Just so you know what to know.
--the difference not, interims of scholarly and other writing, is I know its limits, a popularist really. Black hawk helis in phx

11/13/18 Boistrous Boutrous boutroslopes, lopes lopes lobos, tost one character, sheriff, preacher, revolutionary, assassin, men and women, tont tost reptile artooth to read Boutrol boutrol that genodcide can beby machette and by gas ovens, tony does it with words genocide, do they een know about labs, viruses, bill gates and the the Nebreaska boys?
Stockmaster in a Moment of Triumph. Stelios Faitakis

11/12/18 the woman as the new world is either a denigration as the lit shows, or it a profound statement like Williams kingdom of Logres or the mystical gnosis of union as the new world voyages as platonic allegory. Allegory of the new world, if platonic would be deliverance of the flesh and death. Socrates allegory of death was also facetious. The ship of fools is an allegory,

originating from Book VI of Plato's Republic, about a ship with a ... free with the stores; thus, eating and drinking, they proceed on their voyage in such a manner as might be expected of them.
8 SerialBrain2 -- Q2417 Decoded: Trump's Secret Path Trump as Moses
--That I said I wanted to quit smoking is a symbol established by context of a baptism by fire and walking in kilns.

11/10/18 Sat. Took kids to Bee festival today. Taking them back home Th said, you're going the wrong way! Meaning he wanted to go to our house. hence it is obvious he knew the directions on the freeway, but chose this indirect manner to make his point. Subltey of mind and humorously argued, with a symbol. Interesting way of saying it. After we opened A's car hood, etc. but that Mon the rope slipped off and seriously cracked the windshield. He was at Pappas, needs root canal after three Novocain shots to examine filling, so we wired in after that. At the root canal later he needed three shots again because it wore off, also the dentrite nerves were very long, 24cm.
--In the concern whether pre trib or already done, and Daniel's seventy weeks, the passage can read both as the fall of Jerusalem of 70 AD and now, meaning today again, as in Matthew "out of Egypt have I called my Son" (2.15)" refers both to the Exodus, Israel being the son or the return from Egypt of Joseph Mary and the Child. --I don't like to call to Navajo double weaved blankets two faced, even if when the vision occurs it is complete but the parts that are captured in 3d are incomplete, not two faced even if markedly different. In this they are one view from there and here. Here we bring it to perspective of dimension and time, there it is huge and unimagined until we see it there, but when we do render it here and make rational sense of it it is our best sense however it is guided by itself into those translations. So the foreleg that came from a man's shoulder which was later identified as a centaur is like a weft faced double weaved fabric with a distinct design on each side.

11/9/18 Bridges over D3 to appear at Ghost City Review?
--Orbs of the vurst vessel. But I saw with A and A thousands of orbs go scooting overhead like pigeons used to, a little high though for pigeons. Aey was speechless, like it contradicted. I suppose, say it was just elon musk out golfing. But most of the night worked on the mules and their voyage to the bottome of grand can. Once there were mules, and coyotes, and foxes and elk and eagles and egrets along the canals in winter. And bears but they were …

11/8/18 Woman as American/Elysium, hence the love voyage.
It is getting more and more incredible with the advent of gender, race estudios to consider once again the first thoughts of European explorers of America English and Spanish, French, Dutch explorers whose ancestors so roundly impale them upon their lampstands at night as they try to fumigate way their racist thoughts. Whose thoughts are racist, the fumigators, the exterminors or of our boroughs Burroughs or the explorers is not a subject of our conclusion. Now it seems impossible that not only could "explorers" use native America and the land as they did, but that they made it an analogy of their treatment, albeit facetious, tre=atment of woman. Hence, it we look at them at all we are horrified, but let us localize these European

discoveries to the English here, their very language is now in question, even if the fumigators don't know this, for the language depends jupon the poetry and I speak of as one of those unacknowledged legislators, even if my office is in the basement of the building. It is cool and quiet down here and no one bothers me much. Also the music rooms are down here so it is sometimes melodius.

To get to the point and without exception, English poets of the 16th and 17th centuries of England would to a man be infected with this thought. To a man tells the story doesn't it. There were some women poets but they did not observe that America was a body scanned. Oh ho, ho they called it amatory verse at Cambridge when Marlowe translated Ovid and without exception indulged there in some pattern or other of lovemaking. That women would enjoy or be amused by such amatory possessions is well beyond the margins of our extermination here. Nor should we think that the exterminadors are anti-human, that they deny the cumulative glory and sorrow that all of us partake even if they are a little infected with robotics and entrainments. Isn't that what the illuminatied age must become, a removal of borders of every identity whether geographical, ecomonkic, genderetic but a blend of all. Why even the words are spelled as puns. But do not get out your osterizers just yet, because first these repetitive cycle must come full circle to the politics of literature, the sociology of, the spyscologyn, the physics of you noknow the king where the jack of all trades has mastered the mind. For the identity between the woman and the continent and the world is complete. That the objectives of the archetypes are the technique of lovemaking implied in the poems is offensive to the kitchen counter sex of the Hollywood versions, that are over before the commercial, for this voyager sex is langorous, leisurely, sweeping, passionate all encompassing and tender, the very thing divisive agencies of rhetoric must impugn to make their point. So Marlowe sailing the ocean of love in his ship is already tideful, billowing, sounding, storm and calm. And Donne and they all. There is suggestion of force, but it is by rhetorical seduction, and wiles, and courting that these voyages sail.

--There's nothing soulful about this kitchen sex it being bitter, acrimonious, exploitive, angry, selfish just like its purveyors in the media and the academy, humorless, graceless, as if they had turned into angry centaurs and while they were fomenting fabulous anger, suddenly horse's arms and legs and hooves came out of their shoulders, wild, savage, and lustful but not in any desired sense. This is the deformed centaur that emerged from their Marxist minds, much the way Zeus invented a cloud that looked like Hera to trap Ixion in betraying his loyalty by sleeping with her and when Ixion had sex with the cloud he begot the centaur. So Zeus made a cloud that looked like Hera and while Ixion was sleeping in a field laid the figure, next to him. When Ixion awoke, he thought Hera was laying naked beside him and began to have sex with her. This cloud figure of Hera was later named Nephele, Forget what happened to Ixion after that, stay with the issue of invented progeny, the centaur.

Zeus was so angry when he saw his suspicions confirmed that he drove Ixion from Mount Olympus, struck him with a thunderbolt, and then damned Ixion to be eternally bound to a flying burning wheel that would spin around the heavens nonstop (though it was later moved to Tartarus).

Hera's cloud was an invention of Zeus to catch Ixion in his betrayal. Take the cloud as information scattering and Zeus as the overlord government. But even worse, Cloud Nephele had a child from this phantom union of the cloud and the man whose name came to be Centaurus, but as its mother was a cloud, a crowd, and it was a deformed child who hunched over and found no peace amongst other humans. The only place where Centaurus felt like he belonged was on the mountain of Pelion. Here, he roamed, lived, and mated with the Magnesian mares who resided there. This resulted in the birth of the centaur race. Nothing else was mentioned about Centaurus after that.
This is a first beginning of robot sex and artificial intelligence

Tweet-- TUCKER CARLSON lived there because he sawy--I saw angry ixions fomenting racism attacking homes WHEN SUDDENLY LEGS AND HOOVES SPROUTED OUT OF Their SHOULDERS, deformed children of Ixion and Hera's CLOUD hunched over from other humans. Antifa-Ixion was first man guilty of
KIN-SLAYING in Greek mythology. NAZIS have A NARROW RANGE OF ACCEPTANCE. You can't be a Jew, a gypsy, a Catholic, a believer of any kind. This was THE BIRTH OF THE ANTIFA-FACIST CENTAUR RACE.
The Nazi-Centaur-Kin Slayer is also the beginning of ROBOT SEX since the centaur is a product of Ixion's intercourse with the cloud. This CLOUD APPARITION OF THE FEMININE absolutely touches the highest of human illusions, but it is also first an Artificial Intelligence, a product of this Cloud phantom figure and the kin slayer—because, get this, all acts in the spiritual are real in the physical!
Fb- I saw angry centaurs fomenting racism attacking Tucker Carlson's home in D.C. -- WHEN SUDDENLY LEGS AND HOOVES SPROUTED OUT OF Their SHOULDERS and they became centaurs, the deformed children of Ixion and Hera's CLOUD, hunched over from other humans. Ixion was also the FIRST MAN
GUILTY OF KIN-SLAYING in Greek mythology. aNTIFA-NAZIS have A NARROW RANGE OF ACCEPTANCE. You can't be a Jew, a gypsy, a Catholic, a believer of any kind. This was THE BIRTH OF THE ANTIFA-FACIST CENTAUR RACE.
The Nazi-Centaur-Kin Slayer is also the beginning of ROBOT SEX since the centaur is a product of Ixion's intercourse with the cloud. This CLOUD APPARITION OF THE FEMININE absolutely touches the highest of human illusions SINCE IT IS THE FEMININE THAT ALL MEN SEEK, but it is also first an Artificial Intelligence, a product of this Cloud phantom figure and the kin slayer—get this, all acts in the spiritual are real in the physical! What the fake feminine is, which is the witch…the false cloud of the false feminine engendered the centaur which should never have existed, so it is also a hybrid race, of monsters, endgendered by the gods like the giants…
I saw a man turn into a centaur right in front of my eyes and I saw a rhinoceros run across the keyboard of a piano, these led to different conclusions, the centaur one about politics, the rhino about art. I will tell you about the piano. It does n[t help that in tweeted the centaur I

picture of Pres Obama bending to sight a putt had a link to the Podesta parties, I didn't see this it just appeared as I looked for a pic to go with the treet after the words, first I saw a shoulder and what looked like an arm. Then a leg grew out of the arm all the way down to the hand, which turned into a hoof. So there was this shoulder, arm, leg and hoof when I realized I was seeing remembered centaurs are angry and woke

11/7/18
Gold from grandma is A's plan
after the election: the word the demos use is normalizing. They have normalizing hate, aggression, division, anger in public display, falsity and deception in govst hearings and rhetoric-way beyond selectivity of facts which all do—and they have made the loss of Hillary a permanent stance to the death.

11/6/18 Aeg had his drain replaced today sewer
Self rule is better than passion but the orders of the Father are better yet. Since the passions rule so much, how to act out of charity, freedom without compulsion, from perceived wrongs, willy's lights, or positively, the blue ribbons, Aeg's sewer, seem more than needed.

11/5/18 Aeg wants 2600 plus for sewer patch plus cleanout maybe. Is it covered on his ins? Do Bullens pay half, they see him 4 x what we do. No they have no money. But gave him a 3 oz for his down pay, which he kept opaque. The plumber will finance! A financing plumber! The willy's lights cover the front and back yards. And then the election, good news the dupe at the club desk won't vote. --Bunch of Caucasaphobes!

11/2/18 Pat's B. dinner with kids and grands. Gave her Bernard Leach.
I picked these pieces up today exhibited at the State Fair in October, hoping they would at least emerge unscathed in the handling. They were in boxes on the table ready to travel, but Flower, entered in free standing sculpture was encumbered with this ribbon. The other, Flight, with quail flying, wings extended around it, the detail of the wings from desiccated prickly pear nopales, was in a deeper box. Inside the attendant pulled out a check which seemed double the award, until she pulled out another blue ribbon,with a Best of Arizona too. For their sake I am glad these pieces got appreciated. Flower for its hispid crags and color of flower and Flight for that miracle that so seldom occurs where everything not only goes right but is way beyond expectation.

Oscar Mauer, Oscar Meyer, the grad advisor called me into to say I was headed for academic probation

11/1/18 how many of these scholars are masons?
--Franklin is not a part, even though he published early tracts. The rationalists of later Presidyterians, Methodist, Lutherans, Mennonites and Charismatics are indistinct and pale beside these vibrancies. Sure the charismatics pretend to the flame, but they are so utterly driven to fleece the flock even while they scare them to death. We do not seem to be escaping

our millenarianism., but as the fervors and integrities fade we get primed.   Back to the Journey, Conrad Reiff is a breath of fresh air.

taken from academia edu: --I have given cursory expressions of these ideas at The Way Into the Flowering Heart, which seems to express the next publishing state of these nativist and ethnic materials. For instance.:
-Global Only-https://thewayintothefloweringheart.blogspot.com/2007/12/blog-post_7372.html
-Cultural War II--https://thewayintothefloweringheart.blogspot.com/2007/12/blog-post_9289.html
-Apologizing for Art-https://thewayintothefloweringheart.blogspot.com/2009/03/new-england-vs.html

--As for me, I took a Ph.D. in the language, thought, literature and art of the finest expressions of English because I wanted to train myself in the highest art for its own sake and for what I could do with it, but I was not a prof for long. I sought freedom, above all the way I wanted to tell those many craggy, hispid tales, and write history along the way because it was given to me, but an advantage in all this is the ceramic sculpture also taken up and the way of working without intention, which even more than writing, informs this style of discovery.

From Organs and miscreants: --All this is to say that in rounding possible venues for publication of the essay editors said that Anabaptists, Mennonites and the early colonial period are not considered significant in the general understanding of Pennsylvania German life and culture that was desired, at least as pursued in publications of the Pennsylvania German Society, which demonstrates that the tension between church and sect has not died out. But this masks the real reason which is they are so embarrassed by the end of the story, the blood, which Bird in his Fraktur complains against, with Yoder and.Frederick Weiser, and Richard Wentz and the Pennsylvania German Church Society of business men and professors so much offends. So we conclude that there is an antipathy to the genuine faith reflected in Conrad Reiff's conversion that in a denatured way sums the very nonbeliefs of the New Born that he left behind.

-- Richard E. Wentz, another religion professor, founder of the ASU School of Religion, disbelieves his own folk icons, lending credence to Stoudt's claim that liberalism killed the flower. Wentz's Pennsylvania Dutch: Folk Spirituality describes an introversion of the flowering heart: "at least among scholars and intellectuals, heaven is an obsolescent metaphor (I speak for myself). It is hardly a way to face the darkness" (Der Reggeboge, 2007, 33). It must be hard to face the darkness from the tower. He says, "I have no intention of trying to convince any of you as twenty-first century Dutchmen to reach beyond your grasp and hitch your hopes on heaven" (41). This denaturing of a people, for that society loves studies of assimilation, amounts to assassination, since it was the myriad expressions of their faith that made them a transcendent people 100 years before Emerson ever heard the word. The dilution of ethnic and language groups by assimilation should be called for what it is, assassination. Why did so many people of the Pennsylvania German of the generation before

mine, born c. 1910, feel in their candid moments like second class citizens, the opposite of entitled?
Assimilation. And when completely globalized how will they feel? Soulless

10/31/18 The drought in Europe is revealing ominous messages. Low water levels on the Elbe River have unearthed dozens of "hunger stones" warning of the hardships of drought.
his workmanship—poema
calling an artist the name of a slave is like a lion pulling a warthog from its hold on youtube. Imagine what they call
Kriebel, David W.
Powwowing Among the Pennsylvania
Dutch Wentz, Richard E.
Pennsylvania Dutch Folk Spirituality
A majority of pa dutch scholarship is imprisoned in the schools wentz, yoder, weiser, bird

--the voyage of the thought stream in the voyage of the body in the voyage of the world requires, implies a boat, a vessel of the will, the soul, that I build as I go, for the boundaries stronger or weaker, the integrity of the decisions, the management of the inner currents, cross currents, for these impact, these thoughts generate in these decisions, the other thoughts, memories, and of other peoples thought streams, both personal and corporate in the weather of the world and its ages. The body is the boat in the voyage of the world but what is the boat of in the voyage of the mind, of the thought stream? The navigation of the harbor, the sea, and especially the inland streams the dangers thereof, for there are dangers of weather, the soundness of the vessel, other boats, and especially those beings that live on land as well as in the sea and the stream. Sailing, navigation, position fixing, to sail we have to first know where we are, then have some motive power to embark for there if we will, or we can just sail with no destination, one of exploration but based upon some assumptions deeper down, which we may have only tenuous connection. Where are we on the sea? If we following the analogy we navigate by the heaven and by the maps which must be as much and as many of the accounts of our fellow sailors that we can manage. And by the heaven we mean…well find out yourself. I have left some maps. So those voyages of the Irish sea hermits to bur
Voyage of moving islands, Sargasso seas were different from the Viking ships of purpose of invasion and hunting, but these are more sea based decisions, not land based as modern armies played in buildings of pentagons. Manipulated by the land forces,? You a voyager following th dictates of land? Under orders? Voyage of mael dun. But we don't sai to a delicious or blessed isle, our destination is our voyage and it measure is our praise and thanks, discipline, charity and resistance to the forces of the wold.
Our souls are sailors who have no destination, but to sail is everything and in the thought stream we, numbed to one another's thoughts as we are, we have influence and control to turn our fear, worry, thoughts to compassion and healing and support for those we think of. Sailor what of the islaes/ Soul of Ocean. Not all men will be sailors then, as Leonard Cohen, but all men are sailors now. You get this body this boat at birth, we're on the boat we're bound to float we can't stand still we can' go back what should we do--sail

10/30/18 addictigital here Disconnected: How To Reconnect Our Digitally Distracted Kids Paperback – December 14, 2016 by Mr. Thomas J Kersting
--around my two aunts in childhood, maiden aunts with proper skepticism of the male, I was as brilliant a rhetorician and mind that I ever was for their enthusiasm to enter dialectics combined with their beauty was a joy. My grandmother was too formidable for talk, and her mother also e. Bechtel was also a factor in the transmission of the books, these four leave formidable images inmemory.

1029/30 Aeg stopped after dentist, needs one filling!
 10/28/18 got up at 2am and prepared Conrad reiff, took all day, pat proof a lot, publ in evening.

10/27/18a girl named Cecelia delivered a goya print to blake warpped around a cardboard roll,--Got pneumona 13 shot yesterday.
-- Pat said her mother threw out the some 500 letters she had written home over the years

10/24/18 my gift is that no one can hear me
-- I don't lose any sperm when I talk
--Dragonettes, Demonauts,
--there is a backstory to the ongoing publication of the Taliesin Poems that is still continuing. The first of this was composed in my head, a villanelle, on a long night trip in Texas. It was a more finished villanelle in that incarnation when it appeared in the TQ in 1977. In this more laconic outing of 2018 I have changed the music to break the meter and the meaning further, although the form is still recognizable with a little grace of perception.. The metric of long the days, and there is a harvest however demanded their cadence from the start and could not be altered. On of them was originally dedicated to Bill lee the haikkido teacher who first showed me VandeWeerings two zen books and loaned them to read. He gave me some of his Van der Posts too and the last bushman lingers behind some of these in solidarity. Four O'clocks is a tanka, or was, but in the correspondence below it has its own controversaerry. The plant is obviously a sonnet, one of a number rendered in the worship of God offerings in the Taliessin II, to appear.
While parts of it appeared in print, also in latitude 30, who were eager to get them and called me on the fhone to confirem, they bounced another author in Taliesin's favor, they never appeared online thill now, which means they haven't been read as they outht, for the agonies of war can't be forgot. In 2011 another mag loved the poems but the superstructure around them was souch a problem it threw all three of its editors serially. I tried to withdraw it from the first, but he he would not, so the second and third, academic people bulloxed themselves into knots. The corespondance is relevant for the contentions taken up between the confusion of the literal and the symbolic, still a concern at least somewhere in the U.

10/23/18 Concerned to hear A's next trip to LA I ask that he would call for lunch yesterday. This aM he we had lunch! Theodore can write his full name. he thinks it means Teddy. AB to have first PT conference tomorrow. A to go to Ontario Ca with boss Rob Gen Mgr to visit client Thurs, his immed boss melanie wants him to go to bars with worker s happy hour, but he wont'! His pipes are clogged, maybe from oleanders that were cut down.. told him I don't have any children any more, they are adults, that only a fraction of life is a child the rest is growth, the child is a technicality so to speak. But since he want't to know my child advice to his was to work hard and take the next step and not rely solely on ability to wash every scene with glibness, like a salesman, which he can do as an escape artist, but to develop depth I will know I said when you do, How/ he: I talk like you/ No you won't talk at all. Feel the environ. We ate at the Indian restur, a very sad, depressed overpriced place, won't las a year. He said she won't admit it but Sab like Anadema bread. That they're all coming to Pats Bday! Told hism AB know who I am: dr of the mind

IF THE DEMOBOTS WIN in 2018 AFTER THE ELECTION THEY WILL BE CIVIL BUT IF NOT THEY

WILL CHANGE THEIR NAME TO DRAGOCRATS

--immigration from the souls programmed from the moon into incarceration endless, thousands of iterations, urged by the controllers of that apparatus of the Karma lords, the exodus of the Jews from Egypt, the supposed movements of peoples across the putative land bridge to NA, Immigrants or Invasions, depends on whether you are resident not only. The puritans to NE and the Abenaki (Ken) the forces immigration from north Africa, not even in war, feigned war caused to force the immigration, but not only for that, but mainly to disestablish Europe and weaken nation states, economically and demogratically, the lates being forced marches not of

POWs like the Japanese did at Chosen but from Honduras, with the blessing and aid of the drug cartels to crash the US borders—but this never happened even though there was plenty of impoverishment and political coup caused by the CIA, but only when land, was what, dried up from ice age, no only when interstellar cosmic rays burgeoned around the sun/ , or when it was the gasp of the under state to taken down the nation,--so far anyway the effort to define the masses and mass movements of overpop from 1927! The obesity game, one third blown up and growing! The GMO genomic weakening game to decrease fertility, since planned parenthood and the Rockefellers couldn't do it Bill Gates did with his ag projects,. When the literal human gene is at risk it's bigger than immigration and the causation must be sought beyond the back engineers, but it's not sufficient to cry the sky is falling.

--10/22/18 I put all these allusive black holes in waiting in my writing. Sometimes people get a glimpse, but the cliques that allow them transition and the fact transmitted seem to need translation, so When you travel outside the galaxy it doesn't help to be reading the Grand Inquisitor, needs explanation of the Spanish inquisition tr, to

Dostoevsky. Jesus comes back and is judged by the inquisitor, the scribes and pharisees

--At work in the heat of compulsion and creation the author does not know the relevance of the work, is not conscious of any thing beyond but simply the composition itself. Hence he later comes to discover it's relevance. It could be decade, months or years. It is 40 years since these early works on America that are so relevant now and a year since the Vocab of Opposites sought to explain the problem front and center in politics.

The Opposition of Opposites

For the American scholar the single most poignant fact about America's supposed racism, sexism, imperialism urged against its own Democrat Globalists is Edwardo Galeanos' repudiation in his Opening the Vein that so dramatically gave these foundation. Open Veins was prophetically given by Hugo Chávez to Obama in 2009, who was the seed sower of those doubts to weaken the American government, which now faces constitutional crises of every kind with suspicion upon the supreme court, the executive and the legislature inculcated by those organs themselves. How this occurred can be traced historically if one cared to look, but scholars, historians and agents of news feeding the flames are no corrective voice. No counter history therefore weighs the balance, hence this essay, A Vocabulary of the Opposite, describes the state from the point of view of the 16th century. the essay is a commentary on these subjects as expressed in both Calendar of the New World Planting and Restorations of the Golden Age, combining the humor and chauvinism of the voyage to the new world with the sexism of their effrontery to cast it as a sex act, this domination in the sheets of the seas as Marlowe might say in his Amores of 1582.

Whatever Kafka meant by his spelling it with a k, something about being swallowed up in a sea of machines, there is now a third Amerika which would enforce its facist controls upon the citizen in discrimination of seas, races, women, weather and molecules all charged against white, men, capitalism, and eventually science when it no longer serves that purpose. But before Obama the works of ecofeminism had begotten these wars in the liberation theologies of the eighties. [See - The Fall of the Latin America Mission- https://insightstatutes.blogspot.com/2016/10/the-fall-of-evangelicalism-and-latin.html Oddly however, the avant garde of destruction in literature is preceded nearly a hundred years by the destruction in text theology, as if at base literature is religion, just under another name. To blame white, male, capitalist malefactors is a projection of one shadow of the global to divide and disestablish all nationalism and Christianity by Crisis Management to foster their dream. Many competing accounts of these crimes occur, from the supposed destruction of Aztec records by the Spanish, however all boxed up and and shipped to the Vatican Library along with boatloads of all artifacts of lost civilizations, codexes, relics of space machines to be back engineered. This is an age of the back engineer, a pun to clone those backward souls and dispositions who perform these feats until they are discarded, but all this so scholars can consume the red herrings of the Marxist global to disestablish the nations. Hence there is much more to the Vocabulary of Opposites that therein poses An Opposition of Opposites, "a God who acts in history, Hugo argued, (Assman, not Chavez) would be an "interventionist like the imperialists." Since only the Vatican should be allowed to intervene among native peoples, and it wanted a clear field for this domination, just as we know who the racists, sexist, imperialists are, it is always the tactic to call the conquered what in fact the conquerors are. Those fish hats bespeak their own religion where the concept of native peoples vs. colonial trasnposes to human vs. divine in an invention of…[and that work is in progress] Nimrod and the Mischwessen.

--I'm not sure any more what the word soul means in Donne and the writers who use the term, for the world seems outmoded in light of what is he immediate perception of the Hand of Elohim in life and in the world. That he is called

10/21/18 "the one person who might be able to give some sort of guess at to why God creates anything is the creative artist, and he, of all people in the world, is the least inclined even to ask the question, being accustomed to take all creative activity as its own sufficient justification." Dorothy Sayers, Creed or Chaos, 9 His next work was a translation of the riddles, proverbs, elegies and praises of the 14th century, Llyfr Taliesin in the Red Book of Hergest. These appeared first as Taleisin and the Summer Stars, then as The Taliesin Poems. even natural beauty isa construct there is an aural map of sounds and a visual of sights but if you close your eyes the visual disappears, open them and you identify with it. But if you see the world by notseeing the images shake and dissipate and disappear, leaving… what. No I don't like it.

confronting three sons about who is responsible for their lives. Viz, their father. It strikes me there should be a ceremony, like at menarche, for sons, is it bar mitzah/ to assume their authority for themselves, not an initiation or manhood ceremony maybe, but a formal recognition.

Tour clay pipe, carve in pipe yesterday with az clay club.

10/20/18 Democrats want to kill the babies to make rule for immigrants

Who made the decision to kill the Roe v. Wadey

Who made the decision to take away its life Who made the decision to kill it all, we all did, we all did to remove it lfrom the earth

That's what I call nice

That's what I call nice…species of illuminist first seductions: Pat involved in giving and getting advanced beauty treatments at lakeside beauty resort tells me it wont' be long but it is all day, discontent I drive about am ready to leave, finally she is but car won't start, I look and find a sparkplug loose, traced to a big shot how had the keys according to the guy who owns the salon and his tech with owhom we talk and he gives lowdown on the guy, I say that affluent people have everything but I live on the edges of risk every day. They begin to show affection…this reminds me of the guy at gan's studio nc. 73-74 wo want ed to send me to Trinity U to study acting. He would pay. tis the most erogenous part, I say the, he says take oof your socks, I get out of his car….seduction dreams, sparkplugs?

10/19/18 Pentinentes. It is maddening when trump sponsored the marches from Honduras to win the election, as much as when soros his vp pays them to march. NOW climbs the pyramid in stages, that's why the steps.

Obama was the crust, Hilly the icing but the head was an NPC.

Either Trump has designed the march or that same force greater than CERN that hinders its completion causes the Americans to see a sierge at the border just at the election, making them vote an as ifreferendrum in their vote! Big theatre.

10/18/18 We saw the hermit coming out of his culvert alley blocked with thorns. He said hi.

Treads of Peru
Acrylic paint on bisque, spatter glaze, walter hooper on lewis deuplicityk, lib and J as cia

10/17/18 joined az clay to take the clay pipe tour
10/16/18 eldila Lowell pluto in japan out today
10/15/18 Proverbs 4.19, why cern is opposed

10/14/18 Sunday: had the kids 9-4. Th played in the dry sprinkler. Took wheelbarrow, table, swing to A and S. Saw nikio at end, he had a half smile for me and a look of interest. His corollas are light blue shading to dark blue.superposition is dual position, there is after position and former postioon and present position, but the reason the CERN collider feels it is being opposed by some force is its own creation by this for as they send their collisions to their twin on the other side of the galaxy it sends back healings of the collisions. Mengele experiments with twins in Urugay as a first effort of superpostion and cern. On the way after picking up heard from the back seat in a muddled tone ..surgery on his balls so he can't make seed. Which she repeated. Which explains his discomfort and pjs all day. Leads me to ask what effect on selfhood-being made a eunuch the argument is that after all the woman bore all the reps before-but in response am told the right one can moderate the effect of a period and benefit her. What's done can be undone as Robt found out. But again having no foreknowledge of this or his house he goes his own way. Post Vascret Pain Syndrome testicular backpressure "There is a noticeable enlargement of the epididymides in vasectomized men [8][9]. This is probably due to increased backpressure within the vas deferens on the testicular side following its blockage by vasectomy. The efferent ducts and seminiferous tubules of the testes are also impacted by backpressure, leading to an increase in area and thickness.[10] Backpressure from blockage of the vas deferens causes a rupture in the epididymis, called an "epididymal blowout", in 50% of vasectomy patients.[11] Sperm sometimes leak from the vas deferens of vasectomized men, forming lesions in the scrotum known as sperm granulomas. Some sperm granulomas can be painful.[12] The presence of a sperm . Cf. hystermecty to vascetmacy, diff between organism before and after? granuloma at the vasectomy site prevents epididymal pressure build-up, perforation, and the formation of an epididymal sperm granuloma. It thus lessens the likelihood of epididymal discomfort

10/13/18 what you need to know about the cern experiment woodward more superposition, I am the least of men a worm am made the righteousness of God in Him. And :we sit together with Him in heavenly places! Even while we are here on earth!10/12/18 Orthodox
Holy Archangels Church - 6.7 mi
Russian Orthodox Church Outside of Russia
10030 N 32 St
Phoenix, AZ 85028-4430
10/11/18 the glass transformation temperature. This is the temperature range at which glass changes from exhibiting solid characteristics to exhibiting liquid characteristics. This

temperature is ~580°C for sodalime-silica (SLS) glass (beer bottles, pickle containers and windows are made from SLS glass). The temperature you should be looking for is the working range of glass. This is the temperature range between the softening point and the working point, which for SLS glass is between 700-1000°C. Obviously the proper personal protective equipment is needed when working with glass at these temperatures. Although you can slump glass bottles in a camp fire the temperature is too variable to make it effective for working with glass. Often times you may slump the glass in the fire but later find the glass blown apart once it cools down. This is due to the internal stresses that develop in glass upon cooling. It is important that you anneal the glass after shaping it. You must cool it slowly in order to give the glass time to rearrange itself while cooling. This is done by slowly cooling the glass from its working range down to the annealing point (~500-550°C) and holding there for a couple hours and then slowly cooling down to ~100°C. These annealing curves are dependant on the wall thickness of the glass object. If the object is thick you must cool even more slowly.
I will also caution against using a Bunsen burner for SLS glass. The pipettes that Todd (above) refers to are actually a borosilicate composition (like Pyrex) which has a greater ability to resist thermal shock. A Bunsen burner typically will only heat very small glass objects evenly enough to be able to shape them without them blowing apart. A bottle may be too large for this technique to be useful.

saying that Nikolai is destined, the man in the child formed like superposition, here and there temporal and eternal except the temporal is not the romance of the families. Is humbling to consider their lives and hardships and dedications so it feels to have been given such great blessings.

Eliza Jane Wright was born in Alabama, one of at least six children of Soloman Wright (born 1801 in North
Carolina).-married Amasa Clark in Fredericksburg on July 10, 1858
Momo Sarah Sallie Cosgrove Parsons 29 Mar 1897-5 Aug 1993. Momo considered herself Grandpa Clark's favorite grandchild because she shared with him a love of gardening.
Edwin Earl Parsons
    31 Aug 1899
17 Mar 1975
Father's Name: Edwin August Parsons
Mother's Name: Katie May Matthews
Her mother, Olive Rebekkah Clark Cosgrove (1 Mar 1874-1967) Married john Henry Cosgrove Jr. (10 Feb 1860-1931) from Tweksbeury, AL lived in Lowell, Ma. His father death notice here. https://newspaperarchive.com/lowell-sun-dec-17-1965-p-3/ His father's parents: Mattias F. and Mary
McMahon It carries a love of the land and a heritage of the generations of families)- buried Clark Cemetery-

10/10/18 Galeano: writing about political economy in the style of a novel about love or pirates --the god that failed. Rebecca West: "Arthur Koestler's essay is one of the most handsome presents that has ever been given to the future historians of our time. He is, of course, always an interesting writer. His work is three-dimensional because he is three people. In him there is a believing poet who perpetually changes into an unbelieving critic savagely eager to tear up all evidence of his previous manifestations of faith but never able to complete the work of destruction before he changes back into the poet who is equally eager to fill the wastepaper basket with all the evidences of the critic's skepticism; while another part of him, as tough and jaunty as a racetrack gambler, looks over the wall at this protean struggle quite unimpressed and comments on it with ribald wit. Here he recreates the most formative experience of his life, analyzes it, mocks it."

"We call it the 'wrap-up smear.' it's called a wrap-up smear. You make up something. Then you have the press write about it. And then you say, everybody is writing about this charge. It's a tool of an authoritarian, to just have you always be talking about what you want them to be talking about. Rather than Russia, we're talking about

10/9/18 Aeg in LA all day, 6-10 pm. Prayed for him throughout. stone chisels
--blaming the Antifa mindless demonstrators for their actions is a lot like blaming immigrants dying in the desert or drowning at sea, they are about 20% responsible, the Govt force is another 20 and the news another.
And Soros 20That leaves 10 for you all do goods.
-- goodness in conflict with dialectic is not dialectic, it is judgment.
95-year-old Marvel comics legend stan
lee, 10/8/18 pigeon coin, pigeon bar,
bracelet s,
--clay artist
-- a philosophy of war tells everything about the enemy. Enoch says it and the art of seduction were the main corruptions the angels taught the man and woman. The manipulations for and against war together document effort to control, defeat, and design all men, groups of men, nations and their histories. Any histories of these must be of the angel, 10/7/18 Clif high says he keeps coming back and can recognize his "face' but who brings him back, who are the lords of karma and who put them in charge? eight cosmic beings of the Great White Brotherhood, chosen by God?
--The American voyages as a metaphor for search for truth

Iron city review, pentonville, Doest, Russian writers in outdoor prisons not mechanized along with many polit prisoners, hence a moral
Fyodor, Fedor (Russian: Фёдор) or Feodor is the Russian form of the name "Theodore".

We have to live with it to see the beginning from the end because we are in a struggle with an enemy from the start. To see The finished work in the raw piece, or birth and death in our life, that's heard, better our birth and our eternity first and last, beginning and end, hope and hope. This is very much like Jacob wrestling, and the ladder, and the statement that it was all without form and void, or became so before there was light, which is our beginning and the earth's. We and the earth share the same experience in this, small and great, because it will be recreated as shall we, first in spirit, then in body, so that is our story first to last to live. Many of us have moments of happiness in our childhood and moments when our children were happy, a daughter at the seashore, a son doing a backflip at the Grand Canyon, another son hearing "war guns" when the dumpsters were emptied. The happiest moment of my childhood was the day the sun died.

9/28/18 Put a fall of Jerusalem and Diviation X up on Voat and

9/29/18 Sat. Aey appeared just as I was shown that statement about the Pashtun, which we had considered the previous days in the Hearings. That and the broken rib , trials of the tire, etc seemed to motivate this statement: Intimidation is what makes an abusive relationship, fear is what keeps people in it. Fear of speaking up in self defense, fear of what her family will say, for they have blackmailed by presents his acquiesce. And he has spent way more time with then than with his own. Samson shorn of his hair. The results are no visits to his home, only visits with him when she is distracted, none with Aegand gross obesity and stress, betraying his family, his brother and most of all himself and his gifts. Gave him examples of what E has done. Also what JH did, whose highest value was to honor his mother and be faithful in order to honor her sacrifices. As if that weren't enough Aey appears, but I have to say I am infinitely angry with him. Talk of the abuse of memories like the Dr. accuser of the judge from 15 and her ptsd, which must be much more strong in Sh from her appendectomy, her regret must rule her deep mind and memory with guilt and shame. But she refuses to take counsel of any kind. My point it you must be true, faithful to yourself at all costs, even if you have to go against your word. All the talents, singing, athletics, art, music, film she has prevented, as well as his relation with his two nephews and one niece. All because he is overruled by another's will. This makes me infinitely angry which is a replacement for despair… She has alienated you from everything you love and you are a prisoner of your own choosing. From 9/26 --the ritual desecration of Kavanagh because he might limit r v wade: I know a woman who had an abortion just out of high school who cannot know conceive from complications of her life, but she could have had a son or daughter right now who was 18 and on the verge of being her friend. But she killed them from r v wade.

-- if they were Pashtun these white antifas against their own people and families, Geoffrey, eliza would be put to death. They are traitors to their own blood. And if you betray your own you will everyone else, because there is no mutual respect without self respect. Hence they surrender to the global, the anti human, alien, hybrid. So we know them for who they are. Liars who call others liars, perverts who call others perverts. You name the malady, their chief end is to transfer contagion to all other people because they are traitors, avant garde of the satanic.
.
Meditations on the passage of the phases of a writing life lyrical, middle and long forms, all which I have passed through, but practically none of which have been published in the usual way anyway, but a complete writing life Counting back:

The Colonies of Jerusalem, all the essay stories of the Decaps,

All the exposes of Insight Statutes,
Reviews,
Autobiographies, Chartiers, Spg Springs Criticism, analysis, concurrent with the Pa Dutch, akin to yeats Celts in a fashion, the short lyrical stories in toto, Susan and Orcs, the lyrical poems, of Encouragements geographically the two addresses plus ranchin Tx produced but Phoenix starting with Susan, then orcs, the two addresses wonderful

4821 Spicewood Springs Rd is a house in Austin, TX 78759. This 2,426 square foot house sits on a 0.55 acre lot and features 3 bathrooms. This property was built in 1994. Based on Redfin's Austin data, we estimate the home's value is $653,494. Comparable nearby homes include 4825 Spicewood Springs Rd, 7714 Long Point Dr, and 4405 Walhill Ln. Nearby schools include St Matthew's Episcopal School, Anderson High School and
Bais Menachem Hebrew Academy. The closest grocery stores are Randalls, Savory Spice Shop and Con' Olio Oils & Vinegars. Nearby coffee shops include Nelo's Cycles & Coffee, Starbucks and Galaxy Cafe NW Hills.
Nearby restaurants include Investors Cafe & Stock Exchange, U Sub Inc and DoubleDave's Pizzaworks. 4821
Spicewood Springs Rd is near Bull Creek Greenbelt Park - Upper, Steck Valley Greenbelt and Bull Creek Greenbelt Park. There are some bike lanes and the terrain has very steep hills. 4821 Spicewood Springs Rd is somewhat bikeable, there is minimal bike infrastructure. This address can also be written as 4821 Spicewood Springs Road, Austin, Texas 78759.

9/28/18 Put a fall of Jerusalem and Diviation X up on Voat and

9/27/18 Geoffrey Reiff Mahoi! fixture of the Washington DC tango community and frequently DJs for some of its most popular local milongas.
Double dwarf banana Mahamet hoi poi Ruling family of sierra leone, double banana, tango warrior, tea man. Sufi, BLY: Bill Gaham of chant. Robert Bly's house on Irving Avenue in the Kenwood area of Minneapolis on a certain evening. Perhaps a dozen men, including Bly, met in an uncarpeted room in this house.chants-We started with a core group of singers, some of whom remain active participants to this day. New people joined in later years, and several dropped out when they left Minnesota. Mark Stanley compiled an email list of group members which today has fifteen names: Robert Bly, Glen Helgeson, Kevin Gregerson, Brad Fern, Mark Stanley, Walton Stanley, Duncan Storlie, Eric Storlie, David Ballman, Geoffrey Reiff, Kurt Meyer, Lanny Kuester, Tim Frantzich, Tim Young, and myself. Some attend less frequently than others. I would say the more active participants today include Mark Stanley, Duncan Storlie, Tim Young, Glen Helgeson, Geoff Reiff, Lanny Kuester, Walton Stanley, myself, and Robert Bly, when he is in town. See https://www.podbean.com/media/share/pb-fs2m8-
a0b29a?utm_campaign=w_share_ep&utm_medium=dlink&utm_source=w_share
Jacqueline T. Pham, Jackie Pham PhD candidate in the lab of Dr. Jeffrey D. Rothstein in the Department of Neurology. Thesis work utilizes motor neurons and astroglia differentiated from human patient-derived induced pluripotent stem cells to study pathogenic mechanisms in amyotrophic lateral sclerosis, specifically pertaining to mutations in the C9orf72 gene.

Primary research interests include mechanisms of neurodegeneration, glial biology, neuron-glia interactions, and stem cell biology.

Here is a basket of deplorables. Athens, paris, London, New York, Wash D.C. Managua, Tenochtitlan Austin, Cleveland Seattle We put the fall of Jerusalem in its rank. It's up there with the greatest cities burned to the ground. I'm sure you can add to the list. Tallahassee, Nolon Rouge, cities with their secret names and undergrounds, the tunnels under Dupont Circle, the Paris underground, the abandoned tubes of Seattle. Just to see the physics of fall are not expected.

Try it yourself. The fall is on a fulcrum. The body is spun, lifted to another direction so that where the head was first pointing is reversed and on its side, completes a neat 180 turn in the air and lands with what it was on top of it. I have done this twice, once consummately, so can say that if a city were imagined to be conscious, as it lays there in a heap of itself it first feels terribly embarrassed. I hope nobody saw that, it thinks, as it looks around for spectators. At that point it is in shock and thinks to dust itself off and proceed on its way. It doesn't ever know how bad it's hurt. Adrenalin in the body politic of shock and awe in Baghdad. And yes the fall can be administered also from within like Weimar. The fall, taking of a city, ready or not they said it had a gender too. We can call it a privilege to be in one of these falls. Please add your own experience here!

9/12/18 Duddenhoff Float Academy. Statement to Robt: Soul is that quality attained when consciousness empathizes with as many of the different people of the world as possible, awareness of, identity with, concern for, knowledge of

9/11/ The constitution of the United States is a miracle of liberty for ordinary people. That Bishop Andrew Mack considered the millennium speculative, which tells more about it than him. That year we attended the Conservative Mennonite Church. Pastor: Chris King Overseer: Eddie Graber was another outstanding experiment in social order. Very daring. One in a long line. Foot washing Pastor Yoder! But that is a very tight order and resists all penetration. To have attended the old man school is repugnant to me. They're just business men pretending to be elders. There is an underlying ferocity to many of these men, fear and control they know. So it is natural they would help a stabber of women, the Mennonites and the Phoenix canal murder suspect, Agnes Reynolds, a Mennonite and the Miller's landlord, Bryan Patrick Miller-who stabs women- Miller and his now-ex-wife, Amy, were married by Alfred Yoder, Phoenix police said they used DNA to connect Bryan Miller, 42, to two of the Valley's most grisly unsolved cases. Angela Brosso, 22, failed to return home from riding her bicycle along a canal in November 1992. A headless body was found at 25th Avenue and Cactus Road. Eleven days later, her head was found in the Arizona Canal. Melanie Bernas, 17, the second victim, who also had gone for a bicycle ride, was found dead nearly a year later, in September 1993. Her body was found floating in the canal near Interstate17 and Dunlap Avenue. Miller was accused of stabbing two women, one at Paradise Valley Mall in 1990 and one in Everett in 2002.

Among the Arizona Costumed Revelers, a group of Phoenix-area cosplayers, who wear costumes portraying characters from science fiction, fantasy and comics, or of their own creation. Miller was known as the Zombie Hunter, and dressed to a visual aesthetic known as "steampunk" – a blend of Victorian-era style with Wild West or futuristic motifs. He had goggles, a big fake gun and a tricked-out, decommissioned cop car. When the group met – at local bars – they were always in costume. Are there any more victims? Open cases from the time period include Brandy Myers, a 13-year-old girl who disappeared from her Sunnyslope neighborhood in May of 1992, and Shannon Aumock, a 16-year-old girl whose remains were found near 20th Avenue and Deer Valley Road in May of 1992.
The kill was gleaned as an unknown person's surname by analyzing a DNA profile's paternal lineage through the Y chromosome forensic.

Once after a church dinner I helped the Pastor's wife, Linda Yoder, clean up, none of the men did so. Pastor was an airplane mechanic at the Scottsdale airport? He gave a sermon on the new name once and I brought a back a big bag of fine quartz from the Four Peaks. Washing cuts and abrasions with a very mild salt solution is the most healing. 1/19/15 Linda Yoder, Alfred Yoder's wife.

9/10/18 of Grandfathers, eg. G. Hartmann's or Martin Bubers: Martin (Hebrew name: מָרְדְּכַי, Mordechai) Buber was born in Vienna to an Orthodox Jewish family. Buber was a direct descendant of the 16th-century rabbi Meir Katzenellenbogen, known as the Maharam of Padua. Karl Marx is another notable relative.[3] After the divorce of his parents when he was three years old, he was raised by his grandfather in Lvov.[3] His grandfather, Solomon Buber, was a scholar of Midrash and Rabbinic Literature. At home, Buber spoke Yiddish and German. In 1892, Buber returned to his father's house in Lemberg, today's Lviv, Ukraine. Of the Hechaloth tracts and the names of angels, consider Jacob who cannot get the name of his agonist, hence… Hechaloth tracts, Hershell, the voice of Israel, of Samael.

9/9/18 Rosh Hashana 5779 to 9/11 Merkabeh, EZ, Maimonides, Soncino

9/8/18 tesla's earthquake machine--Teslacles-Yamma ensemble Brian Forester, ancient artifacts in Egypt.
- Dear Zack Wentz, I'm just getting around to asking what in the world you mean in blurb of New Dead Familieses when you say Charles G. Finney…is of our finest, and am more likely to be re-reading…in ten years? I have read all of Finney myself, as justification for the question, which as they go brings another, are you of therefore a Wentz of the family for whom the Wentz Church back in 1762 Skippack was named? I say that because it was, as you know?, a descendent of the Reiff Church of 1730 thereabouts. Please if you get this reply so so I can get on with whatever it is I am doing. Yrs. AE Reiff

9/7/18 Jacob's Ladder: a hallucinogenic drug BZ--chemist with the Army's chemical warfare division where he designed a drug called the Ladder, which when ingested massively increased aggression, to test its effectiveness was secretly given to Jacob's unit before the battle, causing some of them to turn on each other in a homicidal frenzy. Michael's revelation triggers a vision of his wounding in Vietnam, in which he sees that his attacker was a fellow American soldier.

Blake Archive in the last plates of Jerusalem the "Four Living Creatures" (98:24, 42) frame a celebration of resurrection in which everything—animal, vegetable, mineral—becomes individuated living being that appears united in the "One Man" (98:39) of Ezekiel's vision…vows to destroy the tyrannous "Cherub" appearing, like the Cherubim itself, as a man "midst the stones of fire" (Ezek. 28. 16). This satanic being is in Jerusalem the "Selfhood" and the Spectre of self-doubt, the destroyer of brotherhood and prophetic faith masquerading as the true Cherubim (89: 10; 96:8)…after Blake's experience at Felpham, where the imposter pretending to friendship is more dangerous than the outright antagonist.

9/6/18 It is next to impossible to verify John Ruth's notes as the Reiffs of Lancaster vol 2 etc. and p. 123 about Muhlenberg conflicted with journals I 215. Cf funerals 318 with Mittelberger. Heckler says Jacob Reiff took stones from the church to build the mill, then built the serpentine race to irrigate the fields with slaves, but the dam failed anyway.

9/5/18 "Coincidence is God's way of remaining anonymous" = coincidence is God's way of arranging truth --the Oberholtzer Mennonites. The main point of contention was apparently in regard to secret orders. In 1850 the Conference passed a regulation against lodge membership which was somewhat moderated in the same year in the interest of unity.
-Anna Reiff's donation in the Skippack Alms Book was to help fund the new Mennonite Meeting House built on land gotten from Henry 25 Jan 1738. Riffe II, 35
-- Lametaru Amdscales total Carge
Planetary landscapes the title. Large canvases of yellow, red, blue opposed by onlooker student critics dragging thei rpurses over them, in stages of interference. Two of them though in the making.

9/4/18 I am part of the Swiss Palatinate peoples who became part of the United States when it was a British colony. I studied these origins from the point of view of 16th century literature, esp the Elizabethan, to trace the way travel accounts of the European settlement, reflected in poetry as it was then called. This produced a dissertation and a volume of verse that rendered colonization and exploration together with exploitation. Moving further and further west from these Philadelphia origins, first Texas, then Arizona, for its openness and wilds, I was born to Swiss Reformed and Mennonite settlers of Philadelphia, Germantown and Skippack who moved from Germantown, birthplace of that culture called Pa Dutch, an area north of the Perkiomen Valley in the locale of Skippack or Schiweach Schuippach. Nine generations of these families lived in this vicinity from c. 1700 on until just before my birth when that generation returned to the Philadelphia again, after long existence as farmers and traders to be shop keepers and employees. It is an ironic circle that I was born in Germantown after they had come and gone and come back, and I started the first 5 yrs of life there, until that particular family moved again, exoduses that would keep occurring, and resettled in the Chartiers Valley, that massive carboniferous nexus of coal, railroad freight lines and Chartiers' creek that including Pittsburgh, except that it also included weeks out of every year in the pine barrens of New Jersey too, a childhood of complete freedom in open country among ethnically diverse peoples, Italian, Irish, French, for my large family did not particularly notice my comings and goings. All of this is written separately, but at the age of 16 that family returned to the environs it had originally inhabited in Montgomery County Pa, so I was returned to the very place so long inhabited, but ignorantly, knowing little of this identity even though I remained there until age 23, with some time off living in Costa Rica, again a separate writing. Leaving Philadelphia to pursue becoming a writer, hence Iowa and grad study, a path unknown to these ancestors but pursued because of the same spiritual experience that has struck generations of Mennonites, just after my final year of high school. I was deeply attracted then to the allegory of Renn lit, which activities prevented my return, except in visits, in sequence after teaching at a black college in NC, FSC 66-68, provoking my move to Austin where I lived on the Balcones Fault to continue the quest, took up linguistics, was required to switch to English again, from 1970 -75, with again some time off in England and Wales with the woman I would marry, and complete a doctorate of the American voyages as I explored the hill country of the Edwards Plateau. Not drawn to be a professor part time jobs in Austin occupied me for survival, the Clayton foundation and the Drug Garden, for by then I had returned to my ancestors' love of the earth, nature, farming and herbs, and discovered I was a natural horticulturalist and gardener. After the birth of our first child I taught a year at Tx as an adjunct before moving to Dallas for my wife to attend med school while I taught at the black Bishop College. These matters consumed the following years until we concluded we must in the Sonoran western desert, so Phoenix became our home. My interests in exploring this topography, camping, sketching, esp. the grand canyon where we spent much time, the Mogollon, Mazatals and White Mts, developed along side my formed interests in allegory, writing, gardening, native plants, which I pursued throughout her residency while I pursued book scouting to help us survive, Concurrently we sponsored three children into life, liberty and the pursuit of happiness, meaning the desert and the mountains, art and athletics. Major freeways were built behind our house. We moved a little north and the Grand Canal Project was built behind our house. We sponsored these children to adulthood with creativity of all sorts, for we had no TV until the youngest was 10. While my wife persued a solo medical practice she had been given I took up tennis again and our two sons became active, achieving nation stature, again separately written. When that retired I was drawn to ceramic sculpture to pursue Forms of the Formless, again, separate cover, while cultivating a body of written work on the subjects of herbs, native plants, 18th century and 19th century Phila, allegory, fiction and poetry.

9/3/18- Ozark" relates the French term aux arcs. OZ-Orcs

9/2/18 When I first realized and discovered the existence of this family and its community I wanted to reconstruct it from the inside out, showing the relations in as great detail as possible. These start with the identity of names places and biographies that follow. There are two traditions among the folk, one farcical, profane humorous, idolatrous, Balaamistic, celebrated as hexes on barns and hexical signs on barns, and sex magic of abstention and orgy, spiritual virgins and tantric sex, the other high minded, peaceful, struggling against war, much persecuted, agonists of contradiction of Moses or David or Adam for that, standing against the principalities and powers. These two strains appear in the PA Dutch, the angel and the artist in the Germanic sect that practices such ludicrous lawless perversions of their brother's faith, mocking it in many forms while both practicing it and denying it. All of it together is entertaining to the minds we have left in the wilderness that remains. So the history of the settlement of PA by these folk is full of absurdity and sincerity and its understanding will require identifying the names and boroughs of these from 1683 to 1760 thereabouts, which can be further delimited to from 1709 to 1760, about 50 years. So here is list of names that will appear in these findings, but it is obviously incomplete, hence imagine volumes 2 and 3 and one with different selections and names. So be it.

9/1/18 Amar Annus, Inana and Enki

8/31/18 The best evidence of the Lord of lords is the existence of man and the heavens. The proof of the man is he is lost. The proof of the heavens is they are made.
-Aunt Libby always insisted I had surgeon's fingers. Conrad, Jacob, Hans George, Anna left a bigger foot print in 1717- 1756 than many moderns today. Of strength of character and public affairs the trails trace until the present day. The underkeeper.
8/30/18 I went out to do a little juggling and Big Boy came over to my feet, stepping on my toe.
-Tomatoes seedlings, rosemary left in full injury sun after she mows. --On Jacob's wrestling with the putative angel of Esau, we wrestle not against flesh and blood but against principalities
8/29/18 Ezekiel is told not to bow to the living creatures in Ch. 2 which suggests that when all things under his feet, the beasts, the birds and the fish from Gen 2, that he is to have dominion, but here the case in the physical connects with the spiritual, the man in himself interacts with the spiritual beings of the living creatures. What is it Levinas says, the spiritual and physical. So the man does not know his status in the spiritual but is reminding in Psalm 8, and Ez, for these incorporate all living creatures made on the 5th day and specifically included in the Ark have this identity in the (cherubim) but I don't see that Pember's notions of the living creatures has penetrated the thought. Under authority is also a key phrase, for they do not rule the man, he rules them, so also in Christ the man is exalted to judge angels, which would seem to be those not under authority. So Ez is sent to Israel and to the rebellious nations. Ez's living creatures are a superscript of those in Genesis. He is to rule over every living thing 1.28. These intersects involve the celestial and human tribunal, as Levinas in Beyond the Verse 104. Rev 19.10, 22.8-9 "Do not do that. I am a fellow servant of yours and of your brethren the prophets and of those who heed the words of this book. Worship God.

8/28/18 Usage of nephesh chayyāh in Genesis..

8/27/18 Trying to by house warming present, my idea of freezers pat starts her own dialogue after plans made and upsets the cart. Maybe it was the combination of joie de vivre and sadness, deeper down, that made such excellent women love me. I keep having dreams about doing jobs but don't know how, technical jobs, like I never could do accounting or bookkeeping or auditing, All I know anything about is literature and of that not much really

8/26/18 2.35 AM. Stark innocence of the child of Psalm 8. Innocents. A ms. I haven't read in a while but familiar. To encourage me to finish the work on Psalm 8.

8/25/2018 took him truck, anointed A's new house. James Pesrloff, Galaway, Blessingway, World Field, WorldWay, Mirror Way, Proto State.

8/24/18 IDEA OF A SPACESHIP.
A closes today. Had lunch yester.

8/23/18 Pat pulling into drive nearly hits me backing out. Doesn't stop.
8/22/18 Strandbeests, as they are called, are cobbled together from PVC pipes, elastic bands and unbleached muslin. They are the creatures of a Dutch artist. In his videos they gracefully skip across the sand, reminding me of the fifty-foot tall figures crafted by Bread and Puppet, the reactionary performance group based in Vermont. In person they look more like something engineered by Rube Goldberg. Joan Wilking

--He that loves wisdom loves life. Conversations about all different tribal national ethnic identities of the world, the color, compassion experience. So I sent five poems to the Zambia New Ink Review, Stigmata poems.

8/21/18 I SAW this morn that Full of Crow had its account suspended and that the backups I thought were on Wayback don't work. Which led to Pat saying, when Andrew visited July a year ago during the brain episode she had asked him to take a flashdrive of the docs etc, to save them, which reminds that all email will go defunct in a year or less with no use, so I save an archive in docs from blog, of which no electric sources are certain if they can disappear over night as have the FB accts of Jones, etc.

8/20/18 In holding to open source informations of these matters the last instance of this run before the kiln closed until fall was its greatest success, first because of the issue of how to glaze these dark clays without greying them was given a possible solution. All transparent celadon glazes diminish and grey, dark clay—of course in porcelain they are beautiful—so that in awaking one morning the intention was to dust the dark trumpets of this piece with glass frit held on by wax. It was a blue frit on hand but the clay utterly absorbed the color so that it seems any sort, even clear glass would do. Of course there is a danger it would fall on the kiln shelf but this did not happen, instead a magnificent sheen appeared. So that was one. The second on this last and best was the plate-like lamination of different amadors, Black mt, death valley, Jamaica clays affixed before the stretching with serious feldspar crystals rolled in along with some feldspar gravel, pre bisque. This makes the body so interesting in its textures and thicknesses and suggests much use. The coup de grace was when the piece was finished at about 20in upright and because previous ones had fallen was reinforced with paper clay on the inmost slope. So it was finished, covered and left, but again came the message that it had fallen, but not completely, it had bent because one part of the bottom had been compressed, but had not fallen off the table, just bent until the cones were an inch above the surface of the board on the wheel, and there is has stayed more or less, just above the surface, a kiss of five cones bending one over the other. I say all this to urge open source upon us all, for once years ago in a class with the best texture surface maker in the valley, and watching him spray shinos in different strokes and ash between he would in no way explain what he did, but tried to hide his method. Zero sum all the way. Cavet empetor.

8/19/18 chemical in ironwood thorns
-- A Dream Prospectus: TO BEGIN TO FOREBEAR AND NOT. Australian natural resources Cavet empetor. ARMS AGAINST THE SEA. Swedenborg, Boehme.
--A history of the Seventh Day Baptist Canals of Mars
8/18/18 This must be another in the era of Horse and Rider (cast into the sea), the second time in this kiln opening when the best piece fell before or after it got to bisque. I was bored with events before this but not now, and seek to recapture them, for once you see the wild boar you load your gun. At least in the first one, a vase with extensive tares in the middle and bottom, narrow and 20in tall which then had the trumpet figures added to the open top and compressed and there it stood, the most beautiful thing I have seen, so all was well when I covered it, but then the report came 20 min later of its fall, which I reconstituted but it could not be like.
This one here is in the raw after undergoing the same kind of devolution, but this much remained, a kind of cannon off the Triangle at the Fort Pitt blockhouse, its trumpet extending as you see far into the ether. It did bisque, and held, but in the glazing to solidify its meager construction the trumpet fell off. Here in this pic it looks like another horse and rider, which images keep appearing periodically as a kind of Egyptian retrospective.

8/17/18 It invented itself, The way into the flowering is the way the ancestors wove the outside into the in and the in into the out making one seamless garment of their belief. It's mention is a result of dream when asked for a signature I signed the way of the flower heart, part of a long sequence of action that entailed riding atop a box car holding on to slats in a wild ride along dirt roads in Mexico with a 10 yr old boy, which no matter the import is, gather and write it into a book to go with the Psalms.
8/16/18 It took about 7 days to return to no vertigo
8/15/18 revising this three decades after writing makes it read like a tour of London from the top of an open air double decker bus or down a canal in Venice, all extempore and the barker full of asides, but of good cheer so the parties will come back for more. There seems to be a lot of naked speaking herein, which seems attractive and naïve, not the clocked and hispid reaches of the moors. It also reads like a tour through a time long past of innocence perhaps when what we know of the world today had not crept in so profusely. So in the revision the nascent awareness of the chaos become full blown criminal conspiracy of the authorities of all sorts, the critics, the governments, the world. Ample documentation of these produced in the interim, remember the first writing was pre CERN, pre Mandella effect, pre cell phone, pre internet! A totally different world and valuable in the first issue for its being something we will not ever experience again, naivete without overwash, although we have evidence to the contrary. Brainwash of the golden age, the Rhodes scholar, the elite is and has been pervasive since, and everybody has a date, but the 20th century is the century of greatest deception when wars were glorified above and beyond and heroes melted into them. There is nostalgia

but no going back to the era when it was believed the authorities had our back, wanted our good, when for example Jung was thought to describe a universal unconscious of archetypes and not a series of delusions put into the human mind by crazy fallen angels. These awarenesses are kept to a minimum in the retake, which however does benefit from the fast-brain style of the new world in its attempt to set syntax aright for the sake of the flow. Hopefully the asides and injunctions to the reader have survived. So the value of the retelling, which is the spirit of the renaissance, is that the bridge over time between 1985 and 2018 gives a view of the lost terrain below as we pass, but it is anchored in considerations of what these 41 psalms mean to a poet, who however also has been informed by a PhD, and a license. I was not worried with the vibrant interactions with the English text of the psalms first because there have been a thousand translations that differed only a little and second because none of the translators are really native speakers, nor can be, since they live out of time and place of an age many deny anyway and treat the text like an apparition of themselves. Mere intellectual knowledge of a language divorced from itself is always a stilted affair at best. Tyndale and Wycliffe at least preserve the English of their time and place with vigor but to pretend any translation is the thing itself is in error. Only a native speaker can read between the lines. So these uses of the KJV are that too, arbitrary, but at the same time as plausible as any other more or less. What they do preserve from the psalm text is their own take of their time and place and speaker which is why the text is there in the first place an aggregate of every reading ever made. There are two kinds of writing those written after the effect and those before like Psalm 22. Genesis 1-11 is written after the Garden I'm sorry to tell you. It is not a contemporaneous account, but has a purpose to debunk the rival views of creation in Sumer and Egypt. It is subtle and skillful in its refute of the many. The psalms are not rhetorical like this, they are celebratory. 8/14/18 Thinking today of the communities a part of and those belonging to, people seen socially not just in one group or another, in their homes or mine, or at larger affairs, Thornburgh, Crafton, Presby, Phila. Church of covenant, Camerons, Conversion Center, PCB, American viscose trips, Latin American mission, Jim Fallon, Bill Ingram's garret classes, Hollis and Minnis, Ann, Reformed church in Iowa, Herm Nibbelink, Jim
Heynan, Christian lit talk, justice and workshop, Huntley and SNCC Clearing House, Rhodes Dunlap, FSC, Austin, Lib Catholic, Mehy in his Carriage, Bishop Ledbetter, Carl Bowers, Robt Williams clique, dissertation committee, all published in TQ same issue, Cullen and Co., Spg Rd,, Wales, Drug Garden, Bill Lee, Dallas, Bishop and all the books written there, Phx Willetta Clark Reidy life drawing, Molly of Moses Anshem artists, Ed Mell, Foot Dr, tennis events, move office, writing galore, ceramics, pretty much a vibrant participant in all these.

8/13/18 1."it overturns popular, mythical history as if to say, "No, this is what really happened; this is the truth of the matter." As an apological tool, Genesis demythologizes pagan myths. That is, it takes the myths and empties them of their superstition, and corrects faulty and perverted knowledge of the ancient past. AntiMyth In Genesis by Paul Sumner
WEEDS, ADAM HAD'EM
--Foucault's critic of the 16th cent that it was a closed system repeating itself in its infinite relationships and that this relates to the correspondence of man plant and star is not aware that Donne began to see the system lost and anyway it was a much older relation that the med-

renn extended into the oldest Hebrew scriptures fulfilled by its appearance in gospels writers. 2. Foucault's favorite word is infinite, and God all, forever, over and over, so too glib to discriminate grades or even exceptions, especially since he relies solely on alchemists, Paracelsians etc. for the totality of his accounts of plants and stars. Anyway, as the prophets show it is not plants and stars, but plants men and stars, which we can prove at the least by the Pythagorean theorem that things equal to each other are equal to themselves, so if plants and stars have a relation, and plants and men, so do men and stars, even if this is in some spiritual sense, which it is where the object of the contemplation is the plant man who exudes light (implying star). Foucault's unfortunate sex and drug habits compromise the fuzzy things on these and other matters the way Faulkner's daily quart of bourbon did his. That is, it inflames his writing and thought and lengthens his syntax making it much more verbose than is welcome. On the plus side he welcomes Borges and other poets' concision just because they are so accurate and poignant. The first notable to die of AIDS. "Soon after his death, Foucault's partner Daniel Defert founded the first national HIV/AIDS organization in France, AIDES; a pun on the French language word for "help" (aide) and the English language acronym for the disease.[155] On the second anniversary of Foucault's death, Defert publicly revealed that Foucault's death was AIDS-related in The Advocate"
-This reminds of Inuit sculpture where you can have a composite of different elements/beings fused together.
-You have a good eye. From this view it looks a little like a bear.
-It does. Lots of room to slip in new mythologies
-Most poignant phase, new mythologies. I misspelled it first as poingiant. Just as I begin to seek NO MYTHOLOGIES. What would that be: no mythologies? Can they even be escaped? Is Swift anti-mythology? Is Beethoven romantic, that a mythology. Baroque, classical? Is Williams no myth? 8/12/18 A megagon or 1 000 000-gon is a polygon with 1 million sides (mega-, from the Greek μέγας megas, meaning "great").[1][2] Even if drawn at the size of the Earth, a regular megagon would be difficult to distinguish from a circle.
--The usual take on signatures, as in Foucault's, The Order of Things, draws heavily on the alchemists; he cites Crollius multiple times (d. 1609). Pianta Celeste offers extensive biblical metaphors for the relation and the relation of correspondence in the English poets
- Yesterday sensitive to light, sound, headache, vertigo.
8/11/18 To posit a justification for time and place so you might consider your own justified, I lived and grew in the time of end of the later Pennsylvanian carboniferous age and its coal smoke in the Pgh coal seam together with many extraordinary tokens of place that brought the coal to the railroad and the creek. This was a transition from the previous century of exploitation and the rise of the middle class after WWII. After 1947, when I arrived in this place at age 5, the smoke began to decrease and by 1954 was mostly gone with the strip mines of bituminous coal, which ceased in this section several decades before, leaving only the residue of pollution and acid wash, polluting creek and soil and springs as left overs. Not yet justified to live here, unless the whole pattern of life is a series of these pollutions meant to be appreciated, a significant addition to the events occurred in 1950, June the start of the Korean War, September 24, 1950, one of those famous dark days known in history and Thanksgiving 1950 the largest snowfall every recorded in that area, 27 inches. Press accounts, diaries, opinions, scientific explanations for all these exist and can be read, but are they exogenous

events and unrelated. There is nothing like the awareness and sensation of a 9 year old boy on his own who remembers it so long that eventually he traces the events to coincide, correlate with each other. The operations that justify the time before and after these experiences are not to be had. These events might be considered forces, givens that just there appeared and were separate from the degradation of choices that followed them, but were separate from the time. From these givens the 5yr old emerges in the greater environment which as aftermath does not much change since development was curtailed by all the undermined coal seams, but wait and again in a decade the railroad is gone, completely by the 90's with the switching yard, the Korean war and the Dark Day, leaving behind only a visit with an army ranger across the street who boasts his manhood but leaves the question hanging when the boy who fell from the sky the next year knew he did not ever want to kill. And all the cave exploring and river running, Allegheny, Monongahela, Clarion multiple times, not to speak of the guns of Fort Pitt on the point of the joining to the Ohio! confluence of the Monongahela and Allegheny rivers where he spent a lot of time at nine hitchhiking home from Pgh after playing pinball. A quarter for the bus or another series of games takes the games, hitchhike. Thanksgiving weekend report was wildly optimistic. Storms that began on Friday night ultimately dumped 31 inches of snow on southwestern Pennsylvania and paralyzed much of the region for the next five days iconic.

8/9/18 Dark Day Pittsburgh A Dark Day in a similar part of North America to the 1780's occurred in 1950. Search"dark day in Pgh, 1953," black sunday September 24, 1950 mammato forms "mammary cloud", is a cellular pattern of pouches hanging underneath the base of a cloud, Major League Baseball's day games in Pittsburgh and Cleveland played under lights
--"interstellar-interdimensional" devices in our skies—and who, in the concealing of their presence, use unknown technology to envelope themselves in massive cloud formations—so gigantic, in fact, the late American physicist William Corliss Ph.D., in his 1983 scientific research paper titled "Tornadoes, Dark Days, Anomalous Precipitation, and Related Weather Phenomena", documented them being able to cover entire regions, resulting in what he called "Dark Days", as the Sun would be completely obliterated from the sky. One of the most written about "Dark Days" associated with these "interstellar-interdimensinal" devices in near historic times, this report details, occurred on 19 May 1780 throughout the entire region of the United States known as New England—and where, shortly before Noon on that day, the sky turned yellowish, then went completely black.
most infamous "Dark Day" event occurring in recorded human history on 14 April 1561— and was when the inhabitants of the German city of Nuremberg witnessed a massive aerial battle involving hundreds of UFO's in the skies above them—but whose cause of has never been known.
The UFOs were described as being in many different varieties, with shapes including crosses, arrows or spears, tubes, triangles, globes, crescents and other objects, variously flying and darting around the sky.
Shortly after the appearance of the large black triangle, a loud crash was heard.
Celestial phenomenon over the German city of Nuremberg on April 14, 1561 as printed in an illustrated news notice in the same month.

A news report of the incident stated the event started with objects seen on the Sun, witnessed by "many men and women." These various shaped and colored (mostly red or black) objects appeared to be fighting with each other. The report further states that the "fight" lasted over an hour until the objects were "fatigued" and fell to Earth in smoke, though no mention is made of any evidence on the ground. A woodcut broadsheet illustration of the phenomenon was also made, later featured in the 1958 book by Carl Jung, Flying Saucers: A Modern Myth of Things Seen in the Skies. Jung, the famous psychiatrist that was a contemporary of Sigmund Freud, preferred to label the sightings as religious and military misinterpretations of natural events. Natural explanations such as "Sun Dogs," flying swarms of insects, clouds, birds, or other such normal things, have been postulated, but no definitive explanation has been made.

To show how time causes family and generation events beginning in 1949 to coincide with the exploration by canoe of some lakes of the New jersey Pine Barrens, since my mother's father lived there and was visited extensively those summers cause and effect, time, place, family, beginning summer 49.

-The quarry Crafton HS.

Why does dehydration cause vertigo in older people?

Increased Antarctica activity correlated with voyager transiting gas giants, forum borealis. Gabriele Boccaccini the Enoch Seminar.

Psalm 8-- That the lion would lie down with the lamb was a sign of the kingdom of God, the millennium of peace, of Isaiah 35. That the rendition of Psalm 8 in Poetical Reading (1985) ends with a reference to this indicates it was obvious in that verse that is now changed. We don't make sense of this but don't deny the original either. Anther oddity outside the text of the Psalm is the rabbinic midrash that accounts the whole question what is man that art mindful of him as a complaint of jealous angels who suspected they were about to be supplanted as the sons of God, which indeed some were since "all things are under his feet." Much is made of this in the midrash but it is outside the text. So external matters do condition our understanding but not distract from the main account that writes large in minds and hearts. Certain attempts at achieving this event occur with Martin Buber in Berlin in 1900 which sought to establish a "new community," Die neue

Gemeinschaft, not on the basis of blood families of all kinds, especially the 13, but on elective affinity towards "the oldest and most universal community: that of the human species and the cosmos" (Redemption and Utopia, Michael Löwy (1992), 49). The human species and the cosmos is a central subject of Psalm 8.

Another oddity separate from text is the interbreeding of angels with women and their resultant offspring Nephilim giants, men of renown, egregori skaphitee, anshei shem, in the Hebrew, since no new input came to them, for the original offenders of the 200 Watchers were removed leaving only offspring, of which any further reproduction was a diminution of that power divided by halfs or thirds, or eighths until these fractional divines would have had to guard their multiplication lest they breed out of existence, hence they bred among themselves to preserve whatever it was the divine fallen creatures gave them, what the CIA tried to reclaim by staring at goats. Accounts of interbreeding among the government oleanders, the George Bushes related to the other lines ad infinitum, McCains, the mates of the British royals and on, would diminish without strict controls, even as the human would be infected with their genetics. This "people" are the ultimate geneticists who trace to the least degree their ancestry. The flood sought to cleanse this, but some survived, hence initiates like Icke claim all descend from Anunnaki etc, or nomos, but this is as exterior to the human as the genetic proofs they think to raise from chromosome speculation and third strands. Because none of these account for the effect of the Messiah and his elective affinity, not a physical cause and effect, but a spiritual, the one thing the old sons of God lost, the new sons obtain by faith. This is the Reversal of Hermon, the fulfillment of Psalm 2 and 110 and the resultant end of age which opposes the physical with the spiritual, whatever that means, but we find out.

When Buber said that messianism was "Judaism's most profoundly original idea' it meant the yearning for 'an absolute future that transcends all reality of the past and present as the true and perfect life", and the coming of the "world of unity," in which the separation between good and evil would be overcome, as sin would forever be destroyed. Lowy, 49.

Breasted (breastplate0 iconography of scales a theory of armor. Pierre Sabak My Book focuses upon Skaphology

8/10/18 North Korea invaded South Korea in June. I have all the sense impressions of a 9 yr boy living through a grasses. I did not know the dark day was a cosmic event, however to speak of the aesthetic it is to make something never seen before, that is until after it is recognized and called something like the sm=panish armada, the arc de tri;umpt or the guns of fort Pitt. This last seems to fit on a day when I finally identified the day in sept 24 1950 when the world went dak and it iswas pitch back at 2 pm, correlated also for 27 in of snow that thanksgiving 2 months later Nov 24 when there was the largest snow in hisotyr in pgh and immobalizign for 5 days. I have vivid mmores of both but when I look att his piece, photographed in the raw because parts of it are fallen falling off as we speak and no graranteed it will eaven pass bisque let along fire, but will have props and maybe the glaze will holdit,

so it looks Mehy in his carriage. The occult sources of sitwell,
-d. Thomas, Victor Neuburg
-robt Merrill, familiar spirit Ephraim, a Greek Jew once in the court of Tiberius, history of Atlantis, the secrets of Stonehenge, the true meaning of black holes and of the sun worship of Akhnaton, the Bermuda Triangle, and the evolution both of human life and of the universe
-yeats snowfall:
Saturday, Nov. 25, 1950.
Thanksgiving weekend report was wildly optimistic. Storms that began on Friday night ultimately dumped 31 inches of snow on southwestern Pennsylvania and paralyzed much of the region for the next five days. iconic
8/9/18 Dark Day Pittsburgh A Dark Day in a similar part of North America to 1780's occurred in 1950 search"dark day in Pgh, 1953" black sunday September 24, 1950 mammato forms "mammary cloud", is a cellular pattern of pouches hanging underneath the base of a cloud Major League Baseball's day games in
Pittsburgh and Cleveland were played under lights
--"interstellar-interdimensional" devices in our skies—and who, in the concealing of their presence, use unknown technology to envelope themselves in massive cloud formations—so gigantic, in fact, the late

American physicist William Corliss Ph.D., in his 1983 scientific research paper titled "Tornadoes, Dark Days, Anomalous Precipitation, and Related Weather Phenomena", documented them being able to cover entire regions, resulting in what he called "Dark Days", as the Sun would be completely obliterated from the sky. One of the most written about "Dark Days" associated with these "interstellar-interdimensinal" devices in near historic times, this report details, occurred on 19 May 1780 throughout the entire region of the United States known as New England—and where, shortly before Noon on that day, the sky turned yellowish, then went completely black.

most infamous "Dark Day" event occurring in recorded human history on 14 April 1561— and was when the inhabitants of the German city of Nuremberg witnessed a massive aerial battle involving hundreds of UFO's in the skies above them—but whose cause of has never been known.

The UFOs were described as being in many different varieties, with shapes including crosses, arrows or spears, tubes, triangles, globes, crescents and other objects, variously flying and darting around the sky. Shortly after the appearance of the large black triangle, a loud crash was heard.

Celestial phenomenon over the German city of Nuremberg on April 14, 1561 as printed in an illustrated news notice in the same month.

A news report of the incident stated the event started with objects seen on the Sun, witnessed by "many men and women." These various shaped and colored (mostly red or black) objects appeared to be fighting with each other. The report further states that the "fight" lasted over an hour until the objects were "fatigued" and fell to Earth in smoke, though no mention is made of any evidence on the ground. A woodcut broadsheet illustration of the phenomenon was also made, later featured in the 1958 book by Carl Jung, Flying Saucers: A Modern Myth of Things Seen in the Skies. Jung, the famous psychiatrist that was a contemporary of Sigmund Freud, preferred to label the sightings as religious and military misinterpretations of natural events. Natural explanations such as "Sun Dogs," flying swarms of insects, clouds, birds, or other such normal things, have been postulated, but no definitive explanation has been made

8/8/18 Put up Pianta celeste in English
- The Rag
The Licking Dog in three parts, 24 Apr 73,5/1/73, 5/7/73, Take a Sweet with nothing on, 22 jan 73 (not in index because untitled
--Wed. You cannot avoid who you are, your choices, your upbringing, our ancestry. Childhood can be much exploited by disadvantages that you fall prey too, but you give in to them so are responsibly. What makes ou give in? Why are you tempted in that way and not others. No answer, except you were not guarded in this vulnerability. Anyway it's a matter to of inherited character, but to say luck or chance does not account for the underlying theme, It is my responsibility to control myself even while I consult my Master regarding every thing, the neighbor's car parked in front of my house, the music late at night, every annoyance big and small—for no longer shall violence be heard in our land…but we shall call our walls salvation and our gates praise. It is 2.30 am and again from a different

viewpoint I wake reviewing my life, questioning whether I would know myself at all if I met me, reviewing in order: -the life in Germantown till 5
-Thornburg and all that entailed of nature and then corruption, grammer school, high school
-back to Phila, Church of Covenant, Alberta, Al, Alex, PCB, Drexel, Costa Rica and other jobs marriage
-Iowa and Hartman, justice, Dunlap Blake
-travel east coast in between up to maine, fall of 66, visit Matt Pacillo
-Fayetteville, take over of bldg., poems in paper, satires, intoxicants firing
---convalesce in Phila,
-Texas, summer 68, teaching, art, poetry, the Rag, the licking dog, theimpervious counter culture never entered, the roof, spg road, Pat, dissertation, poems move to town, jim bowman, clayton fond, haikido, teaching again, elizbether
--dallas 81, bishop books, psalms, appear in conenza relgiousa unknowingly, aeyrie, walks , Pl3,
-phoenix, chose out of them all. Jane Somers next door, Susan, allegory, fantasy, parody, satire, Andrew, Grand canyon, arches, canyonlands, Mazatzal's, four peaks, life drawing, pottery --today

8/7/2018
--pianta celeste o stella terrestre, search without quotes gets: Le parole e le cose
By Michel Foucault
--Paracelsus stars and plants, herbs and stars
"Every herb is a terrestrial star, every star is a celestial herb"
8/6/18 Even the most austere zen of the contemplative says that eating is itself competition and striving, not resting, for it must obtain food, and that is the best that can be gotten besides death, for Lao Tzu wants Zen to run politics, and Hsien Tao wants it to make immortals, the most corrupt of the three. All this in Creel. To compare China with Mesopotamia and the task of divining the future, whether in the pyromancy or sortilege of yarrow stalks of China, or to liver samples in Syria, or Greek emperors sacrificing animals until they get the answer they want, over and over, beyond the three dove, three sheep limit, whether should an emperor fight or not this battle or Yeats should go to the dentist, the desire to act rightly is extracted from the man who does not know what to do. Among the Jews Zedekiah at the Captivity was told to go quietly and Jerusalem would not be burned, but he was afraid of turncoats in Babylon, and even told it go well by Jeremiah would not go and so all was lost, himself included, all because he would not believe. He would not believe, the Greek /captains would not do their wills unless confirmed by the omen outside themselves. Omen giving and taking everywhere.
Not the fall of Rome or Babylon but the fall of Israel is the most important event in western civ. And the main issue there is it is a symbol of the human dilemma. How to survive the fall, how to remain pure in the midst of corruption. Jeremiah documents the outer tale, pulled up out of the miry prison with old rags under his armpits, kept in the court of the prison until Jerusalem falls, then taken to Babylon but not as Zedekiah, blinded and his children killed in front of him, but in honor. And this not the whole tale but only the start for Daniel whose

answer to the dilemma is water and pulse, dreams of dreams reconstructed, not deconstructed, visited by angels and messengers interfered with in their flight by arch forces opposed to the whole world themselves, but revealing for all time the council of egregori watcher that crowd. Now we know them for what they are. So not to talk as we talk or think but not either in the speech that creates speech, the unsaid that allows the word of God to enter without danger into the language of words, the 120 interpretations of a phrase that lead to the real learning, words within words that begin to receive the real transmission to create, especially in the disappearance of the master whose 1700 analogies and seven hundred doubts given to acquired knowledge emanate from the mind that comes wholly from God unsaid and said in the picture language we call speech, that speaks of itself and we hear the sound thereof but know not whence it comes or wither it goes, as in one born of the spirit, by dictation of the preexisting book written on parchment of white fire with writing of black fire with no punctuation, sentences that neither begin or end, written unwritten, revealed as in Yeshayahu. This describes the celestial to terrestrial, the omens cannot express, the one that becomes many in the domain of reflection and remission, for no sin exists in relation to heaven or earth that cannot not be expiated among men and in the light of day with the understanding that a single bad action can wipe out an accumulation of 1199 good ones, and even that is brought to naught by the severity of the mercy, for free forgiveness is always at the expense of someone innocent who personally assumes its cost, the brother of the guilty who stands in his place and this is the steadfast love good to a thousand generations double. Foucaut the order of things, stars and plants
Pavel Aleksandrovič Florenskij pub by Zolla

8/6/18 neither I nor aey know what level of abuse he is suffering to cause him to say he to S he was going to take time to help Aeg move then to be made to go Yuma that labor day so to prevent it. The same happened 2 Thanksgivings ago when he had her agreement to host thanksg with Robt and Cyn and instead was made to go to Yuma. He is scheduled to go to San Deigo in Sept with her family anyway. How he is so controlled unfathomable. Who knows but tis is desperation so he can finish his degree, because she will take him out? He sprang this on me this am, Mon, without my practice this weekend, so I responded with force. But I am told to let the Worker work! But after a night's sleep it seems like Delilah, jezebel, medusa all the furies against him in one classic tale of domination.

8/5/18 Dream Pop Journal, SPAM Zine, and Obsessed With Pipework. JONAH Magazine, The Oddville Press,
Songs of Eretz, Grey Sparrow Press, Cease, Cows Electric Literature, Words Without Borders, Gramma Poetry, Cosmonauts Avenue, Reality Beach, POEM, Dead Kings Magazine, Funhouse Magazine, The Fanzine, BOMB and Mousse Magazine.
All the really good things happen to a women when she's laying on her back
All the techniques of divination descend from the tutelage of angels who themselves do not know the future even if it is written plainly before them in their circumstances or in scripture that outright reveal it. They want wiggle room and a way around by whatever means that include false legal arguments before the throne that they hope to get somebody to deliver like the Lazurus asking for a drop of water from Abraham's bosom or the Watchers give Enoch

to petition but that are denied. These failures of Appeal leave them with divinations in the short run, their next best option, that being thousands of years for such immortals. There they hope to avoid what evil they can and take whatever advantage is in the cards, the cracks, the throw, anything but cast their burdens upon Jesus which is what we do, for he comes to judge them and they know. The angels use what forces they can to foretell and forestall events in the natural and unnatural for their own sakes so naturally they taught these techniques to their human hybrid successor races among the halfs, which we call orcs in their unveiling. With their clothes on they look like anybody else, even better, the best and the brightest, the most successful, the beautiful, as if they have the power to interrupt our brains and vision to substitute this beauty for what they really are, which we forego for the horror, at least here.
8/418 average tweet: good news, I measured my pecker and its three inches longer than yesterday.
8/3/18 Friday. Relation. Spent even w/ E friends at Aey, faux Pentecostals , young jiving

8/1/18 poem recited by u-boat commanders to enter Antarctica
7/31/18 They lost heir ability to ascend. Angel men mutated into orcs, and things. Like hybrid Egyptian gods. Sent to Three Elements
Cynthia's Gown, that Paragore of the Mind
Much have I traveled in the realms of gold
And many goodly states and kingdoms seen;
Round many western islands have I been Which bards in fealty to Apollo hold.
Oft of one wide expanse had I been told
That deep-browed Homer ruled as his demesne;
Yet never did I breathe its pure serene
Till I heard Chapman speak out loud and bold:
Then felt I like some watcher of the skies
When a new planet swims into his ken;
Or like stout Cortez when with eagle eyes
He stared at the Pacific—and all his men Looked at each other with a wild surmise— Silent, upon a peak in Darien.

I am an imperfect Balboa, but have not traveled in this wandering to give a hoot for Chapman or new planets. I didn't make it into Keats poem either with the bloodthirsty Cortez (Google calls him Cortex). The realms I traveled were counterfeits of states and kingdoms, but since there can be no queens because there are no kings I have even less fealty to Apollo the Imposter. No kings, queens, gods, or seven sages to post below. Likely you will read this since only imposters and their look alikes hype the lord. What's the point? We start out cold and come to this world without mind or memory or disproportionate life that we know, since life is a function of life, and continue in the station of birth until with little prep we come to the renaissance and before with no knowledge of myth, but eventually know them so when William Drummond's poems continually talk of Charon and Morpheus, Phoebe, Doris, Thetis, the Trojan Horse, Adonis or Cupid, Apollo Riboldo, Pamphilis, Briareus, Priapus, Porphyry, Artemis Phoebus, we get no back story. These all stand for what we don't see or hear in the civilized. Names are never spoken, or their standins, so if you want to say good luck, say happy Baal. Baal is luck and time and the disinvention of the past, to fathom when flocks, grass and mead zepher the year with Hybla swarms and wormwood bowers where Cynthia's gown, that paragore of the mind, builds crystal. I got all this from the rocky sea winds and trees with flocks of love parrots whose green shells and orange beaks cover my sunflowers with orange pollen and wings of bees, all which is to say this is where it comes from back to the start.

We keep being confronted in the relation of earth and heaven in the crux, but where did all the idols, gods, myths of the nations come from, the Amorites (Meteorites), Hittites, Perizzites (Preterites), Canaanites, Hivites, Jeubisites (Requisites) of the modern tribes of government intent and inventive technologies that seek to have them all? So as The Future says,

"from the great creeds of the East to the fairy tales of the west, from the gods of Greece to the fetishes of Africa, or the most trivial legends of American or Polynesia, we everywhere find one foundation and one set of laws and are enabled to explain on one uniform system, every genuine myth hereto subjected to analysis." (1 Nov 1860).

This is the belief of the highest and lowest tiers is as if they were just there like caves or bogs or deserts, or flats or gorges or mountains, but they were not. The creeds are not natural, if nature is any concept to be understood. They are hybrids, something already there they are not, idols and so the statement "make no mention of the name of their gods, neither let it be heard out of your mouth" (Ex 23.13). I'm saying that the idols and their gods belong to the angel men who were there first but now have been dispossessed, are being dispossessed. This is not done by all the travel to royal courts of all the purveyors of magic in the renaissance or by any of the secret societies and numerologists who chase their tails. It is done in Exodus by obeying the voice of the Angel,..."for my Name is in him" 23.23. Don't countenance the images, break them! Make no agreement with them, nor with their idols.23.32. I ask again who are they, the idols and the highly evolved religions they prosper that the Vatican has in its basement and the Smithsonian in its, whose wars fought to obtain technology to put to use? How seriously do you take Enoch 10:12? Angel gods became angel men and so diluted their strain that they had to rediscover the technology they built in the first place those eons ago but were lost. Sure a katabole or two intervened, and entropy took its toll, but just the promise that their mentors would be released after 70 generations after they went under was reason to presume."…Bind them fast for seventy generations in the valleys of the earth, until the day of their judgment and of their consummation, till the judgment that is forever and ever is consummated."

-Wordworth says our birth is a sleep and a forgetting. Our birth is an awakening and a remembering!
-your life is a function of yourlife.

7/30/18 goldilocks planet- Not too hot, not too cold, but just right The Goldilocks PlanetThe earth is called the goldilocks planet because it lies in the *goldilocks zone*. It is the region where the distance of a planet is sufficient enough to support life.

As too much hot or too much cold is not suitable for sustaining life.Our planet occupies what scientists sometimes call the Goldilocks zone. Its distance from our star means it is neither too hot, nor too cold to support liquid water - thought to be a key ingredient for life. an Earth-like planet orbiting its star in the "Goldilocks zone

--sabon typeface: burnt book, Princeton the problem of not recognizing your oar, your poem, your wiritng is how then do you know it is your own. In the forgetting, the burnt book, the transmission occurs. So this from Orpheus to Meneads:

7/29/18 acrostic contained in the Hypnerotomachia Poliphili (where the key capital letters are decorated with ornate embellishments). However, acrostics may also be used as a form of steganography, where the author seeks to conceal the message rather than proclaim it. This might be achieved by making the key letters uniform in appearance with the surrounding text, or by aligning the words in such a way that the relationship between the key letters is less obvious. This is referred to as null ciphers in steganography, using the first letter of each word to form a hidden message in an otherwise innocuous text.[5] Using letters to hide a message, as in acrostic ciphers, was popular during the Renaissance, and could employ various methods of enciphering, such as selecting other letters than initials based on a repeating pattern (equidistant letter sequences), or even concealing the message by starting at the end of the text and working backwards.[6]

7/28/18 oh li boppa cow bop cow bop a cow wow o Oh wah, oh wah, oh wah, oh wah, oh wah, oh wah thought, civilize is infected with signs. To name signs seems redundant. That's a stop sign, denotation, the name's the thing… Patch: geomancy & how it is directly connected to the model numbers of D-Wave's quantum computers. Laura on etsy if I say none of my writing appeals to me it smacks of the inflammation of the modern but this is not urge zen but reason, humor, irony and hope. That is worth writing for.' Shorty has recovered well from her surgery Tues. How it must feel to have an unimpeded bladder!

7/27/18 rumplestin the name Talk with Robert.
the misinteretation of reality in the world by omens, divination that creates itself –the insolence and arogance of ignorance why I don't want to teach writing.
--If a piece becomes transcendent it's going to be hard to bear.
--Language thought Reality Whorf says, but it is thought language reality, reality furthest remove, what we say it is. Probability is divination, web bots, science, algorhythm, statistics, names are omens or invocations, What is divination, omens, taboos, not rules for hygiene, law, but what comes to pass, fate, Baal. Gods omen is a sign that is deemed to be significant for foretelling the future. In the first millennium BCE, such omens, based on observation, were collected into long series, such as Šumma ālu TT . but it is not, or it is only if you say it is.Art as omen needs utter interpretation. Not folkways, morays, the predestination, precognition, synchronist, dream that cannot be extrapolated into principles of divination, but only documented, exemplified one by one, Jacob wrestling, Daniel dream, Abraham believing,

7/26/18 –
--long talk with anne
I prefer he had no name but then those who do will think it odd, but who will you think he is and how will we know? He has no name, how could he have a name, he is one who came the

way all of us might prefer to think we must have come, special to ourselves without doubt, trumpets our fantasy of mind, until reason kicks not in and we boast not in the cup of the great. How does anybody escape this illusion? In their public character they seem all humble and empathic who are really interested in ourselves as much as I am in this one with no name, this neuman nhuman who came down from the sun on ice waves and hydrogen fire, swoosh, to forgetful joy.

To the world he is so wrapped up in his coming he forgets there is to be an exit. Then the brain waves change. Oh you didn't know it is coming, takes about seven decades to get the news, lust, peace, hope, death.

So I don't have a name for him, never did and been writing about him all his life. I found out he is a little obtuse in his pretendings and has the ability to dance. There is no need to think him different from any other despite the scientific studies that justify his steps. He's a dancer and when he gets into art he makes onion skins out of paint or some such to cover up the empty. Nothing new, so he has no name, and not much of an identity, all the coverings taken away, although he insists on his dignity.

--He is standing on a 2200 sq ft flat roof surveying the broken skin of roofing. The bare spots where water pools, the cracks in the scuppers remind one of the Gulf coast, but this is his beach where he comes ashore to either do his own work or not, as we all do. Wash the roof, patch, coat again and again with elastometric, five occasions start to finish. He can now go up and down the ladder after knee operations, workouts and stretches. In the 90 degree heat at 5:30 AM sees over the roofs, the roots of the city. For him the roofs are roots with organic superstructures that extend invisibly above him where he stands. The good news is that with a flat roof there is nowhere to fall. But why don't they build a better pitch? Even 6 inches would be double. No. He has cared for this roof 20 years. From Flat Roofs.

Choosing a Format
You may choose from either unbound, shrink-wrapped print copies or PDF files.
Unbound print copies are delivered within three to five business days. Graduate works published prior to 1997 may take a few extra days to deliver. Delivery time to locations outside of the United States may vary depending on customs.
PDF copies are available within one business day
-- it is a sure sign of something when you reread your diss and think it good! the bees are so covered with sunflower pollen their wings are yellow

7/25/18 phone out, visit from aey, picked up Shorty, gone home she drank immensely, peed in the yard!

7/24/18 China wants to use developing countries as a laboratory to improve its own surveillance technologies - CloudWalk Technology, a Guangzhou-based start-up that has signed a deal with the Zimbabwean government to provide a mass facial recognition-- CloudWalk will be better able to train racial biases out of its facial recognition systems—a problem that has beleaguered facial recognition companies around the world and which could give China a vital edge.

--seeing that ball of Shorty's stone woked me. Terra sigillata Woke with Native Texans in mind, but needs a name:

7/23/18 after nursing Short all weekend I made 6 calls but on Pat's advice called Dog, Cat Bird on 7th ave so she was admitted there with large stone, and etc. Heard by 4pm surgery tomorrow.

7/22/18 How can a thing be real and false at the same time/

7/21/l8 three tube piece at kiln collapsed, fused against another, provably preventing the call of all the shelves. Because porcelain weak, Shorty dehydrated uti. The Signal 2104: "perfect integration of human will and alien technology.

7/20/18 had a block of black mt a little dry so cut into slices rolled out, joined into 4 figures and put on a ground of Jamaica, but without paper this time, left the cylinder in all night, in morn pushed the top together, put in the 4 cylinders little ones, and it was beautiful. Some minutes later heard a noise, it spooked the dog, it all fell down!

7/19/18 John Levy

Skeins of onion, schemes. Not too worried about the loss of androgyny of the nomos since I have a woman right here to be the female and I am the male.

- Excellent::Leigh Penman - Intellectual Geography and the Making of the First German Philosopher: Jakob Böhme (1575-1624) and Görlitz. boehme studied occult parachelsus, rosecrucian, Schwenkfelder for 10 yra before his vision

 Nummo Day of the fish, Shannon Dorey

Clif High's origins nemo amphibians, 98% female, change gender, ugly, water beings, can't walk good, like seals, flipper people, shoes of lying platforms, but I got hot caught thigns on fire, owe us because they created hmans, queen of England, accident was they took dna and brought back 8 porto humans, either male or female as in masonry, hempharos,, 2 of the8 fell in love and breeded out of season and the offspring was disturbed, stole a space ship, flew the space medium, powered by ball of liquid copper, like a sun dragging planets, but this guy crashed on earth and polluted it with copper contaminant, new memory of crystal cube and left to considered the damage, but being transmigrant souls they returned to repair the harm, all this is proved by Sirius sun clusters left in nemo lore, they sprayed earth with foam, the flood myth, to fix the pollution, they left the 8 breeds, and made salmon to feed the land creatures, like the raven who were their spokesperson, /cliff thinks he is a nemo, because he has a soul and reincarnates. More nemo, said they would come back when we found out about his enlighten. Annunaki has long life but no soul, nemo have soul, eternal, transposing as it is. Vertebrates nrvous system two systems, spinal cord, wraps the organs, to gut as a transmitter…gut issues effect brain…nemo engineered to water, war of annunaki and nemo a jealousy, destroyed 5th planet, annunaki cast down to earth then, meso amer, aftrican etc different engineered, queens magic stone story says they are offspring of the mentally infirmed nemo, ist psycho. Nemo progenitors…modern homo sapien skeletons out of place in gravel deposits with minitature horses, big dogs. Annunaki divine right to rule, hierarchical,Nemo representative democracy. Jewish people chose Annunaki Adonai to follow, not that they were chosen .32 min.. Salish resisted but middle east had particle war scaring the land, nemo: star people, annunaki: sky people,

7/18/18 together on bike trip in Mex pat has her bike stolen forcibly out of her hands just at dusk, police give us options of airport or car, drive us to one or other, me speaking spanish all along the way, give him 100, much driving along dark ways. Also a bike repair of set with a boy in less threatening circumstance, an open soccer field.

7/17/18 approached by two men at door quasi govst and a commission to write a series on some figure of a war abot 1904 of whom I knew nothing. Toned like man in high castle I was looking at, bleak and dull. This was to be in an empty file later when I looked settle on this and tweeted: Max Spiers: "essentially what they want to do is break the human heart." Words of Peace not in the lexicon, people not putting their hopes on them, that earth all surface, sky and core find peace. No result for the search to come into the body, http://gdancesbetty.blogspot.com/2017/08/the-bright-extensive-will-ae-reiff.html ...
It has escaped from a circus where the language atoms exist just where I cannot see, but see anyway, not with eyes, but with which I transcribe as it enters the same language of facts and chairs, but not language we know, The language atom picture theory of meaning that has no picture nor meaning exists just there where I cannot see it, but I see it anyway. With some faculty of perception transcribed in the same universe where I see chairs, it is not language as we know it. The chairs are thousand pound tested and can hold the millennial weights. Properly transcribed the words will implode, explode, skerry about in letters and syntax and logic—which will be objected to by the world which wants the World to be everything in the case, but it will miss both the thing seen and its representation in words. there were also being three kinds of pot, Momma pot, Poppa pot and baby pot in this cannabinol where the atmosphere hangs like a bong.

7/14/18 moringa clif high to cover up the crypto fiasco takes up the with a sour face, a lot like maiden covers up malfeseace with tirades about the devil. Zecharia Sitchin as well as David Icke" Erich Von Daniken and the whole crowd who turned ancient astronaut theory into the neo-ancient aliens, Anunnaki (watcher) were gods. demigods. True free thinker -Constance E. Gane's 2012 AD dissertation "Composite Beings in Neo-Babylonian Art": apkallu and the genius in human form, as well as creatures based on bulls, lions, canines, winged quadrupeds, fish, birds, scorpions, and snakes. Where do all these instant ancient scholars come from so easily in America, what can they know all hot house language and thought and they breed each other…for all the vaunted cosmic significance all the images are creatres of earth, fish, lion, bird, not cosmic at all except for the overlay. "Watanabe observes that the names of animals mentioned in ancient texts generally carry meaning beyond references to the natural creatures themselves…Each composite creature is derived from two or more species, with each animal part embodying a concept associated with the given animal's natural behavior." Samizdatgane
Mischwesen -composite late neo baBylonigan creatures, easily taken as result of Enoch genetic tamperers, curse of the earth, cf. Pember's animals.
All secret labs under Beltway and elsewwhere must seek apkallu, eph DNA, which they hope to reconstitute with the wooly mammoth, but they really want samples of angel sperm, annunalki so called, but then dna and sperm wats the diff, except who makes angel sperm but

angels themselves, and since they must be able to adapt their bodies in physical form to accomodate their sex wih a woman, so she can give birth, that is, angels make themselves to found their own hybrid race, which of course is the world order, infilitrated by the Reversal. But compare T.H. White's bestiary with these mischwesens and Enoch's condemnation, and Maimonimerkabahdies, and Pember. Also note that as glorious as Babylon was it was disproven by Daniel! Mesopotamian Cosmic Geography, by Wayne Horowitz (1998; rev. 2011), has informed the present study, especially with regard to the "Babylonian Map of the World"

7/13/2018 lunch with A all about the offer. He said all she wants is to be treated...I said that's what everybody wants, like me, so to get it we have to give it. Every tolerance she demands and he gives he and she must give to everyone else in their lives, treat them as they themselves want to be treated.

7/12/18 thurs. build wall with Aey.

10 Reasons Why I Smoke 1.   It's such a clean refined habit.
2. It makes my breath so pleasing to everyone.
3. It sets such a good example for children to follow.
4. It proves I have self control.
5. It makes my fingers and teeth so pretty and yellow.
6. It make me look so feminine, I love the lines around my lips!
7. I love to spit.
8. It starts fires, kills lives and destroys millions of dollars worth of forests and property.
9. I want to see how much poison my body can take before I die.
10. It's my way of obeying God. Who says, "keep yourself pure".

10 Reasons Why I Drink

Written by: Unknown   Posted on: 03/18/2003

Category: Christian Living

Source: CCN
Believers web

       10 Reasons Why I Drink

1. I love to Vomit.
2. It makes my children respect me.
3. My wife loves my whiskey breath and beer-bleary eyes.
4. Drunkards and saloon-keepers make the best citizens.
5. It helps me win the safe-driving award.
6. I want to encourage juvenile delinquency.
7. It helps me think more clearly.
8. It's my way of saving money.
9. I hope to live in a 'flophouse' on Skid Row.

10. It's my way of obeying God, Who says, "Wine is a mocker, strong drink is raging and whosoever is deceived thereby is not wise." - Proverbs 20:1

"I know when to stop!"

Sure. You're smart. You can take it. You know when you've had enough. That's what every drunken bum said at one time. But the time to stop was before he took the first drink. Now he's lost his money, his home, his family, his respect, his health. And his mind's going. Visit him at 5th and Wisconsin, or on the Skid Row of your city. See him begging for money. Look at his eyes, his shaking fingers. Talk to him. He was a doctor, a lawyer, a real estate broker, a college graduate, and athlete. Now he's an alcoholic. He didn't want to be a wallflower. He wanted to sow his wild oats. He got too big for Sunday School. He listened to an atheistic, evolutionist, college professor educated beyond his intellegence. "The Bible? Full of fairy tales. Read Tom Paine instead. Or Robert Ingersoll. Or Eleanor Roosevelt. Or Harry Emerson Fosdick. Or sex books. You're only an animal. Live like one."

Now look in the Mirror!

You are that person - 5, 10, 20 years from now - or sooner. Unless you wake up. God declares, "Whatsoever a man soweth, that shall he also reap." Galations 6:7. You are on the toboggan. So is America. Americans drank 83 millions barrels of beer in 1 year. American spent in 1 year $8,760,000,000 for intoxicating liquors against $5,010,236,000 for public school education. Unless we stop, God will curse America!

How to quit!

Be converted to Jesus Christ, the Son of God. Accept Him as your Saviour. Ask Him to forgive you for your sins and make you a real Christian. Read your Bible daily and urge others to give their hearts to Christ. Write and tell us of your decision. We will send you a free booklet.

The Conversion Center, Drawer V, Havertown, Penn., 19083

COPYRIGHT 1987 by the Conversion Center Anyone is free to use this material in its complete and original form. ANY alterations, deletions or additions to this document violate this agreement!

10 Reasons Why I Swear

Published September 3, 2011 coming in the clouds

10 Reasons Why I Swear

1. It pleases my mother so much.
2. It is a fine mark of manliness.
3. It proves I have self control.
4. It indicates how clearly my mind operates.

5. It makes my conversation so pleasing to everybody.
6. It leaves no doubt in anyone's mind as to my good breeding.
7. It impresses people that I have more than ordinary education.
8. It is an unmistakable sign of culture and refinement.
9. It makes me a very desirable personality among women and children and in respectable society.
10. It is my way of honoring God who said: "Thou shalt not take the name of the Lord thy God in vain."

"SWEARING IS JUST A HABIT WITH ME!"
Sure. Like beating your wife, robbing banks or poisoning babies, Your favorite excuse is –
"I DON'T MEAN ANYTHING BY IT!"
Tell that to the judge the next time you're arrested for speeding! Explain to him, "It's just a habit with me," Try coming in to work drunk for a month. Remind your boss that "I don't mean anything by it. It's just a habit with me." YOU CAN'T FOOL GOD! If you can't kid the judge; if you can't fool your boss; how do you think you can fool God?-It is written, "Swear not at all". (Matt. 5:34). God says, "Be not deceived, God is not mocked." (Gal. 6:7) "The Lord will not hold him guiltless that taketh His name in vain", (Ex, 20:7)

HOW TO QUIT
Pray, right now. Ask God to forgive you for your wickedness and open your heart to the Son of God, Jesus Christ. Ask Him to cleanse you, to save your soul, and make you a real Christian. Read your Bible daily and urge others to repent of their sins and give their hearts to Christ.

from The Conversion Center

). "The 108 Plant Teachers seem to be tied to the grapevine//phone line of 8 cycles per second, which can pass through not only Ormus, but though a faraday cage as well, and it seems to do this by Orthorotating"… Soma Raja considered to be the wild rue plant… these plant chemicals activate the endogenous retro transposons generally located in the thymus tissues (immune tissues), is also demonstrated, the LSD_25 Research. YouTube videos of Ananda Bosman for the 2009 Ethnogens

7/11/18 Andrew offers on house accepted. Looking at the drainage up the alley more slip, left toe, flex thigh, down some mud.
7/9/18 Aey finishing 4 days in Yuma. Took another fall in the drive after/during the flood in the rain, slipped on the silt, fell on right hip, you don't feel the feel of the fall, the heel slps and you end up in the waer wet, or against a rock with the chain saw idling, or on the street when the tire slips. But there is a disconnect in the fall from the moment during it which comes back awake at the end.

--Rubino published some of the lost letters of Freud, and an anthropology study of sasquatch.
-- I'm calling it the connecters of the present when things that happen at the same time interpret each other, o/w synchronicity. It is apparently an unfettered means of knowing the unvarnished because it happens in actions not words leaving causation possible inferred. Like 7/12/17 when a series of events connected the death, move of the bees to the pyrethem

spraying on the street, announced to be "by accident" when Alfred, who I met first time that day, told me of his spraying just after the Ecoshield salesman came to the door to sell after doing across the street. He told me he'd od Alfred, Alfred say he's called them, In that week all the bees were gone. Mike has Blue Sky but no such effects with him.Further just after thinking this below thought, but unremembered, I wake, can't remember exactly what it was, but then searching for Reversing hermon notes, find it at exactly one year ago! Connected thought occurring just below the level of awareness, heard but not heard when we slip up a notch, therefore lost, meaning unremembered, unless we learn to listen better, don't require us to be honest, but to be honest that we are dishonest, which means we stop pretending. --Messiah born Rosh Hashana 3 BC, Sept 11 is not such.

7/8/18 but if we want popular lit we have to have extremes and sensations, cartoons and colors not understatement and reflection gog and magog in turkey turkey iron, libya sudan
Kottke.org tim carmody, Redivider Monkeybicycle. Spork Shya Scanlon
-Guild of St Cooper, rewrite the hist of a dying city,
-Forecast. Seattle is being rebuilt with electricity generated from negative human emotion.
-Border Run: illegal immigration theme park in Arizona
 two paragraphs on the rhino on the piano. Soon the hippo
Out of seq again, phone rings, out of seq, to question Ludwing's reasonable man. So when you go to the doc don't say this hand. Duperflous and apsurd we don't have to insectigate the language game, but if it is not the hand that I doubt but the word of the opposite case where it is not the word that I doubt but the hand. So I leave you with that. Good morning. 7/6/18
Inside the Castle Press

7/5/18 Derek White (Jessica Fanzo) the uncon. "facilitate the ego-purging process by putting my life online" 5cense aug 17i. Written in scientific confused jargon to negate the apocalypse flood. A pagan sumarian tree surmounted the drawings, image of the primal tree of apkallu, largely a spoking for theem. The colors I like at first and the collage, but when interpreted they are polluted, the words, question narrative and syntaxs, both complaints I could make angainst myself. ark codex, "it's strange to me that people "study" writing or art. I think the most important thing in literary writing is having something to write about, otherwise it doesn't mean shit how good a writer you are. Not that I know what I'm doing. Art is also a privilege,… The Fibonacci sequence was first used to explain generational population growth in rabbits" bookslut march 2 The 1 amendment to our new manifest is that going forward Calamari Archive will no longer publish copyrighted works. © is a cancerous snake that bites intellectual property in the foot. As it stands, we can no longer live w/ ourselves being part of such a corrosive + antiquated system that restricts the ability of a work of art to freely copy itself + propagate. At most we will insert the ↄopyleft symbol in books: (ↄ), all rites reversed.
As we've said before: 008
Peter markus, singing fish, eugene thacker, tom McCarthy who boasts on the hearing

**7/4/18 Zachary Scott Hamilton, Norman Lock, George belden --Wold HippoPossum names for children, Democracy. Sarcastic.
Andrew's just kiddin around**

7/3/18 Neom
--We have first hand evidence besides legends of incubus and succubi in the Romantics, tales of Zeus and Apollo taking women and making demigod half breeds, and at that these are all worthwhile experiences for the women, enveloped in showers of golden light, promises of ecstasy and transcendence. So these aren't presented as monsters but what we would all aspire too, to be have intercourse with the gods. The products aren't bloodthirsty terrors but heroes, men of renown. So when we read in the genesis text that these are men of renown that gets our respect and so it goes until we develop something more than childhood awe, for that is the programming of the human race, so easily suggested and controlled. Don't you want to be a god yourself? Asks the guru. Sure just take some of this potion, pscheldic and then from Ginsburg smoke dope smoke dope smoke dope the train leaves the station and little neighborhood parties of dmt spring up for personal enlightenment. The Greek experience for the masses. Canada legalizes it. Not only that but the highest repositories of wisdom in academica and in philosophy and history teach the paths of this wisdom of transcendence, as do the religions. Just look in Krishna's eye to see the universe.

7/2/18 I don't conceive it, I translate it. it's there and I write it down as best I can the image (finished piece) of the vision (Piano Rhinocereus) is like the translation of the text, it's arbitrary, edited. The Rhino is a little big for the piano but time and space are not particularly important in vision landscapes. What if somebody writes or makes something that's not a vision? what do we call that. Imitation. A baby is not a vision, a baby is real.
A vision is indeterminate in its expression,
The playful-weary tone and almost-spoken element the ed Hi, "AE" whomever you might be: Thank you for sending us RECON. We enjoyed the piece's playful-weary tone and almost-spoken element; we feel that it would be a great fit for Metazen. If it's still available, we'd like to publish it.said this infering it diving it from the words of
I too what to find out the spirit of the writer-- spirit of the original author and to reproduce it. Particularly with a first-person narrative, it becomes very important to find the right voice," In sen it said refrain from making dead translation by missing out on all the texture and drama of the text.
"After reading the Bhagavad Gita for the first time, I was shocked. Contrary to my expectations, I found it delightful. In Sanskrit, the tone is different. The Gita has drama, innuendo, humour and there is a dialogue happening between two persons. And in order to bring this playfulness of the Bhagavad Gita out, translators should consider the text as an entire cognitive unit and then use the varied techniques of translation," Rao said. She further said the idea of a Classic is something that is imposed by posterity. People consider Kalidasa as Classic but he was modern in his own time. Translators miss the texture of a classical text by considering it ancient

first part of plainfolking, leaftf walk added to the violin that fell from van gogh's head .Wittgenstein sources

A Martian scientist or Martian researcher is a hypothetical Martian frequently used in thought experiments as an outside observer of conditions on Earth. The most common variety is the Martian anthropologist, but Martians researching subjects such as philosophy, linguistics and biology have also been invoked.

7/1/18 tax cows
--We know that the gold which the devil gives his paramours turns into excrement after his departure, and the devil is certainly nothing else than the personification of the repressed unconscious instinctual life. We also know about the superstition which connects the finding of treasure with defecation, and everyone is familiar with the figure of the "shitter of ducats" (Dukatenscheisser). Indeed, even according to ancient Babylonian doctrine, gold is "the feces of Hell." Lapham's These are the necrophilim. If there is a similiarity between this and nephilim

The only purpose of the continued confession and absolution manufactured by the Ken Burns Vietnamn is the repetition of these acts over and over and over again, from Iraq, Agfanistan, the Towers, the cellphone s, on and on. These anesthetics to deaden, numben the pain into ignorance and rote happiness, all of which, unimaginable as it is, intends to set up an quantum shift greater to come. The psychology is complex, tim O'Brien, Philip Caputo confessiong to atrocities with som many other confessors appointed by their keepers, McCain, Kerry with their rich wives rewarded, the others with mere famej, no Kent Andersons' though, who turn their guns on these spologists. The ultimate cognitive dissoncnee though has to be Kerry throwing his medal and years later jets to Antarctica the night of the election of Trump. Put that in your pipe and smoke it must be the sanity of this absurdism, but it is all to set up the inconceivable, most inconceivable of all. What is it? I keep saying let us go and take our visit as Alex Jones denying and affirming simultaneously.

What Charles Finny says of his departure from Masonry describes the turnspeak:
1. To conceal each other's crimes.
2. To deliver each other from difficulty, whether right or wrong.
3. To unduly favor Masonry in political action and in business matters.
4. Its members are sworn to retaliate and persecute unto death the violators of Masonic obligations.
5. Freemasonry knows no mercy, and swears its candidates to avenge violations of Masonic obligations unto death.
6. Its oaths are profane, taking the Name of God in vain.
7. The penalties of these oaths are barbarous, even savage.
8. Its teachings are false and profane.
9. Its designs are partial and selfish.
10. Its ceremonies are a mixture of puerility and profanity.
11. Its religion is false.

12. It professes to save men on other conditions than those revealed in the Gospel of Christ.
13. It is wholly an enormous falsehood.
14. It is a swindle, obtaining money from its members under false pretenses.
15. It refuses all examinations, and veils itself under a mantle of oath-bound secrecy. 16. It is virtual conspiracy against both Church and State

6/30/18 a man is all along solitary against the enveloping universe and the woman.
--a deflationary style dysfunctional soil disturbance and artifacts: G dh JkearL
results in pre historic structures of wall. --David & Sally Hamilton Indigia
Imports …el interior

6/29/18 surprise visit with Aey, speak of effects of professional training, how it creates its own excellence with work. Of my notion of the line in prose is anglo saxon, two elements with caesura. Sound, rhythm, meaning like string quartets theme, couner theme, etc. against the inflammatory style of Poe, Faulkner etc. to deflate the line
-- Huey Tzompantli Aztec skull rack, but why did they seave the skulls if the reason was they wre anemic? It suggests much more.
--Holly Tavel The basic motivation in all my writing is to not bore myself… The only thing I'd do differently is—I'd hire a publicist! I really have no self-promotion or marketing savvy, so I regret that the book did not get the attention I feel like it otherwise could have.
--watching Ken Burns Vietnam.
My part in the Vietnam. Valley Forge. Costa Rica. Fort Bragg.

6/28/19 doug derbyshire medical missionary to Thailand
The territorial spirit of Austin is very strong and I feel toward it as Thornburg
--Thinking about Willis Pratt who I had on my committee to get his Blake slides, but in the orals I reminded him what we had said about Adonis once and rapped for 20 min, successfuolly. The event befan with
Godron as ing about metaphysical poetry, I said Romjend Tuve…he… what do you think. Perfecto. It all ended with consideration of robt Lowell, like Eliot another emasculated soul, stralling abover her like an elephant, to which they asked what's wrong with thing: I , its metaphysical. And Dr. C =called the hours, full circle he said. It is fun to engage intelligent witty poets and their minds. --Wittgenstein On Certainty

6/27/18 Blake: "I am more famed in Heaven for my works than I could well conceive. In my Brain are studies & Chambers filled with books & pictures of old, which I wrote & painted in ages of Eternity before my mortal life; & those works are the delight & Study of Archangels."
Turquoise forms near copper deposits when water laden with copper and aluminum filter through rock, which is why turquoise veins usually form at the edges of large copper deposits

6/26/17 1970s weird mexican animal ink sketches, tom cranfill Texas Quarterly publishedImage of Mexico: the General Motors de Mexico Collection of Mexican Graphic Artin two volumes Ehrlich selected for the collection was Thomas Mabry Cranfill (1913-1995), ... The coexistence of humankind with the animal kingdom in Of beasts, flora and land- ..... to appreciate the development of the arts in Mexico through the 1970s.
TQ THE GM DE MEXICO COLLECTION
OF DRAWINGS AND GRAPHIC ART
Lolcows

6/25/18 yahoo and Alex Jones declared civil war on the same day, Jones with winged disc beside.

xii--Minotaur. Hapax legomenon, rare rhymes, harsh hounds, counterfeited cow, Pasiphae hides in the cow. Tax cows Labyrinth inescapable corridors, string the meandering passageways. One thing sure these creatures must die, a man with bulls head, a bull with a mans head 169 a semivirumque bovem, myth and demons, biform monsters, topple Masses over which one descends to lower hell, image of a beast berserk, appropriate the classical soruces to their own, and so "we made our way across that heap/of stones, which often moved beneath my feet/because my weight was somewhat strange for them (on this moon). Dante moves what he touches because he is the only living person in hell. Virgil says "that other time/that I descended into lower Hell, /this mass of boulders had not yet collapsed 34-6. That was just before Christ's descent. His walk changes the rabble world, his thought. So the myths change because their supports crumble from the moment of Christ's death. 170-1 "empedocles: " all the elements of the unveerse fire, sir, waer, earth, formerly eld apart by discord were fused by love, recreating the original Chaos. At that time "these ancient boulders toppled, in this way xii, 45. "all the bridges passing to the further ditches or pouches revealed to have been destroyed by this same earthquake. Achilleid of Statius.

Xxxiv:"Hell formed following the fall of Lucifer, when the infernal chasm opened right below the point whee Christ was crucifed on Golgotha." "Lucifer composite of many disconnected parts, his immobility and his grotesque…giant with 6 great wings… negative transcendaence…turning upside down at the center of the univ the topsy world of nT from which Satean seems right side up in hell, but head down from heaven from which he fell. Perspective incongruity lucifer is flight o stairs, but silence. "If God is the World, Lucifer is nonspeech, the non word. In classics hades and Dis without a monstrous aspect were giants.Visions of Tnugdali: giant lucifer and beast by name of Acherons. V: The covetous must enter the gaping maw of Acheron to be tormented with fire and ice. There is ..... Visio Tnugdali: The Vision of Tundale.

6/24/18 trees with 8 mil diameter in Madasgar
--Went to home dept for a flusher nut, not there. Said that's what I need, in a package. He takes it out and gives it to me: happybirthday!
-Put silver bead spacers on mescal bean necklace.
-there is nothng like a man in nature, or everything like a man is in nature.

-- "the Vestibule of Hell, which is populated by souls who lived a lukewarm life with "no blame and no praise," and by the angels who at Lucifer's great rebellion remained undecided… All of the giants, save the titan
Anteaeus, are chained to the wall of the Pit of Giants or the Central Well of the Malebolge. Pit of Giants xxxi. Cocytus, the frozen lake in the "pit of sin."

6/23/18 City of Dis
It became axiomatic that "for Dante hell is a giant projection of the human body" (durling 398) if by that we understand that the body is cut off at the genitals. It has no legs and feet, as if they all were had the 'groin cut off / from that part of his body where it forks (xxx 49f) as is said of Master Adam, "spiritually immobilized by his sines-Master Adam essentially has no legs" Druling 394, but neither does the human torso that spans hell

6/22/18 El Rhino: during a visit yesterday with el sympatico saw a rhinoocerus run across the piano. The upshot was meaning the Ind Health (of the their chief recruit tools as loan forgiveness, up to half a mil) that night and the informant who said NP's have a much lower rate of incidents because they always refer to specialists, their protocol. Inference: that's why the state liscensed them solo, to feather the specialists who have the lobby power. Hence costs rise. Captive population of np and nuse and docs, following protocols, billing 3 mil o get 17o thou, no continuity of care
--I came into the studion last night and a guy at the table asked if I needed both sides. So I said my name is Andy, which was his, which amazed him. I had asked Char about the Ind Med Center for Aey, which Andy's wife Susan over heard asd asked. So I said about Aey, but she is publicist of Indian health on Central, etc. So I got her card to show him.

6/21/18 -- Three kind of apkallu, fish, bird and man, bird and man before the flood fish after. Puru paradu. Two kinds of annunaki, high and low. How different from apkallu/ importance is that these picture Nephilim/ and fallen, buried in Euphrates

6/20/18 Amar Annus On the Origin of Watchers: A Comparative Study of the Antediluvian Wisdom in
Mesopotamian and Jewish Traditions Divine has levels. superhuman / semi-divine beings. "In Mesopotamian king and sage lists, the apkallu occur in the pre-flood era, and in some texts for a limited time after the flood. In general, however, the pre-flood sages are called apkallu and their traditional number is seven, while the post-flood sages are called the ummiānu… The apkallu are semi-divine beings who may be depicted as mixed beings, as priests wearing fish hoods, or who may, like Adapa, be called a son of Ea. Moreover, humans and apkallu could presumably mate since we have the description of the four post-flood apkallu as "of human descent," the fourth being only "two-thirds apkallu" as opposed to pre-flood pure apkallu and subsequent human sages (ummiānu)…It t can be assumed from Gen 6. 1-4 that the nēpīlîm were the offspring of those divine fathers and human mothers, and that it was the nēpīlîm who somehow exemplified wicked mankind in general.

Primeval History: Babylonian, Biblical, and Enochic: An Intertextual Reading By Helge Kvanvig

"apkallus are primor-dial figures, who are variously envisioned as resembling birds, fish or humans, that are associated with the establishment of the cosmic order and the transmission of antediluvian knowledge to Mesopotamian sages (130, 146). ere has been much scholarly interest in the apkallus as mythic background that informs the
Book of the Watchers is book contributes to this topic. For example, Kvanvig, drawing upon the Catalogue of Texts and Authors and the Verse Account of Nabonidus, argues that the apkallu named Uanadapa compiled the compendium of Babylo-nian astronomical knowledge Enuma Anu Enlil is text has strong parallels to the
Enochic Astronomical Book and the author concludes that Enoch should be viewed as a "Jewish counterpart to Uanadapa" (148, 503)" review by Goff

6/19/18 The Nephilim and apkallu identity in Anne Kilmer, the Mesopotanian counterparts of the Biblical Nepilim

--the bird-faced winged genies of Assyrian Palace art may be identified as apkallu -----(see Anthony Green, "Neo-Assyrian Apotropaic Figures," Iraq 45 (1983),
--typhon looks like
-- the uruk list of kings Uruk List of Kings and Sages is best known for its genealogy connecting
Mesopotamian scholars (ummânù) traced their professional ances-try explicitly back to the mythological sages (apkall ù) of antedilu-vian fame --human scholars to antediluvian sages anne kilmer, apkallu. samizdat
Fallen Angels and the History of Judaism and Christianity : The Reception of Enochic Literature by Annette Yoshiko Reed

6/19/18 --Liu Dan (sunflower) does not tend towards a single subject matter, he is known to paint what he calls "uncertain" subjects, since he believes that "the clearer the feeling, the blurrier the image." His best known works depict landscapes, flowers, and what is known as Guai Shi (odd stones) in traditional Chinese art and literati culture. From this, Liu has developed a theory of landscape painting he calls a "micro exploration through macro understanding."
--two images: at a tennis match from the chair a projector casting an image of the cresent moon into the sky so large it filled the whole view, a cresent man in moon figure, as if the moon were a projection! And 2. Mike adams at doubles against conrad ramos on the star court.
Up the Beanstalk suggests the giants are buffoons, part of the control for they are more the board of directors We can document thse techniqus being applied at the personal and the societal level, therefore might speculate beyong that that there are a kind of though blinders at the global, whicdh sounds like Icke and the moon, but that could only be documented as a metaphor of Dante, say.

6/18/18 I'm a natural doctor but I have no patience for it.
All ovals in the human, brain, eyes, sinuses, stomach. The human body a model, a paraeidol of the inferno,

6/17/18 Father's Day, Sunday, went one for three. Aey for tea with a rfid wallet!
Cain in the moon
--Disposition matrix computer algorhytm
The ten circles of the maleboge in the inferno resemble the large intestine, but take the maleboge and transport it into space where it surrounds the earth. All human thought is issued from its anus, which is not physical but the construction of the gregori to corrupt and imprison the earth the way the people are in the inferno with their frauds. The maleboge is a thought form system. It is an allegory of human education in Greece, Rome, England, America. Europe, not to leave out Aztec, and all native worships. liquid evil of cold, end of inferno.
S fears the ghosts of poe but not the owl and dragon

6/16/18 took lunch, Sat, to see Nikolai, gave A Agassi shirt.
Took anoher bike fall, attacked by little dog, turned to face it, slipped on wet asphalt. Canister of pepper spray pocket jammed against ribs, big red spot! Result in wrist, ribs, shoulder.
-Perhaps the greatest advantage I have been given is isolation to do the work, which is mostly done, but not to be noticed.

6/15/18 Pat dizzy, did reply.
-- If a piece is not precarious why should it exist? She is precarious and he is too, but what other reason do they have to be? We have long since fallen away from the norm and even the paranorm. They have become the same. The precarious balances the edge. First it was solid, stable, but taken to where it began to fall, just intervening in its collapse, it was shifted and pulled, for remember it is a hollow cylinder when all is said and done, and while the photograph may not show it, because it is not a photograph, the cylinder, some 27" tall in origin, can collapse from the various strength of its sides, the imprecise pressure of its stretching, and most from the need for it to totter there and be pulled back. Reduced from its origin by even a third, which will be further reduced by the fire another tenth at least, it is a rescue.

6/14/18 Attacked by bulldog.
 6/`13/18 root canal, internists gossiping during.

6/12/18 The best writing comes out of desperation, except Stevens maybe, but there is some repose in Borges and Kafka and innocence in Kerouac vs. Poe's true adventures, misadventures of an anarchist in Beasts, Imp, Man, Bottle. Crane writes with demonic energy of rejection which supercharges his lines with a mass fire of rejection, hence desire for acceptance, picking up seamen. Poe's vindictive glee and ironic jstice. Promethean fire they spark within themselves, but not aganst the gods, rather in favor to them, from them, celebrated all their forbidden fruits, Lingering behind these are shadows of pedophilia, corrupted lusts. All this is the highest complement to empire, domination, the American Babylon. the myth of America. It does not follow that he sought solare with sailors because he couldn't get a job, or lived at home. More Faustian stuff, disconnected intellect from life, the very thing Weimar, empire, feeds on. Crane was a intellectual neurotic as much as Harold Bloom. Truly neurotic verbal fire, the very thing his mentors and peers seek themselves. "12 September, 1927, Hart Crane wrote to his patron, the banker Otto Kahn, asking for financial help. Kahn had already given him $2,000 to work on his projected epic poem The Bridge, which Crane couldn't seem to bring to completion. He was drinking heavily, picking up sailors on the New York docks and getting into terrible brawls that sometimes culminated in a night in jail." Perloff.

6/11/18 Nikolai born at 7.30 am. I made a very specific effort of months to loose joy, peace, health on his life before and after birth, and upon his family. I have held his birth and turning into birth position for some months after praying for S. Aeg told Aey that is the second best name in the world, Aey being first! Even up until the doc confirmed his turning A was planning on C section, according to a text to Aey that thurs before the fri appt. but the birth was vaginal, the baby well. Thou wilt show him the path of life. Ps 16 I sought, and that his election be made sure, his inutero filled with joy and peace. When A called a couple hours after the birth I could hear N cooing effusively in the background. A said he was asleep! He has two weeks off now. Aey visited and said this brings full circle the loss of their child who would have been born a week before this. He and Sh have had much conversation about this. A birth is a miracle. Pat went in a lunch by invite and spent an hour with N.
-- The cold that began last Mon has progressed from throat to sinus to chest to antibiotics to breathing treatment.

6/10/18 Solar Storm Psyche | From Stress to Suicide

6/9/17 in the redevelopment of the Phx Gand canal citizens will participate with the opportunity to dedicate statutes of the Phoenix mayors of their choosing. Skip rimza and Paul Johnson are early favorites. Ev Mechan is fully subscribe on the west portion.

6/8/18 joseph bonanno and billy graham   david hill,
franklin graham did NASA explode a nuke on the moon to
ring the bell
The Apollo 12 mission to the Moon in November 1969 set up seismometers and then intentionally crashed the Lunar Module causing an impact equivalent to one ton of TNT. The shockwaves built up for eight minutes, and NASA scientists said the Moon 'rang like a bell. Ken Johnson, Supervisor of the Data and Photo Control department during the Apollo missions "The Moon not only rang like a bell, but the whole Moon wobbled in such a precise way that it was almost as though it had gigantic hydraulic damper struts inside it." Moon rocks have been found to contain processed metals, including brass and mica, and the elements Uranium 236 and Neptunium 237 that have never been found to occur naturally.

6/7/18 So I was telling Aeg at lunch that names, nikoli Agassi, cover your names with recognition, ground the electric, the creative in the middle! He has completely owned the button I gave him last, natural poet!, lyrical, middle, epic.

-Lot of junior pigeons out today. Cuckoo Finches: Cuckoos cluck to finches: they lay their eggs in the nests of other birds and abandon the care of their young to the hosts. Like wheat and tares. The first act of most brood parasite species' chicks after hatching is to do away with the host's own brood. Different species do this by ejecting their nest mates from the nest, by using their sharp beaks to fatally injure them, or by physically dominating them. One of the most common strategies for brood parasites to manipulate their hosts into raising their offspring is known as "aggressive mimicry". This is a way for the birds to dupe a host by looking harmless, for example by resembling a species that is not parasitic. The strategy is already well-documented in a variety of brood parasite species: some lay eggs that resemble those of their hosts, while the chicks and fledglings of others look (and sound) like the host's own chicks and fledglings. This is necessary, as hosts will reject parasitic eggs, chicks and fledglings, if they can detect them. -"Lord make me a woman.
With your wisdom fill me up …give me a period" song at EN-like service Best conversation overheard was in men's room where I was cleaning my classes with soap at dirty sink by some workers…

6/4/18 Saturn isn't what you think it is either. Who built the moon
--"where a good world is spoiled by human evil, Levinas supposes the world before man to be evil. He postulates the incursion of good into evil…the emergence of faces thar were only heads. " Regina Janes, 190, Losing our heads. She of course is naïve about Genesis where L. is not.

6/3/18 miranda age reversed youtube. Essentrics Aging Backwards #5 - Relieve Your Pain warm up. Essentrics Full-Body Barre Workout- Standing Exercises 15 min

Stan Chuffs. Some kind of black concentrate resin. Go in a h.s. for a leak, chack a break, bell rings for class, bathroom open, go to trough, world's longest high pressure leak, completely unconcerned, an amazing hose, stan in next, later outside he says, what do you chuff? Some kind of chemical, ide? Black wafer? More a lozenge than a vape. What not go ahead and dream of something important, like 9/11?

6/2/18 Clean out line office. Where did the buildings go? Judy Wood
David long 9/11 witness, no planes [john lear no planes hit the towers] airborne holographic projector , multiple explosions, streams of liquid moldent metal straming out of bldg., the fires burned for weeks after, but they began hauling away debris with hours of the event. To cover up Project Hammer
Ion cannon, mechanical oscillator, match the fq of a a mat'l and shake it apart, philosopher oscillator shakes apart ideas, AZ Quotes Rubino del Sur

6/1/18 lunch with A

5/31/18 He said she's as big as a convention center.

--poe, London, crane, harte   the open boat   to build a fire

London the god of his fathers, Neil young stole the nightbirds

chameleons, come into my life the intro: if you believe in fantasy, if you believe in the magical world that we   come with me 3 times,,, then

Come with me If you believe in the mystical world,

--but compare Mahalia Jackson Closer Walk

And Nina Simone, I sing so much better, I dance so much better, …a little bit better, one day I thought I could fly …I looked down and see that I wouldn't know myself, I'd have no hands, I'd have no feet, I'd have new visions my eyes would be open, the Bible says, Be transformed by the renewing of your mind, Be transformed by the renewing of your mind:

-- for these are all multidimensional beings led in the Holy Spirit of God,

--sub-Saharan African music traditions, and find their earliest expression in spirituals, work chants/songs, praise shouts, gospel, blues, and "body rhythms" (hambone, patting juba, and ring shout clapping and stomping patterns clave rhythms   mambo

--A mondegreen /ˈmɒndɪɡriːn/ is a mishearing or misinterpretation of a phrase as a result of near-homophony, in a way that gives it a new meaning. Mondegreens are most often created by a person listening to a poem or a song; the listener, being unable to clearly hear a lyric, substitutes words that sound similar and make some kind of sense.[1][2] American writer Sylvia Wright coined the term in 1954, writing about how as a girl she had misheard the lyric "...and laid him on the green" in a Scottish ballad as "...and Lady Mondegreen".Nightbirds: funk Patti Labelle

-the downbeat—with heavy emphasis on the first beat of every measure to etch his distinctive sound, rather than the backbeat that

Going down makes me shiver…
Going down to your river…
Gitchi gitchi ya ya da da
Gitchi gitchi ya ya here
Mocha chocolata, ya ya
Creole Lady Marmalade
Voulez-vous coucher avec moi ce soir?
Voulez-vous coucher avec moi?
-DuckDuckGo, or Qwant, or searX, or Good Gopher? There is not one news site not complicit. Every form of entertainment is complicit.

5/30/18 The replication crisis "Why Most Published Research Findings Are False".[14] fiction in the guise of science

"studies with incorrect findings are not just rare anomalies, but are actually representative of the majority of published research… Richard Horton, the editor of The Lancet recently put it only slightly more mildly: "Much of the scientific literature, perhaps half, may simply be untrue." Horton agrees with Ioannidis' reasoning, blaming: "small sample sizes, tiny effects, invalid exploratory analyses, and flagrant conflicts of interest, together with an obsession for pursuing fashionable trends of dubious importance." Horton laments: "Science has taken a turn towards darkness." hehr

5/29/18 "to the wohld bludyn world… Pu Nuseht, lord of risings in the yonderworld of Ntamplin, tohp triumphant, speaketh. "593 Arcthuris comeing!...Tirtangel [tinhursay cow goddess of milk]

5/2818 coltane black seed oil
--salk vac introduced at end of bell curve conincidently, does not prove it the cause the end of polio, statins intreudeuct ydfby Keynes an effort at mind control since he threw out half the data to make his point about chlostroel, trump new order to CDC Vulnerable, Entitlement, Diversity, Transgender, Fetus, Evidence-based, Science-based

5/26/18 new glasses pat to get her doc in English--the wall is subliminal
- talk the s out of self and you get elf which shows the bogus self

5/25/18 Kozyrev was corrcct! Entropy/Negentroy can be generated!
-- The term Ōtōkan comes from the "ō" of Daiō, the "tō " of Daitō, and the "kan" of Kanzan). Daitō Kokushi as a Beggar. one sees people crossing and re-crossing the bridge just as they are. This was a single word meaning a frontier-gate or mountain-pass. He told him "Throw your whole spirit into the word 'Pass'. You should have no other occupation ; --List of Troop Loot.

5/24/18 Step 5: Cognitive. Close Calls, passed GMC Yukon up 24th who speeded up , turned in front of him. He Passes within inches. AZ CEF0694. He went to Long Wongs. Had Campensina music sticker on bumper. --back engineered: "Proto-Indo-European "foot" is inferred as *pod-, or*ped- (Fortson, 2010). A reconstructed protolanguage is posited as the evolutionary ancestor of the observed descendant languages, and serves as the baseline from which historical shifts are inferred."   "A protolanguage is regarded as a real language once spoken by a delimited population in a particular time and place, or homeland": but it is a hypothetical construct. Historical linguistics as a sequence optimization problem: the evolution and biogeography of Uto-Aztecan languages Peter Whitley Uto-Aztecan Languages.pdf 2.21 MB The thing is that all these phonemes are based on transcriptions possible inaccurate

5/23/18 A called to thank for boxes, said 9 mo ext on lease was given. Most enthusiasm heard in his voice in a long while. Baby Nikolai flipped and dropped, lease ext: more answers of prayer.

5/22/18 tues: 3rd day grading swale on canal, 10ft wide, 7in deep concrete to be installed as path, talking ot A to arrange delivery of more boxes he said the spasm of last night were the seating to the baby's head into the birth cannel,

5/21/18 all planets on same side of sun july 9 – aug 21. Frequencies, harmonic convergence. Renewal, on all scales! I also realize I've been courting my wife now for a couple years!
--Hebrew has two words, tan, usually translated "jackal," and tanin, usually translated "sea monster" in English and drakon in Greek. The plural suffix -im in Hebrew turns tan ("jackal") into tanim ("jackals"), a word that sounds a lot like tanin. That is, "jackals" and "sea monster" sound very similar.
In the case of Lamentations 4:3, the "written" text is tanin, "sea monster" with a note that the "read" text should be tanim, "jackals." (This is not the only "read"/"written" conflict in Lamentations 4:3. The "like ostriches"
part is the "read" text for the "written" text that has, apparently, as extra
space.) here Kilauea Eruption: Harrowing report from Leilani Estates

5/20/18 N- there is dragon detailed on the wall of the nursery. Robin Bullins has a dragon on his Google plus id. But the next day I read without looking: the beast of the field shall honor Me, the dragons and the owls. Isa 43.20

-- Josiah Lard (1758-1824) descendants - Message Boards
Cecelia Ann Snaveley Lard 657 Po Box Chino Valley Az 86323 Address Search Results
https://www.fastpeoplesearch.com/address/657-po-box_chino-valley-az-86323

1920 census- Cecil E Lard
Birth: abt 1905 - location Residence: 1920 - city, Graham, Arizona, USA

--Ms Cecelia A Lard
Used to live: Concho, AZ, Meadview, AZ, Phoenix, AZ, Chino Valley, AZ
AKA: Cecilia A Lard , Cecelia Lard , Cecilia Lard , Ms Cecelia Lard
Related to: Clifford R Lard , Dixie E Lard
Aliases   Dixie E Land

 Relatives   Cliff R Lard, Dixie E Lard, Ethel C Lard Merryman and Tommy E Lard

Possible Associates: Lauralie R Williams , Janet L Wells , John F Bielanski.
Used to live: Concho, AZ, Meadview, AZ, Phoenix, AZ, Chino Valley, AZ. AKA: Cecilia A Lard , Cecelia Lard , Cecilia Lard , Ms Cecelia Lard. Related to: Clifford ...
--Clifford Ray Lard Lives in: Chino Valley, AZ Used to live: Chino Valley, AZ, AZ, Phoenix, AZ, Meadview, AZ AKA: Cliff D Lard , Clifford Ray Lard , Cecelia A Lard , Clifford Lard , Cliff Lard , Cliff Lord Related to: Dixie E Lard , Cecelia A Lard related to Cecelia A Lard, Dixie Evelyn Lard, and Tommy E Lard.
---Hattie Snively Graveside services for Hattie P. Snively, 84,' who came to Arizona 51 years ago from Ohio and died Dec. 17, 1979, in Phoenix Baptist Hospital, will be 2 p.m. today in Greenwood Memorial Park, 2300 W. Van Buren. Mrs. Snively, 3027 W. San Juan, had been

employed as a housekeeper. Surviving are her .children, Cecelia Lard and . Howard A.; six grandchildren and a greatgrandchild. Grimshaw Bethany Chapel handled arrangements
Jeri Ann LARD (1963 -) & Robin BULLINS (1960 -)
| | | | | | | Christopher BULLINS (1985 -)
| | | | | | | Sabrina Cecilia BULLINS (1988 -)
--Jacob Michael Crockett was born 21 Mar

5/19/18 Theodore won the flop Olympics. He was singing scat to Beethoven while rocking in the chair. On the way home the classical station not on speed dial I asked AB to sing and she did the whole way, Jingle bells, under her breath, TB chiming in.

--abraham b. snavely 5/5/1789 west lampeter twp married Elizabeth Buckwalter 1/18/1809 a bishop of the stricter reformed Mennonite church, d. 1866 p. 587 in the Hershey line Milton S. Hershey's mother was a Reformed Mennonite. bishop in New Danville Reformed Mennonite Church .
"The Reformed Mennonites, though very strict and very conservative, live up to their convictions unusually well. In their daily life they are an upright people, honest, industrious, conscientious, law-abiding citizens. Their religious exclusiveness does not extend to their business enterprise except that there are no partnerships with nonmembers. In this field they are frequently unusually successful. Among those in their line of descent, though himself never a member, was the late Milton Snavely Hershey (1857-1945), the Pennsylvania chocolate candy king, whose mother was a member. His grandfather, Abram Snavely, was a bishop of the church 183067. In the professions open to them, such as medicine and dentistry, they also succeed above the average.
the ruin and destruction not witin our borders is the same words as the katabole, tohu bohu vs barah and asah, created and made.
The words tohu and bohu also occur in parallel in Isaiah 34:11, where King James Version translates with the words "confusion" and "emptiness". Now the earth was formless and empty, darkness was over the surface of the deep, and the spirit of God was hovering over the waters.
The two Hebrew words are properly segolates, spelled tohuw and bohuw.[3] Hebrew tohuw translates to "wasteness, that which is laid waste, desert; emptiness, vanity; nothing".[4] tohuw is frequently used in Isaiah in the sense of "vanity", but bohuw occurs nowhere else in the Hebrew Bible (outside of Genesis 1:2, the passage in Isaiah 34:11 mentioned above,[5] and in Jeremiah 4:23, which is a reference to Genesis 1:2), its use alongside tohu being mere paronomasia, and is given the equivalent translation of "emptiness, voidness".

--Uriah, Mariah, Elijah all the content of the subject content of English is Hebrew from the outset, the anglo saxon period from 600 to 1066, he Norman Conquest. "Cædmon's Hymn" "Genesis A" "Genesis B" "Exodus" toggle Poems about Christ. "The Dream of the Rood" "Christ I" "Christ II" toggle Saints' Lives. "Andreas" "Elene" "Guthlac B" Other Christian Themes. Beowulf. Andrew of the 6th cent. As just the same the greatest writings in Spanish, Italian are Christian in content which is the backdrop of it all.

5/18/18 peter callas: I have expressed life thru art and sought to make a connection of man to nature. A collaborative vocabulary of expressionism that blended both historical references and contemporary intellectual values.
--accident, van de wetering at the monestary in Kyoto, Kazuma Sambe
make an analogy between the layes of plant laid down to make the coal, over and over with the pleating continual pleating of the dna of a family which proudces 1026 sources, layeres in 10 generations, every 300 years.
-- the child in the age of innocence is a great intuitive ocean that dates back wherever you like in this case to the carbonifersic era, the Pennsyalvania period when the steep slopes were sea shore and the swamp and the water buried the vegetation again and again in waves, 300 million years ago, that dried and was covered with and and again and again. The pages of a book they call it, the book of the black rock, and then it lay there horizontal in this zone until furfil changes heaved up the slopes and planted the hills that clapped their hands for joy.

5/17/18 just got a call from Aeg, the baby Nikolai flipped into front position? On thurs he texted Aey that it would be a c section, but….I had put my had on S. belly and prayed for this 6 wks ago, but it hadn't happened so 2 days ago I asked, for the best outcome based on what I didn't know, since Aey had a knot in his cord, That day again asked Him to show his power. Praise the Lord I said to A. Lunch tomorrow, his house is to be sold, out on Jun 30.
all religion is idolatry. Saw a website that doesn't exist from print making days, green and interesting. Seen many times.

5/16/18 emotional distance is evidence of partition as in mkultra,
--Craunch, scythe, marrow bone, broke shin against shell of a snail, spinet, Dionysius Hallearnassensis,, more savage and cruel in proportion to this bulk, trencher, small cider, grildrig splacknuck, eyes like 2 full moon shining in 2 windows, pumpion, scrutore, scrutorian. Effigies, nonfunctional embellishment of an artifact used as a container. Pichrs, mugs, small monty jars. Human effigy bottles, horse effigies. ion sputtering and regolith - JCC gave me a lift to an event for which I was late since he was going too. I had forgot my car keys and would have had to run up the hill to get them.

5/15/18 at one time people judged us very favorably because they saw how our children acted and were. That's how I became a teacher at EN

5/14/18 There was an acceptance at Gambler but I have no record of the submission: Dr. Rubino del Sur is a physiologist who continues to write telling of the invention of soccer. His correspondence on the various identities of urinary speech to those bases in the west has also reached a modern constituency. The mere presence of the jawbone in all these affairs is so important now that the head has been made secondary to the vertebrate. If this seems a pharyngeal twist the science has also been co-contributed.
-- Kurt Weiser, Kazuma Sambe, Puebelo rain Bird, Dali mythologies
--Grigori Yakovlevich Perelman Soul Conjecture: In mathematics, a submersion is a differentiable map between differentiable manifolds whose differential is everywhere

surjective. This is a basic concept in differential topology. The notion of a submersion is dual to the notion of an immersion. "Almost all of them are conformists. They are more or less honest, but they tolerate those who are not honest."[21] He has also said that "It is not people who break ethical standards who are regarded as aliens. It is people like me who are isolated."[21] In 2014, Russian media reported that Perelman was working in the field of nanotechnology in Sweden. pdf

--turquoise tree stumps. John Kredit, wants to kill me (again)? The violence of his getting, lifelong w/o faher, But has these turquoise forms, which later contemplated are stumps. Leading to bloody thirsty nature of reformed people, Jeremeny behond Noah, DeHough, pastors, sudden decisions, church spolits, Lloyd Kredit being atypical.5/1318 to AEy, the world is cover with fallen ageensl that deceive all institutions and systems. How to know truth: feeling, intuition, syunchronicity, Scripture

5/12/18 Onkelos the proselyte

5/11/18 The Confluence Overlook and the East Rim
Adeii Eichii Cliffs near Cameron and Coal Mine Canyon near Tuba City.
--tom --Goodrich hellstorm youtube
- Time going forward from the ever present now, us receiving the future, is malleable as its appearing future is fluid like the present. Taken from any present time accuracy if may change taken from another present time accurately from events that have happened since the first reading. In the case where some diviner predicts the future a collapse of the probability into a reality, and it occurs that may be because they made it occur by ruling out the other versions, ie they made you the subject believe it so it came to pass, like remote viewing targets find what they seek because they pick them out of the experimenter brain and then find what he thought was there. Observer created reality observed itself. An exception in meaning can occur when synchronous events of different kinds confirm themselves in the present, or rather viewed after they have occurred in the present, some day or weeks.
--Waves that crash are escalators up and elevators down. The excess of over trend is the wave long building sudden collapsing.
 confluence of the Colorado plane crash 1956
--east rim little visited overlooks of the Colorado River outside of Grand Canyon National Park. Most of these overlooks are on the Colorado's east rim. These viewpoints lie in the Navajo Nation and a $12 per person per day permit is needed to visit them. Fitzcarraldo transporting steamboat
Les Blank's documentary Burden of Dreams (1982),
grand canyon egypt   site would include multiple restaurants and a cultural center. After visitors took the gondola, which developers call the "Escalade," there would be a 1,400-foot Colorado River walk to a restaurant inside the Grand Canyon, as well as a riverside amphitheater with terraced grass seating.
hawaii 19.5 hyperdimensional latitude one of the tetrahedral points fear is much more powerful than love the tares think they're wheat, the lords think they are sheep, the guilty think they are innocent,

5/10/18 whatever happened to that big sphere of a world in the entry of Eagles Nest on Hayden by Mike Anderson? Or Kim Clement's broken wrists, Franklin Graham, pastor to the Nephs, visits john mccain,.Maiden prays for doug dusey. nephilim are children of fallen angels and women, men of renown, who rule everything. you didn't think evil had a spiritual origin but men of renown rule everything. To call them tares is requisite since tares are sown by the enemy. Counterfeit humans. Wouldn't be much counterfeit if they weren''t beautiful godly and ministering with spiritual gifts and their pyramid structure of authority. All expraticipans fear to speak because they know the appear of these powers is terror and threat. Nothing attracts so, witness all the horror films. All spiritual good is hidden therefore any obvious spiritual good is evil. A wholesale sell out of what were former beliefs and practices motivated by fear, rejection and acceptance, promise of the supernatural, money, favor, prophecies on the part of hundreds of leaders all of who seem to be not only good but greatly good, promising you the Holy Ghost, Salvation, Jesus, God under guise of scaring you to death with fear and death/blessing, curses and rejection if you ever turn on them or turn them in. Just to complex the matter, much of what they say is true and can profit you before it untimely rips. There are literally hundreds of people who have left this oppression who have never said a public word.
https://deskgram.org/_melmaiden
https://deskgram.org/fungirlmm
https://deskgram.org/mcmaiden
https://deskgram.org/timmaiden_

5/9/18 fluid present, now conditioned by then understood
by forever 14th foot
the mist gov't exp

5/8/18Lee Kang-hyo
Chronic wasting disese in deer transmissible spongiform encephalopathy (TSE)
Voth, Traditions of the Hopi and the Hopi. Las Casas. Ken. 5/7/18 Van Gogh Wheatfields
The Wheat Fields is a series of dozens of paintings. In 1876 he was assigned a post in Isleworth, England to teach Bible classes and occasionally preach in the Methodist church. in southern Belgium where he nursed and ministered to coal miners. There he obtained a six-month trial position for a small salary where he preached in an old dance hall and established and taught Bible schoolIt is the nature of weeds to be aggressive. Sheep among wolves. Tares and wheat, Levean. In 1885 Van Gogh described the painting of peasants as the most essential contribution to modern art. The digger and ploughman as symbols of struggle to reach the kingdom "We are not the farmer and we are not the servants. We are the crop." The weeds growing are not simple weeds but close counterfeits. False wheat. "Since the poisonous weeds look so much like wheat, do the weeds know that they are weeds? Do the weeds believe Wheatfield with Sheaves 1885 themselves to be wheat? And since weeds traditionally rob the soil of nutrients and are aggressive at taking over the space in the plot of land, and since the weeds are often said to "choke" the plants, wouldn't Wheatfield with lark, 1883 aggressiveness be a sign of weed rather than wheatness?" Bishop Owles. Roman law

prohibited sowing darnel among the wheat of an enemy. the field is the world. St. Augustine pointed out that the invisible distinction between "wheat" and "tares" also runs through the Church: He was in the world and the world was made by him and the world knew him not. the parable of the Leaven indicates.[5] However, the final judgment will be the "ultimate turning-point when the period of the secret growth of God's kingdom alongside the continued activity of the evil one will Peasant Burning Weeds 1883 be brought to an end, "He who has ears to hear, let him hear," which occurs after biblical passages with a hidden meaning (see Luke 14:34-35 and Mark 4:1-9). According to non-literal readings of Jesus's explanation, "the children of the evil one" and Wheatfield with Crows 1890 "the children of the kingdom" are something else than humans. Origin: the devil sows tares— that is, evil opinions— over and among natural conceptions… those who become conscious that they have received the seeds of the evil one in themselves shall wail and be angry against themselves; for this is the gnashing of teeth. St. Gregory of Nyssa "Scripture means by the good seed the corresponding impulses of the soul, each one of which, if only they are cultured for good, necessarily puts forth the fruit of virtue within us. But since there has been scattered amongst these the bad seed of the error of judgment… the seed of anger does not steel us to be brave, but only arms us to fight with our own people; and the power of loving deserts its intellectual objects and becomes completely mad for the immoderate enjoyment of pleasures of sense… Therefore the Husbandman leaves those bastard seeds within us, not for them always to overwhelm the more precious crop, but in order that the land itself (for so, in his allegory, he calls the heart) by its native inherent power, which is that of reasoning, may wither up the one growth and may render the other fruitful" St Macrina; Van Gogh painted wheat fields: Hidden meanings? Wheat Field with Crows? Yvonne Korshak analyzes the painting and reveals various images hidden throughout the canvas. These images include a giant bird filling the sky, a "cloud presence" and a Gabriel-like trumpeter within the clouds (shown in the detail at right) the pastors say tares are there to practice our tolerance, that maybe they will see who they are. Tare DNA is fixed as wheat and only want to take over, have dominion.

60 pastors. Eagles nest. Chuck Blogett, Carroll Wilson, Dan Telekamp, Mike Anderson, Ken Madden, Frank Luka, Prophet Miller The whole dominion theology of the 7 mountains is a direct input of pastors visit pope
Elijah list Randy Wolf left off his linkin resume his time as henchman and enforcer for his b in law mike maiden, with the Pope John 17 movement, 11 June 2016. Joe Tosini's ministry (www.john17movement.com), which is about bringing the whole Body of Christ together as oneTosini, a Pentecostal Christian, is founder of the Phoenixbased John 17 Movement, together 2016
"Exploring the "divine partnership" as it is described, between the Barnabas Fellowship Of Churches (BFOC) and Michael Maiden's own 'Church For The Nations' (CFTN) in Phoenix, Arizona and 'Church on the Rock International' (COTRI) - a network of affiliated churches of which Maiden is President and CEO - reveals the depth of the Dominionist delusion that Yinka Oyekan has so enthusiastically allied himself with. We need to look at the theology of CFTN and COTRI, noting that Oyekan has accepted the position of European Director of the latter, whose Chairman is Lawrence Kennedy, a known member of the 'New Apostolic

Roundtable' whose Convening Apostle was the late C. Peter Wagner, the "founding father" of the New
Apostolic Reformation (NAR). Watchman4Wales
(See: http://europeanapostolicleaders.eu/welcome/history)
Konvolut erste Ausgaben. Das Totenschiff. (2x). Die Baumwollpflücker. (Buchmeister-Verlag). Land des Frühlings. Der Karren. Regierung. Die Brücke im Dschungel. Der Schatz der Sierra Madre. (2x). Der Busch. Die Troza. (Zürich und Prag). Die weiße Rose. Der Wobbly. (Buchmeister-Verlag). (2x). Der Marsch ins Reich der Caoba. Ein Kriegsmarsch. (Zürich, Wien und Prag). Der Marsch ins Reich der Caobamahogany (caoba) camp

5/6/18 Black Death and abrupt Earth Changes in the 14th Century. Pdf Sacha Dobler
Valentina Zharkova. The electric double dynamo of the sun Carrington Event
Cristian Westbrook, Ice Age Farmer
magnetic double dynamno of the sun. Zharokva-- dynamo effects in two layers of the Sun, one close to the surface and one deep within its convection zone. Predictions from the model suggest that solar activity will fall by 60 per cent during the 2030s to conditions last seen during the 'mini ice age' that began in 1645. Royal Asto Society

5/5/18 gravitubes to be read with such attention and humor gratifying. I was once assigned to teach a remedial grammar class and became to generate a grammar on the board from the present speakers, but was transferred to a lit class three weeks in. Which is a way of saying that the ball is still in the air, rotating slightly as the knees bend and the arm pronates. You also remind me of El Ephod the interlineator.

5/1/18All beings in distress appears.
-Looking at the woman cashier at Walmart realized do not show that you recognize their plight
-exploring the legend of cow, dun cow, how the Celtic church at Clonmacnoise fosters the irish identity and old tales, preserves their history much as h r voth does the Hopi legends: but what to they say of each other to the good in that interface that saves the past, and what does that say of the care of the faith that it preserves them. the cow as a symbol of evil: the alien Nummo were symbolized by both a sun and a cow. In the Dogon language, the sun's name, nay, had the same etymology as mother, na, and cow, nã. In Egyptian mythology the goddess Hathor, shown above, was commonly depicted as a cow goddess with a sun disk between her horns. The Nummo were amphibious beings with long fish tails and when they were on land they stood upright on their tails, making them appear as serpents. cause they were associated with the alien Nummo, cattle were allowed to run free and fatten. The cow and alphabet also appear as symbols in myths about the Greek god Hermes, who I associate with the Dogon Jackal. In Dogon mythology, the Jackal stole the Nummos' spaceship and crashed it into the Earth. The Dogon word for the Celestial Granary (spaceship) was Gouyo, which meant "stolen" and signified how the Jackal stole the Nummo spaceship. The spaceship was likewise identified as a Smithy and associated with stolen fire, a symbol of the alien Nummos' DNA

--RED4ED -if they cannot read and understand how can they be brainwashed? They will revert to the primitive and revolt. Support Public Education Now
--Mike had his 3 mo update sprayed with Blue Sky, kills bugs, bees, bedbugs on the truck. -- the owl is a symbol of evil

4/30/18 dawn chorus. It can start as early as 4:00 a.m. and last several hours Singing loud and proud first thing in the morning tells everyone within hearing distance that you were strong and healthy enough to survive the night
--Buildings are like are bodies, we live in a series of envelopes thqat change u, affect us, the greater is he earth body, atmosphere, to come into the body takes all our doing, to leave it none. lessing

4/28/18 stretch, juggle, sit, cr as of

4/27/18
-(also nabhi at community gardens).jack Brundige took him down. tangentially A puts me in danger, first at the house in dec, now to take the kids while they do birth practice, so I went early to the club and there was the guy I've avoided for 4 months who is so provocative, to him I said, "I'm offering you a chance at a little peace." Patrick Lange to Ancient Exploring in Arizona
The 600 year old ruin at Rogers Trough in the Superstitions is inside a cave. It's a nice trail through trees about 4 miles from the trailhead. It's easy enough to google directions. Interesting as well Angel Springs just a bit farther is where Ted DeGrazia burned a million dollars of his paintings in the 70's to protest a tax situation he was having. what the sentence says is not the same as the sentence saying it. Talk with aey about practice of the Mexican woman w/daughter and granddaughter who came in singing the Name of Jesus, because it was on the door and because she had prayed for a doc, and of Distress to appear in Zambia, but first time talked with Him.
4/26/18 humpty dumpty4/25/18 3rd day of CR, not good sleep, short temper
Bowman Glass: We are relocating to the lovely mountains of Western North Carolina 45 minutes North of Asheville in a small town named Burnsville. One load of equipment has been moved, but we will be in Dallas until the first week of June and then move the rest to stay. Of course we will be back to Texas for visits. Can't wait for our new adventure! 455 Pine Swamp Road
Burnsville, North Carolina 28714

4/24/18 on the way home from Harriet had this irrestible urge to give to the hat under the bridge at 24th st but had to go all the way back around to 7th st and return to do it, feeling some foolish the whole way, but thinking if I didn't I'd feel bad that I'd not. I had asked for support in this impulse of the Spirit, then had to wait for the car in front to move, but he gave, so I said, here's another!

4/23/18 saw ny in riot uproar, even here somewhat, then war in the years 16, 17, then back in ny praying in street with family before dinner, holding hands with And or Th?, as children, sitting on a low stat, street scale?, in this peace that passes, then the cook came to say our dinner would be served in a minute and a halt, P and I took T to potty then. That cook came out to tell us because I had given recognition of his shoes at a turnstile, given him some money too! Do the wars endided in peace.

4/22/18 Mon. finished printing 2017. the wolf does not lie down with the lamb, the wolf is in sheep's clothes casa grande ruins

Hohokam pima nat; mon: this light of mine I'm goin make it shine—AB yesterday singing with the megaphone roll dancing to her own lyrics on the spot and melody, good stuff. Casa Granden today/

4/21/18 had the kids 9-5 casa grande museum, etc. but they locked the door inside and I didn't have my keys because pat's ignition key is bad, ,had to vault the wall and break the door to get in.

these are things I thinki and don't think as a kind of decoder's manual, believe nothing and everything according ot the truth. Unacceptable premises proving and disproving the mythologies of the world from the Europeand apocalypse art and thought to the Pueblo fractal upside down reversed patterns. The world is false, I burn the dross, nothing is revealed.

4/20/18 Print 2016, Lunch with a at Indian. Animosity. Pot on a Rock. just heard the sound of a freight train horn coming from my printer

4/19/18 She believes in car tire but not phone poles in 30 years.

4/18/18 Grand canalscape: water devlivered to hi points 4 per section 640 acres, code for irrigation structures, turn out structure 1-30-50 Head gates 50 number on street. Water from Az canal. Mariacopa Co flood advisory board, flood list of city, dire conditions, storn brain study talk with jim Duncan srp pinncipal analyst waer engineer. Rainbird, puebleo rectilinerar vs europen apocalpyst curvilinear breaghals boshch, fractals reversed and upside down in rainbird design. The complexity mathematical designs of therainbird are a means of explressing fhow ornate their engineering and conceptutual skills.

bleaching effect of phosphates in ceramic bodies.

4/17/18money missing, for maybe a third time, thousands of dollars. You can not correct a thief unless he already self corrects, convicts himself. John Rasco, Mrs. Nigh's nephew could not stop forging. E blames God. The commandments are not clear enough and if they were would be rejected. I was looking for money to build ink to print these journals, started yesterday, when all the envelops except one were empty. A was here Sat while S got her massage I gave her. But this on top of Aey's report of texts about the house A wanted 40K to bid on Sunday, to the effect of my fin status, crypto, finny stuff doesn't make an innocent plea. This happened some years ago too majorly and less one other on the way;. Is it a synchronic tipoff that Willy Sun nite calls to say Mike said he got the flood late and therefore was going to keep in some minutes extra/ they tell you their going to steal from you, then do/. Been trying to ignore the record, faking accounts to steal client protocols, hacking porn sites at PCS, Expelledf or grads after cheating, adultery,, forestry major with b.s., fired from water and ice, porn exposure on cell phone, at tennis center, [digital addictions, implicit blackmail

after calling him on it, didn't speak for …financial irregularity from bank account going back… Malmsine Andrea Mellis: "Noye's Fludde"
(Britten)
   HÄNSEL UND GRETEL (Humperdinck) MHO Vienna

4/16/18 Az lib binding, Dave Hunt, cash is john gardner, long blonde hair Schnützelputz Häusel, 7/13/16

4/15/18 Aey says there is a water right to our deeds. That we pay for delivery, but we own the right to the water itself.
--I am willing to cooperate with my sons in mutual ventures, not unilateral ones, and build from the small to the great, in that order, for the little successes justify larger ones.
1.   Instances of collective delusion, the Foote drive episode as theatre to show the extreme irreality of the bubble thought, its inflation deflation, the cosmic rays penetrating the earth from the loss of the sun's aurora, producing its collective theatre the way the Foote house shows Andrew the bubble thought, right in the face, that since I bought him a car I should buy him a house, not that he should show his gratitude by developing his gifts,
2.   Like the moment of a fall when the balance is lost and consciousness too so that the person has no memory, just a kind of black out until they land. Aunt libby, the hay wagon, the chain saw fall, Aey on Camelback. Is this neurological or psychological 3. This affects the way people drive in their lanes those big trucks and suvs with phones in their hands and computer screens on the dash, and at high rates of speed, also impaired with cosmic rays, mj, drink, whatnot. They think they are driving well.
4. Also that many people came into nursing without empathy from other occupations but left it in a couple of years because they couldn't stand it, meaning the pain. Others become NP as career advancement but without vocation such as Pat has who wants to preserve the lives of the good people who come to her in order not to save the lost, but to save the good.
These matters are compounded by empire delusion, demigod delusion, heroic delusion, domination delusion so that the counterfeit on counterfeit enables the new architecture of buildings and thought like that of the wrecked car or ship, but still they will not hear. Right from the start delusion was factored on the Christians and Jews to defeat the purity of their thought.
Also note that pueblo designs are rectilineal but European apocaphyist art is curvilinear.

4/14/18 acceptance of spontaneous combustion from why vandalism.
--Bees return to tree big buzzing
--The mystery religs, jews, Babylonians had little or no heresies but the Christians had counterfeits and impostesrs from the start. Deliverance devastations of David F. Middleton Bonita Porter? Arizona artist.

4/13/18 Eating disorder, cowboyrhmes, sublimated erosis, quotes from odyssey, sitwell,

4/12/18 byron lewis explains symbolism behind lon megargee zeus and Europa make demigods. Looking for Jimmy, lon megargee https://3.bp.blogspot.com/-CTcwtFZh1F4/WqBWl1RicuI/AAAAAAAANJ0/Z5_sczGoC8wGL4qtDg616dNFrwO2yTjpwCLcBGAs/s160 0/At%3Bamtoc+white+cedar3.jpg

4/11/18 Wed. Faer Press: "The Old English word above holds inside it many meanings. It is a going, a journey, a way, a journeying, an expedition, a road, a passing, a course, a march, a voyage, a path; it is a place where passage is possible, a thoroughfare, an entrance; it is that in which a journey or voyage is made – a vehicle, vessel, carriage, ship, ark; it is a body of persons who journey, a crew; it can also mean fear, peril, danger, sudden, intense and beautiful. [information gathered from the Bosworth-Toller Anglo-Saxon Dictionary]…This word can conjure others too if you look at it long enough: it could be the just-out-of-sight otherworld of færy; it could be a gathering of festive merriments from afar – a fair, or the gift one would give to another at such an occasion – a fairing…"
--Clement alters thermostat to fix a/c.
-zion to vet for split nail.
memory: surface ememory what I said to you just now is forgotten in a minute. There are dozens of layers below it, all the way down to base memory which is the horrible things done to us by the circumstances of the streets of Steubenville for example, that permeate up through the other layers at different times and associations, never forgotten but replayed in different levels. Can anyone forget them, repress them so thy don't play/ I don't think so.
-- the uranium sea.
--Fairy Tale. Hansel and Gretel --ae emblems in this case the poverty of home life prerepackaged culminating in their education at univ where they are completely consumed. The bait consists of the ornate promises of the digital life they lead, the way all nature is corrupted, falsified by its bowers of bliss, instantaneous gratification, lack of ownerships in reality, self driving cars, but the villain is the education system itself which consumes them with false ideas of the world and life even while it convinces them they are superior to it all. Victim consciousness, florea of the golden age, masks.

4/10/18 Tues. "Bibbidi-Bobbidi-Boo talk of abscess at dentist yesterday, body immunity resistant to infection, indibeterics and else where, the AXE swaying the most severe case, that really?? It might not need new crowns, but the life is 10 yrs for root canal, could need to be redone!! both hygienist and Pappas say this might not need, will not need?? "These infections never go away because the tooth that's draining bacteria and is dead because it has no blood supply." Is the tooth dead?
--she says it is a spiritual crisis, coming on some time? No joy. Overworked? Over worried?. All these little problems daily/ Expectations. Id reamed fex acceptance. Now I look for it. Ahead. But even if accepted, until it appears it isn't realized. Even when it appears how long does it last/ "Jacob shall not now be ashamed, neither shall his face now wax pale." Isa 29.22

4/9/18 Aey sees split nail on zion's paw. Tues. dentist

Saw fairy tale appears in preview, kim chinquee does pastels I buy
two boxses for 18 each, tell her of mts and trails pastels with kids, and constellatkln newo
one os sagitarrius seen, here techniques of pouring and burshing, a pueblo book cover like
-Pueblo deisgns by mera

4/8/18 mr M BB333
whimsy for adults, Jonah a comedy
Electric Sisphmyhs

4/7/18 Anu and kids while Sabrina gets massage.
--"I'm deleting all "virtual friends" who are posting things favorable to the mollusk. Including International": soft, unsegmented body and live in aquatic or damp habitats, cephalopod class of mollusks, particularly the
Coleoidea subclass (cuttlefish, squid, and octopuses), are thought to be the most intelligent invertebrates and an important example of advanced cognitive evolution in animals. elusive nature and esoteric thought processes of these creatures. In spite of this, the existence of impressive spatial learning capacity, navigational abilities, and predatory techniques cephelop intelligence

4/6/18 2612 N 25th pl, Jeremy Van Engelhoven car.
-- Supernym. Lucy Lipsey.

4/5/18 AB at office broken elbow.
 4/3/18 Helped Aey clean the purple shed.
 4/2/18 Bid house at end of street?

https://2.bp.blogspot.com/-E31PSE7CJ5k/VrjH0r-g4fI/AAAAAAAALfM/AXuHbTdkJg/s1600/Carrying+Pot.jpg

3/30/18 I saw a combo hike, memorial service of factors, malefactors of Bishop, the women averted their eyes but the men were old, reverend, and pretentious. Also saw a green and bright white ceramic surface.

3/29/18 either a western tanager or hooded oriole feeding on the aloe
-Tom Charles Van Flandern: Every effect has an antecedent, proximate cause, No time reversal, No true action at a distance, No creation ex nihilo, No demise ad nihil, The finite cannot become infinite, Tangible, material entities cannot occupy the same space at the same time

--I saw a river, standing above it on a walk, meandering along pleasantly when it began to increase and course with large swales of current around the bend immediately above, great muscular torrents, clean and deep looking, so that it seems to endanger our position so I said

we should move up the swale of the bed which we did and crossed to a stair where I lived and went up.
-I had been thinking about the cosmic waves coming past the sun from its reduced protective areole.

3/28/17 If you could find an intelligent person who acted dumb that would really be intelligent! Easter is a chief holiday of pagans. If we painted the walls and no one was the wiser how do you know the world has not changed and you missed it?

3/27/18 the trouble is I keep learning, or forgetting on the road to understanding what I have learned, which enthusiasms result in yeserday's fiasco, egged on by folly, aey, aeg, Pand enablers. True, on 3/22, 23 differences in culture: celebration of holidays, pampered rich schools, spend instead of save, totemize children. All your social values are of the Bullins family.
I did DeWoman III, and Sunday the office walls, but how does that excuse the House/ It doesn't. I also cut two recordings of Gravediggers and hawksl call, to find out about their presentation, but they were failing so took them down. Folly 2. Great extremes altogether.

3/26/18 yesterday Andrew and I put 8gal of elastomeric on walls. White buildings! Today, partly from him saying his last offer was a 5 yr flip, and because aey was around he arranged a last min on Lew's old house, at 239, to offer 276, but on inspection it was disgusting, So much for that.

3/25/18 Chill Hours for KAZPHOEN557 for Oct-01-2017 thru Mar-25-2018:
Below 45 Model = 478
Between 32 and 45 Model = 445
First Below 45 day: 2017-10-01 17:06:00
Last Below 45 day: 2018-03-20 07:13:00

3/24/18

--Easu and jacobThe epigraph from Dante Alighieri's La divina commedia (c. 1320; The Divine Comedy) at the head of the first chapter sets the tone for the entire novel. "Dico, che quando l'anima mal nata . . ." ("I mean, when the spirit born to evil . . .") suggests that all characters have a flaw in their spirits or souls that will lead them as humans to do evil. As in the medieval literary epic, the reader of Esau and Jacob is led on a journey through hell in order to be instructed and purified.
--after early bitter satiric versions…"written under the greatest heaviness of heart." In this mood, he softened the satire and recounted details of Tristram's opinions, eccentric family and ill-fated childhood with a sympathetic humour, sometimes hilarious, sometimes sweetly melancholic—a comedy skirting tragedy.

3/23/18 10 gal wall paint for office from HD. Do DeWoman III.

3/22/18 the substance of populatirty of gulliver, Quixote, Tristram is their jocund verbosity and ease of entertainment so the reader need not think at all but be carried verbatim along. The continuing trial of the author is get a style which then is his prison evermore.
-Household tales by the Brothers Grimm Notes: Translated by Margaret Hunt, 1884, this is the only book that contains the complete collection of the Brothers Grimm fairy tales - 200 fairy tales and 10 legends.
--bituminous strip mines: topsoil bushed aside with bulldozers and buried under over burden by power shovels as they uncover coal seams
The raw rock material from just above the coal is placed on top of the piles. These piles of mixed soil and rock are left in long parallel ridges bare of vegetation and possess many extremes of site conditions. Wm bramble, reforestation of strip minded bitunemous coal lands in Pennsy
Mine soils commonly have higher bulk densities and lower porosities than native soils due to heavy traffic associated with grading. This compaction due to traffic also results in increased resistance to roots, impeded infiltration and drainage, reduced aeration, and other factors that are detrimental to tree survival and growth

3/19/18 Life of Lucien Freud, rcd Gulliver and Don Quixote! Mercury craters are named after deceased artists, musicians, painters, and authors

3/18/18 Andrew cancels corporate because he is driving Lyft for St Pats. Meeting held, ledgers. Distribution. Weeds at office, wash walls, Corp meet.

3/17/18 flood at might night, issuing an eco of the corp to its officers payable before this time next year in the form of, and that is the mystery of temptation, whether faith, greed, or some other that incites.
Botanical Garden sale:
-ericameria laricifolia Aguirre-turpentine bush, 3 fit, full sunreflected heat
-blue fescue
-muhlenbergia elmerslevi El toro, drought tolerant, purple flower, 2,3' tall and wide
-festluca ovina glauca, 18" wide growth, tan flower spikes full sun, part shade
-Ruellia brittoniana katie. Shrubby perennial to 1' wide, full ot part sun
-asclepias linarie, pineleaf milkweed, full sun, light shade, transitions to a shrub as its herbaceous stems turn woody from the bottom up with age, afternoon shade
-asclepias angustifolia Texas wild cherry
Flamenco, seme determinate 4' bush leades with highly flavoere 2" red round furits for hot weather Ciudad Victoria

3/15/18 72 Wunderfisch, graffiti at office litecoin.
Crane's use of Samuel Greenberg's Emblems of
Conduct

3/14/18 algory, algier crypto the plant paradox, lectins gold and photon energy Russian SCENAR device (self-controlled energo-neuradaptive regulation

3/13/18 principal Quixote translations

3/12/18 Master. Nobody. looking at katabole, Satan or heifer lucifer is the most beautiful and corrupt of creation Stars take after him. How is the citizen to plumb this. The most beautiful is the most ugly.
JimB says he is moving to NC

3/11/18 lewis alquist studio packup Mingling with Francine Hardaway's five dogs and our three in the street, standing there with no presence at all, like around a bee hive, relaxed.
--it's a little hard to narrative the subtext of the Savior's death, since it is my own. It amounts to a repudiation of the world, which doesn't like to do so, a but whill hardly set this. As Defoe says, "I cried out aloud, "Jesus, Thou son of David! Jesus, Thou exalted Prince and Saviour, give me repentance!" (Cursoe, 117). They only see the questioning of faith, not that faith is so malleable it withstands all.
-benzine rinsings of the moon,
-bluster don reitz hit a tree, went mad twice, so what the cult of the fan base reveres, not The Bridge getting such poor reviews, that Crane's sense of failure crush him, not like the pain of the poets, Eliot world pain or Stevens in old age writing as if a poem were a leaf pile dark within but then you can pull out red oak leaves and maple. the thing about the poets, Hart Crane, so little is known, the images of corruption, transcepts of decay, putrefaction, invocation to Satan's last words, form going to and fro in the earth, in Job, besides in the Garden and in the Wilderness. so we can appreciate the beauty corrupt for itself and not as some puplick relation workshop. Nostalgic, His body was never recovered. Neither was Yeat's. Neither was Sterne's. "in 1969, amongst 11,500 skulls disinterred, several were identified with drastic cuts from anatomizing or a post-mortem examination. One was identified to be of a size that matched a bust of Sterne made by Nollekens.[12]The skull was held up to be his, albeit with "a certain area of doubt". Along with nearby skeletal bones, these remains were transferred to Coxwold churchyard in 1969 by the Laurence Sterne Trust.[13]The story of the reinterment of Sterne's skull in Coxwold is alluded to in Malcolm Bradbury's novel To The Hermitage"
Schputzie is be bookkeeper next door.

3/10/18 the media fast of 12/15 has become a blackout.
Why did Armstrong plant azaleas on the moon.
I will protect him because he acknowledges my Name.

3/9/18 Kids with strep. AB says on phone, MY STOMACH IS ANGRY.
NCECA in Pgh, AWP in Tempe, the same week! Who can decide?

running over, running over, my cup is full and running over. Since the Lord save me I'm as happy as can be, my cup is full and running over. Unless they are in touch with American revivalism they cannot know.

3/7/18 Tues. 5G tera hertz dna breakage shortening
-heat shock protein allow complete unraveling before replication of dna
-are we on the tip of a spear? The Carrington episode concluded yesterday, with their implicit apology, last nite A calls about AB headaches and vomiting twice in past wks. P and A talk migraine. To do exam of eye and hand cord, but I question usefulness of migraine, but Pat says she's had maybe 20, one a week or so ago where she vomited for an hour and was so dizzy she crawled to the bath, was better in morning and one some 4 months ago, o/w none in ten years. I say she is an intelligent sensitive woman, read to here Levinas on the particular in Presence, of the importance of her mission, but the stress of events of these months is suspect cause. AB needs a vacation I say, overnight with us to get off the performer treadmill. I think she is dehydrated. --Later Aey leaves Judah as they are off to Big Sur etc, but in joking I say something like women are made to please men, and have babies. I then see he takes this last hard, so after he has left call him to amend, say I believe Shawna is going to conceive children and bear them healthily and happily to conclusion. He says he believes that too. I have prayed this since Oct. but had never actually told him.

3/6/18 Disney architecture Las Vegas

3/5/18 DNA Sequence Reconstituted from Water Memory? how DNA behaves in water, emitting low frequency electromagnetic waves may be more important with pollution than other: In one experiment, the EM signals were similar in suspensions of E. coli cells …since… Some bacteria do not produce the EM signals (at least in the range detected by the instrument), as in the case of probiotic bacteria such as Lactobacillus… Similar EM signals were detected from some retroviruses (HIV, FeLV), hepatitis viruses (HBV, HCV), and influenza A cultures…in HIV… EM signals are produced by the proviral DNA present in infected cells…hence… nanostructures of water are carriers of the information [this supports that em signals of freq can stimulate and cause various viruses and diseases by transmitting those to DNA]…EM signals transmitted to the pure water that never had DNA in it provide sufficient information would recreate the DNA sequence… also repeated with another DNA sequence from the bacterium Borrelia burgdorferi, the agent of Lyme disease…. Craig Venter's group had claimed to have created life by first reassembling an entire Mycoplasm genome from pieces bought off the shelf… water could store and receive electromagnetic information of such precision that a DNA sequence could be reproduced without a template, which is how it is normally done. The answer takes us on a fascinating journey through decades of research on the exquisite sensitivity of organisms to ultraweak electromagnetic fields, and the quantum electrodynamic theory of water (see [6] Quantum Coherent Water, Non-thermal EMF Effects, & Homeopathy
When Noble laureate HIV researcher Luc Montagnier discovered that certain bacterial and viral DNA sequences dissolved in water causes electromagnetic signals to be emitted at high dilutions, that was bad enough (see [1, 2] 'Homeopathic' Signals from DNA and

Electromagnetic Signals from HIV, SiS 48). Now, new results from his lab appear to show that the DNA sequence itself could be reconstituted from the electromagnetic signal. That has so stunned the scientific community that one prominent supporter was nonetheless moved to remark: "Luc is either a genius or he is mad!" But some quantum physicists are taking that very seriously, and are linking Montagnier's findings to decades of research demonstrating the sensitivity of organisms to extremely weak electromagnetic fields.

--Emanations 7 update: back-channel communications have convinced me to revise the especial thematic request published in the Emanations 7 Call for Submissions. Specifically, I am removing the material suggesting that we "go positive" and seek to write material that in some way advances "affirmations." I am now encouraged to believe this is limiting as we fully engaging the wide range of "possibilities" suggested by the Human Condition. Hence, our chief guiding principle shall be: If a story or poem makes someone say, "Yes, it is good, but what is it?" then it is right for Emanations. I was mildly secure in coming up the scratch of go positive the A Tour of the Vat was ready, but then Magister came along and asserted itself. This contention raises the guiding principle

3/4/18 Sunday. Aeg and fam to celebrate Theo's 3rd. Potato bar, play with dogs, 3 hours, comfortable. --the ethical dilemma of intelligence Still the enemy and avenger with praise from children, Ps 8, prepare a table before me in the presence of my enemies

3/3/18 Baldwin's Book Barn, west chester
— Friday your dept/ contacted us with the information that you need to make a site inspection because your intern, reported biohazard conditons. Which turned out to be that Jacky alleged carried a used needle from the room and did not dispose it there, and that the autoclave didn't work—but Jacky fixed it before the inspection!
ya need to mark up those leaves gawky!
Browns Mills By Marie F. Reynolds cold, iron and Sulphur springs, sailboat regattas on mirror lake, Early 1920s – the club house for the Canoe Club was a popular site for many social events. 1920 – James B. Reilly erected a new dam on Mirror Lake. suffering from tuberculosis. 1913 – Dr. Newcomb opened the first licensed sanatorium in New Jersey. the wonders of the healing spring water. the storms that come up on the lakes in the pine barrens are a sight to see, the lake once placid in a short space would turn to large waves. I would go out in a canoe at 10 in the beginning of the storms to test it just get back before the brunk hit, lightning and thunger largre sheets of sleeting rain, people huddled under awnings in adoration of the wonder, -a million acres, bigger than rhode island,pygmy forests, the Kirkwood-Cohansey aquifer estimated 17.7 trillion gallons – among thecleanest and most abundant source of waterin the world, the Kirkwood-Cohansey aquifer. enough water to cover all of New Jersey 10 feet deep, and equal to nearly half the water consumed each year in the U.S.
In the late 1800s there was a plan to build reservoirs in South Jersey and sell water to the City of Philadelphia. Fortunately, the New Jersey State Legislature had the good sense to pass legislation prohibiting the exportation of water outside state boundaries. Today this area is known as Wharton State Forest

The Cohansey Formation, above, of sand, the Kirkwood below silt and clay which creates a water-confining layer below the aquifer while allowing the top layer of water-bearing sands to remain connected to surface water which at 360 feet deep is active in wells. Largest seaboard open space between maine and florida soils are sandy, acidic, and nutrient-poor, endangered by fracking pipelands --the McDowell mt music fest in the enclosed Hance park looks a shoo-in for an atrocity site. Flume, Flume

3/2/18 Trying to be kind to Carrington the Dr. took an intern, not needing one, after all little Jackiee is only 3 months hired, but the girl, Gloria had wanted a consignee doc and groused, not to get out of the job told Carring that the office was a biohazard, hence she got another assignment and Carring is to send an inspector Monday.
--Chapped Hands, luce, rough skin, pim ples, ringworm, salt - rhcum ttnd other cutaneous affections cured, and the skin made soft and smooth, by using tho Juniper Tar Soap

Reading Times, 25 Mar 1873, Judge, Augustus R Kirlin
Pottstown Mercury 27 Mar 1961. MRS RENA K YEO. Browns Mills, N. J , spent the weekend with her sister, Mrs. Maybel Whitman, Birdsboro The two sisters then visited friends and relatives in Pottstown and area.
-lived near trains all my life, media trains, girls with bright hair and violet hats

3/1/18 long talk with Anne, recom hedge, am, then pm with And about ribs, mourning doves mating on our wall, plantations of candelilla and gyayle
Orphanage of Germantown, pine barrens, Chartier's valley, merion, Jesus: personal evangelism, travel, Costa Rica///

2/28/18 folk tales and legends from the jersey pines the Philadelphia Sunday Pressin
1916 started tosell 80' x 20' parcels in Browns Mills Pineland alliance

2/27/18 Aey cancel work, built mulch pile with one cubic yard and leaves. He and she to vac next wk, decided to cease extraordinary measures. Kurkwold appeared today.

2/26/18 http://www.molecularhydrogenfoundation.org/
Undefined heart. Undefined man. Undefined space of living freedom. the living soul of the undefined man freedom. E-go is trauma based non-sense, ie, image.
Egregore: Arthur Christian FB: Arthur Cristian The egregore of self-obsession keeps changing its guise but it is the same superiority complex that allows the egregore to always be raised above the heart and be King and or Queen over the undefined heart so that the purity and sincerity of the heart cannot be felt and therefore the hearts of others cannot be felt and are not on the radars of those raising the egregore above their hearts.

And if you can't feel/sense the undefined heart holding a magnificent dream of life, then you can NEVER experience true freedom either. You will always be a slave. While the heart remains overpowered, so the MAN remains a subject under the beck and call of the egregore, dominating the real life of the undefined MAN.

--we all have the dream of Kingdom, of do no harm, in our hearts and yet we cannot live it because we are still raising the egregore of our fake personas above our hearts and we have no idea how to be truly REAL with each other, saying it like it is for us, even if we look "bad" doing so, even if we are allowing the full ugliness of the resentment, anger, righteousness, jealousy, bitterness, etc, of our bleeding heart victimhood to be on display for all to see, rather than covered up by our pride and shame that form the "looking good" exterior of an evil monster that we use to deflect the heart from the heart through immense selfishness and greed, the on-going domination of the superiority complex, and from there, perceiving this egregore, of our own portrayal, as being attacks on who we are, when it is just the fantorgasmic bond with the egregore that is being laid bare so that it can be seen for what it really is and be released, allowing the true undefined heart of the MAN/WOMB-MAN to shine

- the child has no egregore to think on behalf of
- we are never dependent on others to hold and be the living dream of... we don't want corruption entering the magnificent dream of undefined life that we hold
- there is more to life than just these socially engineered bodies turned into Freakensteins with implanted, superficial thoughts and that,

-- The moment we project a definition back into the "past", we are also projecting the egregore "back there" too, because the definition IS the egregore. The same occurs when we project a definition into the "future". This is what govern-men-t is all about. In spite of all of the good hearts of every generation dreaming for peace and freedom, everyone raised in "The System" keeps getting stuck in the definitions of the egregore to be ruled by this over-bearing monster, the beast of the apocalypse suppressing the undefined heart.

--All the war, poverty, social engineering, brutality to living nature, injustice, cruelty, etc, comes out of this beast of the apocalypse that we ALL unconsciously fantasise being part of, unable to see/sense the bigger picture of the effects of this fantorgasmic dreaming. The more the definitions form the brilliance of an intellect, the more psychotic we become, with everyone feeding the brilliant intellects that rule us, whether we house them or not. Nothing else is going on.

2/25/18. P did taxes. I planted the apples.
--Insomnia of consciousness. All men are warriors so there are good and better kinds. So the vocation of the warrior is not to kill. We aspire to this vocation and seek to achieve it, obtain it, but cannot trust ourselves in the interim. Must rededicate daily and not to kill comes to mean more and in the end it means not to kill all beings, esp those we know, for who else is there, but our kindness must consist of when we know we are right, having being offended, not only not to retaliate, which is just in its way, but to choose not to retaliated, not to kill, and instead to be kind. Which we then learn wreaks a host of good illusions, benefits, happiness, many names go by this.

--Mad as a hatter, blanche b was a milliner. erethism prolonged exposure to mercury vapors. People with erethism find it difficult to interact socially with others, with behaviors similar to that of a social phobia

--Squalls, calls come along the canals at night over and over ,all, alllll, alll in awhat could be a large child's voice or an older woman from the camps of the lost along the canal. Some times they fire their heavy guns, but they rounds don't sound as if they hit anything. This in a town where the methheads throw bottles in the street in mid afternoon and criminal housing developments everywhere, literally, are to change the structure of this valley forever, but no one chronicles it, films it, mentions it, they are busy. All this while I restructure my sand bags which have grown grass and split in the drive. We need more sandbags because the runoff from all this new housing has eliminated all the vacant lots for cement, need to rearise the level of our berms a foot at least, raise the entry of the driveway, have bags for the back gate from the canal, so I transfer the sand from the old split bags into new ones, but need to keep them out of the uv light this time. When to bed early, now up at midnight. First awoke in early night to the sounds of a mandolin tuning, then the beginning of a tune. Across the canal there is a Saturday night affair, each sat. live.

2/24/18 bought a Fuji and a Gala apple

2/23/18 something about cobalt and Urk
--Mr. Pot or ms. Pot, after Dekooning who I've been looking at all week for Susan. This is a take? DeKooning in clay. I keep trying to make a pot.
-Linkedin searched by collection agency, most deleted:

2/22/18 Why is p so angry. It most be she is tired of taking care.
Slept till 6! When she got up I hugged her. She went to get her hair done in a brilliant yellow sweater and hood. -the greatest art is artless,
60—1st mod lib: From the fifth edition of Tub in 1710, Swift provided an apparatus to the work that incorporated Wotton's explanations and Swift's narrator's own notes as well. densely allusive and sardonic, replete with jibes at coevals and with artificial hiatuses (wittily described –huge, small, well-argued etc.) in the manuscript. It is riddled with digressions, such that the Tale is several, and takes on many subjects. The notes appear to occasionally provide genuine information and just as often to mislead, and William Wotton's name, a defender of the Moderns, was appended to a number of notes. This allows Swift to make the commentary part of the satire itself, as well as to elevate his narrator to the level of self-critic. Robert Hendrickson notes in his book British Literary Anecdotes that "Swift was always partial to his strikingly original The Tale of a Tub (1704). On reading the work again in later years, he exclaimed 'Good God! What a genius I had when I wrote that book!

2/20/18 moon walkers and masons, edgar Mitchel and john Podesta, buzz aldrin --flagler county beach renourishments

2/19/18 Mon so I called Vortex whose name was on the door install, but in error because when we had a glass job they growssly overbid, but at the site the tech said it was a simple pivot, less than an hour and not expensive. I told him to call me if they were was a prob. But the jprob was $207 first half hour, 69 each flowing half hour x 3, pulus cost of jivot, which he had to go get, so did not finish in an hour, knowing he didn't not have the part. The thing is when I saw it was vortex on the door and remember not hiring them for the glass but did anyway I likened it to the architect's blueprints of the bldg. that I hired him for, both backfired from repetition. I DID NOT LISTEN. It was under the same perceived emergency, perceived or real that I hired Zee in the night for the first office flood and their even worse overcharging.

2/17/18
--SUSAN IS DEKOONING DeKooking
engagement of Diane Woodrell to Donald W. Shipley has been announced by her parents. Mr. and Mrs. Dewey
L. Woodrell of Craf-ton. Mr. Shipley is the son of Dr. and Mrs. Earl W. Shipley of Thornburg. He is an aviation cadet in the Air Force, stationed at Bryan Air Force Base in Texas. 1957
-- Nora Woodrell Wed To Donald Shipley' Nora Diane Woodrell and Lt. Donald Wayne Shipley. CSAF, were married recently in the Bryan Air Force Rase Chapel, Rryan, Tex. Jan 1958
-- Mr." and Mrs. Harry Collins Taylor of Vero Beach, Fla., have announced the engagement of their daughter, Florence DeLacy Taylor of Alexandria, Va., to Colin Earl Shipley of Laurel, Md., son of Mr. and Mrs. Donald Wayne Shipley of Bozman.

???Donald Wayne Shipley Sr. was a Fighter Pilot in the Air Force and retired after 30 yrs. as a Captain for US Air. Diane Shipley. Chronological. Andrew Camo B, Brandon Adams, Joe Napier and 411 others like thisBetter bet-- Donald W Shipley MD City: Hagerstown, Maryland Age: 82
-My life is hid with Christ in God who is my Savior. A VI dream, vertial Instruction? Where I was playing tennis with two younger men, high arching shots, serves, but at one point coming forward for a volley to my right which I netted, I closed my eyes to replay the shot, but then apparently blacked, in the position. When I emerged, woke from this peaceful state of practice they were ready to leave. I asked if I was out long, the kid at the club said yes. In the moment there was only peace and rest, no sensation or visuals. A precursor? Like last July the two wks prior to the stroke when everything in that world seemed at peace and rest, when usually it is turbulent to some extent? That afternoon I watch modern painting, like de kooning a lot, whose wife comments on Kline's technique and jasper johns.

2/16/18 Friday. Review Levinas, face at age 2, not to kill 11., do piece, Art Mus lib on Kline, coal and steel. --probably the best gift is the silence to work not interfered with words of praise or solicitations of art. Artist being a revolting term. Populated by nothigs. The tao of it.

Symmetry forced by the wheel, a medieval torture, the wheel of fortune that crushes Boethius' head.

--Kline a six-inch housepainter's brush "the old-fashioned engines that used to roar through the town where he was born." jutting, intersecting beams of black… Lehigh Valley's soot-shrouded landscape — pocked dark forms of coal-breaking towers and steel mills, rived by railroad tracks, trestle bridges and speeding steam locomotives — as if Kline's paintings had some sort of religious significance. Balopticon swift brush drawings, wrenched out of scale by enlargement, white masses and speeds and black masses and speeds meet with blunt force…drawings magnified bodilessly loaded with implications and aspirations and regrets, loomed in gigantic black strokes which eradicated any image, the strokes expanding as entities in themselves, unrelated to any reality but that of their own existence. He fed in the drawings one after the other and, again and again, the image was engulfed by the strokes that delineated it. Meryon I, Tate Elaine dekooning- he began to whip out small brushes of figures, trains, horses, landscapes, buildings, using only black paint. The speed and the weight of the line kept increasing until finally the objective image was overwhelmed by its own outlines.'15
A Belated 'Breakthrough' to Abstraction AnnMarie Perl
The industrial sublime
The miners of fairy town, patchtown, Russian poles Slovaks and rush orange
creeks Anthracite

--THE DIGITAL substitutes a screen for THE FACE, tHE POT, THE PERFECT POT ON THE WHEEL,
MADE SYMMETRICAL WITHOUT TEARS, FOR THE WHEHEEL DESTROYS IMPERFECTION
BEFORE THE FACT OF THE TEAR, THE WHEEL THE PERFECT BALANCE IS UNTRUE TO OURSELVES FOR WE ARE DISPROPORTION AND TORN, AND THIS is our glory for it is our redemption in what is more than symmetry.
Levinas: The Right To Be

2/15/18 elect lines buried parallel to canal 6 ft below ditch

2/14/18 Didn't really plan it but For Valentine's Day I gave her some Yamou H2 fresh brewed hydrogen with purple bubbles! Now she wants to know all the bubbly Hydrogen gossip. Gave gift card to Sabarina for prenatal massae, Had lunch with Andrew.
-John Stam blog 27/1/18:
Antitheses is such a good title! Fierst. Firest. Tera Hertz the world's valentine.

2/13/18--P had dream of Aeg in control of some evil thing, being pulled into deep water by some smiley guy with elf like face who invented some little device, toy. He was going to drown him. Clear blue water. They had been down there a long time. I was looking for some weapon to go after him, she said. we prayed for him just now. Called him now, He's not reading his gut right, there's a disconnect. lunch with him Wed. tomorrow. This weekend, 2/24 he had "night out with boys" Kris, away from family, wife pregnant. Wants acceptance. Low taste.

Sounds like an initiation. How many there. Who is the boss? Is it secret. Where was it held. Like the Angel Pump camp in NM?

--leaky as an unstaunched wench, incontinence or menses?

-- Drive the length of the Chartiers from the Ohio to…

--BRING EVERY THOUGHT INTO CAPTIVITY! every (noema)thought into captivity aichmalosia.

https://biblehub.com/lexicon/2

Logismous—speculations, upsoma—lofty things, Anthrōpois (man-faced) 2 Corinthians 10:5 ▶

NASB © Greek Transliteration Strong's Definition Origin [We are] destroying καθαιροῦντες kathairountes 2507 to take down, pull down speculations λογισμοὺς logismous 3053 a reasoning from logizomai and lofty thing ὕψωμα Upsōma (upsos on high) 5313 lifted up from hupsoó raised up against κατὰ kata 2596 uncertain origin the knowledge γνώσεως of God, θεοῦ theou 2316 of uncertain origin and [we are] taking αἰχμαλωτίζοντες aichmalōtizontes 163 captive every πᾶν pan 3956, all, every thought νόημα noēma 3540, purpose from noeó captive 163 to the obedience ὑπακοὴν upakoēn 5218 obedience from hupakouó of Christ, Χριστοῦ christou 5547 the Anointed One.

logismos log-is-mos': computation, i.e. (figuratively) reasoning (conscience, conceit) -- imagination, thought.

Noema is the reality of de Chardin, upkoen, after the Japanese, logismous is science

He led captivity captive. It says, lego Ephesians 4:8 "WHEN HE ASCENDED ἀναβὰς anabas 305 ON HIGH, ὕψος upsos 5311, HE LED CAPTIVE ᾐχμαλώτευσεν ēchmalōteusen 162 A HOST OF CAPTIVES AND HE GAVE ἔδωκεν edōken 1325 GIFTS δόματα domata 1390 TO MEN." ἀνθρώποις Anthrōpois (man-faced)levinas 444 a man, human, anér and óps (eye, face) Matthew 13:19--αρπαζει verb - harpazo har-pad'-zo: to seize (in various applications) -- catch (away, up), pluck, pull, take (by force).βασιλείας basileias 932 kingdom, sovereignty, royal power from basileuó. When anyone παντὸς pantos 3956 hears ἀκούοντος akouontos 191 λόγον logon 3056 a word from legó of the kingdom βασιλείας basileias 932 kingdom, sovereignty, royal power.

2/12/18 FirstNet The urgency to install 5G is first to establish ist responder 5G secure com network. Secure meaning it cannot be monitored by cvivilians as present 911, fire dept police

calls. No doubt expanded to medical…That is, the gov't gets more private as the civilian become only public. Mrcati ATT and govtybisque, public monitor of 911, fire dept, police scanner prevented by this network
--Thornburg coal. the pervasiveness of soft coal mining on every aspect of life is a sample of the 4G 5G Spacex, Intel, Microost, "savior of the world" meaning its pollution

2/11/18 singularity prosperity 5G Intel, SpaceMusk, Microsoft present themselves as the saviors of the world smart meter guard

--Breuscig. Held title by eagles nest in 1980. Went on bike, found it eagles nest by road sign that changed to geometric symbols as I looked, on the edge of lake in high season, but did not go down the road, but found an apartment where large dogs were kept and a woman gave me a fluffy, red, blue, green yellow bird to ride on my shoulder as I biked, walked. It was playful and liked to flip around, just for the day…

2/10/18 Mars On Pismuth

saw--a cattle farmer, needing to impregnate herds leads starving pop, old bulls by fromping up a great storm of movement in front of them, stomping, puffing, etc to arouse them. Then other farmers come and put down blocks for the bulls to mount on, all to save the community. This puffing and stomping had occurred earlier when the herd was young so it was known to work.

2/9/18 Consciousness transfer: There is a back story also algo driven, that if you buy one here it pops up in your search, all concurrent with even greater dullness by the unreconstituted to whom if you mention cell towers, data mining, full consumer profiling, they arfe openly disbelieving, let alone of cosmic rays or synthetic telepathy. Presumably though they will buy consciousness transfer now. recommends over there Because Robt mentioned clones on TV, and Netflix I'm remembering clones, synthetics, Boys from Brazil (Mengele) and centers from the mainstream announcement at Netflix altered carbon series just begun, with its sleeves etc. an exact take on cloning centers, freemasons, scientolgists, Mormons. Disclaimer: I rejected the freemasons demolay at 12 in very definite language.

Donald marshall, facebook statement
Its not just that he understands Nostradamus, but that N. was written about him-and all the popes too. He calls himself the savior of the world for his reptile revelations, says he will have political power in the future, when people realize. He says this at the end as if he could help not to discredit himself. Gives a caution that Putin is the worst of the worst, pretending to be a savior of the Russian orthodox Christian…so Donald says they want him to reveal this, and did not kill him, which fits the quantum structure, both and neither. Our sympathy runs two waves. In case of 4 vulgar idiots in the wilderness who profance the air with every breath we root for evil to destroy them, but when that has begun we root for their deliverance. Or with marshall, we sympathy with him as a child at the start, through all the tortures, but as he

emerges and groaws prouder and prouder, taking prophetic airs, we root for his just undoing. So it's all true in order to sell the untruth. For ex, Putin as the worst man in the world just at the time the Democrats indict for Russian interference? That's how quantum info works tell the positive to sell the negative Donald Marshall shared Makayla Degler's post.
Makayla Degler sleeves
The Bodies That Went Viral
Trevor Moore - High In Church - Illuminati
Illum drug: ADRENOCHROME
Donald marshall interview 2016 29.00 Hitler found a Viril 1 in Tibet on expedition and learned ot Viril 3 in
Antarctica, hence…
Vinny eastwood interiew FAMMTV sleeve vid james casbolt Acacia-dmt
--I am not an artist. The term is revolting. Take any noun, add ist.
--If there were an analogy of the quantum landscape in this, plus, minus, both and maybe neither then every hill would be a valley, every valley a hill, and both and maybe. This asks whether there is one instance of quantum in the world and if not then whether it is a phantasm, not real, an invention…This is the quantum landscape of Thornburg. Once you start numbering beyond 100 where do you stop? 110? 10?
Two days ago reordered c60, yesterday algo on youtbube rfecommends 3 part dosages series. Connected.

2/8/18 asexually reproducing lady crayfish clones
telepathic "recalibration." search indicates occult old
age, controls:
---You are more sensitive to chemical based products- skin irritations, allergies.
You cannot tolerate synthetic food the way you used to.
You experience aches, pains, colds and flu's, stomach bugs, blurry vision, popping and buzzing in your ears, and unusual headaches.
You are actively filtering out 'news' trying to disconnect from the fear and depression it generates.
You have woken up to much of the lies and deceit played out in global
politics. You are remembering childhood passions, creative outlets you
enjoyed but forgot about You are seeking quieter ways of being.
You are in the process or have shed friends/colleagues/family who bring your vibrations down.
You are drawn to meditation, yoga, healing therapies, being in nature in a way you never have before. You are aware of fluctuations in your perception of time.

Carbon 60 Understanding dosages the invisible and visible, (otherwise 100) are not pairs of the internal and external, present and past 9Existence, 30, 70 in Levinas)

2/7/18. Put up Edwin Yeo Architect, Tues. Show off dinner for Andrew's family. Whatever totem AB is under she acts out. She wore a cat shirt, and crawled under the table after dinner, with T, so I give her milk. This role playing…R and C, Justyn and Jacob, w/ Aeg and Sab and kids, for dinner last light. Shoofly lite. I turn off my wifi at night-toJustyn. Ensuing discussing of waves, Iphone 8 thumprint id, face req, 5G, Silver hats,, cosmic rays, earth expansuion, data evesdrop, etc.

2/6/18 Tues. Magnetic excursion gotherberg HOCUS BOGUS IF YOU DON'T KNOW NOTHIN ABOUT NOGHTHIND you don't no nothing

2/5/18 Mon. lunch with Aey R and C. Converse on slab. Morton toe adjustments. Geofrey had panic attack last summer at visit because they voted for Trump, has severed relations. Wm. Just doesn't communicate. They are elizabethed.
--Viktor Vladimirovich Khlebnikov Zaum. cataclysmic sea battles shift the course of history once every 317 years.
--Anselem Kiefer, Remembering the Future. The borrowing of the stalks of wheat and grasses, tall sunflowers on single stems above with patches of paint a as rock or mud patched brown and greens with blue swirls above, all grainy rhythms of the natural in motion, collage pieces of foil, silver, gold, glued, painted, stock on, peeled off recurrent color notes are black, white, gray, and rust; and their surfaces are rough and slathered with paint, plaster, mud and clay.
Clay artist--These towers I make out of layers of lamination of old and new clay with porcelain interiors but exteriors of lava, gravel and cobalt specks pressed into the new that stretch above two feet, which stretch into cylinders with shoulders and mouths, which taken the other way are cut, compressed, the shoulders lowered into the body, the base informed, all for the climatic event, the vulnerability, the weak spot, prevented as much as possible but inevitable in most, hence the tear, the slump, the complete collapse of the shell so the hands are full, but braces at hand, two by fours and sponges and props combine them all to a landing. The tower lands as play but needs to be put back up on its base, which was made double and triple to support the whole of which by now in diameter is as wide as the tower was high, but it has to touch the ground too, so an edge tilts, otherwise it will fall in the heat of the firing. So there the volcano. Comment on scale: big or small. If big they are a measure of ourselves. If we were big they would be small, so big or small is a slight measure. If we photograph the small close up we make it big in scale. These are the scale they are from the point of view of what will fit in my car when I take it wrapped from the studio to where the real work is done, a garage, not of machines, but of stretching, for when it falls, it can't be moved for a while. They are speed dried though, so in 24 hours after composition are ready to go outside. The scale is the car and the weight carried to the car. Exiting the building they are above the head. I don't have any associates or helpers, hoists or lifts or pulleys or rollers. This work is not a part of any social situation.
--sprinkle cobalt on white satin, etc while wet, oil spot effect.

2/4/18 recover from tree milling

2/3/18 Sat. ram dass expressive aphasia telegraphic speech

-- the matrix illusion as an idea is one thing, but to feel it translated every second on all media productions to exepeience every moment .
-Sat Aey's third alleppo cut, 9-3. Cost was $370 of which I gave 120 plus 100 to transport it.

2/2/18 R and C arrive, take suburu

2/1/18 There are many of us who still miss the The Pittsburgh Press.
Even TechMan, a Post-Gazette guy all the way, remembers with fondness the days when the scrappy little morning PG competed against staid Mother Press. In those days I always thought of the afternoon Press as a workingman's paper.
Well, I have some happy news. The Pittsburgh Press lives again -- at least its archives do, on the Web. With the approval of the Post-Gazette, Google has begun to digitize the microfilm archives of the Press and post them on the Web. The Post-Gazette's permission was required because it owns the Press archives.
But Google doesn't make this material easy to find. To locate it, go to the Google.com home page and click on "advanced search" to the right of the box where you enter your search terms. On the resulting page click on "Google News archive search" in the bottom left-hand corner of the page. On the resulting page, click on "advanced archive search," again to the right of the search box. Or you can just go to search if you're better than I am at typing long URLs. In either case, when you get there, bookmark it.
Now you are at the page where you can perform your search. Type Gilbert Love into the window that says "with all of the words." In the window to the right of "return results that come from," type Pittsburgh Press. Voila, you should get a listing of Gilbert Love columns from the Press.
You can use Pittsburgh Post-Gazette or even Commercial Gazette as your source if you want to go back to the 1800s. (If you just want to browse, use Pittsburgh as your search word). But those archives have been there for a while, unlike the Press.
If you double-click on one of Gilbert Love's columns, you will be taken to a representation of the page. Your cursor is a hand that allows you to click and drag the page around on the screen.
Above are magnifying glass icons to enlarge or reduce the page, a box where you can type in the page number you want to view and arrows to go to the next page or the previous page. My thanks to reader Norma Chase for alerting me to this. Although I knew digitizing the Press was planned, I didn't know it had actually started. Ms. Chase said she spent an entertaining evening reading through Press archives.
Now, into the Press.

--AB's hissing and karate chops and kicks from Disney / anime films?

1/31/18 spectre of maye musk

1/29/18 woke at 2, topography of Chartiers w to Steubenville, n to clarion, ea to Uniontown not much south. We only see the visible when it is remembered o/w it is invisible. So the invisible that swirls

1/28/18 Visit to Kurkwold, acceptance. Sunday
– this search, and Levinas and the sun, began in response to High's space delusions   I woke up attributing to his many changes of residence in youth—ie place—Levinas place misapplied resulting in search produced: Kolonia Qalunya - located near the Jewish town of Motza identified with the Canaanite town of Mozah (Joshua 18:26), Mozah was a Jewish village known for its willows[5] that were used at the Temple of Jerusalem, the village was destroyed in the First Jewish–Roman War. After A.D. 71 Vespasian settled 800 Roman soldiers in the town, which became a Roman settlement known as Colonia Amosa or Colonia Emmaus.[4] Byzantine name, Koloneia, It has also been suggested that Qalunya was Emmaus.[7] The site is the correct distance from Jerusalem to match the story told in the New Testament (Luke 24:13-35) In the 1890s, Jews purchased some of
Qalunya's farmlands, and established the village of Motza, the first Jewish settlement outside Jerusalem. Harry Levin, who accompanied the Palmach force during the assault on 11 April 1948 is an interesting commentary on all of these claims. As he described the even, "Suddenly the village seemed to erupt. Our mortars started it, and at once became a bedlam of answering fire… They fired wildly to all points of the compass… Suddenly an explosion that seemed to rip open the hillside; shrieks of terror. Our shock troops and sappers had reached the houses… More explosions… In half an hour it was over." Levin counted fourteen dead "but there were more." When Levin left, "sappers were blowing up houses. One after another the solid stone buildings, some built in elaborate city style, exploded and crashed." search kolonia Jerusalem. See also the politics of Jerusaleum since 1967. Michael Dumper, 66.
--Illeity From Latin *ille* ("that man; he") + -ity. An external embodiment of the self. Totality and Infinity. Levinas between Ethics and Politics: For the Beauty that Adorns the Earth. By B.G. Bergo. In Heidegger the self oscillates between self revelation and self concealment, but The Il ya, two parabolas intersecting at their bases, open at the top and at the base, transcendence and transdescendence, or the apeiron --Reading Levinas/Reading Talmud: An Introduction
By Ira F. Stone
--Gateway to Heaven, 117- "a rural suburb below Jerusalem called Motza was actually a place called Kolonia but referred to as motza—exempt.
---It is the other human being, not being itself, that summons a response (ethical). The horizon is neither gift nor summons but the open space at the base of parabolic figures, "the heart of the being of the world which we enjoy like a surplus that overwhelms us even as we enjoy the warmth of the sun and the illumination of the morning sky." This must sum the first two commandments. Bergo, 60. See Otherwise than Being or Beyond Essence, OBBE, 8,9
--woke to rooster crowing.
--Had the kids yesterday, Sat., 9-4. AB desperate, mimics karate, shoo goose, hisses, aggressive, throwing punches, leaves? We went to Farmer's market, raked leaves, heard Beethoven, hunted and cracked pecans, made and ate cookies, walked the canal, Th fell in the

potty? Potty at market too, good stream! Wanted to be carried at points throughout. I whispered to him on the way home, he whispered back. We prayed at breakfast, cookies and going home! In the thaw the parents were outside waiting for us. I said I wanted to show them off to Robert! S said Th was not three yet, that she wanted every day. Esp since she was to be 30. I, we'll have to get you a walker. A: you should talk. S, how old will you be on (our) 7/25 birthday. I, a lucky 77! That's a 47 year difference!

--Place, breath. The biography of Place in the identity of breath. Place is a base. For example Frankl exchanging a look with a bird in the camp. Levinas existent/Chartiers I can see the Chartiers valley before the towns and cities and roads when the jpjossomand the bear and the Seneca roamed. Put the roads and mines as an overlap, then add the sentience of a child and you get this tale.

1/27/18 a million doughnut shaped liquid water satellites (with gold fish)

1/26/18 Fleur du Mal because as I worked my sins played in my
mind. cruelty and blessing

1/25/18 Dentist Claud Birk says I need dental op: Go to "Do I need this root canal" (Google) and to "AskMetaFilter" and read the whole thing. Has Dr Pappas compared all of your old Xrays ? It is a question worth asking.
--a day is longer than a year on Mercury. If a day is as a thousand years and a thousand years as a day on earth then a month lasts 83 years, a week 20 years, a day 28 months, an hour 12 months and a second… A DAY IS LONGER THAN A YEAR ON MERCURY. On earth, if as Moses said, a thousand years in Thy sight are as yesterday when it is past, then a month lasts 83 years, a week 20 years, a day 28 months, an hour 12 months and a second-do the math @ Melt for 100
NasaMercury scarps
Bepicolumbo-- October 2018, with an arrival at Mercury planned for December 2025, skipping Stones on the creek, flunked out of Penn State in Dairy, enlisted, Flip Travis dairy farmer, Jay worked for from age 12?
Greenhouses in Merion, Albrecht's, cut cord wood,. I was plopped down and plucked up!

1/24/18 Research Janet Rowland Yeo to see if SRA show in her tree, pretty complete on wikitree, to question whether that's where Jay was contaminated, or was it Flip Travis, wondered previously.
--woke up to Janis Joplin begging a dwave computer for clif high the way Kathereine Austin Fitts wants to crowd source an organ for jos farell. This is cultural retrogression

1/22/18 Masters security screens (623) 466-0136
Sentiment Analysis

Kerf

--I somehow think it immodest to speak in this way, as if the plain clothes of this dress or manner of address were insincere, and I still think it such, but what can we do, whether to walk naked and unclothed were a better course let us all doubt, but some say that the kerf in modern parlence denotes to snuggle in a bed nude, pretending to sleep when in fact in full embrace to kerf the night away, for in the world the world is other only through its clothes. That I should bare this underside as though surprised between, the bare nudity of a body some extraterritorial space to cover in the night, in private, at home, concealed, not turned toward the sun at that, the relation with this nudity is the true experience of the other I seek to show in myself – and not its kief, to ambiguate kerf further as an intoxicating, for I had long before heard this, eavesdropping in the spirit. The ectasy of austerity I suppose had gotten me here to this space that separates the planes, no matter how wide you cut, always the same, the width of the blade, kerf in the thousandths of an inch, the saw that keeps cutting, roars and leaves this space between where the sword cuts asunder, soul and the spirit dividing, the word of truth the width.

I overheard I was a Kerf Baby, and whether I was meant to or not the hearing must be borne, no pun, since all the rest had to be reasoned. Is the kerf something or nothing since it divides worlds or words, whatever cut? Truly the blade is not the kerf's business, since the kerf comes after, some sawdust in case of a saw, or if a sword, part from the whole. But what is the kerf but the fact, since two parts previously exist, the divination of their divide, existent or existence, actor, memory or both?

This parallelism as a construction of the ordinary, where soul and spirit, joints and marrow divide asunder, can there discern the thoughts and intents of the heart. Cut between the heart soul and the spirit breath
In this mode of living, if kerf refers to that, I have nothing in common with Daniel the Excellent except for a divided childhood, for he was taken they say at 12 because they lack the experience themselves, but I ask you what king would expound his culture into a 12 year old, that full form, precipitous and prejudiced being on the brink when he could get them at 6, or 5, as we commend, in the mallable, in the plastic innocence, if such applies. Even saying so is old school and now we know they inculcate alterity from the womb, literally, as they have done with their comprachios from that time. Daniel was spared that and I was too, but there the comparison ceases because he lived in purity and I in pollution. Before overhearing these words I took it that pollutions wreaked upon a five year old were a freak of nature after the nature of a beast in natural form that came up out of the sea and destroyed the earth where I lived, even while all the people around me said how wonderful and good it was to live in that place that felt the iron toes and the clay feet. I don't say I asked for any of it but enough measure was given to me for the impression to last. The memory of cubes of scrap metal and railway cars sunk in the creek, the smell of that first soft coal hauled down at flood from 1850 and later just flooded over whole expanses that froze into a skating rink with dunes and traps and trunks and flotsam and jetsam on the banks with the odor of decay. That was the bottom of this landscape built on a series of cliffs that as you went up at the top were strip mines and iron sump runoff, slag piles and great pits of blue green water surrounded with such steep sides so that if you fell in you would not get out, later all filled in of course as much as the

microhearting and engineers turned the dark black smoke of the freight trains white as they came up the rise where I lived at at 5 and 10 and 15, effects implanting personally worse each year while the wild and natural energy of that stronghold celebrated my contemplation. So I was a kerf baby diverging between saw teeth that lived between the toes that Daniel called the image of iron and clay, a little more that natural as I was shown, when the Fourth beast, dreadful and terrible, and strong exceedingly had great iron teeth devoured and broken in pieces, which stamped the residue with its feet, diverse from all the beasts that were before it; ten horns who can fathom that came up among them and another before whom three of the first were plucked; and in this hourn the eyes of man and a mouth speaking, that Daniel beheld cast down, the Ancient of Days whose garment was white as snow and his wheels as burning fire issued a fiery stream and the ebooks were opened until even till the beast was slain, its body destroyed, given to the burning flame.

Genesis 15:10, he speaks of the sacred and divine Word as cutting through all things, dividing all perceptible objects, and penetrating even to those called indivisible, separating the different parts of the soul. Scripture as a direct divine utterance.
Of course the beast had its own account, that being the Dream of Scipio with all its commentators like Macrobious
1. A kref baby a slit made by cutting, especially with a saw.
the cut end of a felled tree. • The groove or slit created by cutting a workpiece; an incision. quotations ▼
• The width of the groove made while cutting with a saw or laser. quotations ▼
• The distance between diverging saw teeth.
1. • The portion of hay, turf, wool, etc. yielded by a single cut or shearing stroke A schematic drawing of a saw blade looking head-on: the divergence between the teeth that protrude left-and-right is the kerf defines the width of the saw cut. To cut a piece of wood or other material with several kerfs to allow it to be bent. Origin kref, kerf baby, Ophirim, mammonites,

1/21/18 eric Gilmour, unsubstantives, Daniel kolenda, Christ for all nations, all from Floride, slick oil sale reptiles
--"turn left at the apple core" excerpted from The Thornburger in Gilbert Love's Easter Sun column 1953? --Mr. Waitneight will be succeeded by J. Howard Reiff of Thornburg as general commercial supervisor in the company's Western area. Frank P. Atwell has been named to succeed Mr. Reiff as district manager in the Southern districts, Pittsburgh The Pittsburgh Press from Pittsburgh, Pennsylvania on July 3, 1950 ...

J. Howard Reiff continued as manager of the JenIkintown district The Bristol Daily Courier from Bristol, Pennsylvania

Sept 26 1940 High Priest, Fall of Evangelical, False Israel, Jonathan Kleck,

Alabama southerne, retrace the stars, jack dodds, bird house, up high edited, name hard to read classsics, clif high hatred of Israel old and new, wet dream, C60 kicking in, precursor of endrocrine, elect shift?

1/18/18 cf globe, AZ
4d to 3 after 2 unusually open communication with Jared C, dreamed hands cut twice with razors.. --newton's ms came yesterday, a marvel of creation.
--Nat Tecchino in the hall, lunch, sophomore, hits me with rotten pear. I go to wash off, return, his back to me, pin his arms at his side with my arms from behind, throw him in air into ground feet first, over and over, at least five times, over and over, he shouting, who is that, who is that, till finally he is released. Nobody ever talks about it.

1/17/18 root canal eval with Axx, did I want a private conversation with him, one of the intake questions??north of Camelback, the horror, the horror.

1/16/18 Nick Begich says we need distillers of all the info.

1/15/18 correspondance with jared christman
--maximum contrast going and coming, 5-16. The shadown shadow showdown is all of previous confronted, all the coal regions different
1/14/18 Levinas, And God Created Woman, says: Of the psalm, "surely darkness will conceal me, night will provide me with cover," (Ps 139.11)darkness is not dark for you, night is as light as the day. 167 In other words, man's humanity would be the end of interiority, the end of the subject. Everything is open. I am everywhere looked through, touched by the hand. Thus one can understand why Jonah could not escape his mission. This is what it means to have two faces. With only a single face, I have a place in the rear of the head, the occiput, in which my hidden thoughts and my mental reservations accumulate. Refuge which can hold my entire thought. But here, instead of the occiput, a second face! Everything is exposed, everything in me confronts (fait face] and must answer. I cannot, even through sin, separate myself from this God, who looks at me and touches me…167

1/13/18 their opinions are commercials broadcast into their mouths for repeat

1/12/18 Friday termite treat the bldg.
Red Waters, Woods rd. water came down hill after mining with acid from the mind in the natural sprigs 52/ vein 41/2 feet thick 23, coal pits,. Culm dump: hillock of waste matter from coal mining, town celebrated for its beauty to cover it was a strip mine, Chartiers creek, mine dumps, culm dumps, slimes, tails, refuse, leach residue or slickens, terra-cone (terrikon), Acid mine drainage, agricultural and industrial runoff, and sewer overflow made Chartiers Creek one of the most polluted watersheds in Pennsylvania., backbone rd, crafton, waer scorpions in pools under the cliffs high up,
--George Nakashma vs early stickley

1/11/18 Aeg called. It's a boy!
Postpone the milling Sat.
--Trump a variety of crazy emperor Wen who acted nuts to foil his depose by deep state
--neuve ice crystals Appalachia
--"And now it comes, the point of all points, which the Lord has truly revealed to me in my sleep, the point of all points for which there—".last words of Rosenzweig
--as to the lib table from ½ to ¾ planks, taper the legs out of the 4th post to be cut.
--Aey came last night and saved the 153 p ms of the last days. It was lost in another file.

1/1018 Reconstruct: Memoirs: Disappearance of the World, Sky Shadows, Latin American Mission, Jose
Donoso, Ameryca, Methods of Unconscious
--An Aggadah promises the reconstruction of Jerusalem in its glory, a reconstruction by the very means which were used to destroy it, precisely though fire, become protector. But where is the glory of His presence among us, if not in the transfiguration of consuming and avenging fire into a protective wall, into a defensive barrier? Levinas Nine Talmudic Readings 196 false fire, sole with, Faulkner, levinas

1/9/18 December 10, 2017 near Choisy-le-Roi, and here
levinas strausborg 24-29La théorie de l'intuition dans la phénoménologie de Husserl (The Theory of Intuition in
Husserl's Phenomenology; his 1929/30 doctoral thesis), De l'Existence à l'Existant (From Existence to
Existents; 1947), and En Découvrant l'Existence avec Husserl et Heidegger (Discovering Existence with
Husserl and Heidegger; first edition, 1949, with additions, 1967). In 1929 he was awarded his doctorate (Doctorat d'université degree) by the University of Strasbourg for his thesis on the meaning of intuition in the philosophy of Husserl, published in 1930

1/8/18 I once thought Faulkner a great stylist but wondered what the effect had been had he not drunk a quart of bourbon a day. Now I know all this work is inflammatory, self immolating, so that is the bourbon. And his work is drunk and puerile. Compared to Newton's prophecies of Daniel whose syntax is also ornate, but logical and exacting.

1/7/18 the first days she gave amoxicillin, then augmentum, vibrating heating pads on chest, now today a steroid, the cortosteriod prednisone. Last night schedule 2 hydrocodone in syrup, which stopped the cough. --Salvation through Literature Levinas's Carnets de captivity The one-volume collection of Levinas's writings entitled Carnets de captivité suivi de Écrits sur la captivité et Notes philosophiques diverses, published posthumously in 2009, notably collects seven basic sets of notebooks written mainly during wartime captivity de l'existence à l'existant pdf Levinias
--biographic ms. Ameryca, the Prophet is a fool

--the divine gates are beautiful, powerful, corrupt, grotesque, everything that could be said of Cormac McCarthy's writing, which can never vary from its irreality like the orchard keeper "bobbling on one foot like some ungainly bird." The gates of his McCrowley are also overcome with epithets, live on adjectives.

1/6/18 Archie Johnson and The Las Vegas Seraphim Collection
Archie Johnson stopped by and produced pics from the Las Vegas Seraphim Collection. He came to the apartments below where the paintings were but then said he should tour the upper three stories, unfinished, rickety, dangerous with catwalks but traversable. The house had never been properly finished off, just enough so it wouldn't get too wet in the rain. Visited many times in these venues, it had been acquired but never improved much, so to view The Seraphim Collection in situ is a challenge. I Had been up there myself so it was more or less possible. There are so many more parts and pieces he didn't photograph. It's a little like the old Barnes, the only other place I saw pieces crammed and crocked together, crowds milling shoulder to shoulder to pass them. Obviously they can't do that in Vegas. Without apology the name tags are also missing. As for the photography, if was a variable cloudy day when Archie passed through.

-Archie Johnson and the las vegas exhibition of the sculpture of ae reiff. He came to the apartments below where the paintings were but then I said he should tour the upper three stories, unfinished, rickety, dangerous with catwalks but traversable. I had never finished the house off, just enough so it wouldn't get too wet in the rain. Had been up there recently more or less so it was possible. Had gotten this house, visited many times in these venues, but never improved it much the seraphim collection. In situ. The only place I ever saw pieces crammed and crocked together like this was the Barnes, crowds milling shoulder to shoulder past them. They can't do that in las vegas
--easily the best intellectual talk I ever had was with John Cullen at his bungalow fireplace into the wee hours.

1/5/18 sudden money, April 26th, 2018 in Litchfield Park, AZ mary martin loder ph.d, animal person --most of my biblio has great under chassis. Thoughtgoattens?
--saw Aeg etc at office cleaning the last of the branches, AB getting examined, he drove Uber new year's eve, made 200.
-I am going to thaw Sab!
Geoffrey Hartman's trauma. I cough seriously in the night.

1/4/18 Starr bookworks
Panther peak bindery
MP bookbinding 4047 S 16th St, Phoenix,

I ordered the 1733 Newton's Prophecies of Daniel and St John, compiled by Smith this AM for 955. Plus fix binding plus 200 because of reading, reminded of Job, Noah and Daniel in Duties of the Heart, the entry on Daniel in Psalms. Leads into the millennial question and the whole time measure "to learn the will of God, the truth of history, and the understanding of end-time prophecies… in the Jesuit origins of Futurism and Preterism but, few know the role that Isaac Newton played in creating the Protestant Historicist interpretation. All kinds of tales Near the end of his long life, Isaac Newton reached for a scrap of paper and scrawled down the date 2060 A.D. But best is the cogency of syntax just dashed off without revision, that can even suffer excerpt of the profligate smith.

Only one of Newton's books about the Bible ever published.

--on value is intrinsic needs no utility, Job said to his wife, as one of the impious women speaketh, thou speakest.

Newton's half-nephew Benjamin Smith, prophecies daniel, bracht

The contradictions in Newton are fully reconciled in our own.so we take them all as partial allies and judge which to confirm.

A collection of fragments assembled by Newton's half-nephew Benjamin Smith (1700-1776) with a view to publication, and printed posthumously, 1733.

-- Six years after his death, Newton's nephew Benjamin Smith published a small portion of Newton's later writings on the prophetic Books of Daniel and Revelation. For more than two centuries, this book provided the only glimpse into Newton's prophetic thought

--Benjamin Smith (born about 1700, rector of Linton-in-Craven, 1743-1776), one of the most marked specimens of a profligate clergyman at a time when such specimens were more frequent than now by at least twenty to one, to speak charitably of past time; and so notorious in early youth

-- To this nephew, when a very young man, Newton wrote in such plain terms as his conduct justified, describing his haunts and his practices in language which decent people reserve for such occasions as imperatively require it. The clergyman into whose hands these letters fell after Smith's death, destroyed them, for the sake of Newton's reputation. In his disgust at the coarseness of their language, he forgot to consider the necessity of the case. What followed? It oozed out that Newton had written to his nephew letters so objectionable, that a worthy clergyman destroyed them, lest they should damage the writer's character as a respectable man: the clergyman himself furnished the information that he burned them for 'vulgar phraseology.' here

--See also Isaac Newton's Temple of Solomon and his Reconstruction of Sacred Architecture Thomas Pellet, Newton's executor found two areas to publish out of the hundreds, ms on chronology and two on prophecies.

No publishers would buy the prophecies until Smith selected and sold it 1733.

--in the rare books card catalogue of the Library of Congress, I asked to read it. I was astonished when, a few minutes later, I was handed Thomas Jefferson's personal copy. Jefferson would turn to the "J" signature and add a "T" before the "J" and then turn to the "T" signature and add a "J" after the "T." In this way he identified his personal books.) -- The newton Project

--Isaac Newton's Temple of Solomon and his Reconstruction of Sacred Architecture By Tessa Morrison pdf

--the sentences and idea play like sheep all night in my mind

--Diseases of the breath

1/3/18 Edit Neon Genesis Evangelion by Yoshiyuki Sadamoto @ PsalmsofDavid --AZ termites seek cellulous in dry wall so show up early.
--Prune stucco drywall exterior wall away from ground.
--Susan's dizzy heights the elegant precipac
-Alta took mandrake on the plane to Greece and couldn't walk for 7 days

1/2/18 the UN tries to kill the angel because the rulers of the world take counsel together against the LORD and His Anointed who the angel represents. That they also defame the angel, the railing accusations of Jude, is part of their mind set since the angel threatens the domination of the nations.

--things above individual awareness are less programmed in art than in the news. So if we want to get a view from above we look there, so Dante shows CERN.
-- The Dreams of Pantagruel are a series of 120 engravings published by Richard Breton in 1565 under the name, probably usurped, François Rabelais . It is about phantasmagoria drawn probably by the couturier François Desprez

--"Constant consciousness that He contemplates your secret and your open life, that which is hidden within you and that which is seen. [Always bear in mind] that he guides you, has compassion on you, knows your deeds and thoughts—those concealed and those revealed, in the past and in the future, that he reassures you and shows friendliness to you."
33 Duties of the heart, tenth Treatise, The Duties of the Heart, divided into ten sections of the "gates" that constitute human spiritual life. This is from the last, the tenth gate on The Love of God. Rabbi Bahya ben Joseph ibn Pakuda lived in Zaragoza, Spain in the first half of the eleventh century.

1/1/18 Seattle is the capital of the new slavery in this civil war, like Atlanta of the old, purveyor of digital slavery, servitude, crowd sources, clouds, clones, robots, ai, data base, data mining. These know nothing of the primal emotions, so if they speak of lust, it is some pale shade. See Eviathan
--My mother, born with a caul, not something possible any more, taught public school in Philadelphia for two years. She once disarmed a knife from a student,
made more in those years than did her fledging Bell exec husband. She adored her father, the architect E A Yeo, was forced to be the mother-caretaker of their family during the years her mother was incapitated. She once said her mother had tried to burn down their house. This was likely implicated by a post partum stress after she lost her youngest son Donald, after birth or possibly millener poisioning.
--Polato!

2019

1/1/19 layers of succulence

-Hierophantic landscapes in a history of new Philadelphia

The very thing we have been advised not to say, that all the facts are not known, and the case is obscure, which we puzzle and conject, where any one can either be the case or not the case, and everything else remains the same, this which we should not say, we say, but in terms that do not show what we mean.

-The other Side of language

-What can be said at all can be said clearly; and whereof one cannot speak thereof one must be silent. In order to draw a limit to thinking we should have to be able to think both sides of this limit [but don't talk about it] (we should therefore have to be able to think what cannot be thought). The limit can, therefore, only be drawn in language and what lies on the other side of the limit will be simply nonsense. Tractatus Preface

Readers Guide to Wittgenstein

2.15 That the elements of the picture are combined with one another in a definite way, represents that the things are so combined with one another.

--- Architectonics <against the collective> takes accidental design as its principle.

Accident means intent that recognizes what is occurring, but absents external motive.

Accident sees, hears and knows back and forth in dialogue with the person of the creator.

Accident rules out the future, for the present is so delightful as to extrude itself.

Accidence provides an incontrovertible real in the present, made/not made with human hands.

Accident is never apart, never two, but one.

Wittgenstein said his Tractus would only be understood by those who already had the thought.

Accident is a near non-thought.

Its love for its own sake of all species, evident in the "faces" of Emmanuel Levinas, describes compassion.

You can say it is discovered, but it was there when you saw it.

It is bigger than you, but you get to participate, but it is not in a measurable state.

This counters the invoked muse, OUTSIDE the creator that enters and provides inspiration, channeling or invoking gods, engaging a separate intelligence whether editors, fellow artists, zeitgeist or collective consciousness and civilization, but for engineers construction to a norm, contrast engineering.

Consider a map of the stars against drawing free hand.

The engineer measures the angles against the whole to control the precisions of orbits, times and space. In actual space flight joining artificial intelligence to the human, this mathematical function of intelligence outside the person is an adversary of the human.

Accidence says correct distance is an illusion, that perception takes angles differently in every case. Accidence says the map of the heavens is an illusion, for there is no universe in this sense.

All these are synonymous in their illusion with the consciousness farrago of the future and worse.

Architectonics looses intent upon accident and accident upon intent.
Accidental design recognizes what is occurring, absent external motive.
Accident sees, hears and knows back and forth in dialogue with the intent-creator.
All intent is person-al.
The good news is the creator becomes accident-intent.
Accident rules out the future for a present delightful to extrude itself.
Accidence provides an incontrovertible real in the present, made/not made with human hands.
Accident is never apart, never two, but one.
Wittgenstein said his Tractus would only be understood by those who already had the thought.
Accident is a near non-thought.
Its love of all species, evident in the "faces" of Emmanuel Levinas, describes compassion.

You can say it is discovered, but it was there when you saw it.
It is bigger than you, but you get to participate, but it is not in a measurable state.

This counters the invoked muse OUTSIDE the creator that enters and provides inspiration, channeling or invoking a separate intelligence whether editors, fellow artists, zeitgeist or collective consciousness/civilization. For engineers this is construction to a norm, contrast engineering.

Consider constructing a map of the stars against drawing one free hand.
The engineer measures the angles against the whole to control the precisions of orbits, times and space. Accidence says correct distance is an illusion, that perception takes angles differently in every case. Accidence says the map of the heavens is an illusion, that there is no universe in this sense. All these are synonymous in their illusion with the consciousness farrago of the future and worse.

In actual space flight joining artificial intelligence to the human, this mathematical function of intelligence outside the person is an adversary of the human. Architectonics may be sonar or material.

--1/2/19 Dreamed I was sitting in a chair with my arms around my two grandsons standing beside me in light and love. Reminds of of A and A, the same.
--Coming back from walking dogs a. m. talked to Gail in which she feigns to slap my face! Part and parcel. A nice instant block however with improved eye hand.

1/3/19 To listen: The phrase "eye has not seen, nor ear heard, nor has entered into the heart of man what God has prepared for them that love him" will properly mystify us until we read the next, "but God has revealed it to us by his spirit." So what is it that has been revealed? It is as in Psalm 8. The definition of man given there rebuts the Argument. Three qualities endow the man, he is crowned with glory and honor, he has dominion over the works of hands, and all things are put under his feet. The last signifies unseen malign forces as much as any. Since none of this obtains to the present man how is it true? The crown, the hands and feet are Messiah's, called the Christ, which does us some good if he is in us as we are in him, hence we walk in his crown, his hands, his feet.

--- Milkvetch--Your presence softens my pains. Language of flowers. Astragalus, increases the secretion of milk in goats. A few Astragalus species have been used medicinally by humans and have recently been touted as promoting longevity by activating the enzyme telomerase, though little clinical evidence supports these claims. Researchers are also studying milkvetch extracts as a potential drug to combat AIDS. In Greek, "Astragalos" is the name of the anklebone, and was used by the ancients as dice in games of chance (thus the gambler's slang term of "bones" for dice). When shaken, the anklebones made a rattling sound, not unlike that of dried fruit pods of many pea species. Linnaeus applied the name to the group of peas commonly called milkvetches or locoweeds.

--Hard Fern--Blechnum spicant, called deer fern, Blechnum spicant, grows near Deildartunguhver. This fern grows nowhere else in Iceland. Deildartunguhver is a hot spring in Reykholtsdalur, Iceland. Root - cooked. An emergency food, used when all else fails. Young shoots (often called croziers) - cooked. The young tender stems can be peeled and the centre portion eaten. An emergency food, it is only used when all else fails. It is also chewed to alleviate thirst on long journeys.

There is a hazard to the World in this that is greater than medieval compounds where every follicle had a human dress. The sun heart, kohlrabi vegetable, gold its mineral, Brussels its city, Guam its country, why not woman? She lay by her side in Europe, her head in Logres Britain, a breast in France, a hand in Italy, Byzantium her navel, Caucasus her back, Jerusalem below, then her Chin / O'er past; the straight Hellespont between / the Sestos and Abydos of her breasts. Bogs, barrens, white cliffs of Dover, buttocks, hands, Newfoundland! Maps put Jerusalem at the center. Faithful to the world, we love the Centrique part. I found out countries in her!
Language ideation images inlaid with codes of ideas complete only in the sense that they provoke their one thought, as that England populated America with itself, its language, its institutions, unlike the Spanish who spread their language but preserved a difference between themselves and the natives. So England is like Israel and the analogy of promised land, Canaan of the New Englanders is justified by later history when all the natives adopted the English ways, with a few exceptions. The Portuguese language Brazil but the French never did Algeria, Morocco, the religions swept all those worlds and but the Muslim was more

native than the Christian, which was Roman by then in extant. The China and Japan were more impervious and all these nations as Paul calls them had a serparate intelligencia class from the English, not penetrated by these elites. There were two elites in every conquered nation, the governing Engish and the native. In Haiti, Cuba it was curandro based shamem and drug fused. These eventually backfilled the conquerer's homes and infected the deneutered Christian with drugs and rites.

1/4/18
All the shows on how to id the anti, waiting for the beast, subverted, just like brietbart and drudge reporting every lie ever said about.
If you need somebody to tell you you is then you ain't
WAS LOADING GLOBAL WARNING ON TWITTER BUT ANOTHER SOUND TRACK WAS OPEN AND THE NEW TRACKED SOME SECONDS AGAINST THE OLD. VERY EFFECTIVE. "We don't want
Syria. We're talking about sand & death. That's what we're talking about. We're not talking about vast wealth.
We're talkin g about sand and death,"
National security and political version leading the broadcast with every snow storm.
--global Warning-- Mr. Quechua, the putative groomer, here is grooming his sculptures for the next dogshow, featuring Fukushima, Weimar Republic, Civilization Redefined. There is a yoke as they like to say among the soft j mind and egg crowd that The Groomer whispers to his pets as the Weimar has and will whisper to the redeveloped Demonaut America. I also said Behemonaut! This presentation got into the Kurk Wold miniseries and we're proud of that, but hope to see it in the next show coming. Even if that RED Hat honked for it, https://www.redfez.net/fiction/history-oracle-628 Civilization Redefined, next to Weimar ain't so new. It's been fired at least once before, so probably a good talking to helped. This Redefinition is about to be Disclosed. Redemption is too!. That's a pun and not, Ho; Ho. Quechua Man appeared at the Herberger Theatre Gallery besides at Red Hat. I suppose this represents a primitive grapefruit trilogy.

1/5/19 aeg and whole fam to office on Sat for exams. First Sat open. He says to me, asking questions about
Nikolai, "that's why you weren't invited."
 HAARP: January 2019 Time Cross - Farsight

1/6/19 large painting black edge heavy imposto, white cream interior ridges, both sides, another, torso of arms, shoulders, head , extended, both sides one in reds black, yellows,-- suggesting monotypes, but why not paper on paper, save I don't have any paints, or do I?
-Another in a kind of crisis group of people begin to sing chorus, like in a bus station or waiting room. I stand and sing aloud.

1/7/19 thought heart and mind. Kid Kindnapped. No landscape of present only of past. Lost in present, no topography. Past has body of identity

1/8/19 Tues. Aey 18ft trailer, take down one bauhinia, prune two, take to dump. Forklift driver helps me load bags of heavy sodden leaves, the dumptruck driver waves, the roofer jokes, and the guy at the dump eats the red berries. The people I am of.
News is misdirexction, Liberia revolut-I will eat your—raw, but that is what the news is, the news will eat you raw, mercury with a high impact flix https://youtu.be/-3y6tCQpt74?t=1631

1/9/19 thrown off by the effort of the work took this day to recover. Disrupted sleep from the effort, like the 1/6 night after Restore gave those candid dreams

1/10/19 --Emanations Chorus Pleiades (338+ pages) arrived today in the midst of considering and constructing a work in the vein of The Nova Trilogy without the toxins, a kind of cut up style he and Gysin used, doubly reprehensible as that might be, a three hundred page work in completed draft called Transworld Portals.

Nova and the series funded by Burroughs and his beat friends got much play in the pubs. TransPortals is my equivalent w/o any of that and instead of being an addict I am a Christian! And in an era of much disregard of all issues of importance, only distracts and controls.
--Last night put in touch again with this etherial ms. Again, familiar but haven't seen it in a while, a kind of reminder of what is there to do.
--"He uses inspector Lee to express his own thoughts about the world.
-- "The purpose of my writing is to expose and arrest Nova Criminals. In Naked Lunch, Soft Machine and
Nova Express I show who they are and what they are doing and what they will do if they are not arrested. [...] With your help we can occupy The Reality Studio and retake their universe of Fear Death and Monopoly."[7] --As Burroughs battles with the self, what is human and what is "reality", he finds that language is the only way to maintain dominance over the "powerful instruments of control," which are the most prevalent enemies of human society.
"Jack Kerouac says B is .the greatest satirical writer since Jonathan Swift. .
--Without great solitude, no serious work is possible – Picasso—
--angel fire. Angel Saucers. And then you realize that all the apparitions of angels aside from the few canonical messengers, are saucers. That doesn't dignify saucrs it denigrates the term angels—and then that all the various psychic courntery brown charismatics are Saucers! Gives a new meaning to the occdult. Yes there is real power, yes it will completely kill you dead. Keith Haring : future primeval. Future predators
1/11/19 a work in the vein of The Nova Trilogy without the toxins, a kind of cut up style he and Gysin used, doubly reprehensible as that might be. TransPortals, or whatever its final name, is the poetic, scientific equivalent, but instead of an addict drug horde and celebrated lost soul the author is sober and a Christian in disregard of the distractions defined at Memoirs of Athens. The Nova Trilogy funded by Burroughs and his beat friends got much play in the pubs then and now. I take my allies where they are. These answer what Kerouac says of him, that he is the best satirist since Swift, a Satirist of the

1/12/19 How can I reconcile myself to the fact of what I have made?
And its corollary, how can I reconcile myself to the facts that have made me?
-Took theo to museum of Instruments. He is validated to go, only him. A week after this on phone with Anu I said I know him now, meaning how his mind works. Andrew says, Well I hope you like him. How secure can he be to say that?
-- Fiction in the Guise of Science.
--The Replication crisis "Why Most Published Research Findings Are False".[14]: "studies with incorrect findings are not just rare anomalies, but are actually representative of the majority of published
research….Richard Horton, editor of The Lancet: "Much of the scientific literature, perhaps half, may simply be untrue." Horton agrees with Loannidis':
"small sample sizes, tiny effects, invalid exploratory analyses, flagrant conflicts of interest, obsession for pursuing fashionable trends of dubious importance." "Science has taken a turn towards darkness."

1/13/19 Hypothize. Hypotize. Hypothicate, rehypothecate the same as fairyize, farithicate the number from its base rising like smoke, numbers of the pop, ounces of gold, threats to the commonwealth, false informations, news reports, Hypothoize, hypostheisxe or the eagles will come and pull out our eyes.

1/14/19 I have been subjected to divine justice.

1/15/19 Dr. Rubino del Sur is a palantirologist of soccer. His alternate is Rubion del Sure.
Roden Crater --A man's shoulder, a woman's hip

1/16/19 the languages and mythologies of all the nations and prenations, tribals, Israel, Syria, India, Japan, Russia, Turkey, China all have in common their humanity which has always been subverted by the avenger, but redeemed by Messiah, so the war is between the avenger and messiah intervention, to the rescue.
--each of these styles of color and shape represent the nations, rough smooth textured jagged finished colored contrasted: so pray for the intervention!

-if a lion could talk we could not understand him, Wittgenstein Phil Invest, advises 223 And what are the thoughts of a lion? Which is about inner speech, what I say to myself. They bypass language. Knowing them is not hearing them, always. Intuiting them, empathing them. A dog cannot be a hypocrite, neither can he be sincere" -- is a dog sincere because he cannot be insincere.
"remembering has no experiential content…man learns the concept of the past by remembering,"231 —the past comes after the present, not the present after the past.

---Aey comes over, sick second day in midst of composing Apocalypse yourself! Gets apocalypscd…all started when he said he'd talked with Shawna about her smoking and weight-I said what about you, what you think about you..he didn't even know what he felt. I

vocalized his thoughts to him, like he goes to his workshop to get away from her…told him he needs a counselor not me telling what he thinks, he needs to know himself, I am not happy with myself about this…but enough is enough, meaning so many people have accused me of their irrational thoughts from Willy to Doris that when he said he'd asked why I was not welcome there she said, because he judges me, which I do not do at all and have not been there anyway for years except when she is absent or as last when invited for the lights, which she was in a rage, typically about. He is gaslighted continually. In the end if I vocalize his thoughts they are still his thoughts and he is the one to confront them, consciously, not continue to deny them; so I am the favor of a mirror/ She doesn't like his family. He no longer works creatively. Lost his joy, hijacks his life for her own. No singing. No playing. No gardening. No entertaining his family. Worse she denigrates his efforts, from his doors in the house to the lumber in the back, not neutral adverse. No help in the house at all, the attraction not repulsion of evil, like Sabina putting a dragon over Nik when it is the token her father wears on his SCA armor. The thing is when you oppose their gaslighting they retreat, but good people attribute fairness while the GL take that humanity as weakness and exploit it.
---Victor Davis Hanson

1/17/19 Gaslighting and NLP sides of one coin
Pentagon Seeking Proposals on Using Insect Brains to Build Robots
Social engineering feat, reduced birthrates among natives, increase it among immigrants in Europe
--Aey appears, we do the sound track for Little tykes. He assembles the basket so I can burn the office weeds. Make a birdbath at studio.

1/18/19 thurs. Birdbath.
Programable metal
-statue of a musician from the Iron Age with six fingers.
how many toes of clay fail in the european empire. Three. France, Germany…there are not ten toes, giants have 12! six founding member. G6 (Group of Six) in the European Union is an unofficial group of the interior ministers of the six European Union member states—France, Germany, Italy, Poland, Spain, and the United
Kingdom—with the largest populations and thus with the majority of votes in the
Council of the European Union ten horns but 12 toes. how many toes on
Nebuchadnezzar's gold statue
--After this I kept looking in the night visions, and behold, a fourth beast, dreadful and terrifying and extremely strong; and it had large iron teeth. It devoured and crushed and trampled down the remainder with its feet; and it was different from all the beasts that were before it, and it had ten horns. (NASB) Dan. 7:7
--40: And the fourth kingdom shall be strong as iron: forasmuch as iron breaketh in pieces and subdueth all things: and as iron that breaketh all these, shall it break in pieces and bruise.

41: And whereas thou sawest the feet and toes, part of potters' clay, and part of iron, the kingdom shall be divided; but there shall be in it of the strength of the iron, forasmuch as thou sawest the iron mixed with miry clay.

42: And as the toes of the feet were part of iron, and part of clay, so the kingdom shall be partly strong, and partly broken.

43: And whereas thou sawest iron mixed with miry clay, they shall mingle themselves with the seed of men: but they shall not cleave one to another, even as iron is not mixed with clay.

--polydactyly, with 12 fingers and 12 toes all fully functional ... A certain tribe known as the Waorani living in Ecuador has many members who have six fingers and toes. They are normal sized people who are known for their violence, and 50% of all deaths in the five generations were due to homicide. The people of Waorani are classed as an enigma as they have no traces of cardiovascular disease, cancer, high blood pressure, allergies or indeed any other known disease. The members of the tribe are said to also be physically strong.

1/18/19 Friday. Begin office burn.

1/19/19 DQ half price day! Compile Eating Leviathan

1/20/19 the sexual state

----A cement block. A drawer, rubbed w/ manganese etc, cobalt,…streaks

1/21/19 objective correlative John Titor in 2036. Baron Trump's Marvelous Underground Journey

1/22/19 --another definite dream episode in being unwelcome at the aggressive reform church
--"frost heave." As deforested soils freeze and thaw, stones shift and migrate to the surface

1/23/19 rubino in anarctica.
Axx, the sublingual goes straight to the heart o/w shots in arm go to the liver. Tongue to Heart!
Mia's new pair of glasses

1/24/19 Tao Lin some king mango.
--Ryan Groen Principal at Phoenix Christian School
Navigation on Word: control f

1/25/19 --4 hrs kneading stiff clay to make cement block last night and today.
---FBI thugs swat team roger stone in the dark.

1/26/19 Tried Apocalypse Yourself
A Second of Omniscience
Is there a difference between Nazi henchmen "taking orders" and executing horrific acts and the FBI thugs who swat team you home at night to arrest citiheads? To the FBI agents who execute these travesties: THE NAZIs
SAID THEY WERE JUST FOLLOWING ORDERS. You have to quit your jobs or be THUGS OF THE AUTHORITARIAN REGIME. The new Mennonites are Alex Jones and Roger Stone Shunned, arrested in the night. Media and FBI are the the SWAT teams coming to take you away.l What will you do when he tow trucks stop at YOUR door?

--recoverd back gate, added wire to prevent dogs tearing

1/27/19 Sun.
Tried, The Gates of Hell
Pat ill. Burn weeds office, finish back gate

1-28/19 The Blake Flea Scholar.
Mon the hierarchies of society are identical to sports teams and leagues. Owners, spnsoors, athletics, teams, levels up and down with values and coaches and public relations. This is so in education, politics, business
,literature, science, all players try to get to the top, all in service of the system.--microwave auditory effect

1/29/19 hauled branches to dump with Aey. Tale of Two Towers.

1/30/19 Fill the propane tanks. In the Moon-canceled.

1/31/19 Global Warning, the video. The putative WaMer grooms his pets as Weimar whispers to Demonauts. Fukushima, Weimar Civilization Redefine Texts of the jpeg e-mind. Faerie West Roll Up.

Isaac R. Horst — Old Order Mennonite Historian

2/1/19 another boxcar. Chomsky is the left equivalent of Dershowitz for all pizza lovers. Chomsky is the name of a cannibal. If he looked like one you would know.

2/2/19 I asked for a good dream to counter the bad. Hence, reporting to an agency, number …71, short wait, after 70, 72 called. So I ask what happened. Told some stuff about numbers I didn't understand so a supervisor came out and explained a three year policy at Bishop was involved, and, blah, blah, I say it sounds like ASU is a meat market recruiting. He says, always, but this, (you) are better than ASU, friendly like. I say that's the best news I heard all day.
--had the kids 12-6. Walking the empty canal Scion, loose with leash goes right down, sees I'm not there and comes back up, no prob. 6 ft! recovering from cold that got all, Shorty has been coughing 2 days now.
-- messages on the skins of bananas—TAINTED FOOD
"I don't know if anyone's ever tried that — you cannot get shoe polish off,"
I can promise you I'll never do that again in the future.'
A reporter asked Northam if he could still do the moonwalk. After pausing with an "ummm, Northam was nicknamed "Coonman."

2/3/19 JCCIII takes mic to deliver 10 min of paradox and contradiction. Vic leaves in a huff, the room empties except me. I stand and deliver equally impassioned statement about shining with sun. the students coming for the next class began to hum. Later, Aey is smoking coke?

--Trump golfs wih Tiger and Jack. Not all his bona fides are negative.

- eschatology of Viking Ragnarök appeals to the biblical since we shall judge angels. The fallen angels are the gods that are to be defeated in the last battle fleeing the wrath. To quality the Viking must be fearless and strong etc. We fight not against flesh and blood but against principalities and powers, but in that day the least of us shall be as David and David as the angel. Since Messiah shall rule them with the breath of His mouth.

2/4/19 REPHOTOGRAPH LITTLE BIRD TO ENLARGE FORMAT AND MAKE INTO A POSTER

-removal of bridge, three teeth, with saws and grinding at least an hour, like a precision machinist, but with the cough and head cold everyone has had, so engineered antinicotine and cough med to enable the affair. but with the thought of how infinitesimal age proves mortality against all the currents of culture and peoples- monologue--Unhealthy thoughts? What's worse, unhealthy dreams, acts…

2/5/19 Tues. told Andrew has new job in Chandler as director of trucking starts in a week or so, so won't go to Tx, has an hour commute each way.
Got packaged Patriot food 200 cal for a month for 4 people.
-300 6 yr old ginseng
Still recovering from the cold, grinding at dentist to replace old bridge, cold less severe than Pat's, who is still a little under. Daneri out for a week w/flu, Michelle was stuck in Flag for 2 days with car trouble. Aey has scheduled his test.

2/6/19 Fine Grade Angular Crushed Glass
FELDSPAR-CUSTER CRUSHED (PEA GRAVEL)
http://berniesrockandgarden.com/product/peach-feldspar-2/Peach Feldspar - Bernie's Rock & G Decomposed granite
Hnery Maakc

2/7/19 The Hothouse Like taking a boat ride on a train. The translator says it is mentally read aloud while being read, ...
--in the last dream I had a 1908 Eliot at a store on consignment but decided to take it with, but not having id, put it under my arm and walked out, but it was raining hard so put in under my coat and ran to the car but did not remember where it was, then I realized it was a dream and I had neither book nor car nor rain and woke!
--coffe with Andrew and Theo, American Group Logistics, Mike Schember, Daniel Krivickas
2/8/19 the cement block 3 turned into a box of DEMONAUTS -- THE KLAN AND THE COONMAN-- what a title waiting to happen! Here Virginia- DEMONAUTS

DRAGONETTES, DRAGOCRATES Whoops, sorry about that. I think its his wife THE GUY IN THE HOOD IS HIS WIFE!

2/9/19 the office does look abandoned with the metal door and etc.

augusto

2/10/19 asked and axed by Teahouse two pieces.
Samaizdat, the must, Leary, Vacaville—entity separate from the man,
ET, blue T Green T!!
 Volcano East of Los Angeles hit by sudden Earthquake Swarm -- Pisgah Crater Volcano

2/11/19 winter in Antarch, summer? View of street elevation, from inside out elevation, from above. There is no view from beneath, pictures of tree roots, aquifers, strata.—the 4th view is of a biased wholeness of one aspect magnified and instantized, known with comprehenison

In revelation revisited: samizdat.Muse as "a felt engagement with an autonomous entity or intelligence that is separate from the ego."… whether entities of this kind are projections by an apex deity,
… synonymous with the consciousness of the human collective,… whether discarnate entities enjoy independent existence,… whether discarnate entities enjoy independent existence,HGA holy guardian angel, crowely… Crowley initially spelled his interlocutor as Aiwaz. Later, for reasons of numerology, he rendered the name as Aiwass. It was Kenneth Grant (1924-2011 CE) who connected Aiwass with the double star Sirius, announcing his discovery of an occult current emanating from the "transplutonic planet Isis," in a 1955 Manifesto … Leary perceived the entity as telepathic and extraterrestrial. The result: * Timothy Leary, Starseed, San Francisco: Level Press, 1973. * Timothy Leary, Neurologic, San Francisco: Starseed, 1973. * Timothy Leary, Terra II: A Way Out, San Francisco: Imprinting Press, 1974. Leary concluded that humanity was originally extraterrestrial… Kenneth Grant's Lovecraftian synchronicities and Trans-Plutonian communications… Philip K. Dick (1928-1982 CE), also interacted with extraterrestrial intelligence in VALIS (1980)… "The outstanding result was that I entered a belief system, from 1973 until around October 1974, in which I was receiving telepathic messages from entities residing on a planet of the double star Sirius." (p. 277;
RAW 1977 p. 8)…. –Jean Baudrillard, Simulacra and Science Fiction, Science Fiction Studies, #55, Vol. 18,
Part 3, 1991. .. Revelation Revisited, a review of Matt Cardin, "In Search of Higher Intelligence: The
Daemonic Muse(s) of Crowley, Leary, & Robert Anton Wilson," in Angela Voss & William Rowlandson
(eds.), Daimonic Imagination: Uncanny Intelligence, Cambridge Scholars, Newcastle, 2013, pp. 266-831….

---Most musicians, artists, poets, adepts and shamans collaborate with the Muse. The Hindu knew the phenomenon as apauruseya, śruti, and ākāśavāni. We discuss it as prophecy, Dionysian ecstasy, Bacchus, the Jungian collective unconscious, race consciousness, and the Akashic Record. The metaphysics of the multiverses demand that we understand the Muse as an autonomous projection of human consciousness. • Estéban Trujillo de Gutiérrez

Dear Doug,

Sorry to delay in responding. I got wrapped up, just back from being helioed Saturday to a camp at 9108 ft with no amenities and temp shelter to discollect my thought even more after examinations of what was preserved there. I worked at Eau Claire, Mt. McKinley, and Fukushima Prefecture before this, for government, NGOs and corporations, but in this NASA jaunt of dentition, jaw and skull formation analysis, everybody is tasked with everything. I was running a torch with propane strapped to my back! I better send my response before going down for the obligatory sleep they give us after more than 48 hours out. Thank you for your remarks. They are much appreciated even if the effort goes for naught. Your truly, Rubion

--Observations or Descriptions of the Marks is fine for the title.
---Try: "P. 33 looks like the word NIXON has been scrabbled in the margin. That's not the first mark. There is underlining and circling throughout, and on the outside cover there is a disconcerting yellow green sticker with the price of $1.00." ---a bit of trivia intended to lull the reader for the affronts of the H, the M and the O.
---"I'm going into the letter M it says on P. 8, underlined.."
In my mind this suggests 1) a figure poised at the top of the M like a skier on a ski slope about to slide down. How to slide down the M is not illumined except that "they see all life without observing it" and in the margin it says, "buried." We can take this as a caution not get be buried (in the snow) after our slide. Of course from below the M looks like a woman with her knees raised, from one point of view and all that entails, but this is all subliminal, spoken or understood below the mind. At least that is the explanation.
---That need be not capitalized so let it read ---"peek or peak."
---He is not wearing a hair shirt. He is not wearing a shirt. This is intended to save the reader from realizing that he is not exactly human. What kind of animal or hybrid hides there might not be satire.
---about the boarish head, beside the pun on bore, the tusks and snout further the submerged thing below the surface. It looks like a boar head but it is always changing.
---the note in your next comment "admits" in the sense that it "suggests" these bestial tendencies are going on, furthered also in the stork and the goat.
-Whether it should be Ook, and not OOk? My Word program automatically corrects it to lower case so I have to go back and retype the capital. This second capital O references the sexual understory, already suggested in "did you ever look into an O?" Going further into the M we might say is a series that begins to implicate the whole alphabet as symbols. I have

not gotten yet to where symbols, events and journies like George Belden describes destroy all myth leaving nothing beneath the ice but frozen shadows.

--The neurological aeronautics and space administration national
We have two layers of security on return, which is to acknowledge there can be delays, in addition to the relays in transmission before this email address in the States.
Summer here, peak season with nearly 24 hours daylight, with guys claiming they have traversed the ice coast to coast is filled with PR stunts, which Mt. Sustin Primate skull morphology

FAKTA Propitiatory experiments and results of research in nanocomposites, synthesis of grafted polymer, speech to text, text to speech, hybrid environments, conducted at Eau Claire Mayo, Denali, Fukushima Prefecture and McMurdo Station, FAKTA Propitiatory couched as literatures of fact from each of these facilities, occluded with the Futurist playbook opposing Bolshevik society in those 1920's. The new Bolshevik society of the 2020s completely translates from this era one hundred years before, which censorship is again opposed by fakta a continent and an age apart from the original, but the first priority remains to accentuate real material gathered either first hand or culled from documentary sources (Kolchevska). The formalist theories of the faktovivi bypass the controls and translate much of this hidden propitiatory work when read correctly.

Squisquatch.doc
The Gambler, 2018
Connected in the electrolyte excretion of the prognathous jaw, the displacement in function of a posterior heart. Subfornical Organ Squawk Back, 2017
Transformational kidney and third brain queries on the ventral surface of the fornix near the interventricular foramina interconnecting the lateral ventricles and the third ventricle produce in these cases a complex of hybrid speech.
Connected in the electrolyte excretion of the prognathous jaw, the displacement in function of a posterior heart.

Toward a "Hybrid" Literature: Theory and Praxis of the Faktoviki
Natasha Kolchevska
The Slavic and East European Journal
Vol. 27, No. 4 (Winter, 1983), pp. 452-464 (13 pages)
Published by: American Association of Teachers of Slavic and East European Languages Previous Item | Next Item

https://en.wikipedia.org/wiki/Alexander_Rodchenko

Alexandre Rotchenko, who passed through the Soviet revolutionary era, had an abstract

Despite being, it is necessary to survive it as the sole premise of modern Iris Well, it does not bring clues to critically rethink the culture of the 20th century Cow.

2/13/19 wed. Vertigo. Many poems to Frigg

2/14/19 Aey needs to regain his faith. His comments about his poems show that. He has lived with an angry depressed psycho and her friends too long. Box, block 19 complete

2/15/19 Friday. block # 4. Aey passed his NP cert today. Both Aeyrie and Andrew began new elements in their careers this week, after long preparations. So they are back on the same page again!

2/16/19 I taught my natural talent to them, athletics, made them athletes over from nerds, which they still obtain, and warriors of sorts, by hard work, but their gifts, natural artist and natural poet they did nothing to attain, they carry on their own, but I have worked hard for these myself.

2/17/19 Sun. Good news!! ANTHONY WEINERS'S OUT   !!!!!
Accidental delete academia edu site!Taxes.
Lipo somal Vit C. Cancer Ward

2/18/19 early Trump family memorabilia, roll of stamps w/engraving, plus authroizations,, silver cup, etc.
Giant List Of MSM-Fueled Hate-Crime Hoaxes Meant To Frame Trump Supporters

2/19/19 Nachmanide's 10 Dimensions?
Nachmanide's 10 Dimensions
And here in Genesis 1 there are a total of 10 times where the text says "And God said". Each time God spoke, a new dimension was created. I have tried to find an online text of Nachmanide's writing on this topic to find out how he decided that 4 dimensions were knowable and 6 were not, Writings of the
Ramban/Nachmanides:Translated and Annotated
---new bridge put in. Rhonda Patrick Samizdat not a good source.
-GOB Sats upcoding! Good old Boys
--to spank the carp: Rubino del Sur: This is a pretty disconnected new reality piece, or before the new reality, which comes in fits and spurts, bursts of data interspersed with as it were advice to the viewer.

2/20/19 more Trump dreams, I compliment him for being an immoral man. He says his greatest sin is self love. The golden age, the spiritual man is mad, the prophet is a fool. Didn't ask him about his notorious masonic handshake.
 Hidden Egyptian pyramid drawings of the Nephilim kings as centaurs

I heard of you in the credits of someone I know I checked out on Café Irreal and since I have been working about a composition on carp (Squid Hats) thought I'd send this first, to see if this kind of writing appeals to you, since the carp piece isn't quite ready. It does seem to be extreme, but the conditions are such, and for me, in Antarctica with all the stories of underground lakes and all kinds of prehistoric fish, it's more. As credits I have a take on some letters of Freud, a monologue of a scientist at Mt. McKinley, and one promised to appear, soon I hope, on Fukushima.

2/21/19 Liberatum
2/22/19 Jacob's ladder
Rubino has lately documented examinations of faciation zones in the Chernobyl mind which emerged in the irradiated writing preceding these exposures.

2/23/19 rebar the corners with armature wire and metal pegs, then coat the exteriors with metal!! --this guy is running a wire through South AZ, has vid, a booklet, and a plan!!

2/24/19 These takes on the 600 billion invisible beings must have a finite list of subjects even if they vary among observers. What I want is the honest unconscious jake felt in Dante, Goya, Gehry, etc, but do not deny it in Bosch or Breughels, but they are less, Michelangelo not honest, mannered, jpatterned, with a less honest story to tell. All I am trying to do is give a record to myself of what I have encountered as meaningful.
 "the FIRES FOR CORRECTION, DELIVERANCE AND REFININg"

…to judge in finality all things, both evil and good. We ARE here, by God's sovereignty and express appointment, to declare God's true values and ways. I declare to you, that time is here Decades ago, the Lord Jesus Christ said to me that when the anti-Christ comes, people will receive him as Christ, and when the Christ (anointed one) comes, they will call Him anti-Christ. So it has been. the Lord comes in us in this wicked world and we personally identify with Him. Your judgment has come, not by our hand but by God's. He has done and will do His Own "dirty work." We don't need to lift a finger. Watch and see All of you powers of hell, in league, coming at once, are no match for Him, not even close—victor of harvest haven -- murder by decree, kevin annett

2/25/19 alphabelt wind chimes hung as marionettes—first geometryics, bthen letters—so the first from the second—cf soleri
Consider a collection of literature, blake stevens…
Cymatics
Bravo yogurt gfmaf
https://www.orthomolecularproducts.com/

2/26/19 Pat came home clearly distressed last night but didn't know why. This morn she told how Jason had presented having fallen off a roof in chandler

2/27/19 New fiction title, A Rare Burp
-- HELP BUILD the WALL, [HBtW]
What?

2/28/19 from Goya's war: It sometimes happens when the time is right and we aren't listening we hear as when in a mass singing the introit the voices of the whole and not ourselves and this can happen twice, so that the sadness and pain, of joy and love we sing and sign apart are joined as one and we hear at once the beauty and sorrow of all the human song. As though we having felt sorrow and pain of our sins now feel sorrow for the sins of another, our sons, and the sins of the world.
--shungite https://store.shungite.com/?aff_id=4951

3/1/19 a revisit of a dream some time ago, many large, obese men in large trucks I had offended who said they would return show up at Spice spg which is larger than real and work they way through, apprehending and taking an investigation. I sit in a chair eyes averted as this occurs, something about an offense unremembered, the size of the 3 at the porn store that time with TCBundy, but more powerful but it associates with the LAM and Ladoit and Hal, one a ncaa wrestler and the other hatchet man for Tom Gola at Lasalle, like all the men at that mission supremely confident in all they did.
You don't have a present unless you guard and protect , honor the past

3/2/19 burn the weeds office, 2 hrs plus

3/3/19 the after life is filled with vain memories of moments replayed. Bill Russell must replay his epics with wilt chamberlin. The 5 home runs, the one great tennis match against the #2 in college, the one basketball game at ocean City, the list goes on. But in the afterlife life atrophies. Those you knew die and or become estranged.
Some get honors but my parents had every one they knew die
around them. --theodore's b-day at Railroad Park. "It's
everybody's birthday." Sound takes:
Giants and little tykes -2-

1/17/19 forgetMother in law
of the church claims abuse
intimidation
-- This is the raw video cut and stripped so the sound and text could appear in April's AntipodalSF. The conceptual realities besides giants could fill an entry in the new Americana-Britannica. Along with the PupPoets, those Little Types of Mouthful Feeding Anomaly, MFAs and Privileged Professors there are Encephalitic obesities.The best proof this is not abetting the horrid imagination even Swift fled to make these subjects real is that Dream People had it

up a while, but it went around the world rejected until the Australians took it as either visionary or culpable. This proves the hierarchy wants nothing to do with the notions of poppup-poets who tend the giant's mess, the indictment of poetry. Eat and be eaten, they say in Poetry Mind. Here is a rough cut video of the recording from which the final was edited.

3/4/19 Aunt ann says amasa clark wrote to luther Burbank (about peaches?). She used to ride as a child on horseback sitting in from of Poppy in the saddle.
Popous little twits quotes
Land on the sun, at night
Bread goes in toast come ot what happens to the bread.
The Pedophile Hunter DAN REED
Michael Jackson openly kept a boy harem and was approved by all the ring of stars as their exemplar.

--A call to the unregenerate to appear at Outsiders and Surrealists.-fall

3/5/19 there are schools of interpretation that build upon each other, drawing adherents from the top schools, the peer review sources. These define more or less what can be accepted about a subject whether in science or literature. The Gold Age is one os these that has a long history of academic overbelief, a little like biblical literature of the Old Testament which spawned its documentary hypothesis in the 19th cent which became a overbelief. The golden Age has certain shibboleths of acceptance. First of these is the assumption that it is an ancient state in the subconscious mind of all people and therefore represents an archetype of longing. Indeed archetype is another of these beliefs itself which is accepted as factual as gravity. And more recently deconstruction and social justice became accepted norms.
"Hope made the decision to kill the little baby" is today's song. You can hear it on soundcloudhttps://soundcloud.com/ae-reiff/whoo-whoo. I don't like acceptance of the norm. Here are some faces to view.
Quatum entanglement phones not 5 G
Coelescing universe, shrink probability field around each choice
Corporate psychonauts
Violet spectrum
Nmn
Gsmaf cream
Leslie Scalapino, had died. Leslie's most recently published book, FLOATS HORSE-FLOATS OR HORSEFLOWS, is just out from Starcherone,

Seventeen is the sum of the first four prime numbers
Seventeen is the seventh prime number. The next prime is nineteen, with which it forms a twin prime.
Seventeen is a permutable prime and a supersingular prime.

Seventeen is the third Fermat prime, as it is of the form $2^{2n} + 1$, specifically with n = 2.[1]
Since 17 is a Fermat prime, regular heptadecagons can be constructed with a compass and unmarked ruler. This was proven by Carl Friedrich Gauss.[2]
There are exactly 17 two-dimensional space (plane symmetry) groups. These are sometimes called wallpaper groups, as they represent the seventeen possible symmetry types that can be used for wallpaper.
Like 41, the number 17 is a prime that yields primes in the polynomial $n^2 + n + p$, for all positive n < p − 1. Either 16 or 18 unit squares can be formed into rectangles with perimeter equal to the area; and there are no other natural numbers with this property. The Platonists regarded this as a sign of their peculiar propriety; and Plutarch notes it when writing that the Pythagoreans "utterly abominate" 17, which "bars them off from each other and disjoins them".[3]
Seventeen is the minimum possible number of givens for a sudoku puzzle with a unique solution. This was long conjectured, and was proved in 2012.[4][unreliable source?]
There are 17 orthogonal curvilinear coordinate systems (to within a conformal symmetry) in which the threevariable Laplace equation can be solved using the separation of variables technique.
Seventeen is the sixth Mersenne prime exponent, yielding 131071.
Seventeen is the first number that can be written as the sum of a positive cube and a positive square in two different ways; that is, the smallest n such that $x^3 + y^2 = n$ has two different solutions for x and y positive integers. The next such number is 65.
Seventeen is the minimum number of vertices on a graph such that, if the edges are coloured with three different colours, there is bound to be a monochromatic triangle. (See Ramsey's theorem.)
Seventeen is the only prime number which is the sum of four consecutive primes (2,3,5,7). Any other four consecutive primes summed would always produce an even number, thereby divisible by 2 and so not prime.

3/6/19 subvention Calumet Editions
Sarabande bks
Dznac, Sundress, Tin House, Gobbet,

Futhark, Milk Vetch, Hard Fern to be at Gambler,
Blechnum spicant (Hard Fern
 This plant grows in subalpine and alpine climates, often in moist areas, such as woodlands and meadows around streams and lakes. It also occurs on tundra and other cold, dry, exposed areas. It occurs on gravel bars and scree. It is sometimes a pioneer species, colonizing land in the primary phase of ecological succession, such as roads and bare land turned over during frost heave. It has been observed regrowing early in recently burned areas in Grand Teton National Park. It also grows in vegetated areas.[1] Plants occurring in harsh conditions are smaller than those in more favorable sites.[2]

This plant species provides food for caribou, Arctic hares, greater snow geese, small blue butterflies, and grizzly bears
https://www.discoverlife.org/mp/20q?search=Astragalus+alpinus&flags=glean:

3/7/19 Cannes 30
Wallace Stevens, Voices and Visions rubino

3/8/19 served down in the Pentonville Prison but was a model inmate so was released to continue his career in dentistry. He served in the States where his offenses were less known and now in Antarctica at McMurdo. A citizen of three nations, born Argentine, he was made a British citizen through the British Penal Citizenship program at the model Pentonville Prison, served for various offenses in youth but which resulted in his admission to the practice. He continued his education at York and Sussex U in jaw formation and hybrid and synthetic speech. After serving at Eau Claire Mayo, Denai, and Fukushima Prefecture he became a U.S. citizen by corporate contract, being his third passport, to train and embark to his present location where he combines all the above and he is taking further courses in glacierology.

continue his career in dentistry, a little tainted. He served in capacities in the States where his offenses were less known and now works in Antarctica at the McMurdo Station. A citizen of three nations, first born Argentine, he was made a British citizen through the British Penal Citizen ship program at the model pentonville prison, the when he served some years for various offenses in youth but which resulted in lhis education in te practice ef dentistry. Emerging, he continued his education at York and Sussex U in jaw formation of hybrid and synthetic speech to such a degree that after serving at Eau Claire Mayo, the Paracelsus Clinic at Denai, and Fukushima Prefecture he became a U.S. citizen by his employment with corporate status, being his third passport, needed to train and embark to his present location at McMurdo Station in Antarctica, which he comibines all the above dental and penal arts on a contract basis and has begun further courses in glacierology.
--1910 when German chemists Fritz Haber and Carl Bosch invented what is called the Haber–Bosch Process— which remains to this day the only known method to extract nitrogen from the air, and since its invention, has led to an explosion in human population growth that had remained virtually balanced with nature for thousands of years.

3/9/19 all the early writing of elimae is a comedy. All comedies celebrating life
In some odd sense I must have asked to be involved in history, but that is not what I remember, which is instead the progressive uncovering of the feeling of displacement, as though I were on the Kinder transport with Geoffrey Hartman, or prisoner in camp with Levinas, which shows where my sympathies lie. My own displacements were manifold but at the same time their confounding did not exclude a sense of place that forms identity and character and a discovered family. Immersions in successive natural and social environments of Germantown PA, the Chartiers valley valley, rivers of western and central PA, Allegheny, Clarion and Susquehanna, the pine barrens of New Jersey and the sand hills of N Carolina,

led inexorably to the Edwards Plateau of the Texas Hill country, the Balcones Fault, Bull Creek, the Medina, Frio and Guadalupe rivers with points west and south in the range of the madrones and marriage into the families of those who had first settled there when Texas was a sudden and primitive place and time of 1850. Chronicles of these explorations over the Chihuahuan desert and mountains are written in Native Texans, Some Medicinal, Social and Philosophic Contexts of the Plants of Texas and the Southwest.

So there is an identity of place which makes the poem kindle the mind. There is all before the fact where we live, and before realization and consciousness which come after what we make of ourselves, what we don't know, or if we do what courage we have to stick it out in the midst of our misprison's deliberate concealment. Being a child is like a dream where it's possible to be conscious but hard to be an actor. Childhood is like a dream we wake up from. Our misprisons so differ from each other that they are incalculable and incomprehensible, a relentless observation of eccentric borders and analysis of circumstances. Poems of the process of birth, coming into the body that later preoccupy this meditation were begun in the house overlooking the high wall of an orphanage, where from their bars the inmates would taunt at the world behind their literal iron fence. To be given a sensibility and an experience, but not know it, is the essence of discovery of dislocation. These children and their imprisonment, the confounding of the child, preoccupy my imaginations lead to a cultivation of a naive art, peasant if you like, rustic, primitive, but ironically that family had inhabited those regions of colonial Philadelphia of Pennsylvania Fathers and elsewhere pretty much from their founding, which of course we are at pains eventually to discover in the many extensive ethnographic examinations, so I was the opposite of displaced.

Then in the Sonoran desert, in the Salt River valley, in helping to found the solo doc Mcdowell Family
Medical, I pursued athletic, trading and artistic endeavors as a ceramic sculptor @ Forms of the Formless. After the fall of the Soviet regime I escorted the all female McConnell Singers of Phoenix College through the large and small towns of the Czech Republic, Prague, Loket-Elbogen, Cheb-Eger, Karlovy Vary, Horni Slavkov- Schlaggenwald "Impact Gene Forest," and also Vienna, Oberammergau, Ettal, and Munich.

--Jenny Constantine dna
-- dave hunt what love is this calvinism's misrepresentation of god. Calvinism more aggressive 4.31

Interpretations
1. **Understand the nature of the parables.**
2. **Understand the purpose of parables.**
3. **See the parable in its proper context.**
4. **Remember the cultural gap.**
5. **Parables usually have one main point.**
6. **Take notice of surprise details**

7. Not every minor detail has significant meaning.
8. Notice "stock imagery" in the parables.
9. The ending of parables is very important
10. Be careful with allegorical interpretations of parables.

3/10/19 Natsarim

In invented the green new deal ten years in obamaland. When the shititzus ShihTzu were really singing. AOC and her team new comer disaffects from BernieLand. Bernie Sanders retreads.You tink I was kidding with the throwaway lines everybodys goinna be rich and happy, but that was to hammer in WE GONNA TAKE OVER
THE DEMOCRATIC PARTY. AND WAER GOINNA SEE SOMETHING THAT'S NEVER BEEN DONE BEFORE. OH YEAH, DIG IT, WE'RE GONNA HAVE A NEW EARTH

3/11/19
Space Flight
First Preliminary Root of the Mars Waking
Part I of Document B of the CheesE Blocks Mar 2008
Mars Writing the disappearance of the NASA blogs
Ailin Penlight, Sidebrow, May 2007
Spiritual Tour of the Grand Canyon, spring 2009
Writing on the Wall. Why Vandalism Literary and Arts Journal. Nov 2007 Invisible Giants, The Dream People,
Issue 31, Spring 2009 Tom Goat in space. elimae. May 2011.
Herb Cures Of Urk Tongue
Pancake Syntazz, Vulcan: A Literary Dis-Allusion, III, Fall 2009, 66-7.
Sky Shadows. Jack, June 2010
A Christmas Story. elimae, Nov 2007

Children's Stories
Elsie Marley

Histories
The McConnell Singers Czech Republic Concert Tour. Oct 2006
Stick Up! [How To Make a Mennonite Sing] elimae, April 2007
Native Texans. elimae, Apr 2008
Downfall of the Demonots. elimae, Sept 2008
Remembering Jose Donoso (1924-1996) elimae, February 2009
Legends of the Fall, Eyeshot, Aug 2008
Taking Down the Elder, Jack, Spr ing 2009
Sky Shadows. Jack, June 2010
Travels to Byzantium.Eyeshot. 9 June 2012
Opiomes the Domes. Red Fez 66. 13 Apr 2014

The Sixth Landing. Gobbet. 23 July 2014
Oracle. Red Fez 71. 13 Sept 2014
Colonia. Farther Stars Than These. 12 Nov 2015
Forward Blue Superposition I. The Gambler. Summer 2016.
A History of Che Guevara's Hair. Gobbet. 13 July. 2016

SEVERAL MASHES. Mad Bunkers Mash Up Review, June 2010. Issue 11 of Mad Hatters Review

LIFE IN A CEMENT BLOCK #5
You get Digital dual screen TV.
Now you can watch both ways if you like,
as Wordsworth said "to see into the life of
things." What's it like to be on, in and
outside TV? Like eyes! Whether it's
noble to be called the binonomial?

3/12/19 I saw Elsie marley, aka Mylogie Soups made set in word process type with the illustrations jpeged in

Once a Presbyterian always a presbyterian
--take modern investigation os consciousness or some other and set it to the video of the drive to texas
--LIFE IN A CEMENT BLOCK 5
You get Digital dual screen TV.
you can both watch both ways if you
like, as Wordsworth said "see into
the life of things." What's it like to
be on, in and outside TV? Like eyes!
Whether it's noble to be called binomial?
3/13/19 Leda and Swan, m. Jerusalem ms, end p.m.
3/14/19 more Jeru ms edition- ch. edited Next to end and one before
3/15/19 Plasma and ionization, metals sliver and gold from sun. Putting Lasty in book form
3/16/19 wo things. I overheard that one person unnamed but known to be A had been found out and was no longer allowed to practice and
2) Sixth landing and Soul "Spinning together are one chapter in Jerusalem that are pretext for all the rest of the events.

Desert Botanical garden sale atriplex canescens fourwing saltbush Big Sagebrush-artemisis tridentata
Globe mallow, pink- speralcea ambiga Oenotherea elata hookeri Lyceum sp. polymentha

derek broes

There is a tradition that Wold descends from Peter Waldo, founder of the Waldensians, the sect of voluntary poverty and strict adherence to the Bible, who migrated from the south of Europe to the north. Peter Waldo fashioned the Bible into Provencal, the first version of the Bible to appear outside of Latin. There is some confirmation of this in Wold's poetical side, rarely seen, as in his romances of the natural world. Speaking of that world, another explanation of the name, elides to the universal suffering of the man Waldo, the radical Christian of the Poor of Lyons, the Poor of Lombardy, the Poor of God disguised as peddlers taking again the human dimension of a man.

3/17/19 kids for the day 11-4. After running to Grandma over milk and etc Theo leaves his chair climbs in my lap for 15 min. AB in play finally gets out all her joy in yard, built a trail of old cement blocks, then made it into a fountain, sprinkler, on bed in roughhouse , fall, saving,, then walk canal, read, parents come, visit. Nickolai lolls in our laps with big eyes, I say June 11 my only holy day. Tease S. that if the redbud isn't red, buas she says, then the green she wears, barfely, isn't green! Then A. saying A needs a jack hmmer for his wall, she agrees, I mock and say he needs a sledge, I was only kidding! Love is so much better than the rest.

3/18/19 dream a locust nest secreted in house. An extermatior comes smears some salve over it. Some locust begin to exit. I take the nest, a but beehive like bag or box, outside a good distance off. The locusts begin to expolode like firecreackesrs for a long time, scattering like expend shells over a large area. Pat says she dreamed of me dancing in her night.

3/19/19
Steve Almond, William Stoner and the Battle for the Inner Life:
Bookmarked John Williams, stoner

Architectonics may be sonar or material.
3/20/19 best new years eve ever. Silent absolutely. A long reading and memory of Wordsworth's poems. -also consider chage to Parables, put

3/21/19 it seems to me that Genesis and John disprove the divine council, even if Elohim is plural and us occurs, the whole of scripture is the redemption by the Son who made the world, the world was made by Him, and ruled by him not a divine council, Sumerian borrowing.
Lunch in Chandler with Aeg. Begin block 6

3/22/19 Simply, no one was a "Christian" prior to A.D. 325. All the churches that claim to be Christian today are merely daughters of the Roman stylized system of false worship of"Hail Zeus Christna," with their own sanctified spin and variation on doctrinal beliefs. Prior to that year all of the Messiah's obedient early believers referred to themselves as the Natsarim (Nazarenes)

The 1611 KJV spells the Messiah's name as Isous. CHRISTIAN or MASHIAHIYIM So the Jews changed the Name in Babylon and the Natsarim were changed to Christian in Rome.

Scotty's WiFi s threat to health--Repeated Wi-Fi studies show that Wi-Fi causes oxidative stress, sperm/testicular damage, neuropsychiatric effects including EEG changes, apoptosis, cellular DNA damage, endocrine changes, and calcium overload 5G wireless The human skin as a sub-THz receiver - Does 5G pose a danger to it or not?

Betzalel N, Ben Ishai P, Feldman Y. The human skin as a sub-THz receiver - Does 5G pose a danger to it or not? Environ Res. 2018 May;163:208-216.

Highlights

- The sweat duct is regarded as a helical antenna in the sub-THz band, reflectance depends on perspiration.
- We outline the background for non-thermal effects based on the structure of sweat ducts.
- We have introduced a realistic skin EM model and found the expected SAR for the 5G standard.

Abstract

In the interaction of microwave radiation and human beings, the skin is traditionally considered as just an absorbing sponge stratum filled with water. In previous works, we showed that this view is flawed when we demonstrated that the coiled portion of the sweat duct in upper skin layer is regarded as a helical antenna in the sub-THz band.
--proof on how the nephilim will return—all scripture and enoch—mueller report

3/23/19 short bright copper hair—like the wire to use on #6
Solinus, Wunder der WElt
C.IVLII Solini [Polyhistora] Enarrationes. - MELA, Pomponius - Joachim Vadianus. Libri De Situ Orbis
Tres,...
by SOLINUS, Caius Julius (second half 3rd-century AD) - CAMERS, Giovanni Ioannis (1468-1546) Condition: See description

_____

Vienna: Johannes Singrenius for Lucas Alantse, 1520., 1520. THE FIRST AVAILABLE PRINTED MAP TO BEAR THE NAME AM ERICA Two works in one volume. Folio (11 6/8 x 8 2/8 inches). Cordiform woodcut world map, woodcut title-page borders, historiated initials, printer's mark, both works include the final blank leaf. Contemporary limp vellum (sewn on three pairs of pink tawed thongs, early manuscript liners, early ink title and traces of early manuscript paper label on spine, evidence of two fore-edge ties (some minor restoration to covers); modern cloth clamshell box. This volume, actually comprises two works within a single binding, in an instance of a common sixteenth-century book-collecting practice. Both are rare works of signal importance, with the present examples in extraordinary condition. The first is Joannes Camers' edition of the Polyhistor, an ancient treatise on natural history by Caius Julius Solinus (flourished ca. 250 AD). After Ptolemy, Solinus was the classical authority whose writings most strongly informed Renaissance geographical thought. Camers's version of the Polyhistor is quite desirable to collectors, for it contains the earliest obtainable map to name America: Peter Apian's splendid double-page map of the world, at the left of which the new continent appears prominently labeled. Apian, a professor of mathematics at Vienna and Ingolstadt, based his map on Martin Waldseemüller's 1507 rendering, the only surviving example of which is in the Library of Congress.

Waldseemüller's map supported Amerigo Vespucci's revolutionary concept that the New World was a separate continent, previously unknown to the Europeans, and his was the first map to show a separate Western

Hemisphere with the Pacific as a separate ocean. Although Waldseemüller himself had realized, after 1507, that Vespucci was not the discoverer of the New World, Apian's duplication of his predecessor's nomenclature etched the name America into popular consciousness.

The second book is an equally marvelous example of a key work published by the same Viennese press:

Joachim Vadianus's edition with commentary of the first-century AD treatise by Roman geographer Poponius Mela. This 1518 edition also contains Vadianus's letter to his colleague, the Swiss humanist Rudolf Agricola, in which he outlines the geographical problems posed by the recent discovery of the New World and upholds Waldseemüller's decision to name the continent in honor of Vespucci. This treatise, therefore, was also highly influential in directing popular opinion and in bestowing upon the New World the name that it bears to this day.
REFERENCES: Lloyd Arnold Brown, The World Encompassed, exh. cat. (Baltimore, 1952), n. 61; Rodney W. Shirley, The Mapping of the World (London, 1983), n. 45; Philip D. Burden, The Mapping of North America: A List of Printed Maps 1511-1670 (Rickmansworth, 1996), xxiv-v..

But to take this as bipolar is a set up for what of the case where the good is the evil is the good, which is still lineral, not quantum entanglement which would entail a quaternary, which is indeed the immediate cause of all structural states of the Wunder der Welt where the democrats defile trump who sets up the third temple! Who rcognized Jerusalem, the Golan heights, has an apartment like Apollo

3/24/19 The misadventures of Tom Goat
 Skull and bones-Trump
SVR analysts, however, this report concludes, have long suspected that "Skull and Bones" has long had in their possession a secret map of underground Jerusalem showing the location of a mysterious object some believe is the Ark of the Covenant—and which vast tunnel digging under Jerusalem by the Israelis last year (that led to the stunning discovery of Second Temple stones) may have discovered—and if so, would then have to see this powerful and mysterious

ancient religious artifact having to be placed in the Third Temple—that does not yet exist, as it would have to be built on the site of the Islamic religion's most holiest site in Jerusalem called the Al-Aqsa Mosque—and if destroyed to build the Third Temple, would see Israel being attacked by the entire Muslim world it could only defend itself against with American military power and its having full possession of the strategic high ground region known as the Golan Heights—and which President Trump, in fact, did declare fully belongs to Israel yesterday—that was followed by his Secretary of State Mike Pompeo stating firmly that Trump was sent by God to protect Israel and the Jewish people, and his then viewing a model of the Third Temple—followed a few hours later by Special Counsel Mueller announcing his investigation into Trump had ended—all of which combined marks the "Skull and Bones" number "322" as denoting not just one of the most important dates in the history of Trump, but the entire world, too—at least to those who know the full power and unmistakable reality of what the Bible has foretold of the end times.

gods of ground zero by carl gallups
++Skywatch investigates final

3/25/19-dreamed of floods
I saw thrones on which were seated those who had been given authority to judge.-Revelation20:
"mortality's ground floor is immortality" EmilyD The Social Vision of
William Blake By Michael Ferber

apocatastasis
from bear in attic: When those ships set down on once wide ocean I was carried to land. The bark put to shore and toddled up like limestone in a grandfather walking. I wouldn't do it! says somebody, but they do. This constitutes our trebling, the difference vs. real, a County family, myth and para-myth in Homer, in Amaranth, that leaves its seat as "the sons of light haste."
The wilderness is the dappled shade that hides bear, the thing longed for, not the talk of mind, full of hills and rivers, dreams each night that background everywhere the wood. "We have heard of you but now our eyes have seen" could be said of anybody toddling up and down
4chan lit javascript:quote('12827233'); reply to thread 12823770

3/26/19 visit with aey, sent 41000 to Dana dunford

3/27/19 a lunchtime stroll in downtown Chandler? So A will not gaslight himself
--Stark lines of porcelin and black ridges in planes hung in space
--The last clause, "the Head of Christ is God," gives (as is St. Paul's custom, see 1Corinthians 3:23; 1Corinthians 8:6; 1Corinthians 15:25) completeness to the thought. As the Head of the Church--i.e., as the man Christ Jesus--Christ is subordinate to the Father, and, indeed, perhaps the idea is carried farther into the mystery of the divine nature itself, as consisting of

three Persons co-eternal and co-equal, yet being designated with an unvarying sequence as "first," and "second," and "third."

-- The head of Christ is God. That Christ is "inferior to the Father as touching his manhood," that his mediatorial kingdom involves (so far) a subordination of his coequal Godhead, has been already stated in 1

Corinthians 3:23, and is further found in 1 Corinthians 15:27, 28. This too is the meaning of John 14:28, "My Father is greater than I."

Excerpt from: Blue Beamed Aliens Presents
With Nathaniel Hawthorne on Mt Shasta
In case fiction takes a stroll and becomes reality, and the great intellects of 4Chan are right, a Draco Space
Craft is coming to join the Pope to reinterpret the Gospels. True believers will be redefined. To not believe will not be good. Censorship will be beyond your friends disowning you because you voted for Trump, but don't worry, in The Eclipse of the Church, as Malachi Martin says, when that administration announces the alien, there will be Exhilaration! (see Jose G. Funes).

Call it fiction when further on the False Prophet is installed. According to St. Malachy and Fr. René Thibaut, Gentle Francis will make all one together with charismatics and institute a new Me Church. But hurry. The teaching of a hundred thousand divines from the Reformation on have it that if the worship of a morally superior alien comes to earth to evangelize, and you pull down the strongholds with the blood of the Lamb and tread upon the serpent, those multidimensionals will be mighty upset.

It seems a lot to accept, too bad, but as the Vatican said of the film Prometheus, it's a bad idea to defy the gods, meaning the god-forces of Daniel (11.38) that call down fire. When lightning struck St. Peter's Basilica twice, on Feb 11, 2013, following Pope Benedict's resignation that is to say, a new comet, fell from heaven to decree the arrival. Saints given power over serpents and scorpions and over all the power of the enemy and undisclosed reports of Rising parallels between Washington D.C. and Rome, both came right down to obelisk, dome and flying X orb formations.

Technology advanced to the Vatican and D.C. from the Leave It to Obama era to the Trump. Entities want a return match. Navy Commander Alvin E. Moore saw "two huge crosses of pearly white vapor x's of gas or vapor..." (9 Nov) but when giant obelisks, 666 feet in height and base, commemorate the giant phallus in the second round knockout of this war, and fire is called from cloaks, you'll likely be thinking this makes the world safe, until they tell you about the meaning of the X and it don't.

All this emerged from Nathaniel Hawthorne's visit to Mt Shasta. Constant borrowing of New Testament language about the "angel of light," and "do unto others" announced Blue Avians joining in Full Disclosure at the round table of spiritual knights. Then from the lenticular cloud over Mt. Shasta, or from the hollow earth came….

But as somebody once said, since Earth is the Jewel of the Universe and A Man is the Highest Created Being, all the stars are coming here.

Comments

Heather Joyce Ferguson Oh rubbish! (directed towards the master). Your pottery pieces are magnificent, of startling originality. They are highly intuitive. They have nothing to explain or justify. Sometimes happy accidens happen, and one embraces them. This is how we make progress. It's called play. Work which feels compelled to reference itself to earlier works, even one's own, do not break new ground. But you know all this already.

He wanted to get that off his chest. The ceramics world is pretty cliquish, probably from the pressure to sell. I only explore certain ideas give to me, once sold a piece for $50 at the Herberger, keep all the ones that still teach. Cement blocks do le…See More
  Huh? Cancelling a trip? No! Silly ...
•
Heather Joyce Ferguson You must pay attention to my posts if you know I am in Ottawa. You are in or near Marfa, that magical place. I am a fan of Glasstire, discovered that last year.
•
I am about a thousand miles from Glasstire even if the trip drives itself over the flats and mountains, but I am a putative Marfite, so much so that I'm taking off nefarious potting this summer to try to collect the scapulant writings found along the Marfa flats all the way up to Alpine, and others, but, in fact, I am mandated a spot on the Grand Canal here to pursue the ironwood forests prohibited by the colder Chihuahuan desert, which you might say the tortoises demand. I was once an itinerant to Toronto however, some years ago, to the Peoples Church, and had significant connections with Isaac R. Horst in Winnepeg regarding the Letters of Bishop Andrew Mack in much the same way I count KIaus Gerken of your Ottawa a friend for all the kindnesses that Ygdrasil, A Journal of the Poetic Arts has done me--a journal that loves poetry! How rare is that! and besides yourself in Ottawa with such insights of the flow of art once had many exchanges with one who had cut my poem out of a big centerpiece spread in the old Mennonite and put it on her refrigerator door, A Green Tree. All of these I count among the great blessings and treasures of my life.

3/28/19 composed Black hole Down

3/29/19
Dear sir, I respond to your call for 3000 words. I don't know how much mail you get from the south of you and whether you might be inclined to these researches such as they are of a dentist in Antarctica or even whether your advertisement for your issue 250 is open to such foreigners, for I have not made your proper acquaintance, even if I hope to, at least in this formal submission of my Black Hole Down to this upcoming, and if not I sure had fun in writing it. So when the dogsleds pulled in and I read of this I thought to publish my discoveries here in, as it were, anagogical form, hence I address you from somewere out of McMurdo on the way to the Antarctic Mountains and Mt Erebus as long at least as the battery lasts,. Yours truly, Rubino del Sur

3/30/19 Momma don't let your clay grow up into cement blocks! I took her advice. Even though Block #5 got picked up today, and #6, a big boy, is waiting, today's block went bad and turned into a box! Why, why? why me! Can't even make a proper cement block?
Oh course now I have a cement box I have to make a top. And plus the thing slopes looks like its running off to build a garden wall. it must think its a block not a box. This is true identity art

3/31/19 Aey design beams, Judah and Zion, Angel in Sun at Penny, 100 lbs flour

AEY- 1A/2A State Tennis singles champion 2003, state champion and led team to one
Captain Glendale Tennis. Led to 9th place National Junior College Championships
Junior competition. Division I
Unseeded entry in SW Junior Closed, won the Bronze 2006
Lead in Angels Aware,
City Jazz, first trumpet
Honor society
Singing and making music in your heart toward God
The guitar
Model railroad, train hobbyist
Run cross country two years- 20.31.36 1A/2A State Meet, 11/3/2001
Joggy! Prayer and Tyger
Tap dancing
Camping
Hunting with Grandad
Initiative in choosing profession, NP
Emcc of Phoenix College Graduation
All sales and book scout experiences
All trips to ranch and to Philadelphia with and me and take Lib to Barnes with mom
Ben at water and ice
Enable Aegto play at that level and his own tournament play –in the lead-always in the lead --a year off after h.s. photography
All the ceramic statutes in h.s. and after, tolkein
Natural artist,
Earle estate

4/1/19 I don't understand how the world can be the same after Herbert
and Hopkins O the mental intercourse of you Carnalites.
I'm a Joe Biden of the mind
I feel your thoughts

4/2/19 Jericho, Ai and the Reprobate Mind

When Ai came to Tempe she cashed in her library at the rare book stores. I got her proof of Sin and her ed of Creeley's Collected signed and inscribed, but that is not the whole story. Or what it was like when she went to Jericho.

How much is Tempe like Jericho? Besides the singe and the asking Gary Sange? Absurd. The likeness to Top Goat is legion. After all Tempe is the town that wouldn't give a better parking spot to Rita Dove so she went, after the Pulitzer, to Melon. Whether you go to Melon or Tempe or Jericho, and ride the circuit of the jpoet adorato, is not so clear where the walls didn't come tumbling down exactly. They were torn down the way a democrat wants to open their doors to the mauraders and the ppope builds little traveling alters for migrfants in every wayside and restop, the death of nations is that important. Jericho achieve d its death from all records we have seen-but the as a trip to Jericho, overwhelming factior in it, and in Rome, to be so bold, is the reprobate mind designed by tSt. Paul to describe those lminds, which, stop right there, what is a mind that we should addrfess it as such, is it conscious, has it a sould, or is it like some traveling wraith of an AI, not to be diverfse, or is some hybrid reality - HYBRID- hardly is that aworld out when a vast image out of seculary mundi uncovers itself- lionwomanman is more noble sounding than shiny ghibboreth ant or grasshopper, bat and mole, good for all occasions you see, driven into the genes of a man who can function as long as the switch is on to empower the gods to conquer a man. Tlhis man is hard to beat, since he was made to destroy those gods and they know it but what they they do since his day is coming as much as Jericho's is is reprobate. Days man means judge after all and to judge the world, forfend, and Ai, And Tempe with his hydrosonic gene labs busing grafting the tone, what it is to be reprobate is to be given up. This is the one thing the moder state cannot and will not do as long as it is in their interest, but if not it won't. Tlhat's clear. It's like if you go past a certain poin in waywardness, beyond the natural, give yourself to demons, invoke and invite and seek, a poart of your mind, call it your humanity leaves and you look and talk and act like one, but underneath you are roving psychoact with no human feeling, conscious left. Like Joe Biden you may say, full of horror and morality. Tlhe Horro mongels, the horror moguels of Hollywood are like the residetns of Jericho. What were they do during the ominous stomp stamp stomp of the people ringing their city. Selling entrails were no longer a bargain then. Everything went up in price. The Sacrifices, divinations and the temples of Baal were fuoll, not like England and America, Farance and Germany, no only in Russia is the faith strong, And the mogels have turned Russia into the northern horde, when in Washington he beast plans its eternal reward.

Dylan louis Monroe

Incredible Compilation !!! ~ History of the Cult of the Deep State (Baal)
https://youtu.be/0V1O1hhOw7Q
King's chamber: stark, austere, anonymous
Aey's birthday at office

4/3/19 novus orgus secularum

BLUEPRINTS OF DREAM
I'm putting this UP to honor my distinguished sound engineer and all his achievements, and to show what thiNGS WERE in the raw state before it rings in the ear, HIGHER THAN A HORSE, HIGHER THAN A TREE...
peregrine sun guangyi first I like hearing of doings in China of recent decades and today. What I see savors of the past

4/5/19 review mike newcomb for Aey. Haul office branches to dump in the 18ft. Hyper exteneded shoulder thowing branches.

4/6/19 Cement block six is good. Sent Landings to Vision. A and S date night. Sent with kids at their house. Very dear. Pat takes fall unloading pallets there with me. Time to watch our feet.

4/7/19 manxanita for off fungi in space

Nuclear event large epiphanies of light, after effects like rockets at white sands. Four carrions blasted into space or spaceward, effects on mountain sides drifting dust dust, time for more algae pills, provoked by the reins, psalm 139 he shall tell all my reins, kidneys source of dream, wake in middle otherwise no memory of dream, that makes this note

Phoenix bonzai society at valley garden center. Exhibitiions clay
Sweep gravel off parking lot next Sun, fill pot holes, prepared for bid. Found welded wire two rolls, contractor os asphalpt yesterfay

4/8/19 Reflection: all this work is good, Landings etc. but it all begins with the a priori assumption that it will not be known until after.

4/9/19 Mondayi, yesterday, Pat called at 2 to say she wasn't going ot pot because she had vomited three times, which with the blow to her head and Aey consult suggested possible suddural hematoma so I asked for insight and guiding, went to see her, went over the guidelines of observation etc, but asked you Father for help. Slhe is everyting to me.. Aey went with A to get A's new Versa, used then came over to check at my urging, said he had original research viz. that A just said he got home and threw up four times, that the kids had it, lending support to Pat's notion it was flu like etc. and much relieved, she was however still weak, that my prayer was so answered.

4/10/19 DNA triggers. DNA is not immutable but triggers, releases from a host of good and bad effects.Wed

4/11/19 just before I wojem at 6!, we were being ushered to an outdoor pew in Advanced Presbyterian church.

I had a golf bag with me! Ivve been rejected from every body politic I every joined, one way or another. Outre.

-the effulgence of light we surrendered in Eden.

Sabrina FB: Me: Teddy, you should always treat girls like they are princesses!

Teddy: okay, and girls should treat me like I'm a king!

Omg Teddy...you are one of a kind...

people are self censoring their online word use. That part of censorship works. Side effects are/will impact Natural Language Processing bots, chat bots, text analytics, college courses in same, as well as aggregation bots, and wall street algos. And ALL MSM media clif @clif_high 2h2 hours ago

Clif. testing for 5 days now complete. Very bad news. Censorship across platforms has shut down my predictive linguist engine. Too much extreme language. Prescient language reduced to mere drops where used to be rivers of it. Shutting down effort to bring back reports. All MSM 'news' cycles are driven by @twitter activity. Many of the 'news' bots are driven by @twitter activity.

I am finally, at least today, beginning to appreciate the greatness of these pieces I have been looking at for many years. To whoever will embrace it, and you know who you are, it is of utmost importance to keep faith with yourself and your creations, especially when they are unique, because they will be difficult to appraise, until finally you do.

Prescient lang reduction shuts down pred ling engine. Well worth saying

So THERE IS A WORD OF SIMULATANEOUS REFERENCE THAT EVOKES EVERY LANGUAGE, WORD, BEING, HOPE AND DREAM OF THE WORLD!

4/12/19 Thurs. "Cher look at my woman carry a cement block," I exited last nite, thurs. affronting a shock wave of of guarded speech. All speech is masculine, so is all language. Love is a collison of opposites.

--yayoo

--Assaunge arrest staged. In bed with Chelsea Manning, Fist pump, gore vidal book, [Perpetual War for

Perpetual Peace (2002) and Dreaming War: Blood for Oil and the Bush-Cheney Junta (2007)] History of The

National Security State eye wink, all photographed, promulgated

-- The robotic Beresheet spacecraft, couldn't quite make it, crashing, Mission control lost communications with the spacecraft when it was about 489 feet (149 meters) above the moon's surface.Bereshith!

-- the FCC will sell 3,400 megahertz in three different spectrum bands during the auction. the market, not government, is in the best position for privatization and investment the wireless field," Pai. inject $20.4 billion in expanding high-speed broadband networks in rural America over the next decade digital divide

4/13/19 Fri the slanders of the world of eve and the earth in gehry and Stockhausen Licht
"Michael, Lucifer and Eve are, for Stockhausen, more than theatrical figures. They are the expression of a world beyond, to which terrestrial eyes are blind, but which is given concrete

form by The Urantia Book and other sources" (Kurtz 1992, 228) and manga,, the solar system, as in the maleboge, Stockhausen aare all forms of 4D chess, enochian chess which to play is to make culpable, but the son of man who becomes the son of God supercedes all this and is put in the right place at the right time and is given the right words.

AZ Janet at Waco got her spurs, Jan Brewer,

--Literately every thing is symbolic thus cement blocks are of the obtuseneeess of guarded speech as if everyone were a politician, cutting out all prescience and insight which begins with contact with the thought stream

AEy sold the bench, cedar chest, etc. tried to sell Lib's table. Pat said I was angry! A blames me because he is under duress But none of them can either control their emotions or show an honest reaction, they temper it all with shut down censorship

-surveillance capitalism—FROM DUTCHSINSE This just happened today, March 1, 2019 ...The chance of this being "chance" is beyond astronomical, actually in the level of statistical impossibility. I'd have a better chance of winning powerball 15 times in a row actually.I'm into odds, as many of my viewers might know about forecasting probabilities, and other such things to do with averaging statistics...I did NOT have my phone on me in the store, it was in the car in the parking lot...It would appear that every move we make is now being sold, and the turnaround time is 1 hour or less between recording you, and targeting you with something.This means Walmart recorded me, then sold the recording immediately to a distributor or ad company who then has a deal with Yahoo , who then took my IP address at my house, matched it with my identity which was then further matched with the "shoppers profile" or whatever they call it, and then the targeted ad was generated based upon the interaction observed.

Fairview surveillnace

4/14/19 Biz Rate Capital Investment Inquest (ism) Internet
Emotional intelligence is the essense of the human
Sensorvault, according to Google employees, includes detailed location records involving at least hundreds of millions of devices worldwide and dating back nearly a decade.
--google deepmind
- tartaria mud flood.
Age of Disclosure channel, the research was done by a woman named Marcia Ramalho, The Blue.: arch openings, columns, domes and towers, in addition to details such as rose windows and muqarnas, symbols of the vibration of electromagnetic energy, which acts on molecules and changes the behavior of cells. All Tartary power stations, small and large, had pipe organs to harmonize and heal the population through sound waves, what is now known as "cymatics".
"The great dust-fall of february 1903, and its origin"
-- jeff gates youtube playlist
--andrew desantis

4/15/19 Writing is software. One glitch and it won't work. It must be conclusive.
Buzza Aldrin was the priest of the moon

The fire and the burning of Notre Dame.

4/16/'19/ ENIAC (/ˈiːniæk, ˈɛ-/; Electronic Numerical Integrator and Computer) was the first electronic general-purpose computer. It was Turing-complete, digital and able to solve "a large class of numerical problems" through reprogramming 1945
--perceptron- it was quickly proved that perceptrons could not be trained to recognise many classes of patterns, like confusing notre dame fire with 9/11
Due to complications of writing a kind of fiction best described by the category, Content Not to Be Named, the bio of this author became complicated, hence listed as the first person ever named for the chemical process of surfactancy, suitable for all satire. That name itself, AE, stands for those Alcohol Ethoxylate based surfactants, which being non-ionic, require longer ethoxylate chains than their sulfonated analogues to be water-soluble. Unsulfonated, AE transports this hydrocarbon exulate to poetry spills, drops letters in a caustic pot to bioremediate, accelerate and effectively deregulate oils to make them

4/17/19 Dave Robeson who went to prayer 8 hrs a day, climbed to the top of the castle and found king cockroach, pride "in the 21st century men will be machines' Hillie said, his left foot loose for the last time HoHoka bean,cleave to molecules small enough for microbes to digest.

4/18/19 Lunch with A. AB reading wants to take it to school as her own book. After all she says, those are my initials. Andrew said S amazed
E went to Europe as a senior, but she went to D.C. as a junior tooGiving praise forever to you.

CHANGE, OH WORLD

change, oh world! By all reason seen
My friend is to me
A voice in the darkness
A light I now see
Oh, should all light fade
I will hear your voice call A heart's voice, a mind's love And that matters all.

I know, my friend, that the years will pass
And I, I know, will change
But your love for me will forever last
Because, Savior, you're always the same.

change, oh world! By all reason seen
My friend is to me
A voice in the darkness
A light I now see
Oh, should all light fade

I will hear your voice call
A heart's voice, a mind's love
And that matters all.

I know, my friend, that I will fall I'll hurt you time and again. But, oh my friend, through it all
You'll take away all my sin.

change, oh world! By all reason seen
My friend is to me
A voice in the darkness
A light I now see
Oh, should all light fade
I will hear your voice call A heart's voice, a mind's love And that matters all.

I know, my friend, that time will fly
Eons disappear in the night And I, I know, even though I die
Will see you, my heavenly Light.

change, oh world! By all reason seen
My friend is to me
A voice in the darkness
A light I now see
Oh, should all light fade
I will hear your voice call A heart's voice, a mind's love And that matters all.

A SCENE FROM HEAVEN

I can look ahead and see the mountains
Where before was nothing but sky
The stars are shining bright but i do
not see them For there is a tear in my
eye.
My heart's desire at last has been reached,
The mountains are in view,
Soon I will be climbing, ascending in search of
one, Ascending in search of you.

Oftentimes we met on the earth down
below and held each other's hands
and hearts, Now that we are here,
we'll never want to leave it We are
free from evil's arts.

Now that I can see you, at last face to face
I can't think of what to say
Shall I speak of the past or look to the
future Where love eternal's bright as
day?

My last thoughts were of you "Where are you now?"
"I wish that I could see you again."
Oh, had I known how soon that wish would be
granted Now that we're both free from all pain.

I can look ahead and see the mountains Where before was nothing but tears. I look at you, see the grief on your face We are now beyond those years.
My heart's desire at last has been reached I have seen you once again.
Let us now ascend to the bliss waiting for us What we thought was loss is gain.

Memory can play tricks on you

Evil invented evil to call it self good so when you think of evil you don't think of good. All language and concepts coopeted by this

Judd McGraw part 4: call at 9 from office, big truck pulled in on grounds beside bldg. to install sign. Doc went out but no response, called me. Mcgraw not in today, guy moved truck. Pushing women around does not endear me to them. Disrespect, did not ask permission.
Hang up call from CG Law
EU Article 13

4/19/19   Compositions of Joy, by Elizabeth Reiff (1996), were originally performed to live audiences at age 16 in a Capella song. Large crowds were summoned to silence by their power. To hear the melodies doubles the impact. They were delivered without accompliment, sometimes with a microphone, in Gallic folk native
fashion with great projection. since the melodies are indelible and impossible to forget, fruits of a glorious childhood. Since the melodies are indelible and impossible to forget, fruits of a glorious childhood, others in the collection may be added at a later date. It may be recordings of these exist somewhere or it may be they can be re-recorded.

If you think it an unnecessary burden to be the custodian of childhood, of youself and your own children, in addition to being a custodian of your ancestors, bear up. Children need to be reminded sometimes when the pressures of the age hem them in so far they not only forget, but slander and gaslight themselves, blowing out of proportion all the good of their experience. This is most true among the creative. What the age says is the best and highest virtue, creativity, is slams into doubt, conformity and control. I lately confronted this in my sons, both brilliant in artistic expression, but opposed by those who are not so, who want to bring the creative into conformance with the group mind, its expectations, and all the shibboleths of its world. So here is a chance to do this with my daughter, who had such exceptional gifts of song and poetic composition she could not accept them. As a first test of her wisdom and enthusiastic joy in creation I offer here three exceptional poems from her early publication Compositons of Joy. These poems with their themes of mortality and change were originally performed at 16 to live audiences in a Capella song. The testament of faith and understanding of life expressed therein is notable. Others in the collection to be added at a later date, some with expressions of excruciating piety are overwhelmed by the extreme sense of mortality and change, the faith in growth and its resolution of the whole. Compositions of Joy is a series that builds to an end. Seen together it is a great testament of faith.

It may be recordings of these exist somewhere or it may be they can be re-recorded, since the melodies are indelible and impossible to forget, fruits of a glorious childhood.

4/20/19 they literally expired the computer and internet, called it off and everybody was ok with it. A guy with a kialioscope ring said all he had to do was shine it in my eyes and this blue spot appeared. All behavior boundaries were gone. Sons told their mothers to shut up and when I said if they were mine they get something to which the woman was censorious. Thery were floods in bookstores, pranks were played over and over on the unspecting Jorma Jonahs was there to not explain it, so was Pat. Everyone was passive and accepting of like karl hillie in the asylum in the 21st cent man will be machines he said his left foot loose for the last time and every word god speaking

Posted Compositions fo Joy: Hi Andrew! Can I ask you to please I share what was just posted about me? It was not done with my permission or approval and I am not happy that it was posted in this way. Sorry, that should be "unshare" — I'm a bit upset right now.

"anyone who desires may copy any and all pages of this book."
-time of extreme censorship
-species of trump derangement syndrome

They Discovered Something in Luxor and It Proves the Unthinkable!
-webscrapping data-double camel hump replaces normal curve from selfcensoring twitter etc
Bbs systems Many seek the digital intimacy they lost years ago; 373 BBSes still operate, according to the
Telnet BBS Guide, mostly in the United States. ... Sure enough, there are about 20 known dial-up BBSes in
North America. And of those, only a handful have been running non-stop since the mid-1990s.Nov 4, 2016

The Lost Civilization of Dial-Up Bulletin Board Systems - The Atlantic b-line

4/21/19 took down the site of e's poems. That episode caused by S saying to Andrew that E whent to Europe as a senior and he, so it wasn't so bad? I must have thought those poems equal to that trip in not so bad. My mistake, clearly point out. -gcmaf plus
GLYCO GCMAF CAPS ORAL COLOSTRUM MAF 2MG X 60 CAPSULES Natural regenesis Immune biotech papers

4/22/19 what effect the spray on tooth decay etc.
marcophage --in a dream with JH: doing things
without malice.

4/24/19
When he sold the bunk beds Aey gave up his hope to host a party of reptiles for Sh. When he sold or tried to sell Aunt Libby's table he betrayed the past. He traded it for synthetic.

4/25/19 Susan is a parable of the Clintons. Dame Hillary eats Bill.

On Barsoom, the notable' men of renown rule,'the Anshei shem." names,' 'words, and persuasion. Giants in knowledge entangle every key stroke, movement, of 7 billion nodes aggregate link sof UNET. Pseudo sacred writings in the arts of war and magic under cover of darkness. Pseudo, super science is a wonderful thing, airbrushed to obscurify the small to hide the great, not Anshei's words but his mustache.

The hierarchical structure of intelligences and esoteric knowledge in this is a pyramid of intelligences hybrid, hence literal giants and whatever parts were immortal, that is until their deaths. Their immortality was not physical. Hence they fostered every secret knowledge of their blood lines, ascending up the ranks. Hierarchy variously produced predicted programming, but under judgment for their failings, when they attempted to destroy the creation created to supplant them. A chief part of war against the interloper was the invention of civilization, but they evidence their occupation millions of years before. The institutions of religion, government, science, art, all subverted by the anshei shem, perpetrated and increased this structure. If you're going to Titanomachy against Titans, it's nice to see how we got to where what was trusted was betrayed. The less honorific designation of the Renowns is briquitte, From the lineage some say only 15% suffer so. News accounts spread these Barsoomian roars over all the upper class meta-schizo world. Meta schematizo means masquerade, which meta-schizo disguise (meta-schiz-matizo) got sent into the Gadarene swine. The Orcs who fear exposure below are being sent out of the space between the planes (dimensions).

But no meta-schematizos presented oppoistions like men. Dibartolo's uncircumcised medieval frescos of hell (c. 1400) show the play. Transworld salvation and damnation, heaven and hell both accepted and declined invisible writing on the wall covered with codes and control. Medieval peasants saw the saved and damned, saints and devils pictures in churches. right before their eyes. We understand the invisible writing of

Belshazzar's feast as an analogy of hypertext and graffiti of electromagentic lockdown. Transworld Molinism after all is the Jesuit property a person has who would commit a sin in any of the superpositional worlds in which he was or might have been created, that and the 5G microwave transmission of brainwaves. Transworld Superposition is any one of the presumed alternative realities you might have inhabited had you done so. Transworld depravity adopted by Craig and Plantinga, and transworld damnation "is possessed by any person who freely does not respond to God's grace and so is lost in every world feasible for God in which that person exists." So if there are a thousand yous in a thousand worlds only one needs be saved. So much for reincarnation. This is way beyond the Oracle.

Another version of prepositioning in quantum entanglement is no matter what you do you bring about your own demise. So no matter what malefactors do to bring about the demise of the good, they can only bring about their own. The opposite is also presumed. Positive entanglement occurs also in Election. If you are elect you understand that everything Satan has done or can do creates a pre-postitioned end. For example, in the numbering of the people which confirmed the site of the temple, all Satan did, like Balaam, was to confirm its building where time is an anti mirror of itself. Every thing that is said of this process can be copied, falsified and imitated, which the Orc is done, so that what we think we see is not to be taken in.

To wrestle the prolegomenas of our own myths that Oracles are both instigators of civilization and the result its rapine, which accounts for their bad temper and violence, even if they mask it with smiles, inbreeding of oracles with an extra toe, when killed or disembodied broadcast a force field that makes them hard to see. Whether these are orcs cannot be said if orcs mask the human. Since science, history, government, literature are predictive programs to hide effects, and make them seem to be men of renown, the Babylonian captivity is part of a small cadre of documents held true.

It's easy to exhaust the irreality of Barsoom but not the academic science of corporate and government that master its technology which they regard as gods. The modern scheme of of three worlds of illuminists, politicians, prophets and priests in all their forms is paralleled in Artificial intelligence and science mutations, cloning and hybridizing in dark tunnels under Dulce Airport. Modern intellectual and artistic expressions of the vulgar more that all the pantheons of the Roman alien put together is like throwing a bucket of gasoline on the embers. Get Ready. You don't defeat Delta force with a hand gun or the robotim and clones of Psalm 2. the. All civilization   made to example Psalms 145-50.

Baudelaire said "Goya's great merit consists of making the monstrous plausible. His monsters were born viable, but that is true of Brueghel: Nobody has managed to surpass him for a sense of the absurd. All these contortions, these bestial faces, these diabolical grimaces are pierced with humanity." Detail of Bruegel's painting from The Fall of the Rebel Angels: "Pieter Bruegel the Elder's painting The Fall of the Rebel Angels shows us there really is a force to subtraction: you subtract from an angel until you end up with a demon. If you download an image of the painting onto your computer, or better yet see it hanging in the Royal Museum of Arts in Antwerp, you will notice how the rebel angels fall from heaven at the top left of the canvas to hell at the bottom right. Their wings are at first subtracted for the lesser wings of bats and dragons. Towards the earth they are reduced to moths, frogs and other soft things. They are driven together by the golden angels of heaven armed with effulgent discs, lances and swords, whose task it is to sanitise our world. You will see how the rebel angels continue to change their forms as they are driven into a sea, whose opening is an obscure drainpipe. They lose their legs, wings, all hope of surfacing, and become fish, squid, spawn and seeds of trees never to be planted. Underwater they continue to be subtracted from their former selves until they are at last incorporeal and see-through at the bottom." Even in that segment of the life of the mind called fictional and poetic forays, parables want to be fair. The choice becomes however whether to be right is to agree with the meliorists that this is the best of all possible worlds and getting better. Presented with going along or confronting the worst possibilities the senses alert, chronicled more and more in inklings from the start, entertain seriously the notion that the purpose of the literary scientific establishment is to induce sleep, indifference and impotence even while bullets are flying. If a signal is needed from our best and brightest, of course, the Russians, then Victor Pelevin's Life of Insects (1993) serves, for he says businessmen and security agents are really insects.

However the wraiths are anesthetized away. The cherub who originally covered the throne, the Anshei master, not to say father, fostered interbreeding between those princes. In our world that stranger homestead law, that if a house is vacant a squatter can come and possess it gives the squatter the rights of the original. Hence squatters are said to have rights before the law and can hardly be evicted. In the spiritual realms however they can be evicted and dispossessed. Every TV show and ad and literature support this quisling intent. Educated classes co-opt events. Consider the suppressed videos of Apollo 11 and the airbrushing of Mars photos. The men of renown are so smart they can do all these things in open view and then explain them away as if they were nothing. They subvert St. John to prepare their own empire. The whole myth and fact of the breaking dimensions at CERN lines up for destruction. Don't worry about transgressing the prophet by annihilating these spirits. Jude says Michael dared not accuse Satan over the body of Moses, but we do not speak for Michael. For this purpose there was One who said, as the Anglo Saxon remembers the remedy: None of the angels made the world.

Orc[hestro] sto write the textbook of methodeia. Reverse engineering isn't to rebuild, but to piece together with other clues the myriad elements of methodeia design, conflicting disinformations attributed to groups, singly as in Oracle councils or as hegemony among Watchers. These scheme singly and jointly, one hand behind the back, the endgame where three of the ten heads are demolished by the Beast.

That this spilled over into literature is just too funny. The Nanoites ended up doing to themselves what they did to others! once the Orcshave the truth shaken away you never hear such apparatus applied to the celebrated Dogon Nomo, Zulu myth, Moon theories, celeb Castaneda, the visions of Ayuhausca and Tao Lin that pass as intended their uncritical myth fantasies to replace the authentic.!!!—Earth to Max

Jordon Petersen: Not the half of it. See his excuse of pedophilia, explaining away reports in such a glib fashion. More Skinner behaviorism. He is a shill of the peds. He calls children, "those little rats." And notice how he neatly he flips the case to "female offenders" as a straw man, when the HUGE majority of these (outside of Hillary) are male. Note he reports of a "digging for underground satanic layers." Conclusion there actually isn't anybody torturing children in daycare centers." Oh no but everywhere else. See this article at IPP Postal

AQUAPHALT 4/26/19 16 5 ga sealer
Tommie copper
Top roach revised

4/27/19
 P=In preparing to
coat the parking with '
A & a. dehydrated, restless in sleep planninc te job my right leg gave out and I fell then when I stood after walking I did not change position, could not speak mnn   obviously cant type a more

4/28/19 love is the cure for death. Lingering "neglect" on right side

4/29/19 that would be my first fall of 19. TIA I see the world as a ball of noise below, noise and lights and langoong, gonging palpitation, while above I am silent, silent looking down.
That night before I woke at 12.30 and sang Ps 8 aloud on my bed. It is a night scape the moon and stars it has two glories, above the heavens and crowned with glory and honor. Everthing from the angels to his feet are not seen but that above that and below are see seen
When you fall to your knees becasues one gives out in a series of letting go, 1,2,3 and lay on the ground unmoving, then stand and walk a little but stop because without understanding what just happened there says there's nowhere to go and nothing to do so you stop and seem to freeze like a person in a coma you are trying to understand, can't answer questions like how are you, but where is your wallet serves. --Poured out my sinews like water Ps 22--got macrophage.

Ariel the lion of God Jerusalem, Isa 28-9. Most of the angels will be known to the tares.
--Poured out my sinews like water Ps 22
--they're not prawns eating cat food, that 's a disceptat iple lie, the're quids or squids if you like Gordon Brodfuehrer, Collector

Blechnum spicant (Hard Fern
This plant grows in subalpine and alpine climates, around woodlands, meadows streams and lakes. It also occurs on tundra and cold, dry, exposed areas. It occurs on gravel bars and scree. Sometimes a pioneer species, colonizing land in the primary phase of ecological succession, such as roads and bare land turned over during frost heave. It is food for caribou, Arctic hares, greater snow geese, small blue butterflies, and grizzly bears

https://www.discoverlife.org/mp/20q?search=Astragalus+alpinus&flags=glean:

4/30/19 if the the detritus of the gods is shit what must be their life. But that's it is is shit they have no life they are all fallen gods whenerh n. says so or not and that tto say that is the future of man to be a fallen god is shit on the earth of noise which it has become from all the fallen done. Fallen gods, fallen lmamn and the ahe advertised apothosesis is false too too, fallen too Defecations of lIght to Fez -To Thrice Fiction:

Vacunas Guanacos, alpacas by Rubino

Passport for countries that don't exist, by AE

Kleeangel A Fiction of Its art and thought by Augusto Todoele

5/1/19 bring me my bowl of burning gold

5/2/19 dreamed a double blind book(s) kept by corporates etc [the fed?] so that all they owned they bought with phantom money

5/3/19 I may be having a little trouble with this rewiring, a certain impatience and lack of tolerance for fools, always a probolem in this time.

Cynthia has wet macularar degeneration and has both cataracts removed!

5/4/19 Sat. revisit the scene. Put on 6 buckets, cleaned new area parking lot. Outing #3 with A&A

/5/5/19 dreamed opening up new section of house. The old great, tht the new to make a small ampitheatre.

Overlooks in part a valley, river expanse, but overgrown with brush—Fairy

Baumann Patch cracks

Andrew an kids Sun afternoon. Th

5/6/19 dear Cynthia, out weather is sitill in the 60's at night! But the rest of the country has ups and downs.

That's must be why they are all coming here. I was moved when I heard of your cataracts and macular issues. I think you must be bearing up like a warrior but I feel it the more because maybe each of us has something to bear. I decided to do the parking lot at the office on a whim, not have it done, and enlisted A&A, but on the second or third outing took a bad fall right at the start of the day, but enough if the fall wasn't as bad as the cause, it was bad enough. I have been healing very slowly, weeks for a stratch, so was really surprised when this bloody knee and lacerated lower leg healed completely in a week! I have been taking lipo somal C for a couple months, uping the dose till now I take 4 tablespoons a day, about a quadra dose, and that must be the reason I think, except I'd also just started GcMAF, the 8000 NP. It is too early to say what that is doing, but we both take it now, a cream smeared on the lymph glands. Andrew was here yesterday with a sore knee so I put it on the glands behind his knee. It is billed to activate the immune system in stress of colds, up to and including cancers, because the macrophage is neutralized by nagalse generated by those things. Thus it is said to act to restimulate the body's immune response and restore it. Pat thinks the cause of my fall where literally my leg melted beneath me, was much lessened by these and the carbon60 regimen these past years, for the previous occasions were worse. You might think this nuts but I have also raised the head of our beds 5 degrees. The mattress tends to slide a little but it stimulates the venous return, so to speak, which makes sense. The bed looks like it's taking off backwards. We had the four kids yesterday, Sunday, for the PM, Sabrina was sick. Theodore hasn't been eating well, lost 2 lbs, but he ate two tacos, watermelon, strawberries, cheese crips and cooks and three milks, most of while sitting on my lad, he came over from his chair, and after while reclining back, like an ancient Greek at meal, so I has like his bed. Very entertaining. He was silent and ate while AB quizzed me about what tif means in Paraguay. And she says I was right! But I missed the others. I whispered to her a secret at the end that she is the most special of all because there is onoly one of her and two boys. The only granddaughter, but not to tell anybody. Ncrawled all around the back yard and got licked by Shorty many times. Every single life is this precious. I'm going to lunch with Aeg this week to find out what his trials are. It's 38 miles each way to Chandler. P of course sponsored, arranged, and promoted the whole event and loved it. Aey doesn't have an NP job yet, they are a little overstaffed, but in AZ he has practically all the rights as a doc! He's still coming down from the effort, trying to get his new bearings. He saw what happened to me and acted absolutely appropriately at the parking lot. So in the moment I see he has the gift.

--Aeg terminated

Oppheimer Ranch Pjroject

Reported as literatures of fact. Each facility of the Futurist playbook opposing Bolshevik society in those 1920's translated to the new Bolshevik societies of the 2020s completes this era of one hundred years of censorship, again opposed by the fakta of a continent and an age apart from the original. The formalist theories of faktovivi however bypass algorithmic controls to code hidden propitiatory work, read correctly. The first priority remains accentuated real material gathered either first hand or culled from documentary sources.

5/8/19

5/10/19
Explorations of Space
Travel to mercury
Balaams ass
Apulenius ass Diogenes
Angel Space Murdes
The Cry of the Goat
Tales of Saturn

5/11/19 Ch 1 of passport.
5/12/19 Mother's day. Ch 2 Passport, Vats. Nexium indicted

5/13/19 Mon. Patch cracks, fill holes. Endure put downs from aey about office and grounds, finances, ete after he spends days on a boat in san diego with people who put him down with whom he can only lie

5/14/19 Tues after a dream printed Plainfolking reviews of future. Pat insistently misremembers wales dates., picks up Aey vibe from weekend
--george webb sweigert

5/15/19 yshield 5g paint
Jacob's Heavenly Cou 5/14/19 after a dream printed out Plainfolking Reviews of the Future Rabbinic Accounts
Where is the Jacob file?
5/16/19 Andrew a verbal offer from Cardinal Logistics tempe. Wants to enroll Th in PCS I'm an actor performing on a stage I can't see to a script I don't know. After life in life.
Conclude the hardest thing to accept is terrestrial life, tha he has a body and that it matters a whit apart from the thoughts he thinks while in it. Like it should be a pleasure center, ok. That it can perform work, ok. That it a way he can touch other bodies, ok. Center of emotion, feeling. That it is a locus for gratification of fame or success or an end in itself. Excep in general like war there isare no istorical effects or events but it is all looked at both before the effect and after the event and the only matter was the choice first to deny the world and second to comfort the prisoners. And the effort to sustain life to work to find its purpose – provide an identity of children and grandchildren
5/17/19 Aey becomes progressively more bitter as he absorbs S.'s anger.

5/18 Sat. Parking lot, CostCo with A, but Mon call for Pat said the office left unlocked, door open etc. Aeyrie however was the last there, he bought a new Toyota that day or next! !!!
•
5/19/19 Dr Quikley aggregator
Do I look like I need information about the revelation? You can tell you can't see to those who can't see.

5/20/19 Bought 6 55gal water barrels for Aeg Somehow Aey's lapse reminds me of the girl he dated in H.s. Abby, who was schizo and write a tiny handwritten diary to him, whose parents interviewed him to "court" her and wanted to know if he believed in predestination. Also the girl with the child he took, also the girl at Starbucks on Bethany ome
 Anna Vladislavovna Bogacheva - The Moscow Project

 May 20th, 2019
Secret Drilling and Pipelines? No Problem, Rockefeller Has Butinas And Erickson awan diplomatic containers, Charleston dirty bomb, george webb citizen journalist, oleg deripaska, piketon centrifuges, piketon centrifuges shipped to iran, piketon ohio whistleblower, rhoden murders, shipping container radiation testing Plan to hollow out Ohio because of the fracking. I think because it's just a basin and it's all oil and it's just…and they're bring in people …people say it's conspiratorial but what was lisa page doing

5/21/19 in this amazing display of karmic events the following:

Beginning with A provoking the pub of E's poems on line and she really going nuts, and he losing his job in Chandler and Cynthia tells me of her glaucoma and cataracts, Aey goes nuts in a series of selling aunt Libby stuff and machines to make room for a party, looking for a job, interning with Pat, goes to San Diego for weekend with in laws comes back with all putdowns, buys new Toyota and leaves office open while P cannot remember the date of her year in Wales and argues strongly about it, all this while doing the parking lot in many stages, I have a meltdown in parking of office on second repave with a stroke, can't talk can barely walk. In this time I began inclined bed, macrophage, liposomal C, . but it's all about only connect, like with the opoems of Ohio, hearing George Webb refer to fracking Ohio hollow but not conspicuously recording it, going back however and capturing the insight and connecting it to the poem. All these events connect to each other and to other events as well, like Clay, a tragickal saying that o much poetic writing goes "beyond meaning", and it should--wonder if it would be possible or beneficial to have a greater sense of overall cohesion—so the whole thing is like a free form poem, elipses, dips, it's all about aggregation of information and collection for analysis to magnify not diffuse data. All tis occurs while taking time off from clay, adding George Webb binge watching, composing new sections of the the Bridge. https://brassballs.blog/

Kleeangel accepted yesterday. Paint seams with 10 year.

Augusto Todoele's clay angel tests the premise that there is a word of simulaaneous reference that evokes every being, hope and dream of the world. This is the first publication of these writings outside the contemplative order. He is a translator of of 8th century Anglo-Saxon and Latin texts of Lindesfarne.

and curator St. Cuthbert's relics Northumbria when Aldred was priest the when Aldred was a priest, and eventually provost at the end of the 8th century in the Northumbrian monasteries where keeps being mistaken for john Malkovitch

5/27/19

The Enthronement of ISIS, that is, if gets approval. So if it does appear let it be under the listed name of Augusto Todoele. I'm an actor performing on a stage I can't see to a script I don't know—he nonexistence of existence Reported as literatures of fact. Each facility of the Futurist playbook opposing Bolshevik society in those 1920's translated to the new Bolshevik societies of the 2020s completes this era of one hundred years of censorship, again opposed by the fakta of a continent and an age apart from the original. The formalist theories of faktovivi however bypass algorithmic controls to code hidden propitiatory work, read correctly. The first priority remains accentuated real material gathered either first hand or culled from documentary sources. an Enlightenment of Adventure and Lessons Learned in what might be called the literary or fictive aspect of the human sciences. nears completion of his book of angels So After the jump, the fall, the landing, the trek, the privation, the explosions and then back to Ithaca and peace, but where is the peace unless he has left the fight so far inland that they think them winnowing oars.

 5/22/19 the evolution of the wood pile

5/23/19, globaloney (Farrell)

5/24/19 Fri. Blood test. Collect the Little stories. Told Unlikely DeDonald

Rubino del Sur Note on the third revision of Top Roach "Did you ever wander in the cold so long your brain freezes down to the point of bare survival, but then go to sleep and nothing will suffice, but you wake to such clarity you think you're in super brain? That keeps happening to Top Roach changing its story. This latest was so radical it got sent to another mag, since your interest had flagged-goodness knows if they wait too long it will morph again- you know the story of the Bug I'm sure-and this new journal, the Onaldegenany claims it will appear, so sorry, it must withdraw from its adjunct tenure at Unlikely. Hope to see you again though. Del Sur."

Read the Higher Dumb Bunnies. Donald

Removed from Red Fez: AE means Alcohol Ethoxylate. Named for a chemical process, this NON-IONIC surfactant makes long ethoxylate chains water-soluble. Unlike opposing Sulfonated Analogues,

UNSULFONATED AE transports hydrocarbon exulate to poetry spills, drops letters into the Caustic Pot where they are broken down into molecules small enough for microbes to digest. To bioremediate, accelerate and deregulate oils describes the subject of this Content Not Allowed.

5/25/19 Sat. Did the entire second coat on parking lot north side
5/26/19 Picked up metal table and wheeled cart up the street. Andrew and fam for cookout Memorial Day

5/27/19 Memorial Day. the Bay Psalm Book 1640,
the St Cuthbert Gospel, earliest known Western bookbinding to survive, from Saint Cuthbert of Lindisfarne, North East England, in whose tomb it was placed, probably a few years after his death in 687early 8th-century pocket gospel book, essentially undecorated text is the Gospel of John in Latin, written in a script that has been regarded as a model of elegant simplicity.
Codex Leister, a mixture of Leonardo's observations and theories on astronomy; the properties of water, rocks, and fossils; air, and celestial light
1. Magnalia Christi Americana 1702,
2. Hymns and Spiritual Songs for the Fasts and Festivals of the Church of England, by Christopher Smart, Of Plymouth Plantation

Wigglesworth, Michael (1867) [reprint of 6th ed 1715]. "The day of doom: or, A poetical description of the great and last judgment". Google Books.
Passport accepted.

5/28/19 Tues. Plant Folkways
One reason for life is to give hope to others
5/29/19 family gathering. Joe here, aunt danj. On the eway donna fell out of the window of the car long ways and landed in the water, but I had a towel.
5/30/19 Dean from Marjon comes to recondition kiln. T 591!

5/31/19 Print and retrieve The Madness of the Golden Age. Paint the lines with Aey.

It must be an axiom, that the more folk externalized their short term memory into their hand held devices the more they lose the authority over themselves and their power of choice and individuation. The corollary is that the more this happens the more they dogmatically question anything outside their range of knowledge, a knowledge that grows less and less as they externalize their autonomy. These effects mimic early onset Alzheimer. Digital Alzheimer. Loss of the ability to schedule short term memory in the brain but relegated it to an out source in the device, the same with special recognition and mapping. Instead of knowing the route and visualing it on a map the route is outsourced and no memory of it occurs, unless it is the rote cognition of the way to work, but any new destination is outsourced to the device gps, which once resided in the memory and was reasoned out. More prevalent in the abused. Gaslighted.

Aey's short term memory and certitude of his word to himself becomes weaker and weaker. He left the office open, forgot to move the dumpster, had to confirm that we would paint the lines, when it had been agreed, time and place. He becomes more bitter and angry as his wife confronts him at ever point with his so called failings. He said in painting the lines that she got home at 7 and if he wasn't there would face her wrath, esp. since she said he "never does anything around the house!" She continues to prevent his involvement with all of us. He could not come to the reunion Sun, cookout. Claimed he 1. Wasn't told 2. Not soon enough 3. A didn't invite him. 4. But I did, as soon as it was firm. Instead he moved her friends Cory and Alexis Sunday and Mon. He said in the 7 o'clock deadline that it was too late, he'd tied the knot and would go on as long as he did, or not….none of this would have occurred but he brought it up! That he had to be home by 7—or else All this drama provoked further by teasing about my T 591! And capped on the way home with further provocation to him that there are two ways to improve male fertility 1. No underwear, which he said was supported by "research' 2. Cold showers, which he roundly mocked. I of course added 3. Stop taking all the estrogen in food and drink. Told him to get his T checked.

6/1/19 milkcandyreview@gmail.com Culture cult pubs

6/2/19 Finished the lines.
Dear Gambler,
I seek to renew my appeal to restore the public face of the last edition of Feeling Lucky that sponsored my Futhark, as I had written to you then.

6/3/19 Pollard. English Miracle Plays
Everything spiritual has been squeezed, strangled out of his life, song, faith, family, art, leaving only the material
Bruppbacher" first appeared Zurich, in 1580 on the eastern shore of Lake Zurich, There, a wild mountain brook flowed from the mountains into Lake Zurich. It was said that a bridge was constructed over the brook, and it was named "Brugg-Bach", meaning "Bridge-Brook". Near the brook stood a mansion, whose proprietor chose the surname "Bruggbacher" to distinguish himself better from other prominent families of the area. In time, his family

adopted the surname as their own. The townspeople of the nearby village, desiring to create a smoother, more flowing dialect, convinced those in the surrounding countryside, including the household of Bruggbacher, to alter the spelling and pronunciation of their names. Hence, "Bruggbacher" was modified to "Bruppbacher" with the double "g" changed to a double "p".

Another source similarly tells us that "Bruggbach" is a brook with a bridge, and the persons who lived near this brook got the name Bruggbach, which evolved and later changed to Bruppbacher.1

To this day, the name has evolved so as the most common spellings in North America are "Brubaker" or "Brubacher", while spellings such as "Bruppbacher", "Brubacher", and also "Brubpacher" are more prevalent in Eastern Switzerland. upon the arrival of Bruppbachers to England and North America.

Fallstreak Hole cavum,[1] hole punch cloud, punch hole cloud, skypunch, cloud canal or cloud hole) is a large gap, usually circular or elliptical, that can appear in cirrocumulus or altocumulus clouds.

6/4/19 Melichayland , Australia I guess. After sending epancake out of fatigue and not remembering it was johnny cake didn't correct it because the iteration before was so bungled. And it needed airing.

I was telling her this a.m. how significant she is, held her hand, when she told to the patient yesterday, one of the new breed of people, look likes all, like Amanda Kondrat'yev --with CHS, reported by Megan at Mayo and Yessenia in W Valley!

6/5/19 Wed wash the asphalt.

FAKTA Facto Reported as literatures of fact. Each facility of the Futurist playbook opposing Bolshevik society in those 1920's translated to the new Bolshevik societies of the 2020s completes this era of one hundred years of censorship, again opposed by the fakta of a continent and an age apart from the original. The formalist theories of faktovivi however bypass algorithmic controls to code hidden propitiatory work, read correctly. The first priority remains accentuated real material gathered either first hand or culled from documentary source Fables and Fakta Fable Fable

----Flip Fact plip plat fablefact, paddle paddbe flipfact

Eating AMY-why didn't the Aztecs try rice and beans?
How Are You Going to Spend Your Reprieve? My dentist told me he's an alien.

6/6/19 wash again, need pressure washer. Sealmaster.

6/7/19 Fri -- add to Top Roach the dilemma in the society of roaches or groundhogs or rabbits is just that you are roaches, groundhogs and rabbits, even if celebrated by Kafka, t. H. white and Richard Adams. Many more species can be named and celebrated in beastaries. As a bug Johnny sought to overcome the obstacles as a bug.

From Under Ben Bulben

But all this was good cover for the ersatz faux men, who aped masculinity with their beards and rough manner but who had no experience of the rigors that the most menial bug faces, let along the groundhop, that noble creature. Prairie dog, wolverine, fox, but not the cow that factory of meat and milk. No dignity transferred to his animals because there was no dignity in himself, it had been taken from him by his own weakness and conformity. Taught him by the 60 ruling families in one notable nation, that animals were not oligarchs

Men overwhelmed by shock and awe of their gold gods in the formal world religions are as subservient as the primitive. Blood rites top to bottom. War is an invention of the gods. The fact of death is different from the agencies of death, war and the study of war inculcated into earth by supernatural interference. In the Death of Cuchulain at the end of Last Poems Yeats in his resistance confronts these agencies even though he seems compromised with the Titans and the gods. To fight against the divine is paramount in Aeschylus. Aliens turn this as if it were fighting against (the true) God, but this is alien equivocation. In the fight against Saturn, the Titans and all Olympus, men were powerless to effect change even if they resisted to the death like Sisyphus, Prometheus. The recast of this man into a demi-god himself to undermine the man and turn him into a god means he has become his own enemy, has ceased to resist and is completely enslaved. "To those who really believe in a Supreme Being the occurrence of supernatural interference, causing physical convulsions and changes, presents no difficulty, especially in connection with a world the moral condition of which is evidently out of course ages before the creation of our race" (Pember, Earth's Earliest Ages. Preface). Aeschylus, Dante, Yeats lead to wondering how the human fights against the divine, the divine being the fallen, since it has always existed and must have been resisted or influenced long since.

6/8/19 a high on the audacity scale
You have to know the beginning and the end before you appreciate the middle.
God of Forces is baal shaman
6/9/19 Andrew Reiff. Is this the one you used to know. The poet? Probably not. Wash lot twice,

6/10/19 SECOND PREP SEAL nucccess nukesucccess, share holders:
talkshows Non local space
literature and history are a record of confrontations with evil. Fairy tales, myths, epic tales all tell the same tale in different times and place. Balaam and Johny Cake, SF, Lithia—ofter, only tutored by evil itself, an autonomous evil outside the world and in it. Baal Shamen AN "intergalactic bridge" stretching between two galaxy clusters 10 million light-years apart has been observed for the first time he so-called cosmic web describes the gravitationally-bound galaxies through which matter is distributed across the universe.… never before has a radio emission been observed connecting two of these systems. "Understanding the nature of this radio source is a real challenge, since the electrons, during their radiative life time, manage to cover a much smaller space than the entire source. "There must therefore exist some mechanism responsible for their acceleration that operates along the entire filament." a filament connecting the two clusters and this stimulated the curiosity of Federica Govoni and her team, who started investigating the possible extension of the magnetic field beyond the centre former NASA expert Lola Gulomova suicided, (by Jason Rieff, husband)---she was preparing to turn over to Russia information being kept secret by NASA related to the

"mysterious unraveling" of the "Great Red Spot" on the planet Jupiter approaching Earth so close that its moons will be able to be seen with binoculars—and that comes at the same time earthquakes are increasing all along the Western coastal regions of North America, with Los Angeles alone recording over 700 of them since this past Wednesday—and US military forces this past fortnight having begun storming the beaches of Oregon and Washington in preparations for what they call "The Big One".   the big one, unraveling red spot on Jupiter correlated with mercury transit of sun 11 Margery Lewy Rieff You look beautiful...so glad we saw you last summer.
Usha Seetharam Stunning as usual Lola Gulomova! Lots of love from us
Joel Rieff Enjoy your "tiān" and "xing qì" ... say "ní how" to everyone ... and "w(àá)n an" (no v sound). I have been studying. How am I doing?? LOL!!

Lorraine Rieff-Liakouras My beautiful daughter-in-law!!! Love the picture. Hugs and kisses. Mom https://en.wikipedia.org/wiki/Niels_Klim%27s_Underground_Travels 1741 relation to Gulliver? one of the first science-fiction novels in history along with Johannes Kepler's Somnium (The Dream, 1634).   -----Cyrano de Bergerac's Comical History of the States and Empires of the Moon (1656), Jonathan Swift's Gulliver's Travels (1726), and Voltaire's Micromégas (1752). one of David Icke's beliefs.[10][12][13] moon craters are satellite dishes astrophysicist Iosif Shklovsky, who s Between 1972 and 1977, seismometers installed on the Moon by the Apollo missions recorded moonquakes. The Moon was described as "ringing like a bell" during some of those quakes, specifically the shallow ones.[16] This phrase was brought to popular attention in March 1970,[1] in an article in Popular Science.[17] When Apollo 12 deliberately crashed the Ascent Stage of its Lunar Module onto the Moon's surface, it was claimed that the Moon rang like a bell for an hour, leading to arguments that it must be hollow like a bell.[1] suggested that the Martian moon Phobos was an artificial satellite and hollow; Hollow Moon--The absence of any moon mission makes the hollow moon hollow: Between 1972 and 1977, seismometers installed on the Moon by the Apollo missions recorded moonquakes. The Moon was described as "ringing like a bell" during some of those quakes, specifically the shallow ones.[16] Deep structure mass under moon: changes in the strength of gravity around the Moon by analyzing data from NASA's Gravity Recovery and Interior Laboratory (GRAIL) mission.---since no, none news accounts are not CIA composed all of this is to serve the same purpose of intrigue the moon landing did—to be revealed.

6/11/19 white cranny doodles
The whole new order narrative depends on the moon landing and with it all the alt science of ET and space craft and to trigger alien astronauts and theosophic angels with the stars like Orion etc. It might seem contradictory that if you examine a thing you not look directly at it at first, but take periferous views. So to examine the moon question consider the record of wars and deception and if these show a pattern

If no moon landing then no masonic apron and no magic numbers 33. Every layer of the onion infected, no hollow moon and no vibrations of gong on the moon urged by every co conspirator along with, all a façade, a fake, a Hollywood faux, no spaceships on the limb of the moon observing, every one a take giving the lie to Jim Maars and Richard Hoagland and the crystal towers of the moon and the abandoned structures at 19.5—but was there a Jupiter red spot that killed Lola Gulomova

In the model of hyperdimensional physics with their primitive models of angular momentum, the double tetrahedron an illusion made up in Hollywood, that NASA itself "deliberately infected the story that the moon landing was a fake.. dark mission70

--why did NAASA shred every record of its event? And so to verify he moon landing NASA sowing the meme that it was fake—all to hid e the greater discovery? Of the wars of deception to hide the solar system wide civilization that had just disappeared like the Anasazi because it would harm social stability 65 all to cover up extraterrestrial intel next door in Cuba! HOAGLAND IS THE GREATEST CIA PROPAGANDIST OF ALL—the Egyptian meaning of the Apollo patch, Osirisis-Orion—magicians masons and nazis—all left out the cia, cia, cia and why, who oh why----because history is an illusion meant to hide—not an alien reconnaissance and retrieval but….to prepare, prepare the decept of decepts—the red wheelbarrows beside the white chickens glazed with rain

-- all the moon records destroyed

--astronauts ignorance of radiation belt, Grissom's death hit, its all payola which all starts with the gong echo when the lander hit the moon, but the lander didn't hit the moon and the gong echo was a tale from Verne told on WikiLeaks Wikipedia rigged like a bell, that's where it starts, the bell, holy cow the bell THE MOON IS THE COW

My father gave his sin nature to me as his gave it to him, but I know my face, the body is arbitrary

Isaiah 32.19 end is the first to have the city comeing down from the sky,-- that is arguing by anthesis, another form of gematria, argument where the opposite evokes the thesis, requisite in a world where every public event is a fraud, fraud upon fraud, like the moon landing, which Hoagland neatly says was labeled a hoax to justify it, who reports on the masonic communion and the 19.5 Orion Osiris of aldrin and Armstrong, but which is utter fraud since no man went to the moon –proved by one thing THE VAN

ALLEN RADIONATION BELT-- Poulter had been chosen by Admiral Richard E. Byrd as his chief scientist for the 1933–1935 Second Byrd Antarctic Expedition. He had the task of planning and conducting geophysical investigations during that expedition. Van Allen assisted Poulter in those preparations… Poulter invited Van Allen to accompany him as a member of the Antarctic Expedition, but his parents vetoed the idea. He had to be content with listening avidly to the short-wave radio reports from Little America to follow the expedition's progress. He, with the rest of the world, was electrified by Poulter's heroic rescue of Admiral Byrd from his lonely vigil at South Pole Station in August 1934.[8] Poulter and Byrd were honored by a public parade in Mount Pleasant the next summer, and Admiral Byrd delivered the chief commencement address at Van Allen's graduation exercises. geomagnetism, cosmic rays, auroral physics, and ionospheric physics hence before Ezekiel, when translated "peaceable habitation…shall descend itself in the descent of the forest, and far down in the lowlands, the city shall descend…the city shall descend" but cf. Though hail flattens the forest and the city is leveled completely,

Pulpit commentary: The city. Nineveh (Lowth, Gesenius, Rosenmüller); Jerusalem (Delitzsch, Knobel, Cheyne, Kay); "the city in which the hostility of the world to Jehovah will, in the latter days, be centralized" (Drechsler, Nagel) - the "world-power," in fact. The last view seems to give the best sense.

"The prophet then proceeds in the singular number, comprehending the women as a mass, and using the most massive expression. The He introduced into the summons required that the feminine forms, רגזי, etc., should be given up. ערה, from ערר, to be naked, to strip one's self. חגרה absolute, as in Joel 1:13 (cf., Isaiah 3:24), signifies to gird one's self with sackcloth (saq). We meet with the same remarkable enall. generis in Isaiah 32:12. Men have no breasts (shâdaim), and yet the masculine sōphedīm is employed, inasmuch as the prophet had the whole nation in his mind, throughout which there would be such a plangere ubera on account of the utter destruction of the hopeful harvest of corn and wine. Shâdaim (breasts) and שׂדי (construct to sâdōth) have the same common ring as ubera and ubertas frugum. In Isaiah 32:13 ta'ăleh points back to qōts shâmīr, which is condensed into one neuter idea. The ki in Isaiah 32:13 has the sense of the Latin imo (Ewald, 330, b). The genitive connection of עליזה קריה with משוש בתי (joy-houses of the jubilant city) is the same as in Isaiah 28:1. The whole is grammatically strange, just as in the Psalms the language becomes all the more complicated, disjointed, and difficult, the greater the wrath and indignation of the poet." Keil and Delitzsch Biblical

Commentary on the Old Testament

Barnes' Notes on the Bible: Shall be low in a low place - Margin, 'Utterly abased.' Hebrew, 'In humility shall be humbled.' The sense is, shall be completely prostrate. Those who refer this to Jerusalem suppose it refers to the time when God should humble it by bringing the enemy so near, and exciting so much consternation and alarm. Those who refer it to Babylon suppose it relates to its destruction. If referred to Nineveh, it must mean when the pride of the capital of the Assyrian empire should be iratabled by the complete overthrow of their army, and the annihilation of their hopes. The connection seems to require us to adopt this latter interpretation. The whole verse is very obscure; but perhaps the above will express its general sense.

Gill's Exposition of the Entire Bible and the city shall be low in a low place: meaning not the city of Jerusalem, surrounded with mountains, built under hills, and so under the wind, and not exposed to the fury of a storm; but rather Babylon, built in a plain, in a low plain, and yet should be brought lower still; mystical Babylon is here meant, the city of Rome, that should "in humiliation be humbled", as the words may be rendered, that is, brought very low, exceeding low; see Isaiah 26:5 and which, at the time of the great hail, will be divided into three parts, and the cities of the nations shall fall, and Babylon be had in remembrance by the Lord to destroy it, Revelation 16:19.

JPS Tanakh 1917 THE HOLY SCRIPTURES
ACCORDING TO THE MASORETIC TEXT
A NEW TRANSLATION

And the work of righteousness shall be peace;
And the effect of righteousness quietness and
confidence for ever. 18And my people shall abide in
a peaceable habitation, And in secure dwellings, and
in quiet resting-places. 19And it shall hail, in the
downfall of the forest; But the city shall descend into
the valley. 20Happy are ye that sow beside all
waters, That send forth freely the feet of the ox and
the ass

John Bunyan. T H E Holy City O R, The New Jerusalem Donald Kilpatrick, fitz, plaster of paris http://www.ancientpages.com/2016/03/28/fearsome-aztec-eagle-warriors-and-jaguar-warriors-ofmesoamerica/?fbclid=IwAR1IHrgZq8p3lbqJ9gW9KuAv10Epr75u1DJqz_0UE38eQSTOXb58vdTkwfY catastrophism and the old testament amen

6/12/19 two equally old papyri have both readings – 666 and 616. End time C/04 of the fifth century has 616 spelled out with Greek letters as the number of the beast. So, it agrees with P115 as the only other ancient witness of this alternate text. Tyconius recognized 616 as the number of the beast in his 4th century Latin version. In contrast, the writings of Origen and Hippolytus (both of the 3rd century) attest strongly to the value of 666 as the correct reading [Burgon 136]. Most noteworthy however are the statements of Irenaeus, the 2nd century bishop of Lyon, known to be a disciple of Polycarp. Polycarp is believed to have been a disciple of John, the author of Revelation. In his treatise, "Against Heresies,": "I do not know how it is that some have erred following the ordinary mode of speech, and have vitiated the middle number in the name, deducting the amount of fifty from it"

6/13/19 Goethe: ordinary vs supernatural vanity. Macadam comes unglued eventually needs to be recovered, like the universe
James Perloff: war and deception. Matrix: neil's passport expires 11 Sept 2001.6 concepts of "it's just a coincidence: America ruled by oligarchy, America's 60 families, council on foreign relations 2. Olig seek world gov't 3. International in scope, Bilderberg etc masons, 4 .Jerusalem is to be capital of world gov't "BenGurion: supreme court of mankind 5. Satanists in upper level of gov't. Ronald Bernard, Bohemia grove, 6. Oligarchs control the press.
Spanish American Wars 1898- consistent pattern of events. Herz fabricated stories of Cubans eaten by Spanish soldiers. Battleship Maine to Havana harbor, trumped up events, Maine exploded. White gold—sugar!
McKinley, Ohio, Hanna his handler, Nat'l City Bank, Phillipines, Guam, Puerto
Vera Cruz 1914, humiliating 21 gun salute demanded for sailor arrest, invaded Vera Cruz, Smedley Butler: refused to war his medal. War is a Racket of Big Business. Oil! Black Gold. Standard Oil. Regime change, Sinking of Lusatania, Largest ship at the time, May 7, 1915. WWI, 1914. Sunk off Ireland 1200 passengers, Warned 6Mil rounds of ammo aboard plus

huge hoards of explosive, Woman and children used as protective shield, preannounced to go into the war sinking by King George V, a set up to be sunk to bring U.S in war, Churchhill. plus atrocities, Germans cutting off hands, Huns invading America, League of nations

Pearl Harbor, prearranged, designed by Roosevelt

Korean War, Dean Acheson validate U.N. as peacekeeper. No war declaration. Under UN mandate, police action

Tonkin Gulf, Resolution attack on destroyer, Dean Acheson, William Bundy his son in law, wrote the resolution

End of Cold War 1985 Begin war on terror. Russia replaced by

Islam 6/13/19 Book of Gurus, ms.

6/14/19 Unseen Spiritual Realms

The Land of El tovar: Spritual Grand Canyon = Taliesin's house. Penlight = Rock Slide. Mule Song = Espiritu Speech. Marooned Arthropod . Ruby throat The Angel Dog Shorty

6/15/19 New myths: becquerels, Three-lobed Burning Eye Godzilla, /black hole down:Unfit First question of any image, film: what are the the three levels of programming, its propaganda? And the opposites?

6/16/19 supernatural praise: H ALA LE LU YAH !

KIRSTEN KASCHOCK'S SLEIGHT BOOK ~ musings about all things sleight-related

I'm sorry to bother you with this I don't know my age—or do. Doddy do. I saw your arrow tweet this A.M. and this apparently is my response which I absolutely must send right now before it dawns.

6/17/19 Operation Database: if the parameters of search have been altered, reversed, then the results, doctored, will prove just the opposite of what they are and the researchers none the wiser will turn their research into propaganda. 2 examples, but forgotten. Why this is done, who does it is to control the outcomes. This could apply o any universe of data. The thesis selects the data according to the parameters chosen. If the parameters are reprogrammed than the universe of data will give false conclusions but it would not be known. This could apply in polling or any medical examination. Data naif. So in all the metadata stored in all the cell bases, proof becomes the opposite of the real by alternation of the premise. The more this is talked about, the faux, the moe, the farther away it becomes. A muscular fat.

Serial brain 7.45 clowns trump visit, Megan Markle: clowns create their mind controlled assets by targeting select kids through undisclosed programs. The majority of them go through sexual abuse and/or gender perturbation to initiate and facilitate the 'recovery" process. 6/18/19 pain in 11th rib, psychic, psyche, floating rib

Vlad Basarab   Though I am in an abeyance right now the piece at the bottom of the first page in European Ceramics says very well the realization of the planes when they are achieved. I see you work as i do with a knife pretty much only and in paper clay, laminated I take it. I salute you. AE   Hello! Yes, with a knife. Paper clay. I am myself trying to come out of an abeyance. Best to you!

6/19/19 Learned Mark Leon died 18 May 1018. All of our time in the flesh is spiritual. Shadows...much in mind, images, in the retina, in the brain, made with hands, seen in space, imagined at night, every catalogue, photograph, gallery even so that we construe the thing physical changing with light, but to know it must know the spirit. amen.
I got to the 26 level underground before they turned off the elevators
Inspiration is consubstantial. The phrase the moon and the stars, considering the plight of a hollow moon is to be trusted from its consubstantial appearance there. The Word is trans substantial with itself. Beresheth!
6/20/19 Thurs. chateau avoidance, abeyance bid for bath by new urban builders. Lunch in Tempe with And

6/21/19
Dear Diane, It occurs to me to try a small memorial to Mark from his letters which concern religion and philosophy, faith and doubt, and in that they show his humanity raw, which is the true case with us all, unvarnished. I don't know how many friends he had besides me with whom he shared these speculations, but I also don't know whether or to what extent he continued these lines of thought, or whether they were a phase he passed out of.
I think you could set me straight on that, especially his thoughts in the last year or so.
He had called me, last year, I now remember, out of the blue with the information of his plight, but seemed matter of fact about the outcome. His three SF novels are much more disingenyous that the expressions in the letters, which seem sincere. They stem from India, Austin and El Paso, after he met you. The letters conclude about 1993 conicdent with his dissertation. He had visited us in Phoenix a few times after that where we played tennis with my kids, but further contact was desultory. So I guess I wonder what you think of such a venture. It would be necessary to present the letters unedited, except for the elision of only one personal remark, and they would have a natural boundary, being only letters sent to me. The idea of a memorial is that it would reach those who knew him, his family etc., but if they would be offended perhaps it had better not be done. They heavily concern faith, churches, Duns Scotus, faith and doubt, C. S. Lewis, not subjects anybody presently wants to hear, but classically such questions were the bedrock of civilization.
People are either afraid or offended because these are issues that concern us deep down and he vocalizes them in plain terms. For me the bigger picture is that instead of accepting or rejected thoughts like this I think they need to be appreciated for what they are, meaning absolutely human. People only want to be sure and if they can't, they push it down. But he brings it up. It is also honest. Does that have a following?
We all should hope to lead a pitiless life, blade sunk to the hilt in the hardest stone. How did it even get in there our detractors and adversaries will say and, well finally that so and so is gone. Good riddance. So he can laugh at them from the grave, if it holds him, and know he gave it the absolute, absolved and though they grave his name on a stone cannot forget him. But he forgets them, goes on.

Marl Leon, Unified Fields Mind Surfer, The Gaia War at one point in the letters Mark says he is a humanist, so to show the human side these letters are offered

The Dialectic of Truth and News: Implications of Truth in News Narrative

Mark Robert Leon

Dissertation, The University of Texas at Austin (1993)

Abstract   News reporting as a form of discourse has been too long neglected by philosophy. In particular news is a truth discourse. As such it is significantly different from science, philosophy and history, the three forms of discourse more commonly treated in truth theoretic discussions. ;This difference is most evident in the analysis of news form and content.

The top-down, inverted pyramid form of news narrative is specifically designed to feature content that is objective and relevant. After some analysis of this narrative form I turn to the truth theoretic issues of objectivity and relevance. ;Objectivity, in particular proves to be an elusive concept. After examining some unacceptable definitions I characterize objectivity as an inter-subjective phenomenon. I treat relevance in a similar manner. ;These analyses naturally lead into a discussion of truth theory. I examine the two main branches of truth theory, correspondence and coherence. In doing so, I formulate a theory of resonance for news narrative that partakes of both correspondence and coherence considerations. Resonance, in this sense, is not a theory of truth, but a useful tool in the analysis of news. ;Using the resonance theory for news narrative I undertake a case study of a particular news story. Here I test the alethic resonances, derived in part from correspondence and coherence considerations, against a news story that is particularly challenging from a truth theoretic standpoint. ;Finally I take up the wider dialectic of truth and news. The goal here is to use the resonance analysis of news narrative to suggest a basis for a new theory of truth that gets beyond the more intractable metaphysical problems of classical correspondence and coherence theories without sacrificing truth to skepticism, relativism, or solipsism

6/22/19 Yahweh of hosts has purposed it…to bring into contempt all the honorable of the earth Isa 23.9 Demo, sakrete 1000 lbs, first hole
6/23/19 Castration Queen Hat Quonset Hut Clinic

6/24/19 here was a mass evacuation (temporary, so believed) we were lining up to board, I left to find a bathroom, my Dad was concerned I get back, but two bldgs Of campus were closed and I may have missed the flight, but learned Russian forces enforced it. Reminds of all looking for classrooms UT- long elevator rides
(Drexel) unable to find rooms, find roll books
English: ambulance German: KRANKENWAGEN.
The thoughts and intents of the heart: If you do as they say to compose freely taking any thought as valid then you will automatically speak for the controllers of the subcon, the epigones who imitate the true create power of the person sealed with Messiah in the Father.

I was never able to dare much relationship with scholars, even though I wanted to entertain Rhodes D. I never did, but we visited John Lehmann, secretary to Virginia Woolf and Edith Sitwell, in London at his flat in '74. He said we the only students who ever had. But not to be a tourist escapist in their own life

6/25/19 an epigone of Woolf. One sentence in the verse spelderd floor, the entire language at beck and call, so CALL! Consciousness is history, memory.
Ez 13.18 on the Egregori teaching seduction to woman-
But in Aeschylus the inversion of the man/woman in every case and on to Messiah, inverted by Virgil in 4th eclogue And say, Thus saith the Lord GOD; Woe to the women that sew pillows to all armholes, and make kerchiefs upon the head of every stature to hunt souls! Will ye hunt the souls of my people, and will ye save the souls alive that come unto you?
 --This scholarly slapstick is full of jokes upon the lamented loss of the golden age which is found not to be a universal looking of myth but an instance of myth control, a speculative transference of modern alienation. Spokesmen of the rich say that everybody who lives in this Iron Age continually dreams of living in the gold. This golden age, like the later idea of India or Eldorado, was an entertainment, not a piety or a philosophy of improving mankind, the self aggrandizement that money perfects among the wealthy, the intellectual and entitled to empower the sanctions this juxtaposition gives to the ruling order. The golden age was their dream substitute for a cow. The only ones who lost were themselves.

6/26/19 transferred Mark's PDF to doc.
Alethic modality is often associated with epistemic modality in research, and it has been questioned whether this modality should be considered distinct from epistemic modality which denotes the speaker's evaluation or judgment of the truth. The criticism states that there is no real difference between "the truth in the world"
(alethic) and "the truth in an individual's mind" (epistemic) [but thee is, and that's why Mark knew me]

6/27/19 Thurs
--after his interview with banner Aey came for coffee and while making it, with the boiling kettle in his hand, talking about some aspect, tilted his hand and poured the boiling water on the floor, and didn't even notice ..Top Banner ex gets 21 mil compensation for nonprofit. He is to see up to 60 a day, 25 is breakeven, one complaint, but all his with 2 MAs
--The demonic networks are not essentially the media. All this hate of Americans is opposite of Dr. King's effort to evoke humanity esp. in the opposition. The satanic Egregori is all about inversion, everything is inverted from its truth, male, female especially. I conclude I misjudged the value and thought being of Ken and Mark, both of which I now see, with new sight, made mature and far reaching contributions of thought. I never took them seriously in person though—my loss.
Remember is the chi. If you walk in your ki you won't have to try

--Conflict with Teddy---he is to go to PCS I have after school care and before. Throws piece of watermelon across the room on ground. Asks to pick it up, won't. I pick it and throw it at him, Hits in head. He is signed up for PCS kinder. Full of negativity from the start. Refuses to say please. Belligerent always wants the lights turned on Theo says Andrew will die in 12months. That he "hates his name" but he has lot to say about Netflix.

6/28/19 Fri.
--Faith cannot be confirmed by reason, but only by faith and its works which produce the impossible in the world. "I have overcome the world" says the Lord.
-it is as if the Schmann Res is being interdicted by satellite Jetson,' that uses infrared lasers to read a person's cardiac signature. To make the method viable, U.S. Special Forces would likely need to build a database. The method does require an invisible laser to be pointed at a subject for about 30 seconds to get a sufficient read, meaning the technology can only be viably used on someone who is standing still.

6/29/19 Sat.
Rc'd PDF of Restorations, Begin edit. Goldilocks and GoldiPop,
Maybe all the members of my committee were one species of gay or another they did not fully perceive or took for granted the good humor and brightness of what they read. They whole is a peaen to love by the author who organized it, but more on the part of the Elizabethans who wrote it. This does seem now to be a prodigious collection of quotes but at the time I lived, breathed and slept the whole subject for six years before writing. Substitute o for a, scold or scald, and the same connotation occurs, burning. CLOWN MEDIA

6/30/19 Sun.it is a great privilege to have outlived my youth.
lucida, eldorado
 Tagetes This Theological implant of metempsychosis in the Greek mind strains credulity with the idea of one virtuous life let along three, let alone the entity of the soul visiting over and over again this life as a prison, recycled from the chains of the moon as some other Egyptian beliefs proffer throughout the theosophical industry. the child is father of the man in this savagery of the two year old working out its socialization with fear and trembling There was not one biblical figure that let a virtuous life, unless it's Daniel, and therein the one truly virtuous was sacrificed and tortured, not by the mandarins on some distant planet so the rest of humanity could have peace, but tortured here on earth, so they could know the truth of theirf being complete and incomplete in this intermittent world.
The struggle of the man for virtue, to govern his intolerable acts has no end and to know this is not to attain virtue but to wrestle with despair. The madness of the incarnate in every absurd thought and act is honest anyway, to give the lie to the pretense of goodness broadcast from its corrupt public figures in entertainment, leadership of every kind. This denial is so pervasive that to say so is to endanger the self, for the beautiful and the true have betrayed every principle they outwardly profess and virtue is a lie. What thinking man is not vexed with these possessions? What is there to do but admit his fragility with Aeschylus and Shakespeare. Against this backdrop the creations of a man are still extraordinary and full of

acclaim and astonishment but just when they reach their apex his failure of virtue overwhelms the whole. On AB's recital, to A: do you think like it's getting away from you?

7/1/19 saw notice of NCIS and looking for a vita to send found the recommendations that saw I am charming with distinctly original thought. "independence of mind and judgment—a certain originality. Sympathetic, gentle, patient humorous (Cranfill), imaginative and scholarly, attractive and easy to get along with (Pratt). Considerable charm of manner, Gordon, (Committee) Tenure app: joy to work with, Spencer, Then found the ms of the Secret life.I asked for and was given in a recharge this A.M a new image of T, laughing. Pat said that is their reprieve when they visit from the discipline. That we met 50 yrs ago this Sept!

7/2/19 I apparently have access to the archives of the ongoing dream envelope to the EN, CN, Was perusing old bulletins, photos in archive ina metal drawer I found in the huge gymnasium, just vacated as P. Mary was returning to it, then a little lost I came to a men's meeting in a darkish room, then out all of it almost invisibly traversed.
22 Sept 1969 was the day I met my wife! Yom Kippur. Powerful word, wife. Path sharer, comfort, life. University of the People, need vita too. Aey to be offered contact as NP with Banner!

7/3/19 Thought is the bridge between the worlds:::Speech—thought—FAITH
To abstract the simultaneous into a rational rotund perspective is the illusion but on the bridge where the thoughts fly with momentary precision and immediate perception of a constant dream apprehended with a butterfly net and taking the leavings of the net back to your space and paste them in a notebook, spread their wings with pins, the herberian aviary, the ossuary (of thought) is the illusion. They fly they fly and who ever dares will meet them in the bye and bye.

5/25/18 Kozyrev was correct! Entropy/Negentroy can be generated!
-- The term Ōtōkan comes from the "ō" of Daiō, the "tō " of Daitō, and the "kan" of Kanzan). Daitō Kokushi as a Beggar. one sees people crossing and re-crossing the bridge just as they are. This was a single word meaning a frontier-gate or mountain-pass. He told him "Throw your whole spirit into the word 'Pass'. You should have no other occupation ; --List of Troop Loot. Lunch with AEG
--Th Harriot: Many things they sawe with us...as mathematical instruments, sea compasses...[and] spring clocks that seemed to goe of themselves - and many other things we had - were so strange unto them, and so farre exceeded their capacities to comprehend the reason and meanes how they should be made and done, that they thought they were underwater laser weapon system able to heat up and cause fires within submarines --"Sea -- Dragon" was a missile system—but based on MoD analysis, showed it being an underwater laser weapon system based on "Deep Siren" technology—and (seriously, you can't make this up) can be deployed and fired from radical new aircraft that patent documents indicate both

the US and China are actively developing that seem eerily similar to the UFO's being reported by US Navy pilots.

7/4/19 In college I played with a Jack Kramer wood racket 4 ¾ grip strung with gut. Jose Celis, from El Salvador played 1. I played with him once at 1 doubles against Lehigh. He apologized after, said we could have won the watch, but he was not intent. We won a set when they hit an overhead at me at the service, but I went into a crouch and blooped it back over their heads for a winner. We won that set? I came back from CR in May '63, had a knee operation that summer, changed as many classes as I could to English, took an extra term, curtailed Christian activities, played tennis at #4, season 6-6, had a great win in practice against #2, a scholarship player from Mainline.
Put up Psalm 23 / Celine, 1,2,3

7/5/19
I consider in my dwelling place a clear heat upon herbs. Your dead bodies shall arise. The dew of herbs is yours. Awake and sing. Earth shall cast out its dead.

--identifiable features of literary style (such as self-reflexivity, privileging of surface, mixed styles and genre, double coding, and narrative subversion)
McCaffery-postmodern condition. I would trace it back to the 1960s and Herbert Marcuse's analysis of the infinite capacity of capitalism (now late or spherical capitalism) to absorb its own detournement, a variation on previous work, in which the newly created work has a meaning that is antagonistic or antithetical to the original College and (French: [detuʁnəmɑ̃]), meaning "rerouting, hijacking" in French, is a technique developed in the 1950s by the Letterist International,[1] and later adapted by the Situationist International (SI),[2][3] that was defined in the SI's inaugural 1958 journal as "[t]he integration of present or past artistic productions into a superior construction of a milieu. In this sense there can be no situationist painting or music, but only a situationist use of those means contradictions.
--in Prior to Meaning you are developing a poetic quantum mechanics possible cross-pollination of a present to a past fascinates me, that both can be chiasmically propensitive, with the present able to contemporize the past, and the past historicize the present. Thus we find an 18th-century precedent for Gysin and Burroughs's cut-up method in Caleb Whitforde's delightful cross-column reading (first published in the memorable Foundling Hospital for Wit)…
--guessing that clay of tragickal is an anonymous masked antifa Satanist of Edinburgh associates of the new occult Discordia wave. Who ends up next to prick of spindle and wats his name Lish to Carver, would be rewrite artists and opinionated censors like Alex Cigale and unlikely. They think the sum of all life is the number of roles and cameo spots and walk ons played like a Hollywood actor, Dustin Hoffman, not his real offenses berating and victimizing women, words, ideas like Robert dinero how to make metate out of volcanic rock.

7/6/19

Begin with much addition to top
Roamakita chainsaw Jeb Bush 3
presidents die on the 4th
--A and family and Aey for brisket and ice cream and ping pong in the yard. Zion has some aloe off the stalk.
7/7/19 the highest it is possible to reach is not as a cosmic man but an everyman.
Freddie Mercury and Hart Crane are two incandescents who died in their
burning. Kompromate

7/7/19 seriously revise and work Afar Off of the bridge

7/8/19 ---Statues of London, paris, D.C. statues of China of every city and nation exist in the inversion of the inversion where they are inflicted with a voodoo of principalities and powers

Reading this thought stream occurs at odd moments of fatigue and coming in and out of sleep. the terms energy, mass, information, spacetime, field, time, charge, plasma, wave, and others are NOT and do NOT qualify as physical objects Coming in from the spontaneity cha ching, chin ching, cha ching, three steps removed from what was apparent and unspeakable, here becomes the proposition that they maintain statues in that place of all the cites and hence the nations, which they stick with various afflictions, pins and needles is too simple a ruse, but somehow infect the streets and the citizens with their maladies so that London is not London all by itself but withal the tampering and predicament of the kings and powers of that place. Whether any of this is true cannot be said for it is triple translated, but that's what it is in our world to us, in the three envelops, understanding that the envelop is one, two and three, are quantums accelerated from each other and the depth of the third is beyond leaped by the fourth, which is unspeakable spontaneous and self evident there but however is non existent here, except as a passing memory and fancy. Which is really the way a quantum computer works, turn over, turn over, turn over, spit out—bingo so the 4th dimen is the quantum. in math. entanglement: How does one discrete particle over here affect another discrete particle over there?
☐ EN deacquisation about 15 paintings of mine, I take them to my car.
Individuals, sets, subsets, groups, classes
Harry's razor blades

7/9/19 on the road at hotel given room 666 Sick, P leaves w/o giving keys to car and accounts, have to call here…in process
Nieves penitentes are a new habitat for snow algae
Ithe Discolosures Journals: blades of ice found on Earth's second-highest volcano are home to a community of microscopic life, scientists have discovered. Nieves penitentes, snow formations found high up in the Andes, were found to host snow algae. This is the first time life has been recorded in these formations. Nieves penitentes are elongated blades of hardened snow and ice found in some of the most extreme, high-altitude environments on Earth—cold

and dry regions above 13,000 feet. In these spots, UV radiation is high, humidity is low, winds are extreme and the temperature fluctuates dramatically. That makes it difficult for life to exist. Nieves penitentes range from just a few inches in height up to 16 feet and are normally oriented towards our sun. They got their name—which means "penitent snow"—because they resemble praying monks wearing white robes. "The entire back of one of our pickup trucks had to be filled with barrels of drinking water. The penitente fields, found at a height of over 16,000 feet, were found to have red ice patches—a sign that microscopic life exists in the ice.

Shelter among the Pentinmentes: penitentes provide both water and shelter from harsh winds, high UV radiation and thermal fluctuations, creating an oasis in an otherwise extreme landscape," new terrestrial analog for astrobiological studies of life beyond Earth."

Cryosphere close to the Atacama Desert, which is one of the driest places on Earth and is the landscape that is thought to be most similar to Mars.

Nitric Oxide Humann, lozenges, ethetial layers restore, Humann Super Beets, soft chews, True Grit screenplay, Diplomatic underground, scopoline

Rhapsody: Gershwin, inspired by the rhythm of the train, decides he will use what he knows to compose what today is considered one of the greatest American classical works. "It was on the train, with its steely rhythms, its rattlety-bang that is so often stimulating to a composer, that I suddenly heard—even saw on paper—the complete construction of the Rhapsody, from beginning to end. No new themes came to me, but I worked on the thematic material already in my mind and tried to conceive of the composition as a whole. Bernstein's comments: not a composition at all. a string of separate paragraphs stuck together. The themes are terrific–not a real composition in the sense that whatever happens in it must seem inevitable. You can cut parts of it without affecting the whole. You can remove any of these stuck-together sections and the piece still goes on as bravely as before. It can be a five-minute piece or a twelve-minute piece. the journey, expressed in melody, from uncertainty to achievement created by the intermingling of multiple the mesas the orchestra and solo piano parts interact.

7/10/19 THEO GLORIA, TEDDY GRCIA STAGES WATER RESCE WITH FIRE DEPT BUT
ENDANgERES SUBJET WHICH I AM TO RESCUE -CONFRONT CHIEF Exc. MANY MINUTE
VOLCANIC CRACKS SPREAD BT NO MORE ERTHUAKES SINCE RUSSIANS HAVE DEACTIVATED EARTHQUAKE SHIP, BUT TOO LATE FOR CHINA LAKE, PAYBACK FOR ATTACK ON RUSSIAN SUB
New window at office, pat has 2 NP interns, one med student, Aey, in one day—says she likes to teach! I work on bill for no modem, with linesman improve DSL

7/11/19 Mel Gibson Apocalypto
TYPES OF THE GOLDEN AGE The Gold, the Girl, the Soul
Europe reduplicated Greek mythology exactly in the new world, which statement is so underrealized and under represented that this dissertation is offered as a downpayment on the subject of a completely revised writing offered later. I stll think this is the most interesting

subject imaginable, here made accessible to the general reader, even though there is a lot of poetry.

This celebration of the subject of the new world was credited as a dissertation 45 years ago, but looking at it now has never been more appropriate to consider. That's for several reasons, first the beauty of subject and the implicit political commentary it makes, and because it is a model of the native/alien interface! Over and over again these writers cast the new world as a good and bad, a golden age they satire, colonies they see as superficial companies, where natives bedevil or maybe they are noble savages, as all the while they cast the discoveries as the conquest of a woman, when they are not searching for gold. It is a mélange of contradiction with much depth.

They are islands in the sense that they are both/and, meaning vegetable/mineral, real/imaginary, sacred or hellish. Ophir/Guiana, Bermuda, are natives virtuous or hellish, cannibals or practical saints or both, depending. So the islands move and have no fixed position, both as floating islands, which much background in the motifs of travel literature, and in the sense they can reverse identities. They are movables as opposed to the mainland which holds its identity. I

Some members of the committee asked why the spellings were not modernized. I love the language and its ecstasy. How seriously are we to take the rapine and murder of these opportunists/ Just as seriously as all proponents of war do, for war is not a natural human state even if it seems so. That's controversy. England, London conqueror of nations, mythic successor of Rome, is not pilloried in the world court of opinion, probably because it still owns the copyright. If you cannot appreciate the satire of its tactics you miss much of the humor these writers intend.

Milton who has been out of favor for so long for his puritan ways turns out to be the hero here for his restoration of nature to itself and rescuing it from the gold artifice. Otherwise here we see the development of the golden age from an afterlife state to the real world artifice, initiated by royalty, propagandized for the purposes of conquest, allegorized as a moral, immortal good or ill and finally restored again. In this the writing is innocent in the golden sense Lewis defines. Any further elaboration however would be critical considering colonialization as female conquest, chauvism, post modern prejudice and empire. The list goes on. John Donne in this context of coloation, License my rooving hands, is pilloried for anti feminist, colonial thought. Not to speak of them all, all the major white male poets of the renaissance were out to get the gold and the girl! What in modern woo woo is reserved for the annunaki!

One of the standards for good writing being content neutrality there are no preachments on the text that are not in the writers themselves. Mostly this is a presentation of these writers interprets itself. The idea was not to select out proof texts but to capture context and breadth and therein to show development of ideas. The alchemical metaphor of the base matter follows on the vegetable turned to gold. Fictional locations, sources of gold. And Plunder. As Guiana is a reverse golden age, Burmada an anti-Elysium. And island of hell Ken didn't take me seriously because I wasn't a scholar. I didn't take him seriously because he wasn't a poet

Fri. Need to link and relook at sources, take a long revision. Ye hypervibe
One of that cuprous wave of resisters at Abolish ICE on Central st.at the Methodist churl in lawn hairs at the church on central with bags of peanuts and fake astronauts. I see police mobilizing behind the club as I leave. HQ RVs cars, motorcycles. Stop and talk to cop directing traffic. After ward the resistors do get violent. Bob Dylan shelter from the storm 1974

7/15/19 Mon. Philadelphia balsamic olive oil. Violet split gene hybrid children-cynthis
Sauvageaugloia griffithsiana (Greville) in the algae data base of Pycological Society
Note on the marine algae of the Bermudas.   Two species of the genus Polysiphonia Greville (Ceramiales, Rhodophyta)based on morphology of vegetative and reproductive structures. The plants are widely distributed in estuaries and salt marshes attached to substrata such as pneumatophores of trunks of mangroves trees... 1) prostrate and erect ecorticate axes with four pericentral cells; 2) branch initials separating at intervals of more than five segments; 3) lacking or rare vegetative trichoblasts; 4) rhizoids in open connection with pericentral cells; 5) procarps bearing a four celled carpogonial branch; 6) spermatangial branches arising directly from each axial cell; 7) tetrasporangia arranged in straight series on determinate branches and 8) apex is sharp-pointed.

The Demise of Fraktur, Hexes, Chests, Barns.
The Ship Lists, English Public School movement, Ben Franklin, Schlatter are evidences of the prejudice, apprehension even paranoia that fueled the attempt to control the German population of Philadelphia. Before the prejudice concocted by guilt against all so called white populations in the U.S. there were clear social and ethnic divisions between English, German, Welsh, Irish, Italian, Spanish, French peoples of origin. Even as late as the 60s black thinkers called them Caucasoid to put them in their place, but black thought was superseded by Muslim imports in the 21st century. Not that they're the same, but the new pecking order became Black and Hispanic as the old guards and then gay, transgender, and Muslim concurrent with marijuana, opioids, no borders, CIA drug planes, obesity, and digital seductions in entertainment on the outside while the skies chemtrailed aluminum and barium nano particles. Below, where GMO crops, genetic mutations, CRISPRs, https://en.wikipedia.org/wiki/CRISPR_gene_editing sonar and sonic irradiation together made everyone that owned a cell phone a double antenna on the control grid, any attempt to point this out was called Luddite, conspiracy or racist. All media fell. America was clamped down. Christian became an epithet and just as German Anabaptist had been denatured by liberalism, Christian became an outcast socially and churches were undermined by sanctuary movements and ICE demonstrations, FEMA pastors, prosperity for faith and false charism. All the steps outlined in the demise of Fraktur, Hexes, Chests, Barns apply to every folk culture destroyed by assimilation and templates, machine made, from the black colleges of the south absorbed into state university systems, the alternation of the human genome itself, to the obliteration of nations, states and all boundaries, political, social, sexual, except where it served the purpose of division to further divide the folk and their ways. Whether to celebrate the past from the majority point of view or lament the passing as a symbol for the passing of us all, going from the island to the continent of the majority foreordain that the rural folk

benefits were impossible to recapture. Then suddenly wishes for the garden come back again.   Folk Religion×Fraktur×Historical barns×

7/18/19
Sonata: composition in three sections (exposition, development, and recapitulation) in which two themes or subjects are explored according to set key relationships. It forms the basis for much classical music, including the sonata, symphony, and concerto.
Concerto: the two parts in a concerto—the soloist and the orchestra or concert band—alternate between episodes of opposition, cooperation, and independence to create a sense of flow.
Symphony: a work usually consisting of multiple distinct sections or movements, often four, with the first movement in sonata form. Symphonies are almost always scored for an orchestra consisting of a string section (violin, viola, cello, and double bass), brass, woodwind, and percussion instruments which altogether Sasquatch, 5G & Earth's Frequency Grid

7/19/19 this is no history of these events or their likeness before judgment, since all the sources of contemporary information are corrupted. All sort of moral ethical and issues arise form the background narrative Auerbach finds. In the age of Noah and genetic mutation, when Noah goes into the ark and all sorts of peoples surround it beg for deliverance we see them already changing into the bestial likeness of beast four footed and creeping things they have woven into, had woven into their DMA. A wave of crazed half animals, like centaurs, charged the life raft with barks and howls. It sounds like a slander of the living kingdom of animals, the true animals and true men and women however already aboard. For remember the purpose of this salvation and deliverance of life itself is issued in Genesis The Nephilim were on the earth in those days—and also afterward—when the sons of God went to the daughters of humans and had children by them. They were the heroes of old, men of renown.

5 The LORD saw how great the wickedness of the human race had become on the earth, and that every inclination of the thoughts of the human heart was only evil all the time. 6 The LORD regretted that he had made human beings on the earth, and his heart was deeply troubled. 7 So the LORD said, "I will wipe from the face of the earth the human race I have created—and with them the animals, the birds and the creatures that move along the ground—for I regret that I have made them."

Like the half man half angel commanded to be destroyed over and over, not in genocide but deicide, but some seem always to have one way or another survived, perhaps their fins and gills saved them as they took to the waves, it is always between the true men and true animals and the false Men grow horns, and tusks and snouts, fins and bawl in the dust as they lose their legs. They grow hair, scales, every variety of the denatured beasts and who knows what they have been CRISPRd with, branches, leaves roots, they bawl and caw and whistle instead of words, have lost their speech, arms turn to wings but cannot fly, noses are beaks, their fingers are razor sharp, but their minds no longer human, or they are as human as Musk neurolinks with AI, going the opposite way from the bestial to to the inanimate as they enter prisons of virtuality to never escape, not even die, forever tortured except they wll be freed at the destruction of the world and all its woes. All this is in Bosch and Breughels.

So for a while earth life was clean again, "Come out of the ark, you and your wife and your sons and their wives. 17 Bring out every kind of living creature that is with you—the birds, the animals, and all the creatures that move along the ground—so they can multiply on the earth and be fruitful and increase in number on it." for your lifeblood I will surely demand an accounting. I will demand an accounting from every animal. And from each human being, too, I will demand an accounting for the life of another human being.

6 "Whoever sheds human blood,   by humans shall their blood be shed; for in the image of
     God   has God made mankind.

7 As for you, be fruitful and increase in number; multiply on the earth and increase upon it."

8 Then God said to Noah and to his sons with him: 9 "I now establish my covenant with you and with your descendants after you 10 and with every living creature that was with you— the birds, the livestock and all the wild animals, all those that came out of the ark with you—every living creature on earth. Genesis 5:32-10:1 There seem tbe three obvious waves of hybrid invasion, Noahs time, the fall of Atlantis, and our own, but since we are in it we know nothing of it, the sources of information being as corrupt and the false life. The Atlantean Branch Breaks

Many of these "sins" revolved around the crystal implants as discussed, but many others revolved around the manipulation of genetics and other types of implantations. As the dense physicality of the planet began to affect them, they also became overwhelmed by the emotional feeling involved with that physicalness.

 As The Nine express it, they, " became very involved in the creation of larger and more prominent mating organs. They also attempted through their scientific knowledge and understanding to genetically exchange creatures with soul beings on Planet Earth–through transplanting . . . by creating these creatures they would perhaps have the strength of the creature, or the creature could be serving them, or they could develop a means for more physical pleasure (shades of Dr. Moreau)."

"The modern civilization has only attained a part of what Atlantis had attained. They had all the knowledge of using the mind to move objects and themselves (teleportation). If it had not been that below their waist they were always in trouble, then it would have been a fine civilization . . . We have no objections to enjoyment – it is when it become all consuming." The Nine also add that the Atlanteans had great abilities in the field of transplantation of human organs such as the heart and even the brain, but again, used much of this kind of knowledge to improve the size of their sex organs. Life expectancy at times on Atlantis could be up to a few thousand years, and this is the kind of knowledge of 'never growing old' that was transplanted into ancient Egypt and subsequently into the patriarchs of ancient Hebrew culture as well.

This history of Atlantis is "all within the mind of the dolphins," say The Nine, but much of it has also been known to the initiates of those hermetic organizations we referred to earlier.

H.G. Wells' story, The Island Of Dr. Moreau, tells the story of a great scientist in self-imposed exile who creates an island full of hybrids and half-breeds, animal/human mixes, in pursuit of his ultimate goal to create a perfect human by mixing the traits of the two.
In the parahistory of Atlantis and the Cycles of Time: Prophecies, Traditions, and Occult Revelations, By
Joscelyn Godwin "A new exhibition explores supernatural folk traditions from the northern region of Tohoku, Japan. WOW inc., a Japanese design studio, has created large-scale interactive projections with motion capture technology in which visitors transform into characters by wearing special masks. Bakeru transforming spirits, sequel otalku— supernatural folk traditions like the Hopi gods, supernatural folk ghost pi folk belief and traditions of the supernatural: a case study of shimla .. hybrid literary forms
--more hybrids, St John, Spenser, metamorphosis, kafka, john gower, medieval science, gargoyles Hesiod and the gods White's bestiary, thought beasts, St Bernard of Clairvaux, Monoclonal Antibodies Mary Robinette Kowal-space. My Favorite Bit: Clark T. Carlton talks about THE PROPHET OF THE GHOST ANTS a troll that took an acid trip at burning man
John Edward Williams, The Broken Landscape, The Necessary Lie, English Renaissance Poetry: A Collection of Shorter Poems from Skelton to Jonson
Not only are other rhapsodies under construction, The Way Out of Fairywood is all but finished but the final note, but another different form, long, is also well underway, called the Jerusalem Ms. of three parts, less simultaneous but experimental in its speaking of the traverse of the Bridge that connects the worlds. Jose Donoso—NYT-short stories used dark surrealism and social satire to explore the haunted lives of exiles and writers and a world of aristocratic excesses
--empathy depletion
Peter Fenwick, Monica Rentz non jewel give up surrender
7/20/19 went with Aey to Todd langford's

7/21/19 you only know what you are when you were
#Arrowmith, #Austin, #Athens #HillCountry, #philosophy, #teaching, Luminalty is the state between a door, a highway, an airport.
As part of the greater Actor Network of human communications, each cell phone upgrade reinforces globalization, and hypermodernity. If the current trends of technosocial co-production continue, the future relationship of humans and technology will resemble a massive technosocial assemblage that takes the matters of time/space compression into its own hands, colonizing every public space and making it public on a private network. In this new modernity technologies will shrink so small that they will be able to integrate into every aspect of the real world, so that the real world will be interconnected at every point, and everything felt in the real world will also be tallied virtually.

Humans are becoming a single superorganism with a technosocial heartbeat, constantly updating in order to compress time and space closer and closer together. The world itself is exists in a liminal state 'betwixt and between' humanity and technology. A new liminal 'communitas' is emerging with technology as the framework for all social interaction and communication. When this liminality is resolved technology will be free to colonize all human interaction. With the space and time of the world shrinking, the distance between humans and technology will decrease until they are can no longer be understood separately from one another. When the public sphere becomes completely private the social sphere will become public again, but the field of interaction will be global instead of local. Cyborg anthropology Latin limen "threshold, cross-piece, sill" (see limit (n.)) + -al Henry Jones, Palatine families.

7/22/19 Digital and other amnesia of the self is where the immediate history of the perso'ns participation in and the spirit of their life has been misplaced because superceded by one put upon them by exterior forces. They literally cannot remember, they say anyway, acting freely or cheerfully. It is as if they are depressed, esp. if they claim ptsd..
As P says about this, adversarial Aey had an interest in prisoners and prison in sculptures and castles. I thought this was a shared point, that in me it made for compassion for others suffering, that this should help me as a nurse. Now it sounds like he needs a nurse.
Jimmy Dorado was the Methodist camp meeting preacher whose church we visited in vicinity of Overbrook, PA. Too good, too pretty, had temptation on him.

7/23/19 the thing about misfit is that it doesn't fit and that perfectly describes a whole state of beinghttps://www.perpetuallineup.org/   One of the pioneers of 19th-century facial analysis, Francis Galton, was a prominent British eugenicist. He superimposed images of men convicted of crimes, attempting to find through "pictorial statistics" the essence of the criminal face. - "lip curvature, eye inner corner distance, and the so-called nose-mouth angle"-- an Israeli start-up called Faception uses machine learning to score facial images --- face challen https://www.nist.gov/programs-projects/face-challenges
Cf to DNA composites for the same
Donald barr, space relations, Whitney Webb, lee Stranahan, Bannon and the Mercers. Elito Richardson, Larry summers, Dershowitz, Epstein—n.m. age of consent 14 then
Brown clustering: AI- grouping words into clusters that are assumed to be semantically related by virtue of their having been embedded in similar contexts for speech recognition Darpa 1971. Markov chain: a sequence of possible events in which the probability of each event depends only on the state attained in the previous event.[sometimes characterized as "memorylessness"). Roughly speaking, a process satisfies the Markov property if one can make predictions for the future of the process based solely on its present state just as well as one could knowing the process's full history, hence independently from such history. Random walks based on integers and the gambler's ruin problem are examples of Markov processes. In probability theory and related fields, a stochastic or random process is a mathematical object usually defined as a family of random variables. Hidden Markov Model (HMM) is a statistical Markov model in which the system being modeled is assumed to be a Markov process with unobservable (i.e. hidden) states. Hidden Markov models are especially known for their application in reinforcement learning and temporal pattern recognition such as speech, handwriting, gesture recognition,[7] part-of-speech tagging, musical score

following,[8] Melville rewrote *Moby Dick* 82 times. data visualization to web browsers, Jason goodman, David Webb Swigert, 9/11 when hub   time line Studio at a Glance

7/24/19 *hashaymolim hashamalym, Ha earetz ha earetz* That's why they call it redemption. It brings back the lost. --Roy Stemman, vistors from outer space via David Jacobs—albert k. bender and mars, the exalted one from outer space—men were walking on the moon! Hom hoom. Nuke mars, Mars nuke. Runespraggen The words are not enough. They need the presumption of goodness to be accepted.

7/25/10 Went to walk in the Salt River. Worked on Stories.
7/26/19 lunch with A.
7/27/19 coffee with Aey, enter Herberger, frame piece. It's hard to describe feeling good these two days since the river, but there it is. Suspicious. I haven't felt good for years. 6 flaming chords

7/28/19 Sunday. got up at 2 to search for collorary to the piece of the cow of two years ago we just glued to frame. Didn't find it, some reference to U.S.
The Blue Beam is a movie projector from satellite that plays to the auditorium of the earth, tailored to whatever specific myths are famous in different localities and cultures.

7/29/19 We had Nikolai while they went swimming. He is I yr one month, H exchanged greetings with Scion and her bone back and forth. Founded a glass gar many ways. The agony of life repeated again after many reps, the ages it takes for maturity. The care needed to guard it. The fact it is never stable and only realized at the end! If the struggle has succeeded in faithfulness.
Got acceptance at silver pinon of three good poems. But then he only published two.

7/30/19 have Judah for a week while Aey is at Moro Bay.
As George Webb has been saying According to documents filed in the U.S. Federal Court in West Palm Beach, Florida in 2008, Epstein shared the tail number of his Bell Long Ranger 206L3 helicopter (tail number N474AW) with a U.S. State Department OV-10D Bronco. According to the Federal Aviation Administration (FAA) registration database, Epstein's Bell helicopter and the Bronco owned by the ****U.S. State Department**** and contracted to the private military company ****DYNCORP INTERNATIONAL**** both used the same identification number.
4chan
More concepts of the 4th dimension for Klaus Gerken says somewhere he doesn't do bios because they are irrelevant to the work, which must compel on its own. This like what *elimae* said, works of merit.
NASA sniffer aircraft zig zag San Andreas fault
Orcopedia mts. Geology.The dramatic and variable terrain was shaped primarily by movements of the adjacent San Andreas Fault over millennia. Most notably, the Orocopia schist, a blueschist assemblage found in the range, matches the Pelona schist found over 250

km away in the San Gabriel Mountains along the San Andreas fault. Hill and Dibblee (1953) first noted this similarity (a piercing point), and used it to construct the first estimates of the offset on the fault.[3]

Astronaut training

The Orocopia Mountains offer considerable geologic variety and was one of the areas used for geologic field training by Caltech Professor of Geology, Leon T. Silver, for astronauts in preparation for the NASA Project

Apollo Moon landing missions. This training included:[4]

- Apollo 13 Crew Training: September 1969: Astronauts Lovell, Haise and Swigert
- Apollo 14 crew did not train with Dr. Leon "Lee" Silver, they trained with Richard Henry Jahns, a Professor at Stanford at the time.
- Apollo 15 Crew Training: June 1970: Astronauts Scott, Irwin and Worden
- Apollo 16 Crew Training: April 1972: Astronauts Young, Mattingly and Duke
- Apollo 17 Crew Training: December 1972: Astronauts Cernan, Evans and Schmi

Taurofilium Yes Some regions look as they are others not, what happened to the Great lakes, what is that barren bump of a plateau of parts of Ohio, how has the new Madrid fault risen the height, and likewise questions. Yes the darkness around the Mississippi, and what of some regions that look as they are but others not? What happened to the Great lakes? What is that barren bump of a plateau of parts of Ohio? How has the new Madrid fault risen to the height, and likewise questions leave me worried it is a prophetic moral topography on one hand or a restructuring of the geography, geology and morality on the other, as if geography, morality and prophecy could all be combined. I don't want to raise up Ellen White's idea that America is the false prophet of the beast even if it seems here a kind of Taurobolium with the eye and snout -Seattle Amazonia, but maybe parts of CA are gone? The photo could be brighter, "The priest clad in a silk toga worn in the Gabinian cincture, with golden crown and fillets on his head, takes his place in a trench covered by a platform of planks pierced with fine holes, on which a bull, magnificent with flowers and gold, is slain. The blood rains through the platform onto the priest below, who receives it on his face, and even on his tongue and palate, and after the baptism presents himself before his fellow-worshippers purified and regenerated, and receives their salutations and reverence". performed as a measure for the welfare (salus) of the emperor, Empire

He shall lay his hand on the head of the burnt offering, and it shall be accepted for him to make atonement for him. Then he shall kill the bull before the Lord, and Aaron's sons the priests shall bring the blood and throw the blood against the sides of the altar that is at the entrance of the tent of meeting. (Lev. 1:4–5) Women like Leonard Cohen for his monotone chants that touch their perfect beauty with his mind. He says Roshi taught me to love the true person that is there but not there and that made it easier for him to love, with all overlooking of the one who was.

8/1/19 Psychgoats Psigoats

I found this on the sidewalk. I must have slipped out of somebody's notebook. We have no way of knowing who this is.

8/3/19 We speak a patois of a hundred levels of nuance to each other.
George Webb: August 3rd, 2019. Bill Barr Backchannel To Rockefeller Brotherhood?
Uniontown: 8.34f:
Uniontown-a very big part of the national railroad that Lincoln builds out to the west coast, it's where
Rockefeller recruits a lot of his scabs for putting down rebellions, its where Rockefeller for the oil fields there beings a lot of these east Europeans that can only speak Ukrainian or Lithuanian and that's a control mechanism meaning I can get 'em cheap, they'll work all day for me, and they can only communicate with me, I completely control this force… Donavan Worland: Richard Herrnstein and Charles Murray- The Reading! The Bell Curve-Cognitive Elite & Our Future-- high-tech and worldwide economy, where competition is fierce and huge sums of capital are at stake, will require business and government to recruit the highest IQs- here- Coming Apart: The State of White America, 1960–2010 by Charles Murray
They wear culture as their mask, tuxedos, parties, art, opera concerts, gathers are their code for communication with what they are really about.

8/4/19 how many environments from the surface or center of Mercury to the surface or center of earth/ magnetospheres
Ist dream I stop by accident at a place and see Robert and Cyn and fam in a Jewish wedding or ceremony of some sort, right in town, but they had not mentioned it.
The hybrids are democrats and republicans.
One of Ryder's most Melvillean paintings is Jonah, in the Smithsonian's collection. It has become so darkened over time that some details can barely be made out. In the foreground swims Jonah, waving his arms, as the great fish bears down upon him (the creature's eyes and snout can just be discerned in the far right of the painting, about halfway up). Up above, a transcendent God can be seen directing or sanctioning the course of events. It would be hard to imagine a more fitting illustration for Chapter IX, "The Sermon."
Had kids, played kitty, they in hose for hour with Zion, watermelon, made cake, played cars, read books, played piano, mostly all on their own, then to home and A's birthday, gave him genealogy ate meal and cake, opened present, talked then about the makeups of genome, which makes it seem like they need a book wrapping all the strands together on blog, since they have never been to Pa.

8/5/19 Hoverboard over English channel
The size of the bottle has nothing to do with the potency of the pill
Gibson island elite. Gehen netwook to Kissinger. Chenault, flying tigers, al Cameron, wong ping pong in basement.
These killings are cleaning up the rat lines, in Dayton Sayeed selah,

8/6/19 Tues, Aey returns, Has car hit by drunk while parked. Advice: get the name of their agent and talk to him directly not through USAA.
two foxes don't serve the chickens. be direct, aggressive and demanding. 2. Pain and suffering category.

first she is on her vacation and the time and pain of dealing with this cause pain and suffering and detract from the vacation, which must be compensated. second, to come outside to a bang and see here loved new car, a few months old, half totaled, causes dismay and sadness, to be compensated.

3. If she is game, since it's her car, let her make the most impossible extreme demands to set up a close when she says, do you want to talk to my husband? That softens them up for a close. 4. --they must also reimburse you for the rental car you need to replace not having it for whatever time. this is cash. You tell them you want the per diem whether you rent one or not. Mark Kulacz.Mueller contracted sicilian flu to extricate himself, he's so feeble there must be somebody else behind him

Vanishing Area Paradox - Archimedes' Lab Werner Herzog

The peregrine, ja.a. baker, Castillo, discovery and conquest of new spain, the criterion collection

8/7/19 Faith of our fathers holy faith we will be tre to thee till death. The scrpptures of the nations are folly, the Indians mahabarata of the lives the their gods, the muslims of the follies of mohammed are vanity, the Judges, the patricharths are men with their real life foibles of profoundity, it is the trial of men they celebrate and portray and of women, Deborah, jael, samson, Jacob on and on the only real life scriptures in the world. And to compare the mode scientis secular drone hybrids and obscene (warner Herzog) space travels and AI, digital replacement is always inferior

Maya civ ultraviolent Brace yourself! Stone wall coming down! The homeowner was concerned about the movement in this wall over the past 5 years it's leaned in several inches at the top. All braced for removal and repair/replacement.
#restoration #stonework #historic #forge @ Oley, Pennsylvania Hometown carpentry

Owen Kaelen –"I propose, appropriately tentative, that thought is the fourth dimension."
--dentist: thought is different language from speech, if a language. OT biographies of men vs. gods, Soncino

Hebrew texts, illiad and troy, graham hancock and DMT

8/8/19 Thurs, Ruth fell last night there should be MOON
DUST where Buzz Aldrin walked on the moon.

8/9/19 very successful outcome operation, already walking

8/10/19 Heaven's Man. Seek to serve you and to know your word. The know word, ow-wo! Fletcher Prouty awakening from sleep is like descent from a huge cloud of cyclone above down the funnel of connect to the ground, but with decreasing intensity. Best done slowly from the moment of awareness detaching from the cloud but descending slowly to preserve awareness until landing, then making this note.

8/11/19 Sun. Mike confirms the creature to move by
sept three ingreadients of yem

Pat takes Sab and AB to have their nails done, then to Changing Hands

8/12/19 Macduff kennedy airsoft mistake hong kong based airsoft mfg.1.12.20 Coffee with George Webb, Mon. 10am EDT! 8/12/19
Thomas Parr (allegedly 1482-1635) killed by the kings food. Had diet of "subrancid cheese and milk in every form, coarse and hard bread and small drink, generally sour whey", painted by ruebens and van dyck

8/13/19 peregrine.Up periscope me, rising up from
beside dirt patchers to heights makes an awful noise.
the cut eyeball of the Dada boy, but the cut mind of
axe man soul fires to be rescued when their cell
phones fail

8/14/19 Theo begins school today. Preschool. Acceptance of Black Hole Down from Antisf. Change wold to world! These prefaces are a chance to understand that writing of misplaced anthropology from Squisquatch, Subfornical Organ, Concepts of the Subfornical and the Wonk Yaps. here

8/15/19 Straight Arrows. Another notch in this amazingly spontaneous teaching career was when the church had this curriculum called Straight Arrows. The teacher of my son's class, Forest Chaney, was asked to be a supervisor in another area so his wife one day invited herself and their fam to dinner at ours to vet us, which succeeded in my taking his class, which had two of his sones, the son of the Youth pastor and son of the preacher among others, a privileged group, anointed they would say. So I had at the end of these sessions wrestling matches, me against all the boys, they were 5, yrs old, but before that the teaching, which consisted of them all sitting on a large red and black Navajo rug I had got at a yard sale, and facing the board, I would make some marks or they would call out letters and from either of these I would tell a story, unrehearsed, that would tell some moral or scriptural point. In that time my house was burglarized a third time and I told the tale of Psalm 32 that my eyes shall see my accuser, etc, in full faith that they would, and they did, all on the board. But later the guy was caught from fingerprints he left on a metal box he couldn't crack, which had nothing but old papers, and I went to his sentencing. Asked to address the court to a packed room, the lawyer for the guy claimed he was my friend, and etc. on my instructive. So I was able to show the boys two months later this outcome. It was all improv, so much so that the youth pastor's wife felt sorry for me and made an attempt to help, quotes, visited a class and gave me pointers after. But her husband, all these pastors were ex forwards and centers in basketball, like all such biggies are insecure, or was that from their religion, that when he saw his wife, an ex cheerleader, "teaching" me got greal jealous, she was hands on, you see, and thumped around. Another time I arranged a desert hike for the whole extended group early one morning off the Beeline Hgwy, maybe thirty or forty boys and adults, but before at the trailhead I had everybody hold hands in a circle and I prayed thus and so, and the hike came off without a hitch, but the youth leader made it evident he was peeved he had not led the prayer, so it goes I have offended hierarchy among the religious who must stand in their pecking orders, which shows my rrelation to the whole because I never played, just ignored them all. Like the only time in 5 years I was asked to pray at Bishop College English faculty meeting was the last because I did not pray anything anyone had ever heard before, and it was short too, something like, silence and a word, but that was before the charismatic experience, so I can pray good now, and at the drop of a hat, and prophetically it turns out, as the Spirit gives utterance in Rom 8. Another time I had audience with president Vernon McDaniel about a student, Cyril Nweke, who was in Terrel State hospital, but who I had visited, just so somebody would show a care for him.

On vacating all liberal shibboleths, like the sonnet at the base of Liberty. Vacated by your own mouths. Layin there after work on soul spinners, thinking how Theo was the leader when I got him, and needs to let others lead too, but for all time and memory he will have been the First leader, in the half state he comes and kisses me on the brow.

Boner Medical. Doris carrying around a dead rat in a plastic bag

Fletcher Prouty, he was transferred to the Office of the Joint Chiefs of Staff to create a similar worldwide office. He was the Chief of Special Operations with the Joint Staff all during 1962–1963. He was ordered[By whom?] to travel as the Military Escort officer for a group of VIPs who were being flown to the South Pole, November 10–28, 1963 at the United States Navy Base at McMurdo Sound, Antarctica - so he was out of the way during the JFK assassination.[2]

Thank you Lord for the wonder of your Word and Work in the World

Lunch with A and Aey. A given commendation by VP

8/16/19 Jupiter does not have a molten metal core; its magnetic field is created by a core of compressed liquid metallic hydrogen. Uranus' magnetotail — the part of the magnetosphere that trails behind the planet, away from the Sun — is twisted into a long corkscrew.

8/17/19 All in one week: Willy moves out, Teddy begins preschool in our care, A lauded for his work by VP, Sales Mgr, etc, writes account.

8/18/19 at one time the great paradox of evil was how could the people who produced Beethoven bach and Mozart produce the nazis, but now it is patent that evil uses culture as its camelfloge and mask, which further suggests whether culture, Beethoven, Bach, Mozart are not the creation in the first place of that, and all civilization is in question, above and beyond all that we can ask or think.

8/20/20 Tues Black Pearl disclosures I have outlived my knowledge of myself
8/21/19 Christopher Babcock- hyper-mentalism, intention metastasizes into paranoia, emotion into mania, and meaning into delusions of all kinds- the diametric mind
Geo-synchronous orbit 35,786 km (22,236 mi) above Earth's equator and following the direction of Earth's rotation

America's Crisis, Ellen White
"But the reader should bear in mind that there is one symbol, the second symbol of Revelation 13, which is not yet applied, and that there is one mighty nation in this western

hemisphere, worthy, as we have seen, of being noted in prophecy, which is not yet brought in. That is, all the symbols but one are applied, and all the available portions of the earth, with the exception of our own government, are covered by the nations which these symbols represent. To state it in other words, of all the symbols presented, one alone, the two-horned beast of Revelation 13, is so far unapplied, and of all the countries of the earth respecting which any reason exists why they should be mentioned in prophecy at all, one alone, our own government, remains unidentified.

Do the two-horned beast and the United States belong together? Does the former symbolize the latter? If they do thus belong together, all the Biblical symbols find an application, and the whole ground is covered. If they do not thus belong to each other, it follows (1) that the United States is not represented in prophecy at all, by any of the symbols which represent the nations of the earth, which is not probable; and, secondly, that the symbol of Revelation 13:11-17 finds no government to which it can be applied, which is not possible.

Let us then look a little further at this symbol of Revelation 13:11-17, and see if our government has developed any features in its past history, or present character, which answer to the specifications brought to view in the symbol.

1. John calls this "another beast," showing that the nation was a different one from any which had thus far been represented by any of the preceding symbols. But those symbols, as we have seen, cover all the available portions of the eastern hemisphere; hence we must look for the power intended by this symbol to the western hemisphere. And when we turn to this locality, the eye is at once attracted by our own country, the great American colossus here arising.

2. When the nation intended by this prophecy first came to the prophet's attention, it was "coming up." And the point of time is clearly indicated. It was when the preceding, or papal power, represented by the leopard beast, went into captivity (Revelation 13:10), or when, as already mentioned, the Papacy was temporarily overthrown, in 1798. Was our own nation then coming up? - Most emphatically. The Declaration of Independence was issued only twenty-two years before, and the war for national freedom reached its successful termination only fourteen years before. Hence, in the two important points of chronology and location, are we held to this country, and no other, for the application of the symbol of the two-horned beast.

3. It comes up out of the earth. The preceding, or leopard beast, and the four great beasts of Daniel 7, came up out of the sea, that is, arose in territory thickly populated; for waters denote peoples and nations and tongues. Revelation 17:15; Isaiah 8:7. Coming up out of the earth would signify, by contrast with coming up out of the sea, the development of the power in question in a territory new, and previously unoccupied by civilized nations. This, again, points directly to the New World, and to our own country.

4. It had two horns like a lamb. Such horns well symbolize the innocent, peaceful, and lamblike professions of this government. The two great principles of civil and religious liberty, - "a State without a king, and a church without a pope," - have been the great attraction which has drawn the world to America. And this pertains equally to both branches of the really dual government, State and national, which here exists.

5. When first brought to view, it was "coming up". That is, it was in a state of visible, tangible growth and expansion. And it was also coming up in a quiet and peaceful manner,

for the words "coming up" (in the Greek, anabatnon) mean "to grow up like a plant out of the earth." In just this way the United States has arisen. Expanding as it has, from less than three millions of people, when its independence was declared, in 1776, to over three millions and a half square miles of territory, and over sixty-five millions of people, in a little over a century, it presents an instance of national growth that has no parallel in the annals of the world. It has come up, not by conquering and subjugating other peoples, but in a quiet and peaceful manner, so much so that George Alfred Townsend, without any reference to the prophecy, in trying to describe it could think of no better figure than that which the prophet himself used nearly eighteen hundred years before. In his work entitled "The New World Compared with the Old," page 635, contrasting the rise of this country with that of the other nationalities" "Coming up" (in the Greek, anabatnon) means "to grow up like a plant out of the earth." 6. "He exerciseth all the power of the first beast before him." That is, it will be no second-rate power, but as strong a nation as has ever been seen, since empire began. Our own country, as already mentioned, answers admirably to this condition.

7. "He causeth the earth, and them which dwell therein, to worship the first beast." The first beast, as already noticed, is the Papacy; and to worship any power is to obey it in some particulars which are peculiar to itself, and in opposition to the demands of other powers. In the present case it is further explained by the words of verse 16, that (the two-horned beast) causes all to receive a mark, which is the mark of the beast (Revelation 16:2). The mark of any power is that by which it asserts its claim to supreme authority, and by which its followers are distinguished from those of every other power. In the case of the Roman Catholic Church, in reference to which these expressions are used, the worship and the mark are found in the observance of the first day of the week as the sabbath, which that church claims as its special badge of authority. See Roman Catholic catechisms. This comes into direct conflict with the authority of God, who, for reasons set forth in his word, demands the observance of the seventh day. It is impossible for anyone to obey them both; for they are intentionally placed in antagonism and opposition. Therefore, by his course with reference to these two days, as to which he will observe as the Sabbath, every one, with full intelligence in regard to the issue before him, decides whether he prefers to obey God in opposition to the church, or the church in opposition to God. And it is therefore a striking and corroborative fact that the Sabbath commandment is the only one in which the earth - the land, in contrast with them (the people) who dwell therein - as set forth in Revelation 13:12, can be caused to obey (Leviticus 26:34, 35; 2 Chronicles 36:21), and thus worship the beast. And the contest is now on in this country between these two institutions.

8. The nation represented by the two-horned beast is a Protestant nation; for it causes its people to worship the first beast, the Papacy, by religiously regarding some institution of the Papacy, as noted above. Now, if it were a papal nation, its citizens would voluntarily render that worship, or if enforced by the government, it would enforce the worship of itself. But here it is one power enforcing the worship of another power, and that other power is the Papacy; for it is the first beast. Therefore, this power that enforces the worship is a Protestant power, which is another feature by which it is shown that the two-horned beast applies to our own country.

9. "He doeth great wonders, so that he maketh fire come down from heaven on the earth in the sight of men." It is another striking fact that in this country modern Spiritualism

originated, through which many wonders have already appeared, and others, to the full extent of the prophecy, may just as easily follow; for Spiritualism is a masterpiece of evil to deceive; and it, according to the prophecy, is one of the great factors which is to lead the nation on in the oppressive work which it is finally to do. Verse 14.

e 14. 10. It is, lastly, to cause the people to make an image to the beast; and to do this, it says to them that dwell on the earth that they should make an image, etc. By this it plainly appears that the form of the government in question is republican, for appeal is made to the people to carry out whatever measure it is desired to secure, and by their votes the question is decided. Let us now group together these features, and note their significance:-

1. The power in question must be located in the western hemisphere.
2. It comes into view at the time the first beast goes into captivity, namely, about the year 1798.
3. It rises in a quiet and peaceable manner, like a plant out of the earth, and in territory previously unoccupied by civilized nations.
4. It makes a profession which is perfectly just, innocent, and lamb-like.
5. Its progress is so rapid as to strike the beholder with wonder.
6. It is the equal of any other nation in power.
7. It enforces an institution of the Papacy - the first-day sabbath - which, when so enforced, constitutes the worship and mark of the beast.
8. It is a Protestant power.
9. It is a nation in which appear great and super-human wonders to deceive the people.
10. It is republican in its form of government.

And of these ten specifications two things can be said: First, that they will apply perfectly to our own country, the Government of the United States; and, secondly, that if we try to apply them to any other government, they will be found to be utter failures. The two-horned beast, therefore, symbolizes the Government of the United States, and cannot be applied to any other nation. Behind these ten lines of defense the argument for this position lies impregnably intrenched.

But a painful sequel follows; for, according to the conditions of the prophecy, some of them already alluded to, this same power is to commit itself to ways that are dark and inscrutable, and, contrary to all its profession of justice and innocence, enter upon a systematic and legal course of religious persecution against those who would obey the truth of God, according to His word. While the beast has the horns of "a lamb," it speaks "as a dragon." Into these somber features the whole current of this prophecy at last resolves itself. If the first beast represents the Papacy, as is the conviction of all genuine Protestants, and if that system is utterly subversive of the word of God, being the anthropological horn of Daniel 7, the man of sin and son of perdition spoken of by Paul in 2 Thessalonians 2, and the antichrist of John, then to worship that beast is to apostatize from God; and the two-horned beast, by enforcing that worship, shows itself to be an enemy of God and the opposer of true religion.

If Sunday, as a rest day, which Rome claims as a mark of her power to rule the church, is the antagonist and rival of the Sabbath of the Lord, as is proved by the Scriptures, then the two-horned beast, by compelling people to receive such mark, arrays itself on the side of evil, and forces men into a position of antagonism with Jehovah. The image which he causes the people to make is an image of the beast.

We can determine what an image of the Papacy will be by considering what constituted the Papacy itself in its days of power. As brought to view in the prophecy, it may be defined as an ecclesiastical hierarchy, exercising the self-assumed prerogative of defining heresy, and having the control of the civil arm to punish the same. An image of this would be an ecclesiastical organization, having control of the civil power to carry out its own decisions and purposes. This would of course be a virtual union of Church and State.

This the founders of our government intended to guard against, but for just this thing, by a lamentable oversight, they have left the way all open. Such an organization in this country would be a reproduction of the first beast in character, and surely reenact its tyrannical works. The image is not only an image of the beast, but it is an image made to the beast, indicating on the part of those who make the image, an abject deference to, and collusion with, that beast; which, to say the least, is most astonishing in a professedly Protestant country. When people began, years ago, to study these specifications of the prophecy, they were able to draw only one conclusion, and that is that the country represented by the two-horned beast would, in the end, virtually renounce its Protestantism, its republicanism, ignore its professions of lamb-like innocence, and, fired with the spirit of the Papacy, which is the spirit of the dragon the second wild beast supports the former wild beast but with more subtlety, intelligence, and culture Because of this seductiveness, and of his efforts to support his mission with higher sanctions (Revelation 13:13), he is called in later chapters (Revelation 16:13; Revelation 19:20; Revelation 20:10) the False Prophet this beast as self deceit - that form of plausibility by which men persuaded themselves into a belief that they might without harm worship the former beast. assume a plausible exterior, that men may be beguiled.

In Daniel 8:5-7 a male goat with a large horn between his eyes suddenly arises from the west and smashes both horns of the ram. The angel Gabriel tells Daniel this goat represents the kingdom of Greece and its large horn is its first king, which would be shown by later history to be Alexander the Great (Daniel 8:21). After over 200 years of rule, the Medo-Persian Empire came to an end in 331 B.C. This prophecy of a male goat, which represents the same kingdom as the third beast of Daniel 7, takes an unusual turn in verse 8. The large horn being broken represents Alexander's untimely death at the young age of 33

---This is the day Trump said "the Jewish people in Israel love him like he's the King of Israel" and ...

"the second coming of god to Jews. I am the chosen one. "the Jewish people in Israel love him like he's the King of Israel" and ... , Wayne Allyn Root, calling Trump the "King of Israel" and "the second coming of God." Later that day, when speaking to reporters, Trump embraced the prophet identity again, calling himself "the Chosen One," in response to a question about trade dealings with China.

8/24/19 To *Thrice*:" I read this might be the last issue, so while it might breach etiquette to submit again do because in my experience the editorial view of Thrice is hard to find.
I regard endings because I was at the fall of the Latin America Mission, the bulldozing of the Experimental Drug and Herb Garden, the End of Bishop College. I lived on the Balcones

Fault outside Austin that went in decades from wild to banks. I audited the Lewistown American Viscose plant, a huge facility completely swept away by flood.

I always thought these destinies came from the start I had in the Chartiers Valley at five, Chartiers Creek being the second most polluted water in Pennsylvania, and I knew the first too, the Clarion River I canoed. Before Chartiers there was one other, in Germantown where I was born, where the row house backed up against a steep stone wall of an orphanage with bars at the top where the inmates would gather and catcall at the world. The attempt here is to make the reader somehow feel all these events of the Chartiers that the child felt as he became a man.

I wish sometime you had again a call for larger manuscripts of larger as you once did."
Yours truly

-An amanuensis has to be able to hear.
-Battle with the Cosa Rican roach
8/25/19 now I lay me down to sleep, end of Chartiers

8/26/19 Theo Teddy had a time out. He was slamming the inside metal mail slot over and over, gone wild. He said I don't work. Told him I'm a story teller could tell stories about anything. We did musical pencils, straw berrys at the doctors office and getting an appt in the bowl, practiced flops and 3 more. He is kept under wraps in most of his life I think. I'm calling him the little tiger:

8/28/19 Kissinger on the line much silence, tell him I'm going to ring off now. Then email three messages, one it was a something sale, two, it was no sale, 3. blank
It can only be comprehended as fiction that these issues of place are simultaneous with each other, superpositioned together.

-John Daniels father divorced his mother and had another family of many children, but on his 16th, 18th, 21th, I forget which, he came to Daniel's appt to wish him well but Daniels would not answer the door, in a pique, but his father put $500 under the door as a present and left.

8/29/19 Yacobo, Niko, Tigre, Abba, Noah and Augusto
The apocryphal Wold "rehoboth starr"
Vincent Spadea, the pro who finally made good

8/30/19 Nasa lab
I'm ready to go to Pluto today I got a dollar in my pocket and I really got to rocket I'm ready to go Pluto today v. 2 to Zappa: What's the uglies part of your rocket, some say the nose, some say the cone but I think it's val allen, vale allen van allen o, oh told teddy about 2 yr old Ralphie who saw two rockets up high and got in his rocket car and blasted off and when he got to the space machine blasted it out of orbit. Then he came back and had eggs. He got an award. A gold medallion: Defender of Earth

8/31/19 sent in the Democrats yesterday after a dream where Cluckholm was re-spelled.

Cut: I was concerned for the children of democracy when I undid a corner fence. This provoked a break in to my garage. They took all the tools worth mentioning, even the lawnmower from Sears. Since he was their leader I had police address my neighbor, who claimed someone else had dumped them in his yard, but my bicycle was in his room. When he later stood on the corner to glower I burglarized his house.

This and many more rejections convinced him I was a Democrat of the Order, so I pretended to tutor him in the craft. Who knows best its opposition? I gathered these secrets before he went to prison.

This came true::

A true Democrat is a priest of the imagination. I was sixteen when that society first battled evil in the world. But we fell to our own nemesis, truth in opposition to the world. Initial discussions, before corruption, were sworn to secrecy. Those days were leaked as a version of truth, but no one pledged fidelity to such betrayals, much less the twisted later events. Democracy gives that right to everyman. More openness than this is not conceived. Our openness was a cloak.Who else would be deep in the mountains at noon? In full sun, among rocks and under hawks we took orders. The betrayals, if I have to judge interpretations, concern later events. A final disclaimer, I knew nothing of that dread decade of existence.

The Great Inventory The Garden of Earthly delights. Brian Sewell
Grotesque cheatures in last judgement Tripticyh, terrible hybrids of man and beast, fusion of animate and inanimate 26.33 "fantastic waterside constructions in pink and blue, "the hideous ears with their terrifying blade, the harp transformed into a terrible instrument of torture, the lantern that has become fa furnace, …the bird figure swalling the damned only to excrete them into a hole in the ground…a human postiorer excreting coins into a hole, a bird creature wearing a cauldron on its head, the ends of its humanoid legs shod with wine jars, 33.14f, Temptation of St Anthony, 39.53 a winejar turned into a piglike creature, saint's grotto (or a brothel), carved within a hill in the shape of a man on all fours

Koerner: inscrutable enigmas and grotesque antagonists 101, Boschian monsters, ars imitator naturam, Horace 101, Vitruvius, Bernard; contested irreality 103, spindle wold, St Antnony ignoresthem; Jeroon Bos 104, bird catchers, magi, Adoration, bird 106; propulsive furcula, 99, chelonian carapace, antiphilus grotesque --imaginary entities 80- -body bursting with miniature versions of itself 82 -phantom copy of a nonexistent 82 -Aristides, ethike, soul of man -Peiraikos, rhyparographe-idols have taken over the world 93 -hinged shutters 45 -mime the now, mimic 47

-Hay Wain, history of sin 48 Hay history, wagon of nothing, mason of nothin49, I fell off the hay wain down 20 feet on my face. I fell from its history on my fist night out and was sustained, but they wouldn't let me sleep for fear of concussion. I fell from the hay that night at 10, the hay wain of nothing. The—worldscape 55 of optical eternity

--the prose of it: hay is our flesh in the great enchangment of vanities, a wagon of nothingness of the world haystack bundled on a wagon like a misshapen globe the world orb of everyday bubble globus cruciger bobbing in the ocean sea, the world as worldliness of thieves charlatans gypsies propherts soothsays quacks jews Mennonites vagabonds peasants Presbyterians n nuns priests

9/1/19 in the end I wonder if not all of s are guilty of trying to prepare people to live in a world we will not, did not, do not inhabit. The Unspeakable Subject of Hieronymus Bosch - Joseph Leo Koerner

9/2/19 awoke at 1 am and saw the whole body of the downed syncamore on fire The tree was entirely aflame at 1 AM, burning very sedately but serenely over its whole length, inside and out. Causes await the corner's report, but part inferred in autopsy below. Causes cited by ontological experts are lightning, friction, surge, but it was raining when the tree went down. This is what remained after putting it out in the dark. Life on the Canal, so it goes. Inflammation is capable of hiding unseen until later bursting into flame.

---Amar Annus--LOSS describes the syndrome when your reason starts to emerge in your advanced age. It is never too late for LOSS. Better LOSS than nothing (Thanks for this to C. Badcock). Have a nice new school year! Head uut kooliaastat kõigile! C. Badcock, "late onset sanity syndrome"
Bishop Exposes Christian Persecution in Communist Nicaragua
 Smokers were a scapegoat in the instance before, the Libyan pirates Jefferson blamed to justify that war, prima facie amici being cement blocks in nature, whether urged or not, like the face of Jarmere Jenkins burning in the coach's box at the Open among the surrounding pharmakoi.
9/3/19 I saw a river, was standing above it on a walk. Meandering along pleasantly it began to increase and course with large swales of current immediately before, great muscular torrents, clean and deep looking, so that it seems to endanger. This suggested moving up the swale of the bed which I did and crossed to a stair where I lived. and went up. around the bend. Dyan Effir, Beatrice Dotter.

"A Call to the Unregenerate," in *Narrow Doors In Wide Green Fields*. By Surrealists And Outsiders-2019 | Aug 9, 2019

9/4/19 We first appreciate the condition of Benjamin buying the painting after 1920 and writing of it, but after he surrendered it to Bataille on his way to Spain it's real history began with Scholem and his monograph thereon, so full of the nicest speculation it attracted and still does those who care; Geoffrey Hartman was one. All is well as long as we live our lives and expectations according to the lights that shine, but if we see in the dark, for ourselves, then these fine precursors are meet for new substance and corrosive understanding. I mean, if you see reality for yourself, then that pathetic little painting of a hapless kitten blown out to see (sic.) is of no consequence and neither are any of the other "angels" of Klee, but they make fine devils dressed up, which is why so much of the writing concerns the distory of the angelic and the dysfunction of Benjamin. None of these worthies brought the angel of history to judgment. They are still dithering about the would be, taking history and themselves seriously.

9/5/19 Luceitful Lunch with A and A. AB's school etc. Running Wild press Red Planet Mag

9/6/19 Changes. Aeg's contract, Aey's job, Carter dies, Sycamore falls, Willy moves to Quechan.

9/7/19 I had taken my part in Narrow Doors and put it online, until I looked more at the whole, then took it down because I have never before found myself a part of something bigger whose parts affirm the whole, but Narrow Doors is a look at the enemy defined coherently in a world landscape and identity which somehow all the writers seem arrive at independently and the editor has taken their words and formed this bizarre, diabolic, and outlandish painting that Bosch depicts in everyday life in order to reveal it as an alluring trap set by a metaphysical enemy at war with God, whereas Bruegel shows this enemy to be nothing but a humanly fabricated mask.

Attending closely to the visual cunning of these two towering masters, Koerner uncovers art history's unexplored underside: the image itself as an enemy. . Enemy painting is an idea from H. Bosch who I like to call Jeroon Bos, how the painting of everyday life is born from an enemy hell-bent on destroying us. Koerner, Bosch and Bruegel From Enemy Painting to Everyday Life. So just now I open at random and real "I repelled general attacks of invasive sulphur …as a prize in the Babylonian lottery. 99

Narrow Doors is a statement coherently defining The Enemy in the world now, its landscape and identity which the writers have arrived at and the editor at Thrice Fiction Magazine, RW Spryszak, has formed into this Enemy Painting. Memory is like a house with many rooms, compartments with the doors closed that are opened in dreams. I'm not a nihilist I'm a Natsar. Predominant nihilists rule lit. Lily Dale, NY patterncatinfo@gmail.com

9/8/19 Scott Waring, the man gifted with unique powers of pareidolia, is at it again. A scant week after declaring a 10 km tall tower constructed by aliens nestles snugly on the scorching and uninhabitable surface of Mercury, the man who founded etdatabase.com now claims he's discovered another pyramid on the Moon.

P has mishap after two days leg pain cramps can't walk sits down on corner, lady comes to give her water, I go to get car, she passes out, then has most serious bowel eruption--- all from dehydration. Telling S this around a bowl of popcorn elicited via Aeg her fatigue and school teacher bladder syndrome, like doc bladder, not taking the tine to pee so not drinking to control it!

We were to take Aeg and S to Costco, Pat had a foot message for both, celeb of their 10yrs of meeting, but had to send them . I gave Aeg 400 to cover, The kids played while they had their feet done.

9/9/10 dream visit from R and C and G etc. neighbor calls me Caesar, but uses the phone booth on my adjoining strip! Live in old house with panels on borders with vines and murals and rope sculptures in need of restoration, spacious inside, inviting

Nicholas Roerich Nazi Gorman ancient occult missionaries in Tibet. Camp David is a presidential retreat and renamed it "Shangri-La"

Teddy: we ate popcorn with a spoon, taught Zion how to catch them in the air, practiced flops. Judah was here and he said, Zion multiplied! Sobibor

9/10/19 called R and C. c had eye op, resettled here bro
9/12/19 - condominium cement block, whale tale
9/13/19 the dmt entities contacted in nether space are the same insectoid forms that fall are cast out of heaven by Bosch in the Haywain. Brugger

9/13/19 Poe judges the princes of the powers of the air in hopfrog, burns them alive right out of the book of Judges.
On Earth, the presence of regolith is one of the important factors for most life, since few plants can grow on or within solid rock and animals would be unable to burrow or build shelter without loose material. Regolith is also important to engineers constructing buildings, roads and other civil works Soil is a zone of plant growth and is a thin layer of mineral matter that normally contains organic material and is capable of supporting living plants. Regolith is inorganic and lies like a blanket over unfragmented rock. It is typically made up of material that is weathered away from the underlying rock.

9/14/19 the word to Capricorn--From a volume aging in its cellar to maturity water earth fire air

9/15/19 collected fiction It has gone from being called Passports for Countries That Do Not Exist to The Ubu Attorney General and Other Follies to the new settled journey of Pilgrim's Progress. The Progress is updated from its original of 1678.

Dear Spuyten D: These appeared previously before their more permanent forms here. The only sales pitch for this work is itself which if you are disposed to like you will and if not you won't. Your admiration however for shots in the dark, no demand in any market, no map, nondenominational Rilke and Blake invite this submission. Ubu-like forays and investigations gradually develop in the arrangement, which is last first, so Sacred History of Coal will appear in *Thrice* this December. Black Hole Down in AntipodeanSF in November sequentially down the last years.

To Sputyn: " Selling is word of mouth and hands on. I will make Pied Cow available in permanent form so Jimmy Chen can sell it at his cafe by that name in Portland, as no doubt will other such vicinities.

You can eat dinner with a grizzly bear in Pied Cow.
Get eaten by your professor.
This is where you can hear what mules think of you when you get your spiritual tour of Grand Canyon.
Have a conversation with a coyote when you fall down.
Read the Mars writing, and read what Grendel did in the funeral prow of Scyld Scefin. The idea is to give teenagers something to do.

I send publications to people like this so they can display them on their counters and as customers go through they buy them, making bookstores as we speak. This actually works.

Pied Cow is a take from Zarathustra, a kind of Dante burlesque that starts in the neighborhoods with people eating each other and descends into the Grand Canyon to worse, to discover Orcs and youknowwhats down there, talking mules, lizards, roaches, up and down the chain of being, even poets! Poets most of all. It ends with the ritual funeral of Beowulf.

So when Zarathustra came to Pied Cow town founded by Bosch, many folk in the marketplace wanted Uberman so there he came to bode, couched in the principles of of the uncanny and strange everyday of

Fafnir and Hamagmous Coalcrotch Town, ordinare Enginactory Organisms, bicephalic imprints and subfornical necessities, where Blattaria and strudel wagens run mutter sprack, Walto Dog and Tannenbaum, Johnny PanCake and Jack Bommb, Leo O'Hearn, Rehoboth Starr, Pedro Escadero from El Tovar and puppoets of the noonosphere at Hopi House live together in Pied Cow with the Old Burgundian Orders of Causation & Response that broker the Nibelungs." Cheers.

     The general narrative premise is the reporting of literatures of fact that translated into Bolshevik society in the 1920's to defeat censorship. This translated to the new Bolshevik societies of the 2020s completes an era of one hundred years of censorship, transposing the fakta of a continent and an age apart to this new order. The formalist theories of faktovivi tend to bypass algorithmic controls and can code hidden propitiatory examinations if understood. The first priority remains accentuated real material gathered either first hand or culled from documentary sources. I have learned there is a wealth of online readers merely from search algorithms for the fakta blogs I operate, even under new straitened conditions. A significant number of these occur from Russia, Germany South Korea, France, Ukraine and China, besides the United States.

The four author-narrators here have independent existences published under their own names in some pique of anti-vanity. If humor is not corrosive, full of turpitude, how can it be humor? These, in order of appearance are:

Augusto Todoele is a translator and historian of 8th century Anglo-Saxon and Latin texts, the illuminated Gospels and texts of Lindisfarne before the time of the Viking raids until their safe keeping in the Cotton MS in the seventeenth century. Produced when Eadfrith and Ethelwald were bishops at the monastery, written sometime between Cuthbert's death in 687 and Eadfrith's in 721, their scribe, who painted interlaced geometric animal and bird patterns throughout, these are the great masterpiece of medieval book painting. the oldest surviving translation of the Gospels into English.

Dr. Rubino del Sur explores the chattel bindings, the branch of experimental dentistry that references those Maquilas teeth worn around necks of invisible servitude. He served in capacities in the States where his offenses were less known and now works at McMurdo Station. A citizen of three nations, first born Argentine, he was made British through the Penal citizenship program at Pentonville which provided his education in dentistry. Emerging, he continued at York and Sussex U's in jaw formation of hybrid and synthetic speech to such a degree that after the Eau Claire Mayo, the Clinic at Denai, and Fukushima Prefecture he became a U.S. citizen with corporate status, being his third passport, to train, and embark to his present location where he combines propitiatory experiment in Nano-composites, Synthesis of Grafted Polymer Speech to Text, Text to Speech, and Hybrid Environments in Primate skull morphology on a contract basis. He is a palantirologist of soccer. His alternate being Rubion del Sure. He has contributed to the Rueben Crater.

Kurk Wold is not the Norwegian Kirk Wold, married to Petra Wold in the 1900 census, or Kurt Wold, the farmer who developed Seeds for northern Climes or indeed even Kurt Wold the artist of Kinetic sculpture, known for bicycle banging. He is a member of the Woldensian interest group. Whether or not Kurk is Kurt or Kirk under a relocated identity is another matter, as if two or more personas were covalent. We don't know if we have the original papers or if their versions are edited with translations of shorthand and interpretation. Wold was incarcerated in three separate corporate prisons, old mines, ships and abandoned hospitals. It goes without saying people held in these facilities have no notice except if some of the letters online are believed. So gulags, reparations and their revelation are one part of the Wold story. Another part is the reason for his incarceration being those biological experiments in AI which he then overturned, and his role as a quantum chemist, which shifts like tales of the missing microbiologists. To include the dead and the missing makes much longer lists but that these actions stop at any time is naive. Wold's name is not on the list, exactly the point, and his personal records do not seem to exist, another diversion. Cheers, spuyteneditors@gmail.com
New Angel

Molds for grave markers were brought after casting to be cleansed so they could be reused. The names and dates fastened in bronze letters with wax, after casting were soaked in the brine of that super heated bath. Standing at the vat in arm length rubber gloves he removed the letters, wire brushed the blanks loaded on skids to be recast.

9/16/19   Augusto Todoele is a historian of the illuminated Gospels and texts of Lindisfarne before the time of the Viking raids until their safe keeping in the Cotton MS in the seventeenth century. Produced when Eadfrith and Ethelwald were bishops at the monastery, written sometime between Cuthbert's death in 687 and Eadfrith's, their scribe, who painted interlaced geometric animal and bird patterns throughout, and his death in 721, the Lindisfarne Gospels, written in Latin, are the oldest surviving translation of the Gospels into English.

Had the kids Sun and into the night. AB says why do you pray. …don't you believe in magic? …in Santa Christmas, Halloween? AB said she is always sick. It goes like this. Fantasy to cover trauma replaces faith. Fantasy proved untrue disbelieves authorities who said it was. This transfers to the true faith, which is discredited by proxy. No one is at fault for it was done to them.

9/17/19 JCCIII dream visit yesterday and today, some kind of Catholic confirmation before crowds at top of a bldg., he first, me less involved. After, I pass down though various compartments and people and exist at the base. --and with further acknowledgement forever to the joy of life eternal in the accompaniment of Eden to whom these are dedicated.

9/19/19 cryptids. Exaggerations lies and hallucinations: Mike's tale of the roof rat on Willie's shoulder -At least twice in the night I saw Teddy pulling various antic faces. I wake with the thought for the first time that old age is not going to be a prolonged agony of abandonment and isolation.
Twelve monkeys: Cassandra complex is the agony of foreknowledge and the impotence to do anything about it.

I saw a river, was standing above it on a walk. Meandering along pleasantly it began to increase and course with large swales of current immediately before, great muscular torrents, clean and deep looking, so that it seems to endanger. This suggested moving up the swale of the bed which I did and crossed to a stair where I lived.

Compensic, when pay is compensis it is clearly not enough, it includes all that it should have been which becomes the might be.

Stalag Luft I for eleven months, liberated in May 1945. He kept a diary of these trials recorded in tiny script on cigarette papers which he smuggled out and published in book in 2001, Return Ticket, My Diary as a POW Airman in WWII, which went through many editions and is available on line.

9/21/19 There is a hijack code that runs the above and below. Draft proof of Passports

9/22/19 earth and water, sky and water, earth and sky

9/24/19 amid heavy revision of passports big storm, SE corner of office wet, Aey puts up beams, teddy a little sad at pickup, computers down at office, Aeg scratched eye.

9/25/19 at request I went 8 or so times to consult, took ladder, seen as helps to raise beams, but in conclusion hostile territory after pique at one Viga comment etc. and raising the final brick on north wall. Aeg says he is disturbed at the miscalculation of beams, but the same attitude in March selling some Media things, and the bench.

9/26/19 Aleph the foolish inventor
Invented himself into matters
He imagined them in
A transparently thin
And tubular blank formless vapor.

An enlightened adventure of lessons learned. Back cover summary. When thou knowest the Progress of the soul into the body and through the dangers and temptations of life until it comes to its stilling of passion at end, dangers once only personal and psychological, aka spiritual, but in the age of present telling, the soul in its body politic confronted by every sort of interference of sound, waves and super intelligences that never existed in the memory of earth life before. These are identified much like the Slough of Despond and others were, except they have no poetic names and are called by their science. So the journey of the soul in the world is confronted by these attempts to take away its right of origin, and its choice, and force it into a collective of control. The soul that sinneth it shall die, means the person, so we understand that person is another word for soul and the concern of Bunyan from his prison cell to pass through these offences is the same for us when we identify those terrors with our own, as done here. It's the stillness woken up to in the light of the stillness.

Enlighted journey of adventure and lessons, learned sojourn with the authors on a tale of wonder. These intercepts of the Ubu Attorney General surveillance used in prosecutions and for writing in later memoirs of the Enlightenment of Adventure and Lessons Learned in the literary fictive aspect of science, a somewhat semiological elaboration of these hypotheses and journeys of AE Reiff in the writings of Augusto Todoele, Rubino del Sur, Jon Rousseau, Kurk Wold in what might be called the literary or fictive aspect of the human. Todoele is a translator and historian of 8th century Anglo-Saxon and Latin texts, the illuminated Gospels and texts of Lindisfarne before the time of the Viking raids until their safe keeping in the Cotton MS in the seventeenth century. Produced when Eadfrith and Ethelwald were bishops at the monastery, written sometime between Cuthbert's death in 687 and Eadfrith's in 721, their scribe, who painted interlaced geometric animal and bird patterns throughout, these are the great masterpiece of medieval book painting, the oldest surviving translation of the Gospels in English.

9/27/19 An Enlightenment of Adventure and Lessons Learned in the Fiction of literary science, the Progress of the soul through temptations and risk once only personal and psychological, now confronted by every sort of interference of sound and super intelligence.

The Slough of Despond without poetic name is called science. So the soul in the world is confronted by attempts to take away its right of origin by a force of collective control. Person is another word for soul and the concern of Bunyan from his prison to pass identifies those terrors with our own.

At last he thought he heard a company of fiends coming to meet him; he stopped and began to wonder what to do. Sometimes he had half a thought to go back; then again he thought he might be halfway through the valley. He remembered, also, how he had already overcome many a danger, and that the danger of going back might be much more than going forward. So he resolved to go on, yet the fiends seemed to come nearer and nearer. When they were almost at him, he cried out, "I will walk in the strength of the Lord God." So they gave back, and came no farther.

As Christian made his way on through the valley, he thought he heard the voice of a man going before him, saying, "Though I walk through the Valley of the Shadow of Death I will fear no evil; for Thou art with me." Then he was glad, and that for these reasons: First, - Because he knew that some others who feared God were in this valley as well as himself. Secondly, -Because he knew that God was with them in that dark and dismal state. "And why not," thought he, "with me?" Thirdly, -Because he hoped (could he overtake them) to have company by-and-by. So he went on, and called to him that was before; but did not receive an answer. By-andby the day broke. Then said Christian, "He hath turned the shadow of death into the morning."

9/28/19 Formally submitted today to Spuyten, Running Wild, Dzanc, Two Dollar, Blaze Vox, Dalkey, 45K. First ever.

9/29/19 Little Bird Pecking to Fish Food: inspired by the moment and the place. In the best writing wait for the music, which comes little by little in aural and visual accidents of all kinds, continually seeking the measure of the ear to walk and absorb the feeling of place and the found object within those landscape environments. Recent efforts have appeared at Queen Mob's Teahouse and Thrice Fiction. Little Bird Pecking looked like this.

9/30/19 NEW YEAR Momma Noture's newfound Country Runes. How do dentists become hitmen?

     Bio. First born Argentine, Rubion del Sur was made British through the Penal citizenship program at Pentonville which provided his education in dentistry. Emerging, he continued at York and Sussex U's in jaw formation of hybrid and synthetic speech to such a degree that after the Eau Claire Mayo, the Clinic at Denai, and Fukushima Prefecture he became a U.S. citizen with corporate status, being his third passport, to train, and embark to his present location where he combines propitiatory experiment in Nano-composites, Synthesis of Grafted Polymer Speech to Text, Text to Speech, and Hybrid Environments in Primate skull morphology on a contract basis.

     Neven

Labor pains, more and more frequent with greater intensity: doubling exponential growth. 65,536=10th order expansion of 16 geomantic forms. Neven's law supersedes More's law. To decrypt the pit, encrypt decrypt the bottomless pit, doubling as 2, has to do with the # of qubits in a quantum computer 4048 being the highest present, but which will have a threshold reaction in 2020 in which the matter transformed from nothing to some thing, already between stages 5 and 7. BUT BECAUSE THE QUANTUM OPERATING SYSTEM IS GEOMANTIC, 2 TO THE 16, AND BECAUSE THAT IS LIMITED TO 65, 536, ALL THE NUMBERS BEYOND THE FOURTH LEVEL ARE MATEMATICAL ONLY.

Celebrating first day of this new year 5780, just in time access this article on Neven's Law, published this June 21, 2019 and a sequel, just now, September 8, 2019, time down to months, interpretation by Anthony Patch, YouTube today.
https://www.scientificamerican.com/…/a-new-law-suggests-qu…/
https://interestingengineering.com/googles-quantum-processo…

"As more transistors begin to fail and leak their electrons into other components, those too wear down faster and experience higher rates of error, inhibiting the performance of the processor as a whole until the whole thing becomes a useless, leaky sieve of electrons.

Since engineers cannot stabilize the components of the processor if they go any smaller, the silicon chip has reached its physical limit--bringing an end to Moore's Law and with it the expectation that two years from now computers will be twice as fast as they are today."

As maddening as it was, the unavoidable fact is that Schoedinger's cat is indeed both alive and dead at the same time and will remain so until an observer opens the box to check on it…a particle in superposition--called a quantum bit, or qubit-…2 qubits equals 4 bits, 4 qubits equals 16 bits, 16 qubits equals 65, 536 bits…double doubling, 2^{2n}

According to Neven's telling, by February--only three months after they began their tests, so 3 on our list--, there were no longer any classical computers in the building that could recreate the results of Google's quantum computer's calculations, which a laptop had been doing just two months earlier….new algorithms… so Illumined Primate Joe said"

"Once upon a time there were these nukes. A momma nuke, a poppa nuke and a MOX nuke baby. They lost their cores into the earth. Who's been stealing my core, said number four. Who knows where they are? Radiation flows from them like from the woman with an issue of blood. That woman is the earth, the north Pacific is her womb and beyond. This extinction event is now being brought to you that suggests the cure."

10/1/19 Mars shoots out magnetic pulses at midnight every day and NASA is as baffled as the CONNECTION BETWEEN teeth and thoughts, dentrites and dentites.

10/2/19 When the earth was made at Rosh Hashanah in September it was without form and void hence God said let there be light, so here is a kind of light apart from sun and moon and stars and that is the light we walk in when it says blessed are those who have learned to acclaim you, who walk in the light of your presence oh Lord, we rejoice in your name all day long.

Who are the residents of the black hole down, the bottomless pit, their servants are the centarus.

*kintsugi - A centuries-old Japanese art of fixing broken pottery. The kintsugi technique employs a tree sap lacquer dusted with powdered gold, silver, or platinum

10/7/19 Aey reconnects computer.

Steubenville

10/9/19 To inscribe the paradoxes on rooftops and coming out windows and in gardens and on street signs and billboards and written in the sky and in the papers the way Breughel does the folk sayings in his paintings. According to Susan Guy, author of the 2014 book, "Mobsters, Madams and Murder in Steubenville, Ohio," the city's red light district on Water Street drew men from hundreds of miles away as well as underage runaways to Steubenville: "at the tail end of Judy Jordan's operations on Washington Street." "We knew about Judy and worked with the FBI on a case against her. Her operation and the Water Street businesses were all behind closed doors. Judy's girls would actually go shopping at a couple of downtown stores on Saturday morning before the stores open to the public. At that time prostitution was all over town. Judy Jordan was arrested for operating a disorderly house, 133 S. Water St. *Stuebenville Herald Star* 12/Feb/1965, the Modern Steam Bath and Health Studio on Washington Street. It was like the gambling in those days. But there is a different attitude now," declared Villamagna. C. in 2008. Women are all over Fourth Street "Lil Chicago" "In the early 1960s, I had heard that Miss Judy ran a house (of prostitution) on Water Street (in Steubenville). Market Street Bridge is a suspension bridge connecting Market Street in Steubenville, Ohio and West Virginia Route 2 in Follansbee, West Virginia over the Ohio River The bridge spans a length of 1,794 feet with a width of 20.7 feet. It was listed on the National Register of Historic Places in 2019, the Steubenville Bridge. It is rumored that Steubenville businessman Dohrman Sinclair had an agreement with the Follansbee Brothers of West Virginia that if the Market Street Bridge was erected, than the Brothers would create a steel mill on the farm lands of the West Virginia side located less than 1 mile (1.6 km) from the construction site of the bridge. This mill would become known as Wheeling Pittsburgh Steel Coke Works. Of 218 Market St --Paice said. "I am hoping there is someone out there who has some better photos of Judy than I had for the first printing, as well as any photos from the houses and places she would have frequented in the 1930s through the 1970s."

Acknowledge the Thornburg bridge, the quarry on Steubenville pike, those bridges separate four worlds, fairytown, the mountain, at one end, the valley, and the greater world opposite.

--procession on Foote of elephants fancy rich fake solidarity with some travesty but mocking the whole way. I with another way lay, knock one to ground, knee on throat to make the point, they carry umbrellas; Dick Palmer, looks like mike Adams, Andrew Palmer ppg, Libby Palmer, Carol Palmer, country club connect, trip to Bermuda in 6th grade.

"It is wrong, I suggest, it is a misreading of the Constitution for any member here to assert that for a member to vote for an article of impeachment means that that member must be convinced that the President should be removed from office.
against and upon the encroachments of the Executive. Common sense would be revolted if we engaged upon this process for petty reasons… allegations of misuse of the CIA by the President James Madison, from the Virginia ratification convention. "If the President be connected in any suspicious manner with any person and there be grounds to believe that he will shelter him, he may be impeached."
    Anomalous variant light extremes

10/11/19 Alla kinick kanack kanaack, ali kinick canack, the train ran over the railroad track, ali kinich kanack

10/12/19 Lyn palmer dermographology—causes of half of problems are particular to the person, need intuition to diagnose. I am trying to give a record to myself of what I encountered as meaningful.

10/13/19 Public works live, went to back of canal this am to evict, and hauled truck load away some to dumpster of B&G, a king size mattress to good will, feel ambiguous about the dispossessed Lenny Kravitz.
Keystone species, wolf:deer starfish, sea otter:sea urchin wildebeest: grass…large mouth bass: minnows.

10/14/19 Answer! Last patient of day worked for city special forces clearing homeless with police, city council! Got the rundown on this unknown dept.

Wheelchair

10/15/19 Bosch. To celebrate I threw a wheelchair of belief in the canal. Belief is the strongest force in the world. A third of all illnesses are cured merely by belief.

10/16/19 Fairy tales unmake the garden of earthy delight. Parables of sensualism greed, brainwash, cannibalism, Canal-carnal, Pedro Pablo Villa-longa falcon. Misfortune of imaginary beings.
    Paradoxes: fortunate fall, foreknowledge/free will, eternity/time.
Augustine, Confessions: they yeeres are one day; and thy day, is not everyday, but today: seeing thy To day gives not place unto To moooowe, not comes in place of yesterday, they To day is Eternity (tr. Watts, (1631) 754) In *Paradoxia Epidemica*. Rosalie Colie.
    --"the first and most (though insufficient) surmise that ever (as) therein might be raised against me grew thus: When I was first suspected for that libel that concerned the state, amongst those waste and idle papers which I cared not for, and which unasked I delivered up, were found some fragments of a disputation touching that opinion, shuffled with some of mine (unknown to me) by some occasion of or writing in one chamber two years since.' Thomas

Kyd to Sir John Puckering, Lord Keeper (cviii)… of divine prayers used duly in his Lordship's house, have quarreled with such reprobates." The struggle of life and death can become so tedious.

      Blame Submittable for this ms. submission which has been around a little while, but takes your occasion. Kurk Wold as the author is a blind, but his namesake is not known so what's the diff? Words can stand or fall on their own without the author. Who needs them? His namesake did time in Austin too, right there in the premises of Parlin Hall in those years and on top the limestone of Bull Creek, but that was in the day of story told. Your location however beckons it from the far reaches. At one time holding the keys to five (5!) keys to UT bldgs. With a diss in the lib the author does not stand upon ceremonies of degree. This satiric, often fact- based foible of the spiritual gurus gathered in these hot comps when news of Atmosphere came in made Kurk Wold the narrator of our acquaintance most capable of this arena. Obviously the pictures are extra, not needed for the text mostly, but if nothing else this version can go up on Amazon, etc.

10/17/19 P and Aey to Texas. All the Wolds in the world. Lunch with Aeg.
What happened?

10/2019 Pictures descend into words. Coat parking lot with Aeg. Pat returns from Tx.

10/21/19 Bombay Gin. Painted out graffiti on canal.

10/22/19 Monday, yesterday Aey at 5 O'clock, plans situations slabs houses dams we get into why do such, first to honor Carl, do what he had done the many years of maintenance and use, and for P to honor all the sites she and Poppi explored, and of course for the joy of doing it, but all of it for the children, because, to build an empire, forever and a day, when he says, in conversation for confidences, even if he had intended to tell, intuitive relation that it is, says, this will help, and pulls out an ultrasound of a child of 9 weeks! I want one of those! Holy Father, we seek and ask for the birth of this child healthy, whole and blessed in the Name of Jesus, the same as is on the door of our office, In Your Name! He says I said it is a season of change a month ago.

In astronomy, an analemma "support") is a diagram showing the position of the Sun in the sky, as seen from a fixed location on Earth at the same mean solar time, as that position varies over the course of a year and figure eight
Ranch—shipping container

10/23/19 Night Thoughts: Seven Sentences an analemma

10/24/19 Another thought: do you mean my old age is not to be one of loneliness and separation but blessing and children?

10/25/19 No kitchen furniture allowed on the bed.

10/26/19 Fact must be reported free of rhetoric to be fact, but with irony to be truth. long with magnificenza, meraviglia, stupore, and inganno (deception), teatros is one of the most common most beloved words of the Baroque (Unhinged) Banquo
Phoenix Linguistics, Shorty to vet.

10/30/19 To Atmosphere press: Banquo comes because Submittable solicited. The ms. existed, but was given more work. It looks like now further invitations to the event will be given, so this is probably a draft. It could be a series. After all the Warren Report was 26 volumes. Maybe cue up some more witnesses and more transitions. Maybe because you are in Austin it caught my eye, since I lived in Athens long ago, but I'm not much interested in business and markets, I start the fire but need a publicist to attend. I don't know what you do that way.

10/31/19 No need anymore for characters, individuals are swallowed up in the crowd so it only the sociology needs telling and the mass movements.
Lunch with A: entrepreneur discretion.
     Rousseau's view of philosophy and philosophers was firmly negative, seeing philosophers as the post-hoc rationalizers of self-interest, as apologists for various forms of tyranny, and as playing a role in the alienation of the modern individual from humanity's natural impulse to compassion.

11/1/19 Red ribbon for Condo at AZ state fair

11/2/19 P 68, gave her a cashmere sweater. Sun bathe, Aeg and family surprise visit! First ever.

11/3/19 reading Hartman is pleasure because of his gentle handling, but his take of the history of ideas is not made up, the way the first creative is.
--Democracy spelled with an s. the law of the excluded middle. Problem, reaction, solution "we will not recognize America if Trump is elected" means "not recognize America if any demonot is". Final proof coming in the last *Thrice Mag* at end of year, THE SECRET LIFE OF DEMOCRATS. Me too journalist Ronan Farrow like Buttigieg has a gay feline intelligence good with tasty bontits, Merkel is spikey, major voices of the eye in the hand Scriptory.

Susan Stories

11/4/19 This has to be what the Susan Myth is, a corpus of stories interreacting with a commentary-process that continually modifies, updates and syncretizes what is at hand. I am the author redactor critic of these. All poets are redactors, like Emily who worsted God.

11/5/19 A corpus of stories interacting with a commentary-process that continually modifies, updates, and syncretizes what is at hand Hartman (*Third Pillar 27*). All writing is a fusion of heterogeneous stories or types of discourse layered while seeking the appearance of unity. The author is a a redactor and every text seemingly autonomous is a ventriloquist thought which this text and other texts speak.

--Rubino del Sur is a mariner based at McMurdo Station in Antarctica.

--Jon Rousseau is a parking lot attendant who takes after his grandfathers Henri, the toll-keeper against the hyperreal aesthetic so far from the trouble-free nature of Jean-Jacques. His most recent work is Banquo's Safe, an investigation of the psychology of assassination, a repository of who knew what on those private islands of the Chesapeake, castles of Brussels and City of London that made Banquo safe in a ditch with twenty trenched gashes on his head. To Apollinaire and Gertrude Stein at that first banquet held by Picasso he adds Jarry, Bunuel, Cocteau and Satie, and brings Goya, Gehry and Bernini to serve a collection of notables in the spirit of the absurd of those who inherit with the perpetrators the political social intrigues.

11/6/19 Your mind will be eased that Jon Rousseau is a marketing ploy whose output is one and the same with the opposed whose total approbation accrues to the banquet style which came from the name Jean Rousseau from Jean Jacques, then to Henri. That Jon is parking lot attendant is literal fact if we account his trade at writing his stripping, excavation, refilling, asphalting and stripping works around town.

Reading existence and existence, Levinas, there is an inalterable appositeeness in physiology that opposes left and right in and out up and down the day and night that heightens the perception of both.

11/7/19 Make sure Sabrina's cake gets bought. The memory of the good. The woman who was head of the PC board who encouraged us bought the poems I made for the first silent auction.

Fudoki: Oops planetary cow velvet- Just in case you think this is off the cuff, it is not, it is a full developed fairy tale based on the digital multidimensional told out of the fairy tale.

Reverse Fudoki (風土記) future reports also known as local gazetteers on provincial culture, geography, and oral tradition presented to the reigning monarchs of Japan, contain agricultural, geographical, and historical records as well as mythology and folklore.[1] Fudoki manuscripts also document local myths, rituals, and poems that are not mentioned in the Kojiki and the Nihon Shoki chronicles, which are the most important literature of the ancient national mythology and history. In the course of national unification, the imperial court enacted a series of criminal and administrative codes called ritsuryō and surveyed the provinces established by such codes to exert greater control over them.[2]

11/9/19 Let Aldrich speak the 33 degree lat. See civilization in Hartman. Begin with Three OOps. Go to fall festival with A and fam, talk to Bess Bolkema about writing. Ridley's open house.

11/12/19—comeliness, Daniel 10, hod, majesty, glory used of a human natural beauty and grace.

    The limestone lies about the eroded land like the humps of gray back whales sunning at the sky where the backs of these limestone whales surfaced

11/13/19 Dream to learn Spanish for the people in the meantime coconut avocado latin American foods, a cure for cocaine etc—but Spanish with English and Portuguese is the total European domination of those continents. In Latin America the people are Indio with a European overlay. In u.s. they are or were already English and European and the English overlay an easy fit.
In the technique of psychological reverse the hate rhetoric is a tar brush for all white to be tarred black first maybe but the beliefs are more important than the color race. We had an early antifa in E but the antipathy of white men was at FSC in the Upward Bound kids who got their wish and after at Texas in the GSC committee among women. Now the neighbors say with a sign that hate does not live in their home where they are a gay couple upwardly mobile who fix up their house where no hate has touched them. There is no cure for this lamarkian virus hate affect add-gene. A gene of intolerance and rage of which the causes are legion, which is a hint to the cause. --Overlord, amazon prime: J.J. Abrams "about a team of American troops who come face-to-face with Nazi super-soldiers unlike the world has ever seen."

11/14/19 rat bait the A/C
11/16/19 Sat. lunch with Aey at Woodfire, house clean.

11/18/19 Religious charismatics all suspend discretion. Teddy upset he lost his jacket, 20 min worth.
    Rubino del Sur: Just back from being helioed Saturday to a camp at 9000 ft with no amenities and temp shelter to discollect my thought even more after examinations of what was preserved there. I worked at Eau Claire, Mt. McKinley, and Fukushima Prefecture before this, for government, NGOs and corporations, but in this NASA jaunt of dentition- jaw and skull formation, everybody does everything. I was running a torch with a propane tank strapped to my back! I better send my response before going down for the obligatory sleep they give us after more than 48 hours out. Thank you for your remarks.

11/19/19 the film, Assimilation: hybrid prediction program with alien spore
    Writing: To make a wilderness in which he can get lost but with awareness remember where he is. --the vastness the vastness will be said that while boasting of adaptions of space flight to justify DNA modification here below, there was no space flight above the ion Xray belt. Tardigrade DNA Added to Human Cells Could Help Us Survive on Mars, Scientist Says Plastics, metals, Snow turns black, doesn't melt. FAKE SNOW GMB. Hum-animal Japan, working on Susan.

11/20/19 Aey has ultra sound tomorrow. P says when I realized he was to be born I washed the car!

In *Outer Dark*, McCarthy, the travail of childbirth and abandonment with the murders and violence can be taken as prurient or as increasing compassion for those suffering so. It all depends on the reader attitudes. The story is neutral in its fact of this. The meaning emotional is ascribed.

11/21/19 I both armed and then dismantled a nuke.
--yesterday news that the gov will not attach 8K for fin records, thanks to A's work! --Joe Biden: a million whiggers in concentration camps in China. --Incunabula @incunabula

There are four Kartvelian languages (ქართველური ენები) - Georgian, Svan, Mingrelian and Laz - which together form a language isolate, like Basque - of unknown origin, and unrelated to any other language group, including Indo-European. Laz is by far the most endangered today. ½
--a little wain (rain) and they get fagey (flighty?) skip brain language -Joe Biden forever- comment on putting the dogs out in the rain this morn
-she says compared to the past, it's diet, lack of activity, soil bacteria, gut, relationships. JFK Dustin Pickering FB
--both toilets stopped at office, snake in morning, MRI at 6.30.

11/22/19 "I will consider in my dwelling place," lends support to Levinas saying place is the base. Hence the soul finds its identity in the place, and implicitly the time, the language, the people, and other character traits from family, even choice affirmed with them or if negated against, prove the good and acceptable and perfect will of the Father.

Problem, reaction, solution Distributed ledge of information: Blockchain error: The byzantine fault tolerance system: fault acceptance--blockchain, crypto, 1. Data corruption, 2. Dishonest players-sybils, sybil attack, multipersonality entries of ID to hack block chain. Only 2/3 validation of info, Pillar of fire=firewall, Close align Venus, Jupiter in west.

11/23/19 add the children's stories to the Sundress ms. Sunday Parking lot installment. Kids for the day, pool in A barbecue pit. Begin hunger.

11/25/19 see Worthington, schedule for 4/14/20

11/27/19 I was driving home the road dark before dawn when I saw Joggy and opening the door gave him a ride. THE PASSIVIST.

11/28/19 Thurs. Thanksgiving, Late dinner at 5. A and S and kids.
Aey claimed at this affair he is a momma's boy, Sh disagreed. She wants a child with dark hair and green eyes.

Babel Data

11/30/19 Wrestling with the conundrum of massive increase, world population in so few years concurrent with waves of obesity and all swelling, seeking answer to this I made a request to understand the increasing alienation and rejection. Practically in the instant I was presented with world population, Babel and Data. Data, connectedness, 5G, quantum supremacy and triple population size in three generations connect in the notion of the tower of Babel where bricks are considered people, more than ever existed and not just people but their every habit to build the AGI, extrapolate every human genome and amend it with CRISPR implant wedding soul and machine to ascend the heaven on the backs of these eight billion integers. The human is the key to break the heaven! An ascent back engineered from human creation to produce singularity and instant change in consciousness, more than joining it to Alexa, but to the global system of boundless non existence. This is the purpose of the tripling of world population in three generations. See the problem as stated in Doris Lessing, her death.

12/1/19 I could get behind a raven hair Celtic girl with green eyes. There are no blondes in my family, a few red heads.

Octopus passing cloud-change its appearance 1000 times in seven hours.[2][3] As it moves across the seabed it makes changes in its coloring and appearance to match the substrate beneath.[6] The color changes are instantaneous and made by chromatophores under direct control of the brain.

Velazquez must be viewed as impressionistic, from several steps back to see the image. Up close it is fuzzy and muddled as if he painted with a long brush to get the effect. DeKooning sometimes painted with a 12 ft. brush.

12/2/19 Thanksgiving is a time when wives curb their husbands in public and both belittle and dispute the absurd claims that they are mama's boys that they provoke.
--the experimental dog and cat garden -dekooning brushes and technique

12/4/19 The worlds were framed by the word of God.

12/5/19 Art dream talk about dance movement with strong black girls reminds of Stephanie Bowen kissing the impasto painting of Cowboy at Bishop after class, saying, I guess he's a black man!

News of Green Deal to appear at *Queen Mob* courtesy Reb Livingstone. --RW Spryszak: this gift is anonymous but it intends to convey support for your *Thrice* and its editorial point of view. Being so tired of universal puerility in publications your view is restorative, especially since it is so well established.

--12/9/19 Mon. Childhood identity events illustrate memory selected to exemplify the central desire of the person to understand what they think is life long. So the memory of a boy to know people by their faces and the desire never to kill are examples of the remembered events that organize the principle of selection. Only the person involved knows them, but they meditate and revisit them to sustain integrity.

Adam and Eve

Spiritual mantling: -- hunching or arching shoulders, eliciting sword. One of metempsychosis, like birds of prey spread their wings over a captured prey aways elicited by a perceived weakness and pretense of sympathy from the victim.

-- A case of identity transfer when the offer is made of a spirit to trade one body for another, a blind because it is your own spirit elicited, not another's, and it is a disembodied presence that presents this option which ordinarily would be thought impossible. This voice does not identify itself. It sounds authoritative but reasonable, as Satan must seem. What is the purpose of transfer? Happily, if one doesn't find out, but Adam did, the suggestion that the spirits of the two people would be transferred to each other, switched, backgrounds. Intelligence is the right word, even if unknown, since it is spirit engineered, couched in the right circumstance of moonlight, acid, sex, nature or whatever goes with the test to Either accept or reject. But it apparently cannot be forced, it must be chosen. So if Eve had rejected the intelligence nothing would have happened and it would seem to her, as it does here, a kind of hallucination that a beast spoke. Without Consciously rejecting, many must undergo life in a completely different body. --The cases of which proliferate in sex change.

Mantling were not intelligence but powers, a lower force, shown harmful as an even lesser rejection to join the Masonic Demolay about 12 elicited a punch in the stomach and a rabbit chop to the neck, in church.

12/10/19 Teddy touches ceiling with jump from bed. Later says, I'm complicated. The works of His hand!

12/11/19 Middle size high fire ceramic figures and murals with various clays on a laminated surface formed until the eye recognizes what the hand is doing around themes like captives, rapture, boys in a furnace, faces of children.
12/12/19 Aey bringing the propane, says I designed his beams, after vehemently denying it six times. I designed the door between rooms, the rehanging of the outside door and the plantings. Provoked, I told him I can see the end in the beginning. He however carries out the designs which goes for all the video, sound work, etc.
--Picking Teddy up yesterday he says, "you don't have many rules."

12/13/19 Christmas at Arcadia Gospel that night with N.

12/15/19 other interventions, the knee injury exemption and the mantle of peace with the car accident with Chris Scafario in Merion separated me to the new birth coming in which the move from Pgh to Phila was a necessity, to consider all these personal social familial arrangements as designed, for this purpose to nurture a soul is beyond thought. It's hard to be simple but needed high up in order to breathe
--email Sat that Mon privileges revoked because lacking a cover call of credentials from the samite!

-- Jon Rousseau is a parking lot attendant after his grandfather Henri, a toll-keeper against the hyperreal aesthetic so far from the trouble-free nature of Jean-Jacques. Jon's most recent work is *Banquo's Safe*, the psychology of assassination of how and who knew what on those private islands of the Chesapeake, castles of Brussels and City of London that made Banquo safe, in a ditch with twenty trenched gashes on his head. Apollinaire and Gertrude Stein at that first banquet held by Picasso to honor Rousseau, Jon adds Jarry, Bunuel, Cocteau and Satie, and brings Goya, Gehry and Bernini to serve a platter of notables in the spirit of the absurd. To those intend upon the perpetrators of political social intrigues this reportage style of fact like statements in order to reflect obliquely, some science that does not exist is a takeover from the faktovi, a revelation and code of the unthinkable. It's no contradiction that Mengele loved Schumann or Bach; it is axiomatic they are of the same culture of elite control. Synesthesia of the senses, called a mark of sophistication, is a door breaker to disorder the sense and prepare for such travesties as death camps.

Susan

12/16/19 To show that existential threats can be impersonal, like credentialing, or personal, and speaking of Susan as the cow, we also find the famed rhinoceros of philosophy, a re'em, also reëm (Hebrew: רְ אֵ ם), mentioned nine times translated as unicorn or wild ox, identified with aurochs by Johann Ulrich Duerst based on the Akkadian cognate rimu (□ in cuneiform), meaning *Bos primigenius*. Aurochs, progenitor of cattle, translated sometimes as "oryx" as "unicorn," and maybe a one-horned *Rhinoceros unicornis*.

"Will the unicorn be willing to serve thee, or abide by thy crib? Canst thou bind the unicorn with band in the furrow? or will he harrow the valleys after thee? Wilt thou trust him, because his strength is great? or wilt thou leave thy labour to him? Wilt thou believe him, that he will bring home thy seed, and gather it into thy barn?" — Job 39:9–12

In Jewish folklore, the re'em was larger than a mountain and could dam the river Jordan with its dung. To survive during the deluge, Noah had to strap its horns to the side of the Ark so that its nostril could protrude into the Ark allowing it to breathe. King David, while still a shepherd, mistook its horn for a mountain and climbed it, then the re'em got up to carry David up to the heavens.

Linked to the Behemoth it entered politics in the aggada, and Kabbala due to the striking parallels between the -anti Zionist, not anti-Semitic, presidential orders raises the specter of Apollyon stalking Trump's gold apartment with quantum supremacy designing his reelection, a series of performances staged by democrats over and over again, where a 7 year old knows the words to no Christmas carols and 3 members of a class of 8 three women in med school seek only to practice abortions, ruses that conveniently falter, but shore up support for the first white horse that would ride to Jerusalem, but then fails!

Dr. Dee, Paracelsus added to what Pico says, "that Man has no specific nature at all but creates his own nature by his acts." (Lewis, *Sixteenth Century*, 12), "what habitation or countenance or office soever thou doest choose for thyself, the same thou shalt enjoy and possess at thine own proper will and election" (13) which would allow all species of depravity such as enjoyed by pedos, hybrids and ritualists and license of transhuman as a species of the "dreams of power that haunted the European mind" (13) in the effort to manufacture evil and good where the good is evil the evil is good. The old mythical imagination was substituted with a wholly same effects to unite to universe, " the elements and all things sentient" (6) "to awake the sleeping sense" (6) which egregore construct, being "that the region between earth and moon is crowded with airy creatures who are capable of fertile unions with our own species" (10) to construct a "spiritual cosmology" of "the invisible population of the universe.'(11). Ministering angels, seducing devils.

12/20/19 watch your back trail. If nobody calls you it won't be me.

12/22/19 Susan was so big she was like a Taurobolium of a whole country, not to discriminate bull and cow. Bigger than a cow, but not as big as a country, a bull, but bigger than a country, and therein we pay largesse, whole countries and peoples to populate. Census however had not been conducted. Was she literally a whole new world? I, so then therefore, the world.

Wittgenstein and Woman

12/23/19 Wittgenstein. 1889-1951. About 1911 he lived in isolation in Norway for months at a time in a wooden hut he built by the side of a fjord. In the First World War 1914-1919 while serving on the Eastern front a religious conversion part inspired by Tolstoy's The Gospel in Brief (1883) bought at the beginning of the war and carried with him, reading and rereading. Taken captive 3 November, 1918 he spent the remaining war till 21 August, 1919 in a prison camp and wrote the notes and drafts of Tractatus Logico-Philosophicus.

Tractatus account of logic as tautologous. "If only you do not try to utter what is unutterable," he wrote to his friend Paul Engelmann, "then nothing gets lost. But the unutterable will be—unutterably—contained in what has been uttered." After World War I trained as an elementary school teacher, to prove philosophy the synopsis of trivialities," with a detestation of scientism, a "theory of everything" at one time the great writers, artists, and intellectuals of fin de siècle Vienna—Karl Kraus, Gustav Klimt, Oskar Kokoschka, Sigmund Freud—were regular visitors to the Wittgenstein musical evenings also attended by Johannes Brahms, Gustav Mahler, and Bruno Walter. --Three of Ludwig's brothers—Hans, Rudolf, and Kurt—committed suicide, the first two after rebelling against their father's wish that they pursue careers in industry. *(Frank Ramsey 1923)* , …Freud, Einstein, Wittgenstein all live in Germany in Austria, the fez of civilization where indeed, "The world is everything that is the case," and, "Whereof one cannot speak, we must be silent," as part of the code of the civilized.

Tractatus stretches between language and reality. That the world is everything rules out the man who was in the world and the world knew him not, which means the Incarnation proves that the world is not everything that is the case. But the case is not either that the world is not. The case is that the world is a formality that binds to be bound. If we will not be bound the world corollaries, that the gods think they are everything, are overthrown. This is not to install the man as he is, but to prepare redemption of the man and the world. Earth has been long lost. We go with flamethrowers into the dens prehistoric worms of thought to illumine this, but the true flame that is the Breath whose words are truths of immolation of the god counterparts of every complex of Jung who is their fortune teller. The gods in human form and institutions must be overthrown. What, pray tell, is left? Nothing. QED. The world is nothing and nothing is the case. We will have to say every hour on the hour that this will is understood only by one who has already thought, which purpose is achieved if there one in the world. But there were two. Aristotle got in dire straits when he caressed a woman's breast, felt her belly and thighs against his, otherwise he had not known he was social animal. So for the world, the case, the overthrow and the fact, that the world is a woman is entertained for who she is. Who is a woman?

After enlisting in 1914 W wrote "now I have a chance to be a decent human being and stand eye to eye with death." The Gospels by Tolstoy, bought on the Russian front, were always with him, "this world exists,'…but meaning does not lie in it but outside it…good and evil are connected with the meaning of the world….

Some people are gifted with the future, others have to attain it. Wittgenstein paid his price in migraine headaches and imprisonments exchanged for Russell's patronage. But he met the apriori when he said the world is everything. She loves to hear it. This was just complete enough to be given a Puff like the one Billy Graham got from Randolph Hearst, except Hearst was Bertrand Russell. Think of them all singing together, "I love the world," their speech breaking down in complexity. What is the world to Wittgenstein? Does he really think the world is a woman. We know he did, he kept one in a walkup in Cambridge. And of course we know that Einstein thought the world was a woman for pursuing woman was his singular goal. If a woman had the right kind of underwear Einstein was interested. You can substitute the woman for the world. The world is. By 1962 I had the Tractatus, The Future of Man, Allegory: theory of a Symbolic Mode, and Unscientific Postscript and after indulging in the relation between language and reality after my own lights in the intervening took it that there is no special meaning to the word, world Word world in Wittgenstein's *Die Welt ist alles, was der Fall ist*.

It doesn't help that every premise of part 1 is false: but to speak of *The world is the totality of facts, not of things,* is to put abstractions in place of things. No idea but in things, or facts, not things, beside the wheelbarrow, "whereof one cannot speak, thereof one must be silent." Beno longer silent, speak what would have been true had it said, the world is language, and had the whole world been blown away with language atoms, the picture idea of meaning, that is, the world is first an image, has no picture but exists just where I cannot see it the way I see the chair, but I see it anyway, not with eyes, but with imagination the same universe as the language of facts and chair things and woman, is not language as we know it, for language will implode, explode, skerry about its letters and syntax and logic— which will be objected by the world which wants it, the Welt and all, to be everything and everything the case, but will require both the thing seen and its representation in words. But who can judge the world who does not know the world and the word?

Adherents who fight to favor civilization Hegalianly, exist. But it is not either/or, or both/and, and neither/neither/none, to reveal and destroy the world we think we know. Wittgenstein samples the world and acknowledges that everything worthwhile of life and humanity is unspeakable.

Tractatus Logico-Philosophicus GermanOgdenPears/McGuinness1*
Die Welt ist alles, was der Fall ist.
The world is everything that is the case. The world is all that is the case
Die Welt ist die Gesamtheit der Tatsa-
The world is the totality of facts, not of the world is the totality of facts, not of chen, nicht der Dinge. things. things.

Die Welt ist durch die Tatsachen. The world is determined by the facts,.
Was der Fall ist, die Tatsache, ist das? What is the case, the fact, is the exis-What is the case

The unspoken moral, aesthetic and beautiful, or versions of it are known. Only the digital mind asks what is the world and what is it like to be human. The world is like the hood of a car in your driveway that when you wake in the morning has dents that look like the footprints of some large dog. The world like the car hood needs to be covered with a tarp to protect its appearance before you stand on it. The world is like driving to the Good Will thrift store to get some more bed sheets to cover the plants in winter., but while inside the vehicle goes missing because when you come out it is missing. You start tramping the parking lot to find it, an old white pickup, but can't. Reports are that the day before the cops found a stolen car there. Thinking it stolen, you think, if only it was the Subaru then I could beep it. Suddenly you realize it is the Subaru and do beep it. It talks back and you drive off. The one you were to call for help says she does this all the time. Welcome to the world! To begin to speak, the world is Susan.

12/24/19 I carried E in the alleys of Austin singing Psalm 8 and sang it at Bishop College. To recite, sing, perform and shout this psalm with audience participation we would all leave changed. The meaning is the singing.

12/25/19 The floors are paved with translucent lilies, tiles and the walls covered with maps.

12/27/19 some called her Susan Google. Babel Cognition is emotional.
12/28/19 N finds a paddle, brings me the balls to open one pack, finds another paddle and hands it to me to play. We also play soccer. He tosses to Zion, eats all the grapes. On the wavelength!

12/29/19 Observe the god code myths abstracted further from origin as code, the Niki swoosh, maybe, the indoctrination of a child into the owl cult, with full size owls on their wall, owl stories, owl symbols everywhere, eventually just the wing or two wings of the owl, the abstracted symbol sunk into consciousness activated at later stages of sacrifice, unless contradicted.

12/30/19 "The Book of *Ezekiel* contains the first record of the New Jerusalem. Within Ezekiel 40-48, there is an extended and detailed description of the measurements of the Temple, its chambers, porticos, and walls. Ezekiel 48:30–35 contains a list of twelve Temple gates named for Israel's tribes.

The Book of *Zechariah* [13] expands upon Ezekiel's New Jerusalem. After the Second Temple was built after the exile, Jerusalem's population was only a few hundred. There were no defensive city walls until 445 BCE.[14] The author writes about a city wall of fire to protect the enormous population. This text demonstrates the beginning of a progression of New Jerusalem thought.

In Ezekiel, the focus is primarily on the human act of Temple construction. In Zechariah, the focus shifts to God's intercession in the founding of New Jerusalem. New Jerusalem is further extrapolated in Isaiah,[15] where New Jerusalem is adorned with precious sapphires, jewels, and rubies. The city is described as a place free from terror and full of righteousness. Here, Isaiah provides an example of Jewish apocalypticism, where a hope for a perfected Jerusalem and freedom from oppression is revealed.

As the original New Jerusalem composition, Ezekiel functioned as a source for later works such as 4 Ezra, 2 Baruch, Qumran documents, and the Book of Revelation. These texts used similar measurement language and expanded on the limited eschatological perspective in Ezekiel."

12/31/19 Momma Noture's New Found Country Runes: a Walloon municipality located in the Belgian province of Hainaut.

The Government on His Shoulders. In asking what name the angel spoke to Mary, which was then written as we have it in Greek, and then translated to English as Jesus, in order to speak the name as it was spoken, a Hebrew undertext posited by Robert L. Lindsey wants *Luke* as the first document, copied by *Mark*, read by *Matthew* as used in his gospel, but without knowledge of Luke, and in that underpinning *Luke* was first an unknown, but its posited biography of Jesus in Hebrew which itself was translated to Greek is based on the distinctly Hebrew word order of these writings suggesting them first written in Hebrew and then translated, as the Septuagint was.

Pronouncing the Name ""above every name" as a Hebrew name, for though it is said the speaking of the original name of the Father was lost to usage in Babylon out of respect for the unspeakable, it must be other. Countless times injunction is made to hide in that Name, walk and talk in that Name, which means that the loss of the Name was the single-most harm of the Babylonian Captivity to confound. Ever since it has been work-arounds of God and Lord when all along it was the Name Moses learned, YWVH which none hardly speak at all.

2020

1/1/20   A case.
Lungs feel like fire beginning of night, then stop.
We bake two loaves of sourdough before dawn.
Woomga! Augusto Todoele comes out with *Space Malebolge*, companion reading for the age at *Neon Garden* 7.

1/2/2020 One thing owed to democrasy is the many striking proofs of how a lie is not just an opposite of the truth but a multi-layered perversion of it stated boldly with no apology and baldly, with no inkling of remorse. This disservice movie stars have done themselves. Forget DeNiro, a bully thief, Christian Bale, psychopath. What was excused as method acting, identifying with the role, is really typecasting. They have multiple compartments. Their roles are really the way they are. Many instances in congress, the news, and public entertainment of totally made up scurrilous filtholy rages are valuable to us because they show a level of deception so in the face that we easily see it, hence gain insight into other such statements like *thou show not die*, when that is exactly what they did, and *you shall be as gods knowing good and evil*, inadvertently revealing, not that they would know good, but that the fallen cannot know good, but only evil. The lies slant and part parcel themselves out as they enter the chains of belief that bind the populace. The pop is bound politically, socially and religiously, as in religion where the Temptation lie was spoken that *I will give you the kingdoms of the earth*, but the lie is that the voice had these to give. It was a lie that political religion continues to spread, for the tempter has no power except what is given it by the victim. None of the lies are true, all of the lies are false.

--I ADMITTEDLY KNEW SOME STRANGE PERSONS in Austin. HERE'S ANOTHER:
Ron Weddington whose burning advice to Bill Clinton was to abort the poor.

1/3/2020 in 1920, the world's approximately 2 billion peoples had available to them the exact same modern conveniences available to those living in 2020, the nitrogen fixation process of 1918, rocket science of 1926, nuclear fission of 1939, mid-20th century semiconductor to make internet, personal computer of 1970s—all which when combined clearly show why all advancements halted when "*The Golden Quarter*" ended nearly 50-years ago. Now there are 8 billion people.

1/4/2020 I got this cold from T.
Thoughts, memories and infanticide: people kill their own child self by not remembering it when *that* memory is the only identity they have and the sole purpose of a life, no other. I prove this in sons with whom I have extraordinary experiences, but do not know them. Do I know myself or is it a plethora of things? But to not consciously cultivate the child all is lost. This was said to one yesterday. Memories boil down to certain sets and subsets, but thoughts

are impossible, influenced by outside and inside forces that do not belong to the child and which the child did not have. Fears projected as fantasies produce feelings like, I have a cold so Iran will infect NY with the flu as payback.
--Ready for a steroid in the breathing treatment

1/5/2020 Sun. New Augmentin has had good effect after 3 days.

1/6/20 Austerity, singlemindedness opposition to the world is a notable trait of Dar al-Islam. Erratic pulse, afibulation.

1/7/20 A full cardio workup with echo, stress test, Holter monitor in 2005 diagnosed normal but slow heart rate and normal rhythm with B/P treated with Benicar/HCTZ 20/25, 1 tablet a day, with regular strength aspirin and etc. fish oil. Yesterday Heart rate 38, usually 44, but asymptomatic. Rechecked B/P 130/91, pulse rate 107. Sometimes the pulse high, sometimes not, but irregular. Arranged for EKG and told it is an atrial flutter. Given "Xarelto" to dilute, ease blood flow implicated in three minor TIAs 2017, 18, spring of 19. Fighting bronchitis ten days, taking Augmentin, and breathing treatments. Recovered. Not Covid. [?]

1/8/20 Slept from 8 to 5.30 without getting up.
--We have outlived our ancestors and because we're so bored with the faux history and news of the day we invent our own scenarios of entertainment like watch the fluctuations of BitCoin in place of the NBA.

1/9/20 The Paraclete is to have God Himself indwelling in the Word that guides to truth. The Spirit works to give peace, love and joy and comfort in trouble. The power of the Indwelling discerns how "not to gratify the desires of the sinful flesh" which produces that fruit in our lives to the glory of the Father.

1/10/20 Premise: The Linguistic Nature of Reality is a circus.
Under the big top: thought codes, trash codes, language codes. The circus as a metaphor of thought. A Big Top is a large tent in which a *traveling* takes place. First you have to raise the tent. Install the fixtures. Then you cover the ground. Invite the crowd. Perform the acts. Another form is a Gospel Tent meeting.

As for Oliver B. Greene and his Gospel tent afflictions, passions and audacity, at a tent meeting in King of Prussia in 1959, "I knelt down on both knees and then occurred what I have lived since through thought and act, the disappearance of the whole world. The physical manifestation was like a lightning strike. I am still being struck." From that experience incongruities of faith are explained this way: "I wrestled incomplete travesties so as not to celebrate death, but after much pondering saw these giant forms transfer to the thought of the age. The frescoes bloomed and darkened, cracked and spalled, as though in a *War with Neptune* at *Full of Crow* all fight in that moment had been lost, except for the patient's restoration.

--Sculpture is superior to painting which is just a cartoon. Sculpture grapples.

--How brilliant is that? They named the stars after themselves. Which illusion of the earth bound takes some hubris. If you name your children after the stars you name them after these *Hashishin*. That's the point of the archetype universality of the pagan gods manifesting in these forms, but the gods are states of being in themselves.

-Lunch with A., told him of the circus, he is the only one able to comprehend lit that I know, talking of mission. Another instance of negotiation skills.

1/11/20 This is the time of year the worst thoughts/dreams occur. Wondering about it, where they were, this a. m. right before waking the worst! These things first make an environment of doubt, rejection to emerge that gives their credence. Not to say it, it alerts to the importance of blessings occurring, and makes them even more important- Oh. No. Cover. All these torments occur in the desert fathers, St. John of the Cross, and in Bunuel's Exterminating Angel. Plus Hopkins, Smart. Efforts to monitor and observe the thought stream show this. To try to show the stream off, as in mediation, must establish the Barker's existence.

--*Hopkins*. Oxford University Press/Humphrey Milford, London, 1933. Hardcover. Second edition, third impression, with an appendix of additional poems, and a critical introduction by Charles Williams. Edited with notes by Robert Bridges. Blue cloth. Gilt lettering to spine and to upper board. Dustjacket with tissue guard. Extremities of boards slightly discoloured. Cloth covering upper board slightly ruffled in one area adjacent to spine. Bookseller's nameplate to front pastedown. Approximately 20 light pencil marks or annotations throughout the text. Spine of dustjacket tanned. Light tanning to dustjacket otherwise. Two 2 cm closed tears to top edge of dustjacket. Dustjacket edgeworn and chipped and nicked at head and foot of spine. A good copy in a fair to good and scarce dustjacket. Bookseller Inventory # 136 $181

-- Nation-wide decline in body temperature connected to a drop in metabolic rate, environment change, temperature in homes, contact with microorganisms and food.

Cow Language--Liquefacting Language

1/12/20 What is the nature of a cow? There was a moo cow comin' down the road toward Baby Tuckoo and the road had a bit of a sway to it which was the language. Well it wasn't really a moo cow and its wasn't really a road, these two complications aside. The road was more a bridge that waved in the wind, not that there was wind, but there was a natural sway to everything the baby saw, which is the third complication, for what the baby sees or thinks is to be accounted for. Of course the cow swayed while it walked but the road did to. It was not as solid a road as we might like. These two facts or problems affect the baby and he who also sways, which to understand means just that the sights and images and sounds that affront come and go. The ones that stick, well they are the moocow and the road itself waving back and forth in the waving world.

Language is a cow so it is not people eating bratwurst while the big top goes on, it is a herd of cows in feedlot, nouns, verbs, you know the kind where the cow of the language has maxed the mind, but the mind still will not be cowed.

How genius is it that entities, the 200, would engineer all of civilization to celebrate themselves? Taking the Greek pantheon, calling itself the high table as John Wick does is representative of the other five or six pantheons, which as Joseph Campbell says, are of one cloth from which he would prove their universality, but we know that his genius is to reflect their counterfeit.

When a man comes into context with the divine unless he is a typos he cannot exist. Types are molds, templates, patterns, and examples of spiritual realities. Types are historical persons or events that are different in kind from allegory or parable in that typos refer to a literal object pointing to a literal fulfillment or antitype. Demigods love the rules that they create with all their mystic formula to subvert the truth and enslave the man who serves them. But a man is not bound by their rules, especially a man who is a týpos, a mission, an idea, a "pattern" (Titus 2:7; Hebrews 8:5), "form" (Romans 6:17), "print" (John 20:25), "ensample" (1 Corinthians 10:11), "fashion" (Acts 7:44), "figure" (Acts 7:43; Romans 5:14), and "manner" (Acts 23:25).

While comparisons and connections in allegories are more indirect and implicit, types are historical realities. All the old testament figures are typos, but Campbell says myth is a mask of God, but it is a mask of the false gods.

Joyce's last work, HCE ["Here Comes Everybody"] sketches the story of HCE, his wife and children. *"In the first chapter of Finnegan's Wake Joyce describes the fall of the primordial giant Finnegan and his awakening as the modern family man and pub owner H.C.E."* Not comprised of many borrowed styles like Ulysses, but, rather, formulated as one soundscape, which 'language' is based on English vocabulary and syntax, but at the same time, self-consciously functions as a pun machine resisting singularity of meaning. Announcing a 'revolution of the word', is a cultural critique - a miscommunication which, far from stabilizing the world in meaning, constructs a universe radically unfixed by a wild diversity of possibilities and potentials that it represents to bridge. It also remains an hilarious, 'obscene', collection of innuendos.

1/13/20   Finnegan's Wake is a mental translation sole and independent to the viewer, rewritten each time it is read. Every reading of its innuendo soundscape does not have a syllabic, phonetic, semantic meaning, but an experience of sleep and dreaming. Joyce categorizes three epochs from Vico and everywhere: the age of the gods "in which the gentiles believed they lived under divine governments, and everything was commanded them by auspices and oracles, which are the oldest institutions in profane history; the age of the heroes "in which they reigned everywhere in aristocratic commonwealths, on account of a certain superiority of nature which they held themselves to have over the plebs (or peasants);" and the age of men "in which all men recognized themselves as equal in human nature, and therefore there were established first the popular commonwealths and then the monarchies, both of which are forms of human government.

Each age had distinct political and social features characterized by master tropes. The giganti of the age to compare to comprehend, human and natural phenomena require metaphor in the institutions out of idealized figures but in the final age of democracy irony creates rationality which leads to *barbarie della reflessione* or the barbarism of reflection to which civilization descends. Taken together, the recurring cycle of three ages provides the structure that Anthony Burgess lauded in *Finnegan's Wake* as "a great comic vision, one of the few books of the world that can make us laugh aloud on nearly every page."

Language liquefaction. Joyce, Hopkins, Ignatius Loyola.

Here comes Hieronymus. HCE, HCL, HCH. To join in the numinous commonplace, turn language into one of the characters, a language character where poetizing, pastiche, parody deepen the human by adding to their ordinary human dimension history and myth. No face shines through not enlisted in any cause, a man legitimately faceless like Shakespeare with language opaque. Anthony Burgess, *Here Comes Everybody*.

Anonymous Everyman was the same thing over again, not seven, not eight, not nine anonymous Hieronymus Eponymous, but Autonomouses. Hiernomo, Hiero Thomas Kyd, *Spanish Tragedy*, Jerome Jerome Geronimo.

> Lo yonder I see Everyman walking.
> Pilgrimage he must on him take
> the summoning of Everyman so called.

1/14/20 In our medieval bestiary after Joyce, Jacobo Timmerman the Argentine publisher of *La Opinión,* arrested and tortured for criticizing the Dirty War disappeareds, had a regular "chat with Susan," the machine that applied electrodes to his testicles: "It is impossible to shout - you howl" (*Prisoner Without a Name*, 6). For us the phantasmagoria of Walter Benjamin's 19th century civilization comes to roost. Read the appendix of *Arcades* (930f). How else have any bearing in a land of forces, a supernatural zoo, where all the archetype myth types roam at will uncontained? If we don't see them all that's because there is no world enough and time to point the crime, for one of them seen in ours would fill the bill, the mind.

--Subconscious and unconscious are results of the fall. Archetypes occupy, meant to continue loss of awareness. Filled with Medusa, Centaur, Leda, further division occurs when the conscious denies what the uncon says, which hides fears and hopes mixed up together. This opens to control by suggestion, which means that all the types are anti types in effect as nemesis, Aquarius the universal tyrant. Some more obvious than others.

1/16/19 I sent for printed copies of *Thrice 27* as soon as I heard it was ready because I couldn't believe anybody would print *The Secret Life of Democrats* and wanted to get a hard copy before they changed their mind. It is a visual feast with added value of the art and artists who engage with and interpret the text.

Lunch with B. Relayed offer to pay T. kindergarten, talked about his birthday present (*Finnegan's Wake*, FE), verbal facility, S.'s creativity. News to him that AB dreams of writing and illustrating books. As far as he knows T. is not getting a little black kitten for birthday!

1/17/20 The Song potters of Linderhosen:

1/18/20 Ivan Belyaev, Russian artist and ceramist born in Vologda. Since 2105 engaged study of traditional pottery of the Russian North, interior and conceptual art objects, also abstract sculpture of small forms with clay products, engobe (color clay) and glass glaze, because he considers that this combination allows highlighting the nuances of clay. Credo! The feature of work with ceramics is the radical changes from stage to stage: work with raw material, drying and multiple burning. The main ideas are the theme of human nature, movement, silence and calmness, and also the theme of transparency: crosscutting objects, ceramic outlines of vessels or vessels through cracks and holes.

Vlad Basarab shifts focal points from the fluctuations of memory appearances towards questioning methods of transmitting memory, emphasizing to safeguard the past and conserve historic truth. Due to the extreme fragility of memory, knowledge and past Basarab senses the increasing difficulty of remembering, despite memory being the only link to our past, our identity and our heritage.

To Bentley Calverley: On Ivan Belyaev of Vologda and Vlad Basarab of Bucharest: Thanks for your hospitality Friday for myself and my four year old protege. I spoke of Chris Gustin and Jonathan Cross to you but in response to your cordiality let me mention two with whom I share participation in their constructions, Ivan Belyaev of Vologda and Vlad Basarab of Bucharest. These represent the aesthetic of the Russian North and the archeology of memory especially. All the best.

 --The clothing of their salvation was song and light, the tools of their husbandry were thought. This light, these crowns refulgent "take care of," "guard," "watch over" all you Natsar! *That soul, though all hell should endeavor to shake, I'll never, no never, no never forsake.*

1/19/20 The poem "Amarant, or Love-Lies-Bleeding" at *Penny Poetry Blog*, leaves its seat out of season to come "to the world" to "light the mind of spice." This dissonance is what makes the speaker's heart "an aging sack."

--"I found much to relish in "Hierosolyma. The vision alone is truly excellent. Look for the piece in the next issue of *Futures Trading."* --Caleb

1/23/20 Sjon Larsson: in *A Concise Dictionary of Old Icelandic* of derived terms: [Does this not tell us synchronists to look ahead?]

- ("sight")
- n ("the testimony of an eye-witness")
- n ("sharpness of eyesight")
- f ("mirror")
- ("oversight, care, supervision")
- f ("a spectacle (to see)")

--Lunch with B. In effort to give T. continuity in school we offer tuition, but concern for his growth prevents. The very day this was considered he fell asleep in the car on the way home again, and out of sorts the rest of the night. Sleep is more important that continuity! Fri., T, "I did what I want."
- Ultra sound, exam, bubble test.

1/24/20 Progressive revelation is not laying out the case, but dribbling. The collection at Forms of the Formless to me justifies all the aesthetic judgments I am making, where the unthought hand is a prediction of being, the unthought mind as a witness:

--I took a nap and woke in 30 minutes with the image of a clock at six as the cover of a new title, Woops, Oops and Guapa, but in looking for the image online all were fingerprinted, so I looked for six o'clock art and after scrolling down found, "in MU its always 6 o'clock" which is *about what happens if Philip K. Dick takes control of your mind, if time stands still, if ordinary things become mysterious and fantasy creatures overturn the order of your soul. Come and see works of ours now being vandalized by other works of ours, says a young girl peeping through a hole, as Mickey Mouse going through ups and downs might say.* I can't explain, but *MU is located in a former Philips factory at Strijp S in Eindhoven, The Netherlands* NBI. MU explores the hybrid suburbs of contemporary visual art and is one of the creative driving forces of the Strijp-S region.

1/25/20 *Cockroach Orange of StewMasey.* New Title for *Top Roach*, whose epitaph went:

In the bathtub where the funeral was held
for the Nabu leader who died,
Rolls of Coalcrotch crammed them in,
Nabu! Nabu! They cried:

♪ Fellow CoalCrotchians we come,
to honor in behalf,
Remembering with willingness,
Praise Johnny in his death!
Let each one now perform his part,
and sing in praise of Johnny's heart,

And take…this…step to
welcome our Johnny home. ♪

1/26/20 Teslacles. Everyman, Here comes everybody. Everybody goes fishing, to the moon.

1/27/20 Thurs. We took Scion to the vet on Wed because Mon she had a lot of blood and a fever, mastitis, gave her Augmentin which seemed to help. The Vet found two puppies on x-ray and said she was due in 24 hr. Last night with much panting P heard her, thought it was afterbirth, but I took her to the vet because I thought she had had a miscarriage, which I guess it turns out…but now this morning she is lying in closet beside me on the place I made there.

27 Jan 2020. Note the date, first recorded reference to what is coming.

We Order:
 4--3M 6391 Half Mask Respirator with P100 Particulate Filters, Size Large $71.
40 Chaga tea bags. $27.
Copper Sheets $150.
600 black nitrile 5ml gloves. $60.
UV travel wand, plus two eyeglasses

--Bioweapon @ *Lancet*
Kill switch in virus, Palantir, Trump,
Copper handles, counter, Best disinfectant soap,
decontaminate protocols Properties of north birch chaga
Covid 19 sources, dual cartridge & swimming goggles.

Chaga: restrict protease, prevents

The Cockroach in the Castle

Pyramid. You can climb up several layers of the pyramid of these evils and think you know. And if you were imaginatively to get to the top what would you find? David Roberson made this unadvised effort his daily work, spent eight hours a day plus overtime to work the world of prayer. He prayed those forty hours and more a week, week after week, much of it in tongues of course. Those who don't should know this can lead to astonishing revelations just like insight meditation can, or fasting. So Dave made progress, but cut to the end, he got to the top, fumigating the layers below. Of course the top of the pyramid, if it is on, is a rather tight sofit-like dormer structure, but it seemed roomy and ornate on the inside when Dave came in the power to the throne room all gold like Donald Trump's penthouse, and sitting on the throne, all besplendored, was a large gold cockroach.

Descent. I don't remember what happened after that though. I guess you could call Dave and ask if he remembers, but I don't think I will. Dave recognized it was Pride, the spirit of pride.

The point here is that those layers Dave climbed through, and that top he achieved, as opposite, are the same structures in descent that fall through the minds of men, one after another, some above, some further down, to make them all conform. And one more thing. These thought forms, attitudes, opinions, beliefs, evidences, authorities, poets, scientists, architects and others are the immaterial Egregoi in their material states, so hang on. If you think that explains everything from ET to DMT to DARPA you're gonna have to apply for the Bucky Pope Project.

Warfare. Malachi Martin's apologizes for aspects of the castle in the medieval Loyola by teasing that, now "we have drugs for people who talk like that," who speak of "a universal warfare of God-made-man against a Fallen Archangel......" (*The Jesuits*, 182) or "any talk of 'discernment of spirits' or of controlling what enters the consciousness," (183). Pure Pentecostal theology. Charismatics these days go to the Vatican in series to hold hands with Pope Francis, which must be the opposite of such discernment, but Ignacio embraced, "to meet the Risen Christ in person in his glorified...through the very humanity of Christ, was introduced into the bodiless, eternal being of the Trinity--apparently ascending...to participate in the most hidden secrets of divinity for which human language has no words...this characteristic of genuine Christian piety--ascension to a bodiless spirit, God, through the humanity of a real man, Jesus--is a stumbling block for the non-Christian mind...by which you can find out what is authentically Christian or non-Christian' (*The Jesuits*, 156).

Malachi Martin writes and understands this later in life after he has known himself that *the Kingdom* is "'the whole surface of the earth" (157), not disallowing that it includes the sea and the center of the earth, the air and the stratosphere and all these traveling goombahs of space. In the universal warfare the earthly kingdom produces those personal qualities of such characters' resolve of will and resourcefulness no matter what their time and place. It produces a "cut through of the dreadful spiritual trials endured, and result in *Spiritual Exercises"* (158).

Been deceived by a fallen angel lately? Well there it is, like water under a bridge over troubled waters where pop music is a preferred venue along with fairy tales, psychological archetypes, systematic theologies, philosophies, and here's the kicker at the top: it is all good. The good is evil, the evil is evil. So here I am, setting forth on this bridge with my asses, putting explosive charges about every fifty feet. I'll probably have to go back into 3D and get more, but the intent here is to blow the whole structure, pyramid and bridge. Not me. I know a Guy. So in the context if I report what happened in that sojourn to the Mission in Central America I want to arouse in myself and all of us the forgiveness for our sins and for theirs.

"As if the sense of division and pain, of summons and effort…felt the universe as divided both within them and without them to realize single control in the universe; that fashioned demands on themselves and others out of what they held to be the nature of that control."

--It is a very interesting thing to read the unconscious of persons. *Wittgenstein. Philosophical Investigations* 218.

-Talk with sinus: Proper (kinds of) fat intake key to sinus health. Seed oils are drying & leave sinuses prone to micro-cracking & infections. Switch to ghee to repair your FIRST defense system against ALL flu infections...your snout...& sinuses. Turkeytail mushroom tea 2 boost immunity.

--Order UV air cleaners. Inventory masks. Colloidal silver, copper foil.

1/28/20

1/29/20 Wed. Four Peaks Amythyst

1/30/20 Cut into pieces all the railroad cars filled with coal, since it is as likely they have a market like coal. Drive the Dakotas the wastes of Texas and count the cars, it will rob your naivete.

1/31/20 --Dream livin' at Spg Sp with Eden. Realize we haven't paid rent in ages. Lawrence comes, brings ripe peaches, not interested in rent.

Alphabet of a woman. The ABCs. A is for. B is for…

2/1/20 Reviewed family documents while looking for Andrew Mack's civil war. When A has a son he will have reason to remember the past.

2/2/20 went to Four Peaks mine store for amethyst; MIND MINE—to light the mind of spice that fills the heart. Which happened to be their special for that month's birthstone!

Lament for the spontaneous: I would call up T. and sing the super bowl, the super bowl to him but the fathers have lost the spontaneous, only by prior notice and appt approval may you call. Wives. Only the cell phone is spontaneous to lives.

2/3/2020 Mon. Just woke, near 6.30. The antidote: framed copper sheeting, copper arm wraps, copper sculptures, spray colloidal silver. Cytokine storm! Beauty is conditional. Just as nobody likes their first taste of beer, you must learn to love, it is not natural. You must learn the good. The true. Goodness good.

A cannot remember his dream he told of 11 Apr 2014 driving with his son in his arms. Neither can he remember telling me his name which he would not tell me. I recall he had two sons in his arms. At least I did.

2/4/20   Good (Tobh, Tubh, yaTabh; agathos, agathon, kalos, kalon): the entire Bible, old and new is about the coming of the Son and the sons of God.

2/5/20   Wed. Since Mon been restructuring border garden. Added three bales peat.

Whatever replenish the earth means in English, fill the earth in Hebrew has the same sense, fill from being empty, whether it was once filled then empty, as in katabole, to fill means it was empty, without saying whether natively so or from cause.

2/6/20   Grand solar minimum, pandemics, 5G, quantum supremacy and that just this year, last year we had CERN. Commercial minerals.

2/7/20   In the many layers of motivation undercurrent, back and side, lingering in a gift of 33K to the School, three checks of 10k each, plus one of 2K, another of 1K, accidently reaching 33, the thought that this served as a reparation against Jacob's accusers from his second trip to Holland c. 1730 to retrieve funds and when their investment in goods for import to PA to increase them failed from their being put in storage in England and not repatriated for many years and then at a much reduced rate of expectation, Jacob was blamed, which gave rise to the court filings, harassment and finally vindication by Schlatter of his affair of the Reiff Church in 1747.

2/8,9/20   Collect lost tales, shoulder hurt changing water barrels

2/8/9/2020   Worked on stories.

2/10/20   Kirk at office, photo the line, design an answer. Computers down. Order B6, 12.

2/11/20   The name of the collection is Guapa Pop. Like the drink.

2/12/20   Realize dreams of return to Costa Rica many times, and more, of dreams to some place in the north where the first stop had to be some outpost island, then on destination, a little like the top of some Mt. in Wales. It is cold there and I hike.

2/13/20 A Call for Common Sense.

-Chaga a protease inhibitor used in HIV—from fruiting bodies.
-Order Mercola Chaga. Order Nootropics
-Order blow bag for office.

How many people die in their sleep the way several of those ATPs have come on me at 2-4 in the morning? How does it compare to birth, how conscious is anyone at birth? If you know you are dying does it matter in knowing so? Except that you have a record to show for it and the history of a life.

2/14/20   "Fiery the angels rose, and as they rose deep thunder roll'd. Around their shores: indignant burning with the fires of Orc." *America a prophecy.* Blake.

 "Fiery the angels fell deep thunder rolled around their shores burning with fires of Orc." Roy Batty, *Blade Runner.* 1982.

--Order Forzey 48pcs N95 Masks x 2. $30

The accuser falls into his own mouth

2/15/20   Oh-oh yes, the great pretender.
--Order 48pcs N95 Masks. Calgary. $60.

2/16/20   Angus Fletcher *Allegory*, giants, Phillips, Peter. 1994. *A Relative Advantage: Sociology of the San Francisco Bohemian Club*. University of California, Davis. Doctoral Dissertation who began this with investigation at

I desired to write long before the true words came- from where they came, except they were destined if I qualified which qualifying came from my Maker who designed me this way should I choose Him and I did, with vigor to seek the place of the most High, the secret under the shadow of the rock, His wings, then the words came and as the designed grew, produced this fiction and praise poetry to show my debt and honor to Him who sits on the throne and unto the Lamb, all mysterious matters shared with the those gifted with Grace and Truth.

To translate this conundrum of the world I choose literature and language, the best choice it turns out, usually now given to AI to divine, but the take provided me, being arbitrary, especially shows the levels of complexity of the structure of the governing powers, who are unable to discern without a point of view based on the notion that the earth is enemy territory.

Translating dimensions is just this side of the impossible of doing it. For the sake of it let's say a dimension is one quantum step above and is translated down. Could it be translated up? Not to the point.

2/17/2020   Many truths are unpleasant, like total depravity. These stories of *Pied Cow Now* and *Guapa Pop* are my struggle, it can be argued, on a symbolic level with total depravity. They come from the same world. *Pied Cow Now* is a case book without interpretation, *Guapa Pop* has layers and layers of reflection about itself.

There is an analogy between the stories and the ceramics, which displayed show about an equal number of instances. Each is individual one of a kind never to be repeated. They are in different languages though, the stories are symbolic in words, the ceramics are symbolic in images of the same subjects opaquely presented.

2/18/20 Tues. Viral Genomic clusters in U.S. military enlisted recruits and college dorms Newly *enlisted military recruits* are infected by the end of the third week after their recruitment. *Clusters* among non-immune *recruits* occur early in basic training. This phenom spreads in groups as propaganda, prejudice, crowds, mods, lynching, mass hysteria spread, some think, and more and more by commercial surveillance and control of information flows, which infection is as real as in the barracks and dorms. Sorority and fraternity houses. Charles Borromeo Seminary, nunneries, any group houses. Infection happens in three weeks in barracks, so there is a lead time, incubation of that period. Also there is an incubation period for philosophical, political, social contamination. Outbreaks in 60s and 80s in barracks are the signals.

Chaga inhibits HIV protease [ivermectin binds spike protein]

2/19/20 A to sing amazing grace at funeral of 300 Sat. J. is what A has been about, faith and works. The works of faith, the faith of works.

We shall give account of every word we speak. These range behind us in a trail, but in the present we speak the words written for us to speak in the future. After the present passes they are written, but *before* we must qualify to speak the words of our life continually, so each word is important in faith.

T. drew a pic of me and mom and signed with his name, backwards. Hurt shoulder 2 or 3rd time digging. Ice packs at night.

2.20.20 White men trying to dignify black men is like rich men advocating for the poor, piggyback. They ride them like donkeys.

"The Door to Hell" is a burning natural gas field in the Derweze, Turkmenistan fire, boiling mud, and orange flames in the large crater, has a diameter of 70 meters (230 ft). Engineers set up a drilling rig and operations to assess the quantity of oil at the site. Soon after, the preliminary survey found a natural gas pocket, the ground beneath the drilling rig and camp collapsed into a wide crater and was buried. Expecting dangerous releases of poisonous gases from the cavern into nearby towns, engineers considered it advisable to burn the gas off. It was estimated that the gas would burn out within a few weeks, but it has continued to burn for 48 years and is expected to keep on burning. became the first person to set foot at the bottom, gathering samples of extremophile microorganisms.

Birch forests are the most sterile natural environment.

Sewer job finished one day. 11-7 max. After blow bagging the sewer line three times some months, since a snake didn't work, we videoed the line and dug. Jack hammer. Pretty much best case. Beginning, middle, end. After the end, clean up compact dirt and yellow tape. Tree root down there, cut it. Probable eucalypt from neighbor seeking water. Shoulder hurts a lot, don't feel good. What happens in a real emergency? Sewer repaired, shoveled the dirt into the hole before work. Looks like it's just her and me again, like it was.

--Ordered more chaga.

2/21/20 Friday. you get old enough, reach a certain age, and your feeling of responsibility for the sins of the world diminishes. It feels like it's done, the past, a closed book. All you need is realize you went from being author and lead actor to a seat in the audience.

Pied Cow White socks is a symbol of Pied innocence. Trade in body parts is one part of cannibalism. In the mix of truth and fantasy I did review the *Solidarity of Kin* (cited at the end. What is the meaning of fairy tales? Eating disorder/ Sublimated erosis? Ha. The professor's name is Fairy Tale in order to show that it consumes children with the fallen. Hey, the fallen run the world! Why do you think the original English *faer* means to fear? We however are supposed to call that good even while they are eating. In the old language it means an awful horror, a headlong sudden fall, beset by dangers, sudden seizure, apoplexy, pestilence, sudden cold, sudden death. *Faergrygrum* is the rule of these. In other words using Higher Ed Stanford/Harvard do it to convince the children they are something special in order to make them slaves. Hansel and Gretel are emblems in this case of the poverty home prepackaged in their education at the U where they are completely consumed. The bait consists of the ornate promises of the digital life they lead, cake roofs, gold grapefruits, right NOW, the way all nature is corrupted, falsified by its bowers of bliss, instantaneous gratification, lack of ownership in reality, self driving cars, but the villain consumes them with false ideas of the world and life even while it convinces them they are superior to it all.

So in the story that begins *Pied Cow Now*, they go in the house but none come out! Victim consciousness, flora of the golden age, masks Heorot as the Cake House Grendel tears apart. I say we have no kinship with this darkness, its giants, ogres and fairies except to kill them. (John Gardner. *The Construction of Christian Poetry in Old English*, 67f, 70) which result in a series of tales that seemed to require the circulation of a facetious biography, cultivation of several pseudonyms, for it was a consideration of subjects so far from mainstream as to be absurd, ridiculous, unbelievable, with a writing style that bends to this with new words, simple syntax combined with complex—all of which is difficult of audience, but intends to bypass consciousness to communicate with the brain, since consciousness is controlled to such large extent by external sources and no longer by those timeless inquiries into life, death, health and life, love and life it always supposed before.

This is a comment about Bosch to the effect that from the world's beginning until the end of time, the familiar is secretive and strange, the uncanny is the familiar in disguise. That was also the intent of the Lyrical Ballads where Wordsworth and Coleridge each took one end toward the middle. In every momentary surrender of desire, will, action, speech to the provision of the grace which new life utterly supplants in the details of the old confusion, to explore that life outside, beyond the details imposed, might be Bosch. By turning the everyday details upside down, separated against themselves Bosch shows how they are confinement, prison, and are inimical to our being. Parts of bodies hands, feet, heads, buttocks beside ponds flying in the air are all part of the demonstration that later Wordsworth began to celebrate in the rocks and stones and trees and little Lucy flying round her course. The ordinary, the vernacular are our suit that we wear and so doing are manipulated against our interest by this enemy, which is our best interest, but hard to know as snatches of it and the whole life of how it may be recovered occur in instances of self sacrifice, service to others, kindness, compassion, seeing the other face as my face, as Levinas does, to recognize the life we now live in the flesh must be redeemed.

The natural result of this life lived is that my children never slept in front of windows because of stray bullets, and books were kept on the highest shelves to protect from flood, or dam break, or best sculptures stored low on the porch to avoid gunfire. One new year's I did find a forty five slug embedded in the block of the back, so maintaining perimeters, with yucca, ironwood, gogi berry, lantana, continually practicing economies of all kinds conservation inventories, alternative baking, home cooked food always, extreme speculations of all kinds from azomite to buying Enron at its bottom before bankruptcy, as an investment! Absurd as XTND, the first Bluetooth, which made up more half of all tech losses at that time.

2/22/20   Sat. B's party today for T. after moving 44 tons of gravel and A at funeral sings Amazing Grace.

2/23/20 Sunday. My comic narrator has ,been balmy since *Frankie* began anonymously submitted to the *Gargoyle*, nonplussed, aghast awestruck, either that or satiric. The editorial board broke up in laughter, which the author saw, but was masked as Simon Real. This narrator comes in science to excuse these outlandish discoveries about the world, or with fable of his own, calling it myth, but it is more akin to *Mad* magazine and Wall St gone berserk, or to journalism, as if he were ferreting out the facts. A tragic narrator retains elements of this but is way more rational in reporting the events and images of the worlds seen

2/24/20 They did not order masks asked for 10 days ago now, or even inventory them.

--The only semblance is to model the future on every basis, the past, the facts, the speculations and on. But A is way to afraid to do this and B is too busy. I live the future in the present so when it comes I can see it. Any successful model always begins with your own death and the attempt to prevent that of your loved ones and everyone. But the details must be double checked for you will receive covert opposition from those afraid of the future.

--Minestrone soup, what's the memory? Italy, whatever city you ate it in, the meal.

-Massachusetts "the one mile radius between Harvard and MIT is the center of the center of the deep state. Every evil starts between the one mile radius between MIT and Harvard"
Shiva Ayyadurai
 2/23/20

Today we realize Scion has large milk sacs. At noon she is bleeding.
I got a 2nd pneumonia shot.
P. dreamed her mother died. [but she didn't!]
Booked flight to SA.
T. sick from weekend.

2/25/20 T.--White Volcano-yogurt, honey in center, chaga outside.
--Pneumonia shots all round,
--order more breathing machines,

--uv disinfectant light, wand and glasses
Protocols for return from travel

We *operate a trading post neighboring the Diné with exchanges open on the remains of winter night. This particular remain, left by a bearded immigrant, took pickup loads of manure from our stables in trade, which we were easy enough to part with, as well as cottonwood roots dug out of our mud bank, with remunerations to come, depending upon your further reference and consideration.*

2/26/20 G. Bellows! Neighbor early NSA.

41 pneumonia cases by the end of December.
1 Jan 2020 Wuhan sea market closed. Reinfections will be more deadly than initial effects of this protein. The symptoms & causes of death will be different the second time.

2/27/20 Shungite arrives. Cat scan diagnoses coronavirus lung spots in mailman who wonders perm lung damage.

2/28/20 I had a heartbeat of 83 briefly yesterday mid afternoon.

Summary, Jason's crash and burn, new computers, consults, loss of privileges, 8000 questions, computers stall, bandwidth, renegotiate trash, office sewer, denial of n95masks inventory, concern for Ruth finance, dream of mother, Scion hurt foot, admission at vets regarding future modeling: glad I don't have those 2 parts, failure to control imagination, fear.

--U.S. takes same tack as Chinese, downplayed, deny public. Demos turn alarm, Fox says nature, not bio weapon, Sars 2, vaccine soon, no matter no defensive procedures in place

--order 40 n95 masks, $50.

-- Early positive signs from treatment with a combination of the hepatitis C (HCV) medicine Ganovo (danoprevir) and the HIV med ritonavir.

Trump on the coronavirus: "It's going to disappear one day it's like a miracle it will disappear."

"Der Hamsterkauf is a German word used to describe panic buying. It comes from the verb hamstern, which means "to hoard or panic buy" during times of fear, since hamsters are known for filling their cheeks with food."

2/29/20 Weed eat office yesterday after notice from city about 6 in. weeds. Post coronavirus. A furloughed.

3/1/20

Der Hamsterkauf

How the grackles run apace
Look how grackles go
Chow-cho-fu has lost his state
Sung-foo come round
with grackles strange
both proud and great
whose songs to weeping change.

-Spiritual *mischwesen*
-Reisi triterpenoids, polysaccharides and peptidoglycans,
-Honky paper is the paper you put in the oven on top of the stone.
"STOP BUYING MASKS! They are NOT effective in preventing general public from catching but if healthcare providers can't get them to care for sick patients, it puts them and our communities at risk!" CDC.

Apparently Henry driving his Ford to the moon is something that cam be caught.

3/2/20 First sleep: mind of the man.

Globalists: One world government or death. Whatever it takes. Patches in Latin on their sleeves.

Vax me, vac me
I hope that it gets done
Vax me vac me
First sleep is the mind of man
Henry drives his Ford to the moon
Honky paper on top the stone
The millennium and tribulation one.

There are always organized groups behind global events, assassinations of Lincoln, Father Chiniqey, Kennedy, MLK, Rasputin, where programs to trigger on need for the general work of Las Vegas and the 100 one thousand are made. Same with 9/11, Fukushima, Haiti, Wuhan, Ferdinand, for over them "I saw terror advancing, fear from the south (Dr. Oz), but line up to be vaxed. AI, never sees anything but itself and its own operating procedures. First principle is save the program for *The Artilect* (Hugo De Garis). A man sees others instead of himself, and wants to save the weak first. His empathy is foreign to globalist tools. All the AI plots are preannounced by the Nostros, the Chings, and Blavatsky.

Palantir is composed of the data base of the lives of 3 billion+ peoples daily activities and hopes and fears reflected in their tweets, emails, shopping habits induced from there. That is why cell phones are needed to predict outcomes. It is the Otoku to little boy and little girl the world, to de-adult the world away. Homogenize, neutralize of not *aquilae* will come

[All the historical overlays of the sonnets and lyrics in *True Light* were added to mask the impossible fact that these unbelievable thoughts and experiences impossible to obtain, either to think or to have, are made acceptable by their historical or poetical contexts like Taliesin, or in the new world discoveries, or in the prophetic plant.]

First and second sleep are the normal

--Contact tracing and isolation. Lugol's iodine every other day. Two drops on one wrist & rub wrists together. Absorption time tells you how deficient you are, more=faster.

3/3/20 I want there to be repetition. I want there to be redundancy. This might resemble Richard Brautigan slightly and might mean something to those who know the experiences they inhabit but most have never revealed. They have always been outside the circle, but somehow now when we need some consolation of living they give comfort.

Have myself been given a jaded view of the Pennsylvania Dutch language characterized as an inferior pidgin soiling where it landed.
祝福 (Zhùfú)
(Mànpǎo zhě) 慢跑者

Reading B's memo about outlooks and expectations makes me think I have a balsamic consciousness, so none of it really matters. A man who is free will do what he does no matter the circumstances until he is stopped, which doesn't in the end depend on him at all, what depends on him is to act.

"The infection of SARS-CoV has been reported in the brains from both patients and experimental animals, where the brainstem was heavily infected. This is why I was shouting chaga. It stops the HIV part from replicating & being able to get in brain & spinal fluid."

3/4/20 Restoration Breaths

In Qom they kiss the wall of the mosque and die. In Wuhan emissaries spit in shopping carts. In Korea they spread at church but in America they don't wear masks but release the catch in SA to the mall, and in Phx send flu fevers bacteria to the airport to work. You must pay for your own test. In CA the homeless FEMA camps are coming, earth movers novae sound the air. The Pope is negative and Pence for now. First test, second test, release, infection. 24 days incubation, 10 days touch on steel. Try disinfecting your cars people.

3/4/20 Doris called to say irrigation fixed.

3/5/20 Email plumber this am at 11.30 to settle at 1500. He admits disparity by not charging for his first x-ray the pipe. Then he says they got there at 8 but I told him to call me when they started, he didn't but the office did, it was 11. Then he admits he did not know what time they started.

3/7/20 Order six pairs of filters: 3M 2091 (07000) P100 Particulate Filters well suited for a wide range of oil and non-oil based particulate contaminants and provides exceptional (99.97%) filter efficiency against particles. Approved by NIOSH with Advanced Electret Media (AEM), lightweight respiratory protection against lead, asbestos, cadmium, arsenic, and MDA. The filter properly fitted used in welding, brazing, torch cutting, metal pouring and soldering for concentrations up to 10 times the Permissible Exposure Limit (PEL) with half facepieces or 50 times with full.

Time Use Limitation:

- Dispose the filter after 40 hours of use or 30 days, whichever is first, when using in environment containing only aerosols

--Full Moon, the Glastonbury Tor Tues Jan. 8, 1974.

[I never specifically looked up the date before. We were in London to see plays during that series of IRA Christmas bombings, after which we rented a car to stay around Bath, Old Sarum and Stonehenge, which you could walk right up to then there being no guards. Three times with the same regard we visited, as at the Rodin in Paris. The moon being full, that night we took our own rough path up the Tor in the full dark light. She had given me leather hat with a blue band in those times which somehow came off on the Tor and there it stayed. We got to the ruins at the summit, went back down another rough path and looked for a place to eat. Seated at one end of a portico a couple tables away we invaded the space of several conspiratorial men and a woman. There were planned bombings in the Midlands then and much tension flowed from them. The woman kept giving me subtle warning signals to the effect of danger. I went out to the car to get some cigarettes and came back to their close observance. We checked out before them, went to a B&B and the next day went to the Ruins in the bright sun of the morning. I found the Lady Chapel and engraving of Christ above the altar there with the realization danger and blessing walk, their hands knit.]

--The current belief is that is everywhere that humans go. It stays on surfaces, sheds from infected people constantly from all mucoid membranes & can be infectious from surfaces. Anecdotal evidence continues to grow that ppl who take Vitamin C & D do not get it. Synergy provided by Chaga & vitamin C.

The entire elite troop of fools was outperformed by Mongolia and S. Korea. Makes mask high culture beyond corrupt castrato boys singing opera to ponces fighting duels in front of their castle

3/8/20 Longhenge and Shorthenge.

Usney "My encounter with Usney occurred at the peak of the triumph of viruses in various organs, when the virus struck one after another, uniting with immune cells, trying to cause mistrust to its own protective forces, spreading with cosmic speed. And Usney acted and showed herself as befits a warrior, uncompromising and tactically verified. Thanks to usnic acid, and even more than 30 active active ingredients, Usney has a broad antimicrobial activity. Unlike conventional synthetic antibiotics, viruses and bacteria are difficult to reach with natural antibiotics, resistance does not occur. I selected the dosage myself, at that time I was extremely depleted, and therefore I started with 10 drops 3 times a day. I saw the results and it inspired me. An abnormal cough has passed, the maxillary sinuses have cleared! Then he added Olive leaf and Beberin, but that was later.

"High dose Vitamin C kills by electron donation & formation of hydrogen peroxide. Chaga kills by protease inhibition preventing replication. Usnea works by providing endothelial layer & mucous membrane support & increasing cilli function as expectorant."

Sunday--talk with R and C. Since the ACE2 receptors are 5 times greater in the Chinese genome and since China has already overwhelmed the U.S. in so many ways from rare earth to mfg., and since a bio sample of the coronavirus was imported from Canada to that facility months before, and since the seed was more likely planted at war games held at a base near Wuhan attended by 70 nations, mid October '19 where first released, causing the complete subsequent isolation of entire Chinese naval bases and death of entire crews--which incidences are multiple, with hundreds of thousand of deaths thus weakening the Chinese military which was colonizing islands and threatening all countries of middle Asia, and weakening the Chinese mercantile empire in the same blow, the virus, it is argued was not made in China at all -- but planted there, for if we know anything it is that it is never about the appearances, all a show--well where do you think, they say Sars 2 was made? Soho? Except the rebound is never quite well understood by these machinations, for when the elite bind socially together as they do always, they infect themselves and that's peeling only 3 layers.

A brings Xaralto from Mex with 151 proof vodka for hand cleaning. Spray office with ortho. More supplies -P- from stores. Set up UV air for office. Told to take the B prop if offered.

The first cycle is the most infective because it is unknown and too late after and also because it activates in 12 hours. And is strongest. When everybody masks danger decreases.

--People with this Name have a deep inner need for quiet, and a desire to understand and analyze the world they live in, and to learn the deeper truths. The Greek form of the name Jacob (Iakobos) was given to the Latin (Iacomus) which eventually got anglicized to James. The first recoded spelling of the surname came in the 14th century as Jamesson, to which the personality number nine represents completion or ending of a cycle, and a need for perfection. Another balsamatic? This is the personality that moves from "self" to a greater understanding and compassion for the human condition. Nines capable of spiritual and humanitarian achievements, courageous, fearless, able to fight on behalf of worthy causes will not tolerate injustice. They are compassionate people with a strong sensitivity to others, gifted artistically witha keen imagination and enterprising mind.

3/9/20 4 gal 99% isopropyl alcohol
vitamin c at 50mg/kg 200lbs = 90 kilograms

Buy 3 bottles 1600
Merv 13 air filters,
cancel SA flight
Home depot panic, parked at Walgreens

--or every 100 patients seen in S. Korea = 2 PPE Suits per day per medical staff, 4 to 10 masks per day per medico, 100+ pairs of gloves.

Everyone entering Israel will be quarantined for a minimum of 14 days. Israel is 100% closed to tourism.

Albert Bartlet exponential growth,

3/10/20 First Sleep. Now is the time.

possible efficacy of chloroquine in the treatment of coronavirus infections and its role in aiding cellular zinc absorption. China 500mg twice a day, Korea, once.

"Italy had 62 identified cases of on the 22nd of Feb. 888 cases by 29th of Feb, and 4,636 by 6th of March."

-- James Lawler best guess" estimates for

- 96 million coronavirus infections
- 4.8 million hospitalizations from the infection
- 480,000 deaths in the United States

--Vitamin C at 50mg/kg. 200 pounds equals 90 kg equals 5000 mg, (for me that is, with minimal contact). For medicos go up 20% at least. The good thing is you can get liquid liposomal C into children with juice.

--A recipe in addition Minimally:
Probiotic, hyaluronic acid, fish oil, niacin, multiple Vit B, Vit E 400, Vit A and D 1500/400, CoQ10, Selenium, Vit K.

--Exhaustion must be prevented.. learn to use wipes.

--My experience and aggregations now conclude the time of emergency is upon us and all measures available personally must be implemented. This because the principle of exponential doubling indicates that when we think we have more time that is the most dangerous to us. We have no more time because the doubling that is occurring will proceed so rapidly in the U.S and even in states where there is little evidence of infection—it will be an overwhelming cascade, week by month because the virus is most infectious in its early stage. Infectious after 12 hrs, symptom-less for many days up to weeks, 1000 times more infectious that imaginable, all those silent carriers will not show in the first doublings, but when they do they will all have doubled and doubled again and it will all as it were strike at once. Further there are different reports, like young women in their 20's majority affected in S Kora, a hugely disproportionate death toll in Italy, China having shut down all contact the last week, in the affect of the NY subway being closed, all schools, it is too late. Princeton Univ has effectively closed.

So now the regimes of liposomal Vit C, Chaga and Usnea must be active in treatment and before. "*High* dose Vitamin C kills by electron donation & formation of hydrogen peroxide. Chaga kills by protease inhibition preventing replication. Usnea works by providing endothelial layer & mucous membrane support & increasing cilli function as expectorant."

Advanced safe zones implemented. Exposed Clothes need UV cleaning. Clinically they are using earmuffs, goggles, masks, gloves as a minimum in medical conditions, but since the U.S. will never have necessary masks, or medicines, or hospital wards enough, or even the government will to act—until the extreme dictate, as A says, 12 hours later all is shut down, all the medicines especially for a year must be had now, not that that is enough. Won't there be a run on Vit C, chor is it just aga, elderberry, toilet paper? Yesterday, Monday 11 A.M. Went to Home Depot to get some extension cords for the UV, and had to park at Walgreen's and walk! Jam packed..

Princeton University just closed. Curtailing all public appearances not necessary. No club, especially in this 2 wk period now when all seems normal while doubling occurs. More and more conscious sanitation practices, never enough, no restaurants, no churches-not that any do, shopping completed now. Especially stay away from people who travel. As to schools, visitors, visiting friends, the same applies, family excepted maybe, but each must figure it for their own. As to business, shut it down, work at home, or if not go nuts with extreme measures, not enough. We stayed open the whole time. This glue in the lungs is to avoided. Chaga stops the HIV part from replicating & being able to get in brain & spinal fluid. Chaga.

3/11/20 Happy Fukushima Day.

Dreamed *He Was Bruised* exhibited at the Armadillo World HQ / Changing Hands in venue many times. It might have appeared at the Dallas World Fair and did at a Bishop exhibit, Earth and Fire of Adriana Cobo-Frankel, hauled on the top of the car in a rigged up roof rack because it wouldn't fit, 49x59, in any vehicle I had and driven to South Dallas fifteen miles on top of the car, an oil painted in Dallas on an old canvas salvaged from Jim Bowman who had lots of large canvases. H was getting rid of it so I re-prepped and painted over in oils on a covered patio at this gift house, brokered by Fred Outlaw from drug ring pariahs who terrorized the neighbors that we repossessed for the good, just east of White Rock Lake and rehabbed as an answer to their prayers. The owner stoned out unconscious in a middle room when we saw it, her gang-sons rampaging around, I found a loaded pistol under the peer and beam elevated floor. The instant I saw the place it was perfect.

He Was Bruised flashed on screens in partials in all this, sometimes defaced, sometimes turned black and white with lines through, sometimes whole in a light show. Gayle Shanks of Changing Hands was the curator of this now ancient tale, but I still have the painting, get up in the night and go look at it by flashlight to write this. It is the token of the present in the midst of the Revelation for when the lines recite, "over them I saw terror advancing, fear from the south, destruction from the north," all this in the present circumstances where government is paralyzed to pandemic, initially wants to privatize the response, issue test kits from Sonora Quest to med offices where when the afflicted come the staff is unprotected and infected whole because there is no suit, mask or protective gear garb, and then the test is sent back days later while the person infects more and still more if positive and if negative needs to be tested again and again and on. Later they will think of quarantine camps and no vax no food. To ameliorate quarantine they offer payroll tax exemption here instead of direct response the same way of avoiding responsibility as privatizing the tests and the pandemic. But of course it was home grown right there in North Carolina. And when schools close and people can't work at home starve while the government infects itself I asked about all this and was instantly told. Walk.

--Due to Covid-19 Coronavirus No one can be within 15 feet of an infected person without becoming infected. This is a biological weapon Contagious for 37 days now. Check your vital signs swab at home
Querctin + zinc inhibit virus 3000mg

37 days contagious, Brits with a cough or temperature have been told to self isolate for a week as the government steps up its response to the coronavirus. Anyone who has even mild symptoms must immediately self-isolate for a week, starting tonight, Boris Johnson has announced. It is understood the guidance applies to anyone who has a persistent cough or a temperature. Those self-isolating with mild symptoms are not advised to call 111.

Reconstruction Memory

--These Pied Cows account the meeting with the other, neighborhoods in the first case after brother, sister. When Z comes down that is the first incursion form outside, the ET superior, who judge like the Brits in China, Spanish in Mexico, English in New England that they have found a new world. The conflict of cultures is a parable of neighborhoods for Pied Cows since both it and Susan of *Guapa Pop* were immediately so modeled. Both the neighbor in that opening story of the Pied was a legitimate, even profound writer who had extreme insight to the other problem, focused upon the first nation people of his home in Maine and thereabouts, the Abenaki who have everything to do with the conflict of cultures from the outside, red lanterns shining through the fog, the landing of boats, call it space ships of orbs, the subsequent meetings and treaties where the first people are shorn. It always happens this way. No wonder Hawking was afraid of the landings! But the fear is not the profound thing about the Abenaki. They sought to integrate the out with the in. To harmonize, redeem the invader. It was a function of their religion

This automatically poses a comparison of the colonizing Jesuit who came with the other with the Abenaki cultures where the priest supplanted the shaman because the overwhelming famine and disease (initiated by the priest) vitiated shaman authority in the tribes. Who is the priest in this analogy and who the Indian? Who lives or dies? Inviting the priest to serve as kin however is not what happened. The priest was invited to supplant the spiritual governance of the tribe which became its downfall. Consider that the priest cured the disease he himself brought. Amazingly the priest was made over into a new Jesuit Gluskap! "The Jesuit priests then, entered Algonkian traditions sometime during the seventeenth century, performing roles comparable to the benevolent Gluskap" (Kin,76).

This would all be reeducation organized the religion, psychology, physics departments where the ice giant is reeducated to be kin. Gluskap is reeducated to be a priest. Students are re educated to be new members of their global re-tribal society of the new new world, Caliban is reeducated to become a man, Prospero puts down his wand, and your phone is bugged with cookies. So it's a tossup as to who you will serve. You must you will be brought under control.

This is a subject many cases of *Pied Cow Now* explore, as the first of part 2 declares, "I have done what anthropologists want, taken back the native as my own. It admits too much to live the other way. Whether at bus stop or back fence stories pass as found, plain speaking without fiction embarrasses the text. Away with Eskimo, Caribbean divines, myths carried all along. Excavate the Caucasoid within! You will find that primitive thought lost in the forests of homeless scutter wander while fleeing the scutes, troglodytes of leather whose shells scupper an alternate universe, which folktales performed at banquets to large quantities."

The biggest problem we are having with Caucasoids seeking the spiritual is illustrated when Beck and Walters in *The Sacred*, and Gill in *Native American Religions* say the sacred means "something special." They prove then that they know nothing about it, for it is exactly the opposite. Gill saying humans share a "single nature" expressed in "images, actions and symbols" is mere religion of the self, warmed over occult Jung.

Caucasoid spirituality cannot find itself so it must study the other and become it, that is, before it eats it up, which is what *The Dame of Guapa Pop* will do, so here comes Gluskap again and we'd like to prevent him from inviting the social psychosis of those anti-social Caucasoid cannibal ice giants and their Jesuit colonizers Gill, Wenger, Morrison, who in Pied Cow anyway was turned from a tenure professor of religion to a professor eating his students, pretty much what was to Theodore Kaczynski and others in the psych experiments at Harvard and later in the Stanford Prison Experiment, funded by the Navy, based on the Milgram Experiment in enforcing authoritarian measures. The Navy remember was at Montauk and in the Philadelphia Experiment. If there are any ETs they are likely in the Navy for the close quarters that provides and to study the effects on the sailors.

He says the Abenaki believed that inviting the lost, fragmented, rejected and rejecting spirit into the family, honoring him, her or it with family titles, father, father-in-law, implicitly comforting them, clothing and reclothing them, and feeding them real food, which means the food of the soul so they do not have to eat the hearts of the enemies in ritual cannibalism or famine, giving them children to play with, brings them back from their cold into the warmth of the hearth and home and kin. Whether we have any such structures and processes any more as a people, that doubt he says is itself a hindrance to the restoration of the human in lost, separated souls. The 2020s are divisive and separative, on purpose, commanding acquiescence of the individual to the group stereotype that is itself a false windigo pretense of the human is the real danger of the ice giant, the only selfish aggressor. It pretends all too well to be one of us and to compel our acceptance of its eating of the human heart. Many if not all of the Abenaki myths are metaphoric to us, so ritual cannibalism, eating the enemy heart to gain its courage is a metaphor in our language in the saying "eat your heart out," an expression of jealousy, but that is the point, our courage does not lie in the enemy heart but in our own, and our fulfillment is not in the enemy success but in our own. So we are presented with the ice giant verily.

More than Frenchification, this is undermining from within the social structures that had been their means of survival. All this shows the importance of recognizing post contact realities, again a metaphor of the transhuman, technology, modernism, whatever you will, for once the native has been supplanted it does not return, except in reinventions of the modern, which are themselves pretenses of kinship. I see all this as most fertile pollination of the metaphor of contact and multi-dimensionality and take contact as every effect of technology and civilization to bend the will of the (native) person to its empire. Are we the Abenaki? Not if we want to win. Win what exactly? That is the problem the same as where to flee in the Day, to the mountain or to the sea? Well neither, so that leaves, as my interlocutor says, the valley. The worst choice of all. So whether to remain in ignorance in the face of these contacts and be carried by the contemporary delusion or to resist them, alas says Hamlet, that I was born for such a time as this. Well you may think it Hamlet, but it is Esther. I am led merely by the prose in this thought, that Esther has born to intercede for her people against the forces of their destruction, the ice giant Haman, but there was no integration, merely execution, even if Haman was invited to repent. If the priest represents the power of the new contact then the primitive is the tribal, the one on the outs of empire, and appointing the priest to be a Gluskap is absolutely in the vein of baptizing Martians. Inviting ET to a bishopric, everyone else takes the mark of the beast except those in that time who do exploits.

I am nothing if not facetious. This is all reeducation to the religion, psychology, physics departments. The ice giant is reeducated to be kin. Gluskap is reeducated to be a priest. Students are re educated to be new members of their global re-tribal society of the new world, Caliban is reeducated to become a man, Prospero puts down his wand, and your phone is bugged. How's them cookies? So it's a tossup as to who you will serve. Because know this, you must you will be brought under control.

Pied Cow admits to this confession publicly made, that "I have done what anthropologists want, taken back the native as my own. It admits too much to live the other way. Whether at bus stop or back fence stories pass as found, plain speaking without fiction embarrasses the text. Away with Eskimo, Caribbean divines, myths carried all along. Excavate the Caucasoid within! You will find that primitive thought lost in the forests of homeless scutter, wander while fleeing the scutes, troglodytes of leather whose shells scupper an alternate universe, these folktales performed at banquets to large quantities."

The biggest problem we am having with Caucasoids seeking the spiritual, which Ken brings to a head in his intro to *Kin,* citing Beck and Walters, The Sacred, and Gill's Native American Religions, is that when Beck and Walters say the sacred means "something special" they prove they know nothing about it, for it is exactly the opposite. Gill saying humans share a "single nature" expressed in "images, actions and symbols" is mere religion of the self, warmed over Jung opposed by Emmanuel Levinas who says I-Thou is a crock and only we/Thou cuts it. But don't argue with a fool lest thou be like him. Caucasoid spirituality cannot find itself so it must study the other and become it, before it eats it up. So here comes Gluskap again and we'd like to prevent him from the social psychosis of those anti-social Caucasoid cannibal ice giants.

The difference between the native and the colony, the Abenaki and the Jesuit presents the dilemma of identifying the positive, reintegrative forces and processes of creation. The Flower Guys, as AB calls nine large ceramic flowers blooming out of rock, are reintegrative, joining, rejoining the natural and the human into one fabric, human bodies with flower tops, which theme from the initial "way into the flowering heart" involves Sir Walter Raleigh's loss of his son in Guiana and all the Pennsylvania Dutch mythology of the flowering heart.

3/12/20 Thurs: The team begins to wake up. A shaves. P begins to problem solve with notion of a Rapid response team public health van, drive by cop for security, middle part para med fireman who do hazardous waste, keep middle sterile, back of van public health nurse full haz nat suit goes into homes temp, oxy, med problem, whether food water assistance, med and social, patient stays in place, swab Covid-19 influenzas test, all questionnaire published same questions everyone is asked, need financial help/ if transport needed? fireman and nurse in back of van, notify hospital Mobile multiple response team returns to check this gives people motive to stay in because they know somebody's coming,

You Have A Fever And A Dry Cough. Now What?

Jerome Roos, This very interesting finding hints at the potential seasonality of Coronavirus: community-to-community outbreak has so far been limited to "a narrow east-west distribution roughly along the 30-50 N" corridor at consistently similar weather patterns (5-11°C and 47-79% humidity)." Temperature and latitude analysis to predict potential spread and seasonality for COVID-19

--Adjustment Reactions: The Teachable Moment in Crisis Communication
by Peter M. Sandman

3/13/20 Friday. B's boss in Vegas, A n95 masks, goggles, girls mask, gowns for P, at home next week, kids too.

-Death of the President of the Order of Doctors of the Province of Varese (Lombardy) and Director of the Lombard Training School in General Medicine, Dr. .Roberto Stella, a family doctor, died due to the Coronavirus

3/14/20 Sjon Larsson, to tell the truth. Five pieces in four days at *Neon Garden.*

Tools against it: Supreme antiviral mushroom Chaga that blocks the HIV part & Vit C that destroys the lipid layer.
-Pharmacist at U of Vienna study suggests Ibuprofen use in Italy is raising death rate & severity & is the Italian 'go to' analgesic. Their conclusion is that it aids replication of virus, A BIOWEAPON MADE IN CHAPEL HILL AND SOLD TO LEVEL 4 WEAPONS LAB IN CHINA.
--Combined SARS, MERS (Middle East Respiratory Syndrome-MERS) & HIV, SARS-like cluster of circulating bat coronaviruses
-"Here we examine the disease potential of a SARS-like virus, SHC014-CoV, which is currently circulating in Chinese horseshoe bat populations...including influenza A strains H5N1, H1N1 and H7N9 and MERS-CoV—have emerged from animal populations, causing considerable disease."

"Therefore, to examine the emergence potential (that is, the potential to infect humans) of circulating bat CoVs, WE BUILT A CHIMERIC VIRUS encoding a novel, zoonotic CoV spike protein—from the RsSHC014-CoV sequence that was isolated from Chinese horseshoe bats1—in the context of the SARS-CoV mouse-adapted backbone."

3 Feb 2020

Arctic and Alpine Biomes By Joyce Ann Quinn

3/15/20 They go from don't panic, don't wear masks, to call out the military in less than a week. Chicken Little finally came to roost. You remember it was Malcolm X who first said this and it was repeated by Louis Farrakhan. And it was all nicely set up with Y2K and countless conspiracies, scares and magic twangy froggies while the scientificos deliciously CRISPRed their way along the Chimera. They are going to bring back the mastodon remember. They were going to revive King Tut. Remember the transhumans were going to live forever. But now all the elites might be lung-scarred and can't breathe, even if Tom Hanks is happy with his soccer ball down under. Unless they got a placebo. Remember Chicken, do your network, because without that constant distraction of abysmal cows even the drugs they take are not enough. Oh hey! Did you hear, marijuana is the perfect cure for Corona. It kills the virus with its smoke. The sky is falling. Go to your underground bunker.

The virus loves the anti-UV, bro! So following after the American health establishment on the ground the nurse practioner med crowd and the liberal cohort of Starbucks and FB crowing Merz! THIS IS THE FLU. Have they masked up at Trader Joe's? Yes they have masks. No. Liberals! Only the Anitfa are prepared. They wear masks? Search for images of Chicken Little and you find a thousand Little Boyed, Little Girled otaku infantile figures galore. The bomb from above. Genji to the rescue. The U.N. is coming to help. Kill the Exterminating Angel. So many scenarios, so little time.

Hey-I am Chas chicken little galore Erb. My monastic buddy says you never heard. I hate to be heard without the bother of clean air in Houston, To all goofies to dedicate this song I wrote to you. [Chas was in Otherengaged 7 with Alice]

Back to the Mastodon Whoo Whoo

Chicken Little home to roost,Hurrah, hurrah,
remember what ex-Malcolm said, he stick to you like glue,
Tarbaby's up to Y2K,magic twanger's home today
Scientificos will CRISPR you, All the way to Chimera.

Trader Joe is all masked up, Antifas are prepared.
Don't mask. Please mask, Transhonkies living there!
Tommy Hanks is a virus bro, magicjuana cured his lungs
Smoke cures the virus with the flue.

The sky is falling faster now you goofies hear this song
Remember Hollywood net-frogged the King Tut underground,
The bomb below the bomb above,
we all have masks, Revive King Tut
This is the flue they hardly knew, Charlie I never knew ya

Oh hey this smoke kills virus lungs and kills the virus too
Starbucks and FB crow, they loves you bro!
we got Mers beat scarred lungs still breathe
Revive King Tut,.SARs back up, THIS IS THE FLU.
First comes the undoing, then comes the remaking. Without in any way lessening our sit reps, we must get that under awareness. The ammo, alcohol, toilet paper, gasoline runs galore, besides shortages and stockpiles, we prepared long before, as you know, so our contamination now will occur from listening to any of the undoing--because that is intended, so we miss the next and the next. Catch'em? Don't listen to anybody now, the riptides are great and increase. I know you are set in most -- now practice, protect and play ignorant, above all. Cynthia suspended her practice, Sat. and went bowling Sun: riptide.

This is the undoing, then comes the remakin. See the Cockroach in the Castle

3/16/20 how do I know I am alive. Talked to Bea Dewitt in a dream. We met the finest Christian people among the CRC, Bea, Boots, GF Kredit,

--Camostat mesylate, a serine protease inhibitor, partially blocked CoV-2 entry into human cells, and even better when combined with E-64d, a protease inhibitor. Camostat is approved in Japan and "could be considered for off-label use."—but Chaga inhibits protease

New South Wales, Australia 's 171 cases? Because it is the MIDDLE OF SUMMER THERE!!! This virus will not die out\

Normalcy bias, Dec 9., deep web, IRON network, Mar. 1, Chinese chatter, documents, semi trucks crates of ascorbic acid to navy bases NE Wuhan, Dec 9, target vit deficiency, vit d and c never get coronavirus colds, virus match to HIV, Chaga for HIV, stops replication of HIV inhibit Protease, 2 sites in virus resemble HIV, new filter on China internet, evidence that Chaga alone w/o vit c effective, truckloads of bodies in trenches in Iran, 15 ft. spread in air, ten foot pole,

BEFORE THE SHUTDOWN SECONDARY INFECTION RATE FATALITY RATE IN CHINA NEAR 100%

After Gluskap

There are if not countless, many parables of these conflicts with the other self-provoked historical cases and reactions to them. Another notable is the Hiroshima bomb dropped by the self righteous upon the Japan. Was it retaliation for sneak attach on Perl Harbor? Noboyed says, the motives have subtexts below. The result of Little Boy, the name of their first bomb was the invention in the Japanese mind of Godzilla, the other, and the invention of the otaku little boying of their culture, its emasculation, infantizing it by the giant scale, the ice giants again. Always tall buildings are symbols of the gods to dwarf the man who to enter the building, the god, must kneel at the threshold like the Babylonians before the giant statue of Nebuchadnezzar or die. All these things tie together in a bundle. One world just to briefly sketch the result of the bomb on the modern, all the American children addicted to plastic pop toys.

The Evangelion is a monster of a wannabe supernatural civilization, a Babylon destroyed revived. This empire is everything novus ordo seeks to achieve. It plays off against a parody of the fundamentalist idea that the United Nations is like a leopard, with feet like the feet of a bear, and had a mouth like a lion, the beast to be ridden by the Whore.
Willfully reversing the biblical revelation, the Evangelion monsters fight under the aegis of the UN against the angels of Last Judgement. The external justification for foisting this totally western notion upon Tokyo is a pun on the name of the bomb, Little Boy, that Japan was exploded back to childhood. That is, Japanese culture was Little Boyed back to childhood, its antiquity was annihilated for the Chaldean new age.

In prescient manner machines are blended with the human, the very goal of singularity. "Nerve HQ, a bio-mechanical weapon named Evangelion, Man married to machine, the perfect transhuman achievement, a monster piloted by 14 year old Shinji…keystone for the resurrection of the world" (Neon Genesis Evangelelion I, Yoshiyuki Sadamoto (Gainax) tr, /Fred Burke 1980.

There are three versions, the anime, the manga and the film. "As in the original anime series, the first four volumes of the manga deal with the Angel invasions, but from a much different angle. Moreover, several more mundane sub-plot tropes common to Japanese manga occur at the same time at the invasions,"

William Burroughs in his *Nova* series touches the creation of these images as if there were an assembly line production operated at some basement facility churning them out. We only learn that this is another facet of the space Malebolge, Dante running amuck. Who really is producing these affects. Of course it's Hollywood, but how to those writers get so presciently diseased? You have to recognize it is an institution of the fallen, embodied in the strong dope of every kind along with the channeling spirits common in the creation of NASA, DARPA and NSA. Why these government agencies want to create destabilizing literature is as obvious as how and why they created the hippie movement and rock and roll. To rock out monarched children of the American Little Boys, victimized with military microwaves and Laurel Canyon the whole establishment of science fiction should be renamed. What to call it?
"a robot story title that doesn't have a voiced consonant sound in it just isn't catching. So I pushed "Evangelion", which had been rejected once, as sounding stronger. We had talked a lot in the beginning about wanting a title like "Space Runaway Ideon (Legendary Giant God Ideon)", so I think I did push that. And to tell the truth, the story composition is also similar. For example, Nerv can be considered the same as the Solo Ship fighting a lonely battle against both humankind and the Buff Clan, and then there are the incomprehensible robots that can only communicate with children and tend to go berserk, etc. It might not be an exaggeration to say that if you add "Ideon" and "Devilman" together and divide by two, you get "Evangelion". He laughs. (Yoshiyuki Sadamoto interview).

So the bomb created much more destruction in the mind than on the ground. It was in the air and lasted and lasts, taken over part of the Giant called Pop Mind to dwarf the man.

[So you will not ask while all this is being put together for the purpose of publication, why when I take a short nap in the middle of the night, do I see in an unsought vision large rolls of black plastic coffins on flatbed railroad cars. The idea is they unroll like black plastic bags and then turn semi solid for burial of bodies. I was poking the center out of one to climb through, make a hole in the middle like a leather doughnut.]

Pied Cow and Guapa Pop are two peas of a pod except one is a pumpkin.

3/17/20 Buy C Tues B buys sofa, A and he deliver. the real 'tell' that you have is the coating on tongue.

3/18/20 Bought 3 bales peat, get gas

collect Neon Garden anthology of wishes. Upload White Barks.

Wuhan patient suffering from the #coronavirus as early as much earlier than officially announced. According to @WHO, the first recorded case in China was on Dec. 8.

-use Vit C powder from capsules in small bit of water, make a mouthwash. Swish around in mouth hold it in for 5 minutes or so, slowly swallow, coating throat.
-ACE2 receptors found in tongue on autopsy. Highest amounts found on tongue and buccal cavity. That's where it binds.
-Chaga-fungi absorb betulins, a triterpene found in birch species (of the genus Betula), which are responsible for a great deal of their vigorous anti-cancer properties, and famous for surpassing those of most other highly touted mushrooms (including reishi and shiitake). It is hat chaga takes betulin, a potent anti-tumor compound, and synthesizes it into betulinic acid – chaga's cancer-fighting triterpene.
The clincher here: betulin is powerful, but not bioavailable to humans; betulinic acid is, and can be taken orally.

Taxorest to help recover lung function after encounters. This is a peptide that specific to lung repair. Most reported effects in first 5 days or so.
Indigenous ppl in Siberia & Americas used Chaga by keeping small piece in mouth constantly. Saliva extracted some compounds & when soften enough was chewed vigorously & swallowed.
Upload all White Mt videos

3/19/20 Thurs. Stores audit of food supplies
Pwd milk online, TGP

" said Daniel Woodruff, like the comet over the Vatican, the closing of the Wash Monument from lightning
--10k Med students to save Italy, not vit. C

Phase one is when all that will be known is known.
Phase two is when all that can be done will be done.
Now that the gov threw the kitchen sink, part two has ended.

Feels like the end of the age. So I looked up Spring equinox. starts today 8.48 pm. It comes early this year.

Digestive symptoms are the main complaint in nearly half of patients

Chloroquine (and hydroxchloroquine), an anti-malarial drug, is in the news today, prominently mentioned during President Trump's morning press conference. Research does indeed indicate that chloroquine has 'apparent efficacy and acceptable safety against covid-19 associated pneumonia', and has shown to help patients recover more quickly from the coronavirus. Other treatments -- azithromycin, antiviral remdesivir, and Kevzara -- are now thought to make a positive difference, too.

This is what **part three** means. Danger from your household from well meaning people who expose you. Assumptions not practice. Casualty counters who parrot stats. We are beyond stats, only practice. Parrot talk of people who follow orders. Media shaming and kiss assess. If you're going to save a life you can't expect them to like it. corporate emails promoting themselves with Corvid 19 safely plans, news media making us safe, they say. Gov't checks. Whitewash. Now chief among dangers is anger and contempt at the panic stricken officious well meaning who will to any thing to preserve their status quo to please the authorities and will be hurt if you say this to them. A asks me to take down his pic because he thinks "there's patient information in the reflection.. I don't want to get HIPPAA fired…." This as long as he don't rock the boat. Truly gutless attitude that will get him killed along with visits of anybody to his home from the outside. He will sacrifice the life of his unborn son to placate them. It's all shame. Buying toilet paper is. Shame don't wear mask. Shame don't report the hospital. Shame don't buy, don't buy, don't buy until we say, then buy, buy, buy. So with 9/11 patriotism suddenly people are heroes who treat covid 19 cases-"this is my mom. She's my hero. She's a 60 year old primary care physician testing patients for She is putting her health on the line to test patients, get them the care they need, and do what she can to prevent community spread and the overburdening of our hospitals." What travesty trash. Her mom cannot treat them cause it breaks protocol. She can refer them to a ventilator.

Your has many resources at your disposal to help you and your family during any crisis, including

---!!! P had patient from Outpatient Oncology Clinic. Two employees there have tested positive for corona-virus 19 and one has pneumonia at the facility another running a fever was sent for referral. Obviously everyone there has been exposed, patients as well. There are no masks of any kind given. They are infecting everyone who goes there. No warnings are being given to anyone. Stop them. Nobody wants to be contacted. They will either lose their job or their privileges The head of the clinic must be aware. Continued harm to others. Operating a clinic for the sick and making them sicker.

Before I reported to likely authorities this travesty I talked with A who tested 5 today as well as put another 7 on 14 day quarantine. They did not fit the profile to test but still had enough symptoms to quarantine. "All patients were agreeable. The 5 tested were also placed in quarantine until the results are called to them. 3 of the 12 were medical professionals. I also was told today that next week Monday or Tuesday, depending on test availability, will begin drive through testing at multiple locations.. no word on where yet. Tight masking continues.. "my face hurts." Carry on!

Then: apologizing "The point is I guess is that they don't have enough tests to test every possible exposure without symptoms.. this should change next week. So I'm having patients self quarantine.. there is nothing else I can do. If they develop shortness of breath they go to the ED to get admitted and hope there is a ventilator available. I know there are intensive care physicians that are going to be doubling up patients on 1 ventilator, which will essentially double the capacity of units assuming that the patients can survive on the same settings."

--reply. Sorry, for social responsibility I mean.

Completely lacking conscience. I called the AZ rep hotline, and emailed
This morn he wants to buy chloroquine because it made the Trump news.

Then C emails the same article. She suspended/ceased her practice last week after I warned the week before, but taken lightly and this week after suspending went bowling!

Phase three is everything parroted debased distanced twisted and universalized. Never ahead always behind. They can' buy masks or food. And shoe covers! Too late. I gave A N95s, and P, shoe covers, the three zone plans, etc. Like these but worse the govt had game planned the virus Oct 19. I have earned my sleep.

3.22.20 Sunday. 2nd day seclusion. P came up from the melatonin article how Benicar expands Ace 2 cells so to experiment changed BP med, and ordered cinchona from Turkey. Melatonin to be dosed as prophylactic.

Now in Phase Three we see a secular play out of *Matthew* and the Olivet Discourse that a man's enemies, dangers, shall be those of his own household. But these parallels are also both true and false, like Zion, Israel, Washington, America, all the drama, act 3, scene 4. Line 47 …the false messiah and the true. Everywhere the false impersonates the true. Like all the pious outpours over twitter and FB about how things will get better and you only have one life to blah, just what they tell soldiers who get to die "for their deception" and thank them for the service.

3/20/20 The "N95" label stands for the mask ability to filter out at least 95% of airborne particles larger than 0.3 microns (for reference, $PM_{2.5}$ particles are 2.5 microns

Don't panic they said, then engineered the whole American maximum panic like 9/11. "Trump moved from dismissing the coronavirus as a few cases that would soon be "under control" to that he had known all along that a pandemic was on the way. his own administration had already modeled a similar pandemic and understood its potential trajectory…officials have declined to say why the administration was so slow to roll out broad testing or to move faster, as the simulations all indicated it should, to urge social distancing and school closings. Asked at his news briefing on Thursday about the government's preparedness, Mr. Trump responded: "Nobody knew there would be a pandemic or epidemic of this proportion. Nobody has ever seen anything like this before." The work done over the past five years, however, demonstrates that the government had considerable knowledge about the risks of a pandemic and accurately predicted the very types of problems Mr. Trump is now scrambling belatedly to address".

3/21/20 First Sleep. The enemies of a man of his own household. This has been an exercise in compliance waiting till boards, govts decree an action meaning obeying, but if you are ahead of everything they say by six weeks it is a provocation of contempt, because you see how when they could have acted, warned, prepared, they bungled (the tests) pooh poohed (it's the flu), squandered and lied about what they knew from the Crimson Contagion of society in the published research which videos ignored and finally extincted in the changed router: gone. No they will not be forgiven or listened to now since it is obvious they have another agenda in mind. They resisted and continue to resist every preparation to save either lives and health but pretend they do, and they are good actors. They adopt measures late and take credit for them themselves. Pride does not induce humility. They will harbor their bound prejudices and protocols whenever the comfort of their conformity is challenged, over and over. We told them: Let these endangered NPs (nurse practitioners) go half time, scrub up, gown up, goggle up, mask up and scrub down, UV it, reuse it, order it, take this and more, over and over, and after each new protection was layered they resisted with fervor, and as the oncoming waves reached the shore, had to wait till the American Dental Association, the Board of Education, the company authorities gave permission not to travel. Dr. Oz says it's your patriotic duty not to wear a mask. Whatever the authorities say not to do they do and don't do, but always and only wait to be told. If you are out in front of these waves, already preparing for the next and next, since all the info needed to act and to know was available in January, Welcome to the new operation Little Boy, an op for the infantilization of America where the corps and politicians cast themselves as heroes who make you safe and sent you letters to prove it, but first you must become as a little child so they can lead you. A reversal of Isaiah that *a child shall lead them* that imposes the collective with the weight of public might, opinion made weakly by telling them first don't do, then do, then don't do so the poor things don't know what to think except they do know what to think, being that cannot think for themselves, but must rely on the voices, the usual voice prophets priests and king networks, the data base daily figures of their baseball bane like always, the number of cases, the number dead, a running tally to make you safe. You are safe as long as you listen and obey, spouting the public line of the day of the Gov who says all these restrictions are worth it if they can just save one life but who are the leading advocates of abortion of the unborn, ripped from their mother's wombs, a woman's right, but not a mother's because the child is dead.

I lived through the whole of WWII. It colors my thought. One thing, I have seen many planned ops, op after op after op, always progressing toward what we call the Big One. So the question is, is this It, the Kill Virus? Or is it the half It?

Vit C

Got a t.co link check. uses the t.co domain as part of a service to protect users from harmful activity, to provide value for the developer ecosystem, and as a quality signal for surfacing relevance:

Torn limb from limb, you doing good, just relax and breathe, but he has no legs and has been blown to smithereens as they pray for a mutation, but the Dude Fire on the Mogollon Rim was put out by men, inmates! The good news is bad and the bad news is good, Perry Stone got up at 2 AM and heard it was Time of Reckoning for the sickening assurances of the damned and their pathetic jokes.

It's hard not to root for the virus

MrCati:
All millennials are amoral.Think they owe nothing to their neighbors, excuse the murderous intent of their employer. Millennials are not offended by abortion, gays, transsexuals or fairy tales.

Now that I can go to church on tv, go to the doctor on tv I pee on tv

Don't bring your children up in a world that no longer exists. let them adjust they'll get there long before you who must overcome your soft.

drink alleviates hunger, removes tiredness, refreshes, and increases work capacity. Chaga tea is also used as a means of improving the general tone. Research agreed that the fungus has a favorable effect on the central nervous system and metabolic processes, and boosts immunity to infections. The most important components found in those cell-walls are probably the (1>3)(1>6)Beta-D-Glucans. Medicinal mushroom derived Beta-Glucans are notable for their ability to modulate the immune system. How exactly they achieve this is not yet 100% clear. Beta-Glucans can also normalize an overactive immune system *(the cause of allergies and many auto-immune diseases; e.g. lupus and psoriasis)* – this can be compared to locking down receptors that are open for no reason, only re-opening them when needed. This two-way effect is called '*modulating*' and it is exceptionally powerful from a therapeutic point of view.

After all, our immune system is the core of our health in the broadest sense. It is under siege all the time; stress is a major immune killer *(think: physical, mental, chemical – side effects of medication!- and environmental stress)*, age is another one *(after 35 our immune system gets sloppy and after 50 it's simply declining, causing a lot of 'old-age' diseases to appear)*. Apart from that beta-glucans also have a positive effect on the normalization of cholesterol levels and blood sugar, according to research. Indirect, this means it can also have a positive effect on high blood pressure and general cardiovascular health. So, the support one can get from taking a medicinal mushroom extract daily is significant; you help the body to maintain a healthy balance. This balance is what is known as '*homeostasis*'.

Phyto-sterols are powerful therapeutic ingredients; of the phyto-sterols present in Chaga 45% is lanosterol, 25% inotodiol and the remaining 30% consists of ergosterol, fecosterol and several others. In vivo and in vitro research showed a direct anti-cancer effect of both lanosterol and inotodiol. Lanosterol also has an anti-viral effect.

Betulin and betulinic acid are two components unique to the Chaga fungus – it derives them from the birches on which it grows. Betulin and betulinic acid are powerful therapeutic agents *(triterpenes)* that are currently being researched for their anti-viral action *(i.p. anti-HIV)* and their anti-cancer action *(in both cases animal tests showed great potential)*. They also have cholesterol-lowering effects; a recent report found them to be able to break down cholesterol in the bloodstream, instead of just preventing its absorption *(the more common approach)*. A major problem of these two components is their, though.

Chaga will have different properties, depending on where it has been harvested, just like oranges from California have different properties than oranges from Sri Lanka. So far, Chaga that grew under extreme environmental conditions was found to have the highest therapeutic potency. Although Russian scientists were the first to research Chaga, almost all of the more recent research is done in SE-Asia, using samples from areas such as N-Korea, the Changbai mountains *(China)* and Hokkaido *(Japan)*.

It is obvious that the outcome of this research cultivated Chaga should be strictly separated from the results achieved with wild-harvested Chaga. many of Chaga's therapeutically interesting metabolites appear to develop only as a side effect of the harsh environment which it tends to favor and the on-going struggle with the trees defense systems. Cultivated Chaga is not involved in a struggle for survival, and therefore will not develop these secondary metabolites

Washington's first failing to protect against the spread of the deadly coronavirus began on what would be the 'front lines' months prior to the emergence of the pandemic. A lengthy investigative report in Reuters found that the White House ordered the intended to monitor and study disease outbreaks in China. chose to call the scientist home. Dr. Linda Quick

3/24/20 Covid Begins

Tuesday-Twice I woke last night and my heels were on fire, the left especially. Literally burning. Did I see the flames/ No my feet were under the covers. I'm thinking the pain threshold a 7 or 08. Every injury on the left side revived, the epidermis, the two broken ribs, the back, most recent and replayed over again.

Gave A sunflowers. Told him he is made for this moment. He changed subject and said how abysmal Univ. hosp. practices.

3/25/20 when extreme conditions arrive extreme reactions occur. All these pains at night last night shoulder radiating nerves to forearm, lungs feel inflamed but after Vicks and mass c, gone, got pack of corn to put on shoulder. Like the sufferings of the victim soul in the body for the pains of the people now before the wave hits, like the unbelievable alchemical change in the eyes, as if all these things lay just under the surface waiting to be awakened. I hate to say it, but when we finally get to where we forget ourselves so much that we are not conscious then our best work can emerge.

3/26/20 Holy, Holy, Holy is the Lord! A time traveler from months ahead will return and wonder why cures were touted when prevention was faster. Why chloroquine and not masks.

Changed hypertension med to one that does not increase Ace2 Tom Horn.

The third phase disinfo of the virus is a down payment of the 2029 event starting about 2025. Apophis

The lead French investigator and team behind that non-randomized chloroquine paper has a history of faking data and being banned from journal publications.

3/27/20 more phase three: in *Hegel Phase three is the end phase, that's all she wrote, allowing always for further tightening and adjusting. So it goes on and on and on with a whimper.*

-Scare tactic article linked on FB elicited comments of what a hero you are and how you should protect your wife, mother and son are your own self-aggrandizements and play directly into the hands of the projected and caused panic intended. further dissolution of bonds, distrust of authority, prepping for the One Big Man to make it all right.

Step out from behind the link. At least shut up and practice what you know.

what you don't get at all is the practice this event affords you to gear up for the real event that's coming, where the same structure of process will obtain, that is, First phase, all the facts that can be known are known,

Second phase, all the things that can be done have been done,
Third phase, the lies about it all by the parrots ad infinitum. This goes on a long time, the whole length of the event, but 1 and 2 have long been over. 1 and 2 have got a store of oil for their lamps, 3 is running about trying to buy more, meaning confuse the world.

Practice don't preach. It's too late.
--Swiss father is mixing L-ascorbate vit C with gelatin (jello) into ice-cube tray 'shots' for his & relatives kids. No sugar but stevia & acerola cherry powder =vit C too. He makes it loose & keeps cold to sooth sore throat that is first stage of 4many.

-- Talked 2body builder in Singapore. They take mass vit C & collagen together to make good skin & hair & bones. Doses in 10 -30gm daily C for years. Collagen aids absorption of C & C lets body use digested collagen directly. This likely acc'ts 4 no illness.

If you really want to get the rhythm try:

5 grams of sugar lowers immunity 50% for 5 hours after consumption.

All notables get the sniffles when they test positive, Boris Johnson UK, Tom Hanks got the blahs, but all the rest are in desperate shape, so that is an op.

3/28/20 used Vicks last night and tonight
--Docs NOTE Length of Exposure proportionate to severity for health care ppl. This is NOT like any other disease on planet that way. Proof of nature. Proof of anti- protocol of circulating Vit C & antivirals as means of para-immunity.

"By contrast to the prevailing paradigm, our results suggest that up to 4,000 mg of ascorbic acid taken by mouth can produce the same rapid increase in plasma concentration as an intravenous infusion."

We also noticed that the only Asian donor (male) has a much higher ACE2-expressing cell ratio than white and African American donors (2.50% vs. 0.47% of all cells).

While chaga has been shown to aid diabetes sufferers in some ways, other research suggests that it may negatively interact with insulin and other similar medications. Because chaga affects blood sugar levels, it may worsen or bring on hypoglycemia in some users/

At the moment, pregnant women are advised to avoid using chaga due to a lack of definitive information on how it affects child development and birth. While there is no information at the moment to suggest that chaga is harmful to pregnant women, it is better to be cautious and avoid using it.

3/29/20 Sunday chg bp med to amlodipine besylate 10 mg because Benicar increases ACE2 recepto9rs.
--Take Zpak

3/30/20 Rene Daumal died of carbon tetrachloride.
--Fourth night with Vicks. 15 gram vit c
First church of compliance' China twitter drones wars on fauci

3/31/20 Zero hedge, attaching a protein taken from bats to the SARS virus, Acute Pneumonia, derived from mice. The output is a super coronavirus. Chimera – an organism modified by attaching the surface protein of a coronavirus found in bats of the common species called the Great Horseshoe Bat, to a virus that causes SARS in mice, although in a non-fatal form. It was suspected that the protein could make the chimeric hybrid organism suitable for affecting humans, and the experiment confirmed it. It is precisely this molecule, called SHCO14, that allows the coronavirus to attach itself to our respiratory cells and to trigger the syndrome. the information presented in the video is consistent with the information that and that the impact of the virus in the broadcast has a lot in common with mainstream information about the symptoms of COVID-19.

In this latter period alternate voices of fiction developed which took the narrative voice of an anonymous eponymous Everyman, a crying of the human spirit toward redemption. Often in a rational, reportage ironic tone, these personas enabled rapid appearance of the work and he was satisfied to retire somewhat from the active drama of a writer, being occupied more and more in medical research. So Rubino del Sur, Augusto Todoele, Sjon Larsson and Jon Rousseau joined Kurk Wold and Eagin Arthur as mouth pieces whose general narrative premise is the reporting of literatures of fact as had once occurred in Bolshevik society in the 1920's to defeat censorship, but was now revisited to translate the new Bolshevik societies of 2020 in that era of one hundred years of censorship where the fakta of a continent and an age apart were adapted to this new order. The formalist theories of *faktovivi* tend to bypass algorithmic controls and can code hidden propitiatory examinations if understood. Its first priority remains accentuated real material gathered either first hand or culled from documentary sources. A wealth of online readers engaged the speculative fakta blogs that he also operated as an actor performing on stage with no script. So he outlived the knowledge of himself, as if all these things lay just under the surface waiting to be awakened when we finally forget ourselves so much that we are not conscious.

The first priority remains accentuated real material gathered either first hand or culled from documentary sources. an Enlightenment of Adventure and Lessons Learned in what might be called the literary or fictive aspect of the human sciences.

4/2/20 I withdrew my obituary.
THE FeROCITY OF CROWD RESPONSE in full hysteria mode Phase Threes who denied and downplayed earlier data are now in full absolute prevention cry because the govt, equally delinquent, has them convinced with the daily barrage, just like the Got blames china govt for its ineptness. His wife won't let him leave the house.
-regimes of hydrquine
-WuXi PharmaTech to Build $100 Million R&D Center in Wuhan
publication date: Aug 11, 2010
WuXi PharmaTech will spend $100 million to build a new R&D facility in the central China city of Wuhan. The company will construct a 40,000 sq meter CRO facility in the Wuhan National Biological Industry Base (Optics Valley of BioLake). Wuhan sources told ChinaBio® that a cooperative agreement between WuXi and the Wuhan Biological Base was signed on August 9.

short fictional movie screened at the "Event 201 Pandemic Exercise", a tabletop exercise hosted by The Johns Hopkins Center for Health Security in partnership with the World Economic Forum and the Bill and Melinda Gates Foundation on October 18, 2019, in New

York, NY. The exercise illustrated the pandemic preparedness efforts needed to diminish the large-scale economic and societal consequences of a severe pandemic. Drawing from actual events, Event 201 identifies important policy issues and preparedness challenges that could be solved with sufficient political will and attention. These issues were designed in a narrative to engage and educate the participants and the audience

I am either one of the greatest poet alive today or a complete nobody. This has already been half achieved.

Postulate of Prevotella bacterias and Sars cov 2, which is chameleon, protean in shape depending on variant genotype encounters, not mutations, different adaptations to Chinese, Iranian, Italian, etc, some 8 or 9, but it also combines with protean bacillus to do the same trickery, hiding in it and reinfecting later, those who have tested non positive. Like the difference between yogurt and kefir. A grain put in milk makes kefir but the kefir result is not in common with the grain that produced it. So the virus we see is only the result of its production in human cells and not the thing itself, called x. So x hides in the Prevotella in the human and in the horseshoe bat and is in some sense protected there for long periods of time, hence the recurrence, like hanta virus in mouse turds hides within and turns to dust as the turds decay and can be contracted by the dust and totally different form of the virus.

4/3/20 the analogy of the French resistance holds true again when fear is the motive of behavior informed by lies meant to control, the gov of Georgia didn't know about the infected unsymptomatic, China didn't tell us so we didn't know, don't wear masks until we tell, 3M won't sell to Florida anyway, better not let Mera Bank fail, oops, I mean Valley Bank, oops its what bank again? oscillation

Operation fishbowl blows holes in vanilla radiation belt –Chinese masks to CA like smallpox blankets. Oscillating cell towers, of 5G, mask no mask, tesla

4/4/20 the damage that identity politics could not wreak dividing people by race and class, the virus shutdown has by sowing suspicion, turning suspicious, monitoring with cell phones, demo maps among all people who are told, even families, separated keept apart. Meanwhile they are exposed to all the worst Netflix has to condition them into fear. The Food and Drug Administration helped turn the coronavirus from a deadly peril into a national catastrophe. Long after foreign nations had been ravaged and many cases had been detected in America, continued blocking private testing

4/5/20 Dual ISO

prophylactic dose of Hydroxychloroquine--different hydroxychloroquine dosing such as: 400mg BID on day one, then daily for 5 days; 400 mg BID on day one, then 200mg BID for 4 days; 600 mg BID on day one, then 400mg daily on days 2-5

--The pharmacokinetics of HCQ are an important consideration in answering this question. With long-term use of HCQ, peak plasma levels occur 3 to 4 hours after each dose, with a terminal half-life of 40 to 50 days (9). The long half-life means that brief gaps in therapy, on the order of 1 to 2 weeks, are less concerning

Having no new themes I do not seek in vain, seek none at all but the Word trial form of the language of the wheel, of rays of light coming out of a hand Hab 3.4. as the stone shall cry out of the wall 2.11 and the ceramic be booties for them 2.7 that lade thick clay 2.6. Write the vision, make plain 2.1 the sacrifice to a net 1.16, carpenter to a hammer, incense burned to a keyboard, power of an idol 1.11, sacrifice to a gun, prayer to the power of mind, but the Chaldeans coming 1.6 more swift than evening wolves 1.8, gather captivity as sand 1.9. There you go, not thinking for yourself again. Let earth be silent 2.20.

Pharmacokinetics: Following a single 200 mg oral dose of PLAQUENIL to healthy males, the mean peak blood concentration of hydroxychloroquine was 129.6 ng/mL, reached in 3.26 hours with a half-life of 537 hours (22.4 days). In the same study, the plasma peak concentration was 50.3 ng/mL reached in 3.74 hours with a half-life of 2963 hours (123.5 days). Urine hydroxychloroquine levels were still detectable after 3 months with approximately 10% of the dose excreted as the parent drug. Results following a single dose of a 200 mg tablet versus i.v. infusion (155 mg), demonstrated a half-life of about 40 days and a large volume of distribution. Peak blood concentrations of metabolites were observed at the same time as peak levels of hydroxychloroquine. The mean fraction of the dose absorbed was 0.74. After administration of single 155 mg and 310 mg intravenous doses, peak blood concentrations ranged from 1161 ng/mL to 2436 ng/mL (mean 1918 ng/mL) following the 155 mg infusion and 6 months following the 310 mg infusion. Pharmacokinetic parameters were not significantly different over the therapeutic dose range of 155 mg and 310 mg indicating linear kinetics. Following chronic oral administration of hydroxychloroquine, significant levels of three metabolites, desethylhydroxychloroquine (DHCQ), desethylchloroquine (DCQ), and bidesethylhydroxychloroquine (BDCQ) have been found in plasma and blood, with DHCQ being the major metabolite.

The absorption half-life was approximately 3 to 4 hours and the terminal half-life ranged from 40 to 50 days. The long half-life can be attributed to extensive tissue uptake rather than through decreased excretion. Peak plasma levels of hydroxychloroquine were seen in about 3 to 4 hours. Renal clearance in rheumatoid arthritis (RA) patients taking PLAQUENIL for at least six months seemed to be similar to that of the single dose studies in volunteers, suggesting that no change occurs with chronic dosing. Range for renal clearance of unchanged drug was approximately 16 to 30% and did not correlate with creatinine clearance; therefore, a dosage adjustment is not required for patients with renal impairment. In RA patients, there was large variability as to the fraction of the dose absorbed (i.e. 30 to 100%), and mean hydroxychloroquine levels were significantly higher in patients with less disease activity. Cellular levels of patients on daily hydroxychloroquine have been shown to be higher in mononuclear cells than polymorphonuclear leucocytes

--India: aystomatic health workers: 400mg twice a day, day one, 400mg weekly for 7 wks
Asymptomatic household 400may twice first day, 400mg three weeks

Arm	Intervention/treatment
Experimental: Hydroxychloroquine Two tablets (400mg) twice daily on day 1; for days 2-5, they will be instructed to take one tablet (200mg) twice daily.	Drug: Hydroxychloroquine Two tablets (400mg) twice daily on day 1; for days 2-5, they will be instructed to take one tablet (200mg) twice daily. Other Name: Plaquenil

4/6/20 The grammar and sentence structure are cumbersome. Space Colonbus. Dineri says she is going to Banner today, at 15.

4/7/20 TEDROS the electro magnetic signature of a writing. Every piece of work has an e/m signature only perceived by those share that waveleigth. The new urkers

European Union Approves Bugs For Human Consumption novel virus, "novel food," meaning that they are likely to be mass produced for human consumption throughout the continent by the end of the year. secretary-general of the International Platform of Insects for Food and Feed, Christophe Derrien. Since 1997, the EU has required a "novel food" classification to allow the sale of products that had no history of being consumed by humans, meaning that the sale of bugs has been banned in countries like Spain, France and Italy for over two decades. However, with the new approval, mass production of bug-based food is set to ramp up later this year. This means that locusts, crickets, grasshoppers, and mealworms may all appear on supermarket shelves by the autumn. Christophe Derrien -they are a great source of protein and the production of bug food doesn't harm the planet.

libertymavenstock, chris martenson- COVID-19 causes prolonged and progressive hypoxia (starving your body of oxygen) by binding to the heme groups in hemoglobin in your red blood cells. People are simply desaturating (losing o2 in their blood), and that's what eventually leads to organ failures that kill them, not any form of ARDS or pneumonia. All the damage to the lungs you see in CT scans are from the release of oxidative iron from the hemes, this overwhelms the natural defenses against pulmonary oxidative stress and causes that nice, always-bilateral ground glass opacity in the lungs.

4/8/20 "Before the virus hit Europe, Italy sent tons of PPE to China to help China protect its own population. China then has sent Italian PPE back to Italy -- some of it, not even all of it ... and charged them for it," a senior Trump administration official told The Spectator.

The Netherlands forced to recall 1.3 million face masks produced in China because they did not meet safety standards.
In Spain, the Ministry of Health on March 26 revealed that 640,000 COVID-19 tests that it had purchased from China were defective.

4/9/20 *Now this behavior does not sound quite right. It doesn''t sounc plausible. Onder ordinarily circumstances the behavior of Brill doesn't either, or all the eipi shrines of the great books like the faerie queene whereere men are turn ed to pigs and gold prades of sins like madri gras proceed. Not to bore you with more unlikely details. No, it sounds more like the behavior of the gods who were all the time eaing each orther and serving themselves up in ritual sacrifice, like tystes and Saturn and so many of them. But men aren't gods. Sorry to have to say that, but in this case it's a good thing since the power to eat each other is much less. So if its not the gogs and the gods at fault what is/ How explain the behavior south of McDowell, which is an understandment, since in the accounts, Susan wade here her way all over the valley of the Danger Mountains. No little feat in this city of over five million, but a drop in the bucket compared to Rio or Hong Kong or New York.*

So no, research shows they weren't caused by the gods. They were caused by Motorola

An update to your data-sharing settings
The control you have over what information Twitter shares with its business partners has changed. Specifically, your ability to control mobile app advertising measurements has been removed, but you can control whether to share some non-public data to improve Twitter's marketing activities on other sites and apps. These changes, which help Twitter to continue operating as a free service, are reflected now in your settings.

henry woll manoa presbyterian church
carl mcintire world council
It has been obvious for a couple days that something's up, usual sources not functional, or repeating themselves, but last night a reset confirmed –concompetent with the reactivation virus statements

4/13/20 Mon some guy called yakob was swimming in the flood, the old flood, a dangerous critter, fortune teller, part of the population now. Yorma, where is he?

The Brazilian included 81 hospitalized patients, with about half being given a dose of 50 milligrams of chloroquine twice daily for five days. The other participants were prescribed a dose of 600 milligrams for 10 days.

Patients taking higher doses experienced heart arrhythmias, or improper beating of the heart, within three days, according to the study. Eleven patients died by the sixth day of treatment and caused the research on high-dosages to end.

4/14/20 Chest tight one zpak

the interest in computer virus and preventions analogous to Covid, that they are engineered for different covet effects to infect and reinfect programs and states for various nefarious purposes, mainly to defraud and defame, disestablish and defeat, leads to Covid doing the same, three faces MERSa, Sars and Covid, or otherwise actttacks T cells, Ace 2 receptors and bactosis, where it hides, the three at present, that seem to complete deteriorate heart, lung, brain and reactivate themselves show engineering, esp. the chart of Sars and Covid on T-cells in Martinson yesterday.

"The past 48 hours or so have seen a huge revelation: causes prolonged and progressive hypoxia (starving your body of oxygen) by binding to the heme groups in hemoglobin in your red blood cells. People are simply desaturating (losing o2 in their blood), and that's what eventually leads to organ failures that kill them, not any form of ARDS or pneumonia. All the damage to the lungs you see in CT scans are from the release of oxidative iron from the hemes, this overwhelms the natural defenses against pulmonary oxidative stress and causes that nice, always-bilateral ground glass opacity in the lungs.

Patients returning for re-hospitalization days or weeks after recovery suffering from apparent delayed post-hypoxic leukoencephalopathy strengthen the notion COVID-19 patients are suffering from hypoxia despite no signs of respiratory 'tire out' or fatigue."

--The CDC counts both true COVID-19 cases and speculative guesses of COVID-19 the same. They call it death by COVID-19. They automatically overestimate the real death numbers, by their own admission Senator Dr. Scott Jensen from Minnesota who said Hospitals are getting paid more to list patients as COVID-19. *"Right now Medicare is determining that if you have a COVID-19 admission to the hospital you get $13,000. If that COVID-19 patient goes on a ventilator you get $39,000, three times as much* that the Army's field hospital in Seattle, an "epicenter" of the pandemic has closed after three days without seeing one single COVID-19 patient.

Setting forth on this bridge with my three asses and putting explosive charges about every fifty feet. I'll probably have to go back into 3D and get more, but the intent here is to blow that whole structure, pyramid, bridge. Not by me. But I know a Guy.

Pharmacological thrombosis prophylaxis = VITAMIN C = protect the endothelial layers. "excessive clotting in the lungs that appears to be the root cause. Covid-19 causes a coagulation storm that greatly impairs the lungs' ability to exchange oxygen. An indicator called the Disseminated Intravascular Coagulation (DIC) score is emerging as a key predictor of how fatal a covid-19 case will be. If the patient has a DIC score in excess of 5, then odds of a bad outcome dramatically increase. Treating covid-19 patients, even those with mild symptoms, with anticoagulants may be part of the standard regimen going forward."martinson morteums

4/15/20 woke to the sound of poems chiming in the wind, or notes of a recorder. Leads to the notion of Collected Poems.

-- Researchers warn that social distancing measures may be necessary through 2022. Depends on how much you put up with. But still no mention of masks. Of such talk and the close of banks, and hotels and airlines and pet stores and and—by 2022 you will be blind as cave fish. EMF activation hypothesis

Remdesivir, Ivermectin

4/16/20 Took one pill of zpak. Chest tight, elderberry, usnea. Also flood came.
The myths and legends of all of these Native American tribes, this report details, say that an important point to note as all of these Native American tribes had among themselves before European explorers arrived in what is now known as the United States and Canada—and all of whom had the common belief that ""—most particularly of native American peoples, Cherokee remain the largest of the 567 federally recognized tribes in the United States, and who to this day refer to tobacco as" and considered it "" to be used for medicinal and spiritual purposes.
The more than critical importance of noting the Cherokee Nation peoples and their use of tobacco, this report continues,—which was why when they conducted trade ceremonies with other native American tribes along their vast trade routes,—which, in turn, led to one of the greatest mysteries ever to occur in the Americas when European explorers first set foot on these lands—who brought with them viruses that decimated the Native American peoples by the tens, if not hundreds-of-millions—virus pandemics, however, that swept over and barely affected the tobacco smoking Cherokee peoples—as well as many of their main tobacco smoking trading partner tribes—such as the native peoples—who
Bioweapon: gain of function, ace2, t-cell , etec. Four faces

4/17/20 Reset concerns poems, last night much ongoing odyssey like {begin pulmonary distress]

4/18/20 tightness again, Vicks last night.
--All these surveys further increase the flaw of the public domain, its Me self reflexiveness.

Looking for briquette reptile found--
Prominent & Leading Manufacturer from Raipur, we offer Slag Conditioner Powder, De-Oxidizer Powder, Slag Conditioner Briquettes, Black Synthetic Slag Briquittes and Synthetic Slag Powder.

4/19/20 Philosophy of prayer.
Die awake- like twice in sleep, not awake but feeling, as in a coma

Words hold a series of semantic markers Jakobson + geographic + politic
-Airborne AIDs in the least case, a general fatigues

4/20/20 Monday. All night repeated, hydroxychlorine, over and over. Tell her I want to take it but she is concerned about the heart interval, cleared up by Martinson

4/21/20 Swan Arcade - Babylon Is Fallen

4/22/20 I live, work to honor my debt to the living and to life. vas ist du welt und du welt ist this A conscience alive to the world.

```
Was ist die Welt?  What is the world
Die Welt ist das   the world is this
```

You must mear a wask
You must wear a mask

--How many days a work do you week.

--To say the body i live in is a living organism subject to the million vicissitudes of biology is one thing, to say I am a a living organism is another. so it is a full time occupation to meet and defeat the attacks of Wuhan on the body. Imagine if these were upon the mind! So after three such attacks in a succession of some weeks one after another after another, one turns up feeling ok, that means nothing, just a prelude for the next. So what if there were a psycho weapon against the mind, broadcast in an envelop of microwaves with signatures within for different maladies on demand from a keystroke of an operator, more hands on than a bioweapon which only needs a key so it doesn't rebound on the maker?
--

Today's Sign
You must wear a mask in Dr's office.
If you don't have one we will provide it.

4/23/20 One Zpak this morn.
--You must mear a wask ---switch initial consonants

4/24/20

--Vicks again. Max C, 1k an hour. Tickle in chest, dry cough for 36 hours. Second zpak, Ox 96, heart rate flutter 448, down form 460 but not 400, but adjusted 414 maybe HCQ compliant. Expose chest to sun at 11 Pm. Hot. Abou 2.30 pm symptoms of cough and chest tightness abate. Peruvian chincona from Turkey arrives.

4/25/20 Examination of vectors like covid toe after taking……….in treatment @ 5 PM cough gone Ekg reinterpretated for cofactors allows CHQ. Awoke to tight chest took Breath Treatment on porch, double dose isnea, elderberry. P took 2/200 hcq w/augumentum this a.m. but three weeks ago she had it on her tongue. I see it as a continual assault defended by C D and chaga, always looking for an opening, but CHQ is offensive against it.[Antiviral activity of aqueous extracts of the birch on the human immunodeficiency virus].

-[Todoele: I test the premise of a word. Of simultaneous reference that evokes all being, hope and dream of a world. Not separate from that which searches and knows, as if one had outlived the knowledge of himself, as if just under the surface waiting to be awakened where we may forget ourselves so much and emerge.

These studies no longer are exclusively of Lindisfarne. If it seems difficult that the contemplative now speak of the manipulation of the unconscious by eidolia and the fall of the angelic civilizations, this investigation began in the 8th century Latin texts translated into Anglo Saxon from which the current writer takes his name, of Luke 11.22, to plunder the plunderer, painted with interlaced geometric animal and birds, which in the text of the Lindisferne Gospel reads, to "todælþ his here-reaf."]

4/26/20 --the rebuilding of Jerusalem? Destroyed by Babylon, destroyed by Rome

4/27/20 Reactions to the Angel Empires-Burroughs Stockhausen otaku
How does a dry cough lead to a cytokine storm?

This Novus Ordo Portal is a commentary upon the Dante futurum from one sentence,: that "for Dante hell is a giant projection of the human body." The thirteen rings of this Malebolge discover a completely system of sharply focused parodies and concentric circles of the labyrinth of hell with Babylon as its head and Satan at its bottom, overturned, where hell, earth and space are construed as bowel. Dante in this may be a better source of these hallucinatory eidolia than the boasts of that futurm in the Novus Ordo folding the $100 bill into a tidal wave over New York City, .meant to subdue by its giganticism of shock and awe.

3677 /ónar ("a dream") refers strictly to a sleep-dream. It is used six times in the NT (all in Matthew). NAS Exhaustive Concordance. Word Origin a prim.

Nicotine patches. There has been a subdermal perspiration in this period requiring a shower each night, not true before. Defection

4/27/20 Fine culture of the highest and best is always a cover for the depravity of evil. In Django the wonk shakes Candy's hand and wont' let them play Beethoven after feeding a man to the dogs. All the high tables ape high culture, manners, courtesies,

4/28/20 Tues. taken 400 HQL in 50mg over two days. Effects diminishing nearly gone overnight.
--a wife who can walk beside her husband is a rare excellence, not ahead, not behind, but with, and support him too.
-I heard my self breathing as I exhaled.
-So many names, Ablimech 192 times in Genesis, indicate a strata Auerbach does not treat in the back/foreground narrative style, Gk/Heb style. The collective national judgments on nations, sinful people cursing the land itself, is countered by all the plenitude of names all the way through Genesis.
The OT even as collective has as many names as the Greeks; the names are foreground to a background narrative of mystery.
One thing the demos have in common with the China is just as the Wuhan Virus shut down the Hong Kong riots so it shut down the giant Trump rallies.

-- Slag Conditioner Powder, De-Oxidizer Powder, Slag Conditioner Briquettes, Black Synthetic Slag Briquittes and Synthetic Slag Powder.

ACE2--Science Mag: When an infected person expels virus-laden droplets and someone else inhales them, the novel coronavirus, called SARS-CoV-2, enters the nose and throat there is -- It finds a welcome home in the lining of the nose, according to a preprint from scientists at the Wellcome Sanger Institute and elsewhere. They found that cells there are called angiotensin-converting enzyme 2 (ACE2). Throughout the body, the presence of ACE2, which normally helps regulate blood pressure, marks tissues vulnerable to infection, because the virus requires that receptor to enter a cell. Once inside, the virus hijacks the cell's machinery, making myriad copies of itself and invading new cells.

As the virus multiplies, an infected person may shed copious amounts of it, especially during the first week or so. Symptoms may be absent at this point. Or the virus' new victim may develop a fever, dry cough, sore throat, loss of smell and taste, or head and body aches.

If the immune system doesn't beat back SARS-CoV-2 during this initial phase, the virus then marches down the windpipe to attack the lungs, where it can turn deadly. The thinner, distant branches of the lung's respiratory tree end in tiny air sacs called alveoli, each lined by a single layer of cells that are also

--much language from the old colonies suit the new, half breeds, half man, half machine.
--in spring you see the glory of reaction in male and female, doves twittering together, mockingbirds nesting. The Spoiler could make nothing like this, but only a half breed, before a full breed machine in fear that the subverted human half would even then rebel.

--Instinct and cognition. When Biden took his hand in the elevator up and in, where were her instincts to deck him?

Like they say on Battle: los angelos, when a thing is certain< this is war.

Pulling out a spike prevents a wreck in the railway of the future and saves all the passengers and the next town over from gas.

Interview with Bix,virus is sneaky not a cold coming on but building up a viral load over multiple exposures and days and attaching in full force, otherwise it waits for an entry as it does in the bat.
--Individuation: "A longing for that enveloping for safety of group states."
Western denoms feel protected, entitled, illusion shattered.
Body mind, soma—the insects, mantis are behind it.

4/29/20 93-year-old man and his 93-year-old wife arrested:

Five years ago I said that Hannah got her son from the Lord, not from the science. After we had all given it up as impossible God made it happen engineering the life of the mother to every circumstance. Praise be to God.

4/30/20 "This second-week crash, days five through 10, or thereabouts, seem to be so dangerous for some people with covid-19, "There's an early stage of infection and the virus sits somewhere. You can almost look at the virus as a fifth column coming in, securing its stronghold and then slowly inducing more cells to let it in. The virus may be killing the cells that line the air sacs of the lungs, which keep them open and allow for the exchange of oxygen and carbon dioxide,

-Chest tight took one zpak.
D. wants her job back but the girls said no, she didn't work that much anyway. B. put her on a 3 day 30 hr. week. Somebody took out the palo verde in the front, interlopers parked in lot, one guy with probable cause virus.

5/1/20 Sat. Feel good. granaries are round, kivas, religious bldgs square

You'd have to eat a whole refrigeratior of garlic for it to be a medicine. Anything can be a medicine all it needs is reputation, I could be a medicine if you thought I was.

5/2/20 Proning: Within minutes of turning patients with low oxygen saturation onto their stomachs, they saw oxygen saturation levels jump back into the normal range. "Patients who were coming in with oxygen stats in the 70s ... once we proned them, after about a few minutes, they'd be up in the low 90s,"

Jacob Waltz grave is located in the Pioneer Cemetery in Phoenix at the extreme southwest corner of the cemetery. You can actually view his burial site from outside the cemetery by going to the corner of west Harrison Street and 15th Ave.

5/3/20 My sister, my spouse.
 prophlacytic CHQ 200mg.

5/5/20 I had wanted to bonus 500 each to M and J, on Cinco del Mayo as an excuse and planned to. Concurrently we ordered more HCQ even though price was 5 times higher, @$ each, when it was .60 cents three weeks ago, so wanted 100 at the new price but J ordered 500, a $1000 hit, the amt I wanted to bonus. The numbers are too symmetrical, I felt a little checked anyway when D quit last week to take a job that ended up netting her 2.50 less per hr than we were giving –except she got to work for a conglomerate, presumably more prestigious, so withal the unknowns I still want to bonus but prudence gives me a check too, plus the dreams last three nights are identical something about heath practice, but even in the dreams I don't know what they are, let alone now, awake. I had wondered during the D episode what the other shoe would drop about etc, since we already had let the two NPs go.

Amid the scientific flurry about ACE2 and T Cell, there is now a black mkt in HCQ, from Nogales at ^$ 5 a pill.
--chest tight wheezing, took one zpak

5/6/20 chills, night sweat, low fever sometimes, chest tight, double breathing treatment

: A loading dose of 10mg base/kg (four 155mg tablets for a 60kg subject), followed by 155 mg daily (250mg chloroquine phosphate salt/ 200mg hydroxychloroquine sulphate) will be taken for 90 days.

At least three big drug companies, Mylan, Novartis and Teva Pharmaceutical have of hydroxychloroquine, with plans to donate literally tens of millions of doses of the drug hoping it can be used to treat COVID-19.

in Marseille, France, stated, "A treatment with the hydroxychloroquine combination (200 mg X 3 per days for 10 days) + Azithromycin (500 mg on the 1st day then 250 mg per day for 5 more days), as part of the precautions for use of this association (including an electrocardiogram on D0 and D2). "showed a significant reduction of the viral carriage" after six days of treatment and "much lower average carrying duration" compared to patients receiving other treatment.

5/7/20 HCQ 200, zinc/copper, D, C 1:30 AM

Noah built the ark in the land of Eden east of the garden, probably near the garden where one of the rivers ran out from the garden or in the cradle of civilization between the Euphrates and the Tigris rivers around where, after the flood, the tower of Babel was constructed. This was in the "east", which we today call the Middle East. Pepcid , selenium.

5/8/20 Fri Chills, night sweats. Began amoxicillin 3 AM full course of five days 2 a day because the stuff after breathing treatments comes up worse and worse, sometimes black. Wrapped around Vicks last night, again sweats.

Suramin drug for autism, Jespersdatter

Watching Capote I have all the sensibilities of the Pre Raphaelites and before, the artists and 20th cents after. You can learn their ways by aping them, imitation by conformity, but I have natively by imagination, vanity. I just reject it all. Note that abandoned and befriended as he was he still went to the preps, who paid for that? Epstein? Barr? Grooming.

5/9/20 Sat. Tight chest much breathing treatment…etc, maybe lessening PM.

5/10/20 SS shot Reagan inside limo after Hinckley shot Mother's Day

This may be the menu if you ever go to eat at Guapa Pop:

1 - Hors-d oeuvre / Are of spicy in nature in order to stimulate the appetite for the dishes that are to follow in the
 Served from a rotating trolley or a tray a small amount of each variety being placed on the plate to a portion.
Tea: Indian, Ceylon, Earl Grey, Darjeeling, Orange Pekoe

5/11/20 Edwin Earle Parsons was an archeologist tracker, rancher housebuilder. I have one of his tool boxes.

5/12/20 after learning yesterday the NAC breaks up the phlegm I take the breath treatment in two episodes first to open then to break up, which seems to work today

After the breath treat lay down and more will come up.

At 5.30 pm a mother duck and eight small ducklings walked under our kitchen window going south.

5/13/20- So to live without the baggage of the shadow of all collective uncon is to live so that no divination is possible because the moment the thought occurs is the best time to the act and there is no separation between man and nature, but cooperation unspoken, no need to speak of it. In the moment and if a thought is some memoir of a person, that is the moment to intercede peace upon them. So the world and its bag. The flesh we always have with us and must intercede for it too. We reject all siddi temptations and treatments to submit ourselves to the power of the Word and the Name in all things.

 The world is a virus that tries to infect the thought to sin in the body, the devil is a Fauci who deceives and misinforms for self profit and the perverse need to rule because he is overthrown.

The WORLD IS THE VIRUS OF COLLECTIVE UNCONSCIOUS that wants you to shoulder its bag; It wants TO INFECT THE FLESH of your body bacteria with thoughts that cause sin via A GRINNING FAUCI CITING STATISTICS who deceives and misinforms for profit.

The grin they all wear is a cover for their Grimm. The democrats are assault troops to attack and divide what is left.

Words from the plant: thank you Lord that you gave me these lungs to praise you and this breath to sing praise to your Name.

Stephen Kinzer's new book is

  found ways to draw prisoners in interrogation away from their identities, induce them to reveal secrets and perhaps even program them to commit acts against their will. A 'self-contained, off-the-shelf operation' to blast away human minds so new ones could be implanted in their place to implant a new mind in the resulting void

Newk Brupbacker   Die Reaktion in Dreamland Fritz brupbacher
The Knoutogdreamic Empire   Dreamland and Karl Marx
Dreamland Almanac, revoluzze!. revoluzze! If not the eagle will come and pull our your eyes.

The elf executioners carried out a monthly program three times a week. Leo Greiner wrote an *executioner ballad*, to which Hans Richard Weinhöppel composed a march. The stage program very often began or ended with this torture tools seen on the stage, the stage logo consisted of a skull with a judge's wig and a pillory. Mélange of literary chansons, dances, sketches, shadow and puppet shows, sometimes including critical comments on censorship and arbitrary state, is often associated with a morbid and erotic charm. This is the Grizzly Bear Wok.

The Empress of Newfoundland was performed in the cabaret of the *Elf Executioners* .

Good news on the health front for you Covid-19 watchers, Jack Kevorkian has taken a split time appointment with WHO and the CDC to process the after death end game. There were just not that many more hospitalized patients to transfer to nursing homes.

Good news for the Covid-19 watch:
Jack Kevorkian has come back
to WHO & CDC to process after deaths!
They ran out of hospital patients
to transfer to nursing homes.

5/14/20 Covid Cough Ups
Full Systematic Expectoration

Hydrate. In hydration before breathing machine treatment take a drink of Usnea, elderberry syrup, effervescent first, with mucus relief products like Guaifenesin expectorant.

Breath Treatment Albuterol to open up the bronchials, then 20% Acetylcysteine solution (N-Acetyl Cysteine) in series cuts the bonds of the gluey mucous so it will expectorate and is easier to bring up. The Usnea works to lubricate this loosening process and enable it immensely.

Declination. Simple decline 3 degrees or so after this aids the flow out, always taking phlegm up and out. Prone breathing on stomach enables breathe through diaphragm increasing oxygen.

Vibration. If prone and on a vibrating pad this further loosens phlegm. As in cystic fibrosis used to loosen expectorant in concert with Acetylcysteine, cupping strikes to chest and back loosen. The Vibrator pad serves this.

This treatment is pursued concurrent with any antibiotic prescription for bacterial infection in the lungs, followed to the end and to be on wake up in the morning, noontime or mid afternoon and before bed. The whole System, without change, for the desired effect, is meant to produce free breathing.

Summary. NAC and Albuterol are chemically incompatible and cannot be combined, but treated serially, preceded by Usnea in elderberry, then Albuterol, then Acetylcysteine (with a slight sulphur taste), followed by descent prone vibrating, front and back, stimulates expectoration all along is the treatment.

Covid reversals

It is axiomatic in the course of this event, virus or bioweapon that multiple reversals will occur. One morning out the blue you will feel really great, but evening worse than ever. This happens over and over as if the Covid were seeking to lull your defenses to sleep for a fresh attack, which is what this feels like. This may say something about the viral load necessary for the infections to occur, that the Covid is building for a fresh assault. It certainly feels like that when it happens to you. Stay the course of the protocols above and keep fighting. It is long and hard.

Age Related Emmendations

--Because so much of Covid danger is age related some parts of treatment might to be amended, for example the addition of saline to amp the breath treatment would elevate the BP in some sensitive to any saline, and 2, The use of some ACE2 inhibitors for hypertension such as Benicar multiplies the number of ACE 2 cells in the lungs by a factor of 2, thus it would be well to be replaced for some other to lessen the risk of infection there, and 3, In the use of HCQ and Zinc, the EKG interval must be established within bounds and monitored to prevent heart arrythmia and should not be used concurrent with Azrithysim which does the same. A two day interval would be used before AZ is introduced.

Fasting

Since the course of simple bronchitis can be months anyway, and the Covid complication of the lungs devious at every turn with each day and half day of success followed by further and more symptoms of congestion and breathing, the body seems naturally to lessen its appetite in this and should be encouraged, even aided and abetted with smaller options and less frequent eating. This seems to aid the health while a full stomach harms it.

Prayer

During treatments it is well to remind the lungs that they were made to praise their maker, for everything that has breath will praise Him and hence to invite the Holy Spirit to cause the treatments to have their lasting benefit by his catalyst and intervention, for the Holy Spirit is spiritual breath.

Glutathione

The whole purpose of NAC is it produces Glutathione in the body. G IV, women use G in IV for cleansing liver detox and fine wrinkles. A liposomal version which is absorbed through the stomach directly into the blood without digestion is
 500mg twice a day in liquid form from *LipoNaturals.*
Pre Covid These supplements, used as well as Vitamin C and D and quercetin.

5/15/20 at the end of amoxicillian, phelm clearing to clear, still some tightness

5/16/20 Clearly the fix is in.
-some guy has already edited 6 children's books about corona virus, the indoctrination begins, but being in form the start when they all doubted is a measure of how easily they will not be swayed to believe anything that makes them fear.

Distillate psychotropic taken from the bromeliad in homecoming
-Finished the course of Amoxicillian today, continued the CHQ
-Spiritual bandages, Amarant appeared in Penny.

5/19/20 Kids got a puppy.

5/21/20 Go to every other day HCQ

5/22/20 first dream in all this time taken to a Mennonite church with some guy I met they stood up against the wall, facing it and the four sides were preached to in a fashion behind them, one the woman's wall where I first ended up was about the evils of Colinton, changing I went to a spot beside a door, then to a smaller room. Shrangee effects occurred, the site was beside a body of water, Loud booms of drums came across the water. The guy in front of me said to me this is not a usual service. The world of purgatory.

Shadow charts, independent databases, or "orphan systems," as they are sometimes called, are among the most controversial and difficult to manage forms of protected health information (PHI) that exist.

5/23/20 the death toll of 19 is inflated both ways, NY and PA seeded nursing homes with Covid patients so that huge % of deaths resulted there, inflating the total. Drs are pressured to ascribe C-19 as cause of death for which they get an additional 36K in reward, likewise patients with vague cause of death are so ascribed. o/w people are not so ascribed. This opposes prescribing steroids for the immediate relief they give to boost outpatient favorable feedback driving down bonuses.

5/24/20 Finally made good on an omission made in the office of the fourth floor of Parlin hall in 68/9. A female TA, don't remember now her name, was telling her troubles to me and I had the impulse to hug her but did not. I should have and this has never been forgotten, but last night in a dream I did hug her and made her to know my regret for not acting so then.

Sunday So Aey & S visited before the baby this Thurs and the substance of that dream prefigured that visit. I prayed hands on her belly for the birth.

The team identified four promising candidates: atovaquone, a drug previously used to treat malaria that's currently used to treat toxoplasmosis, babesiosis, and *Pneumocystic* pneumonia; mebendazole, a drug that's used to treat several different parasitic worm infections; ouabain, a naturally occurring compound that was used as an arrow poison in Africa and is no longer approved in the U.S. but used in other parts of the world to treat heart failure; and dronedarone, a drug used to maintain heart rhythms.

(The Armed Forces Enlistment Contract) states: "In the event of war, my enlistment in the Armed Forces continues until six (6) months after the war ends, unless the enlistment is ended sooner by the President of the United States."

5/28/20 They go to maternity WATER breaks about 8am but update at 12 pm says heart rate down during contractions which considering the whole trauma of this pregnancy is difficult, so I go to pick up scripture, close it and open it for encouragement, which I only do sometimes, at extremity, and my hand falls on Isaiah 49, amazing encouragement. A few minutes later A calls that the distress of heart rate has eased and the labor continues. So about 7. 40 pm I read Isa 49 aloud to P to celebrate this birth, whose caesarian was to begin at 7.45, born 8.47 pm. Just to show the time in which he is born P's back window was busted out in her parking lot this day, while fires raged in Minneapolis—all these factors of birth tests not needed in countless ultrasounds and fears the baby would be overweight were false, lacking judgment, as much as the transverse position at birth could not be adjusted by an OB they used but solved with a caesarean. All this overwhelmed by the destiny of a child formed years ago in the yearning, struggles, and wrestling of faith which produces the Work of James. Even after hoping had ceased faith kept working.

You thought China was red, but Blue State governors swelled the death tolls by seeding nursing homes with Covid sometimes to half the dead. NY Gov: It's the nursing home's fault if they accepted the Covid positive patients I sent to them.

5/30/20

Bio: Sjon Larsson is still quarantined in Norway north of 65'. He lives in Hammerfest, on the coast of Finemarck where he works for the dictorate of fisheries of Bergen. He has contributed botanical exhibits to the Tromso Museum. This is his first foray into verse

Stole me de skillet, stole me de lead, Stole me de gal that makes short'nin' bread

Had kids for six hrs. T. talks up Mario and Maya vid games. AB a non believer.
To J: Like me you are the only one born in a time of war.

5/31/20 Welcome to Pied Cow is *noir* comedy in five acts of events that occurred in and around a transplanted locale of Pied Cow from which Zarathusta emerged before he set forth on his journey into the wilderness.

Pan MacMillian Australia--This ms. Welcome to Pied Cow is comedy noir in five acts of events that occurred in and around a transplanted locale of Pied Cow from which Zarathustra emerged before he set forth on his journey into the wilderness. But it is set in the now not then. Impossible to summarize, it was cows, cannibalism, talking mules, coyotes of that sort too, spiritual tours of Grand Canyon, Orc, which are often found at the bottom of things, and must of all it has Susan, who is the be all and end all of every dream. Too bad she is eaten. These and etc. themes call back and forth in the array of some 45 stories or so, but which have a oneness withal, especially seen as the Pied Cow of Nietzsche, which detail in their own way his bubble of the Pied. That ties it all together as some kind of new world order take, but never expressly so. No one has ever written stuff like this. it was done over a long long time, considered and reconsidered decades but now is its time. The stories are chosen from many more to preserve the lyrical feel of the best of them. Most have appeared over the last 15 yrs.

It's like First Friday all weekend! And if the galleries aren't open at least there is a good supply of bricks!

Everything is different today. A goes back to work. Aey has his baby. I finished, named and sent Pied Cow.

-- PIED COW is built from the ground up, one brick at a time with no plan as to where it is going. It takes a long time to compose way. The title, the concept are only applied, discovered at the end not only after all the pieces are composed, but then arranged into their coherent structure. Then the question is asked what is it. Pied Cow is civilization. It's motive is to reduce memory to that of a cow, which N. says can't. So the citizen can't remember its unpatriotic to wear a mask (Dr oz), its harmful to wear a mask (Surgeon general, Fauci, CDC, WHO) it won't help to wear a mask towear a mask or go to jail etc. Like the CHQ debacle of risk, too risk, before widespread adoption. The little cow just takes whate'er the present gives without question. Rip tides. Tom Hanks says wear a mask.

1. find a societal fracture point using race, political differences, and apply pressure to it
2. followed by the igniting of protests, where ordinary protesters provide cover for agent provocateurs otherwise known as terrorists and/or saboteurs who perform acts of violence and vandalism

3—the intent of which is to force a government to deploy its police and/or military forces to restore normal order—and if done, sees them walking into a trap—
4. as nearly as soon as these state forces are deployed, a mass civilian death action will be perpetrated by these agent provocateurs, which will quickly be blamed on the government—
5. with the purpose being to ignite enough outrage to overthrow the government before any investigation can be made

Grotowski shared Nietzsche's contempt for much of the insubstantial fabric of modernity: 'The rhythm of life in modern civilization is characterized by pace, tension, a feeling of doom, the wish to hide our personal motives and the assumption of a variety of roles and masks in life . . .. We suffer most from a lack of totality, throwing ourselves away, squandering ourselves' insubstantial fabric of modernity

In Nietzsche's Thus Spake Zarathustra, when Zarathustra visits the town of the Pied Cow, he encounters the townspeople, who mistake him for the scheduled entertainer – the deformed tight-rope walker.

The simplest meaning of the opening quote of this post is this: that mankind is filled with filth and sin. Only a greater being, a more evolved creature, can engage with mankind without succumbing to his follies. Of course, for Nietzsche, that more evolved being is the Overman.

But as mentioned earlier, the Overman, whilst expressed in powerful terms, is ultimately an unattainable ideal. That is to say, the Overman is an ideal that all men should aspire towards, for it is in the striving that we find power.

In the town of the Pied Cow, we see a tightrope walker, entertaining the townsfolk, crossing from one tower to another. Here we see the tightrope as a metaphor for mankind, starting tower representing base animals, the destination tower representing the Overman. Here, mankind is presented by Nietzsche as a "rope between beast and the Superman".

The tightrope walker is unhinged by a jester, who runs out from the first tower, and leaps over the tightrope walker, causing him to fall to the ground. The tightrope walker lay dying, contemplating his life, expressing how futile his life has been, that he is nothing more than an animal. Zarathustra tells him not to fear, that there has been honor in his life – he has lived a life of danger, which is far more than anybody can say about the townsfolk who have lived their lives in safety, superficiality, comfort, weakness: the townsfolk are the epitome of the despised "Last Men".

Here then, the tightrope walker is the epitome of the aspirational man – he who can never hope to become the Overman, but who finds honour and strength in the striving, walking the tenuous path from animal to Overman, and never accepting comfort or safety.

Endlosung

Transporten Norton @ coastal shelf. "This is much too enigmatic for our tastes, and unfortunately because of that there's not a ton of feeback I can give. There are some interesting sentences, but the mixed up grammar and lightnng-fast movement of the piece was a bit overwhelming for our tastes. Some editors at more avant-garde magazines may totally dig it. I'd suggest Otoliths, 'Pider, Juke Joint Magazine, Fence, Cloud Rodeo, Peatsmoke Journal, mutiny!, Bombay Gin and Xavier Review. If the author isn't familiar with those journals I think they'd dig them, and I think the editors would enjoy a piece such as this."

6/2/20 Literary Breughel. Visit with J. Gave me my AER cup. Shawna says looking at Aey's baby book that E had a home haircut, at 5. P does not say but thinks…you try having two kids in med school and driving across the mixmaster every day in an old car that breaks down…. P and I have been consumed with love and justice all our lives. She began in undergrad thesis on love.

6/3/20 Wed Began a Zpak treatment for chest today since the tightness returned even while massive breathing treatments

I don't know J if these stories will make sense to you but they are written in and of the time you woke up in. Since you are a miracle you will have the answer. T went from paw patrol on his birthday to super Mario after lockup.

6/4/20 every single person who has anything to say is crazy they're all infected.
but saying doesn't make it true! It's not just a tweet, IT'S A CALL TO THE UNREGENERATE.

6/5/20 All people who own bulldogs are racist. Covid-19 has infected the grass and now it has spread to the trees.

6/6/20 Variant Bio

"A heavily Caucasian mob burning a successful black man's business while chanting black lives matter." the only knowledge these "Caucasian mobs burning black businesses while chanting black lives matter" have of black people is TV.

Citizens of Pied Cow "leap about, eat, rest, digest, leap about again, and so from morn till night and from day to day, fettered to the moment and its pleasure or displeasure, neither melancholy nor bored, may well ask of the animal: 'Why do you not speak to me of your happiness but only stand and gaze?' If the cow could answer it would say, "the reason is Nietzsche," who supplied these words: "I always forget what I was going to say" - but then I forget this answer too, and stay silent" (*Untimely Meditations*). If you ask why the people of Pied Cow tolerate these offenses it is because they can not remember and go on the next pleasure.

The Pied Cow noir of light and dark has two methods to preserve. A "society of men has grown up among us, bred up from their youth in the art of proving by words multiplied for the purpose, that white is black, and black is white, according to which they are paid" (*Gulliver's Travels*). We write these on the pied skin of our Welcome.

Since a cow in the piebald universe cannot remember, Freidrich makes the moment of black and white a forced choice between the *Endlösung* final solution of the *ubermensch* and the unwashed *utermensh* of the common who does not know what is meant by yesterday. The brain of the herdsman announces what the cow will do and this announcement is tantamount to permission. Just what haven't you been told about what's coming? We hide these events in fairy tales to not disturb the forgetting. Either piedbald civilization is normal or it has escaped from a circus.

The headless herdsman drives the cow. The wiles of the Order of Causation & Response (ORC) with the Laurel Roach sit upon its brow. Arigato Yo, Grizzley Bear, Guapa Pop and Angel poet pull his *strudel vegan* up to Hopi House. Pedro Escadero, Sue Oopsook, Walto Dog and Leo O'Hearn are tempted to jump. Igod's chem to make Peace. Astronautic Poles, Sir Farther Paddington Demonauts, Strum Server taught by Professor Yum are a Rhine Gold Nibelung of Wonk Yaps, MacCoalCrotch Town, Mather Point, Meteor Crater, Enginactory Organisms, Ecoponics, Ecopods, Bazooka Temple and Johnny Cake. When Jack Bommb sends his penlight down to the Oothecan, the uber *mutter sprack* is heard by all. Fafnir, Blattaria, Bill Blake, Leo O'Hearn, Rehoboth Starr, Hotel Damer and the Little Lady of Taiwan, Lipsy Russell, Oopsooks, Nabucodinosaur, Orks, Urks, Orcopoi, OOps, puppoets, Druggist Associations and El Tovar charm the noonosphere. Ice Planet giants, Levi Strauss, Halfling Talk, epubs on Shunt, Undprint ploody popple talk and Hamagmous Johnny feel the bicephalic fingertips of Ubermensch and its subfornical need.

Bosch and Breughel together began   They found the monstrous and the uncanny hid in the everyday. Fantastical forms in the familiar hid a trap set by this enemy. Pied Cow paints these states of the *new* order worldliness of the world. Couched in peasant revelry, grotesque dreamworlds of the everyday show cosmic hostility from the beginning of the world. The gluttons, misers, quacks and libertines are replaced by ravenous superman. These literary Breugels of new worldliness appeared

These Orders of Causation & Response (ORC   ), when Jack Bommb sends his penlight down Guapa Pop and Angel poet pull this *strudel vegan* up. Pedro Escadero, Sue Oopsook, Walto Dog and Leo O'Hearn are tempted to jump. Igod's chem makes Peace. Astronautic Poles, Sir Farther Paddington Demonauts, Strum Server taught by Professor Yum are a Rhine Gold Nibelungs. Wonk Yaps, MacCoalCrotch Town, Mother Point, Meteor Crater, Enginactory Organisms, Ecoponics, Ecopods, Bazooka Temple and Johnny Cake. to the Oothecan, the uber *mutter sprack* is heard by all. Fafnir, Blattaria, Bill Blake, Leo O'Hearn, Rehoboth Starr, Hotel Damer and the Little Lady of Taiwan, Lipsy Russell, Oopsooks, Nabucodinosaur, Orks, Urks, Orcopoi, OOps, puppoets, Druggist Associations and El Tovar charm the noonosphere. Ice Planet giants, Levi Strauss, Halfling Talk, epubs on Shunt, Undprint ploody popple talk and Hamagmous Johnny feel the

bicephalic fingertips of Ubermensch and its subfornical need. with the Laurel Roach sit upon its brow.
of Arigato Yo, Grizzley Bear,
Liner Notes

If symbols slant reference and disappearances emerge, the oldest phenom going and was here before the start. To not interpret what you see in this is reality and to do so is fantasy.

-- Dame and Susan came over and sat on the berm in a true story. They had a basement in their adobe.

-- *Táinte bó,* or "cows," means "driving," or "reaving," or even "a drove" or "herd" of cattle. Patchwork pillow-talk weaving lace, in her right hand was a bordering rod of silvered 14 W. 204.with bronze strips of red gold at the sides. A many-spotted green mantle surrounded her; and a bulging, strong-headed pin of gold in the mantle held her bosom; Also she wore a hooded tunic with red interweaving with a ruddy, fair-faced countenance narrow below and broad above a blue-grey laughing eye. Soft black lashes threw a shadow. Like to those fresh Parthian crimson lips sweet the strings of lutes was her fair speech.

As white as snow in one night fallen was the sheen of her skin and her body that shone outside of her dress. Slender and very white were her feet; rosy, even, sharp-round nails she had; two sandals with golden buckles about them. Fair-yellow, long, golden hair she wore; three braids of hair she wore; two tresses were wound around her head; the other tress from behind threw a shadow down on her calves. The maiden carried arms, and two black horses were under her chariot.

Cattle-preys evidence an early stage of civilization with Queen Mobs fair-yellow, deep-gold, flowing hair down to her shoulders. Purple cloaks embellished with brooches over her breasts, surrounded with curved shields of sharp, chiselled edges and spears as long as silken tunics with hoods, all wore to the instep all together raised their feet, and set them down. "Is that Cormac, yonder?" asked all. "Aye, it is he," Mob made answer.
Snow White and the Literature of the Cow.

-- *A queen sewing at an open window during a winter snowfall pricks her finger with a needle. Three drops drip on the freshly fallen snow. She wishes, "how I wish I had a daughter with skin as white as snow, lips as red as blood, and hair black ebony." The queen gives birth to Snow White, but dies soon after. A year later, Snow White's father, takes a new wife, who is beautiful, but wicked and vain.*

--In the hazard of new Order medieval compounds corresponds, where every planetary follicle has human dress, the sun its heart, kohlrabi its vegetable, gold its mineral, Brussels its city, Guam its country, this woman on her side as Europe, her head, a breast in France, a hand in Italy, Byzantium her navel, Caucasus her buttocks, Jerusalem below and then "her Chin / Ore past; and the straight Hellespont between / the Sestos and Abydos of her breasts

(Donne, "Love's Progress"). Bogs, barrens, white cliffs, lowlands: buttocks, hands, chin and genitals, the symbolic world maps (Andrea Bianco, 1436) put Jerusalem at the center of the globe. Faithful to geography, "we love the Centrique part." "Spherical, like a globe. I could find out countries in her."

They thought it man, the centerverse before Copernicus, (to that world the golden Shiners came to coin Pied philosophy excrete, and art perspire that science galled of government blood, new drug roll gods. New implants and literature hoped to set LIT right with what who knows would read, but the text changes in the day.

--I could have sworn after Grapefruit class when I read in Baudelaire's "The Martyr," that "the head.../ On the night table, like a ranunculus, / Rests," as promised in the ranunculus in this garden with our "golden crocus / fills the cup / of ox law / and ranunculus." These legends of the of Bataille are mere Swiftian Professors in the remains of Lit and Und on Shunt. Maybe an alternate version read, "the names are changed to protect ranunculus." But there it was right in the middle of the page: "Our neighborhood holds the garden principle:

-- Bataille never dreamed the decapitation Louis XVI as a joke, and promising to venerate just like the New Borns of Old Oley did, or Nietzsche, along with discussions of sacrifice so *woderful to intellectuals of the absurd. Alternate herbals list plants of disembodied heads. No matter. The Abenaki giants of the Red Rock predate these taking form in Professor morphs.

--How did the Twelve Steps get into Scyld Scylding's funeral barge?

--That PupPoet heroes of this unworld custodially maintain their giants might be compared to farmers who grow PupPoets at the U to feed and eat, as well as the general populace to consume. If we understand the mind, more is eaten than they need, which requires new planets to devour. Space exploration spreads the disease. It's not as if poets couldn't think of anything to write. "Stated boldly," one tweet: "Today Troy is Freudian in myth, Jungian in archetype and of pagan design, a surrealist combo dream." There's freedom of expression for those lords of Mount Cognentis, Olympus Solipsis. In the Book of Giants "the land is crying out…every animal, every bird." Compare Genesis 6.4. Oh dear.

--That the Moon is hollow we shall not speak, or if it be a cycle in long boots. Our duty then would be to bring a better plight, for we all know oil and water don't, so to mix a tale of the Igod in the Moon, so when the ears fell off and the tongue slides out, and little trees take root in air and the whole turns black and falls with that great hammering, another squirt of that alluric fixer can be administered in return.

-PIED COW is built from the ground up, one brick at a time with no plan as to where it is going. It takes a long time to compose that way. The title, the concept are only applied or discovered at the end not only after all the pieces are composed, but when arranged in their coherent structure. Then the question is asked what is it. Pied Cow is civilization with the motive to reduce memory to that of a cow. This Nietzsche says. So the citizen can't remember its unpatriotic to wear a mask (Dr Oz), or its harmful to wear a mask (Surgeon general, Fauci, CDC, WHO) and that it won't help to wear a mask, but you will either wear a mask or go to jail. Like the CHQ debacle of risk, too risk, before widespread adoption, the little cow just takes whate'er the present gives without question.

6/8/20
all them fathers,
specially new,
crowns wobble, when their bus is due.

In Jan of In '68 at FSC Archie Johnson tiped me to himself and a group of six who were to carry a coffin up the sidewalk of Hay Street as theatre. I went downtown to watch from a deli- with big windows as they went past on the other side, very fast, prudent considering the time and place.

New Taliban-When the Taliban took over Afghanistan in 1996, it imposed a strict, Islamic fundamentalist culture across the country, including wiping out any traces of pre-Islamic history including the of the world's tallest-standing Buddhas. Islamic State likewise in their imposition of sharia law statues in Palmyra, Syria — a site of global historical importance — in 2015 and Farage

In Stalinist Russia and Nazi Germany art and discourse became propaganda and violations went to the gulag or to camp.

6/9/20 A herd is a crowd of black and white mass mind consensus guided by a herdsman with a rope to lead. Pied Cow might be anywhere. In Austin where Raggedly Ann, Dorothy Alice and Johnny Cake live, the author of A Thousand And One Goats said that the hero must leave Pied Cow to find openness of being, but where superman was found, centuries before Bosch and Breughel found the monster in this everyday life and nature a monster too. *Enemy Painting is an idea from* Koerner's *Bosch, how this painting of everyday life is of an enemy bent on destroying us.* Now Pied Cow sees the world as it really is
6/11/20 N. party with all attending. matt Walsh
-- your work no longer has a home at @QueenMobs because the magazine is closing indefinitely due to @RussellBennetts's actions against me, @KolleenCarney of @DrunkMonkeysWeb encourages you to submit there.
Chris Constantine, gorilla, watchman

6/17/20 send the true light to Parousia, seemed to be recovered,
Ichor: the ethereal fluid that is the Greek gods' sometimes said to retain the qualities of the immortals' food and drink, and nectar
You entwine your destiny with that of your children until they are gone, then you are alone.

, our observation that fenbendazole in combination with supplemented vitamins significantly inhibited tumor growth has implications for its use during antitumor studies because it may cause unpredictable interactions with test substances and thus alter research results.

6/18/20 she thinks maybe I have gout in left big toe

6/20/20 I think our sons should take inventory of their possessions that they want to save for their own sons. T and N come while they take AB to dance recital.

6/21/20 Ever body was kung flue fighting
The streets were lockdowned slightly
Masks were flipping and flopping
In fact there was a little less copping

6/22/20 the duties of fatherhood and sonship. A missed another this father's day. Andrew is one for 4 of the last years.

6/23/ Ice age farmer, artecteching the beast system

6/24/20 ancestral EMF level after wanting us to host ricky and the 17people mon after mom's work andrw scales back, doesn't want them in his house either, decides tomeet outside at motel

6/25/20 air feels softer, pat begins ankle wts and jog canale verything changed today, softer air, feel, Pat does a double canal walk,

dreamed a crew showed up, at office, to paint the bldg. with dq. No bid, given, finally though some factor times 20.71, the gal of paint/ they say yes, intimidating,, the j picks up a shears, I take a hammer, refuse the bid and the job.—

6/26/29 P. meets with S and Aey

6/27/20 prison of angels: Dudael (דּוּדָאֵל, compd. of *dud* דּוּד "kettle", "cauldron", "pot" + "deity", "divinity" — lit. "cauldron of ") is the place of imprisonment for (one of the "fallen" angels), cohort of It is described in the chapter 10 verses 4–7:

And again the Lord said to Raphael: 'Bind Azazel hand and foot, and cast him into the darkness: and make an opening in the desert, which is in Dudael, and cast him therein. And place upon him rough and jagged rocks, and cover him with darkness, and let him abide there for ever, and cover his face that he may not see light. And on the day of he shall be cast into the fire.

6/28/20 eric neumann the great mother, *Lambodara* (one who has a pot belly, or, literally, one who has a hanging belly) *Lambodara* (Pot Belly, or, literally, Hanging Belly) and *Mahodara*

(Great Belly). Both names are Sanskrit compounds describing his belly (IAST: *udara*). The *Brahmanda Purana* says that Ganesha has the name Lambodara because all the universes (i.e.,; IAST: *brahmāṇḍas*) of the past, present, and future are present in him. The number of Ganesha's arms varies; his best-known forms have between two and sixteen arms.

Vis with Ricky at plaza pool

6/29/20 dream, a hostel elder health seekers with rules for no clutter, but hard to see. Looking for a bathroom I am packing bag or getting bag to leave. Is this response to I said if he had a church I would sit in last row, but he that it would be in his home and I would "always be welcome" which means of course never.! As per 'explicit critic of John C and the lack of any memorabilia left, or of A's critic of C being too bossy, etc, it is a characteristic of m/ that they demo their past, witness all the sales of Chagall.. That we met at the Plaza pool where women with serpents down their hips in thongs marched in front of us, N, A, etc is a contradiction not to overlook. Patronizing, you look good. Do you write, a courtesy question. He is as fixed as Cor any of them in that mania of self assurance, a coverup for the less. Not playful. When A visited there last fall said he had four locations phoenix, Texas Colorado spgs and Tennessee. R repeated this in the order given. Strange for human mental association will change the restatement of thoughts and speech. R also had high praise for Bezos and amazon! Necessity for an exec but betraying. Gallows humor applied to P he said, he said that P will die of all organ failure except heart, since he had a new one. Health is patronizing, Pwent from walker to cane. The adoptive mother died of meth od. N much impressed with Hamilton!

On religious collisions that occur within a short period of time fuzzy sets: -I' put them down to the strange energies from space …because if they are chaotic occurrence and happenstance appearing by design, any being capable of manipulating at that level across this span of time is far beyond my ability to interact --real phenomena influenced by the vagueness of the colloquial language with rife Streets.

INTERMISSION

"We Look and See."
interacts the commentary-process, continually modifies, updates, and syncretizes a fusion of heterogeneous types of layered discourse, while seeking the appearance of unity, a redactor of every text, seemingly autonomous as a ventriloquist of thought, which texts speak, to be fact fact must be stripped with irony free of rhetoric, along with magnificenza, oh, the meraviglia, stupore, and inganno (deception) to collect those notables in the spirit of the absurd who inherit political social intrigue. The relation between language and thought became a reverse Fudoki of future reports known to gazetteers as agricultural, geographical, and historical records as well as mythology and folklore, chronicles of the most important literature of all, of the future, based upon ancient mythology and history. These FAKTA Proprietaries, couched as literatures of fact operate in a consortium of authors of the Futurist playbook against New Bolshevik society of the 2020s which completely translate from that era a hundred years

before, which censorship is again opposed a continent and an age apart from the first, whose first priority remains to accentuate real material gathered first hand or culled from documentary sources (Kolchevska). The formalist theories of faktovivi bypass the algorithmic controls and translate hidden propitiatory work read correctly, listed as apposite as true of a poet who had the Tractatus in youth long before, with the contemporaries and peers of Wittgenstein in the Principia Mathematica and Physical Principles of the Quantum

The purpose of the meat narrative is to ladder fact into the ether of fact, but there are parallel ladders next to it, counterfacts of false noumena. The meat narrative is to mirror this in order to display, thus it is an awareness tool to bring light. Ho, Ho.

Were this a mystery it might begin: "I meet him at night to exchange outlaw varieties of pigs and corn seeds for white packs of HCQ and ivermectin. We were unobserved, but alter these locations in precaution. He has a farm but none of the pre mutated seed varieties we kept in our freezer of spite before quarantine. I don't ask how he got the white powders just like he doesn't how I got the piglets. He also has clandestine sasafrass, chinchona, shungite, and yarrow stalks, a regular pharmacopeia."

But that sounds more like 2021, spike protein, graphene oxide, nano clots and forced vax. Try to ride a bus without. 2020 preoccupied war against HCQ and obliterated it. 2021 took up the insurgent ivermectin which wiped out the virus in India.
The year 2020 progresses into spring with increasing rumors, media in denial, medical bulletins, and proliferate recipes, but gets rolling in April. We have to bear along the the liquefacting language of stylists and cockroach hustles to prepare for what follows. Events occur in symbolic form. Things that happen in the same place and time have integrity just from the flow of reports. Individuals are identified by initial. Pharmacological herbals touting elderberry, usnea as a kind of general treatment of disease, and Chaga occur.

See Spot Run

What do you call something you don't know what it is, that goes back and forth, part rhinoceros part real. That rhino is Ludwig's who would not not see. Which thought can only be understood by one who already has it.

I didn't make much of this until I saw the rhinoceros myself. It ran across the paino in my study. Then it appeared in a clay form which exists still today, but too big to photograph on the keyboard as I wanted. Also part of the horn broke off when I was moving it around. It hit the door frame, but I snow superglued back on, which goes well with the beaded shino on the head. To the rest of this word-world, "whereof one cannot speak and must be silent" the meta narrative speaks. So the world is not everything in the case.

Wittgenstein bought Tolstoy's gospel in WWI, the only book in that Polish bookstore, and carried it in his pocket throughout those years, but it did not include the passage of Romans 8:26 that "the Spirit makes intercession for us with groanings that cannot be uttered." This utterance is the symbolic purpose of the meta narrative. Tolstoy did allow however "when I, as the spirit of truth, shall be in you, you will not always know that I am there. Sometimes you will, and sometimes you will not, hear me" (Danish Peace Academy, September 2007, (63).. Our purpose is to hear, pretty much like Ransom's buddy, Andrew MacPhee needs in *That Hideous Strength*

Now the absence of a rhino in the Trinity College lecture hall—is harder than proving its presence. In search of this rhinoceros, Wittgenstein travels to Iceland and Norway. Visions of rhino haunt him in the trenches of the First World War and on his secret mission to Soviet Russia and when he said. "what we cannot speak about we must pass over in silence."

Not to compare such a great work towering as the shadow of Babel cast six miles and more depending on the angle of the sun, a meta narrative must be at great length at dusk and dawn, a building by that calculation 7100' tall, three and a half times the present tallest building, the shadow of events that creep so far imaginatively as to be a metaphor of space reflecting earth. It sounds like an antenna, but misstated. For how long must a shadow be to cast a building six miles high to picture the shadow of current events, a strength-lykke metafiction, a meta narrative, meta-reality in symbols that people face who enter the valley of the passengers of Ezekiel in 2020 told as a daily journal.

The skeleton of this work is comprised of entries made more or less daily before and during the onset of Covid-19 2020 to see if thoughts before the event were prescient in symbol or in fact. That was the way a *Calendar* of Poems broke its American year in half between the myth and the real in 1973. The first six months were of 600 years, the last six months the final decades of the 20th century. Prescience is not predictive programming to condition pop mind. *Unlocked* (2017) asks, "Washington will do what exactly? Legalize what's needed for the next time. Forced isolation of all contacts. Quarantine camps and the troops to secure them. Real-time access to private medical records."

Remember, in the first days and weeks of 2020, what is coming has not yet arrived. So take the record, impending or not, as what might have been on our minds before.

The beginning market of the Covid pandemic had three Phases. One and two were gone by April. Phase three was an aftermath, repetition and change. Basic woodsmanship says that when lost the subject should immediately sit down and listen for clues of direction. In the waiting here, among the incidental trivia of contact with the gods, *Finnegan's Wake*, ceramics of light, the zen mind, cockroach hustles, viral genomic clusters, archetypes, Chaga, usnea, CHQ, Pied Cow, antifa, and lockdown, we find a case of someone who actually gets and treats Covid,

The struggle here is with a pathogen, not a pathos. The pity and fear the spectacle stirs is only worth mocking in limericks published on Twitter, which we have done. Our retrospective has no explanation as to how we got to where we are, how government and medicine were so late to address the problem and how they declared war on their own science.

Some recipe and diagnosis is included here too. The narrator contracted the thing about March 20 and in the course of treatment far worse than any previous lung cold bronchitis, for six weeks took treatment with the pharmacology known *before the vaccine*. When Covid became a pandemic absolute the series of small steps a person could take to ease their suffering were forbidden. These are delineated here, if forgotten and denied. Information presented from the present is put into brackets [ ] while at the same time the narrative is mesmerized in the work of collecting and editing for publication a work called Pied Cow Now, and Guapa Pop, fictions the vein of Swift and Nathaniel West.

The manuscript edited here is a found document of past deliriums left to molder its vintage like all the other files over decades. So this has to be treated as found writing from another time and place, but amplified in the present to explain understanding. As such, when the editor cleans and tightens there is no feeling of a right to delete anything except personal matters, leaving what was gathered before to vex and perplex, but that is the nature of the work. To edit further is to prevent its prescience, which in the present seems fictional not situational, and if it ever becomes situational, we will all regret, but that is no reason to deny it may be true before the fact, and if true, let us take steps to overcome. Consider it as proof of Psalm 46, Shakespeare's psalm, the most popular of my scholarly writing,

It's not easy to know when information is skewed against lnowledge. There is a further layer above or below the fact we have no other way to figure out if its mere existence is impossible.

But here, impossible means simply altering time and space. Physics and geography compare to the classical shrines and anti-shrines of the Renaissance heaven, earth and hell (in the *Inferno, Faerie Queene, Paradise Lost*) where time and space, fictionally seen, symbolize forced micro-second nano openings between dimensions for us. Multiple simultaneous layers of time permeate political life. In a stratagem of opposite controls, Prince Charles bemoans populism and compares it to the Nazi state when the Windsor family was the most pro-Nazi of all Europe.

We humor this disability inherited from Hegel to speak of two sides that are opposites. We cannot speak of two sides of a quantum, for a quantum has four. On the 3D side the facetious is the real. That means that information is a deception. When Obama says Americans should be alarmed at Russian hacking they should be alarmed at Obama hacking. These reversals demolish the popular mind with fear, and are meant to, whichis done on every level and speed using the Adibatic Quantum Computer (AQC) of D-Wave.

Given: it is not true that a model of a "real world" runs in sentient Quantum a duplicate reality computing each morning each person among 7 billion "nodes." This can only be true of the 3D mainstream anesthetic. Chicanery had other means in renaissance Italy and England without quantum computing, but we can only accept such things are possible by trying one impossible case.

So does the wolf really lie down with the lamb? Wasn't that the lion? Intrusions like this are possible where the world and people vibrate at higher and lower rates. Anybody who figures out how to fix (freeze) the vibrations alters them, stops them. A car revving outside the door alters your world. Whether alterations come from colliding particles at CERN or from isolation (freezing) of particles in the quantum computers that govern them is moot. Quantum computers send information (combinatoral equations/problems) into another dimension to get an answer/solution back from such unknowns. This makes human culture obsolete.

Alternative realities ripple the globe to create reality for each person as within a river, a "mirror" of their entire Pop or OoP world, which means by means of immersion, POP means both population and the popular cultural anesthetic.

Names are substituted with waivers (avatars) in Sentient World Simulation to outwardly express these inclusions and occultations of text and belief. These are open to programming cause and effect and program predictive algorithms. The "questions" and answers, expressed in combinatorial optimization, are sent through the nano portal to identify optimal targets for alteration in the world algorithm when the answer is returned. This means you see what the algorithm wants you to see and only that [unless!] The cause of change in the 3D world disappears, but the alteration remains. Imposed from without, not from within, the results observed in the Experiments are received through asking:

>Which items and subjects should be altered for best Effect?
>What alterations are noticed by POPulation and to what extent?
>What reactions will this cause and what communication of effects?

Dimensions are altered by *immersing* their aquarium *in another* via a pulse 2 dilution refrigerator. Its creators like to call it an "altar to an alien god" so describe it as a "giant black monolith" of 10x12ft. It sounds like those obelisks found in wild Utah desert. This super refrigerated black box generates close to Absolute zero and pulses once a second, like a heartbeat. Its makers love to pretend it is alive. Its chip, the size of a thumbnail, accesses 2 mutually exclusive states at same time (standard quantum particle and wave), which states are identical except for value of a qubit. In Quantum Computing, each qubit doubles, 2^{500}, 2 to the 500, doubling the number of qubits each year. WARNING: you have to believe all this, and that science is a higher power because it is the nature of intelligence to deceive.

>The more intelligent the entity the larger its neocortex therefore the more likely its deception.
>(maxim from *Liespotting*)

Call therefore the Mandela Effect a Quantum Computing Artificial Intelligence that alters data. The portals that outwardly express these inclusions and occultations of text and belief are predictive algorithms. Corruption of Text in the Palimpsest

As data is altered in texts in books, designs of art and iconic moments, memory becomes the last impediment to alternation. Beyond the altered continuum the lion still lies down with the lamb in memory, but not in the text, to cite the most obvious example of Mandela portals in quantum substitution, which now reads wolf for lion. Literature is naive, art superfluous to these techniques. Memory is then outside the machined and Mainstream text. When written texts are corrupted tradition persists. The loss of this memory is what Zarathustra observed in Pied Cow, so where and how memory is stored is the interest of a new oral age. The corruption of text made invisible or changed also profoundly revisits and affects the layers of palimpsest. There is a negative proof among the latest Yahoo to condition the tribe where ten trivial instances of this are given to disproof the "false memory syndrome" on the authority of an ASU prof, but it proves the opposite. Forget Darth Vader and peanut butter, consider the lion and the wolf.

The cure for this alternation is memory, if there are people who remember the prior state that cannot be erased by combinatorial equation. They can only be made to doubt. This memory of a text that once existed but no longer does, beyond being impossible, is susceptible of evidence however in parallel written expressions of it beyond the altered text. So saying I have one of these myself in a text, *A Poetical Reading of the Psalms of David* (1985), in a comment on Psalm 23, where the lamb does lie down with the lion, the same as it does in Blake's poem, *Night*, where even if the footnote cites the changed *Isaiah* 11.6, that cries wolf, Blake writes:

And there the lion's ruddy eyes
Shall flow with tears of gold,
And pitying the tender cries,
And walking round the fold,
Saying, 'Wrath, by His meekness,
And, by His health, sickness
Is driven away
From our immortal day.

'And now beside thee, bleating lamb,
I can lie down and sleep;
Or think on Him who bore thy name,
Graze after thee and weep.
For, washed in life's river,
My bright mane for ever
Shall shine like the gold
As I guard o'er the fold.'

The important thing here is how memory is an antidote for alternation in this particular case but also in more general cases such as the three hundred year history of a family through all the trials of war, disease, suffering and death, nobly done where the elder gives this gift of memory to the younger, where the birthrite and culture for the child to have identity is protected until maturity. Families inherit a particular genome and experience which if known allays modern fears. If you know of those who made the voyage, survived the landing, settled the land, lived through the Revolution, the Civil War, the ice age, the pestilence of 1918, WWI, WWII, navigated the 60s assassinations, the mills, the universities, the corporations and the computer age, these histories can comfort even as you differentiates in the knowledge dispersed, for there is no testing taken you but such as is common to man, but God is faithful and will make a way to escape so you will be able to bear it.

This Roster of American Families is a testing ground of American history and political theories like the Fourth Turning. All the social dynamic of media listed lettered generations Z, M, X is intended to make them generic, leave them adrift without a ground of being. This ground exists in the ten generations and more here, 1717-2021. By close readings of agriculture and social practices we can judge the impact of the Revolutionary War sweeping over Germantown and out to Worcester, and of the Civil War by Andrew Mack's long walk home from the draft board just in time to attend the birth of his twins, of the coming mini ice age with the Maunder (1645-1715), and the Dalton (1790 to 1830) sunspot minimums on agricultural practices, buildings, barns and cemeteries, the fear of immigrant populations, assimilation practices, pandemics like the Spanish Flu of 1918 which add to Benjamin Rush's accounts of Yellow Fever of 1793, computed with the language diversities by the prejudice against German peoples all along to WWI, II and following. Social practices encompass also the creation of institutions of schools, cemeteries and orphanages from the start in that region outside Philadelphia, settled by Mennonites who were assisted by Hans George Reiff in the founding. Gifts recorded on the first page of the Skippack Alms Book by his wife Anna for the building of a meeting house of that time in the 18th century connect in a long arc to Aunt Elizabeth Reiff, first female elder in her Presbyterian assembly, going on the roof of city hall in downtown Philadelphia to watch for planes in 1942 in the twentieth. These histories go from the draft exercises of the War of 1812, to Philip Mack, would-be second lieutenant and his brother Harvey Mack, conscientious objector serving as an ambulance driver in France, who actually got to the war in France in WWI and remained, working as a carpenter for the Quakers in its reconstruction, but his brother Philip enlisting as second lieutenant just as the war ended did not serve. Segue to the black out curtains in the childhood of AE Reiff in WW II in Philadelphia, to duck and cover exercises in schools, and because every family grows by the accretion of marriage, added to his history marriage with a woman whose father, Carl Carlson, was a waist gunner in a B17 with 24 missions before his plane was shot from the sky and he served 11 months in German prison camps till war's end. If you scratch the surface of any of these lives you can find remarkable events, testings and trials. As every grand solar minimum is associated with 7.0-8.2+ earthquakes as well as eruptions, seismic events and extreme weathers, how to prepare for these and what to expect in infrastructure damage, to keep safe amid crop losses *and intensifications* takes a lot of air out of those dire threats when we see *how these* ancestors thrived. Is it necessary to say they were people of character?

How that character did or did not fare in the midst of paradigm shifts and points of view is paramount. Over 300 years from 1717 to 2021 there have been plenty of shifts of fashion too, from whether to button a coat, drive a car or wear a mask, get a cell phone, get a vax, but the people themselves continue to have been farmers, if you call farming being family practice docs and teachers, and traders who live by their wits, if you think that's what business execs do, and speculative philosophers. The character of these people resisted the philosophy of the world entering their thoughts. They favored *The Wandering Soul* and Arndt's *True Christianity* as encouragements of inner life. Presumably Mennonites still suspect technology in some degree but resisting a does not make "a chosen and separate people!" If Mennonites who charge that the world acts like Mannequins are prophetic to the extreme, mimicking is exactly what Mennonites model to the rest of the wired world, just like they wore wooden knives in their belts in Switzerland to mock murder. Even if they're no longer Mennonites, like attracts like, and the genome, even shorn of faith retains vestiges of these attitudes in the way they protect their children. So we track here too the process of assimilation that has been attempted on every tribal, ethnic group besides the English, which in the end is taken for the modern, a dilution of the culture.

This is part and parcel of the where DARPA advertised for writers to figure out how "narratives," oral stories, speeches, propaganda, books, can interdict, supplant and counter with "better" messages in the public mind, that is, how they could learn to lie better. This is also called hijacking, and is one strain of the Wm. Burroughs' language virus "from outer space" of totalitarian systems used for control. Understand however, that that very statement is a virus. Burroughs used to load his shotgun and fire at targets to design art. He learned to cut up typed sentences and hand written, and put parts willy nilly together and this was composition. He is doing outwardly in this what the mind can do inwardly but at gargantuan speeds beyond comprehension. The mind can grasp and comprehend simultaneous waves and depths of this ocean and hold for contemplation the way a first baseman holds the ball in his glove after the catch, snug, complete. Then he takes the ball out and throws it and the glove is empty. This occurs too with the mind which has at best partial memory of what just happened. Holding it in the mind, stasis, would prevent the next catch. When Agamben says "the very matter-- or the potentiality-- of thought (*la materia stressa o la potenza del pensiero*") is of *language* being thought, not *thought* being thought, is completely wrong. Language is not thought, has nothing to do with thought unless you debase thought into a counterfeit of itself. Language is not either a good translation of thought, even if language, rather speech, is the hallmark of intelligence.

We can have no record of thought. Thought exists on a wholly other plane from language. Whatever the thought is, the language is not, but that does not deny that the language is something. It is like turning a cartoon into a TV ad. The cartoon is what the mind retrieves of thought, the TV ad is language. Whatever it is, language is known. It is a sound signal with deep structures that can be synthetically reproduced. There is no record of thought at all. What passes as the thoughts of great thinkers like Wittgenstein is language. This being said is further complicated by all the false language that passes for true expression. These abound. What is false language? Expropriated. Language used for some other purpose, for commercial purposes. *Media speech, entertainment speech* per se is language drained of meaning, where words become nonsense, untruth, falsity, and purposefully so. This theft, or expropriation, makes language into deceit with all its trappings to be unmasked, for Language, communicates everything, both true and false, in other words *language against itself.*

This permeates every science and is the essence of art. DARPA cannot grasp for a minute that its notion of language is like Doktor Kurt Unruh von Steinplatz, of William Burroughs fame, **a virus.** Let us advance our appreciation of false language by seeing it as a scute, a shell, of troglodytes whose leather shells scupper an alternate false universe. This serves as Burroughs' virus from alien space. But it is a universe not above, but below ours, of the Qlippot, the metaphorical "shells" surrounding holiness. Compare the chaff around the corn of wheat. Literally "Peels," "Shells" or "Husks" represent impure spiritual forces (which have been taken as the material world. But to grasp language as a rung in the physical-spiritual tug of war takes it out the concern for mere language here. Language is a virus of thought. The true redeemed spiritual nature of a man is however worth finding out). That is, the Qlippot anatomical counterpart would be the physiological inner throat structure, the hyoid bone altered, which takes us back to where include large scale systems for language understanding, information extraction, and machine translation, as well as computational linguistics, pretended as the reconstruction of ancient language. What indeed are we speaking? One of the best known results shows that human grammars could be learned by statistical method. What other way was there? Answer: Vertical retraction, mandibular debasement, pharyngular twists. Anomalies that impacted skull structures and jaw formation, oral vs. literal dissociates at the skull base, orthognathous vs. prognathous. It's all in the effort at predictability. Call it scientific method where Faulkner is generated on demand, or who do you like, but not of course those who do not yet exist. The DARPA virus of look-a-likes cannot copy a future state, even if it knows it exists, like the Last Judgment, only mimic it. Hence there are current one hundred thousand interpretations of *The Revelation of* St. Hohn. We know from this that the purpose of science is to prevent any new existence, to control the experiment and predictability. By looking away. The virologists of control select out and bend in anything unreal to make it seem real.

Let's get the difference for the moment. Agamben says that language is "the rendering common of what one thought of as one's own" (181). But is it? I hear language and take it for a fact in itself, not a conveyor of meaning, not some other that it pretends to be, but an overwhelming social fact.

People work at this riddle that language is an infallible lie detector from all sides. This is *not* research which includes a grasp of current scholarship on the subject. All that scholarship is corrupt, a rehash, a rethought of the very control mechanisms of language drained of meaning is an "expropriation of language" for commercial purposes, *for scholarship is commerce.*

Probing beneath the surface of language events reveals no true purpose, whether in the castles of Europe, asteroids, or government. We haven't found out anything except the fantasies of thought mules speaking, mice singing and men on a factory line assembling severed heads. They are metaphors, but the mules, the mice and the men are sublime. The thing at issue here is love of immersion in language. *Language reveals itself in this immersion and discovers and discerns the revelation of language.* **The Word that is a discerner of the thoughts and intents of the heart.**
Out of the abundance of heart the mouth speaks.

"The problem is how to liberate [the means] of communication so it does not again fall prey to the theft of this isolation and separation" (182), but language is already liberated, literate/liberate in itself. It is rather deceit that must be shorn. Something deeper than language is at play if language seems so manipulated against itself. Language still reveals this deceit in all speakers *in common.* "Thought finds itself for the first time, today, confronted by its task without any illusion and without any possible alibi" *(182)...forfeiting every imaginary integrity...of home, race, class."* So saying there is *"no biological destiny that humans must enact or realize (Coming Community, 43).* This could be bad news for evolutionists *and* transhumanists! De la Durantaye says what everyone thinks, "the impoverishment of political discourse, and the increasing reliance on spectacular situations, sound bites" (182) is a crisis. But there are always crises. Wasn't *Crises the name of Antigone's father? [!]

He's saying don't get off the bus yet. The destruction by the global that "empties traditions and beliefs, ideologies and religions, identities and communities" (Coming Community 83) must be carried through to its utter unclothing, "not remaining unveiled in its nothingness [deceit speech]" (183).

Human ethos is "human speech itself" [in Language and Death] and a social relation. Language, death, society are functions of each other and must "become transparent to themselves." Thus philosophy is the attempt "to become conscious of the meaning of the fact that human beings speak" (180). The experience of "language itself" is a joy even if you do not remember acquiring it. You have heard it done in children and know intuitively the language universals that exist in the child's acquisition. The mama and papa of our being are also the first sounds of the child. These fundamental identity factors overwhelm philosophy, but language itself, sound and meaning connect as cells connect to tissue. Language is sewn into a person, tailored with age and becomes the expressive marvel of its being to no purpose other than to be language. That is language itself is "being conscious of the fact that human beings speak." The first human concern is *the fact itself of speaking*, the *event of language.*

So there's no need for some researcher to uncover the occult thing or event. The hidden is already revealed in the event of language. The hypothetical person who can hide language and its ultimate revelation of themselves would be a demigod. For language is the revelation of everything.

--The future walks through the past and the present and leaves a trail. The past is costumed, dressed up. The present is shadowy with sightings of the future, but when the future arrives it too is dressed with what we think we know. Dress up the new, but it is costumed in the old. It looks like we don't know any of them. We think we know and feel the present but it is gone fast. We forget the present and our memory of it, which is what we call the present, but by then is the past. If you were to catch the future walking on the roof of the present built on top of the past it might appear as a series of decisions, timings. To post date your losses to the next new year, so gain equals loss, is a technicality of book keeping, but it is also a bow to Rome the way government counts time as if *January were really the first month of creation.* But it is the fourth!

How to answer any of these dysfunctions in the natural is impossible therefore a kind of meta symbolic meaning emerges in the revision of 132 where they are reviving the heads in the vats of Che Guevarra. That is how to answer the travesties of the virus , its vax and the extermination syndrome to emerge from is answered thus, the heads will roll, that's in the Bible you see, the heads will roll. Followed by Lockerie and the fgov ending in the research of the Marfa sightings, the explositons.

So having come this far we don't' ask what is the rhinoceros in the room lest we be told it is germ warfare on a global scale leading a mass extinction event. When the meta narrative gets to 9/11/20 one year shy of the Taliban severing America from Afghanistan, all will have been done according to Hoyle.

7/1/20 Q they trade so cruelly on hopes and dreams for deliverance, redemption to hold out such false and specious claims.
Pity,the rabbit Privilege, whiteness, racism, gender freedom polyamory, dope and beneath it all the oddult.
Priyamvada Gopal: her dissertation, filled with networks--

--Adrienne Rich's resonant phrase "compulsory heterosexuality", I think we should talk about "compulsory coupledom Insurgent Empire
 Knee cap an English prof on colonialism
– The Politics of Passion: Women's Sexual Culture in the Afro-Surinamese Diaspora. In Wekker fundamentally challenges Dutch racial exceptionalism by undermining the dominant narrative of the Netherlands as a "gentle" and "ethical" nation, showing how the denial of racism and the expression of innocence safeguards white privilege. Philosopher Baukje Prins wondered if Wekker was not alienating her "allies" by asserting that every white person in the Netherlands was a racist class, race and gender--founding member of "Sister Outsider", an Amsterdam-based, literary circle for lesbian black women Afro-Surinamese Dutch focused on gender studies and sexuality in the Afro-Caribbean. White innocence: central paradox of Dutch culture: the passionate denial of racial discrimination and colonial violence coexisting alongside aggressive racism and xenophobia first Dutch settlement, a trading post established by Nicolaes Baliestel and Dirck Claeszoon van Sanen in 1613. Suriname was long inhabited by various indigenous people before being invaded and contested by European powers from the 16th century, eventually coming under rule in the late 17th century. While is the official language of government, business, media, and education, an English-based is a widely used. Planters' treatment of the slaves was notoriously bad—historian wrote that "man's inhumanity to man just about reached its limits in Surinam" Runaway slaves established a new and unique culture in the interior that was highly successful in its own right. They were known collectively in English as located on the Guiana shield.

Gloria Wekker – Beyond White Innocence ——conclusion she is addressing stereo types rather long passed, the white picket fence nuclear one dog bunch. She worked in government. Resorts to Adrienne rich, compulsory actual sexuality

The first premise of racism is Caucasians fighting for blacks. Students always asked if I was going to write a book about them. But I was only there to serve.

Almost made it unscathed at the dentist but he asked what I thought of covid and I said what to you, and he blathered so the short it I told him it was a bioweapon splice of sars and aids producing change good and bad and if he didn't know that too bad. To m I teen said the result would be the activation of fema camps to put alol the ex ary vets who will resist the fall of America without t trump and I expect to be among them. My gums hurt now.

Vist from aey and J. He says a rootbound. Puberty the divide

7/4/20 counter revolution calls to civil war. Alex jons back on youtube to spur it on, by proxy with General Shepherd and others, of zero hedge buying guns.
 All sorts of people moving inland which in absence of gov't order must provide their own. Which effects were the design of the op.
The sun shall not smite thee by day nor the moon by night sun smiten

7/5/20 woke with shorty by my bed and Scion in the hall. Taking safe haven from fire works last night.

--He insisted on his rights faculty as an en loco parentis and they reveled in oedipal hunger and tried to eat him. The Weinstein brothers are the cause, like their ilk of they whole thing. Firset they foster it with the money of their father, elitos, then they queer it by some thought of the first amendment-commandment, then they declare it a war against civilization, a toppling of the Apsu, they don't say, but hat's what civilization is. Surely they belong to be mommies in Egypt ,as educators who argue equity irrational, but faced with evolutional biology as irrational become irate. Appearing before congress he worked hard to make this crisis. Evolutionary biology is a scam. If you think your views are sacroscant…otra vez Benjamin Whorf,

Return current sheet, Boschivitch, three gorges dam

Ygdrasil the white blue pot in the yard

"It's time to Crash land the plane into the control tower." You get the drift. This Dante Futurm was a fiction demolition of that academic system, which got out just before the virus and hasn't been spinor when the Euclidean space is subjected to a slight

So this intellectual dark web is like a Netflix, Joe Rogan, Eric Weinstein, managing director at Thiel Capital. even the evergreen king, the doped psychologist Jordon Peterson all of them hopped up intellects, except Bret's discovery of the mouse telomere, but failed fate. All the intellectual coverup, of academia, they are it!(rotation.n seen since.

7/6/20 bereshith barah in the beginning was the foundation of the world, but it was marred. Barah without form and void.

So Caucasians are doing to white people what they did to black people.

7/7/20 the role of a provocateur has not changed. Attach to group, provoke a disturbance, when order attempts to restore inflame the group by having it attacked by authority to disarm authority to radicalize the group, except what they mean sincerely the agent means cynically, for the agent has no moral or conscience and will literally do anything to inflame the cause. Who are these? Where do they live. The intellectual dark web is perfect example of agent provocateur

7/8/20 A is such a good sales man, skewing, selecting prejudicing the facts I think he has sold himself. Become a nomad between states, like with what he said of schools with kids separated, a stereotype

All these lookalike antifas black and white revolutionaries like Ibram Kendi are the lookalike human surge of the hybrid babies Jacobs writes of

7/9/20 PBA auction sold one for around $500 and others have sold from $350 to $850. My guess is an asking price online should be about $1200-1500.

Torture imprisonment divination corruption aymond chandler mickey spillane

7/10/20 fauci means jaws. Indigo children are the antifa.

7/12/20 d. of Judy D. separate from J. twice! In full

Sweet Dreams (Are Made of This) Some of them want to abuse you

There is no black without white and vice vesa, but there are more or less shades of beige and not black and white at all. Truly black and whites are rare. maintains an interest in iron, cobalt, copper carbonate, feldspar fired in reduction atmospheres and otherwise,

7/13/20 --shungnite in the soil

Fafnir was a drago
He's a bore
He overflowed in micro chips
He wasn't poor
When he wore his helmut
On his head
Fafnir's brain was leaking
Into less
Fafnir was a dragon
And he tried to make that something

7/14/20 the pulled down the statue of Cain in Glasgow yesterday.
- Got to hold James on a short visit by aey. Talked of tattle tales

7/15/20 Dream-irrational anger, civil discord, dream of tennis club awards, me saying some clubs don't even have the prizes advertised and others are worthless trinkles anyway, not like MP where they give you tennis gear, a towel. Many tables in room with tall windows the Take Two table with Linda Brewster says the next time they play me to look out, very hostile as I leave the room.

7/16/20 there are some serious continuing issues of anger and rejection cooking. She just drove off this night. When I called she said I had told her to cut the lawn and disrespected her after, something about putting a cement block on top a sunflower root and my sarcasm. So that comment about checking with the boss to Sabrina should have been a tip of revolt?

7/18/20 Processing discord: 2. this a.m outside the wall pruning the jungle of lantana etc away for ironwood at 5.30 this kid along the path says he will help me, I say nothing, he says he' do it for free. I say beat it.

--The electron Periscope.
--ACCEPTANCE BY PAROUSIA OF A TRUE LIGHT THAT LIGHTS

7/19/20
mike mew, growing your face

7/20/20 Naked Athena" of Portland
Elementary langu school controls
Evolution jaw

7/22/20 today I finished Pied Cow I think. Guapa pop lived in pied cow as much as pied cow lived in pop they were cities or states with cites and states. Was the wold guapa and sate cow or was the world the long ooooo of its cry. We want to know.
So now you've been to Pied Cow we wish you well. This constitutes the record in the pot. We don't know what else to say if you wish that it were not. *Were it not that the time approaches when more distinguished recollections would be based on real events. The mathematical structure of plantation reprise to emphasize the text, choric rephrase, head voice, heart voice, weight of vocal breath on the registers, forward produced enunciation of consonants, mordents and slurs– range, tone, color, pitch and registry breaks, such phonation as appears as if the bottom, middle and top 'voice' have timbre and quality.*
this evil will be systematically opposed by men of greater powers, and with far

7/23/20 enmity between thee and the woman
--Gassing the mayor of Portland
--Speaking of excellence A you don't remember the significance your first and last matches with andy nugyen and jamere Jenkins, for you qualified in and with and against them both to play in the very top realms of usta competition, just like a blue chip, but you were only a four star. The effort of how you got there treasure as much as the results achieved, so realize what you can achieve in spite of y.

will require active measures to flush the virions, particles, & genomic debris from your system. IMO - the MOST studied medicinal mushroom, CHAGA, provides the antiviral efficacy required & ability to consume long term. Dual extracts daily to flush out virus
gas Portland. The jews gas the nazis

-Farrell's book on mccarthy if I have any world view at all about states and internationalse it's Ring-a-round the rosie, A pocket full of posies,Ashes! Ashes!
We all fall down. The theory states that it is in reference to Pagan myths and cited a passage which states, "Gifted children of fortune have the power to laugh roses, as Freyja wept gold." It claimed the first instance to be indicative of pagan beings of light. Another suggestion is more literal, that it was making a "ring" around the roses and bowing with the "all fall down" as a.

The invariable sneezing and falling down in modern English versions have given would-be origin finders the opportunity to say that the rhyme dates back to the Great Plague. A rosy rash, they allege, was a symptom of the plague, and of herbs were carried as protection and to ward off the smell of the disease. or was a final fatal symptom, and "all fall down" was exactly what happened

7/24/20 had a great walk in a light rain tonight

7/25/20 2.20 am item awaken yesterday with sound of tv going off or phone message but tv was mute and phone unplugged. Item: awakened now with high pitched sound like release of steam. Dream: gate left open a troupe of kalakackes ner-do wels invade, one with gun, horsing around, take occupation of house and grounds more or lesss, I am passive alert?- which let the environment of the discord dream a week ago be noted. Resolve Peace and change the lights.

Heard from aey first thing on way to wrok. He came in just as I was ssaying to Pat in bed that he that will save his life must lose and he that would lose his life must find it so that all love and service frow from Him and not ourselves. Hen Anne called and we caought up, told her of the world of Pied Cow etc. then Rob and Cyn called and we went over children boycotts, Minneapolis, Portland, the mind shift, covid, racism. Then last and, loud connection, manic all about moving.

7/26/20 In their attempts to be sperman to be immoral they practice all the arts of meditation and drug not knowing that life and death are the same, these are the immortalites that need a cure.

7/30/20 Forgiveness. Outlaw. Pat's mom wanted her to marry in the ruling class, shriners, masons, instead she took a poet.

Learned how to start my car today. It had post covid osss, not been driven in 10 days in 110 f heat. Tried last night, dead, at 11 on clock. Tried again, dead. This morn before putting the truck battery in, went out the door, but prayed for it to start, I mean I said, Father thank yoyu for starting my car. It started so I took if for a spin.

Radio Show Giants and the Little Tykes Live: 8.37-12.47

7/31/20 got up early to pied clown, memories of phila Christmas 2004 trip with aey, then of driving from Charlestown after last visit with pat…then a and a and their combative wives (at aey's?) and a leaves hurt, lots of kids, friends of somebody one boy in the back yard humming I join him we sing gospel song, he hugs me, later shawna goes home aey stays but his ideas are skewed badly three times. I see one eye is rayed out aflare, the left, I get pat, give him half aspirin, talk to him as Pat brings a black and whte and color mirror so I can see the problem, wake up I realize what I have seen.

Thought Disorder Thinking Process Abnormalities in Schizophrenia
From Distractibility to Incoherence "formal thought disorder"

disorganized behavior and *speech* and includes ... to questions with unrelated answers, say *illogical* things, or shift topics frequently.

Tangential *speech* or tangentiality is a communication disorder in which the train of thought of ... social responses, and a deterioration in pragmatic abilities (including appropriate *eye* contact as well as topic maintenance

disorders that cause disjointed thoughts, a collapse or sudden stop in thought process, randomly spoken words

"disordered thinking" is mild and this often results in *distractibility.*5

A person can begin talking about one thing and then completely shift topics before completing his or her sentence. This is often due to nearby stimuli that interfere with the thought process.

For example: "I moved to New York after college ... what are you eating for lunch?"

connections with one another and become disconnected and disjointed.8 This illogical thinking is called *derailment* or *"loose"* associations.

Clang associations

--So I took the Sub for a battery drive charge and got tail gated by a volvo on mcdowell for pulling out, a long way in front, and speeding up, but they were angry. Need to relearn cognitive driving

Finished and printed proof copy of Pied Cow .

8/1/20 Letter to publishers. You may rub your eyes to see this book a sober certainty in the free and brave thought of Pied Cow. There is such a sense of propriety of incomparable things said absurdly well that can only compare Pied Cow to the Gettysburg Address soaring to declare the goals of nation to whose Western wits grow fat and mean.

8/2/20 Dream, late for dinner at the Wilsons, much to do hurt feelings, like with Ch or any upper class people whose lives you might save, but with whom there is no easy rapport, a list of greats men from Dave Harvey, the Presbyterian. Elder to Alex Dunlap to Richard Foulkes and Carol Wilson involves the Eagles Nest sure, where once, twice there I felt urged to speak prophetically, but did not. Good thing, Wilson declared an unction from the front of the church that, "glory to God, I feel like I can raises it (the money) all by myself," and was de-eldered. I still had Grizzly Bear Wok to write.That's when we took them to dinner! Uneasy rapport because I walked among the poor, so to speak

-- Their wives manage their lives like a PR campaign always looking for angles against the opponent, meaning the opposite numbers. Neither married women have values even remotely resembling their own, so opposites attract. They continually downgrade the other, one can't bring the baby, and another, don't let her hold him.

-Casey Gerald says intersectionality includes planned parenthood abortions and selling body parts and climate change in the ice age to hybrids, then gender swapping when it shows itself the religion of the stars, the smooth and graceful ones who on the other side sound very agreeable in their views.—interview w/ Van Jones about a year or so ago.

When the 1% interviews the 1% to define the thoughts and aspirations of the 90 and 9,Yale and Harvard MBAs are banqueting neo Faucis in the new medieval religion of the talented and corrupt. Casey grew up in the privileged but traditional black society freer of pollution, but stopped it when his mother left. An authoritarian society is hard on women. But then Italian, German, Irish are the same with such old schools while the men are Carbon squatting, sandwiched between their wives prohibitions.

8/3/20
--I had friends in Limon among the longshoreman Jamaicans of the Pentecostal church of Anderson Indiana. We walked at night without streetlights in the dark. I preached a new creation to much mutual affection, like the Panamanian pastor I prayed with in the Annexo

8/4/20 The Jukes and the Kallikaks and the illusive dream of the middle class. The best plan is sleep as much as possible if you're from the Colony of Pastorius where endless checks and body plants are grist for artists buried in the floor. Pills for old age in the last days. The valley of the passers-through was closed. It collapsed at the fall of the *todaelde, which produced a backlog of bodies for ants along the scarab nexus. No wonder passengers held their nose. Beasts crept among fish, fowl and businessmen mosquitoes. Men shook their fists at the iPhone. Devices of hand and eye mythologemed escape to the Iron Room In-between, true children of the instant calculated prescient movement out of spots like fire in restaurants and supper clubs. Sweep the room, mark the exits, never sit publicly with a back to the door. Let's go, no questions, act. Grief counselors are available with burgers and toys.

The *Gogites* won't take a Googist seriously, which is why they made colonists take faerie pills and marched them oberbold to Gaul. Visions of awareness, risky neighborhoods protruding, not celebrating holy days, liberality held captive three nights in the belly of earth, it was a thriller of the lower worlds. Firings, destructions, closings, uprootings of coal and steel, the back severance of contracts, preferments, higher up fun guys of Gogol threw bon mot bottles at the tombs. Fall with rain, they dare. Thousands of workshop writers were trying to find this camp. *"Gyf donne strengra ofer hine cymþ and hine ofer-winþ, ealle his wæpnu, de he on-truwode, he him afyrþ, and todælþ his here-reaf."*"

* jadehelm

Valley of the Passengers

This is *Der stoff* of super colliders cozened open, impossible to reconnoiter, boundary stones of sculptures made like severed heads, *which fantasy of course starts out with arresting strangeness:* S*trangeness, report to base! There goes science in its secret labs. Of course, I in* *my timid body did not wish to have them in the neighborhood, intruding into my relatively safe world, in which it was, for instance, possible to read stories in peace of mind, free from fear* (Tolkien, *Tree and Leaf*). Paronomasia was present in those who passed the land, a play on words, to pun. Commissioners were appointed to search for bones. The notion that it stopped the nose or stench entombed beneath, suggested they were overrun while passing through. Both the searchers, in the case of stepping to elude, and the buriers, who turned faces away from their work, stopped their noses. "Passengers" or travelers were buried in such noisy tumult that afterwards made the valley bear the multitude's name. Sir Gawain's primary and secondary despoilation was incomplete.

I began to contemplate the psychological effect of masses of deaths from any causes like war to be left with those from pandemic as it turns out, but not even that, for these were extinction events that the valley of the passengers stood for, and allowed me to contemplate the real unthinkable event in current terms....

You will understand that it's hard to accept the time of these burials and start over. You will not ask while all this is being put together for the purpose of publication, why when I take a short nap in the middle of the night, I see in an unsought vision of large rolls of black plastic coffins on flatbed railroad cars. There are three insights of dreams and visions. The first is the dream house unconnected to any thought or experience and utterly fresh and symbolically delivered. The second is in the vestibule of dreams while exiting. Here many prompts are given which then lead to the truth of the unspoken within, but unknowing. Third are the thoughts and ratiocinations of plans as we do down the steps that up to the vestibule. This vision was from the first, the house of dreams. The idea is they unroll the black plastic coffins like black plastic bags and then turn them semi-solid for burial of bodies. I was poking the center out of one of these to climb through, make a hole in the middle like a leather doughnut. But of course millions of FEMA coffins are stockpiled at many sites, debunked as merely coffin liners.

That's why we write and also why colonists see themselves in the paradox, to have a thing but not know it, wait a long life for a thing to pursue it, do nothing but wait for the thing to renew it, do nothing but wait for the thing to undo it. Lives and minds drive what we don't know while we think we are doing something else, and for different reasons too, like moles fill in the entrance to their cave and write stone letters in shale below.

All this is the history of our lament, of the living who mourn the dead.

We have seen many things, but pay no attention, our ears are open, but hear nothing. These are reverse timpanis of Beethoven's 9th, Pick a phrase, invert it, splice at will. A drum becomes a word. A word becomes a boom echoing earthquakes. What hubris, to think that after a thousand generations, to say that both sides prevented this revelation. Who says there are two sides? Colonists underground and plain folk. The one to bring it about the other to dissolve, which thoughts compel the verse.

Adverbs come before nouns in the foyer like ballistic glass lacerations with Smart talk on the rug, ambiance, facts and then the door. Liqueurs, bracelets, chairs. Wittgenstein lifts his head on a pedestal at Airpark. Could that head speak it would say the colonist like a mouse is meant to be an experiment to save itself. But inside the colony, no-colony, to serve the greater cause, I cannot We assemble today therefore against this blind cosmick doctrine like Shiites, and have Nostradamus to thank, Nostradamus and Blake. St. John falls on all heads. The colonial underground is clearly not made to recognize. The moon, or Archuleta, take your pick. When the fgov fills in the harbor at night you can read It is an honor to join our brothers there. They come alive from, who only waits to be taken up, but here, now, when the angel looses its vial and Euphrates dries up like a fig, march the Kings of the east.

This is the land of analogue, Mt. analogue if you like, where the valley of Ezekiel the passengers and the deaths of God and MaGog, British and all, are analogues. How do you read it? It is the result of the unthinkable extermination scenario of the spike, the graphene and the nano bits in one.!

This utterance of language, root and alphabet, is the least spiritual power of the Sons. But the meaning is not in the sound, to look in the sound. The meaning is not in the syntax to look at the connections. The meaning is not in language, for the words, the languages were within the still voice that spoke. Indeed they sound like language, none or one or all, and what they say, these impossible words from the deep? "Et erit illa frenans transeuntes" make "a place there, a grave to be buried in; on the east of the sea," a valley through which travelers used to pass a sulfurous lake, allusion perhaps to the sea of Chinnereth, or Jarchi and Kimchi; a passage to the east of the same sea, where the multitude shall fall, but do not hold to the geography.

The reason for their being out of the way notices mountains once magnificent, Rome, Jerusalem, at their best, superstructures falling into rubble, parapets mixed with fountains, better than the organ meat and tissue towers where cardboard crumbled and gave way o dust. We give it that. These were real brick, marble and stone whose parts withstood demise. Not steel skeins tangled, but that's what they sent to China. The city was a paragraph, precognate rubble together, five sentences tangled in one, images broken and misplaced by cranes, except our cranes are accident and sound demolition which pull the parts out to reseat them and the like, the whole city rebuilt as it were, not that it ever existed, but if it didn't how did this mess end up on the ground?

You see the point that out of chaos must come order, as if it described the valley where they bury the army of the Grand general Antiochus, what remained after the fowls. Calmet takes the army defeated, "locum ibi sepulchrum." Starckius: "locum ubi sit sepulchrum." So R. Sol. Urbin. Ohel Moed, fol. 66. 2.((f) "et erit illa obturans transeuntes." These eddas we enjoy in Lindisfarne, Wycliffe, Tyndale, German, Scandinavian or English whereSea captains, gold cargoes, frankincense souls, multinational corps, blondes, City/Woman nations, Gilgamesh star with Ishtar as "the foul goddess" with bond traders, globe internats unmasked. *Alejandro-Nabucodonosor*, mountaintops and rivers, succubi *Christabel* now hold their hands and wait for them to ring. Uncapped pirate samurais with credit cards.

Landings

No one thought from the staging that the technological revolution was staged. "Facts," were broadcast with analysis of the "facts." You could say I came to the grave worlds to ask, "whose is this, which one is this?" Mummies of a thousand years, white to bone to understand the analogy with Maurois' *Tragedy in France* — possess the soul by Vichy confederates and propaganda – or *Why England Slept* — appease by fabrication and myth. New titles for quislings are *Global Science, the Alien Savior*.

The first Quakers of new prose took documentary form, gathered first hand, culled from sources. Literature factura was a lot like pouring a concrete foundation, prosthesis of flat folded sheets of the unspoken. Should words get a public burial? Authorities overruled. The idol of government held bodies responsible, buried beneath and got on, site of some secret. To bury something dead and gone came every word spoken.

The burial was secret because the kill. Watchman Lee used to call it dead Adam. The list of beliefs, poets of influence, heard and unheard, cried in vision to hear the same remixed. Cloud powers split words into sheets.

Like leaves blown into letters on the street, that spell things we do not want to know, I water and tramp the obvious. But word shells wash up. The sea paints pictures in the sand so fast words are futile. I am very busy. The sand is obvious. By the time you read this forest fires will be burning trees into sentences.

Inmates and police had common cells. Their brains were studied to promote robotic sources. Corporations, Universities, hospitals run the arches. Careerists, norm police provoke madness as class rights. The bosses pretend not to notice weekly instances of mutation in the malls. Hospicio Cabañas, built as an orphanage becomes a deconsecrateGaslit doubt is built here. make diseased brainshold trials. Psychopathic auto cut flash clip frescoes bloom and darken, crack and spall. It's certainly too much to believe public events staged. Evidence is an iridescent airbrush. Stagings are incomplete. The needs of further manipulation are a comfort. We are thrown out of the circle.

Arches

There is no obvious connection between these horizons and a series of dreams of arches I remember from the message of the leaves. A colored image of a nose bleeding among honeysuckle. That was under an arbor of bees flying. Yellow and white fragrant tubes. Coming toward me, my brother, blood flowing from his nose. I am four.

Another arch preoccupies the county home of Uniontown, PA. I visited at ten. Who visits an insane asylum at ten? A long whitewashed tunnel extended to either end. A padded door swung massively in on metal hinges. The inmates ranged outside the tunnel and in to stumble and moan. The path was elevated above its gutters so it could be hosed. I didn't smell anything but disinfectant. I am going down this tunnel. There is slobbering on both sides.

Now you see them hunting also in cemeteries at night with spades and boots. Radios, novels, microwaves seek to restore communication with lost powers. Flashlights look for turned earth, but Adam's was secret. were reduced to writing. A cry in the river of light, to write anything human in speech, to navigate a sea so warm the leather hides of the boat smoked on its stretched frames.

I landed just as the freeways were built, ordered my own dump trucks of dirt so children could slide down feet first as I did the original slag hills where I grew up. Houses here had been bulldozed to pavement. Excavation began by flood light at night. There were ringside seats all day. Leave came to walk the barriers, explore the pits, but not one artifact was found. Kmart, at 16th St and Roosevelt, yielded hundreds. We walked the freeway at Christmas that year, picnicked on the bridge over 24th St. before sliding down the berms of shale and dirt.

I lifted one of their dictionaries. *The Social Impact of Technological Slavery* — begins with the European Discovery of America. The new Indian replaced with social, political, commercial new worlds made room for psychics and glands. Discoveries overturned for murder. Ex-terrestrials bigger than Columbus enthroned King Pentagon. Like the arch angel, timing is all.
the invisible image.

8/7/20   Ryoji KOIE
Rod of light in David Paulidies missing, Lima OH

8/8/20 Guerilla warfare in Portland
Rake office grounds

8/9/20 Walter Herzog is a cinematic Bosch
Kids, dq, T. for open house

8/10/20 silver near 30. Fundamentals vs technicals what a people think its worth vs what it is.

8/13/20--T big grin from car.   That we shall abide in the house of the Lord forever meets in the resurrected body.

8/17/20 did Political Li and Fairtales yesterday. B wants to give the kids at 8 tomorrow for new inspection but told no he reschedules.

8/18/20 dreamed of discord, kicking people out, severing relations with crudeness, evil. I hope I get through the work this morn ok.

releasing chemicals into the air at levels that may pose health risks for people in the area. chemicals have gradually moved through the aquifer, tainting a source of groundwater that, if cleaned up, could someday help the fast-growing city meet its water needs. plume of contaminated groundwater, called the West Van Buren site, toxic cleanup sites since 1987. part of a larger polluted zone that stretches across 15 miles of central and west Phoenix, lawyers for the Roosevelt Irrigation District, who say the airborne chemicals may pose health risks in one of Phoenix's poorest areas. On the other side are city water officials and others who disagree with the district and argue the fight is really about a "water grab" — an attempt to take control of a groundwater source once it's cleaned up so that it can be sold for a profit to water-hungry cities west of Phoenix. trichloroethylene (TCE) and tetrachloroethylene (PCE) into the air. These volatile organic compounds, or VOCs, quickly become airborne once the water is flowing through the canals. plume of VOCs.

8/19/20 3 hrs at office palms etc dump-

Synopsis to Austin

A memoir based upon Austin 1968-1980 which shows how the writer got there and ho left has to do with poems composed in the Hill Country, discovery of the new world, and orphans all wrapped in these children being born and flying around. After Erik the Red, Sir Walter Raleigh became an example of new world fooling. Gold in Guiana, piracy and beheading, even more he, who like Erik the Red, lost his son in the new world, went over the sea with St. Branden. That answers what Raleigh says children were doing lifting pretty heads from pillowed beds at the tops of mountains.

The whole piece of this contradiction, some stated and open, as in Costa Rica, Fayetteville, baseball, grammar school, neighbors, cops and high school - where not? nobody's heard - where my Freudian, are you? - ends in its Summer. In the native Amerycan spring and summer, "The Snake," ought to tell us what we have in store in the *coming mist and fogbound bush*, allegories submerged within. I call it Paragorie. The trouble is that they are so deep and repressed, national memories as much as personal, *the snake is squeezing, his eye is teasing*. Not really kundalini, more a deceit of the *rush of dreams*, nightmares. *Run snake run*. If somehow these relations were shown we would see what has been projected in the making of the new world. Ameryca and America were always in conflict. America won. At least until the reversal. Don't you wait for it? In England the natives mock the standing stones. In Texas they bury them. It's all the same as blowing the tops off mountains, part of the America vision too, especially the last six months, September to February, 1950 to 2000. After 2000 the thing is academic.

I absorbed a lot of these antagonisms outside the U.S. in 1963, in Costa Rica, specifically and generally got the feeling from Nicaraguans that America backed the Somozas, from Panamanians that Canal was a worst insult, from San Blas Indians that I was the one to be feared. When the repute of a nation is visited upon its citizens later captured and tortured by

Taliban it makes the citizen know the apple pie. Not to speak of what the Bolivians, or those from Spanish Harlem had to say.

Yet at the same time the national oppositions that visited these privileges could not be denied. As I learned to spread the wealth a little people saw more the heart. Still in the world today, which I know from having taught scores of Jordanians, Kenyans, Nigerians at Bishop, where the worst antagonist apologized, said, Dr. Reiff we didn't know who you were, and add Israelis, Koreans at Texas - would you believe I taught Technical Writing for Foreign Students there at least twice because they heard I had taught blacks in the American south - Is that profiling?- or at Bishop College where the utmost moral authority came about 1982, give or take a year, when Maya Angelou and another poet spoke in the auditorium at Bishop College where we held faculty meetings and Dr. Lassiter would stand on stage and rub his belly as he spoke our responsibilities. I was happily at the back. Maya Angelou was no less outspoken as anytime and had a lot to say about the male white made class of oppressors of women and blacks. The only one represented that day to feel her arraignment, felix culpa me, did not disagree in the slightest with anything she said, but bore it then as much as 20 years before what those Latin American students thought of their American oppressors. I have no doubt her moral suasion and authority of life came from that time when she was raped at seven and after telling her uncle and the man was put to death, she did not speak for five years. She did not speak from the power of her words, so that when she did, it was with this great authority. I did not stay for the Q and A. Hearing her frank obsequies today at her passing, I ask anybody to understand the discomfort of representing the enemy.

There is a heavy sex to colonialism, to the army, navy and air force, and later the drones, a digital sex, *plastic USAs...on Army wheels...out west producing sex organs*. The image withers like a Cialis commercial, *snozzled, in pyknic profile*, as if America were a plastic statue on the dashboard of some spaceship held on with *suction cups that listen in to the beats of a heart*. So when you travel outside the country stay away from the natives or it will spoil your trip. I picked all this up by osmosis. It didn't help that I was reading the Grand Inquisitor at the same time. I would not have survived these disquisitions without the prior years of allowing the true leaven access to heart and mind. Not enough, never enough. So it was *American light, American phone*, American freedom, not light and freedom in themselves, the one species decreasing. Ruben Dario made that impression, *peppermint jelly exploding at night, Alexander, Alexander, Alexander-Nebuchadnezzar is white.* Naive, since the imperial has visited most of the kingdoms, states and nations of the world. But too harshly judged by the light of our worst acts? This Calendar wouldn't cross the water any more than embossed in asbestos on the outer shell of some spacecraft would be grokked by the Albigensians on Betelgeuse. Little still life bookmarks were paged into these satires, *a 1584 London maple chest saying, GIVE THE GLORIE TO GOD ALLONNE,* a phrase carved into a sideboard at the Folger, but the context sullied and doubted, when the enemies of GLORIE took over. This is civilization. American light, liberty, the chest which is really mocked in the portmanteau of th while Hesper is singing I love you, I love you, a little like the dream princess, except *merchants dream of new Americas...nose the Bermudas, ravish Virginia*, as Thomas Randolph says. This cover, off, reveals nothing at all, stolen from Allen Ginsburg on a boxcar somewhere *pressing nudely on the honey tube.* When I read that one for the radio station the tech was so convinced he bought the book, but the Christian values are two edged in the context of everything else. Would that be they produced *a falling off of stretch on the stalk of* sexual colonialism. *Spring to the arms of burlap, poke a stitching, jam a smock. Nothing must be covered up.* Not that these cannot be as vulgar as a Volkswagen Puppy in production, or corpses *sprouting out in the snow in winter* that *come up with crocuses.* So it says among the vulgar, *this rose gives many a care of its dying.*

Synopsis: Bridge, Get Away

If it is possible to have a novel without a character so called, the character here is ourselves en masse, as a collective and a society of the world wherein certain mythological conflicts overwhelm. It is important not to spell these out but to let them creep into our consciousness as in fact they have done over the years. New Philadelphia is a colony, an out post on a Hadrian's Wall inhabited by refugees who are confronted in their new environment not so much by nature but by myth and this is the record of their adaptions backgrounded by salient features of the first settling of Philadelphia by those mystics of the Wissahickon *Creek as it passes through the gorge to merge with the Schuylkill* River into the Delaware and then the sea. The series of transfers of water are like the transfers of culture from that old world the colonists abandoned to the new one they know nothing of. Who could know of it, inhabited by monsters worse than the Odyssey and with no heroes or overarching great cause like Helen or Troy or Truth. They thought they were reliving elements of the Odyssey, descendants into hell or hades let us say, signature of that hero. In the beginning their obtuse recommendations were as confusing as scruples against geese. They excitedly questioned each others nerve. But the five microcosms did not notice either set of believers. Since the mystics were predominant, Leviathan was invited which introduced extreme oddities of topography. The majority in that town patterned their lives and homes after this sea monster they saw in the stars and in the cosmos, if not actually in the sea, casting omens of earth and fire and trying to foretell the future, for all the good it did them. They sacrificed to Poseidon right out of the Greek, so though they believed a child was born pure and innocent it was not scrupled to live among tens of millions in the womb. These contrasted with the harbor seal Baptists as they were called, who would begin speaking along the jetties and walks with their eyes closed and go so long that even after their audience had long departed they kept on with their antiphonies. They anointed themselves elders in a Council of Watchers to oppose the intrusion of their so called nemesis from the sky as much as Leviathan was the mystic nemesis from the sea.

There are many ways to offend those who have not seen the cracks radiating from centers of implosion of fissures like Tycho in the Moon, colony craterlets, orbits of phyllotaxis, divergences perceptible as the shape Ohio once was, or became. It too existed after proof of some finite intelligence at work, occurring passim, the a priori rendezvous-proving rule, circle down to circle for one who descends, crossings seen in the meeting-places of more than one canal.

To call them canals is a faux pa from the planned obsolescence of intelligence that once existed, like thinking the world flat mistaking rivers for canals, spheroid for flat, something as if Gilgamesh below the Euphrates Beltway to which people dug tracks and underground trains in their temples to convince themselves theirs was a perfect world. These tracks, taken apart, were not seen, for this they did not do.

Every effort to conceal the one cell organism known as Mammon-Oranus, a huge intestine of money governed in Secret with its primitive media nerves, multilayered in a newfound. For you know the gut has a brain stimulating the tribes with "wow pulses," This *Stockholm-Munchhausen mosaic of tribes caught between the coasts of the present-day fabulous and history would digest money, excrete money, displace other processes of being. After exposure that the Secret mind could produce these impulses on its own would gurgle would not be spoken full in words.

8/2020 B calls last nite second inspection needs new roof, decking, maybe a/cs and not done yet. He's worried he and A won't camp if Sh forbids. But he can only call me when he's walking the dog. "A woman wants the self-same sovereignty over her husband as over her lover, And master him; he maist not be above her," said the Wife of Bath.

Maybe all this is to prevent him digging the hole even deeper, 400k vs 200

Maine

Finally got rest in second nap, was standing at high tide of the sea boiling up into streets cleaning the fog of the mist off my glasses.

8/21/20 C W Doerr

Bio: I washed the letters off of tombstones, washed dishes in biochemical research lab, couldn't stomach the dish job I got at a gas pump one time next to the HR of that old folks home. You had to pressure wash the half empty plates in the air by the hundreds. I went down the rivers of w. Pgh a lot and explored the caves. I have fought the surf off the coast before a storm, walked miles up storm drains until I had to crawl. I walked many miles down the Rio Grande in the river, swam Mariscal Canyon, free ran in the Chisos Mts. among the salvia regla, built erosion dams in the Texas Hills, lived on Balcones Fault before the fall of Austin, been in and out of these delivered from all my troubles, but what I really I do can't say because it is too important to be noised about. I still live near water, submit this ms. among others because I once had a friend who was so close to me he was never two steps from his mistress whose life he saved. His first name was Tramp, but when he came to me I called him Joggy. He was a black Athabaskan chow.

This ms. runs about 40-60K depending. It is novel if you allow a novel to be novel, undertakes the events in and around Pied Cow, it's name, where due to the remediation of VOC compounds into the air the community saw the giants that surrounded them fluoresce in mid air. This is about those people, the giants, their ways, you know giants will eat ya, from the effects on the lives of those people who can't see them, like in the first story here, but many more. Bye. There is lots more.

--The way they control the thought of Pied Cow is with the myth countermyth and supermyth even anti myth anything just so the people don't see. Their mistake was spraying. They thought all the VOCs, a downpayment on the airplanes vocs that filled the sky for decades would do one thing but they did another. So it was as if a social experiment like the Milgram had gone awry and everyone was electrocuted with a PC.

8/22/20
-- He that speaks in an unknown tongue speaks mysteries… ICor 14. 2, 9, except you utter by the tongue words easy to be understood, how shall it be known what is spoken, for you speak into the air, There are many kinds of voices in the world and none of them is without significance, 15-16. I will sing with the spirit and I will sing with the understanding, else how shall he that occupies the place of the unlearned say, I understand?

--When the effrontery of Pied Cow is gone, worn off, the brain rewired sees what all these things are, the light and bright gets reflective into the philosophy of this cow becoming a Taurobolium of Geography, Morality and Prophecy

--Combined in this the use of language of a highly ornate symbolic style is far beyond the denotation. Virginia Woolf. "In reading we have to allow the sunken meanings to remain sunken, suggested, not stated; lapsing and flowing into each other like reeds on the bed of a river. But … very rudimentary words … come fresh from a human brain… without the writer's will."

It doesn't take long to realize that if the world is a Host, a sacrifice is about to be offered up. What is surrendered? Catching away the self, called transcendence [stage 4]. In this Ordo Seculorum religion, a prelude of the coming into full "cosmic consciousness" [stage 5] Teilhard de Dragon and the Pope concur. Enrapturement, transcendence of the body with the mind, leaves earth behind got interested in these "paranormal" projections from his experiences in Yoseikan aikido. He says his transcendence outside himself began when he saw himself practicing the exercises in slow motion as if he were watching from the sidelines. He called it "the pure Zen state of aikido," "the complete aikido oneness." It led to his investigations of UFO materialization, thought forms (cf. "tulpas"), telepathy and the entire "entity nature of collective human unconscious," a vast "psychotronic Manhattan Project." Compare the Soviet psychotronics turning "the minds of all men into a great super mind having absolute psychokinetic mastery over time and space–truly a godlike being... the collective human unconscious has a collective conscious instead of four [eight] billion fragments of individual personal conscious minds" We call these people, each one are bits in their quantum supreme world. I've never met a single person who cares one way or the other. Never even met anybody who knew about it. So give it up for amnesia and entrainment, and Give it up for The Globe! Teilhard de dragon

8/23/20 I told her yesterday that the woman is the glory of the man, as I Cor says.
- Today I said that if there is such a thing as karma exists then she has transformed herself in service.
--For sons this is the case that when all things shall be subdued unto Him. Then shall the Son also Himself be subject unto Him that put all things under him, that Yahweh may be ALL IN ALL. 1Cor 15.28

8/24/20 A is now exposed not as proof of a superior education, but simply the purchase of a cattle brand to separate one's future career from the herd. The Sixties generation is going out as it came in: gross, loud, and cowardly, destroying the very institutions for others that it so selfishly consumed for its own benefit. , opposite of Kesey's bus, mystery tour rampage of towns of stops of their caravan.

--Before words, things and images got all svelte and dressed up to fashion on the stage they existed inchoate and broken, illiterate in every way, which automatically is edited out by the finished on stage, automatically covered up. It redoes it with dress. Which veils the savage state of this translation from thought to speech, call it dream, but it is not.

8/25/20 To love is see yourself not as a thing, a mountain, a robot, but a person. This person has depth so that a v above them is a v below where the raw energy of youth enthusiasm that knows only itself grows and assimilates the highest and the best as it will, Christopher Smart let us say, who Geoffrey Hartman loves, and these highest and best thoughts, the entire Bible, and persons it brings into its own life and expresses below in thought, deed, work and understanding are absorbed.

-I putatively, Lord willing, will be the first of my family's generation to reach 80, but I see in my sisters a growing breadth of understanding in their lives, even if they are more isolated now form me.

You will like *The Pig*. It is more close up and personal that imagined. It is idyllic. Driving the pig to its last destiny among people who can receive it and ending up in the last shot-I'm not giving it away- create images unseen elsewhere. A keeper.

Christopher. Smart had extensive background in botany and his knowledge of taxonomy.
--He, James, is fearfully and wonderfully made in your Name. fallen from 50 to 12 percentile weight, spitting up, I told P to visit last Sat and she began to treat this, smaller feedings, hi calorie form. Get ultra sound Thurs.

8/26/20 after working from 2, in a nap I was singing a song with B before I woke
-Retribalizing Goths and Visigoths of old Europe, do they really want to bring back Rome? What's Joe Rogan's call on Goths vs the Assyrians? Depends on the home town? In Europe Hammurabi's dead, even in Mesopotamia it's not sure!

--Am I allowed to say that. for now the sun's turned white, The corona ltd. Boys miss the old yellow sun. Do black suns matter?

8/27/20 Telling her of the comic writing of Sterne, Flann O'Brien a la Dalkey archive, Swift, Borges. Read to her Dylan Thomas, Child Mourning, Child's Christmas.

8/28/20 Pied Cow represents the kingpins of a community of individuals who nonetheless are joined by many ideas and events in common, taken together, taken for +granted, they represent any other like society, and all societies alike in their rural, tribal, community structure of families, whether rural or urban, in apartment houses or small towns. The events are the same only the names and the cultures have changed. When I was a young I traveled on a circuit of these communities from large cities like Toronto and Roanoke to small towns, farming communities which take up much more of the landscape and whose names blend together, but individual actors stand out. Let it be certain that every one of these, large and small, had kingpins, authorities, powers and each of these had as it were daughters which they treated jealously to protect. These daughters might be girls or they could be boundaries and ideas, and one of a hundred fraternal, social community clubs, players, Elks, Rotarians, along with volunteer fire departments and implicit militias. This deep interrelatedness is less known to a fast paced mobile nation, but it is its backbone and only invisible because the information services are heavily biased against. As a young man I visited these communities self assured and full of energy and those daughters were easily enamored of such a one, hence he was viewed by the fathers and kingpins with suspicion that was palpable, whether this was in Strasberg PA or Conway Wales. and of course this was the better known when I was the one who had a winsome wife, confronted on the Paris Metro by dozens of rapacious young Arab Moroccans, who played the role I had a decade before, except more extreme. All this is to say the ring of communities goes out from any and every center of one person, including family, street, town, state, nation in every nation of the world. So whether break dancing in Horní Slavkov *Schlaggenwald* CZ or walking the street early in Limon, Costa Rica among prison cast offs, beaten and desperate, the same must be true, we are all caught up in the social milieu, and it is not cotillions and balls, dinners among the rich in party dresses, it is the communities of souls who do not know who they are.

To talk about these phenomena it is as though a *deus ex machina* is employed here in the form of aerosoled volatile organic compounds cleansed from the aquifers and bedrock that underly that region. How they got there, where they are going, because all is in motion in the world, is not so much the case as simply saying that they are there, but this is omitted from discourse and what it might mean for the inhabitants. While this is a real effect in many cites and communities not to be denied, because it is under our feet and in the air that we feel the *deus ex machina* in the VOC as an example of all the pollutants, nuclear and not, downstream from Hanford or sprayed in much disputed trails that linger and spread in the sky to improve the transmissibility of the cell. None of the electromagnetics can be seen and there is a great range of them from ELP antennas to the world net of Pied Cow, which is the world where giants rule the kingpins who rule the men.

--The whole point of passive resistance was to afflict the conscious of the oppressor by their own humanity. Present protestors have no humanity like this, transfer their inhumanity to all they oppose, who really have it.: "At first I was trying to look in their eyes and trying to have any kind of reason or to see someone as a human being and I realized they did not see us as human beings," she continued. "I am furious," she exclaimed. "You tell me if you are surrounded by a mob, that will not let you move, that is screaming in your face, that is holding you completely hostage, and you cannot walk to your hotel and you are on a dark street, you tell me that's not violence. You tell me that is not an attack."
: the police union is "like a bunch of dudes that pay dues so they can go someplace and meet and get away from their wives."

"only Marxists view violence as an acceptable tool for social change. It is their first, last, & only tool, in all its forms, subtle & overt. Marxism is the rust that attacks the social order when necessary corruption maintenance has been neglected for too long." High 8/27/20
--Hours after Nancy Pelosi labeled Republicans as "domestic enemies," leftist mobs harassed, intimidated, and tried to incite violence against Republicans in the streets

--B called to check antibiotic prescription, asked about roof said many bids 8-12k, ins. good to 13k, asked what about the overage since 8 is well under, said many contractors solicited him to double invoice and keep the overage, I said the cost of that is greater than the reward, scrupulous honesty for his sons, character and repute. S looking the other way. It's up to him to be honest. I need to tell him he has to work on his karma, even if this is a built in something for nothing fraud that everybody does and ins builds into their rates.

8/29/20 Entomologies of Oops, to use the vernacular, think back to the Greek and to Sumer where in the first picture writing the Oops were long headed giants, then forward to Mt Hermon where they were even older than that. This is the accepted wisdom of anthropologists who the further they retreat from time and space the more certain they categorically state the millions of years gone.

Internal Klan

And since oops is a translation at best, and not even that, for we don't know what El Ephod knew -- these monastics often master the obscure--the original name was, far seeing goat serpent, Draco, Cetus, like those known to that Trojan priest who threw his spear at the old horse of Troy, Pyrmonidies wasn't it, as we read PostHomerica for which we need more than etymologies but entomologies, or so said the auction clerk in Hong Kong when he rang up the next batch for auction, being a complete set of the books of insects of offered by Gorham with pictures in color of each known then, which are analogies, in=sects for sects back to when they had fiefdom of assembly you could google as you pin their canceled wings to the page, as every herbarium and butterfliarium does along with physics and Matter, useful with the compliments of von Beutenmuller, *Taxa hierarchy,* for the taxonomic classes, the same as protesters on streets of the various phyla, are anything but human, their hybrid natures known to the great Russian entomologists attested in his modern update to *The Life of Insects* by Victor Pelevin, a work of fiction.

Butterfly butterfly on the wall who's the feariest of them all? These evoke with the tunnels of earth those moments of our youth we dreamed pre Tolkien, and not just storm sewers, but full fledged treks in the bowels, sorry, of the earth. Many on these same treks as an Inman have found their kimberlite ancestries retrieved from some old blog and worth repeating here in order not to affront the greater with the rest. Kimberlites…diamonds are forged by pressure miles down. After they are carried to the surface by volcanic act, shot into kimberlites high. Lodging in the diamond pipe enables them to be found. Vannoccio Biringuccio thought gold mines a kind of kimberlite that took the shape of tree roots of gold. In times of the human forging of these, they are made, by translation, of unspeakable memories, like those POW's and released prisoners, deep things, but then we wake from sleep. The exile does not show his heart as he sits in the diamond tubes forgot, the sparking jewels. Depth mining round the descents brings them out. Look.

Clean office. Talk: everything connected told of Port Arthur/Lamar crash, Tionesta/ punch in side of head [see "Morning Star," *Otherwise Engaged* 7. Grace Chapel, $600 pledge.

8/30/20 ---It's as if the flesh of the *Little Stories* were like the inside of pomegranates and running around inside were species of swift paramecium bugs elusive, impossible to catch against the red flesh and the seeds, but need to be heated to a certain temp to remove, but does this compromise the life of the stories? The life in the flesh with the paramecium, like after making coffee, grains get into the brew, revealed as you put milk in and hard to catch out with just a finger, except the pomegranate story is neon red and glittering and the bugs microscopic. These are all among the effects that we overhear as we eavesdrop in the words and sentences of the psycho laminates.

Psycho laminate means to describe the connection of multi layers of associated meaning in among the vortices and convections of human emotion, thought sensation and intuition, especially when it is left to mature without interference from psychotropes, drugs or anything that interferes with its sobriety. Then meaning emerges little by little to be overheard. It is not visual it is aural. It is not thought it is a reality impossible to cognition. It calls itself the psycho laminate, so stay with that and don't try to improve it later with analysis or myth. It has to be what you hear when you pin your ear, which the slave would do when he stayed, when your ear is pierced with the awl so that it is dedicated sole, a listener. If you want it you have to pay for it. Lip service won't do. *Morning by morning I listen as one being taught (Isaiah 50.4)*. Laminates of the word overhear the concept, all the rest is applied.

[The cultivation of the vocabulary of history, literature and science in its interstices is a laminate, it has layers to be understood as one. A caveat concerns its philosophy of evil, Bataille, Rimbaud, Huysmans, etc for the French seem to express the most overt philosophy of evil in Europe, which may seem astonishing, thinking that it was the German or the Dutch, much more castle covert, hidden underground. The point of these writers is that even though they may warn that their practices are a danger, Bataille, for example, is still the more pronounced pedophile of Europe, even if he as librarian secreted Walter Benjamin's with the Kleeangel inside valises in the Bibliothèque nationale de France through the end of the war, [online, PDF] so his disclaimer smacks facetious, the same way Wm. Burroughs in *Naked Lunch* cautions the drugs he uses, but uses them. Hunter Thompson does the same.

None of these felt the awl.]

--Words to an executioner: did you know the blood of Jesus Christ, God's son, cleanses us from all sin?

-Version of the Chartiers. [See "*Thrice Fiction 27*. PDF, online]

8/31/20 The white van and the black van, the coal and the snow.
Slight twitch in left thumb feels like nerve radiates down from shoulder. Left index finger stiff in second knuckle.
Travels to foreign places indigo.

9/1/20 Hardy board, y shield.

9/2/20 Get bike from B, get kids Pm. P to hand surgeon. Guten noggin.

9/3/20 She sees Ch., worried about disappearance of J, lost job, girl, house! Last seen at J's birthday where Ch left J to be entertained!
9/5/20 Finished Recon. Cover of True Light out.
Sang Ps 23 to J. A and A to camp, Rosh Hashana

9/7/20 Offense given provides license in return.

9/8/20 direct energy eweapon Dutch Sinse to Silver Creek OR—diamond craters volcanic center MALHEUR NATIONAL REFUGE to CA fire or from.
-Word hooligans
- demons -Video of an arrestee at violent BLM-antifa Portland protest overnight allegedly having a seizure. Others arrested at past recent Portland riots suddenly shaking rapidly.

9/9/20 Went to office to clean, found iron gates, called a 4 times, went over just as he leaves for work, he later gets 30 min cover, we load gates, come home.
-Order cashmere sweater for P all before 10. Paid for it though with rotor rt arm and back pain.
--"I think I'll have to put it on the slab, need to weld new feet so it can be properly set in concrete, probably won't happen today. Fortunately it's so heavy, it's not going anywhere, have to move the trailer to get the truck in the back. Keen to measure it. It's close. Both ends need hinges.

9/11/21 A and B move it to slab. It's 10 feet. Exact width for the driveway
-- I think you should put strong castors under each of the posts to give it mobility, which anyway might be way to proceed to open it when installed, also to support the frame. So tracks, castors, and swing.

9/10/20 -History of Pyruvate Phosphatase

Revolution does not dialogue with itself. The thing that made this clone was that the shared experience was gone. Each Day brings out the test tube shot, to play it all again, but it doesn't make you trust this narrative where heads detach. The hallucinated have come to tell you that your utilities are being shut off.

To spark such riddles the thing is not quite in the middle cloud of nuclear explosions being dodged. And, another decap, the thing that is, is not. Another decap! Just two guys on the assembly line making heads and who trade barbs of inward glory that few can share. "Our mistress thigh is nothing like her bum." It's the same metric, and all, and the same rhyme. Only the words are changed.

"Two little babies was sittin in bed, standing on the assembly line assembling heads, they sent for the doctor and the doctor said, yammering (in italics)…"

F Gov

If you wonder why I'm telling these staged events as real, they're not. Clues thrown out of the circle discover a consciousness no one wants to know. It's not the eyes that see any more than the ear that hears. The brain fools the eye, the eye doesn't fool the brain. If the scene is unremembered is never "seen," never was, even if passed directly into consciousness from Control.

 Somewhere undergrounds monitors turn blank. That slogan, *all institutions are demonic*? Three hundred pyramid levels below, Hawthorne found the government roof failing. The history clone died talking. No outside sun, new to many. If colorless, it gives no sign. Watching algorithms, cameras, microchips, blood pressure, heart rate, brain shift, *It was conceivable they watched everybody all the time.* Et Tu duty, outside Revelations 18. After losing their first encounter on earth the gave out drugs and meditation.

The unconscious anybody can see these Ararat divines in the EU parliament and in Breughel, or in the Guggenheim and Denver. The FEMA train beast, animated within, originally carried cargo manacled end to end. *There must have been a market, there must have been a market.* Rocketing down the night tracks sealed, no cracks in the floors like Weissmandel, rabbi of Slovenia, cut with a dull blade through the bottom of his Nazi box entering Auschwitz and escaped like Lockerbie.
When it comes to planet, who gets this base? The daemon Blum recruited when the trolls

fanned out. *Wenn du also sagst, du habest.* Natives tranked, stored random guineas, the best and brightest genes of f gov know the calculated ehad Selective Service complements. They tranked.

                        Infrastructure trained in faculties underground.

                        Programmers foresaw that iconoclasts must go.
                        Presume you go where none has gone before.

It is necessary to distinguish two governments in this, but the government Underground did not forgo the home market guillotine use. Who would not want a guillotine they grant, where a stray rooster could be dealt, or cut bread. All who join the guillotine throng assume the honor of Sir Thomas More, and if his head is not yet battlement be a subject for Madame Tussaud.

Forty foot containers have a guillotine end. You find yourself in the Amtrak Branch Beech Grove of the Jersey Report among those martyrs who oppose the gods, who lift the veil, as judged by Psytarch. Even though Lockerbie escaped the Gundersons cars, the airports and underground bases, it hardly seems a bridge to a peaceful mind. Under that circumstance the Psytarch revealed those tin men and undersea rebel tentacles, half human, half animal crabbots, mutants with scaled arms, paramecium, parts of butterfly wings, scales, hydra, fish with bared teeth, snakes that look like Klansmen, defecating upturned eels, fins, helmets, wasps, falling geese and shattered eggs, clams on half shell contending, angels with red and gold armor, a disc of white above, against the creatures of the water below.

                                  Before the semiotic tip of DuPont Circle the left ear of a head of secret architecture inhabited by the entertainment patriot matrix, you can get cozy if you want. They said he was a good New Order guy, aught Virgil before Homer, a revival of the old Apollyon nee Abaddon Altar Pergamos Denver CERN. Screwy acronyms like MOAB, Mother of All Bombs, tipped mine shafts nine craters deep. Locked in the ninth vault of Virgil was the Seal of the United States. It still needs to manifest. Various feedback loops connect this last to what the spinners in formation say. Read these texts asleep and then awake.

Note: hat at
All disbod speech is in italics.

9/11/20 what is the effect of earthquakes on the roots of plants?
Go see Roe v Wade.
The E in the Biden sign is the same E in the logo ENRON.
NANCY PELOSI SPEAKS FOR MOTHER EARTH.
SHE'S THE HURRICANE OF THE WEST
SHE'S THE FIRE IN THE MOUTH
SHE'S A WEATHER SYSTEM ALL HERSELF
If you turn hell upside down like a spit hood you get traitors at the top and then the giant's well.

Birthday call. C writes off the present with astrology as an excuse not to intervene a transit of US natals and M's condo. Defensive that J is emotionally like her, house, job travel loss, didn't dare say J is worried about him, out of contact.. She's thinks it's Pluto. Everything is connected and everyone is responsible. It's like they're shell shocked like a planet is some autonomous force and not a design of the Lord of all ages. A SARs victim of the gods in Shakespeare killed us for sport, all good theosophists. Then they come out of their golly cages and snap at you with their mask off.

9/12/20 Saddened at inability to positively effect teenage girls in medical practice, soliciting prayer from godly patients is suggested to effect healing.

9/13/20 They look at houses. Kids clean toy ceramic pieces, walk canal, muffins and pizza. Now count to three.

9/14/20 if you don't buy a thing you haven't lost. Panic is as panic does, they go over the cliff so you compete with them to see if you can go first? Make list of assumptions and question the Hamesterkauf. Watch the back trail, if lost sit down and listen.

9/16/20 B takes truck for moving to apt. A visits second day. Brings traps. Martinsen ceases his Covid work, says unless its not over. It's over

Corrections: P. 5   The feet of the coming King need to appear not in a single line, but broken in order to show His approaching steps.

P. 8   "we go our way de-verbalizing verse." Not verses. This completes the consonance with deverbalizing:
P. 11 "That pierced the cloud where I had hidden my fear." Not hidden, but "hid my fear."

9/18/20 last day of 5780 send Jaky dutch out.
 --Truly an American classic, to be read in literature classes of the absurd until literature is no more.
-More end of year: A fixed outdoor faucet, new valve stems indoor shower and sink. A and B camp tomorrow, same day as the 3 of us 11 yrs ago. Ruth Bader Ginsurg dies.

New Year

9/19/20 A and B camp Rim

Since giants come in two forms palpable and impalpable, physical and spirit it is an error to identify them with personalities like George Soros, Bill Gates, Rockefeller, six new hearts, and all the potentates who rule the world, for the personalities are mere serial habitations of giants in their impalpable forms, turned always to the zeitgeist, gist, geist, ghost, like in ee cummings little ghostlings twinkle toe, so giants seem to live and die but in no ordinary sense. They reincarnate, come back as Genghis Khan, Nero, in an unbroken chain from the first discard they were back before the days of Rome. So if you like history conspiracy in a series of retr=tards harvesting the world which of course is not to be allowed expression, when the personalities gather before Moloch each year in San Francisco, or at any of the many hunting lodges, drawn there by the spirits that inhabit them to worship from time past, presidents cut their middle fingers and have to wear band aids at the head of the Podesta line, but sometimes when they golf the fingers show and the mask falls as they are seen as all sorts of mythological animals, minotaur with hoofs growing out of their shoulders, then full legs, and from horses to apocalypse, whinny and moon, then literally have to trample off the green. Their putts fail. Quantum moles come out then and soil the cup, just the same as giant carp tangle themselves on bridges over the Mississippi the spiritual reality surrounds, not just in the buildings of government t slave buildings of the giants. It is unfortunate that this continues out into space, but there it is.

- Technology allows biological processes to be controlled remotely to open the door to manipulation of biological responses and, ultimately entire existence called

9/20/20 Durham helps care for exhausted or stranded bats, and trains staff to use 'bat ambulances'! to bring nature into neighborhoods, and make them more congenial in other ways - each bat can eat several thousand midges in a single night.
--biked today
--bye bye roof rat

What's the ugliest part of your roof rat?
You pigged and ate your fill now laying
Where all good roof rats go.
Good rats for justice
running up and down the field
We lost a roof rat today,
services will be held in on Tues at the green barrel
How's your roof rat!

9/22/20 Another rat dead in street. Paul concurs the green barrel.
--Read finished proof of True light
-Talked to B about S. Hill, made room for his water barrels

9/23/20 In Dutch slang, some folks call cobblestoneskinderkoppen, which translates to "children's heads.
P's hand operated.

9/24/20 Anne calls, fell off ladder in kitchen.

9/25/20 We don't smoke Kenosha in Wuskogie.
B is an escape artist. As soon as he gets out of one hole he digs a deeper, leaves his dog, fish, Baja warrior EMP proof.

" With scientists having long known that there is no genetic explanation for what Monarch Butterflies are doing, their attention turned to "self-organizing systems" and the learned "habits" within them —which has led to one of the most amazing and remarkable discoveries ever made, the new therapeutic method called—that views a human family, to include all of its past and future members, as a "self-organizing system" whose "bad habits" can be changed, and "new habits" learned—even to the extent that past family members having "bad habits" that died even generations ago, can be seen as being changed into "new habits" able to be passed on to future generations. Baptized for the dead.

9/26/20 If we attempt to penetrate the ruse and counters of the fuselage of these mome rathe wraiths, for this is how it sounds when they speak, that is to recognize they are like bombers dropping ruses and counter ruses into the public mind, carpet bombing to prevent anyone from knowing what is really on. Like *mischwesen*.

Mischmasch and illustrated for the amusement of his family from 1855 to 1862. It is notable for containing the earliest version of the poem " which Carroll would later expand and publish in It was collected into *The Rectory Umbrella and Mischmasch*, published in 1932.

In German, *Mischmasch* (masc.), also refers to a disorderly mixture of things.

Political Theory is the closest I can come, but the process of literature here is common to science and all intuitive thought. All writers seek this but few find it, which is also the subject here, that is, what counterfeits are settled for in place of direct access. Boethius, Dionysus the Areopagite, St John of the Desert, all seek to find the origin of things, but to do so is at the cost of certain loss and much pain so not recommended.

9/27/20 Dreamed again of a car, parked on public street, stolen, a red and white olds convert, red olds coup stolen so the perps could have a festival, Italian festival in it. [Now I realize! It's Susan's car in Guapa Pop!]

In other words whosoever shall call on the Name of the LORD shall be saved. Many occult sources have sought that Name to use to their advantage but could not find it, did not know it. You may put that Name on your door. That Name is the door for as many as received Him. For as many as received Him. Casting down imaginations and every high thing that exalts itself against the knowledge of God, I bring every thought into captivity to the obedience of Yeshua:

term: horizons unlimited bookstore, Austin Tx, article on goodreads
-Find four metal bookcases
B returns truck, clears 50k. also returns the genealogy given him at his birthday and inscribed to him. He is ambivalent about his background?

Now for the America part of the story *in brief*. There was an Old Catholic Church in America that entered the Orthodox Church via the American Exarchate of the Russian Patriarchal

Church (MP). Its leader was Metropolitan William who was named the Exarch of the Western Rite within the MP in the 1960s. This was all accomplished via the MP's American Exarch. Therefore the MP required Metr William to present himself in Moscow. Being during the Soviet era there was suspicion as to this requirement. Metr. William resigned from the MP and led his Church to the Ukrainian Autocephalous Orthodox Church in Exile under the leadership of Abp Palladios in communion with the EP. Those who know of the history of SCOBA know that Abp Palladios was one of its founders. Under the Ukrainian's spiritual protection, this Western Rite community was granted autocephaly (independence) that was recognized by the EP in 1967. In that same year Metr. William & Abp Palladios consecrated Abp Joseph of San Francisco. Abp Palladios reposed in 1969. In 1973, the EP & Rome declared their mutual recognition, at which time the Orthodox Synod for the Western Rite ceased any communications with the EP. In 1977, the Orthodox Synod for the Western Rite received the former Old Catholic Diocese of Texas and its leader bishop Hilarion was consecrated anew as Archbishop of Texas. You all know him from St. Hilarion Monastery in Austin, Texas. In 1979 Metr. William reposed and Abp Joseph was installed as Chief Hierarch. Archbishop John (a former Roman Catholic Jesuit) was named "locum Tenens" prior to Metr Joseph's repose in 1990. By 1997, what remained of the Orthodox Synod for the Western Rite was Abps John (Eastern USA) and Hilarion (Western USA). It was under Abp John's leadership as locum tenens that they entered the Milan Synod in 1997 and both American Hierarchs were accepted, with correction to their ordinations.
http://forums.orthodoxchristianity.net/threads/the-synod-of-.4577/

https://jwwinfree.wordpress.com/2009/12/20/st-hilarion-monastery-austin-tx/

9/28/20 The bride-elect is a graduate of MacArthur high School, where she was a member of National Honor Society, Forensic League and the school band. She graduated magna cum laude from the University of Texas at Austin, and was awarded a graduate fellowship by Rotary International for Study at the university of North Wales in Bangor, Wales, receiving a master's degree in 1974. Her fiancé is presently employed at the University of Texas at Austin as an experimental horticulturist.

9/30/20 –Organizing a trip to Iceland, another, late again.

10/2/20 B gets battery. *Lumen*. Christi is a catholic press

10/3/20 Trump covid, unexpected happenings, Venus Regulas conj 1/2/ degree, all the fixed stars are malefic. Horrible as it sounds high culture, high art, classical music, sculpture are all the furnishings of the royal Egregori illuminati castle folk of Europe, the mass, Wagner, are celebrations of their evil hand me downs from mischwesen.

[*Mischwesen* are composite late neo babylonigan creatures, easily taken as result of Enoch genetic tamperers, curse of the earth, cf. Pember's animals.
All secret labs under Beltway and elswwhere must seek apkallu, eph DNA, which they hope to reconstitute with the wooly mammoth, but they really want samples of angel sperm, annunalki so called, but then dna and sperm wats the diff, except who makes angel sperm but angels themselves, and since they must be able to adapt their bodies in physical form to accomodate their sex wih a woman, so she can give birth, that is, angels make themselves to found their own hybrid race, which of course is the world order, infilitrated by the Reversal. But compare T.H. White's bestiary with these mischwesens and Enoch's condemnation, and Maimonimerkabahdies, and Pember. Also note that as glorious as Babylon was it was disproven by Daniel!
by Wayne Horowitz (1998; rev. 2011), has informed the present study, especially with regard to the "]

-Constance E. Gane's 2012 AD dissertation: apkallu and the genius in human form, as well as creatures based on bulls, lions, canines, winged quadrupeds, fish, birds, scorpions, and snakes. Where do all these instant ancient scholars come from so easily in America, what can they know all hot house language and thought and they breed each other…for all the vaunted cosmic significance all the images are creatres of earth, fish, lion, bird, not cosmic at all except for the overlay. "Watanabe observes that the names of animals mentioned in ancient texts generally carry meaning beyond references to the natural creatures themselves…Each composite creature is derived from two or more species, with each animal part embodying a concept associated with the given animal's natural behavior."

If there were karma then everyone one of the illumined would return as a maggot which proves there is no karma since they would know this and seek self sacrifice and service to the least in order to come back as the great. If reincarnated the great come back as maggots forever:: therefore there is no karma just heaven and hell.

10/4/20 A and B were talking nephs on camp. Does he know nephs invented lipstick, and female adornment?

10/5/20 This is the draft *The Red Portfolio*, mailed 9/26/05. Looking at it as of 10/3/20 it seems to be two different books. Why wasn't she surprised when I sent a bound first draft to her following the news of her terminal illness?

10/6/20 Dream---visited once again the ramshackle bldg that once housed the las Vegas seraphim collection of Archie Johnson, which I own, but it has deteriorated hugely, walls missing, gangs hanging out, mostly Latin's--which I suppose to be my literary estate.

10/7/20 AB and B stay over last nite, for his first day of work. AB goes with P to work.

10/8/20 Sterate, the red in shino

Since Z first came down to Pied Cow I thought it instructive to show what he found there and so to start out by speaking of the orcs and half orcs might seem astonishing but they are as true to life as any in that benighted town considering the divine origins and their kings whose codices and wall murals and clay tablets embody the histories of such as we have come to know them. Whether in Mesopotamian Sumer or Mesoamerica Mixtec, the elite always want us to know how they are descended from the on high, I mean the Z himself, who while he does not recount this exactly must have been busy flourishing to repopulate with himself all those races that populate the earth. The only difference of the records of our time to those before is in the transmission in codes, not codices, and in language familiar to us all, the king's English so called, even if the king is dead and long lives Ubu Roi, his successor. This like those before is both a history of the kings, the elites and their petite estates which always divide so that what was one or a few became hundreds and shortly millions of division, which descriptive events occur again and again and prescriptive images may take place at some future time and place, all of course designed to obscure what will really occur, which they know in part and labor all the more to obscure.

These repetitions of history and myth over and over whether on animal hides or tablets, or digital cartoon history and just that, cartoons in full figure Disney narrative form wedded to the mold of the absurd and thus they descend from their gods, quote. The conventions therein that so inspire notions of fallen societies of the defeat of their empires, again, again and again, whether Tututepec or Yanhuitlan, post classic, post modern, post human, so shoot these societies that the transformation that reemerged could only be taken as the new Pied Cow, but in fact there was no old Pied Cow even if those who migrated away from there still return for the festivals.

10/9/20 Life gets harder as you approach eighty from the weight of memory and introspection. Countless actions and reactions weigh the soul so at some point it is good to forget whenever that point is reached, but for when you forget you are at death, cessation and then the afterlife. So better to reconcile here than there. The injustices of pride, the inability to change, to bring peace to others as well as your own wrongs all become magnified and emotionally sensitive, like old injuries in the change of weather at night in ruminations of memory, fasting contradicted, deliverances opposed, well intended but mistaken acts because following the supposed rule the law of the letter contradicts the spirit, and then to meet the opposition of other minds incapable of sympathy or understanding, who insist upon their rights to abuse, lie, exaggerate, declaim, you suspect whether you yourself are not doing this too. Sin. So to put others ahead of yourself, give money away to cleaning ladies, fly Russian

Jews to Aliyah, stray rabbis like Marty, halve your salary to give opportunity to another, give away new cars, making faith promises in youth and fulfill them, giving to schools and Dana Dunford tokens of the least, but how to give the great eludes social prayers and prayer rings in churches at six in the morn, left out by an encounter with the one they are praying to. I saw a Kim Clement tape where he says he heard the voice of old and young at the same time in 2027 (Feb 2, 2013) while he describes light and lights, but what significance, just words, when the light of lights is seen every moment if remembered. That and the lack of human ideation in what is written and read, the other in the self, intercession intercede between the present, a bridge to deliver, call out blessing for curses, call for conviction upon the earth's tribes and nations.

10/10/20 Dream--did three paintings in the night plus one modeled suit of clothes painted, taken off, mounted, painted more. These last days I have sudden arrhythmia of heart, 32, then 45 with pretty wide range of blood pressure from 174/75 to higher and lower.

10/11/20 Had the kids overnight while A and S take anniversary break.

10/12/20 There is no empiricism left, all the facts are churned, up and down, spike and trough, explanations of the big top.

Peradam, *Mount Analogue*, puerile Rene Daumal's Mount Analogue will recognize the reference to the only real means of payment in that far-off country. The peradam was described as "a clear and extremely hard stone . . . a true crystal . . . harder than diamond," so transparent that it was almost impossible to see and extremely difficult to find. The discovery of a peradam was never accidental, but resulted from some kind of inner effort. At such a moment, its "brilliant sparkle like that of a dewdrop" might catch the eye of those who truly and sincerely sought the truth.

In the world of Mount Analogue, all authority came from above. Since these peradams were the only currency accepted as payment by the mountain guides, those who wished to climb the mountain would need to find some in order to move on. Most peradams were found on the rough and dangerous trails up the mountain. However, to everyone's astonishment, the leader of the band of adventurers whose story is told in the book uncovered one in the sand on the beach, seconds after he renounced his authority over the group he had gathered together and led for many months. Tr. Roger Shattuck

10/13/20 Donald Barnhouse, walk/stand
-Captain John Diemer led a British colonial expedition into Quebec against in 1746 to 1747.

10/16/2 Rick Shabi Eighth day speaks of that which comes after the end. Day after the Feast of Tabernacles. Rev 10 the mystery of God finished-- 7th trump.   Adam/Eve to 7th Trump. When thousand years ends Lev 23 ---36 feast of tabernacles—v. 39 1st and 8th day sabbath rest

Sabbath means temporary shelter until the temple built. World not permanent residence.

—Cahn-- *Shemini Atzeret* means *the Gathering of the Eighth Day*. The Feast of Tabernacles is the last of the holy days appointed by God, the final feast. So it speaks of the end, the end of days." "It's the very last day appointed by God . . . the mystery day. And those who belong to God belong to the Eighth Day. And when the creation ends, they will enter it . . . the day beyond days, when the finite yields to the infinite . . . and its limitations are no more . . . the age beyond ages . . . eternity."
Go beyond the end . . . beyond the end of yourself . . . and you'll find out."

--Revelation 20:11 Expanded Bible People of the World Judged

¹¹ Then I saw a great white throne and the One who was sitting on it. Earth and ·sky [heaven] ·ran away [fled] from ·him [ᴸhis presence/face] and ·disappeared [ᴸno place was found for them].

--Leviticus 23:39 Complete Jewish Bible

³⁹ "'But on the fifteenth day of the seventh month, when you have gathered the produce of the land, you are to observe the festival of *ADONAI* seven days; the first day is to be a complete rest and the eighth day is to be a complete rest.

-- Romans 6:11 Expanded Bible

¹¹ In the same way, you should ·see [count; consider] yourselves as being dead to ·the power of sin [ᴸsin] and alive ·with [to; with reference to] God ·through [*or* in; in union with] Christ Jesus.

--2 Corinthians 5:1-6 Expanded Bible

5 [ᴸFor] We know that ·when [if] our ·body [ᴸearthly house]—the tent we live in here on earth—is destroyed, ·God will have a house for us [ᴸwe have a building from God]. It will not be made by human hands, but will be an eternal home ·in heaven [*or* in the heavens]. ² But now we ·groan [sigh] in this ·tent [*or* body; ᴸone], longing to be clothed in our heavenly ·home [dwelling place], ³ because it will clothe us so we will not be naked. ⁴ While we live in this ·body [ᴸtent], we ·have burdens [are weighed down], and we ·groan [sigh]. We do not want to be ·naked [stripped; unclothed], but we want to be clothed with our heavenly home. Then ·this body that dies [ᴸthe mortal] will be ·fully covered with [ᴸswallowed up by] life ⁵ This is what God ·made [designed; prepared] us for, and he has given us the Spirit to be a ·guarantee for this new life [deposit; down payment;

Goya, Blake, Crane, White Buildings Hopkins, Smart, Breughel, Bosch

10/17/20
Biden voters furl their wings up

like microwave towers waiting for dark

10/18/20 The Light published. P gets 8 wheelbarrows of red sand from Brian, has battery in truck so when it failed at Trader Joe she and clerk with crescent wrench installed it there, then she returned the old for credit!. One half Benicar makes bp go from 180 to 108, weakening.

10/19/20 76f and the Mystery of Lawlessness
p.23- "Amused by the gamobols of these monsters of the deep some having the form of calves others of horses others of whales…these former bodies in such a manner that the new covers the old, as hides or pelts cover the hut of Moses the dolphins wedged between anchor and poop..with huge bulk and 7 ft length ticked either our eyes so much nor our taste for the dolphin filled out both cherubim would be the companion of our way and our protectors in danger, p 24

Compare the signs of the times and be able to make a resolution to hide yourself that you would believe it would rain manna in your tent

All criticism of puritans fear of the trees and the dark pales against the modern in his neighborhood of light.

10/20/20 FB to close 10/23 at disc to 355k

10/21/20 one reason for pseudonym is the automatic mental downrank to the name
--Pulse 32 for a while

10/22/20 Kelpius three- fold wilderness to Hester Palmer 86
Barren wilderness
Fruitful wilderness
The valley of Achor Wilderness of the Elect of God 89 of Moses,
-- Elijah John the Baptist Jesus the Messiah, David, and Paul—all of the Wilderness—that "God has always prepared his most eminent instruments in the wilderness"
Childhood and manhood may both consist of the second state

10/24/20 Kelpius, Restitution of All Things, 181, birth of eternities,
h. t. hillbrook, George Washington Shadow of time hit job

10/25/20 palpatiatons last night to 84

Political Theory is the closest I can come, but the process of literature here is common to science and all intuitive thought. All writers seek this but few find it, which is also the subject here, that is, what counterfeits are settled for in place of direct access. Boethius, Dionysus the

Aereoplogite, St John of the Desert, all seek to find the origin of things, but to do so is at the cost of certain loss and much pain so not to be recommended.

10/29/20 My mother's name is Beatrice so I have a title to what I write

10/30/20 bubba buber uber ubu. True light banned on FB. The cows will moo as Nietzsche but they won't fight.

Dear Willum: with this impression that I must put into an envelope, find and address and sent it along with the wishes that you might write something beyond the four specimens of this character who afterward spent all nights in his garage to wit and leveraging the many volumes forth that have not yet appeared but are threatened any years now from his remains I could not resist in these characters of the Glass your voice which whether Buddy or Seymour, poet or novelist you decide but in any case especially well worth reading again. As such, your AE

Matthew McConaughey-Minister of Culture-Austin
--after his drugged out, scum bag suicidal crazy man act McConaughey praying with you would be like Anne Rice taking your pulse.

/chances you get this slim saw etc. Here is vision of Austin as Ameryca, etc. free
The funnel, the burning bush, the naked speaking then.

11/1/20 House party at B's new house at mesa. Truck blew out hose on way. Three people stopped, one with a gal of coolant, left the truck there, hitch home with A.

11/2/20 <He Covers my head with oil> P's b. Heard from one in three, got a pony express banner and party with Jackie. Like me, out of date

11/3/20 in big bold letters: WITH TUESDAY'S ANNOUNCEMENT

11/4/20 <no weapon formed against me shall prosper and I rebuke the tongues of my accusers> Trump's comments come after several key states mysteriously stopped counting ballots on election night for the first time in perhaps ever, after which large batches of votes - seemingly all, or mostly all for Biden - tipped the race towards the former Vice President in Michigan and Wisconsin.--- So while everyone was asleep and after everyone went home, Democrats in Michigan magically found a trove of 138,339 votes, and all 138,339 of those "votes" magically went to Biden? That doesn't look suspicious at all.
Joe shapario, Jordan petereson, joe rogan, math McConaughey alex jones, tucker carlson stalking horses of…
On waking up from afternoon dream: <"Im a propheta nd my names is Jesus
I became ugly to my God and king.>. heard after returning to an apt bldg. after being sent to retrieve retrieving a .45 fired by a fat woman in a panic before the police etc came

If a Biden victory bodes these votes my promise in result--THE BANQUET OF GOD--still fresh at Ygdrasil: top billing that issue, with some improvements reads:

http://users.synapse.net/kgerken/Y-1305.pthat

11/5/20 <bind the lips of the accusers enemies and avengers and loose your rivers of living water>
Shut their mouths bind their lips you still passivist electonalists, accusers, enemies and avengers roar,

Plants of Texas new mex and az AE Reiff is a poet of Austin, Texas who when completed a doctorate in literature became the horticulturist of the Experimental Drug and Herb Garden of the College of Pharmacy.

11/6/20 AMERYCA—a chapbook Orpheus born in ameryca
<the resurrection of Jorma, the anointing of the ones, derision of the enemy.>

A woman is an apple device
There was always two Americas but never laid so bare now the ballot baggers and engine stackers stickered the election so baldly and openly. They were always the ones in complete control they just missed in '16, but never again. The showdown is on.

11/7/20 Momma Noture goes to the Academy. The feminne person of Momma Noture shows a motherly compassion for her animals and children.
called uncalled for Schlegel Friedrich Sméagol elected

11/8/20 Smeagel goes to Washington. Smeagol made the White House in reality what it had been for long, a puppet. ?Smeagol took his orders. He literally changed the climate in making it what it already was. Smeg's orders were to dumd down the questions. Core the nubbin. <you prepare a table before him in the presence of his enemies> sent ms.

-- FaceBook banned my poems. so I turned to Twitter to publicize an Arizona tweet, paid $50, but got an "AD POLICY VIOLATION: Your promotion has been stopped because it did not comply with Twitter's Ad Policy." You people hear me now?
ARCHY, HOW BAD IS ARIZONA?
AE, ARIZONA IS SO BAD IT'S THE ONLY STATE WHERE EVEN THE MAINSTREAM MEDIA ADMIT THEY WERE WRONG IN THE VOTE COUNT. I'm so proud.

-- PRAYER MANUAL TO ALL THE UNCALLED.
BAGGYJOE IS FALLING!
Falling! Is falling!
BAGGYJOE IS FALLING! to rise no more.
E. Pluribus Unum loses its heads

seven headed hydra comes to roost
BabbyJoe is fallen -- BabbyJoe is coming down!

-- The informant I talked to only vosted forty times.
If that seems impressive. Forty times for each state
VOSTing for American (u)Nity and the prophecy coming soon.

-- We must be interested in this new practice of VOSTING since it obviously involves raising from the dead, multiple incarnations of the same person both before and after death and very probably the emptying out of old folks home in the VOST. These are major social phenomena to be studied at length in coming years. But for now we must include also the need to employ more and better machines to ease the pain to all these displaced VOSTERS. We propose and offer as a referendum that all subsequent elections avoid such contaminants.

--We need a song for this new age: Mario Lanza's, Come Prima
VOST OR NITY
VOST FOR NITY
VOST OR NITY

--I do not appreciate the volume of texts received that call VOSTing a new form of GHOSTing. Surely in this new democrat age where the promises of uNITY are so great whether by means of stealth or o/w by removal of those incalcitrant irritants of the peace and unity of the whole we must all be made SAFE. Peace and safety I say, the way the Bible does when they say peace and safety. Indeed I have myself written in praise of this new system and its rewards in The Secret life of Democrats, which is not so secret anymore now with this return to Power of G. W. Friedrich Hege up the Intelligence top. Indeed, down from that mountain descended once another and greater Friedrich super-entity to those lesser prodigies of Pied Cow. To which all us we may be sure shall soon attend.

--Don't defame the mouse, even if the usual phrase is mousetrap. It's better stated RAT TRAP?
SO I'D LIKE TO TAKE A POLL;;; MOUSETRAP OR RAT TRAP?
I CAN'T MAKE UUUP MY MYYNDE. PLEASE VOTE!

---GOOD NEWS, I HAVE BEEN APPOINTED TO THE NEW TRUTH AND RECONCILIATION COMMITTEE BEING RUN BY DARPA TO BUY BIDEN.
Much obliged to you voters and vosters on Instagram and message texts for your BUY BIDEN response, but many were muted from true societal response. Many voters defended the mouse, but the rat did not fare so well. Mousetrap = 15, Ratrap = 40. Much concern about the use of warfarin bait, vs the clack method to save predatory birds and kats from poisoning on the dead carcasses occurred, which if you see any dead ones they belong in the green barrel not the blue barrel, and may be disposed without ceremony. If you think any of this is allegorical and that DemocRATS are rats, even if that's what the name says, that just shows how far we come down this prophetic highway. And yes, the prophecy is coming, unless you turn away.

Many mouse posters claimed literally a verse from Psalm 23 would do, and a landslide majority after that phrase of walking through the shadow of death spoke out loud to prepare A TABLE BEFORE ME IN THE PRESENCE OF MY ENEMIES. Each day of these two weeks of shadow, while the rats luxuriate greater and greater, may be profitable spent in anointing the head with oil. Finally, as to the prophecy and its reward this one tip: buy up all the used Biden signs that have disappeared because there is going to be a hot market in two weeks in the Biden rebound -so yes, BUY BIDEN, buy as much used Biden as you can store to resell. They'll also be hot collector's items along with the ubiquitous KN95 Chinese maskS. BUY BIDEN BUY BIDEN BUY BIDEN

11/9/20 Monday. towed truck in Aey's trailer to Nissan, jump andrew's suburu

11/10/20 Dream---at an art class, had 3 narrow plastic fishtanks, fooling with one it got narrower, an inch wide and most of the water came out the fish had an inch at the bottom wrestling to restore it enlist another guy, a book dealer of adrenalin books/ whe go for water, but each time I return with a container but no water. The fish tank wavering back and forth in prolonged moment of collapse. A 2 dimensional fish tank where the fish can only swim back and forth, but can turn around or go up and down maybe add another side so it is round and hollow in the center so the fish can complete their circuit. Momma nature would b proud. So would la belle dame

Philadelphia instead of Jerusalem, could easy be London, all eastern cities in a manner. But Phila because all the connections of the past it is an abstraction of an American city with a past, and it encompasses all tits history expanded to the greater city that defined it originally, now divided into serv=eral counties.

11/11/20
Wednesday. piano on canal by old B&G club hq, now Imagine school, being discarded, one castor on top, without a front, painted white a honky-tonk piano (a piano in which one or more strings of each key are slightly detuned). $^{\text{Aand A piano}}$ movers The Cable Company produced the Wellington line as a more budget-friendly option for those that could not afford some of their higher-end brands; however, Wellington instruments were still superior in quality and well made. Made in 1915 192242. Recruited A and A to put in the white pickup, just back w/ new rad, drive to front door and with dollies move to porch.

11/12/20 Dream--with many others, but in front, I climb a very steep parapet of a ridge, but the bridge is gone. At the top looking over I can see long way to the water, 500ft. 100/ who knows. I am holding on there thinking about how to fall in order to survive, one does not want to pancake or swivel in the fall. Then I woke.
<the Holy Spirit inhibits the spirit of lawlessness>
BAD NEWS FOR BIDEN:
There is one who inhibits the power of lawlessness
And he will continue... II Thess 2.7
But it's not Trump.

11/13/20 Friday write Beatrice entry.

It's one thing to be ignorant but another to embrace with a face mask that has letters and ID on it in place of your number.

<sharper than any two edged sword, piecing even joints and marrow dividing soul and spirit and discerning even thought and intents

Aey says the aliens are landing in dec they've already landed if you look at Obama piracy.

Section: Westlawn
Lot: 466C

11/14/20 Sat, Kids. <grafted into your holy nation I speak as Moses, Ezekiel, Isaiah, David, in your Name for you are a lamp unto my feet and a light unto my path. Saw Auriga, clear sky ---After we took the kids home the parents weren't back so we waited. In the course AB came up to me from a few feet away and sneeze/coughed directly into my face, with intent, as if an assassination, As if she wanted to hurt me, as if because she was acting from another intent to harm me, not her own. We had talked earlier about Satan, devils, Halloween, owls, she said she id not believe in god as did teddy, that their dad used to but not any more, I talked to her about prayer and protection that her dad wants to protect her for what, bad men, ie evil that life is continual temptation between good and evil. Teddy came on board then when I spoke of the creation, that God made everything.

11/15/20 Sunday. Book out in pb on amazon. Order 7. AB is alienated from herself. Says she only wants to do what she wants I ask, what? art, dance, books? then show her the Pelop Wars etc, , but not math, so show her Principia on classes, she reads the title pages. Dogmatic about everything I say to her her thought is controlled, manipulated, that evil is everywhere in the world. She says she can't see God or prayer. I say you can't name one star in the sky all the eternal sounding world, later drawn some constellations for them, not interested. She mentions ASU. I say it is third rate, tell her of Cambridge and Oxford, mean to to tell her of traditions of learning etc, Erasmus…also spoke of her genome, rare as 10 to the 26th, she wanted to hear of the American rev, told her of Reiffs there

---in this context , checking how the fly in the fly bottle was doing, (I heard a fly buzz when I died) I read, that Wit on meeting Russell "He won't admit that it was certain that there was not a rhinoceros in the room. 1 Nov 1911

(A&A, S&S, a constitutional nation, (exceeding abundantly above all I can ask!) Wittgenstein's paternal great-great-grandfather was Moses Meier, and became Moses Meier Wittgenstein

11/16/20 Monday. Cardiology, vegus nerve singing herald songs all night, maybe a second ed to come later? Then was shaving some root or whatever to snort or eat, with others, bin neared view felt heart beating fast or faster? Then heard outside in the year a mild clanking, like a racoon? Turn on light, event. Got up at 4 for dr. appt at 7.

Obama calling Trump a dictator is like scientology calling Mccaviage a saint [speaking words to heaven and earth]

Usually look at the sky before dawn. But took the trash out because the car would block it. There, Jupiter seen before, but faint above Mercury, no, Saturn to 1/5 degree conjunct on 12/21 Pluto between, about 23 of Cap Mar transit Ares 15 now. Don't' take out the trash in the night.

11/17/20 Tuesday
How is it there is not one planet not inimical to man. Mercury runs dominion voting, Venus every lewd industry, mars, war, Jupiter our horrid govts, Saturn every prison system, Uranus every under ritual, Neptune all deception and snakes and pluto death. That's the lineup around earth. But who invented this system of oppression. Man against the gods since the gods of the planets claim they run space and time, seems out matched and that must be why his only hope is in the one who conquered them all, and conquered the stars that fall, the gods the stars and the system of idols they use as figureheads of themselves of not jut wood and stone and thought and art, the idols of art and thought.

It is a measure of the inimical that the planets have thus been slandered by the earth, which invented these notions without reference to anything but the deception of the fallen.[since all things were made by You and You do not exist] they must be recognized for what they are, corruptible beings that will pass away [in the new heaven and new earth].! ', Wittgenstein once said of Schopenhauer 'philosopher', he replied: 'A teacher of manners-- (In a diary entry from 1930, Wittgenstein judges that beside good and authentic things the Tractatus also contains
some 'Kitsch' (D 30). One may suspect that some of the purple passages from the end of the book belonged to what he had in mind.), more critically, wrote of this period in Wittgenstein's life: " as a village schoolmaster is surely a piece of perversity. who gave penance for his millions, gave them away, was an ascetic, a POW, on the wrong side! I have noticed a little torque on my fly swatting.
!
Walking Zion,' there were two Americas then, and three and four to account half.

Private Sprache

Andrew goes to Ohio. Walking Zion, she running but coming down foote a long hair shepherd, man and woman dog between afraid, gesturing, so I walk back ot get her, walk because they are clearly hysterical over nothing, passing them I say, she won't hurt you, he barks, keep your dog on a leash, but he]s not wearing a mask. His tone makes me say, aren't you a bad ass. He keeps walking. Pat says the demographic is changing. At 8 a dozen dog walkers.! The entitled millennial MSM white class. B/C 17k because of them so maybe I shouldn't shoot them. Plan, develop protocol demographic with Pat. A couple days after notice from city about leashing, so he is fearful, vindictive, censorious and knows my address.

Scrubbed bio for opacity: Andrew Edwin Reiff wants to read the face and know who he is talking to. After he was apprehended by Immanuel his gifts were loosed and he was given instruction among the finest poets and scholars of the age. After a PhD in the English Renaissance he took service among people who stirred his heart.

The place as the face in the Chartiers Valley, three of the major rivers of PA, the Jersey Pine Barrens, the Edwards Plateau of Texas and the Sonoran desert where he abides. He is an explorer, gardener, teacher, parking lot attendant, contemplative, father, husband, son and brother who has held positions in the Latin America Mission of Costa Rica, on two traditional Black college faculties in the U.S., as a horticulturist of an Experimental Drug and Herb Garden, written of native plants and his Palatinate fore-bearers in early Mennonite Pennsylvania, and with his wife founded a medical practice.

Subsequent to these the executed ceramic sculptures and murals explore the not quite bringing into existence as a parable of what really exists but cannot be seen. Throughout raising a family, taking on the national tennis tour, books on plants, the Psalms, prerevolutionary Philadelphia, essays, satire and poems. A collection of poems in praise of the King of Kings, titled The True Light That Lights, composed in the ballad-like forms of older traditions, like those sung by court bards to welcome a King, take the court as heaven and earth and the King as the King of Kings and Lord of Lords conveyed in the images of flowers, plants, stars and creation which participate in the song in their embassy of the King.

Concluding that fiction allows a greater open expression, or what is called fiction even if it is as the Russians say, factura, being born for such a time as this, all the above themes are concentrated in myths of refuge and escape that in time became an extensive work with the sense of afterlife therein.

To obviate automatic algorithmic downranks of these ideas, pseudonymous identities employed to enable and speed publication, which Every-men may be inferred from links of index, as appeared in the mags brought into unity of purpose in the record of direct perception face to face with the Word in observation of the invisible.

All this is in the middle of the great election fraud of all time, AEY chastised for moving the piano for me, AB sneezing in my face, the disorder of lives, the appearance of True Light, Heart issues, the Cardio appt.

11/19/20 captivity without visible bars.

11/20/20 $250 to Sidney Powell

11/21/20 as in the berst there is
 were taken for education: those for abortion, climate violations, violated covid public health, made unfact checked speech,

11/24/20 SLEEP SLEEP today
WHY ENGLAND SLEPT by JFK.
Killed that day by the same assassin
Shot from the sewer.
Except if it's UP to you! from the Embassies of Delight
-Tucker Carlson is part of media Big Tech dumping Trump. He complimented and dumped on 5 Nov. Tucker capo, sympathizer, commmandante, quisling, like Alex Jones saying I love God to flashing the horns. Can't you read Hegel? Mitrocondrial rna vaccine not speaking.

11/25/20 AB exposed to virus. What is that karma? Payback?2616-24 n 27th st
Welcome to Vichy Fox. Tucker wants to know what Biden believes now that Trump is gone from Fox. Thrown all sources to interviewing not the fraud, interviewing, digging naught and you know what he found? A Fox. Hegel for two? At least Banquo's Safe

11/26/20 Thanksgiving, aey brings dog. Told him I will tfr title to him for promissory note. Soonest. Aeg doesn't go to Chino, calls to tell of his turkey, tell him of planets in the southwest. Ask if he doesn't miss having philosophical discourse. He says he does with S. I say phil discourse has no emotion. That women first get anger or depressed at the thoughts of a man.
-HERE's WHY DEMOCRATS DON'T BELIEVE THE BIBLE.
It says full restitution of a theft requires that if "he have nothing then he shall be sold for his theft" (Ex. 22.3)
The price of a Biden, the whole kaboodle, is that enough for the theft of a nation?
-I like Biden as much as you, but the Hegel works are obvious. Overturning Biden to mask backdoor compliance is a blind for sacrosanct vaccine Overturn of your DNA. bye, bye mitochondrial RNA.

11/29/20
what when it really is childhood's end and the parents don't even know?

11/30/20 Ceramic dream: Piece in 5 pieces, volcanic black, blue red after working, on board. Preceded by another which cut on a saw through, in some kind group setting, cited by the one in charge, Vassily, who spoke of it. Not having dreams of note for two, three days,--even got out the bottle of Restore but didn't open it, put it on the counter though, in the environment of hearing about Daniels dreams etc and Rev. prophetics, but this like a painting some weeks ago is what mine are composed of. Last nite began another cut of OOps.

12/1/20 dream: Rebellious preteen boy and younger brother living in very ramshackle place of drugged out carloads of whites and blacks in the back, no security. The boy redecorates the house, digs a pit for a/c, but no discernment, moves the phone, runs from home when I seriously upbraid him, like some kind of failed old folks etc community with parasites living off it.

All the history I know and the vast I don't and all the experiences of everyone and every word collapsed into one drop speak at the start and then explode out into space and time where it came to exist and be and I met up with it here today.

-I was reconstructing events of the open door from the church of Philadelphia, first to appear, the elders, living creatures and the throne and before it then, the lament to open the scroll, and its opening, 4 horsemen, the souls that were slain, the 6th seal earthquake, fall of the stars, flight of the great, the four angels, sealing of the tribes and then the Great Multitude of martyrs of saintly past crying, and told they must wait until the finished number of the great tribulation, then the 7th seal, the Apophis of Ch. 8, looses the key of the abyss, locusts, scorpions, lions and their king Abaddon, then the 4 angels buried in the Euphrates and on to the Little Scroll which he ate and the angel said; **there shall be time no longer 10.6**—whereupon I let out an unexpected whoop, so loud in a minute she comes in asks if I'm ok, but by then I had put the Bible on the table and was sitting in the middle of that whoop and the picture which swallowed up it all. Praise, honor, glory, power and might to Him. Because to me time has been the great goal of the elite and the evil to wreak their ways, and they are about to lose it!
--In our neighborhood the ice cream trucks play La Cucaracha, but you have to buy from the curb side.

12/3/20 the point of Wittgenstein's cut up, hair cut (*Philosophical Investigations124*) style 121f is that autonomous elements independent of each 396 of them are arrayed in relation after much juggling right out of Tractatus, but in Phil Invest the monopolar 139 blue vs the red.
--Thoughts are like fish against a background of the same color, you see 'em when they move.
-The nation is captive of forces that take a hostage to make the good surrender.
-The only people fame sees are the ones the camera is on, the actors, the film, the script, the rest you never see. Does that make the actors valuable or puppets?
Sterling Morrison is dead.

12/2/20 Wittgenstein's three brothers died from the Werther effect, imitation.
She must think it makes her virtuous to confess that though she has two pianos she does play a few chords. What say, why not just glory in the piano itself. Same as when she says she tries hard to love, so many, and seems to fail, why not just glory in the ones you love?

12/4/20 the gay boys across the street are more afraid of me than the blacks.

12/5/20 the time of the dead when time shall be no more is for the elite of the nations. Those who turn to life then will be the lesser, not the great who sought these times to make themselves immortal and who **control all the media with their umbilical.**

12/6/20 dream–there is no blood for blood. Mike Anderson was the sales attendant. I was looking at shoes but when asked the price they cut it up. I had wanted it to sculpt but the cut versions had everything for everyone on the sides.—so when I bought nothing I offered him $5. He declined and let it fall to the floor, wrapped four ways the top left quarter I caught it on my shoe, thinking that would be a good design for a **five dollar shoe with the bill embossed on top.** ---all this is to say further awake that the Swedish Carlsons of Elgin, Hannah past and Ossian's, their son a POW and daughter a mission doc are noble, which together with the Parsons Clarke make the primordial Texan saga.

Smart house: Vacuum blender doorbell casts blender votes for Trump then pulls the cord
If your blender votes for Trump pull the cord out fast, if it persists go the last and pull the plug. If you vote for Biden last and best put on defrost. Biden, turn on, the chumps will come out last.

We are **not a zoom practice**, why so many FPs cease, work for conglomerates or don't see patients in the black market for saguaro ribs.

12/7/20 DREAM PACKAGES, such as might be produced by NPR, broadcast periodically on different subjects, assumed received by many, bulk passages that play two or three times in sequence in a night, indoctrinations of different intents, but which do not translate to 3D from 4, nonetheless the pattern is observed.
Proposed by media, governors, boards and judges, but even so
THE HILLS ARE FULL OF CHARIOTS OF FIRE "open his eyes O LORD that he may see." II Kings 6

--REBUKED THE TONGUES OF MEDIA YET TODAY? Isa. 54 Praise be to the LORD MY ROCK He trains my hands for war my fingers for battle Ps 144.

TO ALL YOU GOD FIGHTERS lift up eyes to the hills—You second story Jacobs:

"Many of us feel vulnerable, imperfect & frail. That is why the example of Jacob (Yaakov) is so fitting to inspire. Jacob highly valued the blessings & wrestled & struggled. In GEN 32 he struggled w/ the Angel of the Lord in the dark, and persisted even though wounded in the hip until he was blessed. We can to work hard for blessing, not to let go God in the dark. "Now faith is...the conviction of things not seen".

It may be permitted to add to this GOD FIGHTER the struggle for the Text, "the doubleness and duplicity out of which Jacob emerges a divinely inflicted bruise to replace a flaw of character to make straight, as opposed to the one whom God limp."

12/9/20 Bobby Brightflower

12/11/20 -**Shibumi** understated beauty, or quiet excellence, achieved through simplicity, subtlety, and the balance of complexity within restraint, **first is recognized by the born warrior as that moment the perception of the enemy becomes clear. It never fades & its awareness of** approach of battle. Shibumi is consciousness of the threads of time & being conscious of the realization of one's purpose in universe.

The flag symbolizes the sacrificed body of the citizen

-Found children's school table/bench

12/13/20 <your kingdom come in our families on earth and it is in heaven> Kids: N fell asleep sitting up on me laying down watching Carson. T digs runs, wants to stay over. I after reading Psalms to AB to show her **the Lord going out coming in is birth and death, Teddy says, I think about that.** AB says she thought it was a riddle until she "breaks her back" falling off the bed. Best thing that happened to her.

Doesn't it seem fitting that Susan would come out in pieces? I'll wait to see it.

12/16/20 woke up just now and saw Zion at the inside living room door with an **alligator** in her mouth.

12/19/20 Words over heard when awaking from sleep.

12/20/20 When Solomon's Preacher says vanity vanity he is the best example with riches of gold and slave labor. Sheba says his wisdom was greater than her imagination by half, apothegms and math, botany and Qab conclude that the Holy One allows great latitude of partnership with his creation to fellowship together the individualist. That how wisdom and vanity, gold and baboons go together.

12/21/20 there were shepherds abiding in the fields keeping watch over their flocks by night. These are things we don't see and might hope not to understand.

12/22/20 -New creche: Frosty, unicorns and little plastic pines in the yards of Red for Ed school buds. Angels replaced by Santa, wisemen by little snowmen, Mary without a child. Joseph replaced by a second Santa.
--Dr. Richard Urso: evidence that Hydroxychloroquine KILLS CANCER CELLS by 'suffocating' them. No wonder they are SO DESPERATE to bury this drug!
-- I invented five identities because the time was short, which thoughts need to be resaid so they link up here, as usually offered to those who have already thought them, said Ludwig in *Tractatus*. This is the case of understanding.

12/23/20 --And suddenly! Do you remember? there was a great light! If any man is in Christ he is a new creation, old things are passed away, all things are become new

12/26/20 Teaching synchronicities, perceptions and reflections combine with dreams. At one time people sang Christmas carols door to door, now you don't hear them even in church because there is no church or gathering. We sang them ourselves around the piano with Grandfather Carl playing.

12/27/20 Another parable. In the ff the New Jersey Coast, 1854, English captain and crew abandoned 500 German immigrants in the far surf of Asbury Park. The night was wild. The west wind was cold. Rigging and cordage made a dismal howl. Rescuers shot a line to the New Era off the coast except the sailors commandeered the life boat and saved themselves, then cut the line so no one could get off. The ships bell seconded by the griefs and prayers, sounded for the frozen and dying abandoned by the Yankee crew. That's proved. 500 Dunkards drowned in the surf.
-Step to the Bridge Nous Delphica appears at *otherwiseengagedjournal* vol 6 in this regard: "I am not squandering words. We pray on Sunday for those at sea."
--To obscure its mythic name in the Leviathan community add Seattle and Florence to the taurobolium.

12/28/20 -- The Hebrew word for "happenstance" is "kerry," and implies chance occurrence. For example, Rashi uses a form of the word *kerry* to distinguish between the prophecy of Moshe Rabbeinu and that of Bilaam (Moses and Balaam) is *And He called to Moshe . . . (*

A calling preceded all statements and commandments. It is an expression the Ministering Angels use, as it says, "One called to the other" However, to the gentile prophets (like Balaam) He revealed Himself with an expression of happenstance and uncleanness, as it says, "God chanced—vayikar—upon Bilaam"

When it comes to a "random" appearance of history, there is only *hester panim*, the hiding of God's face. *Hester panim* is when God makes things occur in a way that disguises the patterns of history, making events seem random to us. They are anything but random, but not seeing the pattern, even after seeing the "answer," minds beg to believe that a pattern does not exist, that history is random, and that God is not actively involved in the affairs of man.

--If you treat Me as happenstance, and you do not wish to listen to Me, I will add seven punishments corresponding to your sins. Leviticus

12/29/20 A little dizzy in waking dream couldn't find A's house. I was carrying his baby chair and lost motor bike—dehydrated some days, now realize, took a two weeks course of Lipitor and one baby aspirin. The message is the dream telling you the fact. Wake up and treat it with aspirin and get in bed with your wife.

Booleying is Irish transhumance for– taking cattle up to the high country to graze during the summer months. High pasture. There are words for the higher summer pastures, and frequently these words have been used as place names, like. in Wales and in Scotland. Chorrbhaile combines *corr* – round hill, pointed hill, hollow, pointed, conspicuous with *baile* – townland, town, homestead, but the alternative suffix *buaile* means cattle-fold, or summer-pasture. Other Irish names derived from the *booley* are Coill na

Buailidh, Kilinaboley, Kilenabooley, Both Théith, Boheagh, Knocknaboley, Buaile h'Anraoi, and Cnoc an tSamhraidh (which actually translates as Summerhill – a place name associated with transhumance in Britain) and the Hear @ The Booley House

LIGHTHOUSE your BOOTHY
Get ye up into the high mountains.

     A dozen years after, this Puzzle Palace, (James Bamford), of an underground mammoth computing center that lies beneath the mag-lev trains has reached the surface. As if were on city sized platform elevators supported by huge screws the size of many giant sequoias, it all appears as an outgrow of a two mile high Babel pile of eyes, an internet software that predicts future events by tracking keywords on the Palantir. Fore and aft, these Explodition aftershocks reflect the eight year pattern of once upon a time search results, vanishing domains, censored sweeps.

This fictional version of the academic joined Netflix to Thiel Capital, and the hopped up new intellects of Laocoön, the Trojan priest and his sons strangled by sea serpents,.as if it were a painting of Bosch of hideous ears that convert all repetition, echo, and progression to simultaneity.

A Mercator Projection

www.ingramcontent.com/pod-product-compliance
Lightning Source LLC
Chambersburg PA
CBHW081156230426
43666CB00016B/2831